To Morrie
What more can
I say than you
were always someone
on whom I counted
for support — — and you
were always there!
Best wishes
L. Mulund

PRAISE FOR *LEO MELAMED: ESCAPE TO THE FUTURES*

A well-written, fascinating memoir of a remarkable man of many parts who arrived in the United States at age 9, fleeing the Holocaust. Almost single-handedly, he transformed a minor commodity exchange into the leading futures market in the world. His influence was and remains worldwide.

> **Milton Friedman**
> Senior Research Fellow, Hoover Institution
> Stanford University

A grizzled old Merc trader once assured me that nobody ever lost by being long on Leo. Why that's so, this endlessly fascinating personal history makes clear. It shows how an immigrant boy, after surviving unimaginable horrors, drew on the "elan, combativeness and sophisticated conviction" learned from his equally remarkable father to build the CME and to lay the foundations of the modern, Chicago-based, financial services industry.

> **Morton H. Miller**
> Nobel Laureate
> Emeritus Professor, University of Chicago
> Graduate School of Business

There are only a few people who have revolutionized big portions of the business world. Warren Buffett did it in investing, Bill Gates in software. Leo Melamed, author of this book, is in that same league. He truly revolutionized futures trading in the United States, and in the world. This book tells how.

> **Ambassador Clayton Yeutter**
> Former U.S. Secretary of Agriculture
> Former U.S. Trade Representative

Leo Melamed is one of the architects of modern markets, and his memoirs will provide great value to those studying how financial markets were developed in the last half of the 20th Century.

> **Richard A. Grasso**
> Chairman & CEO, New York Stock Exchange

Escape to the Futures tells the remarkable story of a young boy's escape from the Nazis and the impact of his life on the financial markets of the world. It also serves as yet another poignant reminder of the immeasurable losses—in the arts, sciences, professions, and everyday life—humanity suffered because of the Holocaust.

> **Benjamin Meed**
> President, American Gathering of Jewish Holocaust Survivors

It's an amazing success story about a brilliant entrepreneur and businessman who did it the old-fashioned way. Leaving Poland at an early age, he came to the United States via Siberia and Japan with nothing more than determination and an uncanny ability to make good things happen. Although starting humbly as a runner at the Mercantile Exchange, he has become the father of international monetary exchange—a fundamental figure in the development of what is arguably the largest futures exchange in the world. A truly remarkable story.

Donald P. Jacobs
Dean, J.L. Kellogg Graduate School of Management
Northwestern University

Leo Melamed takes you into the pits which becomes a path through an exciting jungle. The jungle animals are people who care to fight, care to love, care to live, and care for those left behind in the Holocaust.

The hidden theme of the book is "timing is everything." As Leo says about his decision to leave the practice of law for a life as a trader: "I made the decision a thousand times. But I always stopped short from actually executing the trade." In this book, Leo does not stop short and neither will you.

Wayne B. Angell
Former Member, Board of Governors, Federal Reserve System
Senior Managing Director, Bear, Stearns & Co., Inc.

Leo tells it all. To say there would not have been a financial futures industry without Leo is probably only a *slight* exaggeration!!!

John Damgard
President, Futures Industry Association

Leo Melamed tells the story of the futures market as no one else could. *Escape to the Futures* is both a fascinating personal memoir and a lively contribution to the policy debate about these critical markets. Anyone interested in where the futures market came from and where it is going should want to read this book.

Martin Feldstein
Former Chairman, President's Council of Economic Advisors
President, National Bureau of Economic Research

LEO MELAMED

*Escape to the
Futures*

OTHER BOOKS BY LEO MELAMED

Leo Melamed on the Markets
The Merits of Flexible Exchange Rates (Editor)
The Tenth Planet

OTHER BOOKS BY BOB TAMARKIN

The Merc
The Leader Within
Rumor Has It: A Curio of Lies, Hoaxes, and Hearsay
The New Gatsbys
The Young Executive Today
Hefner's Gonna Kill Me When He Reads This (ghost author)

LEO MELAMED

Escape to the Futures

Leo Melamed

with Bob Tamarkin

JOHN WILEY & SONS, INC.
New York • Chichester • Brisbane • Toronto • Singapore

In memory of
Isaac and Faygl Melamdovich,
Who gave me the opportunity

Preface

This is not a book about my life although there is a lot of my life in it. First, with all due respect to time, I trust I have enough remaining to undertake some other missions. Second, as the title explains, this book is about an *escape* that led me to the futures markets. While the early part of the book has quite a bit about my personal life as a child and young adult, the balance of the book—indeed, its greatest portion—is mostly about my love affair with futures markets. And while one could make the case that my life was consumed by my work and therefore they are one and the same, I submit there is a substantial distinction between the two. Indeed, I believe that nearly everyone has at least two lives, the private one and the official one. In recent years, more and more of our two lives have gotten mixed up because we live in the information age when much more about each of us is likely to be known, recorded, and reported. Still, the dividing line is intact for most people; for me too. *Escape to the Futures*, if you will, is the story of my official life in the markets.

At the risk of belaboring the obvious, I must state that no *one* person can accomplish what this book records *alone*. In building the modern futures market, I was assisted by thousands of individuals both on and off the exchanges. But there is no way I can name even a fraction of all those people in this book or any other. In today's world, I suspect that many people who reach a significant role in society, particularly those in government, are conscious of the fact that they might someday write a book about their accomplishments. Thus, they maintain a diary or keep other forms of notes to chronicle their actions. I kept no such diary or notes. Indeed, I had no idea during most of my undertakings on behalf of futures markets, that I would someday be writing my memoirs. This book, therefore, is mostly from memory. Oh sure, there are official minutes, brochures, books, and gobs of newspaper and magazine articles, but these can in no shape, way, or form, identify all the people with whom I dealt during the two-and-a-half decades involved. I name some of them. But to those I inadvertently omitted, my deepest apologies.

For similar reasons, I no doubt missed some interesting occurrences and encounters. To some degree, I was limited by the amount of time and space

allotted by the publisher to this undertaking. As every movie director will
tell you, there is much on the cutting-room floor. And what is memorable
to one is not necessarily meaningful to another. Nevertheless, I believe I
hit the high notes of those events that I remembered, that mattered to me,
and which, in my opinion, were important to this story. To the degree I really did omit something of value, I again offer my sincere apologies. Perhaps I will make it up in the sequel.

It is imperative, however, to single out and publicly thank my dear
friend, esteemed mentor, distinguished teacher, and singular beacon of
economic thought, Milton Friedman. I cannot help but reiterate what I
stated in *Leo Melamed on the Markets:*

> Without Milton Friedman's support, without his intellectual blessing,
> without his assistance in opening doors and without his consistent and un-
> wavering belief in our mission, I could never have had the courage or tenac-
> ity to achieve what I did.

It is equally essential to underscore that without the complete backing
of my wife, Betty, and my children Idelle, Jordan, and David, I would not
have had the foundation on which to build my career. My family, particularly Betty, understood the importance of the role they were to play, even
though I would be the one to get the credit. But surely without their devotion and understanding, without their willingness to sacrifice the inordinate amount of time that I would spend away from them, without their
unequivocal support for the dreams and battles I encountered, I could not
have done it. And while the world generally does not sufficiently credit the
value of such support, I was fully conscious of its worth and eternally
grateful for their sacrifice.

Similarly, but in a different vein, I am forever beholden to the labor provided by Alysann Posner in assisting me in the production of this book. Her
devotion to this undertaking, her organizational proficiency, and her technical skills were indispensable in bringing this publication to a successful
conclusion. It also goes without saying that the professional talents of Bob
Tamarkin, my personal friend and literary guide, were vital to the process.
Tamarkin had spent the better part of six years writing the official history
of the Merc and as a result represented a resource and an institutional memory that is impossible to duplicate. Finally, I also wish to express my thanks
to Myles Thompson, John Wiley & Sons, and Nancy Marcus Land, Publica-
tions Development Company, for their expertise in producing this book.

What this book attempts to record is a most exciting and revolutionary
period in world markets. It represents a metamorphosis in futures markets
that nearly defies comprehension. As I tried to explain in my 1983 speech
entitled *The Future of Futures:*

Our markets, which since time immemorial were the unique and exclusive domain of agriculture, seemingly overnight became an integral mechanism of finance. Our markets, which for more than 100 years were strictly limited to tangible and storable products, suddenly shed these fundamental requirements and embraced live animals, foreign exchange, government instruments, and stock indices. Our markets, whose defined boundaries precluded entry into the sphere reserved for securities, brazenly transgressed the dividing line by inventing products that blurred that age-old distinction. Our markets, whose birth-right necessitated a system of physical delivery, broke their genetic code and engendered products without a delivery. Our markets, which only yesterday were viewed with scorn and considered barely at the edge of respectability, are today an indispensable member of the financial family.

Indeed, the phenomenal success of financial futures during the past two decades has few equals in the business world and symbolizes the power of an idea whose time had come. Statistics are an inadequate measurement but serve to dramatize the story. In 1971, on the eve of the birth of financial futures, 14.6 million contracts traded on U.S. futures exchanges; there were no foreign exchanges of any consequence. Twenty years later, in 1991, the total transactions of futures and options on U.S. futures exchanges was 325 million contracts, an astounding increase of over 2100 percent, with agricultural contracts representing a mere 19 percent of the total. In the same year, the burgeoning number of new foreign financial exchanges traded an equally impressive 230 million contracts.

I was fortunate that fate afforded me an opportunity to participate in this story.

LEO MELAMED

Chicago, Illinois
March 1996

Contents

LEO MELAMED

Escape to the
Futures

PART ONE

The Siberian Express

1

Peace and War

Aboard a screaming train somewhere in Siberia, I learned my first lesson in strategy. I was eight years old, peering over the shoulder of my father who had encouraged me to do so. He was engrossed in a game of chess. His opponent was a brooding old man with hunched shoulders and long white fingers constantly stroking a bushy gray beard. Slowly the old man shifted forward in his seat, muttering to himself and showing a measure of passion.

"*Shach!*" he blurted in Yiddish as his knight snatched a pawn checking my father's king. The pause seemed forever. My father sat there, he later explained to me, searching for the best strategy between three options.

I do not remember how my father countered or who claimed victory. What struck me, however, was the calmness of the men and their focus as each methodically took his turn. They did not seem to hear the rattle of the train's wheels that vibrated through the car's frail underbelly. Nor were they bothered by the sleet slamming against the windows, then moving slowly down in rivulets.

Looking back to that day in late 1940, the scene seems almost surreal: Two men playing chess, leisurely pondering each move as if they had all the time in the world, nowhere to go, and nothing to worry about except the chess game when, in fact, time was quickly running out. We were a train of nomads driven by a sense of survival, escaping for our lives from the Nazis. Ironically, we were pawns in someone else's game.

The scourge that had swept Europe turned everything upside down, severing the tether of genes, language, ideas, and ideologies and sending families like mine into exile. We were among the fortunate ones. The main part of my family was still together—my mother, father and I—and we were healthy though sometimes cold and hungry. I wondered about my grandmothers, my favorite Aunt Bobble, and friends who had stayed behind in Bialystok, unwittingly taking their chances with what the gods of war had to offer.

The trip was filled with the unknown and fraught with danger as we moved along Siberia's spine, the 5,800-mile Trans-Siberian Railroad, begun in 1891 to connect Moscow to Vladivostok among other Asian ports. The rickety train was a pinprick against the vast wilderness, utterly untouched, where you could travel for thousands of miles without seeing traces of man or beast. There was beauty in this frigid frontier, but a harsh and muscular beauty, where bear, tigers, sable, reindeer, and wolves roamed freely among some of the greatest physical treasures on earth. A cash cow, they said of Siberia, that accounted for one-fifth of the world's gold and silver, a third of its iron and timber, along with an immeasurable wealth of gas, oil, and coal. It was the largest region of the world's largest nation, four million square miles—the size of the entire United States—a bewildering kaleidoscope of marshy plains, dense forests, desolate plateaus, and craggy-peaked mountains where time and place were lost.

With few roads, the train, on its single track, was the ubiquitous carryall, the workhorse of the Siberian transport system, like the oxen-pulled wagons stacked with children and battered household utensils that were moving other streams of refugees in flight all across rural Europe at the time. While they fled in panic, somehow the oxen never realized just how critical time was for them. Nor, it seemed, did the engineer driving our train have much concern for our simmering anxieties. The train kept at a steady speed, its rhythm lulling us into a false sense of security, perhaps to conserve fuel, or because of weather conditions, or the fact that we were crossing treacherous terrain. There were no shortcuts. Indeed, because there was only one track, we would often spend lonely hours at designated switching points (at Oms, or Novosibirsk, or Irkutsk), waiting for our westbound sibling to pass so that we could continue our trek to Siberia's most Eastern point, the port of Vladivostok.

During the 1930s, men with shovels and wheelbarrows built steel mills as part of Joseph Stalin's plan to industrialize the Soviet Union. And when the war broke out, millions of workers and their factories would be transported to Siberia from the vulnerable areas, retreating like a turtle beneath its shell. It was also where Stalin banished criminals and political prisoners to work in mines and build in forced labor camps, and where untold millions died long before and after the war.

I don't, however, want to get ahead of my story. That's the trouble with memory; once it uncoils, it tends to race. But there's magic in memory. You can stop and replay it at almost any point, rubbing old images together for sparks of new meaning. And one thing more about memory in passing: it's a safety valve; you survive by memory.

Everyone sooner or later broods about the difficult parts of his or her life—the hurts, the failures, the injustices, all the things we like to believe we can let go to move on with our lives. But you can never really let go of personal history because it is what shapes you and shades wisdom.

It was nearly a year-and-a-half before I ended up on that train in Siberia, a year-and-a-half of my family playing hide-and-seek with the Gestapo or the KGB. I was too young, or too shielded by my parents, to fully realize the consequences of being caught. But I sensed our plight. While at times it seemed like one glorious adventure, there was always the feeling we were running from something very evil, from a boogeyman breathing down our necks. Indeed we were. While most children my age, especially those in the United States, were busy learning the three "Rs," my early years were shaped by the three "Fs"—flight, fear, and fate.

I was the only child of Isaac and Faygl Melamdovich. Both were teachers in Yiddish-speaking schools. Mother taught first grade in the Grosser school, Bialystok's first government-approved parochial school sanctioned to conduct its entire curriculum in the Yiddish language. The *Grosser Folks Shul*, as it was called, was named after the founder and first principal. My father taught mathematics in the higher grades and was the author of three books on the subject. His books became the standard mathematics works for grade school classes in the Yiddish schools of Poland. The schools were secular, in that there was no religious training. They were the showcase and pride of the modern Jewish society that was emerging throughout Eastern Europe. These schools had offered a full curriculum and were accredited by the Polish government. This meant that graduates from these schools could go on to *gymnasium*, high-school, or even in rare instances college, although Jews were seldom allowed to enter.

My parents would leave the house in the morning when the light was still soft and shadowy. They'd return late in the day. During that time I would wait under the watchful eyes of my maternal grandmother, or sometimes to my delight, my father's sister, Aunt Bobble, an exceptionally beautiful woman in her early twenties. Itke Cyrla Barakin was my grandmother's name, but to me she was "Babba." We all lived together in a house on Zieben (No. 7) Fastowska street in Bialystok, a city in northeastern Poland known for the production of textiles and finished goods, near the Russian border and roughly midway between Poland's capital, Warsaw, and Lithuania's, Wilno (now Vilnius). Bialystok was a political football. Founded in 1310, it was annexed to Prussia in 1795, to Russia in 1807, and returned to Poland in 1921.

However, it wasn't the weavers of Bialystok but its bakers who exported a bit of the city to the world. Over the years, Bialystok would leave its gastronomical mark, especially on the United States, where bakeries, delicatessens, and food stores would sell the "bialy," a flat breakfast roll—the creation of Bialystok bakers. Unlike its more popular cousin, the bagel, the bialy had no hole in its center, giving more surface on which to slather the cream cheese. As a child in the city of the bialy, I loved bialys and ate them with herring, the tail of the herring. I also loved my grandmother's homemade *challa*, a soft braided loaf of bread glazed with egg white.

Sitting in the middle of the kitchen, like a headless dark Buddha, was a potbellied stove that used coal and wood. Plenty of it. In the morning, well before dawn, my grandmother would stoke it up in preparation for breakfast. The wood burned like a miniature forest fire, crackling at first, then exploding into yellow flames that shimmered through the front vent on the door to create odd shadows in the darkened room. The stove did double duty. It provided our heat during the long winter months and cooked our meals. But we were fortunate; we also had a white brick modern oven that dominated the dining room. It was modern because it had its own brick chimney built into the wall. At times, a huge pot of cholent would be simmering inside its mysterious door, which I was admonished never to touch. Cholent was a thick stew made with pieces of beef, potatoes, onions, carrots, beans, and a host of spices mixed with water, and cooked. And I mean cooked. Babba cooked cholent overnight and until noon the next day, careful never to stir the concoction during the entire time. It was manna.

A teacher's life was relatively comfortable and carried a certain amount of prestige in the community. My father was one of the few elected Jewish city councilmen. We lived in a small wooden bungalow that had been inherited by my mother from her father, who died before I was born. There was one bedroom, a large dining room with a daybed, a kitchen, an upstairs attic where my grandmother slept, and a seldom-found luxury in Jewish homes, an indoor bathroom. My father, who I was convinced could do everything, had installed the plumbing himself and took great pride in showing me how to pull the chain that released the muffled explosion of gushing water from the overhead box.

As a preschooler, I was pretty much left to my own wits. Most of the children on my street were older and were in school during the day. I would wander around outside, living in my mind and letting my imagination soar to wherever it would take me. I made up games and acted out stories my mother had read to me at night. Sometimes the daybed would be a ship at sea with pirates bearing down on me. Other times I would become an explorer and sneak about the narrow opening between our house and the next.

Finally, it was my turn to go to school. In August 1939, shortly before we were about to be swept up in the turmoil of war, I entered first grade. I had just turned seven and very much anticipated seeing my parents during the course of the day. But they had other plans for me. It wasn't proper, they explained to me, to go to the same school where they taught. They didn't want students, parents, or fellow teachers to perceive me as having an advantage or to be perceived as a "teacher's pet." Thus, to my dismay, I was enrolled in another Yiddish grammar school. The pangs of separation were painful. For the first time, I was away from my parents and my Babba. I felt fear and, to some degree, rejection. When I was introduced to my new teacher and she offered her hand, I did an unthinkable thing; I slapped it. My mother was terribly embarrassed and furious with me.

Nearly three and a half million Jews lived in Poland in 1939, making it the world's second largest *Diaspora* community. They were heirs to a Jewish culture that had thrived in Poland for a thousand years. Of Bialystok's 1.6 million denizens, some 40,000 were Jews. We were integrated, although Jews generally lived in what became Jewish neighborhoods. There were no ghettos, but there was anti-Semitism. While it wasn't notorious, even as a child I often heard, "Jiyd, go to Jerusalem." I recall my puzzlement at the slur. Where was Jerusalem? Why should we go there? But it was tolerable. After all, my father was a Jew and a member of Bialystok's City Council — Poland was trying to enter the "enlightened era."

To the south of Bialystok, about a hundred miles, was Lublin, the "Jewish Oxford" known throughout Europe for its Talmudic and Cabalistic scholars. One of the first Yeshivas was established there in the sixteenth century. In 1939, Lublin with a population of 2.4 million also boasted a Jewish community of 40,000. After the war, there wouldn't be enough Jews in either city to make a "minyan," the 10 Jewish males needed to form a quorum for prayer in accordance with Jewish law. Poland had always been bullied by its neighbors. Poland's name comes from the Polaine, or "plains people," a Slavic group that settled in Europe before the birth of Christ. With few natural mountains and rivers on its borders, Poland constantly fell victim to the territorial ambitions of the surrounding countries. In 1795, it was partitioned between Russia, Prussia, and Austria—erasing Poland from the map altogether. It reappeared as a sovereign nation at the end of World War I in 1918. Then, in 1939, came the German invasion of Poland to spark World War II. Again, Poland was overrun. First it was the Germans, then the Soviets. (In the wake of the war, Stalin would end up moving Poland westward by annexing more than 50,000 square miles of eastern German territory under Polish rule and another 100,000 square miles of eastern Poland to the Soviet Union.) During these periods, when Poland ceased to exist, it was the Roman Catholic church that became the bastion of Polish nationality and the protector of the language and culture.

Similarly, the Jewish community and culture were kept intact through its synagogues and Rabbis and scholars. However, I was born into the secular Jewish movement that had taken hold in Europe since the early 1900s. My parents were emancipated Jews. They had left the "shtetl" ways of their parents to become the new Jewish intellegensia. They were rightful citizens of the world. They were worldly Jews who had the inherent right to live as citizens of any country. In their world ideal, race and religious distinctions no longer mattered. All humans were equal. One of the first songs I remember my mother singing was Friedrich von Schiller's words to Beethoven's Ninth, *Alle Menchen Seinen Breeder*, "All Humans are Brothers." (How ironic that this monument to equality was written by a German poet.) Indeed, in our home, I was raised to believe this philosophy as gospel. It wasn't until much later in life that I learned to my chagrin that the world wasn't really quite as my parents taught me.

Thus, orthodoxy and religious rituals were not part of our daily life. They were replaced by worldly precepts—intertwined with Jewish ethnicity, its history, literature, culture, holidays, and especially its Yiddish language. My mother and father were fervent *Yiddishistn*. Following World War I, the Polish government, under a treaty guaranteed by the League of Nations, recognized Yiddish as a language and granted Jews the right to use it in their primary education. It also assured the Jews civil and political equality as well as their cultural autonomy.

Although among the gentiles we spoke Polish, Yiddish was the first language I learned. We spoke it in the house, and in school, and on the street. But it was a literary Yiddish—that is, pure and grammatically perfect—after all, my parents were Yiddish teachers of the highest order. (It wasn't until I became an adult that I learned to my amazement that Yiddish contained swear words.) My parents were the products of Eastern European Jews who for hundreds of years were subjected to poverty, persecution, and harassment by czars, cossacks, and a host of local officials whose favorite pastime, it seemed, was to plan organized riots known as pogroms. Despite the poverty and violence and the fact that Jews were forced to live in designated areas called the Pale, they clung to God, a memory of greatness and a messianic hope. "For them the Bible was a living reality," is how historians Irving Howe and Kenneth Libo put it. "It was a token of promise, a source of wisdom, a guide to conduct."

Here is where my father departed from his ancestors. While he fervently believed that the central value in Jewish culture was learning, he saw no glow of messianic hope. He was an agnostic, and as such felt no spiritual pleasure in the reenactment of ritual. My mother, although drawing the line with respect to eating of non-Kosher foods, was among the early emancipated women in Jewish Poland. Indeed, unlike most women of that day and age, Faygl Melamdovich was an equal co-worker in our household and a professional member of the teaching fraternity. She, no less than her husband, embraced the new emancipated philosophy with zeal and fervor. In their crowd, some of whom would occasionally gather around our dining room table, there seemed to be little distinction between the rights of women and men—all were considered equal. Everyone had a right to voice his opinion, and did, as they drank tea from glasses, ate my Babba's honey cake, and discussed the dawning of a new era for Jews in Poland. Still, it was an oddity of cultural European life that, in company, a woman referred to her husband by his last name. Thus, when my mother spoke of my father, she would speak of him as "Melamdovich." First names were reserved for private conversations. My mother called my father by his middle name, Moishe.

I am uncertain at what exact age my father rejected religion, since his early youth was spent in the religious upbringing of a *cheder*. (Indeed, he was steeped in religious lore.) I suspect it was sometime in the early 1920s when many of Europe's young intellectuals with a sense of idealism turned from the dogma of religion to science and humanism. They wrestled with the conflict of traditionalism, as embodied in a Hasidic inheritance, and modernism, the trend of secular-progressive thought that was sweeping through the world of East European Jewry—a legacy of eighteenth century philosopher Moses Mendelssohn and dramatist Gotthold Lessing. Together, these two pioneers of modern Jewish thought forged the concept of Jewish emancipation and were first in denouncing Jewish separatism. Moses Mendelssohn, a little hunchback from the Dessau ghetto in Germany, the grandfather of composer Felix Mendelssohn (who was born a Christian), made it his mission to lead Judaism out of the ghetto and into the new Enlightenment in which the practice of Judaism would not conflict with life in a non-Jewish world. Mendelssohn's revolutionary thought evolved into the modern Jewish secular movement whose by-product gave the world artists, writers, musicians, and scientists—the numbers of which were out of all proportion to the tiny percentage of Jews within the general population. In the early 1900s, this secular movement, although still in its infancy, was an irresistible force to the young generation of European Jews, snaring the likes of my father and mother in its current and causing them to leave the ways of the shtetl. My father graduated from the University de Liege on November 26, 1923, having completed a full course in modern studies, mathematics, and humanities.

Thus, it wasn't surprising that my father's favorite writer (and later mine, too) was the Yiddish author Itzchok L. Peretz, regarded as one of the giants of Yiddish literature along with Mendele Mocher Sforim, "Mendel the Bookseller," the pseudonym of Shalom Jacob Abramowits, and Sholem Aleichem, "Peace be with you," the pseudonym of Salomon Rabinovitch. Peretz was a so-called *maskil*, or enlightener, who had deep-rooted love for Jewish history and its folklore, but found bridges and commonality between traditional religion and the growing new secular cultural movement of the emerging Jewish masses. Indeed, Peretz gave new meaning, new interpretation, and new practical application to age-old religious precepts and rituals. Like Peretz, my father no longer believed in divine metaphysics or in the orthodox concepts of heaven and hell, or in the notion that there was subsequent reward and punishment for a person's acts in life. Rather, my father believed in an even higher morality than that contained in the Ten Commandments. Indeed, my father's morality was embodied in Peretz's short story, *Oib Nisht Noch Hecher*, "If Not Higher." Morality for him was an inherent necessity of one's being, as was the concept of equality between human beings.

My father was a idealist, a mathematician, and teacher by trade; a skeptic by nature. On top of that, add stubborn. Taking a stand in what he believed became a leitmotif in his writings and personal philosophy. Small in stature, but ramrod-straight with receding hair, he was an independent man who followed his own conscience throughout his life. Sometimes that path took strange turns, as it did shortly before the Nazis marched into Bialystok.

Germany's attack on Poland on September 1, 1939, all along its frontier brought on World War II. And though Bialystok was hardly a military threat to the Third Reich, German bombers were sent over the defenseless city. Their bombs were randomly dropped on "to whom it may concern" targets. One of them was City Hall, an early nineteenth century edifice, which had been reduced to cinders. It was only a matter of time before the Blitzkrieg would be storming the city gates. The mayor hastily called a meeting of the city council of which my father was a member. There was only one problem: There was no longer a city council chambers. The city's major synagogue, *Die Groyse Shul*, still stood intact, and the mayor asked its rabbi if the council could gather in its hall. The rabbi consented on the condition that all the councilmen wear hats or *yarmulkes*, skullcaps, as a sign of respect before God as prescribed by Jewish religion when entering a synagogue. The mayor and the other councilmen all agreed. There was only one holdout. My father, who happened to be one of a handful of Jewish councilmen, refused to enter the shul if he had to cover his head. In principle he wouldn't acknowledge any form of religion, and to wear a hat was to reenact ritual. Vintage Melamdovich.

Although he boycotted the meeting, he went along with the consensus for an escape plan. The mayor and the entire city council, which made up Bialystok's political backbone, intended to leave the city along with the other prominent citizens before the Nazis showed up. The city fathers had been advised that the Nazis would use Bialystok's prominent citizens as hostages. If anything went wrong, the hostages would be held responsible. In their naiveté, they believed families left behind would be safe. What we didn't know was the Nazi scheme to isolate Jews from the Poles by expelling them from small towns and villages, forcing them to make their ways to the larger cities where eventually they would be concentrated. Bialystok along with Warsaw, Lublin, Cracow, Wilno, and Lodz would become the major cities where Jews were confined to ghettos, and later six million of them would be transported like cattle and exterminated in the death camps. But this was long before the world had heard of Dachau, Buchenwald, Auschwitz-Birkenau, Maidanek, Bergen-Belsen, or Treblinka. By late September 1939, Germany and Russia would divide Poland. While Stalin was banking on his nonaggression pact with Hitler, Russia concluded pacts with Latvia, Lithuania, and Estonia, obtaining rights to set up military bases. In return, Russia ceded Wilno, which had been part of Poland, back to Lithuania. Wilno, hard on Poland's border, had been Lithuania's historic capital. Europe's geopolitical machinations were in high gear.

I, of course, knew nothing of my father's escape plan until the middle of a moonless night, a few days after the council meeting. My mother woke me and dressed me.

"We are going to say goodbye to your father," she whispered, taking me by the hand and leading me out into the deserted and totally blackened streets of Bialystok. While I couldn't see any traces of war, I could hear them: the constant echoing throughout the buildings of the ack-ack of gunfire around us.

On an empty lot we came upon a group of people milling around a large canvas-covered truck. There were other children, wives, and family members of the councilmen saying their goodbyes. I saw my father and ran to him. There were tears in my mother's eyes. There were tears in everyone's eyes. My parents clung to each other for a brief moment. Then my father and his fellow councilmen piled into the truck and left. No one knew their destination.

I don't remember my father's precise words that night, but he said his goodbyes in a tone that tried to be reassuring. Politics had driven him away. Perhaps it would bring him back. But the world in the 1930s didn't work that way. The norms of safety, the norms of self-respect no longer mattered. Europe had been swept up in the momentum of politics all right, but power politics backed by the machines of war—tanks, planes, and mobile armies—swept across lands like the Mongol hordes that once stormed out of Asia.

Before I heard the bombs, my own vision of war at that time centered more on the swashbuckle than on the swastika. I imagined the war would play out as sword fights in the main streets of Bialystok. The brave Bialystokans against the barbarians, up one avenue, down another. But the war would take place only on the big streets. Life on the side streets, such as the one I lived on, would carry on as normal.

Such childish thoughts were soon jolted by reality. Suddenly the world was noisy and frightening. The noise of church bells. The noise of air raid sirens. The noise of rumors. The noise of bombs and gunfire echoing throughout the streets. The dark and shrouded nights. The fear evidenced on faces. The tumult of agony and despair with the crushing armies of the Nazi war machine.

My child's vision of a fantasy war, it turned out, wasn't that far-fetched. Unfortunately, the Polish military machine was a relic of the nineteenth century like many of the buildings in our town. Slogging through mud and cold rain, the Polish cavalrymen charged Nazi tanks with lances and sabers. Poland fell in 27 days.

Now we could only wait for our conquerors and our fate.

2

Eluding the Intruders

I was in the barber shop waiting my turn. The barber had sat me on the special children's bench so I would be high enough. Then he wrapped the white smock around me and smiled. Suddenly there was shouting in the street. *"Lozt arop die shluzen, der gast iz do . . . Lozt arop die shluzen der gast iz do."* "Put down the grating, the guest is here," a man was screaming as he ran by outside the shop's window, "Put down the grating, the guest is here."

My mother grabbed my hand and pulled me out of the chair. Quickly she put my coat on. The September air was chilly and our hasty departure didn't give me time to button my coat. There were many others in the street scurrying, slamming shutters, closing doors, pulling down window shades, drawing curtains. The entire city was in a crouching lope.

"Gicher Leibl." "Hurry Leibl," my mother urged, pulling my hand. I had never seen her move so fast. Though she didn't say another word, I could sense her frenzy. But I couldn't figure out if we were running to something or away from something. It took us a while to get to our destination because we had moved out of our own house to my father's building which was at the edge of the city. It was a brick two-story structure, where he grew up and where his mother, my paternal grandmother, and his sister Bobble, lived. My father made us move there just before the bombing began, only days before he left Bialystok. He felt that not only would the brick structure be safer during the bombing, but we would also be together. There was safety in numbers, he had told my mother.

By the time we reached the building, my aunt Bobble and both my grandmothers were already anxiously awaiting us. All the windows and doors were tightly locked. My father had painted most of the upstairs windows with black paint so no light would shine through during the blackouts. Like everyone in Bialystok, we were hiding, too.

The Germans were marching into Bialystok. And word of their arrival had spread throughout the city like an unchecked virus. All of Bialystok had hunkered down under an omnipresent fear. The Poles had been easily

13

outgunned and outnumbered. It was hardly a contest, and now the victors were claiming their spoils without any resistance from the Polish army.

Because of our location on the outskirts of Bialystok, we were among the first to witness their arrival. One shutter was ajar so that we could catch a glimpse of the arriving intruders. The tanks came first. You could hear their thunderous roar long before you saw them. There were countless numbers of them moving slowly into Bialystok like so many alien robots. As they passed our building, they made a strange squealing and eerie noise. Oddly, they were followed by five horsemen. I sat in wonderment peeking through the shutter. They were in officer uniforms and one of them raised his hand as if to give an order to the long convoy of trucks carrying thousands of soldiers who were silent and grim.

We were being forced to look at the world in a different way. There was still a semblance of humanity. But that didn't last long. Immediately, there were orders. No one was to walk outside with their hands in their pockets. No one was allowed to congregate on the streets. Six o'clock curfew for everyone. Anyone violating the curfew would be summarily shot.

Across the street from father's building was a cemetery with neat rows of gravestones among tall trees. Some of the graves, my aunt once told me, were as old as the trees. For the dead, it was the final stop. For the living, it was a shortcut into town, a way of saving a good 10 minutes. During the day, it was a well-traveled route. After curfew, it was mostly deserted, although on occasion I would sometimes spot some brave soul hurriedly sneaking through the gravestones. Often after dinner, around dusk, I would sit upstairs at the living room window and gaze outside through a peephole I had secretly scratched in the painted window with a key. I had nothing else to do but to watch and think. Things were turning ugly, and inhumanity became the enemy.

It happened in front of my eyes. One evening, my eye had caught a teenage girl turning quickly into the cemetery on the way into town. It was near curfew time and she walked very fast. She held down her head as if that would prevent her from being seen. Suddenly, I saw not far behind her two German soldiers. When they caught up to her, they grabbed her and threw her to the ground. They were laughing. One of them held her arms down and placed his hand over her mouth, but not before she screamed out. The other fell on top of her. Over the years, that vision flashed into my memory off and on. I didn't understand what I had witnessed until sometime in my early teens, but I could never forget the incident. It kept turning up—and still does—like a recurring nightmare. I suppose I remembered the episode because it was my first encounter with violence—I had heard the girl's scream. It was the only time I ever witnessed a rape.

Not long after the German's arrival, we moved back to our own house. Because the bombing had stopped there seemed no reason to remain in the outskirts of the city. Besides, my mother feared that our empty house would attract looters. It was good we returned because not much later, they came to look for my father—just as he had anticipated. He was to be taken as a hostage. In the event anyone disobeyed their orders, he would be held responsible and shot. Once they entered our home, it made the war a personal affair. I saw their boots, their black clickity-clacking boots, but I don't remember seeing faces. Perhaps I was too afraid to look up. There was also the sound of their stern and bellowing voices. Several of them milled about the house, poking into drawers and closets. One began to shout when he saw my father's clothes. Where was he, they demanded. They spoke in a language vaguely resembling Yiddish. I had never heard that kind of shouting nor had I ever heard anyone yell at my mother before. She tried to remain calm although I saw tears welling in her eyes. Her fear was transmitted to me and I squeezed her hand.

Something had permanently changed. After the Gestapo left our house, there was always the fear that they would return. Dinner that night was eaten in total silence. From then on, everyone seemed to whisper. There was little conversation between my mother and grandmother.

Their apprehension permeated my being. How foolish of me to wait for sword fighters. There was hardly any fighting at all. Where were all the Bialystok fighters, I wondered. Had they left with my father? When would they return? Would I see my father again? Where was he? My mother said everything would be all right and that my father would be in contact. But the alarm in her eyes belied her words. I was afraid.

Although my mother began working at school again, she would not let me leave the house. I stayed inside every day with my Babba. Sometimes a friend would come over and we played soldier. Rumors and stories circulated among the children about relatives and neighbors who had been taken away for work somewhere by the invaders. Myron, the grocer, was dragged out of his store and had both of his hands broken because two German soldiers accused him of overcharging for bread. Rochl Wiseberg was taken away and never heard from again. The Goldberg's house was set on fire and burned to the ground.

Two more weeks had passed, and by now all over Poland synagogues were going up in flames. Senseless violence against Jews had become habitual and commonplace. And though there was an overwhelming dreariness on the streets, the situation in Bialystok had not yet erupted into the insanity of the Holocaust. One reason was because Bialystok had become part of the prewar tinkering between Hitler and Stalin. Teutonic Knights, Prussians,

Germans, Russians, and Poles; it made no difference who dominated. They all did so with a heavy hand as far as the Jews were concerned. There would be little sympathy generated from the locals for whatever plight the Jews faced. In 1934, for example, the Polish government denounced a promise made in 1919 to guarantee civil and political equality to its minorities. At the time, Jews represented about 10 percent of the total Polish population. Pogroms became more frequent. Jews trying to get into universities and professional schools faced a strict quota system. Such discriminatory regulations and restrictive practices became an economic noose that had tightened even more in 1935 with the death of Poland's premier, Marshal Pilsudski, the old revolutionary and diehard socialist. By 1938, a torrent of anti-Semitic legislation swept the country that included even withdrawing citizenship from Polish Jews living abroad.

All its promises to respect the rights of minorities were scrapped. Anti-Semitism was a ready-made lightning rod to divert revolution. But the Jews persisted with their religious, educational, and cultural institutions. They even managed to organize politically. And in the late 1930s, Jews shifted their support in municipal elections from the Zionist parties to the socialist-minded "Bund," which in the elections of 1938 and 1939, claimed sweeping victories in many large cities including Bialystok. That's how my father won his seat on the city council. He was a Bundist who abhorred the Bolsheviks not much less than the Nazis. For him, Communism was as bitter a pill as Fascism. By whatever name, totalitarian states stole a person's mind, my father would say. For him there could be no compromise of intellectual freedom.

As a child, I did not have a grasp of what anti-Semitism was all about. I knew that we were moderately comfortable and my parents were respected teachers and that there was a parallel world in which the gentiles spoke no Yiddish. There were rules that people played by, but the political leaders kept changing them, my father would explain to me. My mother agreed. Sometimes there would be heated discussions between my father, my mother, and their friends about the inevitability of war and how Poland would be the first target.

History, geography, and politics were some of my father's favorite topics. He knew quite a lot and kept me informed about everything. My parents always explained what was happening around us. Children, my father said, should understand history and political matters because they kept repeating themselves. Children must always be aware of what is happening around them so that they are prepared. One is never too young to learn, he stated. But it was my mother who did most of the teaching. We were close, because it was easy to be close to her. She was not only smart and insightful, she had the sixth sense one hears about. She knew my questions before

I could ask them, and always provided the answer. Later in life, no matter how hard I tried to keep it from her, she always knew when I had a bad day trading the market.

Thus, even as a kid, I knew there was something about history and politics that aroused passion in grown people. Although I was by nature quite shy, I was comfortable around adults and I had learned to listen to them closely. Though I might not always understand what they were saying, by the time I was six, my ear was tuned to pick up on the emotional ebbs and flows of their conversations. The decibels in their voices would rise whenever the topic was politics. Later, my parents would explain.

If, however, there was any lesson to be learned, it was never to ignore politics, even at a tender age. I and my schoolmates were removed from all of it, until Nazi madness became a child's war, too. Like our parents caught up in war-ravaged Europe, we also found ourselves coping with the rules of chance and probability and distorted codes of conduct. The world had unwittingly taken Hitler's bait and was paying the price; Jews were methodically being annihilated man by man, woman by woman, child by child.

To survive took wits—and luck. And time. But by September 1939, the fate of Europe's Polish Jews had been compressed into a matter of days. When the Poles refused to give up the port of Gdansk, Germany invaded, touching off the war. The Germans attacked from the west. Seventeen days later, Russia sent its troops in from the east. Two days later, the German and Russian armies met near Brest Litovsk, and Poland was pulled apart like a piece of taffy. The partition sent Jews scurrying in every direction; some 300,000 of them fled into Soviet-occupied Poland that now included Bialystok.

In just weeks, Bialystok had moved from the hands of the Poles to the hands of the Germans to the hands of the Russians. Bialystokans were wringing their hands in frustration. The town elders, who long ruled Bialystok, were now emblems of Tolstoy's view of history in which the most powerful generals often have less freedom than the foot soldiers, becoming prisoners of the events and forces they have sought to strenuously manipulate.

After the acrid smoke had lifted and chunks of stone and brick lay scattered, after the whir and whine of incoming barrages, after the clatter of machine-gunfire, after the whomp, whomp of mortars in the countryside, a strange calm settled upon Bialystok. It was as if the old city had paused to gasp for breath. Perhaps a last breath. The day had arrived when Bialystok was to change hands.

My mother took me to witness the strange ceremony. We were among thousands who had lined Bialystok's major boulevard bisected by a carefully manicured grassy parkway with a rainbow of flowers. It was an historic event: the German troops goose-stepping down one side of the avenue on their way out of the city, and a little later, the Russians troops marching up the other side as they triumphantly entered the city. Although there was clearly a festive mood, the crowds stood silently watching the Nazis leave. No one publicly dared to display any pleasure at seeing that hated enemy depart. Later, when the Russians soldiers appeared, the crowd broke loudly into cheers and, suddenly, red flags appeared everywhere to welcome the incoming "liberators." Looking back on that scene, it is easy to understand that the Bialystokans were welcoming what they perceived as the lesser of two evils; two of the most repressive and cruelest regimes in history had been shoved down Bialystok's gullet. The Poles seemed to be saying the odds favored the Russians as far as their chances for survival. After all, the Russians had been to Poland before. They were a better choice than the Germans. The prospect, however, left a queasy feeling in one's stomach.

Even the Bialystok elite who had fled with my father showed their confidence in the new conquerors. Bringing up the rear of the Soviet troops marched the returning councilmen and other prominent citizens to the relief and delight of their families and friends. But not my father. Only he and one other close friend were not part of the returning entourage, much to the sorrow of my mother. Why had he failed to return with the others? Did he not miss his wife and child? Had something terrible befallen him? Why did all the others know to return with the Russian army, but not my father?

What had happened to him, no one knew. Those who returned told my mother that he was a stubborn fool, that his anti-communist views had clouded his good senses, that his refusal to return with them sentenced him to a life of hiding and fear. They said these things, until they learned of their mistake.

How strangely things turn out. Even before the week was out, all those who had followed the Russians back into Bialystok were rounded up by the GPU—the precursor to the dreaded KGB—and summarily arrested to be sent off to Siberia. We never heard from them again. The Russians, it seemed, no different than the Nazis before them, wanted no part of the hierarchy of Bialystok. In effect, by returning to Bialystok, the councilmen and others were turning themselves in. Now it was painfully clear. My father was right not to trust the Bolsheviks. He could not return to Bialystok. In effect, for him to remain in Poland meant either a Nazi firing squad or a Siberian outpost. He was now truly a man without a country.

They came to look for him just as did the Germans. These were not soldiers, nor did they wear boots. They were in plain clothes, but the stern language was the same. My mother could speak to them because she knew Russian fluently. No, she didn't know where my father was or when he would return. Yes, she would advise them as soon as she heard from him. Fat chance!

Of course, we did not hear from him and had no idea of his whereabouts. He seemed to have vanished from the earth. Had he gone underground to become a partisan, my mother wondered? Was he safe? Had something befallen him?

"Why do you always fear the worst?" my aunt Bobble would say. "You need not worry," she said to my mother. Father was too smart, too shrewd, she insisted, to be caught. After all, hadn't he avoided the fate of his fellow councilmen?

It didn't help. "What about those who returned?" my mother pointed out to Bobble, "They were smart men, too." My mother always thought the worst. To her, disaster lurked around every corner. Especially for Jews.

What were the chances of a fugitive Jew escaping two enemies bent on destroying him? And where do you run in a world at war? Obviously, what my father needed if he were still alive was time, time to figure things out. To come up with a plan. Even Stalin had bought himself some time with the nonaggression pact. And Hitler also bought time by not having to open a second front by facing the Russians in the east.

If only my father would contact us. Once again, I found myself waiting and afraid.

3

The Mission

Two weeks had passed since the Russians took over Bialystok, and still no word from my father. A restlessness set in, and life, as I had known it, had unraveled. Although my mother valiantly tried to mask her desperation from my eyesight, she was too emotional a person to hide the truth. In front of me, there were smiles and chit-chat throughout the day, but at night and behind my back the mood was somber. There were whispers and questions. How, my mother wondered out loud to Aunt Bobble, would my father contact us? We had no telephone, mail had stopped completely, and travel in and out of Bialystok was limited. The war had changed all normalcy, trains and depots were being monitored by Russian soldiers and its secret police. Even for a child, the atmosphere of repression was fully evident. In her reassuring manner, my Babba told us not to worry. But we did.

I don't know what time it was, but night already had fallen when a loud knock on the door came. It was Chaike London, a neighbor who lived several blocks from us and a close friend of my parents who would visit from time to time. She was one of the few neighbors with a telephone. After a brief exchange in hurried tones, my mother rushed out with Chaike. I watched them through the window as far as a thin crescent of moonlight above the trees allowed me to see. They vanished into the darkness.

My father had made contact. He called Mrs. London to alert my mother. Within an hour my mother had returned with the news: my father was safe. She had talked to him. And, as expected, he had a plan. He had made the only decision he could. He couldn't return to Bialystok, not with his track record of opposing Communism and now, no doubt, he was considered a fugitive from the Russian regime. Over the years his views had been extensively expressed in speeches and articles under his byline in the *Bialystoker Shtime*, our city's Jewish newspaper.

My father was born to Gimple and Faygl Melamdovich on January 2, 1904. Gimple was a carpenter who at an early age was killed when he accidentally fell from a scaffold. They had two sons and a daughter. My father's

20

younger brother died as a teenager. My father was reared in a typically religious environment. From youth, his left arm was frozen at the elbow as consequence of a severe bout with smallpox. But the infirmity was unnoticeable and did not prevent him from being extremely capable with his hands. He had inherited his father's dexterity and craftsman's skills. Isaac Moishe Melamdovich's life changed dramatically upon becoming a member of the *Skif*, the Socialist youth organization of Central and Eastern Europe, and the precursor to his eventual membership in the Yiddish Socialist Bund. The Bund, which remained his lifelong ideal, gave his existence purpose and direction. Although on the outside he appeared small and fragile, inside he had tensile vitality and the cachet of a banker who takes the long-term interest-bearing view. He was an excellent speaker who had more than a touch of dramatic flair. His voice was strong and assertive. It projected no doubts about his views or opinions. An independent man in thought and deed, there would be no compromise in my father's life at this juncture or any other. Looking back, I see a man striking a heroic pose, a man defending his beliefs in an effort to avoid the shackles he perceived as clamping down on him. He wanted no part of the barbarians from the east or west. His instincts were accurate, his resolve unflappable. No one, not from Germany or Russia, least of all some commissar or commandant, was going to run his life—or his family's. He was, after all, independent, emancipated, an intellectual, a nonbeliever, and a *Bundist*.

The Bund, the party of the Jewish proletariat, was a socialist Jewish labor organization that evolved in the late nineteenth century when the Czar ruled Russia with an anti-Semitic hand. Anti-Semitism had deep roots in Poland, too, often forcing Jews from their villages and hamlets to urban centers. And while many relocated and many more abandoned their religious lives, all clung to their Jewish identity. The Bund movement became the bridge from the past to the future. It also served to bring my parents together.

As Bundists, my father and mother leaned toward international socialism and abhorred communism. They supported trade unions and a Jewish working class that had a sense of its own self-worth. By rallying the working class, they and their colleagues argued, the stigma of shtetl passivity could be dissipated. Instead of religion, they believed in a secular and modern Jewish culture based on Yiddish as the language of the masses. And while my parents were fiercely committed to Jewish national survival, they dismissed Zionism—the return of the Jews to their historic homeland in Palestine—as a utopian dream that could not serve as a practical solution for world Jewry. In the Bundist view, Jews must remain citizens of the country in which they resided and join in the universal struggle for the rights of working class—irrespective of their race, ethnicity, or religion.

Instead of moving to Palestine, they advocated living in harmony and with equality within the world.

Although I didn't understand the entire Bundist movement until many years later, I was able to sense the intense feelings it generated in my parents. I will never forget being wedged between them standing rigidly erect at Bund meetings in Bialystok that opened with the *Shvue*, the Bund's anthem—an oath of allegiance. My mother held my hand tightly as she and my father sang, and I could feel the emotional choking that gripped both of them as they fervently swore never to forsake the battle on behalf of the working class. There among the mass of people with the decibels ringing in my ears, I knew something was going on, something big, something awe-inspiring, something eternal.

As an only child, they had taken me everywhere, and I was growing up quickly in an adult world. They brought me to the Bund meetings for a simple reason: I was being indoctrinated. I was the next generation being groomed to carry forward the torch, being prepared to enter the *Skif*. Alas, fate would not cooperate.

I was much closer to my mother, although everything my father did in life made an impression on me. However, he wasn't the kind of person you'd run up to, jump into his arms, and hug when he entered the house. My father didn't intentionally demand an arms-length relationship, it was just that, in this respect, his attitude reverted to old-world culture: bringing up a child was more the wife's obligation; the father's role was as a disciplinarian and a teacher. He was always the *melamed* and I, the pupil, which allowed me to grab the ideas of the man but never place my hands around the man himself. Thus, I don't recall having too many heart-to-heart conversations with him the way some sons did with their fathers. He left the doting and nurturing to my mother. She was fully qualified on that score.

My mother, Chay Faygl Barakin, was born on April 16, 1902, to non-professional parents. Her father, Nachman Leib, after whom I was named, died in 1917. He was a *Kashnik*, a grain merchant who owned his own store. My mother once related how her father would use bags of grain as a shield to protect the family when it was rumored that the Cossacks were on their way for a pogrom. She was the youngest of three sisters. The other two, Sarah and Bertha, emigrated to America while my mother was still quite young. The three sisters were, of course, reunited when, after our nightmarish journey, we arrived safely to their open arms in Brooklyn.

My mother had set her sights on teaching from her early teens. She succeeded in entering the Wilno Teachers Seminary, the most prestigious institution of its kind, and graduated with honors on May 28, 1926. It was there that my parents first met. They were married in Bialystok four years later, in 1930. From her youth, my mother was an ardent member of the

European movement for women's equality and rights and thus was a most likely candidate for the Bund, which espoused a similar philosophy. Like my father, Faygl Barakin left her religious shtetl ways of her parents, but remained devoted to the Yiddish cultural movement in Poland, immersed in Jewish literature and secular studies. Although an emancipated woman, intelligent, well-educated, and outspoken, my mother was the gentlest of souls. Extremely sensitive to others' feelings and exceptionally perceptive, she was everyone's favorite teacher. To this day, adult men and women come up to me to say that they loved my mother, their *lehrerke*, teacher. It was no different for me or my children. My mother was always easy to talk with and come to with one's fears and needs. Lehrerke always understood.

Still, there was a strong bond between my father and myself. It is from him that I inherited my love for the Yiddish language, as well as his tenacious commitment to ideals, responsibilities, and promises. My father also passed on to me an insatiable attraction to salty foods, particularly herring and sour pickles. The taste for pickles actually ran in my father's family; his uncle was a pickle farmer whose small tract of land lay just outside of Bialystok. My father sometimes took me there, and his uncle, whom I also called *fetter*, uncle, would take me out on a rowboat on a small lake to inspect where his cucumbers were being pickled. Wooden barrels loaded with pickles, salt, dill, and other spices were sitting in the lake in their brine waiting to be perfected for the market. We would row out to those barrels, open their covers, and uncle and I would taste them to see how close they were to being ready. I became a pickle connoisseur at a very tender age.

But mostly my love for my father was based on respect and admiration. He was a man who deserved great deference, and, though he was an iconoclast, in my eyes he was an icon. He was the smartest man I ever met. I saw him not just as my father; he was a somebody, an important person who had an ideal. He was devoting his life to doing something for the world, for the *kehila*—the community—and for Jews and for Yiddish. The "mission." He was a self-assured man, honest to himself, his family, and his friends, and his advice to me was pure and simple: live for the greater good, never turn away from your mission, or your back on a friend. Most of all, never forget you are a Jew. My father possessed what scholar Irving Howe would later attribute to the Bundists who came to America: elan, combativeness, and sophisticated conviction. But even more than Bundism, it was the rich body of Yiddish culture and the language itself, as it is embodied in Yiddish literature, songs, folklore, stories and poetry, that became my father's first love.

With all its nuances and psychological subtleties, Yiddish was the language among Jews that immediately bonded them whether they were Poles, Russians, Latvians, Rumanians, Lithuanians, Germans, or from New York's lower East Side. There are few languages that can arouse humor and pathos with a single word, and Yiddish is one of them. Scholars estimate that only about 40,000 words were ever printed in Yiddish. You should hear Tom Sawyer with a Yiddish accent! To this day, in spite of Hitler's Holocaust, you can travel to the four corners of the world and still find someone to communicate with in Yiddish.

Yiddish, *Mamme Loshn*, "Mother Tongue," had become a language of the masses—11 million people spoke it throughout the world before World War II. Hebrew remained the word of the Bible. In America, Yiddish had aroused political impulses that were harbored in class resentment. Many German Jews considered Yiddish a "low-class" language, a ghetto vernacular that held back Jewish assimilation. There were even those among second- and third-generation American Jews who viewed the Hasidic waves of immigrants as a source of embarrassment. With their beards and long sideburn-locks known as *payess*, garbed in black caftans and phylacteries, they were perceived as a group of Yiddish-speaking medieval throwbacks practicing an ancient religion in Hebrew. But the Bundists from Poland, Lithuania, and Russia had been the socialists and social democrats involved in the Russian revolutions of 1905 and 1917. And their language was Yiddish. They refused to use Hebrew, opposed Zionism, and behind a new Enlightenment pushed for secularism. Most were agnostics.

Most important, they had a vision on behalf of humankind. My parents wanted me to carry this mission and the Yiddish torch. The notion of mission would be reinforced several years later in Chicago when, as a 10-year old, I was taken by them to listen to one of the world's leading literary figures and famous Bundists. The lecture was at the Labor Lyceum of the Workman's Circle on the West Side of Chicago, the largely Jewish section of the city. The speaker was Shloyme Mendelson standing before more than 500 who had gathered to hear the great man. Reputedly, he was an actual descendant of the great Moses Mendelssohn himself. Many in the crowd were Bundists, but mostly they represented a cross section of Chicago Yiddish-speaking "intelligensia." There were teachers, doctors, lawyers, actors, artists, writers, college students, laborers, lowbrows, middlebrows, highbrows—people who still lived in Yiddish, revered its literature, and believed in the mission. The audience's attention was riveted on the speaker as if Mendelson had cast some kind of spell. In Yiddish, of course, the eloquent sounds of Mendelson's sonorous voice bounced off the walls and ceiling in a lecture that left an indelible impression on me.

"The only way to achieve immortality," he said poetically, raising his hand to the sky, "is to connect your life to something that transcends mortality." He paused for a moment. What was that something? I wondered. "And that something," he answered "is an ideal."

I could see heads around me, including my parents', shaking in agreement. If one connected to an ideal, a paragon, a movement—a mission—and devoted one's life to it, Mendelson explained, the ideal's inherent immortality would carry one with it forever. Certainly the founding fathers of American democracy had felt that way. Why shouldn't the Bundists?

Perhaps it was my father's single-mindedness to carry out the mission that got us to America. Windows of opportunity for escape were shutting tightly in the late fall of September 1939, and it looked like we weren't going to get out of the trap that Europe represented for Jews. My father's mission then was to save the family, and his first rule was to keep us together. In a world that was gearing up for genocide, where people were reduced to survive by how clever they were, to stay ahead one had to plan each move with the worst possible scenario in mind should things go wrong. Instinct became more important than intellect. Decisions had to be hard and quick. To stay alive, who knew what kind of Faustian bargains were going to have to be made? Years later, the insanity of the Holocaust would bring to memory a story by Peretz called the "Joy Beyond Measure," in which God trades the world to Satan in order to save a Hasidic rabbi. Perhaps that's what happened: for a brief crazy moment, Satan ravaged what he could before he lost it. And in the wake, the Jews who remained emerged stronger and more resolved than ever to carry on the tradition and culture.

The day after my father's telephone call, the information he had acted upon became public knowledge. The border between Lithuania and Poland was to be closed that very evening as my father had told us. The Russians were returning Wilno to the Lithuanians. There was no time to lose. If we were going to reunite, my mother and I would have to leave Bialystok that very day for Wilno. After that the borders would close. Lithuania represented a haven for my father. We packed frantically but lightly because my mother was sure we would be returning in a few days.

We said goodbye to my two grandmothers and aunt, all of whom escorted us to the depot, and boarded the night train. It was to be the last train out of Bialystok. We were becoming nocturnal creatures moving with ease in the dark. It was strange: Darkness, once a child's fear, now represented safety. It was daylight that European Jews feared more. We were running from darkness into darkness; our world was being turned upside down and we had to adjust, to move in shadows, through blackened corridors, along lightless streets, down murky roads.

The scene at the train station was pure bedlam, a madhouse of people loaded down with suitcases and bags, jostling and shouting. Where were they all going? Jews from small towns were fleeing to big cities, and Jews from metropolitan areas were in flight to rural villages. In reality, most of them would end up moving in concentric circles facing the same fate once the wheels of the Nazi death machine churned into high gear.

The train was packed beyond capacity, forcing some to sit on their luggage or boxes. We were among the fortunate who actually had seats and I was privileged to sit at a window. The trip, normally several hours long, took all night. There was no normalcy. The train moved at a snail's pace, stopping incessantly for very long intervals. I would wake at each stop and peer out the window, although there was precious little I could see in the darkness. I sensed that for the adults each stop was nerve-racking since no one could be certain the train would ever move again. Sometimes, the engineer would use the train's piercing whistle, screeching at something in the way; other times, shouting and angry voices could be heard; once or twice, there was what sounded like gunfire, but most of the time the stops were filled with silence.

In the morning we arrived. The Wilno station scene was a duplicate of the bedlam we left in Bialystok. Indeed, one could not be certain we had gone anywhere until suddenly I saw my father. There was his face among the sea of people who were rushing about frantically trying to catch a glimpse of someone through the train windows. He was wearing his *kapelush*, hat, and for a split second I thought our eyes met. I shouted to my mother, but our train was still in motion, so that by the time I could point him out, he was lost in a crush of humanity. It was a scene that kept repeating itself throughout the European continent.

4

Sugihara's Stand

My father had rented a one-room loft for us on the second floor of an old building on Straszuna Street in the heart of Wilno's historic Jewish quarter. The neighborhood was a warren of narrow streets pulsating with commercial vitality. Our street was within the city's butcher section. Its frenzied pace was a collage of scurrying shoppers, horse-pulled wagons clippity-clopping, and rickety trucks belching black smoke from their exhausts loaded with freshly cut carcasses of beef and veal for the city's butcher shops. In their windows hung slabs of meat, ladders of sausages, limp-necked geese and chickens. All week long a stream of blood from the meat ran down the gutters in a constant flow until Friday afternoon when the bustle slowed down in preparation for the Sabbath.

I had never seen a sight like Straszuna Street before or since. It captivated me. Our flat's only feature was a tiny terrace overlooking the street. It had an iron railing and just enough room for one person to step onto. I would often stand there staring at the scene below with its busy shoppers carrying their *koshiks*, shopping bags, its many butcher shops, its hairy-armed butchers in blood-splattered aprons wielding their cleavers with scalpel precision while they yammered in Yiddish with customers. There were no slicing machines. Instead, the sharp eye and steady hand of the butcher would saw off cuts of meat in perfect slices, each with the same thickness.

Over the centuries, Lithuania—the last stronghold in Europe against Christianity—had been pulled and tugged at by the Poles, Russians, and Germans until it became a remnant of its glory days when its domain stretched from the Baltic to the Black Sea. It regained independence again by taking advantage of the Russian Revolution in 1918 and proclaiming itself independent until June 1940, when the Russian troops took over. A year later, Lithuania would fall into German hands until 1944. Then the Russians were back in control again.

Wilno's Jewish population was much larger than Bialystok's, with nearly 80,000 Jews. In all of Lithuania there were some 155,000 Jews,

27

about 8 percent of the population. Nearly three-quarters were in the retail trade or industry, some 10 percent were in the professions, and another 10 percent in farming. The Jewish community was active and very visible. For nearly 150 years, Wilno was the center of Eastern European Jewish cultural life that traced its origin as far back as 1568. The city became renowned for rabbinical studies and religious lore that produced texts of the *Mishna*, the commentary on the Talmud, still in use today. In the nineteenth century, Wilno became the center of Jewish enlightenment and later a flourishing source of Hebrew and Yiddish literature, with Yiddish and Hebrew secular schools, and a diversified Jewish press. It was in Wilno in 1925 that Dr. Max Weinreich, and historian Eliyohu Tsherikover, and several other scholars founded the *Yiddish Visnshaftlicher Institute*, the Institute for Yiddish Research, known as the YIVO. The YIVO (since 1940 situated in New York City) has remained the conclusive authority on the Yiddish language, a bastion of Eastern European Jewish history and culture, a center housing Jewish historical and linguistic documentation, Jewish art and ethnographic treasures, a laboratory for Jewish scholars, and a scholarly publishing house.

At the time we arrived in Wilno in late September 1939, although there was anti-Semitism, as there was throughout all of Europe, Wilno Jewish communal life was still thriving. By the middle of 1941, however, that would change. Wilno and Bialystok were destined to fall into Nazi hands. The entire Jewish population would be herded into ghettos, their lives eventually to be snuffed out. By the end of the war, 90 percent of both Poland's and Lithuania's Jews would be murdered. There would be but 6,000 Jewish survivors in Wilno.

For a brief moment, normalcy returned to my life. My family was reunited. Soon we were visited by friends, the Manns, who lived nearby. They were Yiddish schoolteachers like my parents; both women had been together at the Wilno Teachers Seminary. Mr. Mann was a tall lanky man with a thin face. Mrs. Mann was considerably shorter and much fatter. The Manns had a daughter my age named Esther. Esther was about my height, slender, with chin-length, dark blond hair, and striking blue eyes. Although I had never made friends with a girl before and was naturally quite shy, Esther made it easy. The smile that lit up her whole face the instant we were introduced made me feel welcome. I had arrived with virtually the clothes on my back. Esther shared all her things with me from the start, and we became inseparable friends.

After about a week, my parents told me that because my father was safe here, they had decided it was best to remain in Wilno. They were able to secure part-time teaching jobs in a Yiddish school, and I was to begin school as soon as possible. This meant I would enter first grade under Lithuanian rule. The thought was terrifying until I learned that Esther would be my classmate. She shepherded me to first-grade classes that were taught in Lithuanian, the oldest surviving Indo-European language that closely resembled ancient Sanskrit. (To this day I have a little notebook scrawled in Lithuanian saved from that class.) It was to be the third language of my life, and one of many as fate carried us around the world. Once again, our lives gained some order. I attended school, and my child's ear began to pick up Lithuanian to the point where I could communicate in the classroom. Also, my social life began to expand as a consequence of where we lived. The backs of all the buildings in our block poured out into one huge courtyard. This became the neighborhood children's haven where all the kids would gather after school. Outdoor games were played, fights were held, and friends would gather to talk or walk or argue. In this courtyard, I learned about sex, about love, and about life. Here I began to mature. I even attended my first birthday party, held for one of my classmates, whose name I cannot recall. But I still have a sepia-colored photograph from that party. Seated around a table are a dozen children, wide-eyed and laughing, enjoying the moment. Most of them never had a chance. However, next to me is a young girl, Masha Bernstein, who, like me, would become one of the fortunate ones to find her way out of the trap. But not her father, Mordechai, known in political circles as Matvey, an active Bundist who was arrested at the last moment in 1940 and sent to Siberia.

Masha and her mother, Zelda Bernstein, followed a similar route to freedom as did the Melamdoviches, coming to Japan two months after we did, and to the United States via Canada in August 1941 just ahead of the ax man. Masha (now Masha Leon) and I remained good friends over the years. Our paths would often cross in adulthood as she became a reporter for the *Forward* in New York. To this day, she authors a highly successful and popular weekly column, tracking the worthy events and personalities of the Jewish scene. She never fails to mention my exploits.

Life had settled into a routine during the next six months, and just as I began to believe that things were normal again, fate intervened. The war was closing in on Wilno, and the city's life lines of goods were being squeezed along with the psyches of its inhabitants. Rumors of what the Germans were doing to the Jews and other nationals in the west had reached Wilno, striking panic in the hearts of Lithuanian Jews given the limited options of escape routes: to the north was the Baltic Sea already dominated by German submarines and patrol planes, and to the east stretched the vast Soviet Union.

Wilno's transformation began when Stalin had a change of mind in July 1940. He wanted Wilno back from the Lithuanians, and while he was at it, he took back all of Lithuania, along with Estonia and Latvia. The three

Baltic states were now in the hands of the Soviets, and they wasted little time rounding up thousands of politically suspect Jews and non-Jews for deportation to slave labor camps in Siberia and elsewhere deep in Russia. Surely my father and his friends were on one of those lists.

Overnight our world changed. Russia's reappearance dropped like a heavy drape over the city. Straszuna Street was no longer manic. Its shops and stores displayed few items. The pickle barrels and herring vats stood empty, the evaporated brine left a white chalky film on the inside of the containers. There was no meat. No butchers. The sharp smells that would spear the nose were replaced by the odor of abandonment and neglect. For weeks during the summer of 1940, hoarding became a way of life. Long lines for essentials such as bread and milk snaked around corners. If you didn't rise early enough and wait long enough, you'd walk away empty-handed.

Again my father went underground. He had joined the partisans in the forests outside of Kovno (Kaunas), about 80 miles northwest of Wilno, leaving us in the second-story flat overlooking a forlorn Straszuna Street. Our small terrace became a signal post. When my mother hung a towel over the iron railing, my father knew the way was clear and he would visit. No towel meant danger, stay away—someone was either unexpectedly paying a visit or an authority was grilling my mother on the whereabouts of my father. No one, my father said, could be trusted. In any case, the crude signalling system worked.

I remember the night my father left. He took me by the hand to explain why he was leaving and that he had to open my mattress. I surprised him by saying I understood. Once, after we first moved into our flat, when my parents didn't think I was in the room, I watched as my father made a deep cut in the mattress on which I slept. There I saw him hide what looked like some paper money. I never said anything about it. At first when I slept in my bed, I would be conscious of the money beneath me, but as time went on I forgot about it. Now my father told me, he needed some of that money. It was not much, he said, but it was all we had to save us from whatever fate awaited. So he explained that he had hidden the money there because my bed would be the least likely place a robber or the police would look. The money was still there.

Although life around me changed, my personal existence remained nearly the same. I continued to attend school on a daily basis, all of the courses remained the same, all of the children were the same. Esther and I hardly left each other's sides. But there was one big difference. Everything in school had changed to Russian. Once again I was learning a new language, my fourth, and I was barely eight years old. There was a children's Yiddish song we used to sing that went, "one, two, three, four, small children are we." Suddenly, the words changed to, "one, two, three, four, Stalin's children are we."

Like everything else in the world that was unravelling, Lithuania's precarious independence collapsed that summer of 1940. After last-minute negotiations between its leaders and Moscow, followed by arrests of dissidents who opposed the deal, on July 14, the Lithuanians voted to become the fourteenth Soviet republic. The United States refused to recognize the new regime, even froze Lithuanian assets, and allowed the old legation in Washington to remain. But that didn't help us. Lithuania's president fled, and there were some 12,000 Jews and other war refugees also scrambling to get out. We were among them.

The key was the transit visa. The escape routes to and from Poland had been cut off. That meant there was no way back to Bialystok to reach my grandmothers, aunt, and other relatives. It had been months since my parents had made contact with them. Now the only route open was through the hinterlands of the Soviet Union to reach the eastern port of Vladivostok. I couldn't imagine the distance, but after overhearing my parents discuss the prospect, I knew it was as far as the moon. But my parents told me Vladivostok was a place where ships sailed away across oceans to Japan, China, Australia, America. What they didn't tell me was just how slim the chances were of making it. What we desperately needed was a transit visa, a piece of paper that allowed a refugee to leave the Soviet Union and enter Japan in transit to somewhere else. (Ironically, two years later, the Hollywood mythmakers would use the transit visa, or "letters of transit" they called them, as a dramatic device in the classic Bogart movie *Casablanca*.)

In late July, there was more drama tied to the transit visa being played out on the streets of Kovno than any screenwriter could conjure up. My father played his role solo but gave his wife and son a word-for-word, moment-to-moment description of his fears and dangers, his exploits, and encounters, as he struggled with fate and the hand he was dealt.

Every day for weeks, my father would steal into Kovno to find himself milling among hundreds of Jews in front of the Japanese consulate. There was a collective exhaustion outside, and as I learned years later, inside as well. It was a desperate scene: infants coddled in the arms of mothers, young boys nervously moving in place, sullen-faced men with their arms draped over the chest-high fence surrounding the consulate. It was a crowd of despair, but not a hostile one.

Like everyone else, Isaac Moishe Melamdovich was hoping to squeeze through some bureaucratic crack for a dash at freedom. Perhaps he was too frightened—or dazed—to be angry. Even my philosophic father couldn't explain how a person's life was reduced to waiting in line for a slip of paper that could mean the difference between living and dying.

The crowd began to form at 5:00 A.M. Less than an hour later, the quiet street was choked with jostling bodies as it had been at the train station in Wilno and in Bialystok the night my father left. Now the only hope was Japan's consul general in Lithuania, a 40-year-old soft-spoken man named Chiune (Sempo) Sugihara. When Sugihara peered from behind the curtained windows of the consulate that morning and saw the crowd below, he was shaken. So shaken, in fact, he woke his wife and three children and hid them in a closet. He feared the crowd would storm the consulate, but soon realized there was no danger. It was the typical crowd in Europe at the time, made up of individuals who seemed as if they were about to fray. Although I didn't witness it, by accounts written years later, including Sugihara's own memoirs, I learned there were those in the crowd who tried to climb over the fence, and others who put their palms together in a prayerful gesture when they saw Sugihara as if they had gazed upon a divine vision. They showed no self-pity or sentimentality because they couldn't afford to break down. But their drive to escape bordered on ferocity as they lined the streets, waiting for days outside the Japanese mission.

With so many lives at stake, Sugihara knew something had to be done, but he was caught in a dilemma: the choice between conscience and duty. In a world where duty already had taken precedence over conscience, Sugihara showed extraordinary courage. Beginning July 31, 1940, and over the next 28 days, he defied his government by issuing transit visas to Jews. My father, along with the other applicants, pleaded his case before Sugihara. He never told me what was said. But it made no difference what rationale was given, my father later explained, because Sugihara wasn't making judgment calls on individual cases. The pleas were passionate; the analysis dispassionate. No one had to tell Sugihara the sky was falling. He could see it in the bloodshot eyes of the applicants, hear it in their hoarse voices, and read it in the cable traffic from Tokyo.

There was no bickering or arguing. If you were a Jew, that's all that mattered to Sugihara because he knew full well the fate of all European Jews. Should he fail in obtaining a visa, my father saw only one possibility left: to become partisans. My father was prepared to take his chances as a guerrilla fighter on the run in the Lithuanian wilds with his family rather than join the Red Army and leave us behind or be herded by the Nazis and cooped up in some Jewish quarter with death waiting on the doorstep. I tried to imagine my parents toting rifles—the notion shouldn't have been that far-fetched given the fact that it was Bund members led by Leon Feiner, head of the underground Jewish Socialist Bund movement, who organized the Jewish resistance movement and the fight-until-death uprising in the Warsaw Ghetto in April 1943. Similar Ghetto uprisings led by Bundists, Zionists, and members of other Jewish organizations, occurred throughout the cities of Poland. In Bialystok, the Ghetto uprising, led by Mordecai Tanenbaum, Adek Rureks, and Daniel Moshkovitch, reached its high point in August 1943.

After the war, I remember the emotional meeting of my parents and Feigele Peltel-Miedzyrzecki (now Vladka Meed) at our Chicago apartment at 3210 West Haddon. Under her assumed Polish name, Vladka, at the age of 17, she had achieved fame as one of the heroes of the underground movement, smuggling weapons to the Jewish Fighting Organization in Warsaw, helping Jews escape from the ghetto, and acting as a courier and resistance organizer. Upon meeting Vladka, my mother, Faygl Melamdovich, confided to me that Vladka was her personal heroine. How close we were to that fate. Vladka now lives in New York with her husband, Benjamin Meed, who became one of the founders of the United States Holocaust Memorial Museum and is president of the Association of Holocaust Survivors.

The pressure on Sugihara was inordinate. The Jewish refugees had learned about the Japanese transit possibility from the Honorary Dutch Consul, Jan Zwartendijk, who was the only other foreign diplomat willing to help the Jews. Zwartendijk continued to issue visas to Dutch territories such as Curacao even after Holland was occupied by Germany in May 1940. But you couldn't get to Curacao except via Japan.

Several times, Sugihara cabled his government for permission to issue visas. Each time the response was in the negative: *"Concerning transit visas requested previously Stop. Advise absolutely not to be issued to any traveler not holding firm end visa with guaranteed departure ex Japan Stop. No exceptions Stop. No further inquires expected Stop. K Tanaka Foreign Ministry Tokyo."*

The reason was obvious. The Tripartite Pact between Japan, Germany, and Italy was in the process of being completed, and the Japanese Foreign Ministry would not consider anything that would upset the Germans. Helping Jews was high on that list. The Pact was finally signed on September 27, 1940.

Sugihara was in anguish. He canvassed his family at the consulate, which consisted of his wife Yukiko, her younger sister, Setsuko Kikuchi (who was nanny to the children), and their three sons, five-year-old, Hiroki, three-year-old, Chiaki, and three-month old, Haruki. The family was unanimous in urging him to help the Jews. He searched his soul and made up his mind. He told his wife, "I may have to disobey my government, but if I don't, I will be disobeying God." His decision to defy his government orders became known in Japanese Foreign Ministry circles as the "incident in Lithuania."

But first it was necessary that he get a travel permit from the Soviets to let the refugees pass through Russia. He had already received instructions from the Russian government to close his consulate doors. But unless the refugees were permitted to ride the trains across Siberia to Vladivostok, they could never get to Japan. Sugihara personally went to negotiate for the Jews. He impressed the Soviets with his ability to speak near-perfect Russian. But what clinched a favorable decision is when the Russians realized they could charge the Jewish refugees more than double the fare and pocket the difference.

The next morning, at dawn, Sugihara addressed the Jewish throngs waiting outside: "I'll issue visas to each and every one of you to the last, so please wait patiently." It was a magical moment as word passed through the crowd. People began rejoicing as they hugged and kissed one another while others looked toward the sky in silent thanks. Then in a hurried and harried state, with the help of his family and staff, and even some of the refugees who pitched in, Sugihara began issuing visas, literally scrawling them out day and night. He lost weight, became exhausted. But he kept writing the visas.

The number of visas issued is uncertain, but Sugihara tried to issue 300 each day. An entire family could travel on a single transit visa. Thus, historians have since credited him with saving the lives of over six thousand Jews in that frantic month of August 1940. The visa recipients included the entire student body of the *Mirer Yeshiva* which today boasts of a branch in both New York and Israel. From Japan the refugees immigrated to many parts of the world. A few lucky ones got to the United Sates. By fate, two of those families ended in Chicago—the Melamdoviches and Rochelle and Berek Zielonka and their daughter Julie, who was three-years old at the time. The Zielonkas had escaped the Germans by the skin of their teeth from Sosnowiec, a small Polish town 40 miles from Auschwitz. After receiving the Sugihara visa, they traveled the same escape route to Vladivostok. It wasn't until they were United States residents and their son Sam was born that the Zielonkas changed their name to Zell. Sam Zell is today one of the most renowned real estate entrepreneurs and probably the single largest private owner of property in the United States.

Even after he closed the consulate and moved to a hotel to wait for the train that would take him and his family to Germany, he continued issuing visas. As the train he was on moved slowly out of the station, Sugihara managed to hand out yet more visas through the open window to the refugees. Unfortunately, it still wasn't enough. Hundreds on the platform without visas watched their last hope pulling away. He would later recall his words as he bowed to them. "Please forgive me," he said, "I can't write any more. I will pray for your safety."

Forty years after the war was over Sugihara would tell a reporter he acted out of humanity. For his defiance, what could his government do to him? Fire him and call him back to Japan. A small price, he reasoned, for saving lives. But he wasn't dismissed, not immediately anyway. He remained a diplomat during the course of the war, serving in various posts that included Berlin. On January 18, 1985 the *Yad Vashem* Memorial Museum in Israel gave Sugihara a medal and a citation naming him one of the "Righteous Heroes" who saved Jews during the Holocaust. He was similarly honored by the United States Holocaust Museum. The most celebrated among this elite group of non-Jews are Raoul Wallenberg and Oscar Schindler.

We received our transit visa to Japan on August 31, 1940. The cost of securing the transit visa was an administrative fee of only one American dollar, the price of a lottery ticket today. But the odds of escaping were as great as any lottery. The visa was no guarantee to freedom. It was a one-way ticket bounding and bouncing on a tightrope without a safety net, and there was a catch: no one left Stalinist rule without explicit permission. To do so, my parents had to decide whether to apply in the only way possible—as refugees with a visa to Japan, running from the Nazis. The danger was very real; there was a saying that went around in Wilno among the refugees, "A visa from the Russians is a one-way passport to Siberia." If in the confusion of those chaotic days, the Bolshevik official reviewing the Melamdovich application *did not* catch onto the fact that this applicant was Isaac Melamdovich, the anti-communist rabble-rouser, and that we were really from Bialystok—running not from German but from Russian rule—then permission might be granted. My father had shaved his head completely in an attempt to change his appearance on the photograph necessary for the Russian application form. If the truth was discovered, my father and his family would be arrested as political prisoners to end up either in some Siberian gulag or in a Wilno prison that was soon to be snared by the Germans. After a great deal of soul-searching, during which my parents even consulted me, we agreed to take the gamble. There were no alternatives.

My father once again took to hiding in the outskirts of Kovno, and my mother and I remained in Wilno to await our fate. Every Friday the Russian Foreign Department would announce the names of those to whom permission to leave was granted. With fear and hope in her heart, each week my mother took me by hand to the Russian Ministry to read the list of names posted. Each week we left discouraged, only to return the following Friday. The process lasted four and a half months. When our name at long last appeared, the joy was beyond words. At last we had our chance. But our euphoria had to be checked; freedom was still a long and treacherous way off.

First we had to travel by train from Wilno to Moscow, where we would again be at risk from the authorities, then cross a daunting frontier on the Trans-Siberian Railway. After the 6,000 mile journey to Vladivostok, there would be more authorities to deal with and more questions about who we were and where we were going. And why? At any point in the journey, my father could be stopped and arrested. In every minute along the way, we lived a year.

Up against time, people, distance, and a relentless enemy set upon destroying us, we were banking on being swallowed up by the motherland like Russia's generals when Napoleon invaded. They would do it again when Hitler broke his pact with Stalin and attacked the Soviet Union on June 22, 1941.

Just days after the German invasion of Russia, Jews began to be slaughtered by Lithuanians, White Russians, Poles, and Ukrainians under Nazi orders. In Kovno, 10,000 Lithuanian Jews, one-third of the Jewish population, were rounded up, taken into the fort overlooking the hills of Kovno, and shot by German murder squads. By mid-July 1941, nearly half of the Jewish population of Wilno—some 20,000 people perished. Among them were Esther and her family. It was only the beginning.

Several days after permission to leave Russia was granted, my father risked returning to Wilno in order to arrange our departure. There were plans to be made. When I left Bialystok, it was so sudden there was hardly any time to say goodbye. Besides, my mother had told everyone that it was only a temporary separation. But we knew this time our departure would be permanent. However, since it was impossible to place any calls to Bialystok, we instead left word with everyone in Wilno to pass on our good wishes and love. We also said our goodbyes to our Wilno friends, particularly to the Manns. I remember telling Esther that I was confident we would see each other again—as grown-ups. The Germans made certain that Esther would never grow up.

Our world was flying apart like a disintegrating galaxy, and now we were defectors, immigrants, people who no longer had personal ties to Europe and, if we made it to Japan, were destined to fade in the anonymity of a new and strange culture.

After we boarded the train for Moscow, we became like a troupe of actors performing improvisation in that there was no script and we were reinventing ourselves from moment to moment. And like actors we became impersonators, hiding behind whatever facade fit the circumstance. Yet with each turn of events, there was a faint hope that somehow we could gain control of our lives. But that is all it amounted to, a flicker of a chance that was quickly snuffed out. The strange thing was that everybody was acting. The whole world seemed like a tilted stage on which the lights had gone out, plunging the actors into darkness and confusion as they bumped into one another, groping for some director to enter and reset the scene. It could be lonely on the run. And while I never felt as I imagined an orphan to feel, there were times I felt like a loner in the universe, despite my parents always being near—like falling into a dream and forgetting where I was. But this feeling of disengagement never lasted long.

And so there came a sense of displacement as each experience was to bring with it a concomitant loss of innocence. The pulse of the times was coursing through me and I was gaining a strength that I could not understand during a dark period in history when the world seemed doomed to go to hell, a period no one understood.

5

The Bialystok Syndrome

The war had not yet reached Moscow. When I got off the train and stepped outside the station, I thought I had entered another world. The streets teemed with Muscovites and traffic moved in every direction. There were towers and spires and golden domes and gardens and plazas and blotches of red on tunics and flags. There were soldiers everywhere, too, the same kinds of soldiers I had seen goose-stepping along the streets of Bialystok.

There were rich layers of history all around me but I didn't realize it. I knew nothing of Nicholas II, or Alexandra, or Tolstoy, or Tchaikovsky, or the Red guards, or the Bolsheviks, or John Reed, the leftist writer and the only American ever to be buried in the Kremlin. Of course, my parents did their best to explain everything, but there was so much to take in. I didn't even know of Vladimir Ilyich Lenin, until I saw him in his tomb as we silently marched past his embalmed body lying life-like and fully uniformed in the Mausoleum built in his honor. The soldier-guards, stiff, stern-faced, and zipper-mouthed, reminded me of the lead ones I had once played with. My father took pains to explain about the October Revolution of 1917, and who Lenin was, adding for good measure that he opposed Lenin's views. But he respected him because Lenin had an ideal. He had been a man with a cause—a mission—that was living long after he stopped breathing.

The words hardly sunk in. I was too busy craning in every direction. My father explained that throughout its history Moscow had survived riots, plagues, revolts, sieges, and foreign occupations. He told me of the Mongolian Tartars as well as the armies of Napoleon in 1812. But I was more interested in what I saw before me. The city's sights and sounds had captured my eyes and heart, rendering me like a kid plunked down in Disney World for the first time. Moscow was massive: great wooden doors, chunks of stone, tall pillars and lofty ceilings, a giant bell, and a cannon into whose bore I could have squeezed my body. And those awesome and frightening red walls of the Kremlin. They left an indelible impression on this eight-year-old refugee. I often dreamt about those red walls in the nights that followed. Who would have ever have imagined that almost to the day 50 years later I would return to Moscow— this time as a conquering hero of free markets to be hosted within those very Kremlin walls by the successors of Joseph Stalin.

During our mandatory three-day Moscow stay in late December of 1940 as we awaited the east-bound Siberian train for Vladivostok and perhaps freedom, we had the run of the city, more or less. However, our movements were monitored by Russian *Intourist* agents who had made all the arrangements and who my father believed were GPU. We stayed at the Novaya Moskowskaya. And while I have since learned that this was no more than a third-rate hotel (and a fifth-rate hotel today) to me at that time it was a palace, with its mirrors and chandeliers, and carpeted lobby with overstuffed chairs. What most impressed me was the floor show in the hotel's pretentious ballroom to which my father treated us one evening in celebration of our impending freedom. It featured scantily dressed female gypsies, who sang as they cavorted about the stage offering their ren dition of belly dancing. But, of course, we weren't tourists out to buy knickknacks as a reminder of our trip. We were refugees, moving about cautiously. My mother's anxiety was unceasing, and my father expected to be apprehended by the secret police at every corner. For me, Moscow was a diversion; for my parents, it was a potential sinkhole. I was traveling light, toting a child's curiosity while my father lugged a fugitive's suspicion. As we pretended to stroll leisurely along the streets like other tourists, we never lost sight of the fact that the hangman was no more than a few feet behind us.

Finally, it was time to leave. We packed and cautiously made our way to the railway station. The closer we got, the more soldiers appeared. While Russia was not yet at war with Germany, it had already fought—and defeated—its small northern neighbor Finland. Stalin had taken a page out of Hitler's book by bombing the Finnish capital Helsinki in a blitzkrieg-style campaign waged in temperatures of 60 degrees below zero. Still, there were no traces of war like I had witnessed in Bialystok. Muscovites were going about their business as usual, and buildings stood tall and untouched.

We departed Moscow on a bitterly cold December morning. I remember the conductor shouting what I assume was "All aboard," the brakeman waving a lantern, and the train at first hissing, then picking up speed, and roaring. Snow covered the countryside, and within minutes the windows were glazed with moisture. It was a powerful locomotive, pulling a rickety chain of wooden cars that rumbled over narrow tracks. We had a small compartment to ourselves that could be converted into sleeping quarters. There was also a dining car that offered two sittings for each meal. We could afford tickets only for dinners. At various stops my father would get off the train and buy bread or milk or other foodstuffs for breakfast and lunch.

The trip from Moscow to Vladivostok was scheduled to take 10 days. It actually took two weeks. With every passing mile it began to sink in that we might never again see the world we were leaving. Still, we could not possibly know the absolute horror that was to unfold behind us. My mother often told me she never forgave herself for not taking my Babba along. But at the time who could know what our fate would be, and who could ever imagine theirs. There were rumors, of course; stories of Nazi atrocities circulated as fast as the Siberian chill. But Europe had not yet turned into the Jewish slaughterhouse it would later become. In late 1943, Heinrich Himmler, chief of the Nazi SS, sent a letter to Heinrich Mueller, chief of the Gestapo, in which he emphasized the importance of burning and destroying all human remains so that there would be no evidence of the genocide.

We were the fortunate ones, fleeing on a transit visa, frenzied hope, and a glimmer of dignity. At first it was a milk run, stopping at every village depot. But the deeper we went into Siberia—"sleeping land" its natives called it—the stops were fewer and fewer. Siberians knew what Muscovites apparently didn't care to know—there was joy in staggering space, providing you didn't mind battling the permafrost, the elements, and the emptiness.

Siberia—where the Mensheviks made their last stand before retreating into northern China in the 1920s—could freeze a traveler physically and mentally. Its vast stretches and solitude, coupled with the short winter days, made one lose track of time—like man's ancestors who lived in a kind of "timeless present" with a diminished sense of the past or future. In essence, our train was a sort of time machine transporting us backward in man's timeline. Clearly, Siberia was forcing us to live in the moment, despite the fact we—the retreating Diaspora—were speeding through eight time zones from the Urals to the Pacific. From Vladivostok, we were to sail across the Sea of Japan to Japan and, from there, to the far-flung corners of the world. My family's heart was set on America. Others sought to reach Canada, or South America, or Australia, or whatever country would let them enter.

Much of my time on the train was consumed staring at a landscape whitewashed with winter, my face pressed against the window like a picture locked in a frame. The birch trees that glowed orange in the autumn were now invisible, and I could have sworn the clouds were lavender as we moved through the lofty Urals heading toward Sverdlovsk, Omsk, Irkutsk, Khabarovsk; cities I could not then pronounce. While passing a frozen wasteland just after Omsk, the Melamdoviches, together with the other kindred refugees on our Siberian express, quietly welcomed the New Year and silently toasted a better tomorrow.

With every stop throughout the nights, I was awakened by the jerking and screeching halt of the train. I would gaze upon the depot from my bunk and look at the people wrapped like mummies to ward off the cold. Siberians, or Sibiryaki as they called themselves, were a hardy bunch. They grew their own vegetables, picked berries in the forests, and ice-fished. Patriotic Russian writers had lauded the Siberian way of life for its close ties to nature.

When I wasn't surveying the landscape, I focused on my father's chess games with fellow passengers, careful not to interrupt him with questions until a game was over. By the time we would reach Japan, to my father's astonishment, I could play the game. At other times, he would tutor me, mostly in mathematics. Being the mathematician-teacher he was, he thought I could learn quicker with practical application. He taught me, for instance, how to convert degrees Fahrenheit to centigrade by subtracting 32 degrees, then multiplying by five and dividing by nine. He would draw scales and graphs and lines to make a point. Both Fahrenheit and centigrade, we figured out together, converge at 40 degrees below zero.

With this exercise my father was preparing me for our visit to Birobidzhan. Practically in the middle of Siberia, about 300 miles north of Manchuria, Birobidzhan's temperature, it was rumored, was so cold that a person's breath could instantly become an icicle upon exhaling. There was constant danger of frostbite, and at that temperature a stiff wind could freeze eyelids shut.

This ice city, where the Biro and Bidzhan Rivers met, had been a gift of the Russian government to its Jewish denizens. Here, they were told, they could create their own subzero paradise. Indeed, there was a community of Jewish poets, authors, journalists, and professors who had been exiled to Birobidzhan. Many among this disaffected group, however, believed it was a far better option than ending up in the frozen grips of a gulag, or labor camp, for which Siberia had become synonymous. (Stalin had sent 17 to 25 million people to these camps from 1928 until his death in 1953. But the system's horrors didn't reach the West until the 1970s with Aleksandr Solzhenitsyn's *Gulag Archipelago*.)

By the time our train pulled up to the Birobidzhan station, my parents had wrapped me like the mummies I had seen at depots along the way. Besides a heavy coat, a hat, and boots, my face and nose were covered by scarves with a small opening left for my mouth. A contingent of Jewish people we didn't know waited to greet us. They had gotten word a train-load of Jewish immigrants were passing through and they wanted to know about relatives and what was happening in the war. The temperature that night was minus 40 degrees Fahrenheit and centigrade—and dropping. (I'm sure the howling wind made it colder, but who knew from chill factors back then.) The scales notwithstanding, it was frigid. As we stepped out onto the platform, I was stunned by the blast of air that seeped through every fiber on my body. The rumor was true. I could see it with my own eyes; my breath had turned to tiny droplets of ice.

We milled inside the station for about an hour. It was a bittersweet reunion. We intermingled with *landsleit*—fellow countrymen, fellow Jews— whom we had met for the first time. But there was instant rapport and a festive mood. People were laughing, smoking cigarettes, and drinking hot tea. The Birobidzhaner were hungry for news, any news about the real world, the world from which they were exiled. I lost count of the number of friendly pats I received on my head from the adults. As we were leaving, a certain sadness struck me over the thought that they would be left behind like our family and friends in Bialystok and Wilno. But in Birobidzhan, they struggled against a different enemy—the cold. This was hardly a land for dreamers. Or maybe it was. How else could one get through long winters without untying the melancholy knots of the mind? Back aboard the train, it felt like the tropics. I suppose to the average Birobidzahian, minus 20 degrees was a balmy day. I have never forgotten the chill of that evening, and whenever I've been cold since, Birobidzahn comes to mind.

We arrived in Vladivostok on a cold, windy morning. Founded in the nineteenth century by Russian sailors, Vladivostok was built on a series of hills overlooking a bay. Life in Vladivostok centered around its port, which was the largest in eastern Russia. The great Russian playwright Anton Chekhov had worked in a museum there. And the streets had the same kind of hustle that I had seen in Moscow. I find it no small irony that today Vladivostok boasts of an international stock exchange containing the most modern trading floor in all of Russia, located in the cavernous hall intended to house the regional archives of the Soviet Communist Party.

Carrying all our belongings in three suitcases and a number of little cases and packages, a freezing wind ripping at our clothes, the three of us walked the length of the train to the Vladivostoker *vagsall*, the station house. My family along with the other refugees stood in endless lines to be processed in the large and smell-ridden depot at the end of a dock. The place was bedlam. But refugees get used to being crowded and squeezed into small spaces. It was an endless wait, and people sat on their baggage, on the floor. Immigration officers searched each bag as if they were looking for gold. As it turned out, they were. They would search for valuables and confiscate them in the name of security—their own. Once the immigrants got wind of the shakedown taking place, they became inventive.

Yosef and Lola Brumberg, close family friends and Bundistn, came up to my parents with a request. Their son, Amik, who had just turned 13, owned a gold watch. The Brumbergs were certain he would be searched and that the watch would be found and confiscated. They were hopeful, however, that little children might not be searched. Would my parents ¬gree to let me wear the watch? My father acquiesced. The worst thing that could happen is that the watch would be taken away. Amik quickly placed his watch on my wrist, gave me a pat, and went back to sit on his bags with his parents. I proudly wore the watch for several hours as the Brumberg's meager belongings were dissected. It was a big moment for me because I had been part of the Brumberg conspiracy—a huge victory for an eight-year-old child. The Brumbergs remained friends of the Melamdoviches all of their lives. Amik became an official of the U.S. State Department, an expert, appropriately enough, in Russian affairs.

We were still on Soviet soil, and losing a watch to a corrupt official was the least of my parents' worries. Up to this point, we were on a roll, but the wheels could come off at any moment. My father had depended on the confusion and chaos of the times to evade the authorities. Fear and propaganda had overtaken Vladivostok because of its strategic position in relation to the Japanese mainland. Japan already had bullied its way into China and Manchuria. Moreover, Soviet-Japanese relations had been simmering since 1905 when the Japanese soundly defeated the Russians in a war. It wasn't surprising that Soviet secret police were everywhere. Control was rigid. Just a few feet ahead of us, one of my father's political friends from Bialystok, who was also on a fugitive list, was caught and literally dragged away by the police. A frightened look overcame my mother's face. Disaster is about to strike us too, she thought. It was a nightmare to have come this far only to be captured by the Russian police.

But we got through the questioning and probing. For whatever reason, my father's name did not appear on any list. And nothing materially had been taken from us, which meant we possessed nothing worth taking. It was past one o'clock in the morning when we were permitted to walk up the gangplank to board the boat that would take us to Japan. The sky was black, the sea was black, and the waves smashed against the side of the boat rocking it violently. The icy wind was fierce, and my mother clutched my hand with one of hers while the other was wrapped around a suitcase and a package. I too carried something, although I never remembered what it was. My father, behind us lugging the other suitcases and packages, never uttered a sound. Inside the boat there was a peculiar smell; it was, after all, a Japanese junk. It was a small vessel but because of the darkness I didn't realize how small. I also never knew when we left; all I wanted to do was sleep. We all laid down on straw mats in the hold of the

Japanese boat, together with a dozen or so other passengers. It was to be our community bedroom.

It was a wooden tub, my father said. A wooden tub that was never meant to haul human cargo. For the next three days it groaned and creaked and the horizon never stood still. We were at the mercy of the sea as we had been at the mercy of the cold. The relentless waves leaped high above the bow, drenching every inch of the deck. I awoke to the sight of scores of passengers vomiting into buckets, and the stench was gagging. My mother took me up on the narrow deck for air, and there were more heads hanging over the railing. I don't know why, but I never got sick.

We reached Tsuruga, a tiny port just north of Kyoto, a bit groggy. But the agony of the rough crossing was replaced by sheer joy. Suddenly we were free. We had escaped the Germans and the Russians. We had survived Siberia and the sea. The fear that I sensed from my father and mother in Wilno, in Moscow, on the train, and in Vladivostok had dissipated in the salt air. Now instead there was an odd sense of wonderment. There were snow-covered mountains like in Europe. But that's where the similarity ended. I was somewhat disoriented, truly a stranger in a strange land—like a left-hander in a right-handed universe. People in straw hats walked around pushing snow with funny brooms. They seemed so short. The language was fiercely strange to my European-Yiddish ear. The buildings were strange, too, so unlike those of Eastern Europe that were fancy and tall, built of stone with columns and porticos. Most Japanese structures—more delicate in decoration if less monumental in scale—were made of wood, with paper walls and wooden walkways and delicate gardens. In contrast to Russia, where everything seemed enormous, this California-size archipelago felt constricted and fragile. Yet there appeared to be more order and a sense of more calm than I had felt in a long while. The imperial army notwithstanding, there was a kindness on the part of the Japanese people toward strangers from the West. It was truly remarkable. They were so considerate and friendly to us. As we departed down the gangplank, I heard some strange language pointed at me from some onlookers. "Japanese boy, Japanese boy," they snickered in a language I did not know. Someone later explained to my mother that I was mistaken for a Japanese boy.

It takes time to get into the rhythm of a system, whether it's a trading strategy, an organization, or a foreign culture. But by January 1941—less than a year before the Japanese attack on Pearl Harbor—time had caught up with us, and there was not a lot of it left to soft-pedal and massage. Of course, we didn't realize Japan was to become the enemy as it geared up to attack the United States. We saw Japan as a haven, not a prison; the Japanese as liberators, not captors. After all, it was by the grace of Sugihara that we escaped doom. Oddly, the Japanese saw the Jews in a different light from the fascists and communists: as potential allies with financial clout. Some historians believe there was a plan to create a haven for Jews in Japanese-controlled Manchuria in exchange for financial aid in helping to develop the region. A question remains, however, whether such a plan ever existed since it was never executed. Nevertheless, when other nations were closing their doors to Jewish refugees, Japan continued to allow them to settle in Shanghai.

It was difficult, however, for my father to reconcile the nation's natural jingoism with its Zen Buddhist emphasis on passionless calm to gain *satori*, the insight into philosophical truths. We were among a people who coveted inner peace and austere beauty, for whom the stark simplicity of a rock and sand garden held a mystical relationship, where tea masters conducted ancient tea ceremonies, where poets recited the traditional poetic forms *haiku* and *waka*, and where altarless shrines were built with space in which to feel. But for centuries, the Land of the Rising Sun had also been the land of the samurai and authoritarian shoguns, and now imperial order under Emperor Hirohito who bowed to the generals. By the twentieth century, Japan's culture had created a nation with a strong sense of community and collective mentality: it was better to play on a winning team than to shine as an individual star. That same sensibility would help turn a defeated Japan into an economic titan—"Japan, Inc."—in the decades after the war.

So far, my father had been remarkably right in his every move. If he had been a commodity trader, he would have been well ahead of the game. He had an uncanny instinct, a sixth sense, for making the right decision under pressure and in critical situations. He did it when he left Bialystok before the Germans captured us, when he refused to return with the Russian army, when he smuggled my mother and me on the last train out of Bialystok, and when he managed to get a visa from Ambassador Sugihara. He showed it again when we reached Japan and were confronted with yet another critical fork in the road to freedom. A decision had to be made about where to apply for a visa to the United States. The options were Tokyo, Yokohama, or Kobe. Each city had a U.S. consulate but the trick was that you had to live in the city where the application was made. Why did it matter? It mattered a lot. Our new friends who had arrived in Japan before us had a variety of opinions about which U.S. consulate, which foreign officer, would be more likely to issue a visa. First, there was always the question of who was more anti-Semitic, the eternal question for Jews on the run. There were also rumors about which foreign consulate favored single people over families. Then there was the most critical question of all: once in America, to work or not to work? One theory was that if you said you would seek employment, it was good because then you wouldn't be a burden on the state. On the other hand, there were those who claimed that if you sought work, it was bad because you would be displacing the job of an American citizen. And, of course, the theory you embraced determined the U.S. consulate to which you should apply.

My father ultimately decided to say he and my mother would seek employment. As Jewish schoolteachers, he reasoned, they couldn't possibly be displacing many jobs. Of course, given the influx of Jewish refugees to the United States, he had no idea if there was a need for any more teachers of his type; or for that matter, if there was a viable Jewish school system in America. Regardless, their application marked them as educated people who could become useful to society almost as soon as they reached the shore. They were teachers, and my father decided to capitalize on that fact. We had also heard there were quotas in various countries and that the United States was about to close its doors to Jewish refugees. Stories circulated about how the United States had refused to accept a shipload of Jewish refugees who were then forced to return to Europe. The odds were definitely against us. But they had been before and my father wasn't going to be deterred by that prospect.

The obvious choice was to settle in Kobe since that was the cheapest place for refugees to live. Tokyo was expensive even then, and the Jewish Labor Committee, the agency in Japan that helped the incoming refugees, could only afford to provide a limited amount of funds. But my father concluded our chances were better working through the consulate in Tokyo. Since we couldn't afford to live there, it was decided my mother and I would live in Kobe, and my father would become a commuter. He would move to Tokyo, a seven-hour train ride from Kobe, to share a room with two other friends, in order to establish residence and apply for a visa there. He would return to Kobe on weekends aboard what he called the Refugee Express. He wasn't alone. There were many others using the same strategy. And as in Kovno, there were thousands of refugees who faced a weeding-out process that seemed arbitrary. It wasn't a first-come, first-served basis. Nor did political asylum carry any weight.

We moved into a small one-bedroom apartment on the second floor of a wooden frame structure. We had no idea how long our stay would be, maybe permanent. A million people lived in Kobe, which was a principal port that shipped nearly 40 percent of Japan's exports. Its big rubber plants and steel mills belched smoke 24 hours a day leaving thick gray clouds to boil over the city. But there were rural parts of Kobe, such as the Tarumi district in the southwest where farmers cultivated terraced fields on mountain slopes and bred cattle they massaged with straw to produce leaner meat. Within minutes from the city's center were beaches and mountain ranges that were part of the Japan Alps, as they were called. The Japanese revered their mountains and made pilgrimages to them, but during the 1930s, few climbed them for sport.

By now I was used to change—quick change. In a matter of 18 months, my travels had taken me from Poland to Lithuania to Russia and finally Japan. During that period, I had attended two different schools, adding Lithuanian and a smattering of Russian to my vagabond's lexicon. Now I was to enter the International School where instruction was in Japanese. Another school, a fifth language to cope with. My parents had to cope, too.

As it turned out, our first linguistic struggle was with English rather than Japanese. My parents accompanied me to enroll me in school. The teacher was not Japanese. She was an American missionary, a Quaker I believe, who spoke fluent Japanese and, of course, English, as well as a smattering of other languages. Within minutes of meeting, my parents and the teacher had created their own Tower of Babel. Despite all the languages at their command, they could not find a common one to bridge the communications gap. Small wonder my parents were confused when the teacher told them to pick me up when the class ended at "noon."

At first my mother thought the teacher had said "moon," an English word she knew to mean earth's celestial satellite. But, clearly, it was impossible for class to let out when the moon came out. When it became clear that the teacher had said "noon," my father felt he had the answer. "Noon" is a letter in the Yiddish alphabet. But at first my parents couldn't figure out its cryptic use by the teacher. Then my father started counting. Noon was the fifteenth letter in the alphabet. That's what she must have meant, he reasoned. "We will pick him up at 3:00 P.M."

To her credit, the teacher actually waited with me the three hours after my first day's class until my parents finally showed up. Then the comical conversation between my parents and the teacher began again as they tried to straighten out the mistake. I could sense the frustration in their voices. It was right out of a story by Sholem Aleichem. After the shouting subsided, the teacher pointed to her watch and the confusion was cleared up. Sign language and symbols had saved the day.

Figuring out the length of the school day was the least of my worries. It was the length of my hair that really caused me grief. To conform to the Japanese school code, my locks were shorn to within a quarter inch of my scalp. But by now my parents welcomed a school for me even if it would have meant becoming totally bald. As my parents viewed it, a head of hair was a small sacrifice for a chance to interact with children my own age. They were right. It had been nearly three months since I attended a school of peers, since I had heard the shouting and giggling of children. Having been with adults for such an intense period at first made it awkward to deal with my new classmates. I easily could have withdrawn, but I adjusted quickly despite the language barrier. This wasn't your ordinary group of neighborhood kids. It was a class of foreigners who shared a common rootlessness. And our ages belied a certain sophistication acquired as world citizens. Their fathers were either part of the diplomatic corps, or business community, or refugees like us, and they came from Europe, India, Africa, South America, and the Middle East. In many cases, their families had settled in Japan for a lengthy stay. For my family, Japan was to be a way station on the road to somewhere else. But for how long, no one could say. It depended, my father said, on the right answers and paperwork.

Meanwhile, life became fairly routine. In an instant, Japan had transformed our frightened and freezing existence into a warm land of blue skies. No one was following us, no one was after us; instead, there were friendly people, colorful kimonos, wooden shoes, and so much to see. There were the Japanese performing arts, originating from ancient religious customs and Buddhist rituals to become the captivating *Kabuki* and *Bunraku* puppet shows. There was the wondrous trip up the Fujiyama, its volcanic fumes mysteriously rising from the top. The mountaintop included my first encounter of a genuine Budddah sitting benevolently in its holy shrine. There was the Ginza with its multitude of shops, its breathtaking bustle and foot-traffic, laden with kimonos of every color in the rainbow; beautiful women with their wide *obi*, or the short *haori* coat, or the *yukata* with its stencil-dyed patterns in shades of indigo. It was difficult not to be impressed and awed.

Once, in an unusual burst of enthusiasm for the unique new culture around us, my father insisted that we partake in some Japanese cuisine. Opinionated, set in his ways, and not much of an experimenter when it came to foreign foods, it was out of character for him to walk into a strange restaurant and order from a strange menu. Nevertheless, he did it, pointing to several items shown in pictures on the Japanese menu for a smiling waiter who spoke only Japanese. My mother sat there shoeless on a straw mat, tight-lipped, holding back a laugh. The pickled cucumbers and cabbage were familiar tastes. And some of the raw fish reminded my father of herring. We even got through the rice wrapped in sheets of seaweed. It was the rubbery little creature my father began chewing that turned his dark complexion to white and brought a quick end to our gastronomical adventure. Suddenly he looked like those people who had buried their heads in buckets on the rocky ship that brought us to Japan. It was the first time—and last—he ever dined on octopus. My mother had not touched a crumb. From then on, it was home cooking. There was plenty of salmon and tuna. And since Japan lived on rice and fish, so did we—as long as the fish had scales. Even in Japan my mother was able to maintain her abolition of nonkosher foods. For instance, only those animals that chewed their cud and had cloven hoofs were kosher, as were fish with both scales and fins. Shell fish were a definite no-no along with things that crawled. Eating kosher was the kind of ritual my father abhorred. But to his dismay, my mother did it, as did her mother, and her mother's mother, and so on.

Although my father vowed never to venture into another restaurant until he could read the menu, he still had a hearty appetite for exploring Japanese culture. This time we literally immersed ourselves in it. Again, my father took my hand, waved goodbye to mother, and the two of us went to a public bathhouse. The Japanese bathing customs had grown out of Shinto purification rites. But to the average Japanese, the baths no longer had ritual meaning. After a hard day in the office or in the field, they would use the baths for both cleanliness and relaxation. I didn't quite understand why we were there, because we had a bathtub in our apartment—but not as big or as deep or as crowded. I remember steam rising from the water's surface and the water at first feeling hot, unlike the chilling ocean that had sprayed us on deck during our crossing from Vladivostok. The water, we were told, came from thermal springs. With only a veneer of lather to hide our modesty, we plunged into the miniature pool, welcomed by an entire family: the father, mother, children, and assorted cousins. Yet another family jumped in after us. We washed and soaked in the same water exchanging glances and smiles for the better part of an hour. Communal bathing wasn't for everyone, my father conceded, but as he later explained to my mother, indeed it was a fascinating means of bridging the language barrier.

The Japanese, I decided, were the most courteous people on earth. One early morning when we were going to visit a friend, we got lost. My father used sign language on a passerby, showing the Japanese gentleman the envelope on which an address was scribbled, and asked for directions. Seeing that we could not understand the language, the man disregarded the fact that he was on his way to work, and stayed with us for the next hour or so until he found where we were supposed to be.

But there were unpleasant moments as well. One evening, as I sat by the window watching the people below, suddenly the earth began to rumble beneath me and the walls moved. It wasn't much of an earthquake and it did little damage. But it startled my mother who grabbed me and ran from the house. By the time we were out the door, the ground had settled. Furniture moved and what few dishes and pots we had rattled off the cupboard whose door had flung open. Beyond that, there was no damage. Just a quick scare, another threat to worry about. We had been told about the devastation of Tokyo that was ravaged by fire in the 1923 earthquake, and that we would grow accustomed to the tremors. Of course, our encounter in Kobe was routine and a full five decades before that city would suffer the catastrophic 7.2 Richter-scale earthquake of 1995. In any event, as refugees, we were used to being on shaky ground anyway. And besides, coping with Mother Nature could be a lot easier than coping with a bureaucrat who held your fate in his hands.

One Friday afternoon in late March, my father had returned to Kobe in a depressed mood. He told mother that the outlook was bleak for reaching America. Numerous applicants were being rejected, and Jewish agency officials told him to consider other alternatives. Perhaps, he suggested, we should settle for Shanghai where a Jewish community seemed to be thriving under the Japanese. We knew we had to move on, but didn't feel the desperate sense of urgency we had in Lithuania. While we still had no inkling that the Pearl Harbor attack was but nine months away, my father and his friends would often discuss the political tensions mounting between the United States and Japan. Such discussions always left my father with the same uneasy feeling: that people like us, swept up in currents beyond our control, were the floatsam and jetsam of war and what we did mattered little.

On Sunday morning, the currents unexpectedly shifted. We got word that we were to appear at the Tokyo embassy the very next day at 2:00 P.M. It was the prelude to receiving a visa to America. The long shot had come in. But here we were in Kobe. If we missed the appointed time, who knew what consequences would follow. The American authorities might even discover that we were not residents of Tokyo. My father panicked as we rushed to the train station. We took the night train for Tokyo and didn't mind traveling third class, packed like sardines all the way. We ate some fruit my mother had brought, and we watched the other passengers regale in rice, raw fish slices, and an assortment of vegetables in little boxes bought from hawkers at the various depot stops. We reached Tokyo well after 2:00 P.M., and I could feel my heart pumping as if I had been running up hill. I can only imagine my parents' hearts and the adrenaline flow. Weaving our way through the heavy traffic in a taxi, we arrived at the embassy, across from where the Hotel Okura now stands, a good hour late. I remember because my mother kept looking at her watch and giving time reports at five-minute intervals.

We got the visa. Try as they did, my parents could not hold back their elation, even though my mother thought of a thousand horrors that could yet befall us. To this day, I live with my mother's apprehension, which I carried with me from Poland to the shores of America and subsequently into my professional and private life. I call it the Bialystok Syndrome: take care—disaster lurks around the next corner! But on that day in Tokyo, we had beaten the odds once again.

6

So Long Japan, Hello America

For my parents and me, the light at the end of the tunnel had often flickered, but never failed. There remained a long voyage across the Pacific and then resettlement in a new country with a new culture and a new language. But that was weeks away, too far in the future for us to deal with. Our immediate worries were of a financial nature. In the face of war our concerns were economic, not military.

It was several days before we were to board the Heian Maru out of Yokohama. But before we could leave, we had to become financially solvent. At the time, U.S. immigration laws required that every family entering the United States had to have at least $50. By that standard, my family was destitute and had been so for a long time. Fifty dollars was a fortune. Thousands of other Jewish refugees ready to leave Japan for a host of countries faced the same situation. Like us, most were penniless and needed a stake of some kind.

Though I didn't realize it then, I was about to encounter my first experience with the black market of foreign exchange. Officials of the Jewish Labor Committee, the agency that helped newcomers and refugees around the world and had booked and paid our passage, hit upon a scheme to get around the currency restrictions and add to its own coffers in the process. A resident of Japan was not allowed to hold any foreign currency. With a valid visa, however, a traveler could exchange yen for dollars the day before departure. Dollars were a valued currency, and while the official rate was, say, 500 yen to the dollar, the black market rate was perhaps as high as 900 yen to the dollar.

Here's how the scheme worked: The day before departure, the traveler accompanied an official of the agency to the bank where he presented his visa as proof that he would be in transit. Fifty dollars' worth of yen was then withdrawn from the agency account, converted into dollars, and given to the traveler. Aboard the ship, the traveler would register with the purser by showing that he possessed $50. The purser in turn would log it to indicate that the traveler and his family wasn't destitute. And the matter was settled. The traveler would then slip the money to a "friend" who had come aboard to wish him bon voyage. The friend was actually a plant from the agency whose sole job was to retrieve the $50 and then sell it for yen on the black market at twice the official exchange rate. Such currency dealing between the official and black market rates of exchange helped the agency sustain itself—and the thousands of refugees during their stay in Japan.

As soon as we boarded the Heian Maru, my father quickly made his way to the purser's office. Behind him was the man from the Jewish Labor Committee. But the purser was nowhere to be found. And before we knew it a whistle sounded for visitors to leave the ship. The agency representative demanded the money from my father. "I can't give you the money," my father pleaded, "they'll come looking for me and throw me off the ship." Refusing to be foiled by a technicality, my father ran up to a crew member seeking directions to the captain's quarters. It was an emergency, insisted my father. He tracked down the captain as he was preparing to settle in on the bridge just prior to departure. By now, the whistles were more frequent and their sounds piping from every direction seemed more frantic in the ears of my father and the agency man. My father found the captain and plunked down the $50 as proof that he wasn't destitute—at least at that particular moment. Naturally, the captain didn't understand all the fuss over a matter that could easily have been handled by the purser once the ship was under way. But my father and the agency representative understood. This was a business deal and a link in a system that saved Jews. Every individual who was part of it had an obligation to ensure it worked. My father understood that. I, of course, was too young to realize any of this until it was later explained to me. All I saw was a man dashing about in a frenzy, a man who happened to be my father. That's what the captain saw, too. He dismissed my father's tenacity as that of an overly conscientious immigrant who wanted to start his new life in accordance with the law. The captain himself logged in the $50. My father thanked him profusely, slipped the money to the agency man, who left the ship with minutes to spare, heading for a black market money changer. And we were off, too.

The Heian Maru wasn't the QE II, but it wasn't the Bounty either. It was, in fact, considered a luxury liner by modest standards. My mother and I shared our own cabin and my father shared a cabin with another man. Our course was set for the United States, and the port of entry was to be Seattle. It was a long trip, my father told me, like crossing Siberia. There on deck looking out at the mighty Pacific, he turned from father to tutor, trying to teach me something about the world I was quickly growing up in. My father's scope of knowledge never ceased to amaze me. Reading was the key, he would constantly emphasize. But unfortunately we were no longer surrounded by Yiddish books and hadn't been for some time. So my father became a resource in my early travels that I never hesitated to tap. He was the "answer man" to my child's curiosity, turning my journey of escape into a journey of discovery as well.

He started with geography. We were, he explained, on the biggest and deepest ocean in the world; and that most of the earth was covered with water, and most of that water was salt water, the kind we were sailing on. I had seen the deepest lake and now the deepest ocean. Tides, weather patterns, ocean currents—he tried to squeeze it all into a mind already spinning like the earth. For a nine-year-old whose geographical boundaries were expanding exponentially, time and space were far too difficult to contemplate. But that didn't stop my father from trying to explain the international date line and how we would live through the same day twice. Like the concept of temperature my father had taught me, time was also an enigma worth considering.

Time is probably the one thing measured most, yet remains the greatest riddle. Maybe the guy who said time was nature's way of keeping everything from happening at once was right. I don't know. To the Buddhists and Taoists we had left behind in Japan, time was but a circle turning back on itself. For some, it is a healer; for others, it prolongs pain. It purveys wisdom, or as one philosopher jocularly mused, it is the best teacher, but unfortunately kills all its pupils. There is no way to outwit it, or to outwear it, or to catch up with it unless you're moving at light speed. Time—and timing— had been crucial in our race against the Holocaust. Into the two years on the run we had packed a lifetime, yet the notion of efficiency and speed wouldn't catch up with me until 20 years later when my life would be synchronized in the seconds of a futures trade. Aboard the ship in my child's mind, I had all the time in the world.

On the second day of our voyage, I met a youngster my age whose name I don't recall. And though we didn't speak the same language, we communicated through child's play well enough to spend most of each day together exploring the ship, making up games, and watching the ocean. A citizen from India, he spoke Hindi, and I, Yiddish or Polish. Our banter of strange sounds forged a traveler's bond that made us fast friends. We had scrounged up a chess set and I tried to teach him the game that ironically was invented in his homeland. The two weeks at sea was a happy period. And while we weren't passengers on a holiday, we were relaxed. The worst was behind us. We were all going to the United States. Everyone aboard had survived the ordeal of escape. The mood among the adults was upbeat, everything in the past was over, gone, and I had a friend. Oddly, it was a stormless trip, the sailing was smooth, and the salt air refreshing. For the first time in a long time, I heard my parents laughing. At what, it made no difference. We were heading for a new world.

We arrived at the Port of Seattle on April 18, 1941. I'm not sure what Christopher Columbus and his men aboard the Santa Maria did when they thought they had found the Orient, but they too must have jumped up and down, and clapped, and yelled with sheer joy like the passengers on the Heian Maru when the American shoreline came in view. We were, however, my parents explained, entering the new world from the "wrong" side. Historically, European immigrants enter the United States from the Atlantic and were processed in Ellis Island.

It didn't matter to me. Now we were about to become part of some vital immigration statistics. We were the Old World meeting the New World, anxious to become part of a dream that spoke to us of freedom rather than wealth. We had reached the land of capitalism, but without capital, hardened to the hazardous ways of the world. I didn't care that we had come from the wrong side of the world. I was glad to be here, mesmerized by what I saw and thrilled beyond words to be part of this adventure. Again I felt very much like Sholem Aleichem's Mottle in *Paisse dem Chazn* arriving in America, and, like Mottle, I was curious and proud, and full of the concepts that their friend Pinye had constantly vocalized—Columbus, democracy, freedom! "The land of liberty," he would say, waving his hands in praise of America, "where everybody is equal, no more poor, no more rich, hooray for Columbus, Shakespeare, and George Washington."

Was I really here? The land of milk and honey! Now it was our chance to trade in old ways for new logic. At last my parents could resume their lives as teachers. For me, though I didn't then realize it or even think about it, there were all the possibilities a new world had to offer in which to pursue private dreams and demons. Nor did I think of something far more profound: my parents had saved my life.

Being on the run at such a young age, I'm convinced, gave me the ability to cope with the serendipitous nature of life. It embedded a rhythm and pattern in ways I am just starting to understand. True, from Bialystok to Chicago was a long, and sometimes hellish journey, but for a child, it was a grand adventure, the kind that plants seeds somewhere deep inside that bloom later. Taking risks, living on the edge, adapting to change, understanding people, and learning to get around the obstacles grew out of those early years. There are some people who spend their entire lives trying to find shortcuts over familiar territory. We had covered three-fourths of the world, moving across continents and oceans without figuring out the shortest distance between two points, without being intimidated by lines and legends that scaled the distances in miles or kilometers. We weren't bound by parameters, neither the ones on paper nor those of the mind.

Now we were bound for our final destination: to join my mother's two sisters, nieces, nephews and cousins. They represented not simply family but were also our guarantors and paid the cost of the train ticket to New York. Another long train ride awaited me, across another continent. But, my parents assured me, nothing would again be as long as the one across Siberia. It was long enough. Four days and 4,000 miles. The trip aboard the Northern Pacific was overwhelming for the three of us. The scale of America jarred our senses, leaving us literally speechless most of the time. The people were different, so self-assured, so happy. Their eyes exhibited none of the fear we had become so accustomed to while encountering other travelers along the way. The train was different too: longer, bigger, faster than the one that crossed Siberia. Even the tracks were different. The gauge between the Russian rails was wider. Russian rulers knew that if Russia were invaded, my father explained, the broad gauge would keep locomotives and cars of other countries from being used there.

Winter still gripped the nation, and the snow-covered Rockies with their sharp spires and angled faces chiseled by the wind, rain, and glaciers seemed as grand as the Urals. The vast plateaus went on forever. The cities were different, as well. They were all so big. From Seattle we angled southeast to Helena, Rapid City, St. Paul, and Chicago, and then the final leg of our trip.

But nothing prepared us for New York City as we pulled into Grand Central Station where our family waited to greet us. Once again, there were hugs and tears but not the kind in Bialystok or Wilno. There was relief to go with them. We were together as a family, and everyone was genuinely overwhelmed with joy to see us. It was a moment of security I had not felt for two years. But it was the city that jarred my senses most. When I stepped outside of the station and New York hit me, I immediately felt dwarfed, as if something gigantic had opened its mouth and swallowed my entire family. I had seen tall mountains, but never buildings as tall as mountains. There was a rush of people, of vehicles, of noise. This vertical city was restless and neurotic, swaying to the rhythm of a thousand different cultures and faces to match. In an instant, it had cast its spell over me like no other city I had been in. It is a spell that has remained throughout my life. Sure, I was tentative and even frightened at first. But I was instantly in love. Here was constant wonderment; here was uninhibited strength; here was unlimited adventure; here was the pulse of America; here was freedom; here I could prattle on in Yiddish and be understood.

From Grand Central it was a quick subway ride to Brooklyn. My aunts Sarah and Bertha, my cousins Norman Tursh and Janet Isaacowitz, and the others, were unbelievably outgoing, embracing us and instantly taking us into their lives as if we had been intimate family members our entire lives.

To our amazement, there was a postcard waiting for us from my Babba; somehow she knew that we would make it to the new world and she sent us a greeting—or was it a goodbye? It was to be the last contact we would ever have. Two months later, on June 27, 1941, the very day Hitler recaptured Bialystok, both my grandmothers, my Aunt Bobble, and all our other relatives along with hundreds of other Bialystokan Jews were jammed into the *Groyse Shul*—the very synagogue my father refused to enter when he was a councilman—which was hosed down with gasoline and ignited. No one survived the inferno. We would not know of their fate until long after the war ended.

Everyone had come to meet us. I didn't know who they were but they were relatives and they loved us. We sat around a big table covered with a fine linen tablecloth, and our new relatives toasted our homecoming. Afterward, my parents began to tell the Melamdovich odyssey. To hear my mother tell it, she had held my hand for nearly two years. Then my aunt Sarah gave me a bag of potato chips. "Imagine that," I thought, as I devoured them with delight, "thin little *latkes* in a bag." God, did I love America! Later, my cousin, Norman, already in his twenties, became my personal hero. He took me under his wing until the United States entered the war eight months later, and Norman joined the navy.

I guess the warmth of the greeting we received in New York paralleled millions of similar greetings throughout time that refugees of every nationality—Jewish, Italian, Irish, Polish, and so forth—received from their families when they finally made it to the safety of America. It was genuine, unaffected, and spontaneous. Almost instantly I felt I had known them all of my life—a tangible lesson to a nine-year-old that explained why they say blood is thicker than water. Our families remained close from that day forward.

After a few days, we moved into a hotel with a Riverside Drive address. It was the international refuge for newcomers on New York's West Side hard along the Hudson in the upper eighties. It was a one-room affair, but it spared us the indignities of the waves of immigrants years back who had to settle in the lower East Side tenements along streets called Hester and Orchard. Back then, they were packed as steerage passengers and then repacked as residents using communal faucets and toilets and rooftops for children's playgrounds. But there was a trade-off. Most of the Jews who came to America in the late 1800s and early 1900s were not escaping poverty so much as persecution. (After the war, more Jews would be living in New York than in any city in the world.)

A few weeks later, now seasoned New Yorkers, we set out to pay a return visit to our relatives in Brooklyn. My Aunt Sarah and her two children, who had adopted us as if we were their own, offered to pick us up, but my father refused. He wanted to show his independence and skills as a citizen of New York. We would take the subway. By now, he boasted, he could read a street map of the city. We arrived all right, and spent a wonderful day with our family. Before we knew, it was night and time to go. Again, we were offered a ride home. Again, my father refused. We took the subway and sat back to enjoy the ride. But we were too relaxed. My father had made a classic mistake, and we took a subway that carried us to the other side of Central Park. When we came to the surface, we were aghast. "Oh my God," my mother whispered in Yiddish, "we are in Africa." We were smack in the middle of Harlem at 1:00 A.M. on a Saturday. It was a new world once again, this time completely black. It was the first time we had ever seen a community of African Americans. While we were startled by the sight, so totally foreign to immigrants from Europe, people were cordial and very friendly. There was no hostility, but much curiosity on our part. Directions were provided, and we retraced our steps to our hotel. That night we learned about territorial boundaries in New York and that there were pockets of culture within the culture.

Because my parents were well-known teachers, Yiddishistn and Bundistin, they were quickly welcomed into the social structure of Jewish cultural life in New York. There were innumerable get-togethers and welcoming events at which my parents brought fresh news from abroad. They would tell of our travails and encounters during our long journey to safety and offer an insight of Europe at war. My father would also publicly speak of the precarious nature of Jewish settlements that had been snared by the Nazis and urge the New York Jewish community to find ways to rescue those that they could. Usually, my parents would take me with them to these functions, and I would entertain the gathering with my Yiddish tongue because even as a little kid I could speak such "pure Yiddish." This was a rarity in New York. Unfortunately, Yiddish had become corrupted with an infusion of English words and anglicized terms. Always the teachers, my parents would mimic what they heard and politely correct the speaker whenever they heard Yiddish that was less than their literary taste could tolerate. They would sometimes repeat privately the so-called American Yiddish phrases they heard and laughed about them. *Lozt arop die vinde*, a totally corrupt Yiddish phraseology for "let down the window," was a favorite of my father's—the real Yiddish word for window is *fenster*. Yiddish in our house remained literate throughout our life in the States and, to this day, my Yiddish has maintained most of its innocent purity.

One particular night, when they knew they'd be out late, my parents decided to leave me at the hotel and I became the home-alone kid, left to my own devices, which meant listening to the radio then falling asleep by nine o'clock. In those days, it was a safe enough situation with neighbors just a few steps away in every direction and a 24-hour manned desk in the hotel lobby. There was little mischief a nine-year-old could get into. But just so I wouldn't panic in case I awoke to find my parents gone, I wrote myself a note as a reminder that they were out for the evening. It was a restless night. Maybe it was the traffic outside, or the honking of horns, or noisy neighbors; whatever it was, something woke me at 2:00 A.M. and my parents weren't home yet. I dressed, left the room and walked down to the lobby to wait for them but must have missed them when I wandered outside. An hour or so later they returned to find me gone and the note. It was the note that confused my mother. With the Lindbergh kidnapping still fresh on her mind, she fainted, convinced I too had been kidnapped. The police were called. I showed up at the same time they did. After that episode, my parents kept a close eye on my wanderings.

Perhaps that was the reason my parents enrolled me in the summer camp where they had been hired as Yiddish teachers. That way, not only could they look in on me, they knew the camp experience would help Americanize me. They were more right than they could have ever imagined. It was one of a number of children's camps just outside New York City set up for children of families whose middle-class background was theoretically close to our own. The campgrounds were sprawling and offered all sorts of activities and games. There were scores of children. I was placed in a cabin with other nine-year-old boys. The name of my counselor was Freddy. Although my parents were nearby, I hardly ever saw them. I was alone for the first time in my life. I felt abandoned and more alien than when I landed in Japan. Here were middle-class kids, healthy and happy, every one of them steeped in American culture, and every one of them speaking English, a foreign tongue to me. The children played all kinds of American games, none of which I had ever encountered; but most of all, they played baseball. The game was a complete mystery to me. They swam, which I had never learned to do. They wore short pants and high-top sneakers, which I didn't have. I was totally out of synch with the world. I was hurt and miserable. Freddy tried to help and teach me things, but it was difficult, and the other kids were impatient. I became the loner, the brunt of kids poking fun at the greenhorn who didn't know the difference between a strike and a ball. There were taunts and gestures, but I couldn't steel myself to them as some kids do with humor because I didn't know the language. I was totally vulnerable. And trying to fit in, I laughed when they did, which meant I was laughing at myself.

How could I have known that baseball was America's pastime and that practically every nine-year-old already could swing a bat, or catch a ball, or run a base path. I couldn't. To make matters worse, I was short for my age. I was the greenhorn runt who couldn't swing a bat. I cried every night.

And while my counselor understood my plight, he wasn't equipped to handle the situation. He would try to console me with words I did not yet understand. I couldn't run to my parents because I didn't want to be perceived as having favored status. Had I done so, now looking back, I'm sure I would have been pegged as a "mommy's boy." I was miserable and that was after the first week.

I grit my teeth and stuck it out for the two months of that summer. And when it was time to go home, I had learned a thing or two about American culture and the pain of nonconformity. But more important, I learned to speak in English. My parents were right. Somehow, in some way, the two months of harassment in English clicked. It was a crash course worth enduring. I even learned a little about baseball. My greenhorn status was dissipating quickly.

The one thing I never wanted to do again was to move. After traveling three-quarters around the world, it was glorious to find normalcy, where there was family, and where I had a chance to become like everyone else. Never mind the problems I encountered with the kids, I loved New York. In just three short months, I had become an ardent disciple of the Big Apple.

There were cities that grew out of specialization. Detroit ran on the combustion engine; Chicago was once moved by cattle power; Los Angeles sprawled by its dream factories; but New York seemed to have it all, as diverse a place as you would want. I was especially happy there, now that I could finally speak the language, my sixth in two years. If it had been up to me, I would have stayed there forever, but who can understand fate? A month after we returned from camp, we were packing again. My parents had been offered permanent positions as Yiddish school teachers in the Sholom Aleichem schools of Chicago. My father assured me I would love Chicago, too. I had little choice anyway. Shortly before Labor Day 1941, we took off for the Windy City.

7

The Chicago Connection

I fell in love with Chicago, but more important, I became an American in this city. We had moved to the heart of Chicago on its northwest side, across the street from Humboldt Park, settling in a third floor walk-up with one bedroom, living room, dining room, kitchen, and bath. Having lived in cramped quarters or on boats and trains for the better part of the last two years, our new quarters seemed palatial. I slept on a daybed in the dining room and was allowed to use the bedroom when friends would visit. It was our first home in more than two years. We would live in these quarters at Kedzie and Haddon for the next decade and a half.

By the time I enrolled in Lowell grammar school, in fourth grade, I had a lot of catching up to do. I had missed two years of primary education and, of course, knew very little of reading or writing in the English language. The kids knew I was a foreigner since it was impossible to hide this fact. Not only did my accent still give me away, my "greenhorn-ishness" was like my alter ego, which for the next several years would never leave my side. Everything was different and new to me, and I had to learn it all from the bottom up. Summer camp had taught me to talk in English, but camp life had not prepared me for life on the streets, in the alleys, in the park, or in school. The inner city of a large American metropolis is a very strange place even for people who live in its suburbs; for a foreign kid who had no knowledge of American culture, the inner city was like Mars. It has its own codes and mores, its own way of dress, its own do's and don'ts. Once again, I had to regain my sense of balance. Once again, I knew no one, did not speak right, did not dress right, did not walk right, did not think right. My next several years were often filled with a misery reserved for children who for one reason or another are outcasts.

And there was the special curse of baseball. It followed me from New York to Chicago. Sure, New Yorkers took pride in their Yankees, but the Chicago Cubs were also a hot team in the 1940s. And if you were a North-sider, you became cursed as a Cubs fan for life. (They were actually a contender and won the National League pennant in 1945. They have never won another since. But I suppose any team can have a bad century.) Cub fever is generational, and I have passed it on to my children and grandchildren. I had become a triple threat to myself: I couldn't hit, catch, or throw. Although I still hadn't gotten the hang of baseball, I began to understand its significance in the lives of my peers. Every kid had a favorite ballplayer he emulated—a Babe, a Joe, a Stan, a Ty. (Well beyond my teens I would view baseball as a metaphor for discipline, pleasure, and ambition—the same elements that give any job its satisfactory spice.) Once more, my ineptitude at the plate became a source of personal grief. I was taunted and laughed at. Although I often withdrew into my inner consciousness, somehow I never became rebellious. In my awkwardness, I grew determined.

If nothing else, my early experiences, truly alien from those of my peers, set me apart. (As for my first name, my teacher who was of Polish descent, instantly knew that it was translatable to Leo. But I remained Leibl to my parents, relatives, and their friends in the Yiddish-speaking community then and to this day.) Amid the scrap drives, and rubber drives, and bond drives, victory gardens and, of course, rationing, the war was everywhere. It was in newspapers, on the radio, on signs, on billboards, on movie theater screens. Some of my classmates' fathers were fighting in it. But in spite of all that, the war seemed so far away in America. I never quite got the feeling that Americans believed their freedom was in danger. It was impossible to explain war to children who had never felt the impact of a bomb that reduced a building to a pile of stones; or who had never seen masses of people fleeing in panic from armies that made no distinction between killing soldiers and civilians. Sports, not politics or war, held the interest of most of my grammar school friends. But as a child who escaped war's horror, I couldn't ignore it. My parents wouldn't let me. The war, the plight of the Jews trapped in Europe in the unfolding Holocaust, was a constant source of discussion during meals in our home. There, around our dinner table, growing up, my feelings about democracy and self-determination crystallized.

My parents' professional lives drove a wedge of isolation even further into my life. Though they provided a comfortable home, I spent a good deal of time roaming the streets as a youngster. I wasn't a waif who pandered to get by, nor was I a Dead End Kid from out of Hell's Kitchen. I was a "latchkey kid," the pet phrase of the 1980s that would later be used to describe the household of two working parents who leave their children to fend for themselves after school. Indeed back in the 1940s, it was an oddity to have two working parents unless they owned the corner ma-and-pa store. The Henry Aldrich (and later the *Leave It To Beaver*) model of a mother in a frilly apron pushing a vacuum cleaner around the house was the way people lived then. Even Rosie the Riveter would retreat back to the kitchen once the war was over. But that didn't coincide with my parents' view of life. My mother cooked and cleaned, but she also taught. Like my father, she was a professional teacher and wasn't about to let household chores hold her back.

My parent's workday at school began at 3:00 P.M., just as mine ended. When I returned home from school, they were gone. They were *melameds*— elementary school teachers—with a cause. It was far nobler and more liberating to slave over a class than an oven, mother believed. There was the practical aspect to consider as well. We needed her income, given the penurious wages of a teacher. My parents were not the type of *melamed* encountered in childhood by the immigrants who found their way to the *goldene medina*, the golden land of America. Back in their old hometowns of Russia or Poland, the *melamed*, who was usually a rabbi, taught the *Torah*, Bible, in a *cheder*, a religious school. It was a strict orthodox religious training, pure and simple. Beginning in the late 1800s and growing in number throughout the 1910s and 1920s, these immigrants fled their pogrom-ridden impoverished life of Eastern Europe. They came to America, seeking freedom and opportunity, and bringing along a deep spiritual and cultural heritage. Like my parents, many of these immigrants had left their shtetl ways and the idea that religion was the only avenue for Jewish identity. Although they maintained their ties to the Jewish faith, they were more comfortable with their cultural heritage, their holidays, and their Yiddish language. For their children they wanted more than the cheder could offer, demanding reinforcement of their separate identity as an ethnic group and not simply as a different religious group. The answer for them was secular Yiddish schools. In the late 1890s, the leaders of the Jewish intelligensia decided that it was their obligation to respond to these demands. At the international conference held in Tchernowitz in 1908, which included such literary giants as Scholom Asch, Abraham Raisin, Dr. Chairm Shitlowsky, I.L. Peretz, and Nathan Birnbaum, Yiddish was proclaimed the national language and schools were proposed to teach the children.

Two types of Jewish schools developed side by side on the American shore. First, the traditional Hebrew school, often sponsored by a synagogue, whose curriculum was the Torah, some Hebrew language, and precepts of Jewish religious practices. The second type, the Yiddish school, was totally secular and specifically excluded religion. Its curriculum included Yiddish language, Yiddish literature and songs, Jewish folklore, Jewish history, festivals, and holidays. The *melameds* of these schools were, like my parents, trained teachers. In Chicago, beginning in 1912, the first of these secular Yiddish schools was opened under the name National Radical Yiddish School. Many other schools followed, each representing a different sociopolitical segment of the diverse Chicago Jewish population that sponsored them.

Ultimately, two main Yiddish schools systems survived: those of the Workmen's Circle, the *Arbeter Ring*, and those of the Sholem Aleichem Folks Institute. The Workmen's Circle was a powerful national labor and fraternal organization founded in 1892 in New York by a group of socialist-minded Eastern European immigrants. Its purpose was to provide the working class with sick care (it had set up a tuberculosis sanitarium in Liberty, New York), burial service, and intellectual nourishment through civic and cultural activities in Yiddish aimed at clearing the worker's mind of factory dust. By the 1930s, the Workmen's Circle had more than 80,000 members, was a major force for spreading secular Jewish culture, and had promoted a chain of Yiddish schools throughout major American cities. But its strong ties to socialism brought a political flavor into the classroom that was hotly objected to by a number of academicians and intellectual leaders. To maintain political purity in the classroom, the Sholem Aleichem Folks Institute was founded in Chicago on May 25, 1925, by Jacob and Sarah Dubow, Dr. M. Brownstein, and Chaim Pomeranz, and dedicated exclusively to a nonreligious, apolitical literary curriculum.

The Yiddish secular school idea worked; the schools grew in prominence throughout the 1930s, 1940s, and 1950s, and continued their existence into the early 1960s. At their height, they included many schools in the Chicago area, a Yiddish *Mittleschule*, (a three-year high school), postgraduate study courses at the College of Jewish Studies, as well as holiday school-sponsored events, which included a citywide "third-seder" festival celebrating the holiday of Passover and drawing huge audiences from all over Chicago.

In September 1941, my parents became teachers for the Sholem Aleichem Folks Institute schools. My father eventually became the principal of its school system and its chief operating officer. For the next two decades, these schools flourished as they followed the migration of the Jewish population to the north side of Chicago. In 1962, together with Janet Faber Meyers and other parents who had studied in the Chicago Yiddish schools and now had children of their own, we led a successful effort to launch a combined offspring of the Workmen's Circle and Sholem Aleichem schools. The North Suburban Yiddish School in Skokie, a northern suburb of Chicago, was successfully maintained for the next dozen or so years. Many of the funds to run the school came from annual donations from my Chicago Mercantile Exchange trading cronies. In fact, the North Suburban Yiddish school had the unique distinction of having part of its budget covered by trading of pork bellies. For years, Marlowe

King, one of my closest trading buddies, and I maintained a joint trading account for the benefit of the school. Nevertheless, it was a struggle against a changing tide, and most of the secular Yiddish schools went out of existence some time in the early seventies.

Jewish secularism, Yiddish culture, and Jewish ethnicity in America would gradually be transformed; its original constituency becoming older. The Golden Age of Yiddish culture, Yiddish literature, journalism, criticism, and theater, which began in the middle of the nineteenth century and spread from Europe to the United States and South America, and reached a new high in the early decades of the twentieth century, was dealt a deathly blow by Hitler's march across Europe. The breach in its natural progression was as deep as it was permanent. Along with the six million Jews who were massacred, there perished the vast majority of authors, philosophers, academicians, and intellectual leaders of the Yiddish-based cultural movement. The intellectual foundation upon which the new secular culture was built had been decimated. It caused a dysfunction in the normal evolutionary chain of Jewish ethnicity.

And there were other factors. Along with the prosperity that followed World War II, there was a perceptible lessening of systemic anti-Semitism, and with it a commensurate increase in assimilation. Most important, the second generation of American Jews were taking over and with them came the State of Israel. This fledgling new democracy, born in blood, had a profound impact on American Jewry. Nationalistic pride, religion, and the synagogue would slowly begin to replace the need for a secular Yiddish identity. If a post-war immigrant generation—my generation—was going to change the world, it would have to do so in the context of the New World and not the old one. While my parents understood the sweeping changes swirling about the Yiddish community, their philosophy remained steadfast. Although they allowed some changes to enter their lives and their schools (Bar Mitzvah preparation eventually became part of the curriculum), they never embraced Israel with the same zeal as did the American Jews. They lived their lives surrounded by their books and memories of a fading Yiddish world, which they would devote their lives to sustain over the next 45 years. But like other first-generation immigrants who waited for their children to grow up to become lawyers or doctors, they waited, too.

And I waited for them. Three days a week after grammar school, I would attend the Yiddish school. The other two days, and the hours after Yiddish school, I was on my own to jog along the paths of imagination with radio heroes Tom Mix, Jack Armstrong, and Captain Midnight; or scamper through the warren of gangways between apartment buildings, and down alleys hiding and seeking and tagging with my pals—"buck, buck, how many fingers up?" Across the street from our house was Walther Memorial Hospital that flanked Humboldt Park, the neighborhood's backyard with its grassy hills, bicycle paths, climbable trees, athletic fields, and a bowl built (and accidentally burned down) for bicycle races. Often, I would spend time with an Italian family who lived around the corner. There were four children in the family and they treated me like a fifth. I also met my first boyhood chum, Jared Specthrie, whose family embraced me and with whom I spent countless hours. But mostly I was on the streets, and sometimes there were uncomfortable moments. The northwest side of Chicago was a melting pot of Jews, Poles, and Italians. For the most part, the kids of each ethnic group stayed with their own, only coming in direct contact with members of other communities during school hours. Although there was no overt anti-Semitism, there was often a beneath-the-surface feeling that sometimes would burst to the top. As kids on the street, we would inevitably encounter a "you dirty kike" from time to time. I had developed a give-no-quarter, take-no-quarter stance, forged over years of encounters with foreign cultures and foreign situations. Each new experience was a new challenge and a new source of potential problems. Each challenge was another lesson. I learned soon enough that to survive I had to stand my ground; that to back away from a taunt, threat, or fight was to invite still another taunt, threat, or fight. Long before I arrived in Chicago, I had discarded from my arsenal of defenses the idea of retreating or shrinking from a social confrontation. Thus, at each threatening encounter, whether in school, on the streets, or in the playground, whether over a perceived taunt, an actual offense, or a verbal slur, I instinctively took on the adversary and gave as much as I got. There was a particularly nasty kid named Louie on the block (everyone has at least one Louie in their lives) who rarely let an opportunity pass without some personal attack, either with a rock or snowball or with "hey, you dirty Jew." And I never let anything he did go by the boards—an eye for an eye. It honed an inner toughness, but it didn't make for a wonderful time.

Shortly after 7:00 P.M., my parents would return from school, and we would have dinner, conversing in Yiddish about our daily lives in America. But there was always the strong influence of our European past. The war in Europe, the fate of Jews in Europe, and the fate of Yiddish culture in America were their primary concerns. My parents did learn the language rather quickly, due in part to the classroom where a kind of lingual reciprocity took place; they taught the kids Yiddish and the kids taught them English. Somehow it was easier for my mother to accept American ways—she was more pliable, more adaptable. It was harder for my father—he never wanted to became Americanized. In his head and heart, my father really never came over here, and he was mostly European to the day he died.

My parents resided in a parallel universe of Yiddish culture, consumed by the secular Jewish life in Chicago and embraced by many organizations—

educational groups, political groups, theatrical groups, musical groups. After all, they were part of the intelligensia of old Europe who had been leaders in Poland's secular Jewish movement. Our household evolved into the Mecca for Yiddish cultural events in Chicago. Not only was it often the hub of whatever important Jewish secular activity was taking place in the city, it was the must stopping-place for most important Jewish dignitaries and literary figures who visited or lectured in Chicago. Drawn into a very active social life, shortly after dinner, my parents usually would be off to attend some meeting or gathering in connection with the Yiddish community. Again I was left to my imagination and my own devices. On weekends they would sometimes take me along, but on school nights, I stayed behind with a simple rule that I be asleep by 10:00 P.M., a rule I usually violated by listening to the radio until well past midnight.

When I attended various Yiddish cultural events, it was not as a member of the audience, but as a performer. The presentation would usually include a singer, a pianist, a reciter of poetry, a speaker on politics or social issues. Like stage parents, my mother and father would haul me before a group to recite poetry in Yiddish. The poetic themes dealt mostly with the war and the Holocaust. There weren't many children my age with a command of Yiddish, and fortunately I possessed a modicum of artistic capability. My parents became my dramatic directors, not only providing and arranging the artistic material, but spending hours with me to make sure that I knew the recitation by heart, that I understood its meaning, and that I correctly emoted its message. With time, my recitals became more frequent, and as I gained confidence, I became better at them. Sometimes I was provided the unique and highly thrilling experience of reciting a poem in front of its author, who was either the featured speaker at the event or visiting our home. Eventually, I gained a reputation within Yiddish Chicago circles as a "talented young actor." It was a great experience in that it evolved into a speaking skill that was to serve me the rest of my life, and it gave me a certain sense of poise and confidence to communicate before audiences. From the age of nine into my late teens, hardly a month went by without a recital. Some were held in Milwaukee or Detroit, but mostly in Chicago, which had a thriving Yiddish culture. Eventually, my poetic recitals led me to the Jewish theatrical stage and actors such as Dina Halpern, my stage mentor. Halpern was an international star, who, in 1988, at age 78, gave her last performance to a packed house in Paris—eight months before she died of cancer in Chicago.

Yiddish theater began in Romania in 1876, and by 1887, it had reached Chicago along with the wave of Jewish immigrants who flooded into the tenements of Maxwell Street on the city's west side. Ironically, many of these immigrants, who would relax at the Yiddish theater on nearby

Roosevelt Road, were among the butter and egg merchants who became the founding fathers of the Chicago Mercantile Exchange. They, along with the other Yiddish masses—peddlers, sweatshop workers, laborers, and small businesspeople—attended these theatrical performances with relish and joy. It gave them a touch of the Sabbath, some songs, poetry and dance, epics of Jewish heroism, tales of ancient kings and prophets, dramas of real life, as well as memories of their old home. A number of Yiddish performers broke away to become mainstream actors; one of them was Chicago-born Muni Weisenfreund, who became an Oscar-winning screen star know by his Hollywood-ized name, Paul Muni. But Halpern, a niece of the famed European actress Ida Kaminsky, driven from her native Poland by the Holocaust, devoted her life to the Yiddish theater. In 1947, in Chicago, Halpern had played Portia to Maurice Schwartz's Shylock in Shakespeare's *Merchant of Venice*.

At the time we were fleeing Poland in 1939, Halpern was making her American debut to great critical acclaim at New York's Yiddish Art Theater. It was a bittersweet triumph. The war had broken out in Poland, and she was alone in the United States. She was saved, but her father, brothers, sisters, and scores of other relatives were killed at the Treblinka concentration camp. A beautiful woman with dark hair and sensitive features, Halpern and her husband, Danny Newman, the publicist for Chicago's Lyric Opera, founded the Yiddish Theater Association in Chicago in 1960. I was recruited for substantial roles in plays under the critical eye of Halpern who was the Yiddish Theater Association's director. Among the successful productions in which I participated—along with Yiddish actors including Manya Ghitzis, Jose Borcia, Chaike Fox, and Maurice Mason— were Jewish classics such as *Die Kishevmachern, Mirele Efros,* and *Doña Gratzia Mendes.*

As a teenager in the late 1940s, I was lucky enough to be invited to participate in several of the professional productions staged at the Douglas Park Theater on the west side of Chicago, and was privileged to be directed by renowned actor Maurice Mason. During those years, for a fleeting moment, I considered a professional career as an actor and even traveled to live in Greenwich Village, New York to get the feel of "Bohemia." But my parents would not hear of it. An amateur acting status was acceptable, even desirable, but as a career, acting was not one of my options. I could not consider anything less than a doctor or lawyer.

Chicago's Yiddish culture extended to the airwaves as well, which offered another venue for a budding actor. Until my voice changed, I portrayed child characters on Yiddish soap operas that aired on Friday nights and Sunday afternoons. I would listen to the episodes since they had been prerecorded during the previous week. I didn't tell my friends about the radio shows. Childish modesty was probably the reason. Besides, none of them understood Yiddish sufficiently, so there was no point. With poetry recitations, radio, and theater, my ties to Yiddish culture grew stronger than ever, and I hardly ever said no to my parents' demands as they related to the Jewish world.

Even when I reached the age of Bar Mitzvah, my father stood his secular ground: he wouldn't permit me to have a Bar Mitzvah ceremony. Instead, I had a special thirteenth birthday party for which I spent nearly a year in preparation. While most Jewish kids at age 12 were under the tutelage of a rabbi teaching them the *Haftorah*, a reading from the Torah that coincided with the day of their respective Bar and Bat Mitzvahs, my regimen was quite different. No rabbi. No prayers. No ritual. Only my father and mother with a single assignment: write an autobiography, in Yiddish, of course.

In my own words, I described events, people, scenes, cultures, war, the escape, life in America—all I could remember that had touched me. It was a glorious adventure for a youngster, but a mournful one because of family and friends left behind. The war was winding down and the Holocaust's grim statistics were being tallied. Europe had been turned into an immense graveyard of massacred Jews. With their elaborate transport system, slave-labor camps, methodical murdering and incinerating processes, and maniacal economic plan to recycle human hair and gold fillings from the teeth of their victims, the Nazis showed the world for the first time how to industrialize death. The war in Europe would be over two months after my thirteenth birthday. I had been geographically isolated from the war for four years, but emotionally had never let go. In the years ahead, I would meet many Holocaust survivors who had felt the brunt of Nazi barbarism far more severely than I, and after listening to them and looking into their eyes, I knew that the pain of memory doesn't diminish with age.

I labored on my memoirs every day after school and on weekends. The world according to Leibl Melamdovich in 35 handwritten pages was presented to a packed apartment of my parents' friends, colleagues, and various dignitaries of the Yiddish community. Even the Yiddish press—the esteemed *Forward*—out of deference to my parents and their stature in the community, covered the reading and gave a full report of the event. There were my parents *kvelling*—beaming with delight—over every sentence I read aloud with dramatic flair. It was a party more for them than for me, and, as such, none of my school chums were there. I was still very much the child among adults, a role that fit me only too well. But unlike most youngsters my age living in America at that time, I had a sense of the world—its good and evil—and a sense of self. But, I wasn't fully aware of how the world had changed me. How could I at that age?

Today, as I reread that autobiography, I realize that young Indiana Jones had nothing over me in my first 13 years. And I can't help agreeing with the ancient Greeks who believed a man's character is his fate. Chance may take us places, but it's character that keeps us there. I had grown up quickly, perhaps too quickly. While the Yiddish memoir of a youth on the cusp of manhood brings on tears and laughter, it tells me something I didn't know back then: I wasn't brought up to see my fate reflected in the destiny of others.

I never really felt comfortable throughout my grammar school years, even though by eighth grade I had lost my accent, mastered English and math, and was among the top students in my class. Together with Jerry Specthrie, I had even been a patrol guard who helped children cross the streets before and after school. The patrol force, led by Mrs. Galvin, was a big deal at Lowell School. It was a prestigious group with caps, belts, badges, and a hierarchy of officers, to which I had been promoted to second lieutenant. The Lowell patrol force even entered some of the city's marching competitions. I had also become a Golden Eagle, a member of an after-school social club. But at meetings, I would often drift into a self-imposed censorship, reluctant to talk because I didn't want to come off as sounding ignorant. It would be the last time I played it safe in that manner.

It was in high school that I soared. By the fall of 1946, when I became a freshman at Roosevelt High School on Chicago's north side, I shed my refugee image forever. It was a rebirth. No one knew of my immigrant history; no one cared. Although I continued my Yiddish education, attending Yiddish high school on Sundays, it was Roosevelt High that consumed my life. About this time I consciously realized my dreams were no longer occurring in Yiddish. Not only did I sound like an American, I thought like one, dressed like one, and dreamed like one. The world had been in transition and so had I. My awkwardness and shyness was replaced by confidence, ambition, and a group of friends who weren't a bunch of sensitive adolescents fighting a world of conformity. Anyway, not yet. People, for the most part, were still obsessed with the American dream of prosperity. The Cold War jitters had not yet taken hold of American psyches. That would happen in the late summer of 1949 when the Soviet Union exploded its first atomic bomb.

I became a voracious reader and blossomed as a student. One of my earliest decisions was to carry out a plan that had matured into a mission. It was the result of a thousand conversations that I had overheard as a child sitting quietly on a window sill or an out-of-the-way chair whenever grownups gathered in our household. My young mind, thirsting for knowledge of every sort, would hang on every word as my parents' guests assembled in our living room or around the dining room table and spoke with reverence of authors, of books and philosophers, often quoting passages and phrases and sometimes arguing for hours over their meaning. I secretly vowed, as soon as I grew up, to learn for myself what they were talking about and why it was so important. Upon discovering the library on the first floor of Roosevelt High, I brazenly walked up to Mrs. Walters, the school librarian who sported blue hair, and asked if she could direct me to the classics. I guess it was a somewhat unusual request since Mrs. Walters spent considerable time discussing with me exactly what I had in mind. We settled on a list of books that she provided, whose authors, in alphabetical order, she considered worthy of my quest. Although I confess that I didn't read every book on the list, I did do it justice, beginning with Aristotle and four years later ending with Zola.

Somewhere, in the course of those literary travels and the ones that followed, I encountered a multitude of writers who hadn't made Mrs. Walter's list, but held an even greater attraction for me and became my favorite companions. Authors like E. Hemingway, Aldous Huxley, James Joyce, Eric Maria Remarque, Thomas Mann, Philip Wylie, John Le Carre, and my all-time favorite, Lawrence Durrell. And early in this literary career, I also discovered Jules Verne and H.G. Wells, which opened for me the special world of science fiction, a world I never left, and which led me to the likes of George Orwell, Arthur Clarke, Larry Niven, and Ray Bradbury.

Now that I caught up academically, I could compete. I became an associate editor of the school paper. I also became socially accepted and active. A memorable event was my first encounter with music that was not the product of the Jewish world, the Yiddish stage or my mother's Jewish songs that her wonderful soft voice would treat me to as she did the dishes or cleaned house. Although I never could jitter bug, I discovered Frank Sinatra and Frankie Lane and Peggy Lee. I also discovered Satchmo and the world of jazz, a genre of music in which the unconventional sounds of Coltrane, Hawkins, Mulligan, and Brubeck seemed for me strangely in synch with the imaginative wandering of my favorite authors in the Sci-Fi world.

Most important, baseball was no longer the only sport; basketball had come into focus. And in basketball, although I was still short for my age, I was an equal, since we were all beginners. I became a member of a high school fraternity, the Phi Kappa Tau, not only gaining a large group of friends but also the security of knowing that I belonged—plus a club jacket that I could let a girlfriend wear. The friends you make in high school are among the closest you will have the rest of your life, and it was no different in my case. Meyer Seltzer, Jerry Specthrie, and I became inseparable during our four years at Roosevelt, and we have remained the closest of friends to this day. Jerry Specthrie and I dreamed about becoming business tycoons and taking over the Midwest. He actually became an extremely able and highly successful attorney. Alas, because he went to Harvard and married a girl from the East Coast, Jeannette Kotler, he ended up in New York, and our dreams of togetherness remained strictly social. Still, we are as close today as we were when we roamed the halls of Roosevelt High or cut classes together. Friends like that are irreplaceable. Meyer Seltzer, on the other hand, remained a true-blue Chicagoan, and our lives continue to intertwine in many ways. Seltzer is a commercial artist by profession, specializing in children's book illustrations, but for me he is my confidant, my intellectual maven, my compatriot, and my best friend.

Every one of my buddies had something to contribute toward my development and each had his own idiosyncrasy. Zave Gussin, for instance, was the guy with the tie. No matter where we were—at a movie, playing basketball, eating a hot dog—Zave would be wearing a tie. Some guys walked around with their shirts out, some wore tight jeans, some had black leather jackets. But Zave wore that damn tie as if he were a prep school brat.

The streets were relatively safe then, and we were still living in an age of innocence, making the most of it. We had lived through an era that glorified violence, an era in which millions of young men were trained to kill and destroy. It was only a matter of time before the atmosphere of a hostile world would be reflected in the nature of its youth. Street gang life with its private language, peculiar rituals, and deadly violence wouldn't sprout in the big city until the mid-1950s. But every once in a while, we'd face a dicey situation like the time three of us, Specthrie, Gussin, and I, were walking home from Meyer Seltzer's house late one evening. We passed a small group of guys sitting on a stoop in a rather secluded section of the street. Instantly, they rose to stand in our way. I sensed there might be a "hey Jew" confrontation, but instead they focused on Zave's tie. The tie was indeed out of place in that part of Chicago. It was taken by our rivals as an act of hostility. Was this guy with the tie sending them some sort of negative message, they wondered out loud? One of them pulled out a six-inch switchblade as the others grabbed hold of the tie. Jerry Specthrie and I were about to intervene when Zave said the unthinkable. "Ah, come on guys," he pleaded, "it's my father's tie." That was the dumbest thing he could have said. His statement was taken as some sort of hostile challenge. It even made Jerry and me pause for a second. A moment later, the tie was cut in half. Some minor pushing and shoving followed, but the wrong to their honor having been righted, our rivals lost interest in us.

The incident reminded me just how willy-nilly the world worked—as it did when we ran from Bialystok. Had we crossed a different street, Zave wouldn't have ended up with half a tie. The next day he wore a new one.

High school meant many things, including girls (as a senior, I dated nearly every Jewish girl in the sophomore class), homework, movies, sports, and the like, but for me and my group it also meant a "set of wheels." During the war, automobiles were hard to come by, and only old clunkers were around and very expensive. But after the war, when Detroit started to replace tanks with new model autos once again, the price of used cars built in the 1920s and 1930s came into pocketbook range of any teenager who had a part-time job. And I had plenty of those. The entrepreneurial spirit grabbed me early, and the notion of how business worked was highly appealing. I began to sell magazines door-to-door in my last year in grammar school. What kid wouldn't turn capitalist for the incentive of earning a dollar and a Captain Midnight decoder ring?

Once I got to high school, however, my ambitions could match only my maturity. I had grown a year older, and decoder rings and box top toys were the stuff of grade school kids, not a high school freshman. So I moved into rockets, cherry bombs, and assorted firecrackers. My pals, Jerry Specthrie and Zave Gussin, and I became partners in a fireworks business. Fireworks were already banned in Illinois at the time, and they were no longer sold. But we got around the problem in the same way as the Chicago bootleggers did in the Prohibition days. We became importers and ordered the fireworks from a manufacturer in neighboring Indiana. Each shipment was carefully stored in the shed of my basement. Then we would sell them to kids on the streets. And with every sale came my verbal instruction: "If you get caught, make sure you say you bought these from some kid passing on a bicycle." Business was booming until fate stepped in. One day, shortly after I had completed a sale, a police car spotted the kids with a fistful of firecrackers. Where did they get them, the officers asked. The kids said exactly what I had told them to say. The cops looked around, and there I was on my bicycle furiously peddling down the street. They nabbed me and brought me home.

Flanked by two tree-sized cops, we climbed the three flights of stairs to the apartment. My mother opened the door; her mouth, and eyes convulsed at the same time in an expression of bewilderment. Just behind her was my father on a ladder hanging wallpaper—we did our own decorating. The cops told them the story. First my father nodded, then came that icy gaze. It was the look of the Jewish father who had no doubt his son would end up on the ash heap of society. Suddenly, I felt like Al Capone facing the hanging judge. I vowed never to stray again. The police never found our firework inventory stashed in the shed, but Jerry and I had a devil of a time disposing of it. The fireworks eventually found themselves at the bottom of the Chicago River, a common graveyard for all sorts of contraband.

My next highly profitable joint venture was with Meyer Seltzer and came a year later. Careful to stay within the legal limits of the law this time, we went into the wholesale condom business. We knew every guy in high school would want to carry one in his wallet, just in case, if not for a practical reason, then as a badge of manhood—even if it rotted inside the wallet, which it often did. We bought two-gross cartons from a pharmaceutical distributor at a quantity discount of a nickel a package—there were three rubbers in each. We sold them for fifty cents a pack, well below market value, and minus the embarrassment of having to face some cynical pharmacist. Profits were rolling in. But as word about our enterprise spread, we began to feel paranoid. Around every corner lurked a cop waiting for us, or there was one tailing us ready to make the pinch. Though the enterprise was legal, our age made us feel guilty. We became scared and decided to retire from the business. There was only one thing to do—dump the goods. Meyer and I drove through Humboldt Park one afternoon, and I flung a carton of the condoms from the car window. It hit the street and splattered open, sending rubbers in every direction like pieces of shrapnel from a hand grenade. The next thing we knew kids were scrambling in the street to pick them up. Quickly, we changed our plan and hightailed it to the forest preserve where the remaining cartons found a resting place in the bottom of a lagoon.

My earning power throughout high school was clearly reflected in the kind of car I drove. Arnie Warshawsky taught me to drive. He was a buddy who owned a jeep—stick shift, of course. For fifty cents, just enough for gas to drive around for an hour or so, Arnie would give me lessons. Once I mastered the art, I yearned for a car of my own. For $6.00 I became a one-fourth owner of my first car, a Model-T that needed to be cranked and pushed to get it going. Then Meyer and I became partners on a smoke-spewing 1928 LaSalle, minus brakes and a gas pedal. The car was a road hazard and could be stopped only by pulling up the emergency brake. A busted throttle caused it to die at nearly every stop, so it had to be kept in perpetual motion, rolling through stop signs we came upon. It also meant we were dodging ticket-happy traffic cops at every major stoplight. One day, after limping to Milwaukee and Kimball on our way north, there was a traffic jam. We prayed we would make it through the intersection where there was always a traffic cop, but fate would not cooperate. The old girl died, and the throttle unhooked. I had the presence of mind to jump out, lift the hood, which instantly fell onto the ground, and manually pulled on the gas lever as Meyer restarted the engine and steered us through the busy intersection, the cop's whistle behind us. We pulled around a corner, stopped the car at the curb and ran away, leaving our woes behind for the city's auto pound. We were confident that the old LaSalle couldn't be traced to us since it had no license plates. In my junior year, I owned my first car outright, a 1936 Chrysler that worked better in the winter than the summer, but it served me well. The next year I moved up to a sleek 1941 Pontiac, the last model built before the war. Seltzer proudly drove a 1934 Ford, and Specthrie got a brand new Thunderbird for graduation.

My romance with cars, especially fast ones, never ended. Speed and the ability to maneuver a car through traffic at a very fast pace, epitomized my experience with life—there was always danger, there was always the need to make the right turn at the right moment, and there was always the necessity of speed. In the 1960s, when I could finally afford one, it was Corvettes. My 1965 green Corvette convertible exemplified my dream car. By then, of course, I was married with three children who learned to love the car as well. On weekends, when I wasn't taking Idelle, Jordy, or David for a ride, I was racing other Corvette owners. Later in life, my ultimate dream of owning a Porsche was realized. It is a dream I never stopped enjoying.

I was a city kid at heart, but during the summers I became a country boy. Every summer, beginning in seventh grade, my parents rented a cottage in Beverly Shores, Indiana, among the sandy dunes along Lake Michigan. I would go for long walks alone on paths that were narrow and steep, and bicycle rides on bumpy back roads. It was heavenly and provided some of my fondest memories from childhood. For my parents, summer life was pleasant and settled. They neither hiked nor cycled. They read and talked politics with other friends, who similarly had come to the shore for the summer, and strolled the sandy beaches along Lake Michigan. Mother cooked, and father could always find someone with whom to play a game of chess. The Dubows, my parents' friends and professional colleagues at the Sholem Aleichem schools, owned a beach front home in Beverly Shores where we would often gather to spend a Sunday afternoon. The days were idle and quiet, and the air was clean, and the blue sky stretched tautly across the lake reminded me of how it had been crossing the ocean—a span of sky meeting a span of water.

Those wonderful summers got even better as I grew older. The summer after my seventeenth birthday, I became a counselor at a Workmen's Circle camp called *Kinderland*. It was located just outside of South Haven, Michigan, a popular resort area for Jewish families who flocked there from all over the Midwest, like the New Yorkers who spent their summers cooling off in the so-called Borsht Belt in the Catskills. The camp director was Avrum Gurwitz, a Yiddish schoolteacher whom I loved and respected—and since the death of my father, my last personal connection to his world. One summer, my father took over the directorship, making it a bit awkward for me, but I loved working with youngsters and found that they liked me too. I was always inventing another game or contest for them, and I was especially adept at getting everyone involved. But Camp Kinderland meant more to me than taking care of kids. It became a way of life, a place to make strong new friends, a place to sit under the stars on the green tables in front of the cabins and dream of the future. It was a place to be free, a place to grow up, a place to fall in love. Oddly, camp romances between counselors were often more than fleeting affairs, and sometimes blossomed into lifelong commitments. This was true for many in our group. Our head counselor, Sheldon Mantelman, with whom I formed a lasting bond and who quickly appointed me second-in-command, married my counselor pal Joanne Diamond. Nina Schwartz, our arts and crafts expert who was forever making lanyards with the kids, ended up with fellow counselor and fraternity pal, Jack Bell; and my buddy Simon Golden married camp compatriot, Marilyn Kalish. As for me, my love was Cece Sigalowsky. She was strikingly beautiful and it was love at first sight. We had a torrid affair that lasted two whole summer seasons. Alas, she lived in Buffalo, New York, and love letters could go only so far.

In my junior year of high school, I got my first taste of politics when I threw my hat in the ring for class president. I was popular, and by then had a reputation as an accomplished speaker who could emote with ease before the hundreds of students in our class. Not to leave anything to chance, however, my mother helped me make "Leo the Lion" campaign signs. I was easily elected president. In my senior year, I was expected to again become president but I chose to run for vice president instead. That would make me chairman of the senior prom—an honor without equal in high school. I was on a roll, and the momentum carried over into my social life when I was elected president of my fraternity. I had gained unusual stature with my buddies when I inadvertently expressed some provocative views about sex. It happened after one of our members proudly confided that he had "made" his most recent girlfriend. Such a happening was widely regarded as an incomparable badge of honor, a conquest to be applauded and admired. Without thinking about it, I suddenly blurted out "She made you too, you know." Everyone looked at me as if I had broken some sacred trust. But I persisted. Women, I offered, were no different than men in their desire to explore sex. The conquest, I proclaimed, was equal to both parties. I had no idea where or how I had come to this uncommon thought; however, it labeled me as a deep thinker. But the most important position I acquired as a senior was doling out lockers to the senior class. It was definitely a power post; I controlled something people wanted. There were plenty of lockers to go around, but it was the position of the locker in relation to a student's class schedule that gave it its value.

It was also in high school that I met Betty Sattler, cute, blond, small, perky, and bright. As it turned out, Betty was a greenhorn, no different than I. I didn't know it at the time, but Betty was born in Berlin, Germany, and escaped with her mother Marlene and her older sister Leah to the United States aboard the Ile de France in 1938 at the age of three. Shortly after, her father Harry also managed to escape the Nazis, as did her mother's brothers Seymour and Sam. Her mother's brother Phil later made it to the United States after surviving Auschwitz and Dachau.

I was the big junior on campus; she the wide-eyed freshman. We rode the Kimball Avenue bus to school together, and I couldn't take my eyes off of her. Somehow, she got a swell locker right next to mine. I guess it was love at first sight, although, in the beginning, I sometimes mixed her up with some other cute blond. Betty was smart, easy to be with, and someone the other guys turned around for. Although from time to time we had other romantic attachments, we went steady "on and off" throughout her four years at high school.

We also became part of a clique made up of a number of our friends who hung around together, partied, dated, made love, fought, and grew up together. There were classes to attend, homework to do, and sororities and fraternities to belong to; as well as sports activities, rivalries, hops (dances), movies, and clubs. In high school, mutually encountering for the first time so many of life's notable experiences creates an unbreachable bond that lasts a lifetime. My pals Meyer Seltzer and Jerry Specthrie, and I would double- and triple-date and hardly ever let a weekend pass without tooling around together. Betty's girlfriends became my friends, and their boyfriends, my best buddies. Eunice Novinson, for instance, married Abe Chervony who became one of my closest friends and eventually my personal physician—he ended up running the Rush North Shore hospital in Skokie, Illinois. Dr. Chervony's ability to talk Yiddish qualified him to become my parents' doctor as well. And their son Steve Chervony and daughter Lynn became my son Jordy's friends. Steve ended up as a trader at the Chicago Mercantile Exchange. In similar fashion, Betty's childhood friend Gloria Steinberg married Sheldon Welstein, which qualified him to become one of my close friends and end up in the gold pit at the International Monetary Market.

Perhaps it was simply the fifties—with the war over and the feeling of rebirth throughout the world—that produced this intense comraderie at Roosevelt High on the north side of Chicago, but whatever it was, life seemed good as we bonded, planned, schemed, and dreamed about tomorrow.

In my mind, from the very moment I met her, Betty was the one I would marry. There were plenty of stormy moments, however, because we broke up just before my senior prom, and my special reason for becoming "prom bigshot" was for naught. Still, our love was stronger than any dance. Our high school romance blossomed into marriage, and Betty and I have been together ever since, just like in all the romantic movies of the fifties that we watched on Saturday nights.

8

Law and Chaos

I never had the ambition to follow in my parents' footsteps as a teacher. Nor did they expect me to. Like most Jewish parents they aspired medicine or law for their son. As for me, I hadn't really made up my mind when I entered the University of Illinois at Navy Pier—the precursor of the Chicago Circle Campus—in the fall of 1950.

I found magic in the Pier's historical aura. Built in 1916 for $4.5 million, the Pier was a horizontal colossus that extended 3,000 feet into Lake Michigan on the Near North Side. It had been one of the most visible symbols of Chicago's prewar spirit and part of visionary planner Daniel Burnham's grand redesign of the Windy City. But its destiny as the greatest inland seaport in the world was never fulfilled. By the early 1920s, it had fallen on hard times and, subsequently, like Chicago's great stockyards, steel mills, and railway system, the Pier was overtaken by time and technology. But it wasn't down and out, left to rot in the wind and rain. The old Pier had been recycled and revived. Now its skeleton wrapped around a center of learning, and it was in the business of importing and exporting human cargo. In 1995, it was recycled once again to become a magnificent city recreational center.

The academic environment was no-nonsense. Most of the students were returning veterans on the G.I. Bill eager to resume their lives. They were serious, bright, and highly competitive in the classrooms that flanked both sides of a nearly three-quarter-mile-long corridor, accounting for the Pier's sobriquet: "Harvard on the rocks" (or as others, less respectful but more descriptive would call it: "Hardon on the rocks"). The 10 minutes between classes from one end of the corridor to the other offered the best aerobic workout around. For the vets, the makeshift campus was friendly enough. Some of the buildings were vintage Quonset huts. Many of my friends (sans Jerry Specthrie who actually could afford to go to Harvard, and did) were also attending the Pier, which offered a two-year program. From the Pier, students would transfer to other colleges or go downstate to finish up at the University of Illinois main campus in Champaign-Urbana.

The Pier was the best of all worlds; a wonderful view of Lake Michigan and a good urban college in the heart of a big city that worked, if you believed its politicians. In winter, it was also the coldest place on earth; fortunately, this was before we knew about the windchill factor, or it surely would have lost half its student body. There was no student union to speak of, but a coffee shop that was a gathering spot between classes. It offered the strongest cup of coffee on the North Side and a place to hustle up serious players of hearts, a popular card game with our group of guys at the time. We played often, sometimes between classes, sometimes instead of classes, and always for money—a nickel a heart, 35 cents for the queen of spades. One of my stellar laudits was graduating "cum-sum-laude hearts 103." The coffee shop was also where we compared class notes, talked politics, made dates, rated the women, and shared dreams about the future.

I began as a pre-med student. But any ambitions I might have had for becoming the next Albert Schweitzer ended with biology. It began with the rat caper. One weekend, Meyer Seltzer and I prepared to cram for our midterm exam in biology that was to be given on a Monday. Since the exam was to focus on the anatomy of the rat, it was imperative that we know every part of the dissected rodent. On a wintery Friday afternoon, we sneaked into the laboratory, chose a nice fat rat pickled in formaldehyde, and made off with it. Wrapped in newspaper, we threw it into the trunk of my 1941 Pontiac for safekeeping until Sunday night when we planned to study. It was the dead of winter in Chicago, and when I opened the trunk two nights later the rat was frozen solid like some ice age woolly mammoth preserved in the tundra of northern Siberia. The last time I had seen anything that cold was in Birobidzhan. We couldn't even unwrap the paper.

Meyer had a bright idea. "We'll cook it," he said. We took it up to Meyer's apartment on the third floor to defrost. His parents were out for the evening and we had to work fast. Wrapper and all, Meyer threw the rat in a pan and began frying it. His mother kept a kosher kitchen, which meant that only certain pots, pans, dishes and utensils could be used for meats; a separate set was for dairy products. He made sure the frying pan was the one used strictly for meats. As the rat began to thaw, the worst odor I had ever smelled singed my nostrils, and both of us began to retch. Soon the smell permeated the entire apartment and we opened windows. No sooner had Meyer turned off the fire and tried to dispose of the rat than his parents walked in on us. I thought it was best that I leave. I couldn't face Meyer's mother for months. I'm still not sure what his punishment was, but Meyer said it was the worst he had ever received. As for the exam, we did okay, but clearly not as good as we could have had we been able to study the rat.

The next semester I shifted my major to pre-law; everyone was certain I would become a great barrister. I also learned that my avid imagination could be put to good use and that I had a flair for writing. In my English Literature course I was given an opportunity to let my mind wander and to write short stories. It was the first recognition, by an outside authority, that I had some talent in this direction. In two instances, my teacher encouraged me to publish my stories in science-fiction magazines of that era. Too bad I never saved a copy of the pulp publication, something called *Amazing Adventures*, in which my first work appeared—authors received no pay. The first was a story about an ant civilization. The second was influenced by the prevalent 1950's fear of the coming world conflagration. It was a sci-fi rendition of a past civilization that reached it height just before it was destroyed in a nuclear war.

But again my background caused me a bit of academic grief. Because my father was a mathematician, it was an obligatory requirement that I continue with math courses come what may, as I had done throughout high school. Until Navy Pier I had actually done quite well in math, but by then I had run out of desire, and college calculus was far from a breeze. As was my style, I did little or none of the assignments and rarely opened the book. When the midterm came, I didn't even understand a single problem our professor presented. Realizing there was no hope, I spotted some chalk-written algebraic gibberish on one of the rafters in the classroom ceiling. This immediately became my answer. I waited for the inevitable, and finally the professor called me to his office.

"Melamdovich, I don't understand this," he said. "According to your records, you're a straight A student, but it's obvious you never opened the book in my classroom. Besides, you're in pre-law, so what the hell are you doing in a class full of engineers?"

I was suddenly overcome with remorse and really embarrassed. I decided to find protection in the truth. After I found my voice, I whispered, "My father is a mathematician; I have to take math."

It got very quiet in the room and I was afraid to look up. Then, after what seemed like an eternity, the professor spoke. "I understand," he said in a fatherly tone. "I have a son about your age. I'll make a deal with you: I'll pass you with a C if you never show up in my classroom again." It was the last math course I ever took. It's a story I never did tell my father.

When I wasn't in class or playing hearts, I would sometimes sit in the lounge at the rear end of the Pier and watch the ships, dreaming of adventures in faraway places. Or I would go to the movies. Our group had established the "movie club," which required that we keep abreast of all new releases in the movie houses around Chicago's loop. I also worked odd jobs to pay for tuition, car expenses, and for my social life. At one time or another in my school years, both graduate and undergraduate, I drove a taxicab; delivered telephone directories; was a stock boy at Marshall Field's department store; a Fuller Brush salesman with Jerry Specthrie; a catalog server at Montgomery Ward; and helped my pal, Al Surgal, run Freddy's Hot Dog Stand at Chicago and Grand avenues. Every time I'd come home from the hot dog stand, my mother would make me undress before I stepped through the doorway because my clothes reeked from the oil and french fries. Then she directed me into the bath. The hot dog stand was where I had my first experience with marijuana. It was then known as reefer, and the first drag cured me for life. The accentuated smell of grease around me instantly brought me to a point of extreme nausea. But it was a great job, and Freddy, who lived in Florida most of the time, paid us well. I even managed to parlay my summer counseling experience into a job and later brought Meyer Seltzer onboard. We would teach children in an after-school program at the Jewish People's Institute on the west side of Chicago. When I had filled out the application, I stated that I could teach nearly everything. I figured I could take out a book and stay one day ahead of my students. One day we'd be acting out plays, the next building birdhouses, a third day conducting Friday night services. I was once asked by a little black child in class what color God was. "All colors," I replied without a moment's hesitation. My parents had given me the answer long before.

Nothing, however, compared to driving a Checker cab on the boulevards and back streets of Chicago and beneath them along lower Wacker Drive. Chicago was truly the city of neighborhoods, as I found out firsthand. Hacking taught me the city as no other job could. It was a gritty job, a tough one, and this was long before cabs were air conditioned and a safety shield separated driver from passenger. I was constantly under pressure to find a fare so as not to waste gas and time by "deadheading." There was also the problem of finding one's way via the quickest and most direct route without having a passenger scream at you for being dumb. Once in a while I got lost and, out of embarrassment, declined the fare. Then there were the big tippers and no tippers, the drunks and weirdos, the bad guys and loose women, as well as every other form of humanity. You learn about life quickly driving a cab. Once in the middle of a steamy August afternoon, I found myself in a long line of cabs beneath Union Station waiting for passengers. The temperature outside was 105 degrees, below ground 140 degrees. My clothes clung to me with sweat. And there was the horrible rotten-egg stench of the sewers that combined with the urine from the cabbies who used the underground ramp as their private toilet. To this day, I'm sympathetic to cab drivers, especially when the days are unbearably hot. My cab driving also taught me that cabbies can be a good barometer of opinions, be it a political or social subject. Cabbies are exposed to a wide cross section of opinions and become

wonderful teacher and,
...eze. Not only did I be-
...utomatic four-hour A.
...ushed for John Mar-
...ai Stevenson had
...where her husband,
More important,
...ol entry from 60
...'t enroll in law
There was no
...her defining
...oing to be
...en, I had
...gh hon-
...ddenly,
ll the
...ke it
...es,
sy

...ng a cabbie was that I could
... a college student. While
front of school, attend
...ne.

...an way of life, but
...Old World strict with
...e, I had to be home by a
...were not beyond calling the
...On Friday and Saturday nights
... of my friends would meet at the
...f California and Division streets. It
...great place, noisy and crowded, and the
...e doorway, your nose was attacked by the
...rlic-laced salamis shriveled like giant prunes
... the counter. Over corned beef sandwiches and
...we'd sit for hours talking about life and women. The
...ectual and argumentative and even pretentious. (You
...as reading Plato and Walter Lippmann at the time.) We
...or authority or prestige, but more or less expressed our feel-
...the world as we saw it and how it felt growing up in a dynamic
...ere you could still walk the streets at night. For me, time sort of
...a still in the Humboldt Spot. But not for my father. When the clock
...ruck 2:00 A.M., I turned into a problem for him.

Dressed in his pajamas and a coat, he would drive across the park to the Humboldt Spot. Without uttering a word, he would stand in the doorway playing Jiminy Cricket to my Pinocchio. The instant he knew I saw him, he'd do a quick about-face and return home. Although embarrassed and angry, I'd follow shortly thereafter. It wasn't that my father was a tyrant; he was reacting to the Bialystok Syndrome. If I didn't show up at a designated time, something terrible must have befallen me. In any case, I did my level best to abide by the house rules as long as I lived in their home. However, I did not bend out of fear, but out of respect. This respect for my parents was a strong European heritage. And terribly inhibiting. Even in my college years I couldn't consider moving out of the house and into my own apartment like some of my friends had done.

The summer after my second year at the Pier, I was set for a high seas adventure. The great seagoing authors Joseph Conrad and Jack London had gotten under my skin, and so had Alan Surgal, my high school chum, who convinced me to sign on as a deckhand aboard a Norwegian freighter. He and I decided to cross the Atlantic and spend the summer of '52 exploring the back roads of Norway and the other Scandinavian countries. It would be a blast. But my seafaring plans abruptly changed after a conversation with

my German professor, Frau Nauman. She was
with my Yiddish background, German was a bre
come quite proficient in the language, it was an a
Since she knew I wanted to attend law school, she
shall Law School in the heart of downtown Chicago
Professor Braunfeld, taught tax and constitutional la
Frau Nauman advised me that Illinois Governor Ad
signed a new law, changing the requirements for law scho
hours, which I already had, to 90 hours. In short, if I did
school in the summer, I would need another year of pre-law
choice. I would have to sacrifice my sea adventure. It was and
moment in my life.

I entered law school in June and quickly realized that it was
completely different from my previous school experiences. Until t
found school a breeze. Without trying too hard, I graduated with h
ors from high school and got nearly straight A's at Navy Pier. But su
there were no shortcuts, no way to finesse a course without doing
required work. It was a shocking revelation. There was no way to ma
through Contracts or Torts without doing the reading, preparing the ca
and taking copious notes during the lectures. And those were the ea
courses. In fact, for the first time since grammar school, I occasionall
found it difficult to keep up. Suddenly, I had to become a serious student.
Like other law students, I became part of a study group, four men and a
woman—Larry Mayster, Merwin Lichtenstein, Leroy Levy, and Mildred
McNairy. Of the group, Levy was the only one who didn't make it. Merwin
Lichtenstein, who I loved because of his sense of humor and ability to tell
jokes, practiced law but also followed my path into the markets, first with a
job at the Merc, later as a member at both Chicago futures exchanges. The
study group met on a regular basis at my parents' house, gathering around
the dining room table. A study group is a defensive mechanism for law students and the only way to survive law school. We divided the various subjects among our members so that each became an "expert" in a given field
and then had to transfer this expertise to the others. My subjects were constitutional law and taxation—usually backbreakers at law school. The group,
however, did more than merely study. It became our extended family. We
got to know each other as if we had been siblings of the same family: our
habits, our tastes, our likes and dislikes, our capabilities and shortcomings.
My mother, as expected, became attached to the members of our group,
treating them like her own. Everyone took to her, no different from all her
students during her entire professional career. She would serve coffee and
pop, and get to know everyone on an intimate basis. It never mattered to her
that the group stayed until the wee hours of the morning.

Of course, my base of operations changed when I got married. To get out of my house, marriage to Betty was probably the healthiest thing I could have done. The bond with my parents would forever be there, forged solidly when we escaped Poland. But I needed independence, and marriage was the only legitimate route to freedom. She was 18 and I was 21, in my second year of law school; we were madly in love, and for the first time in our young lives, we were on our own.

The wedding was a vintage fifties affair, complete with a *chupah*, brides-maids, ushers; and Meyer Seltzer as best man. My bride was radiant, her ex-quisite white gown seemingly right out of a fashion couturier. The maid of honor, Betty's sister Lee (changed from Leah), looked so proper and pleased. Lee later married Nate Slutsky, who became a broker in the Swiss franc pit. Poor Harry Sattler, Betty's wonderful and gracious father, an in-stallment salesman who couldn't afford to take his wife Marlene on a proper vacation, paid for the entire event without a word of complaint. Much of it was a scene right out of Barry Levinson's *Diner*, replayed time and again throughout American history. The ballroom at the Sheridan Hotel on the north side of Chicago was bathed in flowers and filled with relatives who came from faraway places like California and New York. There were friends from the neighborhood, buddies from high school, and the crème de la crème of the Yiddish world of Chicago. The toasts were funny, and serious, and corny. My parents never stopped beaming with pride, although I de-tected an occasional tear in my mother's eyes. It was the first time my father wore a tux. It wasn't the kind of thing Bundists do. But for that night, it was okay. His immigrant son had grown up and on his way to becoming a great lawyer.

Instead of a honeymoon, Betty and I used the $600 of gift money to buy a nifty four-door Ford that was only three years' old. It was a bright char-treuse, but the price was right. After the wedding, the study group met at our apartment on Juneway Terrace just off Sheridan Road, less than a block from Lake Michigan. We lived in a fourth floor walk-up, and with-out air conditioning the summers became a bit much. So hot, in fact, that we often slept on the beach soaking up the sand, water, and lake breezes.

It was an interesting time to be tackling the rationale and rhetoric of con-stitutional law in law school, given the nation's political climate. America, obsessed with national security and the threat of communism, had fallen under the spell of McCarthyism. We spent hours debating Joe McCarthy's tactics and the wobbly constitutional ground on which he stood. After Pres-ident Eisenhower, Joe McCarthy had become the second most powerful man in the country. For a while the Senate was afraid of him, and so was the media. In the end, Congress regained its senses and rejected McCarthy. For me, the McCarthy affair had become a lesson in leadership gone awry. Joe

McCarthy was an example of a demagogue, and how absolute power can de-range the person who possesses it, blurring the boundary between fantasy and reality. Gunner Joe had faith in his false whiskers.

I had a love-hate relationship with law school. Like most students, I hated the constant homework, the case-briefings, the time it took to study, and the pressure. But I loved the intellectual demand of the law courses. It made me think, and think with precision. "What was the underlying principle in-volved?" "What were the real facts?" "Ignore the superfluous—embrace only the consequential." I became a believer of this academic regime, and to this day believe that law school offers the best education irrespective of what occupation one eventually seeks. But it is tough. Of the 70-odd students who started in my class, only 34 graduated. I ranked eighth in the class at graduation. I enjoyed the challenge of coming to terms with a case, under-standing its essence, and attempting to determine the legal principals in-volved. It was like solving a difficult puzzle. I had become an excellent student and aced the killer courses, Taxation and Constitutional Law.

And I learned something more of my natural talent. Early in my first se-mester, I cut my first class—nothing really unusual about that; it was my norm. But this time I felt really guilty. I mean, this was law school; what if they threw me out? I decided to use the skill I had developed at Navy Pier and write a letter of apology to the dean, concocting a story about a flat tire on the Outer Drive. The language was flowery, overstated and overwritten, but spiced with humor and quite convincing. And as I expected, the dean called me in. Dean Noble Lee was a personality in the city, a representative to the Illinois Legislature, and known to be both eccentric and demanding as a professor. I believe his father had been the founder of John Marshall Law School. I sat in his office waiting for him to appear and not knowing whether my ploy had worked. He entered the room and stared at me. Then he smiled. "I ought to give you an A for the course, for pleading your case as you did." Because of that letter I could do no wrong in the dean's eyes, and for the next three years I was his favorite student. Subsequently, he confided that I graduated with the highest number of cuts ever recorded at John Marshall Law School. For the first time, I understood the power of the pen—in my own hand. Dry legal briefs were one thing, but words that stirred emotions, another. Even when I ran the Merc, I not only wrote my own speeches, but in the early years, also all the material produced by the exchange, its annual reports, its marketing materials, and even to a large measure its congressional testimony. In the later years, when the exchange grew too large for me to write all its material, I wouldn't permit material out of the Merc unless I, at least, approved it. It was labor-intensive given all the responsibilities of the chairmanship, but I knew what I wanted the Merc to be, the image I wanted to project at each stage of its growth, and I knew the power of words.

Then there were times in law school when I couldn't conjure up a single word. It happened in Administrative Law, a course that dealt with procedures at governmental agencies. I hated the course. That fact became obvious when I took the final exam. I had three hours to answer 10 questions. I was stymied on the first. The second one didn't look promising either. Nor the third. It wasn't until the fourth question I had something to say. By then it was too late. Frustration had overcome my ability to think straight. Now I was driven by sheer emotion and dashed off a note at the top of the paper: "This is not a good exam. And since I did not learn anything in Administrative Law, I cannot take it." I handed in the exam and walked out. There were others in the class who had the same feelings toward the professor, but they weren't as blunt. I had to take the course over again at night school.

But of all the courses, the one that nearly gave me the most embarrassment was Library and Research—a course nobody took seriously, was pass-fail, and didn't count in your grade point average. Taught by Ms. Shaw, the daughter of a Circuit Court judge, the course focused on the fine and boring points of research. At the end, we were to submit a fully footnoted research paper on any subject we chose. I let time get away and, before I knew it, the paper was due in a few days. I went to the Newberry Library, one of the great private research libraries in the country, and began roaming the stacks, a panicked law student in search of an idea. On one bookshelf, tucked behind some books, I found a pamphlet with fading writing containing an article with an intriguing title: "Is Baseball a Sport or a Business?" It had been written back in the thirties by an unknown author. It was an excellent paper loaded with all sorts of annotations and references. Just what the professor expected. I caved in and did the unthinkable. I massaged it here and there, rewrote some passages, wrote a new introduction, but copied most of it. When the papers were returned, in place of a grade I found a reference number. I prepared for the worst, my stomach knotted. I went to the library and looked up the reference the professor had provided. It was a book entitled *Plagiarism*. I went to her office shaken and ashamed. Fortunately, I knew this was not a credit-based course and didn't really count. I stood there embarrassed, caught redhanded without a plausible defense. I pled guilty. Ms. Shaw, upon reviewing a transcript of my law school grades, which were nearly all A's, reasoned that my academic lapse had been an abnormal blip in what otherwise was a top-notch performance. I accepted my sentence with equanimity: to write a major original paper over the summer. I should have known better than to mess with baseball. That old childhood demon had gotten me again.

During the summer, I worked on the paper. It was triple the length of the first one, and while it included the business of baseball, I also compared and contrasted the businesses of four other sports. In September, I handed it in and, three weeks later, received it back with the grade of A. Today when I write, whether it's a speech, a book, an editorial, I'll meticulously reference every thought and phrase that isn't mine. I learned my lesson well, and never forgot it.

Why do I speak of these failings? Because I know it's human to make mistakes. It's how we rebound from mistakes and what we learn from them that matters, that indeed shapes us. Out of mistakes comes humility. I didn't fully understand this in law school, but I did when I began to run the Merc. I could better cope with others who made mistakes around me and deal with opponents on a more rational basis. I learned to reexamine my ideas again and again, in order to avoid a mistake. But I didn't hesitate to admit it whenever I made one. In fact, second chances often prove more worthy than first chances, as I was to discover time and again.

With the pressure of law school came financial pressure. Although my parents had helped with my law school tuition, I was strapped. I needed to work. As was common, I wanted to work as a law clerk for one of the downtown law firms, and I got my first job at Defrees, Fisk and Thompson, a prestigious old-line law firm. In no time, I was promoted to sharpening pencils and watering the flowers. I was bored out of my mind, and the summer was hot. One scorching morning I called in sick and promptly went to North Avenue beach to meet my buddies. As fate would have it, my immediate boss at the law firm also took the morning off, and, lo and behold, among the thousands of beachgoers ran smack into me. Bad luck. It was a quick end to my career at D, F & T.

In the fall, my classes didn't start until 2:15 in the afternoon, which left the entire morning open for another try as a law clerk. Knowing I was looking for work, Meyer Seltzer called me one day with a lead. He had seen a want ad in the *Chicago Tribune* by a law firm for the exact hours I wanted. I looked up the ad. The firm in question, Merrill, Lynch, Pierce, Fenner & Bean, was looking for a "runner" between the hours of 9:00 A.M. to 1:00 P.M., which was perfect for my class schedule. With that many names, how could this firm be anything but an established old-line law firm seeking a clerk to run to court. This was long before Merrill Lynch would spread the word in newspapers, magazines, and television that it was "Bullish on America."

The next morning I showed up at 141 West Jackson, the address provided, and was somewhat puzzled. The building I was about to enter was the Chicago Board of Trade. As I made my way to the second floor, I didn't quite understand why a law firm would base itself in the Board of Trade building. Even when I walked into the office, I still had no idea that Merrill Lynch was not a law firm, but a brokerage firm that sold stocks, bonds, and commodities—I hadn't gotten to the back office nor the main room where the clerks sat receiving orders from customers or prospecting for new ones. But even if I had, I would have been disoriented; I had never been in a brokerage house. I filled out an application in an anteroom, handed it to a secretary who disappeared behind a door. Minutes later she ushered me to an inside room where I was interviewed. I must have satisfied the requirements because I was given instructions to show up the next morning at 9:00 A.M. at 110 North Franklin and ask for Joe Sieger. Of course, I told myself, this was merely the hiring office, and I was being sent to the law offices. It all made perfect sense until I arrived at 110 North Franklin and saw the name in stone across the face of the building: Chicago Mercantile Exchange.

Now I was truly mystified. I had never heard of the Chicago Mercantile Exchange. Perhaps the firm practiced business law here. Then I went to the second floor as instructed and in total bewilderment peered through the glass doors at a scene I had never before imagined. I was Alice stepping through the Looking Glass into a world of not just one Mad Hatter, but hundreds. The shouting among the traders, the movement of their bodies and hands, captivated me like nothing before. Dumfounded, I watched the clerks—the job Joe Sieger hired me for—darting across the floor at roadrunner pace with buy and sell orders in their hands for brokers in the trading pits. If it wasn't the Looking Glass then it must have been the Twilight Zone, a dimension of sight, sound, and mind. Maybe it was both. Whatever it was, there was a life force on that floor that was magical and exciting, and though I didn't understand what was going on, I wanted to be a part of it. I had no doubts or illusions that this wasn't a law office. It was whatever it was, and it paid $25 a week. I was thrilled beyond words. In the morning, before entering the floor, I would touch the bronze rooster that stood magnificently on a pedestal before the old doorway. It was the Merc's mascot. Years later, as the Merc began its move from old quarters to new quarters, I hung on to that rooster for dear life. Finally, when we moved into our ultimate structure on Wacker Drive, I had the rooster glass-encased, put on display in the VIP gallery, and labeled "Our Founder" so no member would forget the Merc's humble origin.

Eggs and onions were traded at the Merc when I began running for Sieger, then chairman of the Exchange and head floor broker for Merrill Lynch. In the mornings, it was the Merc; in the afternoons, law school. Apparently I learned well, because after a month, Sieger paid me an extra $20 out of his own pocket, boosting my salary to $45 a week. With Betty's $55 a week as a switchboard operator for Beatrice Foods, we were now doing all right as newlyweds. Marriage or law school, my romance with the Merc never let up. I was enthralled with the open outcry system of buying and selling contracts, with the speed at which things happened, with the colorful players in this arena of capitalistic hope and sweat. For me it was an open laboratory to study human nature as I had never seen it before. What I was seeing couldn't be taught in a classroom or read in an economics textbook.

Granted, the Merc was a small exchange dwarfed in trading volume and prestige by the granddaddy of commodity exchanges, the Chicago Board of Trade, its smug and arrogant downtown neighbor where wheat, corn, rye, barley, and soybeans were traded. But the Merc was still the second largest exchange in the United States. And though it was a rough house of trading cliques that grew out of the early days when the Merc traded futures contracts on butter and eggs, beneath the surface something rumbled; but I couldn't figure it out yet. I was a novice, a beginner, an observer.

During the first six months, I didn't say much. Diligently I went about my business. The Merc was merely a means of getting through law school, I kept thinking. But I knew better. I had fallen in love with the place. I kibitzed with my fellow runners, and even played Ping-Pong with some of the traders at the table set up in the back, off the trading floor. Some of those games could be as heated and competitive as the trading in the pits, and they caused me to be tardy to my law classes more than a few times. But mostly I watched, listened, and learned, soaking in the lore of the marketplace like a sponge.

Joe Sieger was chairman of the Merc. And there was no doubt in my mind—or in anyone else's—he was the power of the exchange. When I first began working for him, he intimidated me, but I was so awed by the promise of the Merc that it didn't matter. A nail-tough Dutchman with a strong tenor voice, Sieger gave no quarter to anybody. He was smart, autocratic, demanding, and wanted things done his way. And his temper was mercurial. Once he threw a steelcase chair at one of the phone clerks who made a big error. I felt sorry for the kid. But that's the way it was down there; the chairman could do anything he wanted, and no one argued. Yet, as Merc president E.B. Harris used to say about Sieger, "He could charm you out of your britches." I learned to love my boss. I observed Sieger and how he related to the membership. They loved him and hated him, and I wasn't sure that's what leadership was all about. Still, it was the first time I had seen a chairman of an institution: what he did, how he was treated, how he operated, what he thought, and the power he represented. It taught me a lot, particularly that the chairman had a great deal of responsibility. Joe Sieger ruled the exchange with an iron hand in those days.

At the beginning of my last year of law school, in 1954, I made a decision that would have far-reaching implications on my life, although I didn't know it then. I had worked at the Merc for 15 months and was now a full-fledged phone clerk with serious responsibilities, but I wanted much more. I desperately wanted to become a member so that I could trade. Actually, I had already traded. Kenneth Birks, the other Merrill Lynch broker and I had become close friends. It was a friendship that years later was instrumental in catapulting me to chairmanship. We were much closer in age than I was to Sieger and our chemistry was right from the start. Eventually, I became his phone clerk. Ken let me trade by taking small positions in his account. It was probably against the rules, but in those days many of the brokers let their clerks trade like that. The problem was I could never take a different position than that of Birks, and he wasn't much of a trader. Pretty soon I was deep in the red, and Birks asked for some money, $150 to be exact. It was far beyond my means, and I had to borrow from about five friends to meet his margin call.

The cost of a seat was $3,000. Assuring my father I would go into the practice of law when I graduated, I asked him to lend me the money to buy a CME membership. It was a measure of the man that he even considered my request. I was asking for an amount equal to about half of my parents' savings. Before he decided, I brought him to the Merc to show him what I was doing and why I wanted the membership. I explained the egg and onion contracts and what went on in the trading pits. As I knew he would, he quickly grasped the idea of the marketplace. He could identify with the action. The haggling between buyer and seller was similar to what went on in the open markets in Poland he remembered as a boy. He lent me the money. And I entered my last year of law school as student-cum-futures trader.

In the morning I traded eggs and onions, and in the afternoon I studied taxation and probate. It was a profitable year both academically and economically. I was earning A's in the classroom and a nice income in the pit. I soon had made $12,000 off my budding trading skills, enough to pay for my tuition and to get by without Betty's income. I even offered to begin paying back my father, but he said it could wait. Subsequently, I would repay my father by buying him a seat on the International Monetary Market—the IMM—when it was launched in 1972. The membership cost $10,000 and I made certain my father's trading symbol was "IMM" which, appropriately enough, stood for Isaac Moishe Melamdovich. He, of course, never traded himself—I traded for him from time to time. Although I encouraged him to sell the membership at any time he wished, he never did. At one point, when the seat was worth a quarter of a million dollars, I told him I thought we were even. He agreed, but still wouldn't sell. When he passed away in 1990, the value of an IMM seat was $330,000.

I graduated in the summer of 1955, and began to prepare for the bar exam in October. My student status had kept me out of the Korean War, but now my draft deferment had expired. Though the war was over, Uncle Sam was knocking at my door. I was eligible for the draft. If I had to serve, I was resigned to it. But the thought of taking two years out of my life when I was about to start a family and a career hit me like a sharp jab to the solar plexus. Actually, I had constant stomach pains during my senior year in law school, but I ignored them, fearing that somehow they would prevent me from taking finals. Upon graduation, I went to my doctor who gave me the works; upper and lower gastrointestinal tests and various x-rays. He confirmed what I guessed all along: ulcers. I had two of them, gastrol and peptic. Only one question remained: Would the ulcers keep me out of military service?

I showed up for my army physical with the X rays of my ulcers tucked under my arm. But no one seemed to be interested in looking at them. I went through a battery of tests and, at the end of the psychological exam, the doctor asked what I was carrying. "My X rays to show I have two ulcers," I answered. "Really," he said, "let me take a look." He muttered to himself for a couple of minutes and said, "Oh my God, there're two craters here." He shuffled off, and I went to a waiting room, sitting conspicuously naked.

Here's where things became a bit weird. Still naked, carrying my X rays, I was ushered into a room. At one end was a table at which three fully clothed officers sat. To me they looked like generals. Embarrassed and feeling highly vulnerable, I sat in a chair in front of them. The scene had all the earmarks of a kangaroo court. But I refused to let my imagination send me into a frenzy. One of them began reading my report aloud. "So you have ulcers," he said. I thought that was why I was there, but it wasn't. Then came the pitch. "For what we are going to offer you, it doesn't matter if you have ulcers because you'll be able to eat whatever you want and you'll be able to be on a diet, so don't worry about the ulcers." I had no idea what he was talking about.

As it turned out, I was being recruited to work in army intelligence, in Germany, of all places. After basic training, officers school, and special intelligence, I'd emerge as a lieutenant and spy. In their eyes, I was the perfect cold warrior, fluent in German, an attorney, a Holocaust survivor, and a man indebted to the United States for opening its doors. Well, they were partially correct. True, I was all these things. But I lacked any desire to go to Germany. I had enough ulcers and I didn't need a couple more. Halfway through their pitch I realized that the only way they could get me was if I volunteered. If I don't volunteer, I told myself, I'm either drafted, or 4F, and that's that. I decided to leave matters to the Almighty. After an hour of subtle brainwashing in the nude, I left a free man.

Not long after I took the bar exam, I changed my name to Melamed. My parents had Americanized Melamdovich four years earlier in 1951. Legally, they became Melamed, but in the Yiddish world they continued to be Isaac and Faygl Melamdovich. But I had refused to change and held on to the ancestral name. Even though my professors in law school broke their teeth trying to pronounce Melamdovich, I didn't want to give it up. I was Leo Melamdovich on my marriage license, my college degrees, my driver's license. But now that I was going out into the world, I found that clients had too difficult a time pronouncing it. Clients were much more important than professors I gave up. In 1955, I joined my parents and became Melamed.

There are some who plan their lives like a military campaign with a strategy, a contingent strategy, and a counter strategy. I didn't want to be one of those people who are so deliberate in life that they squeeze out any spontaneity. Yet I needed to define myself, and I was hoping that somehow the practice of law would give me definition. I had no illusions about becoming the next Clarence Darrow in the City of Big Shoulders. Sure, I wanted to make a difference, but my first priority was to make a living. All I wanted was to earn enough money to support my family. So I hung up my shingle and went to work.

PART TWO

The Beauty of Markets

9

The Revolution

I opened a small office on LaSalle Street. My partner was Larry Mayster, who had been in my law school study group. Mayster & Melamed we were called, but it was slow going at first. On top of that, my trading turned sour and I again went into the red. I was trading at Miller & Co., a small local trading house that was run by Daniel Jesser. Jesser was an excellent trader—some said a "money machine." He was a methodical spreader. Spreading was a trading technique that eliminated much of the trading risk but it also limited one's upside potential. He tried to teach me how to spread, but it wasn't for me. I was an "allsy," either all long or all short. I guess I was an allsy in most respects. Whatever I did, I did with completeness and total commitment. When I drove, I did it very fast; when I smoked, it was nearly four packs a day; once I quit, I would not even take a drag on a bet. Fortunately, Dan became my friend and "carried" me through my difficult periods during my early trading career. I guess Dan figured that if I didn't make it trading, I could always earn a buck as a lawyer.

For the next five years I was an attorney and a commodities trader. But I could never get both disciplines in synch. In the beginning of a law career, you make precious little money. And in trading, every time I got something going, the market would suddenly turn dead or erratic and I would soon lose what I had made. During this period, I went broke twice trading eggs. One of my problems was that I couldn't keep track of the market. If I had a hearing in court, a deposition to cover, or had to see a client in the morning, there was no way to follow the market action. In order to feel the market, I had to know its every move, watch its trend. But the biggest problem was much more profound and had to do with what the Merc was trading. There was hardly any play in the egg market, because modern egg production had become a year-round business. Eggs, it appeared, were headed the way of the Merc's once thriving butter futures market, which died after the war with support prices for butter. I had a wife, two children, little money to bring home, and was deeply in debt.

And things kept going from bad to worse. One afternoon, I hit rock bottom. It was the weekend, and we had no money for food. I took a jar of pennies we had saved to the American National Bank and cashed them in for $26.30. It got us through the weekend.

While initially I wasn't making it as a commodities trader, I wasn't wasting my time. I looked at my effort as a kind of apprenticeship. I was learning about trading, about myself, and about the exchange and its members. Some of it I liked; some of it I didn't. As a runner I had spent most of my time with the other clerks sharing a collective ambition: to become a trader. When I became one, I entered another level. Now I was one of the guys, one of the members. And some of the older ones took me under wing. I was young and likeable, but they never really looked on me as the up and coming generation of trader that would replace them some day. No one in the exchange leadership thought too far ahead. The old guard was in control. The floor was a cutthroat world where might was not always right, but it prevailed. If a trader or a group of them cornered a market and got out on top of the corner, to the victor went the spoils. I witnessed how traders would corner the cash market in order to manipulate the futures market, and how they would use certain brokers to get them out of their positions. I learned the essence of trading from high rollers like Joe Siegel, who took big positions in onions and eggs and knew how to frustrate supply and demand; from Dan Jesser and his brother Martin, who as spreaders, dashed to buy in one contract month and sell in the next; from Albert MacKinzie, who taught me to apply *time* as a factor of price charting; and from Marlowe King, a fundamentalist who had all the statistics in his head and understood supply and demand better than anyone.

I also learned that often emotion is more important than facts. I will never forget that lesson, which was exemplified when the 1967 Six-Day War between Israel and Egypt broke out. War is always bullish on commodity prices, and the hog and belly contracts instantly rose until they reached the permissible daily price limit. When the market couldn't go any higher, the traders stood in the pit and frantically shouted their desire to buy at the limit-up price. Suddenly, Marlowe King, who was heavily short the market, came down from his office to the floor, ran to the edge of the pit, and shouted at the traders at the top of his lungs: "You guys are crazy. Don't you know that neither Arabs or Jews eat pork."

It was also from Marlowe King that I learned that superstition was an integral part of trading. Indeed, as a rule, most traders, whether they admit it or not, are superstitious—after all, who really can be certain what makes this great cosmic universe function. Some have a lucky tie that they must wear every day, some use a lucky pencil, others drive to work down the same streets, and so on. I have even heard of lucky underwear that had to be washed every night so that the trader could wear it the next morning. Once, for 13 consecutive days, Marlowe King insisted that a bunch of us have lunch in the same restaurant, at the same table, sitting in the same chairs. A bear market move in eggs had begun after we first ate there, and we were all short the market. So there we were, every day. Unfortunately, I had picked up the check on the first day, and Marlowe insisted that I must do so every day so long as the streak continued.

Ever since my days as a runner, I viewed life at the Merc as a series of stop-action photographs tucked away in the gallery of my mind. One minute it could be a wild west show, the next a ship adrift in deep doldrums. The place ran hot and cold, and there was always some sort of struggle going on. And while there were no lives at stake, there were a lot of livelihoods on the line, which often turned tempers as volatile as the commodities themselves.

At times, the Merc trading pits gave meaning to Darwin's theory of survival of the fittest. One day Sol Rich—one of the princes of the egg market and a Merc stalwart—bullied his way into the pork belly pit, pushing and kicking traders aside. I was one of the traders he kicked, and I would not stand for it. So I made a formal complaint before the Board. It was an unheard of maneuver. Some of the Board members pressured me to back off and to forget about it. Milt Rich, Sol's son, whom I respected, also thought I should back off, but Sol Rich's arrogance and disregard for fellow members had gotten to me. He was reprimanded, and he apologized. It enhanced my reputation as a tough fighter. To me, Rich's attitude was symptomatic of the old guard who often placed self-interest above the reputation of the Merc. The roughhouse of trading cliques would squeeze and corner markets, driving prices up one day and down the next, and in the process, the Merc's character suffered to the point that outsiders dubbed the exchange the "Whorehouse of the Loop."

Perhaps there is no better example of how the old-timers abused their positions than when Miles Friedman bought the entire egg market. It took place long before I arrived at the exchange, but the incident was so blatant it became a part of the Merc lore. Miles Friedman was a tough, barrel-chested Merc powerhouse whose trademark was a flower in his lapel. Like many of his contemporaries, Friedman came out of the butter and egg era and gained a strong grip on the exchange for years. He was Merc chairman in 1939, and his son-in-law, Nathan Werthheimer, was chairman in 1966. They were the heirs of the Mandeville, Isadore Katz, Saul Stone, Hy Henner, Harry Redfearn, and Barney Schreiber era that had ruled the exchange with an iron fist.

One morning, Friedman walked up to the boards (there was no pit trading) that listed all the egg prices for the near and distant months. The bids were listed on one side, the offers on the other. He planted himself in front of the offer side and waved his hand. The board marker chalked a slash through the month and initialed "M.F." to indicate Miles Friedman had bought all the eggs for that particular month. Friedman walked to the next board and yelled, "Buy 'em." And so on down the line. When he was through, Friedman had bought the entire offering of the exchange. He owned all the egg contracts. As news of this happening spread, the traders were stunned as they gathered around. He walked off the floor without saying a word and returned to his office. The egg market was limit up.

What did Miles Friedman know that no one else did? Enough to make a small fortune. Inside his pocket was a telegram from the United States Department of Agriculture addressed to the chairman of the Chicago Mercantile Exchange, Miles Friedman. That day the Agriculture Department had announced a nationwide school lunch program, which meant the government would be buying a lot of eggs in the coming months, and prices were sure to go higher. So Friedman promptly went out and cornered the egg market.

Afterwards, the Board called an emergency session to figure out how exactly it was going to deal with Friedman's blatant indiscretion. There was no fine. No reprimand. No threat of expulsion. The only solution was a settlement of some type that called for him to sell out some of his position and accept a reduced profit. After all, he did buy the eggs before anyone else and was entitled to a profit for his trouble. In short, his unethical behavior had been duly rewarded, and he remained chairman.

That's how it went in those days. By the time I got there in the 1950s, things hadn't improved much. When I bought my membership in 1954, the Merc was a third-rate marketplace with a total of 500 members, roughly half of whom ever came to the floor. And a trading floor comprised three sunken octagonal pits of which only two were used: one for eggs, the other for onions.

Eggs were the big market, but they were extremely vulnerable to manipulation. I used to joke that on any given weekend a couple of housewives could get together and corner the market. That was an overstatement, but not by much. Cornering the egg market was usually the pastime of the likes of Harold Fox. Fox was an executive of Fox Deluxe Foods, a national firm that processed poultry, eggs, dairy products, and even its own line of beer. The firm, started as Peter Fox & Sons, was run by the nine brothers of the Fox family. Fox Deluxe was sold in the late 1970s to the Pillsbury organization. Harold's uncle, Michael Fox, had been Merc chairman in the late 1930s. Harold Fox, a four-pack-a-day smoker who always had a cigarette dangling from his mouth and ashes on his vest, was one of the Merc's biggest egg traders. The Fox family of that era was notorious for its alleged manipulations of the egg markets. Fortunately, time passed and things changed. While the Fox family remained permanent citizens of the Merc, Harold's cousin, Joe Fox, became a pillar of the new CME and my strong ally. Joe's wife Ann is a Merc member, as are his sons, John, Mark, Thomas, and Timothy, who do business throughout the floor as brokers, with Joe Jr. working for the exchange.

Within four years of my becoming a member, the Merc would be reduced to a one-pit exchange, teetering on the brink of extinction. The onion debacle was the primary cause. Onions had come to the exchange with great hoopla and anticipation. Onions were a volatile commodity greatly affected by weather, which provided the Merc members with lots of action. Unfortunately, the onion contract was poorly designed and prone to manipulation. It immediately became a source of trouble. It had attracted to the Merc some new produce wheeler-dealers. If it wasn't a corner, it was a squeeze, or some other attempted manipulative activity. The Board in those days did little to discourage the questionable business that onions were bringing to the exchange. Live and let live, so to speak; after all, as brokers, the Board members were all benefiting from the income generated by the manipulators. I remember once, when a manipulation went beyond even what that Board could stand, the governors came out with some ridiculous action to liquidate the contract without endangering the price to which the manipulation had driven it. I had just become a member, and Joe Sieger, who was still chairman, gave me an order to stand in the onion pit and bid 3.59 for all who would sell while offering at 3.60 for all who would buy. In other words, I and a few other brokers were given an unlimited order, something unheard of in the annals of markets, in order to allow all open positions to be liquidated at a price set by the Board. This was a new definition for free markets, and a new low for the Merc Board.

Then, in 1957, these cutthroat manipulators, acting on an imagined onion shortage, drove the price of onions to unparalleled heights. In the process, instead of hedging their crops at profitable prices, onion farmers were counseled to put on what is known as a "Texas hedge"—they bought the futures market for speculative purposes. The result was predictable. When the bubble burst, the price of onions came crashing down. Onions ended up selling for less than the price of the burlap bags in which they were delivered. The onion farmers of America were outraged. They had lost money on their crops as well as on their futures contracts. They drove their tractors to their congressmen and demanded retribution. On August 28, 1958, Congress took an unheard of and historical step: onion trading on the Merc was outlawed by congressional edict.

In an unprecedented action, Congress had actually passed a law to ban trading a futures contract on an exchange in a given commodity. It was an unbelievable shock for the membership, and engendered a humiliating low point for its self-esteem. While I would not attempt to condone the Merc for its ineptitude, which produced the onion debacle, I felt that Congress overstepped its legal bounds. And to this day, I believe that the congressional onion ban, at a minimum, breached the commerce clause of the U.S. Constitution, which guarantees unabridged commerce between states. But after the Merc's lawyers lost in the U.S. Appellate Court, they backed down and were afraid to challenge the law in the Supreme Court. The Board was counseled by its lawyers and other exchanges not to go further with the appeal process lest the onion legislation become a terrible precedent for all futures exchanges. Never mind that, if allowed to stand, it was already a precedent. The Merc was now reduced to a one-pit exchange, teetering on the brink of extinction.

I was bitter and in the camp that believed the Merc should have appealed. But I was then very young and only a small part-time trader. My early rabble-rousing against the Board had no effect. By then, the membership was so disillusioned that no one had the appetite to take on the United States Congress. The shock of having the U.S. Congress single out the Chicago Mercantile Exchange was of such embarrassment that most members just wanted to hide. So the membership took its punishment, brooded, and tried to go about its business as if nothing catastrophic happened. Of course, this proved to be nearly impossible, and membership prices eventually sunk to $3,000 where they had to be subsidized by edict of the Board. It was hard to believe that this bastion of free markets would decree to support seat prices. But then again, this was the same Merc Board that paid homage to the past, that countenanced egg corners year after year by the same traders, that allowed the debacle in the onion market, and had cut a deal with Miles Friedman.

But those early days on the Merc floor gave me a great deal of knowledge and insight. I watched and listened. I peeked into all its nooks and crannies. I learned of the Merc history, its heritage, its strengths and weaknesses; I learned how the Board operates and rules the membership; I learned of the Merc hierarchy, about its cadre of untouchables; I learned the codes, the mores and the rules; I learned how expert brokers fill their orders and how successful traders make their money; I learned the do's and don'ts, the good and the bad, the tricks of the trade, the underhanded tactics and the shenanigans; I learned how to scalp the market, how to live in the pit, how to evaluate reports, how to read traders' minds, and how to feel the market.

But mostly I learned from the old-timers who roamed that floor. Take Elmer Falker, for instance. On any given day in the 1950s, he'd stroll across the floor, an elderly, cigar-chomping bachelor just under five-feet tall, still wearing spats and driving to and from work in his spiffy 1932 Franklin. He could send an oyster into the corner spittoon from 30 feet. I don't know how many fortunes he had gone through, but by the time I met him, he was broke. Rumor had it he lost all his money waiting for a gap to be filled on a butter chart, but the market never came back to fill the gap. He was one of the early chart technicians who took me under wing and dispensed all sorts of tips and advice. In fact, Elmer believed he had the secret technical formula for making commodity fortunes. He would lead me to the chart room in back of the trading floor, peer at the charts that were pinned to a bulletin-board, write some figures on his cards, do some mysterious calculations, and confide to me what the day's high and low would be in, say, September eggs. At other times, he would point to the charts, spit into a nearby spittoon, take the cigar stub from his mouth, and point it at an area on the chart and say with complete confidence that from that level a sale was a sure thing or a buy was money in the bank. Elmer never dealt in probabilities; he was always dead certain of his predictions and chart theory. When they were wrong, as they often were, he would not refer to them again. If in my naive thirst for knowledge I would ask for an explanation, he would in no uncertain terms explain what went wrong, and leave me with the impression that the reasons were so obvious that I was hopelessly stupid. The funny thing was that Elmer was treated with respect by most on the Exchange floor. You see, Elmer's predictions were sometimes dead right. It was uncanny. Besides, Elmer had a store of knowledge that many deeply respected. So even the most hard-boiled fundamentalist—who, like my boss Joe Sieger, considered charts nothing more than "chicken scratches" and chartists nothing more than tribal pagans—would at times come to Elmer, tongue-in-cheek, to ask his opinion about the market. These fundamentalists pretended to be mocking the little guy, but deep down, I knew they were seriously interested in Falker's answer.

A few years later, after I had taken a leadership role in Merc affairs, Elmer Falker sidled up to me and in an ominous whisper warned, "Don't let our futures market get too successful."

"Why not?" I asked.

"Because futures markets tell the truth and nobody wants to know the truth. If the truth is too bad and too loud, they'll close us down."

I nodded in agreement, amazed at the deep philosophical thought uttered by this old man. I had a pretty good idea what Falker meant, but it would be more than 30 years and the stock market crash of 1987 before his words would come back to me. The Merc's stock index contract was first to tell the world the truth about the crashing stock market, so the Merc was blamed for the fall. The little guy was truly a sage. He died with the unwavering belief in his secret formula for trading. He was, however, practically penniless when he died, proving there is no magic formula for trading. It is from

Elmer that I learned the hardest lesson of all: a good trader has to admit when he is wrong. I learned to discard my ego.

Roy Simmons represented the other side of the trading spectrum. He was one of the Merc traders, who would always get in on a squeeze, be it eggs or onions. Besides being an outstanding trader, he was also a professional "coattail"—someone who hung on to the coattails of the manipulators for the market ride it provided. On one onion play, Simmons and other big traders locked themselves in a hotel room so they wouldn't be tempted to sell out of their positions and break the squeeze. Simmons, the stoic and foxy trader that he was, hedged his bet. He had arranged a special signal with his clerk: if the window shade in the room was pulled down, that was the signal to sell out of his position—and damn the others. After listening to the others in the room, Simmons decided their manipulation would fail anyway, so he calmly walked over to the window and pulled the shade down. And the market went down with it. But not before Simmons got out with big profit.

And there was Sam Schneider. Like Miles Friedman, Harold Fox, Saul Stone, Izzy Mulmat, and Bill Katz, he also was an egg merchant and trader. On days when egg trading was slow, Schneider, in his heavy Jewish accent, would walk around shouting, "It's lackity, it's lackity," his personalized description for a lackluster market.

Schneider owned an egg-breaking plant that supplied bakeries, restaurants, and other commercial users with egg yolks or the whites, depending on their needs. The eggs would be broken by hand. He was a tyrant with a sweatshop mentality who perched himself on a stool atop a table in front of his workers and tapped his cane in a snappy rhythm to keep the production line moving. One time, Schneider told me how he handled government health inspectors. "When the federalists came to inspect my plant," he said in his heavy eastern European accent, "I threw them down the stairs." There was no doubt in my mind that he did just that. The Schneider family spans three generations on the Merc floor, his grandson Jimmy, became a close friend.

Sam Schneider could be as cunning as he was tough. At the beginning of each year, he'd borrow $100,000 from the First National Bank of Chicago to operate his plant. During the Depression, no one was buying eggs, and Schneider needed more money. So he went back to the bank for a second $100,000 in the same year. This time he got turned down. "I'm sorry," the loan officer said. "We can't do it, you don't have the collateral." Schneider stood up, extended his hand and said, "Congratulations, you now own an egg-breaking plant. Goodbye." He got his $100,000. It was my first "too big to fail" lesson. In 1995, the government of Mexico tested that axiom to its limit with the United States.

The Merc floor was a biosphere of humanity, and I never knew what was going to set someone off. But whatever it was, fists and insults would fly. It was against the law, but that didn't matter. I got my first glimpse of a near-death confrontation in the early days when Johnny Jung, a big Swede with muscles, got Bill Henner in a headlock on the floor, and Henner's face turned white. If board marker Billy Muno hadn't broken it up, Henner might have choked to death. Billy Muno was a very good friend of mine who went on to become a Board member himself during the so-called Melamed era. "From board marker to Board member," Muno would say. "Only in America," I would reply.

Bill Henner was Hyman Henner's son; Hyman was a Board member and a major domo on the exchange. (Little wonder the Henners were in the egg business; "henner" means chickens in Yiddish.) His son Bill preferred being a cynical naysayer who was always mouthing off. His other son David was an excellent trader who made "touching-off stops" into an art form.

Louis Urban, was another hard-to-forget floor character. He was a successful broker for one of the legendary onion squeezers, Vince Kasuga. Urban's fortunes unfortunately went with onions. He ended up flat broke, and years later, the exchange members held a collection for him. But in his heyday, Urban's tongue could lash out with the best of them. He walked up to me one day and whispered, "You know, the more I see of Izzy Mulmat, the more I love my neighbor's dog." It was the type of nasty and hateful statements that were prevalent around the floor, especially when another trader made you lose money. The Mulmat brothers, Izzy and Jack were powerhouses on the exchange. Izzy was an outstanding trader who often influenced the direction of the egg market by simply walking into the pit. But he had a deep-seated cynicism and a mean temper. Once during an argument, Izzy chased Charlie Keeshin around the trading floor and right out the door of the Exchange in Keystone Cop fashion. And his brother Jack, (Maury Kravitz nicknamed Jack, "King Farouk") with arms crossed, stood at the door blocking Izzy from going after Keeshin onto the staircase. We were certain that King Farouk saved Izzy's life, because if he continued to go after Charlie, he surely would have died from a heart attack. Violence on the floor is a tradition that has continued on through the years. As activity heightened, so did the type of altercation. For instance, not long ago in the S&P pit during a hectic trading session, a broker who had become overwrought, lost it and bit the finger of a fellow trader whose hand motions had gotten on his nerves.

The place was always full of siblings, then as now. Besides the brothers Mulmat, there were the brothers Katz, the brothers Siegel, the brothers Fox, the brothers Henner, the brothers Schneider, the brothers Keeshin, the brothers Schreiber, the brothers Schulte, among others. There were fathers and sons and grandsons and cousins and son-in-laws by the droves. The place was a web of dynasties—a vassal state presided over by a board of lords that grew out of the butter and egg culture, which supplied a hungry, tough city in the late nineteenth century. If anyone had tried to construct a family tree of the Merc's 500 members, it wouldn't have surprised me to find everyone connected in some way. In a way, this was a Chicago tradition. Both at the Merc and at the Chicago Board of Trade, the trading profession was handed down to one's children. Today, the Merc floor is full of the offspring of my generation of traders: the Munos, the Boyles, the Schneiders, the Moniesons, the Foxes, the Millers, the Carls, the Cahills, the Schillers, the Shenders, the Zeidmans. The list is endless.

It was the kind of place you would hear "goddammit" muttered in every other breath. Outsiders could casually walk on the trading floor because a badge or a pass wasn't required. There was no dress code, no trading jacket. And smoke was everywhere, thick acrid clouds of it, billowing from cigarettes, cigars, and pipes that hung from the mouths of the traders in the pits. Obviously, neither was there a no-smoking code. But as a chain-smoker myself I wasn't about to complain. In fact, nobody complained about anything. And that was the problem. The prevailing attitude seemed to be that, if it was broken, ignore it. As a clerk back then, I was hardly in a position of influence. And even after I got my membership in 1954, no one was about to listen to a part-time trader. Still, I loved to walk the floor listening to the stories and gossip. Sifting through the accounts, I never knew what was true and what wasn't. But it didn't matter. It was a place that kept me guessing. I never knew from one minute to the next what was going to happen. Once, a trader keeled over in the pit with a heart attack. The traders kept right on trading. Another time, a jilted wife stormed onto the floor and attacked her unfaithful husband in the trading pit by slugging him with her purse. People drank, swore, played cards, and Ping-Pong.

I seldom drank, but I did all the other things. Before I became an avid bridge player, I was an avid Ping-Pong player. I had even won a teenage championship in Humboldt Park. During slow trading days at the Merc—and there were plenty of those—usually a hot Ping-Pong match would be going on. A table was set up in a back room off the trading floor (later it became the statistical department under Walter Kowalski), where I would play with Ruby Carl or Robert Redfearn, or get thoroughly trounced by Marvin Prager. Prager and I went back to our teenage days when we were both at Camp Kinderland, near South Haven, Michigan, and I was a counselor and the camp's hotshot Ping-Pong player. One day, this thin, tall, gawky guy showed up and waited for his turn at the table. I should have known something was up when he took his own paddle out of his back pocket. But I thought it was just a one-upmanship gambit, as was his offer to spot me 10 points on the game, which, in a game of 21 is a ridiculously large offer. I judged it was done to irritate me and psyche me out of winning.

All the kids gathered around to see the challenge that was about to un-fold. After all, I was their hero, and they wanted vengeance. I, of course, refused the spot. And then the roof caved in. Prager beat me 21 to zip. I mean, it was unheard of. For a seasoned player not to win even a single point was unbelievable. Not to mention how humiliating an experience it was for me, the camp's Ping-Pong champ, devastated before all his admir-ers. Of course, none of us knew at the time that Marvin Prager was a na-tionally rated U.S. table tennis champ. Clearly, I was no match for Prager as a teenager or as an adult. But we became good friends, and he proceeded to teach me the game so that by the end of the summer I could actually score 10 points against him.

Later in our lives, I got him a job at the Merc with Bill Rankin, who was the chief broker for Bache & Co. and quite a character. Rankin had a mean temper and was seldom sober. Reputedly, he drank his breakfast, as did plenty of other brokers on the floor. After several years working as a phone clerk, Marvin Prager asked for a week's vacation. Rankin gave it to him. When Prager returned, he found someone else sitting at the desk.

"Where do I sit?" Prager asked Rankin.

"Who the hell are you?" Rankin retorted. It was vintage Rankin and Prager never did get his job back.

These are the kind of sensibilities I was exposed to in my early Merc days. They were imparted by people who taught me about the markets they lived with. I knew how a market was supposed to work, keyed to supply and demand; they knew how to work the markets keyed to their advantage.

The one thing the Merc did have going for it was energy, but it was pent-up energy that needed uncorking. There were fits and starts, but no dramatic change until 1964. Butter was dead. Onions were dead. Eggs were gasping. At one time or another, the Merc had tried to trade, or considered trading futures contracts on apples, cheese hides, chickens, turkeys, pecans, and orange juice concentrate. The exchange even broke stride and tried to trade in scrap iron and shrimps, the latter effort led by Gilbert Miller, whose two sons, Alan and Bruce became steadfast cattle brokers and members of my elite corps.

Fortunately, by the time I became a full-time trader, the Merc had made some important and impressive strides to change its course. In 1961, it began trading contracts on the pork belly, a frozen slab of uncured bacon. It was slow going for a few years, however. The size of the contract had to be changed a couple of times until suddenly it hit a home run. But by 1965, the public craving for bacon and eggs had dramatically boosted the Merc's fortunes. Nearly 90 percent of 1965's first-half volume was accounted for by pork bellies. And the boom was reflected in seat prices: a membership now sold for $8,500, up from the $3,000 price support. The Merc was fast becoming known as the house that bellies built.

The Merc, in 1964, had also taken another dramatic step. It began trading live cattle contracts. For the first time in the history of futures trading, there was a market in a nonstorable product. And wonders of wonders, it was a market in a product that was alive and kicking. Under Stephen Greenberg's rule, the Merc had broken the age-old tradition that futures contracts had to be storable. Unfortunately, cattle weren't an instant success. Again the specifications were wrong. A few years later, as chairman, I directed a revamping of the contract and appointed Glen Andersen to do the job. Within a year after Andersen changed the specifications, the cattle contract came to life. In proving that we could succeed with a non-stored product, we broke the futures genetic code for the first time.

While the Merc had become a brew of inbreeding, old-boy cronyism, and moral ambivalence that was becoming harder and harder to swallow, it was a paradox to me. Pork bellies and live cattle were clear signs that the Merc had the stomach for change and innovation. Yet with these successes, the Board seemed to grow more insular, which was contrary to the times. The Merc's intimacy and its lack of pretense should have led to an openness for fresh ideas from the rank and file. Here, among the open outcries, was a place driven by a staccato sense of time toward the future, yet its leaders were in a time warp somewhere in the past. There was no doubt, at least in my mind, that the Merc cried out for political reform. We wanted our voices heard.

The battle lines had been drawn, and the first skirmish took place in 1961 while I was still a part-time trader. The need for change began to echo around the trading floor. It's one thing to sense a need for change, quite another to harness that change. It's a lesson failed leaders learn the hard way. That's what my colleagues and I faced when we took on the Merc Board in June 1961. So I looked at the Merc's arcane rules, which had been neglected since their original creation with little update.

One rule in particular caught my eye. It centered on the quorum needed to hold a membership meeting. Of the Merc's 500 members, 300, or 60 percent, were required to hold a meeting. The percentage was so high that it effectively prevented a membership meeting from ever being held. Consequently, the leadership of the exchange was virtually controlled by a small group of members. The rank and file literally had no voice in the process, and the quorum rule prevented them from ever introducing their ideas.

I became a member of the Brokers' Club and, because I was an attorney, I was asked to be its legal advisor. Initially formed in the early 1950s, the

Brokers' Club was primarily a social organization, but it also had activist ambitions that unfortunately fell short of intentions. It had hoped to exert pressure on the Board to adopt constructive policies and, at the same time, get new members elected to the Board. Among the Club's founding members was my new boss, Kenneth Birks, the Merrill Lynch broker for whom I worked as a phone clerk after my stint as a runner for Joe Sieger. Birks was honest to a fault, had a sharp mind and an iron will. Another member was Dan Jesser, by profession an electrical engineer who was a skilled trader with a moral fiber difficult to match. Jesser had carried me through my sporadic trading days by lending me money to keep my trading account alive. And there was Marlowe King, my close comrade-in-arms, an excellent trader, level-headed and logical; and there was even Bill Henner, who, while often difficult to get along with, had good intentions and knew quite a lot about the inner workings of the place. There was also Robert O'Brien, a straight-up guy, who became the first CME chairman sponsored by the Brokers' Club. All in all, there were about 20 members. The Club had remained dormant through most of the 1950s. As a social outlet it was redundant because, in those days, the Merc was already like one big club. There was less competition, more camaraderie, and the place was small. So there was really no need for a club within a club. But now the Brokers' Club had been revived and reshaped into a den of dissidents. And Birks and O'Brien, who preceded my generation of traders, were two of its loudest voices. Ken Birks eventually became the primary force to catapult me to CME leadership, and Robert O'Brien would help me take over at the end of his chairmanship term. After I became Merc chairman, I campaigned to elect Dan Jesser and Marlowe King to the Board, as well as others from the Brokers' Club. By then, of course, my relationship with Dan Jesser and Marlowe King had moved beyond the trading floor to a personal level. The Jessers, Dan and his wife Pauline, had become family friends to the Melameds. Marlowe King and I have remained lifelong friends who could trust each other with our lives.

In the beginning, the Brokers' Club members met to gripe to each other in private. There had to be an air of secrecy, since some of the members depended on their livelihood from the very people about whom they were complaining. Besides, the Board was all-powerful, and if word of our dissatisfaction leaked out, who could tell what retribution it might take. I loved the place, and the others felt the same way. But I had deep convictions that something was terribly wrong. I saw might make right. I saw rules given lip service and a wink. I saw the Exchange run by a rotation of chairmen who were in office to benefit themselves, who were set in their ways, who relied on antiquated rules and discredited concepts, who ruled the Exchange with an iron fist, and who were stone deaf to new ideas or

the needs of the members. I saw market corners, pit chicanery, and commission kickbacks. I saw the rule of the jungle, and the rule book become a
mockery to the rule of law.

One could legitimately wonder why the membership tolerated these
conditions. After all, they had the power of the ballot box; a Board member
had to face reelection every two years. Why didn't the membership simply
throw the rascals out? I guess the answer is ubiquitous to politics. It is not
easy to effect change. It would take a revolution, and revolutions take a
long time to foment.

For instance, when Franklin Roosevelt introduced the New Deal in 1933
he set in motion a philosophy that sponsored growing government involvement into the lives of U.S. citizens. At the time, it was what the nation
needed and wanted. But after many decades, there was a growing dissatisfaction with that philosophy. There were demands for change. Still the Roosevelt philosophy continued unabated. Finally, 1994 rang the bell on the end
of that era. Good or bad, right or wrong, an era of less federal government
intervention seemed to have dawned. This political revolution, like every
revolution, needed certain ingredients to coalesce before it occurred. It
needed time, it needed initiative, it needed a special issue, and it needed
leadership. It was no different at the Merc. Member dissatisfaction had been
growing for years, but the other ingredients had not yet been incorporated.
In the meantime, the membership continued to hobble under the old set
of rules.

Indeed, if it weren't for Kenneth Mackay, the Merc's executive vice president, there might not even be a rule book. Mackay was a kindly man, a Mr.
Peepers type, a man who knew right from wrong. But he was the only one
who knew what the rules were. Mackay had the rule book in his head, and
one never knew from one day to the next if he rewrote a rule to fit his interpretation or not. I liked Mackay because I knew he was not malevolent, and
his motivations seemed always to be good. But nobody else had a record of
the Board's actions. Nobody else knew the history or intent of a given rule.
And E.B. Harris, the CME President, never dared to question Mackay's
memory, so there was no arguing with Mackay. There was only one rule
book and he had it. Of similar importance was Mrs. Dewey, E.B. Harris's
administrative aide. Mrs. Dewey, too was a kindly person. She had the keys
to the front office, and could do favors—if she liked you. She could also
bend the rules with a wink and a smile, and Mackay would go along.

Membership in the Brokers' Club was a dramatic contradiction to the
makeup of the existing Board of Governors. We were then relatively young,
aggressive, and without a stake in the establishment. We were, for the most
part, financially insecure, had nothing to lose, and were dissatisfied with
the status quo. And, at the moment, status quo meant an annual transaction

volume that had fallen to a low of 25,000 contracts; the CME's market share was at 4 percent of U.S. futures.

I recall that we were seated around a large table at the Bismarck Hotel where the Brokers' Club often rented a room for its dinner meetings. There were about a dozen of us and it was twenty dollars a person to cover the costs. I had everyone's attention as I tried to explain that we could change nothing at the Merc until we lowered the quorum requirements to a realistic level. That was step number one.

"Listen, guys," I said, warming up to the subject, "If you can't hold a meeting, you can't change the system. I come from Poland where the voice of the individual wasn't always so important. But this is America, here everyone's voice counts. Except, that is, at the CME. At the Merc, our voices have no meaning because we need three hundred members before we count. That's a joke and the Board knows it."

Everyone agreed. But to no one's surprise, when we demanded the quorum change, the board rejected the notion out of hand and we were literally laughed out of the boardroom. I then called Lee Freeman, the Merc's attorney. Although we had once met, he really didn't remember me. He actually chuckled over the phone. "If you do what you propose," he told me in no uncertain terms, "it will be meaningless."

What I proposed was basic. I even obtained a copy of the Merc's original by-laws filed with the Illinois Secretary of State to ensure that I was on solid legal footing. All we had to do was call for a members' meeting and offer a resolution to lower the quorum requirements. If such a resolution were passed by the members, then it would necessarily have to be accepted by the Board.

"This is the United States of America," I said, waxing eloquently to the members of the Brokers' Club. "The Merc is an Illinois corporation no matter what our Board members think. No way can the CME Board or its attorney Lee Freeman ignore the laws of the land." And if they do, I ventured, "I am prepared to take it to the courts."

At this point, we weren't yet caught up in any grand scheme to create a sleeker institution with a youthful air. The strategy was driven by a more practical sense—survival. We recognized that another onion debacle could drive the Exchange straight into oblivion. It wasn't exactly a palace revolt, and we certainly didn't set out with a sweeping series of management changes. Instead, I aimed for one specific target. The strategy I devised with my colleague-in-arms Ken Birks was to call for a special meeting of the Merc membership in order to revise the quorum requirements under Rule 109. The number we wanted was 100, or 20 percent, as opposed to 60 percent in the existing rule. But there was a catch-22. To call the special meeting required a quorum of 300 members.

There was but one solution. We had to obtain a sufficient number of proxies to hold a duly qualified meeting. Such a task had never before been attempted, and it primarily fell on the shoulders of Ken Birks. I authored the proxy, and Ken Birks, who had strong credibility with the membership and good credentials because he was the Merrill Lynch broker, headed up the proxy effort. To this day I marvel at his accomplishment. Methodically, he wrote, called, and cajoled the out-of-town members for their proxy. The rest of us rallied the Chicago-based members with the cry of reform. All the while, the Board was sure the meeting would never take place, and if it did, it wouldn't matter.

Although our group was small, we were well organized and managed to do what our opponents thought impossible. Thanks mostly to Ken Birks, the Brokers' Club had gathered 120 proxies—enough to pull it off. The first milestone in the journey to the new Merc had been reached.

On the warm, humid afternoon of June 14, 1961, the annual Merc members' meeting was called to order at the Bismarck Hotel. But at this meeting there was the required number of members present—in person and through proxy—for a legal quorum. It was unique to the history of the Chicago Mercantile Exchange. Per my instructions, the proxies had been duly registered with Ken Mackay prior to the meeting. I spoke to him personally and trusted that he would report the truth to the chairman when he was openly asked whether a quorum was present. It was the required ritual before the meeting got underway. For the first time in Ken Mackay's tenure, he responded in the affirmative. Hands shaking but voice steady, I presented the proposition to the members. Then I held my breath. It was adopted by a resounding voice vote. The young Turks had won the first battle. Or did we? There was a great deal of nervous anticipation. No one knew how the Board, under the chairmanship of Bill Katz, would respond. Katz was the ultimate power, having been chairman throughout the early 1960s and having led the Exchange with an iron fist for the past decade. Bill Katz, a lawyer who never practiced, joined the Merc in 1930, beginning as an egg dealer and trader. His business was founded by his father Samuel at the turn of the century when he opened a butter and egg store at 14th and Carpenter in Chicago. It grew into an egg-breaking enterprise, one of the biggest in Chicago which Bill Katz and his brother Isadore ran from the floor of the Merc.

Speaking for the Board, Katz publicly stated the next day that nothing the members did at this meeting had any validity. The quorum requirements were not changed until the Board chose to do so. That was the edict of the Merc's general counsel Lee A. Freeman and endorsed by the other 11 members of the Board.

At the next Board meeting, the Merc governors immersed themselves in the matter. Debate lapsed into argument. Tempers were hot, and there was plenty of cursing. There was a great deal of sentiment that the dissidents should not get their way. *If they win this one, who knows what they'll ask for next?* Left to their own devices, the Board would have probably rejected the members' motion. But Lee A. Freeman knew better. Although he had publicly stated that the members' action was invalid, I always thought that his private view was different. While I was nowhere his match in legal ability, he must have known that I had led the Brokers' Club onto solid ground. If he tested our will, he would lose in court. So at the Board meeting, behind closed doors, he adopted a different posture. He argued that the way to avoid any confrontation was for the Board to adopt the members' quorum change voluntarily. That way the official record would show that the board chose to lower the quorum requirements of its own volition. More than two hours later, the Board adopted the amendment to Rule 109. The quorum requirement had been lowered to the realistic number of 100.

After the Board meeting, there appeared to be no hard feelings between the camps. But I knew full well that you can make peace with enemies, but not with memories. The victory of the Brokers' Club wasn't a case of generational chauvinism or the iconoclasm of the sixties; the Merc simply had to keep up with the times, and that meant change and compromise. Overnight, I had become a hero.

As for the members of Brokers' Club, we were feeling pretty good about ourselves. The quorum victory had served as a warning to the Merc's elders of what to expect in the future from its younger members. As spokesman for the dissidents, I was perceived as being defiant. Thinking back, perhaps it was part of my nature to be so. I had defied the odds by escaping the Holocaust. I had defied more odds by reaching the safety of this country. And a few years later, I would defy my partner's plea not to leave law. I would even defy my father at the painful cost of rejection. And again I would defy the Board.

Still, as I said, revolutions don't happen overnight.

In 1961, we had taken only our first step in a revolution that would take the better part of the next five years. My timing couldn't have been better when I settled at the Exchange in 1965. While I knew full well that soldiers don't start out as generals, I also knew that it helps to have front-line action when the time comes to move higher in the ranks. I was ready for the next battle.

10

Into the Pits

By 1964, my law practice was eclectic, and I was handling everything from personal injury and divorce to real estate and bankruptcy. A few years earlier, I had left Mayster for a new partner, Maury Kravitz, who I had known since my days at Navy Pier. A good-natured, raspy-voiced dynamo, Kravitz could walk into a room with 50 strangers and within an hour come out with 49 "best" friends. Like me, Kravitz also was an only child. His parents had emigrated from Eastern Europe, landed in Cuba where they met and married, then moved to Philadelphia. Maury Kravitz was born there. In 1939, at the time my family left Bialystok, Kravitz's family moved to Chicago. Like my father, Kravitz's dad was scholarly and heavily involved in the Yiddish world as an editor of a Yiddish newspaper. It was natural for us to become close friends.

After a three-year hitch in the U.S. Army, having spent most of the time in Germany, Kravitz enrolled at John Marshall Law School at about the time I was graduating. When I was promoted to a telephone clerk at the Merc, I got Kravitz my old job as Joe Sieger's runner. He also was quickly bitten by the trading bug, and in the mid-1950s he bought a membership and traded full time. But after losing his trading stake, Kravitz sold his seat and went back into law in 1957.

I had introduced him to my first secretary, Mona Wallace, and told him that she had a good head on her shoulder and a great body. If I wasn't already married, I said, I would go after her. Kravitz took my advice and it was love at first sight. Eventually, they were married. Kravitz was an idea man, lovable, and innovative. Sometimes his ideas were very imaginative. Once he tried to start a Sword of the Month Club for all those "can't live without it" sword lovers of the world. Another time he tried to sign up all the Seminole Indians of the State of Florida in their would-be land claims against the United States government. We had a lot of fun. At first, times were difficult, but when they got better, we bought a boat. It was a 33-foot cabin cruiser that we christened the *Dellsher* after my daughter, Idelle, and his daughter, Sheryl.

One bright Monday morning, Kravitz walked into my office with another idea. The rumor on the street, Kravitz said, was that Cosmopolitan Insurance Company—a big automobile insurer—was on its last legs about to go belly up. It was a period when the insurance industry in Illinois was mired in fraud and the courts. Some insurance companies, like Cosmopolitan, had been set up to milk the premiums from policyholders without ever intending to pay any claims. The insurance companies knew time was on their side. If their policyholders were sued as a result of an automobile accident, they would refuse to pay and let the claims linger in court. They used every available delaying tactic. It took nearly six years to get a judgment, meanwhile they would continue to receive the premiums. Eventually, the company would go bankrupt before the caseload of claims against their policyholders had to be paid. It was an outright scam and the State Insurance Commission had begun to crack down. If Cosmopolitan went bankrupt, then the State would appoint a liquidator to liquidate the assets of the insurance company and claims against it. The way Kravitz figured, the lawyers named as liquidator, would have access to a potential client list of policyholders that numbered in the thousands. He became excited as he explained the plan.

"You see, Leo, it's a cinch. With Cosmo bankrupt, their policyholders will need to hire a lawyer to defend themselves in the accident claims that have been filed against them in court."

"And that will be Melamed and Kravitz?" I asked.

"You bet. We will be the first to notify them and call them in to explain that Cosmo is dead."

While I told Kravitz not to be so certain about his scheme, he was already counting the thousands of clients we were about to get. We would become big-time, he insisted. His exuberance was infectious and won me over.

The insurance liquidator was a fellow named John Bolton who had been appointed by then Illinois Governor Otto Kerner. Kravitz went to work on him—charmed the very pants off the guy and underbid everyone else. Finally, Bolton appointed us as attorneys for the liquidator. Melamed and Kravitz were on their way. In our haste to get the business, we were willing to work for a song. Actually, it was more of a whistle. We had asked for only expenses, two secretaries and two typewriters. We took a chance with a low-ball bid, figuring that if 20 percent of the 5,500 cases became our clients, our law practice would thrive for the next decade.

One evening reality set in. It came in a truckload of files from Cosmopolitan delivered to our office. Our suite of two offices and an anteroom overflowed with file cabinets. We hardly had room to breathe. At first we were thrilled and celebrated that night with a champagne dinner together with our wives, Mona and Betty. There was even some welcomed publicity in a newspaper article that stated we had been appointed to handle the Cosmopolitan case. Working 15-hour days, our secretaries typed all the documentation in order to file everything with the clerk of the court. All the cases against the policyholders had be notified that we were now the *Attorneys of Record* on behalf of these defendants. We also notified all the policyholders of the bad news about Cosmopolitan and to come in to discuss the fact that they would now need their own attorney to defend themselves. If they didn't hire Melamed and Kravitz, it would have to be someone else. Shortly thereafter, the defendant parade began. Day after day, a dozen or so people would come to our office. Soon it became clear we had made a giant miscalculation. The people filing in to our office would plead poverty; they had nothing. Besides that, they blamed us and threatened us, thinking we worked for Cosmopolitan.

"What do you mean I don't have an attorney? Who are you?"

"Well, you see, we work for the State liquidator. But its only temporary."

"Oh yeah? Well, I got no money and the whole thing is a rip-off."

Sometimes it would nearly get violent as they would storm out of the office in complete misery. We got a lot of sob stories, but hardly a client.

Months went by and we never saw daylight. Then things got worse. As attorneys on behalf of the defendants in all those cases, we were in court from morning to night, walking around with hundreds of files tucked under our arms. It was a mess. There were cases in courts in every Illinois District. If we weren't there to answer the plaintiff's motions or defend them in the trial, then default judgments would be entered against the defendants, the policyholders. Never mind that the defendants really weren't yet our clients, never mind we weren't paid for our efforts, technically we were now responsible for the defense in 5,500 law suits. It became an unending rat race as I drove my car from circuit court to circuit court trying to stop the flow of motions and judgments. The truth was a bitter awakening. Melamed and Kravitz had bought the proverbial "pig in a poke."

During this period, I continued trading at the Merc. And at times, it became untenable. Once, for instance, I was in the courtroom waiting for one of my cases to be called when I realized I had to call the Merc. I had a position in the egg market and needed to know the price in order to figure out my next move. I had no dimes, so I borrowed one from a court clerk who warned me that if the judge called my case and I wasn't there, the case would be judged against me. I took the chance and dashed out to the hall and made the call. Old-man Miller, the 80-year-old founder of Miller & Co. at which I traded, answered.

"Mr. Miller, this is Leo," I shouted to make sure he could hear me over the din of the traders in the background.

"Leo," he answered in his thick Jewish accent, "just a minute, I'll get him."

I left the receiver dangling and ran back to the courtroom to see if my case had been called. It hadn't. I scrambled back to the phone in time to hear Miller say, "Leo's not here. Goodbye." And he hung up. Again, I ran back into the courtroom. Still my case hadn't been called. This time I ran out of the courthouse across the street to a drugstore, got change for a dollar, and ran back. I called Miller again.

"Mr. Miller, Mr. Miller," I pleaded, "don't hang up. This is Leo."

"Leo," he said, "just a minute." A few seconds later he returned to say, "Leo's not here" and promptly hung up. I nearly died. I was living an Abbot and Costello routine. I made it back to the courtroom just in time to hear my case called. I won that particular case, but took a loss in the egg trade, which more than offset any fee I had earned for the day.

So went a typical day when I tried to intermingle law with trading. The timing was never right. I knew I needed to be in the pit if I was going to make it as a trader. A year after handling the Cosmopolitan cases, the situation had become worse. Now we were up to three secretaries, furiously typing just to keep up with the motions. And we were losing our paying clients because we couldn't give them proper attention. Something had to give.

We went to Bolton and explained the situation. He listened carefully and offered to raise our fee. It sounded plausible. But when he offered an additional $50 a month, our hearts sank. We told Bolton that he had to help us out of the mess we were in. We had to be relieved of this burden or we would go broke. Bolton was sympathetic and agreed. But there was a serious problem. We were attorneys of record on every one of those 5,500 lawsuits. An attorney of record must answer to the court; if he is not officially discharged from the proceeding, he is responsible for the result. In other words, we were stuck real bad. I figured it would take us the next 20 years to dislodge ourselves from the Cosmopolitan obligation. Bolton suggested we tell our story to the chief judge of the Circuit Court. When we asked to be released from the case, the judge asked if there was an attorney to replace us. Of course there wasn't. The poor Cosmopolitan defendants couldn't afford a lawyer. The judge shook his head. Then it was too bad. He wasn't about to let 5,500 individuals loose without legal representation, he told us. And he turned us down.

We were ruined. We would forever be doomed to running around the state without getting paid. My legal career was in shambles. I had nothing to lose but go to the highest level, the Illinois Supreme Court. With Bolton by our side, we went to Springfield, the state capital, and pleaded our case before a Supreme Court justice. He listened sympathetically, but told us that only the Governor could help us out of the dilemma. We didn't hesitate. Bolton called his pal Otto Kerner, Governor of the State of Illinois, and set up an appointment. I gave the most impassioned plea of my career. It worked. The Governor called the chief justice of the Circuit Court and asked him to give us help. The judge agreed but wanted to know how we would physically notify all those opposing lawyers. At first, the court wanted us to withdraw on a case-by-case basis, but that process, I pointed out, would have taken a good three years. Instead, I had a brilliant idea: we would publish a notice in the *Chicago Law Bulletin*, the official law publication, listing all the 5,500 pending cases, and announcing that at 11:00 A.M. on a designated day, Melamed and Kravitz were withdrawing from all of them at Motions Court before Judge Ward. It was the first time in Illinois history such a notice ever appeared in the *Law Bulletin*. On the day we appeared as expected, the courtroom was jammed and there was a hail of objections from the plaintiff's lawyers. But to no avail. Judge Ward hit the gavel and our motion to withdraw was granted. Maury and I ran out of that courtroom like two boys let out of school for summer vacation.

The result, however, was no fun for the poor souls who had bought those worthless insurance policies. Those who had money hired attorneys who settled the claims. Those who couldn't, ended up with default judgments entered against them. In some cases it forced the defendants to go through bankruptcy proceedings. But in most cases, the judgments were themselves worthless because the defendants never could pay and after a while the plaintiffs stopped trying to collect.

The Cosmopolitan withdrawal, in 1965, became a turning point for me. I was 33 years old, had a wife, three children, and a profession that hadn't given me the kind of satisfaction I had hoped it would. I had been an excellent law student and thought I had the potential of being a good lawyer, but life hadn't provided the opportunity. Without preparing a speech, I walked into Kravitz's office one morning and said, "Maury, our lives are ours again. I'm leaving. The entire practice is yours. Pay me what you think it's worth. I'm through."

I had caught Kravitz off guard. "You can't mean it," he said. "You can't leave me. I can't do it alone."

"I don't want to be a lawyer anymore," I said. "There is no satisfaction. I want to do something else with my life. I'm going to trade full time."

Kravitz realized that I meant what I said, and he wasn't about to talk me out of it. "How do you know you will succeed?"

"I don't," I admitted, "but I have to find out."

Suddenly, Kravitz asked, "What about the boat? I can't afford it alone." Out of my trading profits, I bought his half of the boat and its name,

Dellsher, and headed for Franklin Street, leaving a courtroom for a trading pit.

Eventually, Maury Kravitz would abandon law, too, returning to the Merc. I loaned him $25,000 to buy a seat again, and in the late 1970s and early 1980s, he would make his reputation and fortune as the Exchange's most aggressive broker—some said too aggressive—in gold futures contracts. He joined RB&H, Jack Sandner's firm, and published a newsletter "View From the Pit." Later, in partnership with Jimmy Kaulentis, he developed the concept of Broker Groups—an association of brokers to service floor business—and formed one of the most powerful and successful groups at the Merc. Broker groups became quite controversial over the years as a result of their unified power and influence. It represents an ongoing controversial Merc issue.

Years later, Kravitz would become an expert on Genghis Khan, and his fertile imagination would lead him to organize an expedition to search for Genghis Khan. I cheered when he was successful actually in persuading the government of Mongolia to give him an exclusive license to lead such an expedition to find the burial grounds of this Mongolian emperor. Now that the University of Chicago has taken a serious interest in this project, it wouldn't surprise me if Kravitz found the guy.

In truth, my decision to give up law in favor of a life as a trader was not a decision I made on the spur of the moment; in fact, I made the decision a thousand times. But I always stopped short from actually executing the trade. First of all, there was my father. To say he would be furious if I gave up law was the understatement of the century. We had talked about it often. As a lawyer, his immigrant son was a somebody, *an advocate*. As a trader, I was what? *Nothing but a gambler*. He would not listen to the rationale I provided. It was out of the question. Then there was my own self doubt about my ability as a trader. After all, I had already proved that I could be a fairly good lawyer, and the law always provided me a living—and I had a family to worry about. Who could tell if I would be as good a trader. The jury was still out on that. Up to now I had learned that I could make good money in trading, but I also learned I could lose it as well. Still, the appeal to trade full time was nearly irresistible. All my senses told me I could succeed in trading if only I had to depend on it exclusively. Law was my hedge against trading fiascos. Knowing I could always earn a living at law, I believed, diminished my discipline in trading, and discipline is the foundation of good trading.

But, most of all, there was the overwhelming magnetism of the trading environment as a way of life when compared to the life as an attorney. Law was interesting, but boring in the sense that things happened slowly, according to rhythm set by procedure in a system that could be manipulated by delays, postponements, appeals, and technicalities. It could take months, even years to win a case. Besides, lawyers were tiresome. And for every victory, there were a hundred thank yous: thank the client, thank the cop that referred him to me, thank the clerk in court for assisting me, thank the judge for being fair. By contrast, the trading pits existed for the moment, caught up in a swirl of information and instant reaction. You knew where you stood at the end of each trading day. And there was nobody to thank. It was you against the market. If you figured out the direction it would take, you had only yourself to thank. The market was a daily challenge. Each day a new adventure. There was neither certainty about the direction of the market, nor was there a guarantee that I would be able to figure it out. The challenge of this uncertainty was an overwhelming attraction. Law was so terribly predictable by comparison. So I took the plunge.

I had timed my decision in 1965 to the departure of my parents on their summer vacation. They were driving through Colorado and weren't expected to return until September. By then, it would be too late for my father to talk me out of it. I wanted to avoid confrontation and the feeling of guilt that he could impart in his eloquent Yiddish. I was still under his influence, and I felt as if I had done something wrong and was skulking off into the night to escape his wrath. In fact, I had made what would turn out to be the most important decision of my professional life.

When I broke the news to my father, he didn't blow up, because that wasn't his style. He sat there, stunned, unable to fully comprehend how a person who was educated and trained could walk away from his profession. He had seen his son become an advocate, and suddenly I was throwing it all out the window. I also believe he was frightened for me and my family. I wanted to allay his fears and tell him everything would work out, but I never got the chance. He stopped talking to me. Not for a day or a week, but for almost an entire year. That's how angry he was. My mother was quick to forgive, showing a mother's confidence in her son's judgment. For the next 12 months, my father recognized my presence only with a nod, speaking to me only when absolutely necessary. His anger dissipated in 1967 when I was elected to the Board of the Chicago Mercantile Exchange. There were stories in the newspapers, and that caught his attention. Perhaps the Merc *was* a place where a person could enhance his dignity and earn a dependable living as well. After all, capitalism was an ideal just like any other. When I became chairman of the Merc two years later, he forgave me completely. By then he became convinced that my decision hadn't been all that "off the wall."

I was no babe in the woods. By the time I turned full-time trader, I had spent a decade at the Exchange from my humble beginning as a runner. It was like starting as a copyboy on a newspaper and ending up as a full-fledged reporter with an eye on the editor's desk. Everyone knew me by my first name. And I knew everyone.

There were some members who couldn't understand why a person would give up the life of a lawyer for the life of a trader. But nobody asked me to explain anything. In fact, I had a certain cachet; there weren't many college graduates, much less lawyers, in the Merc's trading pits in those days. (Since giving up my practice, the legal profession has grown at four times the rate of the nation's population to reach a ratio of one lawyer for every 290 Americans in 1995.) I was pretty glib and could be one of the boys. And, hey, if the place could attract an educated young Turk, there must be something going on.

Indeed, there was a lot going on. Some of it to my liking; some not. The pits were no longer torpid. The meats were much more alive than the eggs. There was yelling and buying and selling. The markets were moving. It was still hellish to figure out in what direction, but that was part of the lure. Up or down, you could make money, providing, of course, you were right. The wonderful thing about the markets was their surprise. No matter how long you played the market, and how many times you won, it could never become transparent, that is, predictable. Shifting from its lulls to its outbursts, the market could be steady, depressed, neurotic, even schizophrenic—all in the same day. Every trader had a theory of what was happening in the next five minutes. But no one really knew. It could never be boring, and, because of its nature, you could never take a market for granted. To this day, when I am asked my opinion about the market, I give it with the caveat that my opinion is good for the next 30 seconds.

I was a so-called local, one of the regular pit traders, who traded for his own account. There were other floor traders who, as brokers, bought and sold on behalf of customers for a brokerage fee on each trade. Most of them also traded for themselves because so-called dual trading was allowed; but brokers traded a lot less than did locals. The locals were the "market makers" of the securities markets, who provided the necessary pool of liquidity for the buy-and-sell orders that came together on the floor of the Exchange. Unlike stock market specialists, whose buying and selling supports a particular stock or stocks, we were not bound to support any particular contract. We could roam the floor and trade anywhere. And unlike specialists, we were not under contract with the Exchange. We used our own capital, and we speculated.

No question about it, futures traders speculate. In fact, futures contracts will not work without speculation. A futures contract is a risk management tool, like an insurance policy. The idea of futures contracts is quite old. I used to lecture about how in biblical times, Joseph was the first to put on a buy hedge. He convinced the Egyptian Pharaoh to buy grain during the seven years of plenty and store it for use during the seven years of lean. Historically, in this country, futures contracts were widely used by farmers and producers to protect against crop failure, against commodity price rises, or against falling prices in years of oversupply. After the advent of financial futures in 1972, these contracts were also used by money managers and corporate treasurers to protect against inherent financial risks, to hedge interest-rate exposure, to hedge exchange-rate fluctuations, or to assist in the management of assets and liabilities. And speculators provide the necessary liquidity to lubricate the competitive market machinery that brings buyers and sellers together. Without speculators, the hedgers would have no one to whom they could transfer the inherent risks they faced.

But I wanted to be more than simply a trader speculator. I went one step further. I decided to open my own clearing firm. It was an obvious move. A clearing firm had the right to process business through the Exchange. Every futures transaction in the pit had to be "cleared" through a clearing firm, which received a small fee for the service. Each buyer and seller would report the particulars of their transaction to their respective clearing firm. At the end of the day, the clearing firm, in turn, submitted the trade data to the central clearinghouse of the Exchange. If the data supplied by the buyer and seller matched, the trade would clear. Otherwise, any discrepancy, known as an "out-trade," would have to be resolved between the traders involved before the beginning of trade the next morning. That was the most unique characteristic of futures markets and hardly known to the outside world. Futures markets are based on a no-debt system. All trades are "marked-to-the-market"; in other words, *evaluated* at the close of business every day. And everyone is required to pay—in cash—for his positions, based on the price of the market on the close. In that way, each trader begins the next day without owing anybody.

The commissions paid by local traders to a clearing firm to guarantee and process trades ate up some of the profits. If I had my own clearing firm, I figured, I could save money. Besides, since the commodities business was my life now, a clearing firm was the establishment. You didn't get anywhere until you were a clearing member firm, and I wasn't going to be just a local. My ambitions were sky-high. A clearing firm had to meet certain financial requirements—$50,000 in cash at that time—and had to own as least two seats (memberships). I opened my clearing firm, Dellsher Investment Company—using the name of my boat that I had bought from Kravitz—and, as was the custom, took on a partner, Anthony Marterano, who provided the second membership.

Marterano was quiet and easygoing. I got to know him when a few years earlier he asked me to handle a personal injury case on behalf of his son, who was in high school at the time. It was one of those awful malpractice situations. His son needed his knee pinned, a rather routine orthopedic surgical undertaking. But the doctor botched the leg cast, and it caused the boy's leg to gangrene. Tony's son lost his leg. I instituted a malpractice law suit, which ultimately resulted in a settlement at the limit of the insurance policy. We remained friends until Tony's death.

As traders, we shared the fascination of technical analysis. Albert McKinzie, an astute trader and technician, took us under his wing. He had wonderful charts on his desk and would roll them out as if he were the captain of a ship setting a course. At that time, the markets, for the most part, were uncharted waters. McKinzie's explanations were precise and logical, and he wasn't reluctant to share insights. He was the first to introduce me to the concept of *time* as an element in technical interpretations of charts. Like Elmer Falker, McKinzie believed fervently in the technical approach to trading: *The charts say it all.* But for Tony Marterano, technical analysis meant something different. Marterano was one of those early stargazers who believed the markets are influenced by the movement of the planets. He had stacks of charts showing the movements of Jupiter, Mars, and Venus. Today, in fact, there is a rather large number of traders who follow the predictions of stargazing market gurus. I agree that it's silly stuff, but I don't argue. Whatever works. Marterano was a pioneer in this field.

Al McKinzie and Elmer Falker were only two of many who took me under their respective wings to teach me about trading. They were the technicians. Marlowe King and most others, on the other hand, believed solemnly that all that mattered were the underlying fundamentals affecting supply and demand of the product. Ruby Carl was in this camp. The Carl family began Merc operations as egg merchants in the earliest Exchange days, and they were tough and savvy traders. Ruby Carl was one of my select floor friends, with whom I could converse in perfect Yiddish. I loved him for his contrarian views, which always questioned sacrosanct dogma. He eventually moved to Tel Aviv and used to commute to the CME floor.

Still others believed that what counted most was not analysis but technique. For instance, Sidney Shear was a legendary Maine potato trader on the New York Mercantile Exchange, the precursor to today's NYMEX, who had made and lost several fortunes in his lifetime. I had become good friends with his son, Fred Shear, and one spring he invited me to come to New York and trade potatoes in the May contract, the most active trading month. I went, together with my buddy Dan Jesser who was a member there. We rented an apartment in lower Manhattan and stayed for the summer. Even though I wasn't a member, I was able to stand near the pit and give orders to brokers. Rules on the New York Mercantile were practically nonexistent. I remember the traders eating corned beef sandwiches in the pit as they jostled to trade with each other. Sidney Shear took a liking to me, and one day confided that he had a huge long position and it was time to sell out. "Watch and learn," he said as he entered the pit and everyone rushed to see what Shear would do. The traders knew that Sidney Shear could move the market and thus respected his every motion. Shear raised his arms and in a loud voice started to buy. The pit went with him, and everyone started buying pushing the market higher and higher. After a while Shear walked out of the pit with a satisfied smile. "I thought you told me it was time to sell?" I inquired respectfully that evening over dinner. "It was," he responded with a large grin. "You see, kid, my brokers were all in the pit with my sell orders. I unloaded on the locals."

See what I mean? It's not in the analysis but in the technique. Actually, what I learned from all those early tutors was that trading is a most difficult profession that requires not just technique, but experience, information, and sound business judgment. As for methodology, I learned that there is no such thing as a pure fundamentalist or a pure technician; a good trader learns to apply both.

To run my new clearing firm I chose Valerie Turner, my legal secretary for years who replaced Mona Wallace when she married Maury Kravitz. Though only 18 years old, Turner was bright, articulate, and full of confidence when I initially hired her straight out of YMCA secretarial school. I couldn't use an employment agency because I couldn't afford one. Even if I could have, I doubt I would have found a secretary as competent as Valerie Turner. She was one of the few black secretaries on LaSalle Street in the late 1950s, but what mattered to me was her ability. Unfortunately, that factor made little difference to some of my colleagues in the legal community at the time. They were more concerned with status quo. I once took Turner to lunch at the Bar Association restaurant. Shortly thereafter, I started to receive a number of nasty letters calling me a "rabble-rouser." It was a rude awakening that the real world was not the idealistic one my parents had conditioned me to expect. They had left me with a legacy that was mostly blind to distinctions of color, religion, race, and gender. And I was stunned. This wasn't the deep South. This was Chicago, the deep North.

Valerie Turner became my confidante and one of my closest personal friends during my entire market career. She would not only end up running Dellsher—which she ran with authority—but she became one of the first women, and certainly the first black woman, to own a membership on an exchange. In May 1972, at my insistence, she bought a seat on the

International Monetary Market. She also purchased a minor interest in Dellsher, and under her direction, the firm became a model for the futures industry. Today she is one of the most respected experts in futures operations, and, since its inception, has served as Chief Operating Officer of my firm, Sakura Dellsher, Inc. She only recently announced her plans to retire and get married.

Not to get too ahead of the story, after I became Merc chairman, I had my second lesson in prejudice in the real world. High on my agenda was to create departments and staff them with the best people our budget would allow. The Exchange I inherited had little structure and no departments. I was hell-bent on creating a real organization. I wanted a Research and Education Department, something unheard of at the Exchange; I wanted an official Compliance Department to enforce the trading rules; I wanted a Public Relations Department to lift the CME's lowly image. I began interviewing and hiring. After the first five hires, E.B. Harris, the Merc president, called me one day to meet. He wouldn't tell me what it was about, but he said it was important. Harris was always a bit nervous around me. As the new chairman who had beaten the establishment, he thought I was going to clean house and him along with it.

"Promise me you won't get mad," Harris said, pacing the floor around my office. I assured him I wouldn't.

"I support everything you are doing," he continued. "I am totally on your side, please believe me. Do you believe me?"

I assured him I believed him.

"Okay," he said, still pacing around my office, "So everything you are doing is fine with me. New departments, new personnel; I think that's great."

I began to get impatient. "E.B. get on with it."

"Okay, Okay, so I just have one question. Don't get mad, but why are you hiring only Catholics?"

I drew a blank. I had no answer because at first I didn't even understand what he was talking about. I didn't know what religion the new Merc employees were. I had no idea they were all Catholics. But apparently Harris did and was keeping some sort of scorecard. "Don't you know Catholics are cliquish?" Harris said. "I wouldn't blame you if you hired Jews. You're Jewish, but you're hiring Catholics."

I was both stunned and mystified. Throughout the sixties, the Chicago Board of Trade, whose founders were primarily wheat farmers, had always been perceived as the Irish Exchange and, yes, it had fewer Jewish members than did the Merc. In contrast, the Merc, whose founders were butter and egg merchants, was referred to as the Jewish Exchange in those days. Actually, only about one-third of the Merc's members were Jewish. Harris had been executive secretary of the CBOT before coming to the Merc in 1953 as president to replace Oscar Olson. He was neither Catholic nor Jewish.

"Everette, I don't know what to tell you. Religion has never had a bearing—nor will it ever have—on who I hire at this Exchange." I nearly shouted as I said those words, my temper rising. That's all I could say, and he never brought it up again. Harris was no bigot. Just overly cautious. He was a gentle soul who had grown up on a farm in Norris City, Illinois. At 17, he hitchhiked to Detroit and worked on the loading docks for Kroger & Company. He then attended the University of Illinois and graduated with a degree in economics. Afterwards, he scrambled to survive the Depression, and worked for the New Deal government in the war years. Behind a big smile and strong handshake, he knew how to network in a cutthroat age of competition. He was more than 20 years my senior and a product of his times. And I was a product of mine.

But his views reflected the way the Exchange was run. Its members never understood its potential; they never wanted to change. I didn't look for idealism in the trading pits. Only realism. In the open outcry system, you traded with the first person to meet the bid or offer. It was noisy, but efficient since it allowed everyone in the pit to receive the same market information at the same time. Sure, the traders could be intimidating with their shouts and glares and growls and snarls. But it was all part of the pit culture. And like all dens of capitalism, it was a culture that embraced the principles of wealth as the measure of power. Money was the score. The prestigious traders were the successful ones. But, theoretically, the Exchange was no aristocracy whereby the rich deserved the political power. To the contrary, the Exchange was a meritocracy and deserved to be run like one. While some eked by and others made fortunes, we all had a share in the place. And the Exchange leaders had to understand this. But they didn't. No one really counted unless he was powerful. To add to this inequity, there were traders for whom the rules did not apply. They were bent on manipulating markets, and the system allowed it. And in doing so, it limited the potential of the place and everyone in it.

The Board was staid, nepotistic, and deaf to its rank and file. My history books had taught me that when one stops listening to everyone, one begins listening only to oneself and begins operating by fiat. That, in turn, leads to operating by the law of retribution. No one, in his right mind, wants to be any part of that kind of process. The key, especially in a membership organization, had to be consensus. But the Merc leadership in the 1960s was smug in its inertia. This applied across the Board: to trading, to members, to customs, to hiring practices. Through a set of arcane rules, it had a tight hold on the Exchange.

We needed to create a culture in which the speed of change constantly rose and questions were allowed to be asked. I was a young Turk, but old enough to have witnessed the Exchange at its worst. No doubt reform was needed. But what kind of reform? This was a member-owned institution, not a private club. And it dealt with a public and business world outside of its doors. It had to be accountable. That meant that the Board had to be accountable to the members, to the Exchange, to the users of the Merc. That notion teetered on a fault line. On one side were the younger traders like myself and a public whose confidence was shaken; on the other, the old guard satisfied with the status quo.

11

Chairman Leo

I was first and always a trader. A good trader, by definition, must be willing to admit he makes mistakes. And he must do so quickly. Otherwise, he goes broke. Once I learned that lesson, it was rooted in my trading culture. I then applied it to all spheres of life. As a leader, I had the same mind-set. If I made a mistake, I couldn't wait to correct it. If I was wrong, I wanted to know fast enough to head off any potential disaster.

I was bemused by the fact that the Merc leaders in the 1950s and early 1960s who were also traders, and pretty darn good ones, ignored their instincts when it came to running the Merc. Somewhere in my history books I remember Thomas Jefferson saying, "Each generation has to make the country over again" and "A democracy must always be working out its destiny." The same notions could be applied to institutions that have been around a long time, especially when their bureaucratic machinery creaks from age—like it did at the Merc in 1966. Back then I was a Jeffersonian in spirit, believing in the rights of the common man. But I was up against a board that seemed more closely tied to Alexander Hamilton's belief in government by the privileged.

While I had no cache of notions waiting to be tested, I watched and listened. I knew when I heard a good idea and when I heard a lousy one. I had also figured out my ambitions. Beginning in 1965, when I knew my career was the Exchange, I had a mission: to become thoroughly immersed in the political framework of the Chicago Mercantile Exchange.

Since the quorum rule adopted four years earlier, there had been no new member-driven idea to challenge the Board, so the quorum rule now seemed like an empty victory. There was no recognition by the Board of the needs of my generation. Still, there was uneasiness across the country, and young voices from every quarter were being heard and tested in marches and sit-ins. Whatever their motives and causes, people were basically striving for one thing: more control over their lives, more say in their destiny. That's what I wanted for myself and the other Merc members—a say in our future.

Our moods were changing along with the times. The so-called Silent Generation of the fifties had been replaced by the Beat Generation with its bearded poets chanting their coffeehouse gospel in free verse. And the flower children weren't far behind. Institutional investors were playing the stock market and driving the Dow Jones Industrial Average to new highs. There was inflation and a war in Vietnam and the sweeping domestic changes of President Johnson's Great Society all tugging at the economy.

It was obvious to the rank and file members that the Board disregarded the views of the membership and ruled the Exchange as if they owned the institution. Our ideas, thoughts, and criticisms were totally ignored. We didn't count, and we knew we had no way to make our voices heard. It was clear to me that the Brokers' Club had to be rejuvenated. In doing so, some of the junior members and veterans in the rank and file formed a we-versus-they alliance. What was needed, I thought, was an equalizer. Something that would force the Board to listen to its membership. This time we were going to push the Board for one of the most basic principles in American democracy: the referendum. A referendum rule in the Merc bylaws, I believed, was the only way to give the membership a meaningful voice in running the Exchange and to make the Board fully responsive to its members. At the time I believed such a rule would probably never be used except under extreme circumstances. It would, however, be an effective threat and force the Board to pay more attention to its membership. In essence, we were looking for moral equilibrium.

Where to start? Once more, the proxy played a role in our strategy. But unlike our first effort, we didn't have to gather proxies for a quorum; the lower quorum rule was in effect. Now we needed to rally a majority number of votes to propose and approve an amendment to the bylaws. Word got back to us that the Board would fight a referendum rule tooth and nail. In the Board's opinion, such an amendment, if passed, would not be binding on them. That remained to be seen.

We were facing off against a Board chaired by Nathan Werthheimer and backed by President E.B. Harris and, most notably, Merc attorney Lee A. Freeman. Freeman was still a strong voice in Merc affairs. Katz, of course, was still on the Board, along with the other hard-liners. And Katz was still very much in control. Werthheimer, who was considered a very weak chairman, took his orders from Katz and Freeman.

As before, Ken Birks and I strategized, and he spent weeks soliciting proxies in preparation for the members' meeting. Letters had been sent to the entire membership about the meeting. It was held after the close of trading one afternoon in mid-December 1966 when the snow-packed streets of

Chicago looked like the Siberian landscape I had crossed as a child. Every member who was a floor participant came. So did many of the other Chicago-based members. Huddled in groups on the trading floor, the members listened to the debate, which at times became heated. Standing before a microphone, Werthheimer opened the meeting and turned it over to Katz. Katz spoke in loud and angry tones, telling the membership that what we were planning would ruin the Exchange. We were being led by young members who didn't know anything about Exchange matters. His comments were followed by those of attorney Lee Freeman who argued that the referendum rule had no legal justification in the context of the Exchange's bylaws. Muscular and good-looking, with an expressive face with heavy eyebrows, a full head of hair, and fiery rhetoric, Freeman paused for a moment, cleared his throat, spoke confidently and with authority, and concluded with a threat. Any motion passed by the membership at this meeting, he stated unequivocally, was meaningless. It was a rogue action and illegal, and would have no effect on the Board or the institution.

It was my turn. I had used my acting ability in the classroom and in the courtroom, and now I used it in the trading room. I was center stage and, to be honest, I liked the role. Like Thomas Paine I was there to talk common sense. I was Leo. A trader like the rest of them. And the Merc was where I earned my living today—and tomorrow. I knew the membership and it knew me. We were in this boat together. We knew each other's families; we knew each other's hopes and dreams. We had placed our future in the hands of the Board, and our future was not very bright. We had already been to the brink of destruction and barely survived. Unless new ideas and a modern order was instituted, the Exchange could again face its demise. The Board had rejected all of our demands and ignored all of our ideas. We were tired of squeezes and corners. We wanted a fair market where not only the rich and powerful could succeed. We deserved better. We wanted a voice. We wanted rules that applied to everyone and were administered fairly to all. We wanted our ideas to be given a fair hearing. We didn't want revolution; we wanted participation. If indeed the Merc was to be a solid democratic system, it needed checks and balances in its framework. It was now or never.

Political success in any organization, I believe, is rooted in personal discretion, discipline, restraint, logic, candor, and, to some degree, courage. That day, whether I showed any of these qualities or all of them, I cannot say. I felt my heart beating and heard my voice booming across the floor as I explained the justification for the referendum. I was comfortable doing it, although I didn't particularly like the dissident role. But it was necessary to assume in order to bring about change. I didn't view myself as a revolutionary espousing a different form of government; rather, I was promoting change from within the existing framework. Effecting change from the inside of a system requires a subtle rather than a heavy-handed approach. The system couldn't be severely shocked. In the wake of victory—especially an intramural one—fences have to be mended, egos salved, new alliances formed, and all in a relatively short period. But as I addressed the members, my mind was focused on the moment, not on its aftermath.

I used all my skill as an actor, as a reader of Yiddish poetry, as an attorney before the jury. My language wasn't eloquent, but direct. I didn't want words to get in the way of reason and logic. But I didn't talk down to the membership either. Simply, the referendum was a basic American tenet. What we were asking for was not something earthshaking, something untoward. It was an American tradition. The Board should not fear its own membership; rather, it should welcome and embrace its participation. A referendum rule would encourage dialogue, and allow ideas to circulate, to be discussed, and examined. My words were strong and had the ring of truth to them. I spoke them confidently, knowing that I was on solid constitutional ground irrespective of what Lee Freeman had said. I was convinced that, if passed by the membership, the referendum rule would be legally binding to the Board. This was a duly sanctioned membership meeting with a quorum of the membership present. If the Board rejected the referendum proposal, and if the courts had to decide it, our side was prepared to go the distance. Apparently, it was a palpable speech. Immediately after I finished, the membership voted on the referendum, or Rule 206 as it was called. It was overwhelmingly adopted. The entire session had taken just over an hour.

A court battle never ensued. In fact, the controversy, for all intents and purposes, had ended there on the floor that afternoon. Although Rule 206 wasn't officially adopted until after the next Board election, which took place the following January, the members had won and the Board knew it, whether it openly admitted it or not. Ironically, in subsequent years, the referendum rule would be used more times by the Board than by the membership. But the dissidents didn't go around smugly proclaiming victory. That would have been counterproductive and would not have served to ease tensions between the camps.

The momentum of the victory became obvious the following month. In January 1967, I was elected to the Board of Governors with the highest number of votes of all the candidates. It was a huge victory, not simply by virtue of the large plurality I received, nor the fact that as a nonincumbent I led the ticket, but more because I was the first of a new breed to be elected to the Board—one who was not a son, son-in-law, or other relation of the establishment. The first gusts of wind ushering in the new era had swept through the floor of the Merc.

The new epoch had further confirmation when the Board elected its new chairman, 48-year-old Robert O'Brien. Not only my good friend, O'Brien was a key member of the Brokers' Club. The son-in-law of one of Merc's founding fathers, John V. McCarthy, O'Brien was the link between the old guard and the new wave of members like me. I was elected secretary. In doing so, the Board again broke tradition by electing a freshman Board member as an officer of the Exchange. Any office on the Board was important, but the office of secretary, which I coveted, had special significance to me. My father, who never became chairman of the Sholom Aleichem Folks Institute, led the school organization for many years from his position as secretary. I had similar designs and knew that O'Brien would support me. Indeed, he was fully supportive when I used my position as secretary to write official reports to the membership, a unique use of a Board office. Although this was a huge departure from the traditional secretive custom of past Boards, O'Brien recognized that since I had run for election on the platform of openness, I was bound to keep my promise. Besides, openness and candor was the hallmark of O'Brien's administration. Not only did Bob O'Brien welcome my close collaboration, he was receptive to my ideas and encouraged my leadership role during the two years of his tenure as chairman. He wanted me to succeed him.

Under his rule, the Merc began to regroup its forces and to set about broadening its ambitions. He took the first step toward decentralizing administrative power by forming an executive committee made up of board members who were Merc officers. This committee became a steering force. To his credit, O'Brien wanted the new board to fashion a moral code, as he put it, while leaving the old-boy network behind. Referendum Rule 206 was a big start. It was one of the most dramatic policy revisions since the Merc's founding in 1919. At my suggestion, a three-person committee, which included Michael Weinberg Jr., Gilbert Miller, and me, was selected to write and refine Rule 206. In addition, the Board doubled the number of annual meetings. A list of the various committees and the names of its members were published and sent to the out-of-town members to keep them in touch with Chicago. I even produced the first official annual report. Members and machines were doing some adjusting as well. Capital improvements were underway to increase the trading floor space by 25 percent. The translux tickers were relocated in units at the end of the floor with a set of catwalks and ticker booths. The former boardroom became a temporary coffee room, and the coffee room a committee office. Though a new IBM data processing center was set up that included a 1401 processing unit, the Merc was still a long way from full automation. But a groundwork for the major changes ahead had been laid.

In 1969, on the eve of the Chicago Mercantile Exchange's 50th birthday, I was reelected to the Board by an unprecedented nearly 90 percentile vote of the membership. It was no surprise. I had been highly visible in my role as secretary, I was popular with the rank and file, and I was a good trader. I also provided an unending stream of new ideas to Bob O'Brien, who delighted in their implementation and was totally honest about their origin. We made a potent combination. Besides, I had kept my promises and was listening to the members while serving on a host of committees and intermingling with my pals in the pits. Everyone knew Leo.

By then, I was on a steady diet of endless cups of black coffee and three packs of Winstons a day. One journalist described me in a feature article as having the intensity of a tightly coiled spring. Indeed, my pace was manic. Half the day was spent trading, the other half and into the night was taken up by Exchange business. But I loved it. A week after my reelection to the Board, it was a foregone conclusion that I would become the Merc's 23rd chairman.

As I said, my father had long before broken his silence and forgiven me completely, and by no means was he a stage father. He had never had any intentions of guiding my career as did, say, Mozart's father. First of all, I was no prodigy. But looking back I now suspect that part of the motivation that drove me into the Exchange limelight was his tacit expectation that I should do more with my life than simply be a trader. I've seen too many sons and daughters end up in a lifelong bondage tied to parental expectations of career and money. I didn't fear my father in that manner nor did I need his approval. But, I was beholden to him and always would be. Our escape to America had bonded me and my parents in ways that I'm still coming to terms with today. After all, my father was the man who saved my life.

One of the first things Everette Harris learned about me was that I could forgive and forget. Harris, certain I was going to fire CME attorney Lee Freeman, my chief adversary, wanted us to meet in the hope that we could perhaps smooth things out. Of all the Merc lions, none roared as loudly as Freeman. And I liked the sound. "Everette, what makes you think I want to fire this guy? He's a bulldog," I said. "Why wouldn't I want a bulldog on my side? He's a hell of a lawyer."

At this point, neither Harris nor anyone else knew my management philosophy. I had no intention of turning the boardroom into the last act of Hamlet. I wanted to create a "we're all in this together" bond rather than let paranoia and anxiety turn the Exchange into a culture of betrayals. To do that takes forgiving, forgetting, and friendly persuasion. I have never cared who a person was, or how great an enemy he was, I always had an unshakable conviction that a person could be reached through logic. This became the hallmark of my philosophy. I would not act until I convinced enough of the membership that it was the right thing to do. On the other hand, if someone could convince me I was doing something wrong, then I would immediately attempt to correct it. I was always testing myself against the so-called enemy. Consequently, I was never afraid of the opposition; rather, I welcomed it to join me.

I met with Lee Freeman. He too expected to be fired. Looking straight into his steel gray eyes I said, "I have no intention of firing you. I want you to fight for me like you fought for them." He laughed a loud and boisterous laugh, and he knew exactly what I meant. It was instant rapport. It was one of my best decisions. Over the years I would lean heavily on him for advice and counsel. We became friends and ardent admirers of each other's respective talents. No matter what idea I came up with, no matter how revolutionary or difficult, Freeman supported it with unconditional fervor and stood at my side in every battle. We never lost. Had I cut the Merc ties with the Freeman firm in 1969, the Exchange would have been the loser.

When Lee Freeman died in 1995, I lost a trusted friend and incomparable ally. His lovely wife Brena and his son Lee Freeman, Jr. honored me by asking that I present one of the eulogies. The memorial was held at the Bond Chapel at the University of Chicago where performers from the Lyric Opera offered song and music to his memory. Chicago's Lyric Opera was the Freemans' passion, and he and his wife Brena were its special angels. To a standing-room only audience I offered that Lee Freeman, who became CME general counsel in 1946, rose to all occasions, shrank from no danger, and ran from no challenge. "Tenacity," I told the assembled, "was his middle name, perseverance was his ancestry, determination was his legal oath, loyalty was his blood." He called me a Don Quixote. If I was Don Quixote, I could not have chosen a better Sancho Panza than Lee Freeman as we encountered the giant windmills of an unwilling establishment, an antagonistic financial world, a hostile legal environment, a cynical government, an intransigent local community.

Not long after we made peace, Freeman assigned Jerry Salzman, a young Harvard-educated attorney from his firm, to work with the Merc. It was an outstanding decision. While Freeman provided me with strength and connections in the early years of my tenure, Salzman, who was much closer to me in age, was a brilliant lawyer who became a trusted collaborator in advancing the radical and innovative ideas we were to initiate.

While I didn't hold grudges, I didn't mind settling old scores. Thirteen years earlier, when I was a struggling attorney-trader, I had a checking account with the Northern Trust Bank, whose moniker Gray Lady of LaSalle Street reflected both its stone facade and conservative bent. I was constantly rushing over to the bank with fresh deposits to cover checks I had written, careful not to be overdrawn because I didn't want a deadbeat credit rating. After one particularly good day in the market, I made a hefty deposit, and paid all my bills. But a week later, the checks were bouncing. I immediately went to the bank and pointed out to one of its officers that a bank error had failed to properly record my deposit. At first, the bank denied it had made a mistake and gave me a hard time. Later, reluctantly, it admitted the error. I insisted the bank write an apology to each of the recipients of the bounced checks and, threatened to sue if they did not. The bank sent notes acknowledging its mistake and my credit rating escaped blemish. But the bank's irritation with me showed when they asked me to withdraw my account. And I did. I tried to open an account at two other LaSalle Street banks, but was refused. I could have sworn I was on a blacklist of some kind though I could never prove it. Eventually, I opened an account with American National Bank. That was in 1956. I had forgotten about the incident until 1969 when I became chairman of the Merc.

Although we were a small exchange then, we were a major client of the banks. I made sure we spread our deposits around: American National, First National, Continental, and Harris Trust all got money. Northern Trust got nothing. Then one day, E.B. Harris asked me why we were spurning the Gray Lady. I told the story to him and the two officers from Northern Trust who came to meet with me for an explanation. I could see them wincing as I told my tale of a struggling LaSalle Street attorney in need of a friendly banker and that I had been rebuffed. They got the message.

"Is there any way to mend the past?" one of the bankers asked.

"I don't carry grudges," I said, "but if your chairman will send me a letter of apology for that sin, I'll consider it a case closed." The letter was sent and we opened an account.

From those early years on, I always had a small group of people who were my select inner circle. They were the closest to me. They were individuals who were smart, who were honest, and to whom I could turn for advice; they would tell me the truth and weren't intimidated by me. They were my sounding board, my friends, my advice givers, my truth squad. While our conferences were sometimes held over the telephone, it was mostly a face to face rendezvous. We would meet in an assortment of places and usually after hours. Sometimes it would be in one of our offices, sometimes in one of our homes, but most often in some all night cafe where we would eat sandwiches and sip endless cups of coffee. There we would scheme, discuss and argue as we explored or planned a strategy, an innovation, or the next stage in the evolution of the Merc.

These were people who never put their personal interests above that of the Exchange. These were people who were always ready to work and to whom I could trust my life. These were the people with whom I built the

Merc. With them ideas could be examined and tested before they moved to the next level, which was basically the establishment level—members of committees and the Board as well as executives of the Exchange. At that second level, the ideas would be examined for the purposes of refinement and implementation. After that, I went to the floor. There too, I had an elite corps of loyalists who would advance the cause and carry out the plans. Whoever belonged to this group of floor partisans would willingly lay down their life for me and I for them.

Although the members of my first-level inner circle changed somewhat over the years, sometimes expanding, sometimes contracting, it remained relatively small, and there were some who were always included. I leaned heavily on Barry Lind almost from the beginning. His facile mind for numbers was an extraordinary asset. In 1970, I placed Lind in charge of the Merc's Clearinghouse Committee, the nerve center of our financial integrity. Under his guidance, the work previously begun in reorganizing the clearinghouse and reshaping the financial structure of the Exchange went into high gear. Requirements were upgraded, higher financial standards were adopted, modern guidelines were developed, and a formalized system of surveillance and audits was instituted. With Lind's assistance, the Merc was set on a course of unparalleled financial strength and integrity.

Lind, son of a famous Jewish Chicago cantor, Phil Lind, began his career as a clerk for Sam and Phil Becker, but rose quickly through the ranks to become a valued and respected member of the CME Board, and most important, my best friend. Enormously successful in business, Lind was the farthest thing from a yes-man you could find. After his service on the Board, he directed his talents at creating the first futures discount firm. Lind-Waldock & Company is today the counterpart in futures to Charles Schwab in securities.

We often disagreed, but we always respected each other's views and remained the closest of friends—brothers describes it better—during the many years and often difficult times that followed. More than that, our families became close. I was best man at his marriage to Terri and instantly fell in love with her for her candor and depth of insight. Betty, Terri, Barry, and I became a steady foursome. Together we adventured around the world—Acapulco, Rio, London, Paris, Burgenstock, Venice, Scottsdale, Aspen—and loved every minute of it. Different in many respects, Lind and I had one special common trait, we both drove Porsches—fast. Upon my retirement, he paid me the greatest compliment possible, admitting that I made it from his house to the Loop in 19 minutes and 34 seconds, thereby establishing a world's record—and beating his record by 58 seconds.

In the beginning, my inner circle also included the members of the Brokers' Club, Ken Birks, Dan Jesser, Bob O'Brien, Marlowe King, and Bill

Brodsky (no relation to the current Merc president). There was also George Fawcett, my partner at Dellsher, a shrewd trader with an exceptionally insightful intellect. And Raymond Nessim, my friend and market advisor from Philipp Brothers who later became a director of my firm, Sakura Dellsher, Inc. From the start, there was also tax guru Ira Marcus, whom I brought in as tax counsel for the Exchange. He was positively dazzling at finding just the right legal umbrella under which to institute some of the ideas that we would bring forth. In later years, there was also Jeffrey Josephson with whom I connected both on an intellectual level and as traders, until his untimely death in 1989. He and his wife Sybil had become family friends on whom Betty and I could depend for support and diversion.

And there was Les Rosenthal, a Chicago Board of Trade powerhouse and trusted friend of countless members at all Chicago exchanges. In 1976, Les Rosenthal had the unique distinction of serving as a director on my CME board, on our rival's CBOT board, and on the board of the Board of Trade Clearing Corporation at the same time. After he became CBOT chairman, he and I worked in harmony to lead our competitive institutions and the futures industry through many revolutionary changes. We even toyed with the idea of a merger. Les Rosenthal, like Barry Lind, became an extremely close personal friend, whose sense of humor I relished, and on whom I relied for advice and assistance throughout the years. Indeed, the two of us could trust each other with the most intimate details of our lives—and always did. The fact that we were both refugees—Rosenthal came from Hungary—provided the foundation for a special bond that extended to a social level and resulted in his gracious wife Harriet becoming a good friend to Betty.

Brian Monieson, a math and computer maven, was the first in our group to genuinely understand computer analytics. In later years, he became a Merc chairman. A horse racing devotee from early childhood, Monieson was the first in Chicago to design and program a computerized handicapping system that he sold for a nice profit before applying his skills to trading at the Merc. He never gave up his horse racing hobby though. Later, he and George Segal, an extremely successful trader and a mutual friend of ours, became the owners of *Artsplace*, winner of the world's record for two-year-olds and 1992 horse of the year in standardbred racing. Monieson and I became inseparable friends, and I greatly valued his opinions as we launched some of the Merc's untested contracts of finance and traveled uncharted territory in establishing the world's first futures trading link with the SIMEX of Singapore. The fact that the two of us were first and foremost traders cemented our relationship and extended it to the social sphere. We also learned that we were both bridge enthusiasts and became bridge partners. Eventually, Brian Monieson and his wife Doris followed our lead and bought a second home in Arizona where the four of us enjoyed jogging and the movies and just letting our hair down.

There was also Henry Jarecki, a New York psychiatrist turned precious metals arbitrageur as head of Mocatta Metals Corp. His depth of intellect and business acumen was an inexorable attraction for me. He became my trusted confidante from the start, an unending source of provocative thoughts and discussions, a constant member of my inner circle who never failed to provide an enlightened and candid critique of my ideas, and one of the original directors of the International Monetary Market. Once, in an exuberant burst of passion, he publicly declared that he "would have followed me through fire." For many years, I had no idea that Jarecki, too, was a fellow refugee, having come to the States as a child from Germany. This discovery caused Commodity Futures Trading Commission (CFTC) chairman Jim Stone, who got to know us both, to say, "While your origin is common, your lives took dramatically opposite paths . . . Jarecki operates almost exclusively as a private entrepreneur, while Melamed applies his talents almost solely on behalf of the public sector." As the years went by, Henry Jarecki and I extended our friendship to the social level, philosophizing about life, exploring ideas, and running around Europe together.

As chairman, I not only wanted to keep the momentum going, but I also concerned myself with the long-range view. You can short the market, but you can't be shortsighted running an exchange. I was certain that, in business, to stand still is equivalent to retreating. But I was realistic enough to know that rebirth was certainly more difficult than continuing old policies. I didn't want to flout tradition, but merely to tease it, which dictated a flexible management style and language that was tough, blunt, and even philosophical. The first letter I drafted to the membership expressed my feelings: ". . . I submit that our choice must be to use our momentum for continued forward motion. The problem with forward motion, however, is that it has no magic formula, particularly when it relates to a large institution. What may be good for one business may be fatal to another. . . ."

I asked them to forget the old model of an exchange for a progressive one whose leaders could look ahead to the next 50 years. It is no small task to instill long-term thinking in a culture of traders, who for the most part, earned their livings in the short term. But that was part of the challenge. I had to find an anodyne for the management-by-crisis syndrome from which the Merc suffered. To do that, I set three goals I would pursue as chairman: to rewrite and update the Merc's bylaws; to change our image by cracking down on those traders who tried to manipulate markets; and to diversify the Exchange by creating new markets.

First, I evaluated personnel. My preference was to keep people in place, especially those with an expertise and a sense of history. I believed in

preserving every resource the Merc had. It wasn't that easy to find re-
placements in an industry that was still emerging. To most outsiders,
despite their financial sophistication, commodities trading was an enigma—
and would remain so into the 1990s. Everette B. Harris was an unknown
quantity to me and the fact that he had been president for 15 years had substantially prejudiced me against him. But I vowed to reserve final judgment.
He, too, had his doubts about my ability to run an exchange and wondered
whether I was diplomatic enough to bridge the generation gap that existed.
Instinctively, I concluded that Harris had been caught up in circumstances
beyond his control. He seldom got backing from an often vacillating and
sometimes diabolical Board. Under such conditions it was difficult for him
to develop a leadership role. Nevertheless, he offered experience, practical
wisdom, and to some degree, statesmanship. He was my reference for past
eras. But often Harris gave more than I needed. It was an ingrained habit.
He would run on and on, digressing to the point that the subject at hand was
lost in a haze of recollection. He was, nevertheless, an important sounding
board who knew how to deal with Chicago's old-boy network. There was
more going for Harris than against him. He endeared himself to me one day
by pointing to the huge Calder sculpture in the lobby of the Sears Tower,
which is composed of moving wheels, steel arms, and a giant steel screw.
"You know what that describes?" Harris asked me. I shook my head, having
no clue. "It's what Sears has been doing to the public for years!" How can
you dislike a guy with such perception.

So I kept Harris in place. We formed a kind of partnership that bridged
the generation gap and served notice to the membership that the transition
between the past and present would be harmonious. I also made it clear that
one person would no longer serve as the whipping boy for any future failures
in Exchange policy. The Board and its chairman would be fully accountable,
not just the president. What I did establish was a top-to-bottom reorganization of every department. Positions were created and redefined, as was conduct. I instilled a devotion-to-duty attitude and set a personal example by
tireless labor. The Merc was to become not simply a place to work, but a
place to love, too. I wanted the members to participate as well, to feel the
Merc's new energy and zeal. The newly formed committees were to make
meaningful contributions. Committee chairmen would be Exchange governors, and they were urged to work closely with department managers and
to report their work to the Board. Trying to build a more participatory organization meant giving the committees more power. Members' ideas would
be heard.

It is difficult to visualize the Merc in 1969 when I counted every penny
as I hired staff. My annual budget was $180,000. When I left the Merc 22
years later, the budget was in excess of $100 million.

In a sense, great leaders are like great actors who are able to master the art of transformation to take on any role. Eisenhower was a general, university president, and president of the United States; varied positions, yet he led in each. I'm not saying I'm in a class with Eisenhower, but that I felt comfortable in the role of a chairman although I had never been one. I followed instinct, logic, and conscience, and fought to prevent my ego from clouding my business judgment. I saw myself as the protagonist in a drama being played out on a stage somewhere; and at the same time, I was directing the scenes, moving up close, then standing back for perspective, in an effort to gauge the depth and emotion of my characters. In reality, I was a director and the Merc was my stage. We opened in Chicago. And it would be three years before I took the show on the road with an original production billed as the International Monetary Market.

12

By the Book

As a chairman analyzing the flaws of an organization, I was not all that different from a psychotherapist who deals with a patient's problems that stem from internal pathologies that need to be identified, scrutinized, and corrected. The Merc was my 50-year-old patient: dour, manic, suffering from crisis of identity. Something had to be done quickly. Unfortunately, I didn't have the luxury of time that a shrink normally has in dealing with a patient. Change had to be both dramatic and quick, and in an era long before the "re" words—re-engineering, reinventing, reorganizing, redeploying, repositioning—crept into the business rhetoric.

"Can a market work without squeezes?" I asked Harris shortly after I became chairman.

He was somber, almost melancholy, uncharacteristically serene. Obviously, it wasn't a question easily answered. And the fact that the normally loquacious Harris was silent for the moment told me what I needed to know.

"I don't know," he said stroking his chin. "I just don't know."

"Then, we're going to find out."

If he had said no, I would've been scared. As the Merc's new chairman I was fresh, untainted, and without money. And I couldn't be bought. That's not to say I didn't want money, because I did. But I wanted to earn it by virtue of trading a market that dispenses reward and punishment based on market forces, not from people who were out to make a buck using the Exchange solely for their selfish purpose. It was challenging enough to be right just on the basis of supply and demand in futures. No extra kicks were needed.

I was in love with the beauty of the free marketplace. Although never trained in economics, I intuitively and fervently believed that, in a free market, the true price wins out. But there were too many people at the Merc who believed that might makes right, people for whom the Golden Rule had perversely come to mean those with the gold, rule. In other words, with enough power and money, they could thwart the truth. Some were the pillars of the Merc, and they owned the Board members or they could get to them. As trite and old-fashioned as it might sound, I wanted everyone to play by the same rules. I wanted to give the market a chance to work.

We were the second largest commodity exchange in the nation, but that was nothing to boast about. The Merc's share of the futures business was only 6 percent of the overall volume. That statistic matched our lowly stature in the financial world. We were nothing but a backwater shop of dubious financial value in which market sharks had an opportunity to pounce on an unwitting prey. E.B. Harris once confided, "Leo, the exchange is a whorehouse. The administration provides the beds, the traders do the rest."

If we were ever to reach a level of substantive national value, if we were ever to attain the possibility of a secure future, we needed to change our ways and image from the inside out. The foundation of a new Merc had to be based on new regulations and a new era of enforcement that put an end to manipulations, corners, and squeezes. No more market bullies. We had to free the market from the chains of illegal controls.

Historically, all the commodities markets suffered a miserable image anyway. Futures markets were considered nothing short of illegitimate distant cousins of the financial family. Our purpose and function was not understood. We were the target of innuendo and derision. There were always a few politicians who were trying to close futures exchanges as gambling dens. In fact, there were laws on the books that could jail futures speculators as gamblers. There was even a government prohibition on options. Fiction writers found fertile ground on the exchange floors as well, producing novels about the evils of market manipulators. Among them was the Frank Norris classic *The Pit*, about the cornering of the wheat market on the Chicago Board of Trade in the 1880s. A lot of educating needed to be done, and it was up to the exchanges to do it. This became my mission. I could start with the Merc.

I know that the strongest tool a governing body can have, whether it is a corporate board or a congress at odds with the President, is inaction. Unfortunately, it's a self-destructive tool, because the result is institutional malaise. As chairman, I represented members who felt the Board had done nothing for too long. With my election came an explicit promise of change. Everyone who starts out to lead has a vision of something new: Thomas Jefferson's Declaration of Independence, Teddy Roosevelt's Square Deal, Franklin Roosevelt's New Deal, Harry Truman's Fair Deal, John Kennedy's New Frontier, Lyndon Johnson's Great Society, and the current Republican Contract with America. Each generation is a world of its own and, as such, has what it perceives as its own unique vision. One generation wages war, and the next forgets why it was fought. Time chisels away perspective.

I, too, had my vision. I wanted a model exchange. To achieve this vision I needed a committed and willing Board. In my first "state of the CME" message to the Board, I tried to set the tone and tenor of my administration. We were no longer governors of the same institution as it stood a decade before, I said. Now we were directors of a business that would soon rank among the nation's biggest. This carried a grave responsibility. What I tried to convey was a sense of pride and a desire to rise above the average. "It is a wretched waste to be gratified with mediocrity when the excellent lies before us," Isaac D'Israeli had said. I not only spoke those words, I tried to live them. I worked day and night at it. I created numerous committees and set their goals; I would visit them during their deliberations; I would encourage others to participate; I would make suggestions, offer ideas. I tried to show that everyone's thoughts were important. Soon Board members began putting in a full day's work for the Exchange. Soon, becoming a member of the Board was not simply a matter of prestige, but a commitment. It meant devoting time to scores of meetings and conferences. It meant listening to members. It also meant being responsive to new needs and broader goals. It meant building for the future. In my first annual report to the members, I told them "we have only two choices—to retreat or move forward." I had no intention of retreating.

As for federal authority, there wasn't any to speak of, except the Commodity Exchange Authority (CEA), which was part of the Agriculture Department. Headed by Alex Caldwell, and staffed by his deputy director, Charles Robinson (who became the first general counsel for the Futures Industry Association (FIA)), a couple of secretaries, and virtually no one else, the CEA operated on a puny budget that matched its power. But I knew that this would change. And if we didn't want the government dictating our actions or breathing down our necks à la the onion scandal, then we had to prove we could police ourselves. After establishing a Department of Audits and Investigations, I put a pragmatic attorney, William Phelan, in charge. I wanted to create the model of a modern futures exchange from the inside—governed by those who understood the business and its nuances—rather than bend and twist to the whims of outsiders. When Franklin Roosevelt cast Joe Kennedy as the first chairman of the SEC, he didn't pick a career bureaucrat, but an insider who intimately knew Wall Street's many facets, including its dark side. After many years of outstanding service to the Merc, Phelan went on to become an Illinois Circuit Court judge.

Two years before, as CME secretary, I finally got a full picture of the rule book. I had known the rules were dated, but I never imagined they were downright archaic, and often cryptic. There were bits and pieces of rules, as if each had been added in a vacuum without regard from one decade to the next. They were all bundled inside a single ragged book held together by yellowed Scotch tape, paste, paper clips, staples; and included the intentions of boards dating back to 1898 when the Merc's predecessor was called the Butter and Egg Board. Some of the pages were typed, others were scrawled in faded ink that required the services of an Egyptologist to decipher. I had blocked out a long weekend to plough through the hodge-podge, and found it full of contradictions that absolutely made no sense when taken together; particular amendments in the context of others often meant something different. It was clear to me that the history of each change was neither understood nor explained. My suspicion that the Merc's institutional memory and its bylaws were tucked in the head of one man, Kenneth Mackay, was confirmed. At one time or another, and all at once, he had been the executive vice president, secretary, manager of the clearinghouse, and administrator of the Exchange. Mackay, who was then in his late sixties, could have garnered a couple more titles—that of historian and keeper of the relics.

As an attorney, it was clear to me that our legal house was beyond repair. It needed a new foundation. The existing rule structure was hopeless. Without hesitation, I launched what was best described as a constitutional convention. The process lasted a year and a half. I organized dozens of committees, scores of members, and legal counsel who toiled over numerous rules that were examined and revised. Night after night we met in a rented room at the Bismarck Hotel, just as the members of the Brokers' Club had done years before. Input came not only from Exchange members but industry experts and end users. Sometimes, over weekends, our attorney Jerry Salzman and I would meet at my house, where, with papers and rule books strewn about the dining room table, my children Idelle, Jordy, and David would watch in respectful silence as the two of us argued over the wording of one or another rule. They were watching a new structure in the making, the birth of the new Merc. The painstaking process had Salzman reviewing hundreds of Exchange rules, many of which had to go through five drafts before they were accepted. It was the first time the rule book was comprehensively rewritten since its original adoption in 1919.

When we finished, the Merc's bylaws were at last clear, up-to-date, and authoritative. The foundation in the political machinery of the new Merc that I was fashioning was in place. I placed Dan Jesser in charge of the Rules Committee because I knew he would interpret the rules as we intended and without regard to whom they applied. In June 1970, I proudly made sure a copy of the Merc rule book was given to each member. One of its main features was a Business Conduct Committee—with teeth. Back then, I had no way of knowing how the Merc's future would play out with me at its helm.

But I knew where the Merc was at that point and, more importantly, I realized its enormous potential. And I knew something else: the days of winking at trading violations were over.

It wasn't long before the new rule book was put to the test. It came in my confrontation with Saul Stone. It was clearly a clash of the new era against the old. Stone had emigrated from Romanow, a small town in Russia, at the age of 22, directly after the Russian Revolution. His career in eggs began as an egg-candler for sixty cents an hour at Becker Brothers, an egg-breaking plant on Fulton Street in Chicago. Stone had been a Merc member since the late 1930s and had singlehandedly built the venerable Saul Stone & Company, a major clearing and brokerage operation. Although Stone's operation began in eggs, he quickly transferred his knowledge to the relatively new pork belly market. And when it came to squeezes, it didn't really matter what the commodity was, the methodology was the same. All one had to do was own the bulk of the deliverable supply and, presto, one was in control of the price of the futures market. But not this time. My personal maven, Marlowe King, who was more precise than a computer when it came to statistical information, confirmed that Stone had a virtual corner on the deliverable supply of bellies for the expiring contract. "Lee," Marlowe said ("Lee" was my pit acronym), "if you don't step in to break it up, Stone can drive the price up to wherever he wants."

"That's it," I told E. B. Harris, "I'm going to stop it." Harris responded with a quizzical look. "Good luck," he muttered.

With deference to the age difference between us, I met with Stone in his office. "Saul," I said, "you can scream, argue, bluff, and shout, but the truth is that you own more than the visible supply of bellies."

Silently he sat beaming an icy stare at me. "Did you hear me, Saul, it's against the rules to own more than the available supply."

"I wouldn't know about that," he said with a slight smile on his lips.

"Well, I don't know who knows, if you don't," I responded. "But anyway, you must get out of half of your position by next Friday. You have a whole week to do it. I won't bother you or say a word to anybody. No one will know. But I want your pork belly commitment down 10 percent each day next week, beginning with Monday."

"You must be crazy," he said softly and chuckled. "Who's going to make me do it? Nobody!"

I opened the rule book and pointed to a passage. "Saul, it says here in black and white that under the new rules, the Business Conduct Committee can force the margin up on you until it will cost you more than even you can afford. Don't make me prove it."

Again he laughed. "I don't think so," he said.

I didn't know if he was bluffing or not. But I knew I wasn't. I was prepared to carry out the threat and accept the consequences. This was the new era, and we were playing by new rules. Not my rules, but the Merc's rules.

By next Tuesday morning, nothing happened. I called Stone. "I'm not bluffing, Saul," I said quietly. "You're going to get official notice tonight. The margin on your belly position is going up 25 percent a day until you liquidate half of your position."

There was silence on the phone. "Did you hear me, Saul?" There was a click. Stone had hung up on me. I was completely flabbergasted. *What would I have to do to make these guys believe I meant business.* Fortunately, I didn't have to wait long to see if he believed me.

Things started happening fairly quickly. The pork belly market on Wednesday closed limit down, the maximum price movement allowed in a single day. Down again on Thursday. And Friday. The heavy selling by Saul Stone & Company had spiraled the market downward. By week's end, Stone had reduced his position by half.

Emotionally I was drained. It had been a wrenching few days. They had to have been just as bad for Stone who lost several hundred thousand dollars in the sell-off. I had won an important victory, but made a powerful enemy in the process. Believe me, I wasn't in a celebratory mood; instead, I was racked with anxiety. How many more Saul Stones would I have to stand up to, I wondered. Old E.B. Harris was amazed and somewhat shocked by the whole episode. From that point on, I feel, Harris began to believe in my judgment. And to be honest, I was feeling more confident about it myself.

But again it was generational. We had to prove that the old ways were over. Tom Stone, Saul's son eventually took over the company and was straight as an arrow. Saul's son-in-law Gerald Hirsch was an executive of Saul Stone & Company, a governor of the Merc for a multitude of years, and a very good friend of mine whose sense of humor was supreme. From the beginning, Hirsch would tell everyone that he was going to get ahead by marrying his boss' daughter. He did. As for Saul Stone, it was the measure of the man that he not only forgave me, but became one of my admirers.

But confrontation was always part of my management style. That is, I refused to run from a difficult issue or allow the Exchange to ignore a problem. As an Eleanor Roosevelt fan, I too believed, in the motto of the Christopher Society which she often quoted, "It is better to light a candle than curse the darkness." That's not to say I believe a leader imposes a decision on his constituents. Rather, he nurtures a consensus by shaping and molding and being a keen listener who carefully notes each person's view. A leader leads the discussion in the desired direction. I would smile, shake my

head, remove my glasses, maintain direct eye contact. I didn't want dead-
lock, but compromise, and that took patience. Sometimes I had to wheedle,
flatter, and humor people to form an acceptable solution. Sometimes I was
downright ruthless in demanding that a given issue be examined, but I never
stifled or silenced opposing views. Real consensus can occur only when everyone's voice is heard. John, Viscount Morley of Blackburn's words, "You
have not converted a man because you have silenced him" are prominently
displayed before my office door. It is my credo.

A year later, I had another opportunity to prove that my resolve in
stopping corners was not limited to Saul Stone. In what became known
as the pork belly trials of 1970, I took the Merc another step forward in
cleaning up our image. For the first time, a group of traders who attempted to corner a market were made publicly accountable to the Exchange. In October 1970, they appeared before the Merc board to answer
charges. We were neither a kangaroo court nor a moot court; but we were
a jury of peers. If I was to be a reformer, I wanted to be a cautious one, especially with livelihoods and reputations at stake. But the Merc's reputation was also on the line.

The alleged violators in the case involved David G. Henner, who had
masterminded the plot, and a host of other members that included the old-
line clearing firm of L.D. Schreiber & Co., and Ann Cuneo, who had inherited her membership from her deceased husband. Others who appeared
before the Board during the inquiry because they were considered co-
conspirators included Sidney Maduff and L.D. Schreiber, two of the most
prominent and successful traders at the time. In a bill of particulars prepared by the Business Conduct Committee, Henner, Maduff, and the others
were accused of acting in concert to corner the 1970 July or August pork
belly contract and manipulate the price.

I remember looking into the tired eyes of L.D. Schreiber, a founding
father of the Merc, then in his eighties and asking him about the squeeze.
The transactions in question had been cleared through his firm. In a rising hoarse voice he said, "Sonny boy, ask me about something that happened 30 years ago, I remember that. Ask me about yesterday, I can't
remember anything."

Fortunately, Bill Phelan's office of Audits and Investigations had been
monitoring the positions taken by the Merc's bigger traders, among them
Henner and Cuneo. He had the facts. Jerry Salzman was brilliant as pros-
ecutor. First the accused had cornered the cash market by taking delivery
of the available supply. From that moment they were in a position to manipulate the futures market in small—but highly profitable—swings. They
had failed to establish bona fide hedge accounts and instead engaged in
speculative trading that whipsawed the market to their advantage through

day trades and changing positions. The conspirators were found guilty and punished.

The Board meted out both record fines and penalties. One broker was fined $10,000 and suspended from the Merc for three years and another for two. At the time, these were considered severe penalties. One clearing firm was suspended for two months, and the principal owner of a second firm was suspended for two years, and his firm's clearing privileges were revoked. The member rates of an associate firm were revoked, and a fourth individual whose membership remained intact was fined $30,000—the biggest fine ever assessed to a Merc member up to that time. Our reform image had taken a major step forward.

Because I had served as chief justice in the proceedings, there was a personal irony to cope with, because I actually liked David Henner. He was unquestionably a brilliant trader who could be hugely successful playing it straight. He was both a fundamentalist as well as a technician, one of the first to use point-and-figure charting successfully. In my early trading days, Dave and I were often on the same side of the market and complemented each other's trading style, as we took turns setting off stop-orders in the direction we wanted the market to go. I always believed that he violated the rules just for the fun of it. There are many traders like that; they can win almost any race inside the track but something always made them run outside the prescribed perimeter.

I'm uncertain how the individual Board members felt in the aftermath of the pork belly trials. Collectively, though, there was a sign of relief. And, without question, it changed the nature of the Exchange forever. We had crossed over a threshold into a new era that no longer tolerated nonsense in our markets. The hearings, along with the new bylaws, were a leveler and a reminder that all Merc traders were created equal. For the first time in a long time, I felt the Merc was what it was meant to be: a place where one could discover one's true mettle in a test with the market—and be able to survive economically.

The members had taken pride in the hearings, which had been held two to three times a week in the clearinghouse office. Open to any member who cared to observe (as long as there were seats), the trials sensitized the entire Merc membership. Some were stunned, others irritated, and more than a few were ebullient. During the hearings, Eddie Cahill, one of my floor loyalists, liked to say that the board of governors would put on their powdered wigs and robes before retiring to chambers to sit in judgment. But everyone knew the hearings were no laughing matter, considering the fact that a market squeeze hurt everyone's wallet.

In a sense, the hearings freed the Exchange because it freed the markets from the hands of the manipulator—at least for the time being. As for me,

I had strengthened my leadership role. I had never suffered the nervous strain of trying to live up to an ideal because there had been none. Before I became chairman, the Merc was a sorry place, burdened by moral ambiguity and loaded with irascible old men whose competitive streak often crossed the lines of fair play.

The hearings also served to answer those critics who had given us poor marks for self-regulation. However, I wasn't so naive that I believed we had silenced our detractors forever or that market schemers would never again appear. There would always be noisy and forceful criticism, quiet and subtle criticism, or some combination of the two. And there would always be someone out to squeeze a market, someone with deep pockets for whom control was a pathology. I just didn't want them on our turf.

At times the chairmanship became a balancing act. I had to know how to lead and when to follow. I had to be sensitive to the advice of others, but by no means become totally susceptible to their influence. I wanted achievement, but not at the expense of an ego that shadowed the contribution of colleagues and even the institution itself. While the institution was bound to give me fame, I could never use the institution as a means to achieve personal gains. I could never do anything to demean or disgrace the institution. Most of all, I wanted results.

I tried to set an example. And I was always examining my personal performance. If I made a mistake, I wanted it corrected immediately. If I perceived a problem, I sought a solution as quickly as possible. Too often, problems can become a noise so loud that eventually you can't hear yourself think. And if you put them on a back burner, they smolder, only to burst into a raging flame later. My predecessors never thought that way. I vowed that my legacy would be a clean slate with no debt to past problems. And I had an early test of this resolve. One of the first problems I encountered was an antitrust suit for huge damages resulting from the established practice of fixed-customer commission fees. It was a debt of a previous era. Ironically, the lawsuit was brought against us by a grammar school classmate, Aram Hartunian. In a conversation with Merc attorney Lee Freeman, I quickly concluded that rather than fight this unwinnable battle that could drag on for years, we should settle and get on with our business. It was a winning decision. It wasn't that this was a brilliant solution; it was realistic. The judge rewarded us by suspending damages, depriving our adversary of the additional fees he was counting on.

This early encounter epitomized my style. It was the methodology I would apply during the white-knuckle years that saw the founding of the International Monetary Market in 1972, the introduction of cash settlement in 1981, the launch of stock index futures in 1982, the $150 million construction of a new Chicago Mercantile Exchange building in 1983—

complete with a spare trading floor—the Singapore SIMEX connection in 1984, the launch of GLOBEX, the stock market crash in 1987, and the U.S. Justice Department's floor practices investigation of Merc and CBOT traders in 1989.

There can be a wonderful by-product of solutions that are based on realism: innovation. I realized that long before I became chairman. As a newly elected Board member, I had challenged the more problematic bylaws. One in particular I immediately wanted dropped discriminated against women being members or even employees of the Exchange. This, too, was a debt of a past era. Bob O'Brien, our chairman, was totally in synch with this cause but not so the other Board members whose average age was well over 60. The year was 1967, and miniskirts were in, which became a source of argument in our Board room. In order to drop the female prohibition, I had to agree to a dress code. The question of the day: How much above or below her knees should a skirt be in order for a woman to be allowed on the floor? Bare knees, the argument went, would give the members problems—distract them from the solitude of their thoughts while on the tumultuous trading floor where, in truth, no one really cared if you were a woman, a man, or an alien from Mars. "You'll have the traders walking around with erections," one of the Board members warned. After a three-hour debate, we settled on a hemline two inches below the knees, which was much more than adequate for the political correctness of the time. Sandra Stephens, who worked upstairs for R.J. O'Brien, the chairman's firm, appropriately enough became the first female to clerk on an exchange floor anywhere in the United States. Later that same year, the New York Stock Exchange admitted its first female member and, in 1968, the CBOT also changed its bylaws to allow female traders on its floor.

In breaking the female barrier, we had become innovators. Unwittingly, I had become a charter member of the women's rights movement. My daughter Idelle likes to remind me that I was a member of that movement long before the Merc Board. As she tells the story, on the day of her brother Jordy's 7th birthday, I came home from work with his birthday present. But as usual I also brought presents for her, she was 8, and for her younger brother David. When she asked me years later if I remembered what I had brought for Jordy, I didn't remember. "It was a baseball mitt," Idelle emphatically declared. "And what was my present?" she asked. I'm afraid I didn't remember that either. "It was a baseball mitt, too!" she proudly stated, "I was an equal in your eyes."

In 1972, the barrier fell completely. I sponsored my friend and bridge partner, Carol (Mickey) Norton to IMM membership, where she became the first woman to actually trade in the previously all-male pits. Barbara Diamond, Dorothy Harris, Terry Savage, and a number of other females soon followed and took to the pits. I encouraged Savage, who was a quick study, to parlay her acquired trading skills into a career as a national business newscaster. But the floor wasn't easy for them. It was a male-dominated world, and the members gave no quarter. Kim Hough started clerking in the cattle pit in 1973 as a young woman. She became a member and class-B arbitrageur five years later, and gave private briefings to female members and employees on what to expect and how they should conduct themselves. "No crying in the pit," she would sternly warn. "Never give those bastards that kind of satisfaction." Many years later, Kim married Sherwin Kite, a former IMM governor, carrying forward the Merc's tradition for floor romances that began when the gender discrimination ended. In the late 1970s, Dorothy and Alan Press and Nina and Tom Curtean were the first husband and wife teams on the floor. And Janet Disteldorf, who attributes her success to the fact that as a theater major at the University of Illinois she learned voice control, has, since 1982, been an active broker in the cattle pit. Today, nearly half the CME clerk population is female, and many a lady trader can be found in the pits. Still, it wasn't until 1988 that Norma Newberger, a retired schoolteacher-turned-trader, became the first female to be elected by the Merc membership to the office of governor.

At about the time we attended to women's equality, we also turned our attention to automation. The CME process of recording trades and clearing them was still quite primitive, its past history still in control. When I began trading on the floor, there was Sammy, a thimble of a man perched on a high stool in a glass booth. Next to him stood Joe, a tall, burly man whose eagle eyes would gaze across the trading floor at the board markers, scribbling the prices as they heard them. Joe would then call out the change in prices as Sammy's fingers went flying over a keyboard to record the transaction on a continuous tape that would end up in the traditional wastebasket. The system was about as low-tech as you could get. As volume grew, for all their dedication and long hours, Sammy and Joe could hardly keep up. At the end of a trading day, the brokers would get a pink buy-transfer sheet and a blue sell-transfer sheet. They would then record by hand each transaction by price, quantity, and the trading parties involved. These transfer sheets would then be handed over to our computer, Harvey.

Harvey was straight out of central casting. A tall, thin, elderly man, slightly hunched at the shoulders, he had a perpetual frown of concern. Harvey wore a green eyeshade and black armbands. What was Harvey's function? He was the clearinghouse and did all the logging and calculating of the daily records that determined the net amount to be paid by the loser or received by the winner. Many nights, Harvey would finish at 2:00 A.M.

and be back in the office by 7:00 A.M. It was a grueling schedule. If Harvey, God forbid, did not finish his calculations, the Merc would not open the next day.

Harvey's solution to the surge in trading volume was a simple one. "Maybe we'll have to cut back the trading hours because the volume is getting too big to handle," he once said to me. That wasn't exactly what I had in mind when I took over. Granted, it was the dawn of the computer era, and hardware and software programs were limited. But while the Merc was a major futures exchange on-the-make, and volume was booming, and trades had to be settled before the next day's opening, we were crawling down the automation highway. In the early 1960s, the trading storm that overtook Wall Street had buried the back offices of brokerages houses in a blizzard of paperwork and resulted in a temporary curtailment in trading hours on the NYSE in order to dig out. But that was hardly a solution for us. There was no way I was going to tamper with trading momentum even if it meant hiring an army of Harveys.

I didn't have to go that far. In about 1963, the CBOT, our big brother exchange, had made the first move toward automation in the clearing process by going to "mark sense" cards for trade recordation. This was a major move in the right direction, but the Merc Board viewed it with suspicion.

Fortunately, William Goldstandt was one of the Merc's pork belly traders at that time. Billy Goldstandt, who was way ahead of the crowd when it came to technology, became the in-house Merc computer guru. His advice to the Exchange: follow the Board of Trade. Fortunately, the Board listened, and the Merc took its initial steps, primitive as those were, toward automation in the clearing process. Where and how Billy got his technology knowledge remains a mystery to me, but I know that he was the only one on the floor to actually spend $600 to purchase the first portable calculator. It was as big as a briefcase, and he showed it to me one day with great pride and some secrecy. At about the same time, another trader, John Geldermann, came over to the Merc from the CBOT where he and his brother Tom had established a fairly prominent clearing firm. John Geldermann was connected to the old-line Merc establishment because he married into the Fox family. A tall, quiet man with a knack for computer technology, Geldermann had started at the CBOT shortly after his return from World War II. When his trading firm expanded in 1964, he moved over to the Merc to trade pork bellies. Several years later, Geldermann, along with his partner Art O'Grady, founded CIS, the computer information service firm that was one of the very first private sector companies to provide bookkeeping to futures market participants. By 1984, CIS had become so successful that it was taken over by the giant ADP. But the knowledge attained by Geldermann remained in the family. The following year, John's oldest son Jeff

Geldermann founded GMI, which today is arguably the largest futures market trade-processing organization in the world.

John Geldermann was elected to the Board in 1968, and his computer skills became an invaluable Merc asset. During the following year, Robert O'Brien and I pushed Geldermann to lead us through the initial stages of clearing automation. By 1969, I vowed the Merc would never be prisoner of Harvey's clearing mechanism again. I put John Geldermann in charge of the Floor Facilities Committee as well as a newly created special Computer Committee, with the goal of automating the Merc's trading and clearing operations.

I wanted to get away from the system of blackboard trading. This antiquated process was not only an embarrassment to the modern Merc we were building, but it ended up in something of a scandal. Since we could use only a limited number of blackboards, we introduced a technique of taking Polaroid pictures of a blackboard's record of previous transactions so that the blackboard could be quickly recycled for use. One day we discovered that the Merc's manager in charge of the photo operation had decided to apply his own innovation to the process. He was using the darkroom to develop pictures of women clerks in the buff. It was a rather ignominious ending to the blackboard era.

This led us to the first automated quote-boards built by Ferranti-Packard Electronics Ltd. Before I approved it, Geldermann instructed the Canadian-based company to provide me with a private demonstration on the floor. It was about this time that we hired Glenn Windstrup. Windstrup was kind of an odd young man, a loner who used to sit in his office without ever turning on the lights. But Windstrup, who was totally self-taught and quite brilliant, became the technological expert for the Merc, and Geldermann's right-hand man. Over the next three decades, Geldermann, together with Windstrup and his assistant, would ensure we got the latest and spiffiest electronic quote-boards, mainframes, and high-speed communication systems available. We were soon plugged in to the world, and the world in to us. Technically, we never again looked back to the dark ages, although we struggled through the middle ages with punch cards and handheld devices before the fully automated reporting systems became standard. There was a period of time when Geldermann and I were totally dependent on Ed Lowendowski, a techie who had written the Merc's first clearing program software. Whenever there was a breakdown, which was quite often, we would frantically search all the nearby taverns to find Lowendowski, then try to sober him up enough so that he could patch up the problem before the next morning's opening. The more sophisticated our automation became, the more volume we sustained. Perhaps that represents yet another unwritten market law: transaction volume will grow proportionally with your ability to clear it. Notwithstanding Harvey's suggestion, we never had to shorten trading hours to catch our clearing breath.

Information is the soul of any market. I applied this principle in two ways: providing information to help our traders and disseminating information to build the Merc's image. The members began receiving a daily bulletin of market statistics—the previous day's high and low, the open interest, and so forth. They also began receiving a formal executive report as well as a monthly newsletter so that they were apprised of Board actions. I institutionalized an annual report and, under the guidance of Ron Frost, manager of our newly organized public relations department, turned it into a marketing tool. Why should the annual report look dull and shabby? That's not what the markets were all about. There was color and pace in both the markets and the Merc. Prior to Exchange elections, I also instituted booklets that described the qualifications of perspective candidates for the Board. It was only right the members should know the people for whom they were voting. Most important, I directed the creation of a series of educational booklets, which became one of the Merc's most valuable marketing tools. It is a legacy that has been adopted by every exchange.

But for me, education went far beyond daily information, booklets, or annual reports. Education, from childhood, was instilled in me as the essence of life itself. In part, this is a classic Jewish canon prescribed by the *Torah:* education is the avenue to life's fulfillment. But in our household, it went beyond that. As our family name—which means teacher—suggests, my parents were teachers first and foremost. The Melamdoviches took their profession very seriously. As a child, education, school, homework, and grades were ingrained tenets of my existence. A day did not pass without my parents taking time to teach me about some aspect of life. This mind-set became a permanent characteristic of my being and made education the critical path to whatever I undertook. Instinctively or intentionally, through subtle nudges or overt actions, in private ways or public pronouncements, I made education a permanent fixture of the Merc—whether it was directed at staff, the members, the users of our markets, the regulators, the public at large, or all of the above. It didn't happen all at once, but in little or big steps over the next two decades, education became one of the defining characteristics of the CME. And because education was so obviously intertwined with the Merc's success, to one degree or another this idea has been followed and copied by other exchanges in the United States and around the world. Over time, the Merc involved itself with every form of education: workshops and seminars, a regular schedule of global symposia, the publication of books, funds for the establishment of permanent programs and courses at colleges and universities (Columbia Futures Center at New York's

Columbia University, for years headed by professor Franklin Edwards, is a good example), and grants for fellowships and specific studies; it provided lecturers and speakers, promoted joint educational programs, created a Merc motion picture, encouraged radio and TV programming, and, beginning with the University of Chicago, established permanent chairs for a course in futures markets.

Another departure from the past was an overt attempt on my part to develop rapport and interaction with our brokerage firms as well as with the industries whose products we traded. I was determined to prove to our clearing member firms called Futures Commission Merchants (FCMs) as well as our end-user community that we represented a new breed of traders and that this Merc was a new Merc. Their input was welcome, their calls would be answered, their representation on committees was desired, their criticisms would not fall on deaf ears. In time, it earned the Merc a reputation that distinguished it from the CBOT, which was then known to listen only to its own floor community. Sometimes I created advisory committees composed of nonmembers who would meet on a regular basis to offer ideas and input. This proved to be a most effective means of opening lines of communication with experts who had something to offer our markets but never before had the opportunity. In doing so, we served notice that we were no longer the black sheep of the financial world. Commodity futures, we proclaimed, had shed their Rodney Dangerfield image and deserved respect. Our markets, we insisted, provided an important function to the national economy. It was a new message to our members, our traders, our end users, our regulators, and the public at large.

I explained to Ron Frost that my goal was to create a new image. It was to be his primary mission. He responded by getting us involved in community affairs, by developing a working relationship with the press, by connecting us to local agriculture forums and radio talk shows. Together, we deliberately forged an open-press policy. It was a first in Merc history. No longer would we shy from responding to difficult questions from the media. No longer would actions of the Board be a secret from the membership. We welcomed media interviews, we accepted criticisms, and we issued press reports. For Merc members who were used to silence from the boardroom and a hunker-down mentality whenever things went wrong, it was yet another revolution.

To shape our advertising program I called on a number of Merc governors who had a flair for what was needed: first Michael Weinberg, Jr., then Larry Rosenberg, and later on Gerald Hirsch. The budget, which in 1965 was $1,600, was boosted to $700,000 by the early 1970s. We contracted a small outside firm headed by Martin Cohen whose highly creative mind fashioned some of the most provocative and award-winning ads the business world had ever seen. The first Cohen ad, which appeared in *The Wall Street Journal* featured the photograph of a hefty pig with the caption "Capitalist Pig." Simple, but so clever, effective, and sassy. Another one, touting our lumber futures contract, even took a good-natured swipe at our arch competitor, the Chicago Board of Trade, with a picture of a two-by-four and the caption "The Chicago Mercantile Exchange presents the board of trade."

The Merc was serious business and, similar to my former boss Merrill Lynch, was certainly bullish on America. But that didn't mean we had to be staid, stuffy, stiff and devoid of attitude. No, we weren't Wall Street. And we weren't stocks. We were something else that grew out of the nation's heartland: pioneers, we told ourselves, fueled by ingenuity and guts, and dedicated to preserving the spirit of the frontier. As far as I was concerned, the futures industry was still a vast business frontier waiting to be explored and developed. And maybe all that pioneering talk sounded corny, but this was Chicago, the tough, big-shouldered city with nerves of steel. In futures, Chicago was the first city in the world. It was where futures trading began in 1848 at the CBOT.

Although the Merc was the second largest futures exchange in the United States in 1969, it was light years behind the Board of Trade, whose grain market was an immensely important product line for not only the nation but the world as well. The merchants of grain bought and sold enormous quantities for exporting and often hedged their positions on the CBOT. Among the various grains was a difference in pricing affected by inflationary factors, weather conditions, and supply and demand in the marketplace. While, say, wheat was in a bull market, corn could be in a bear market. The CBOT was well organized and easily had half of the futures business in the world. Its Exchange never had to endure the embarrassment of a subsidized membership price. In the early 1960s, while Merc transaction volume hovered around the 550,000 level, the CBOT boasted a volume of almost 2.5 million contracts. It was my dream and goal to achieve parity with our crosstown rivals.

Of course the Merc wasn't exactly a Johnny-come-lately. It could trace its lineage back to 1874 when the Chicago Produce Exchange was formed to attract buyers of eggs and butter from the eastern and southern parts of the United States. It had undergone various stages, including a 1898 spin-off called the Chicago Butter and Egg Board, which was reorganized and renamed the Chicago Mercantile Exchange in 1919.

Part of the Merc's ethos had been its ability to survive, a skill I could readily identify with. The Merc had proved its resiliency. It had withstood the collapse of its butter and egg markets, following shifts in the production and marketing patterns of these commodities. It even managed to edge back from the brink of extinction after being driven there in 1958 by the loss of its onion contract. Now, a decade later, the Merc was known as the house that pork bellies built. The pork belly contract had kept the Exchange alive. But no one knew how long an exchange could survive trading a single commodity. I didn't give it high odds.

I knew that, to survive, we would have to diversify. Having witnessed firsthand the danger of a one-product exchange, I was hell-bent on not repeating that mistake. This mission became a priority. In 1969, we revived the dormant hog market, which had been initiated in 1966. With the help of Board Governor Glenn Andersen, we changed the specifications of the cattle contract, added new delivery points, and breathed life into a contract that was going nowhere. Those revisions were the key ingredients that made cattle the premier Merc contract for the next decade. We then ventured into a new field by opening a lumber market. And we finally dropped the storage egg market, replacing it with a fresh egg contract. In 1970, there were new contracts in boneless beef, grain sorghum (milo), and feeder cattle. We also revised the Idaho potato contract and tried once again to resurrect it. On one occasion I required Barry Lind, chairman of the Potato Contract Committee, to travel to Pocatello, Idaho, for a weekend (he says it felt like a month) to a potato convention. According to Lind, he was the first Jew they had ever seen, and he barely got out with his life. But I was not overly optimistic about any of these new contracts and continued my search for something dynamic; perhaps even a new dimension.

There was yet one more innovation introduced in 1969 that was clearly revolutionary and that catapulted the Merc's financial status above all others. The CME became the first futures exchange to create a public trust for the purpose of protecting customer funds in the event of a failure by one of its clearing members. It was unique to any exchange in the nation. To accomplish this feat required the talents of Ira Marcus, whom I had installed as the Merc's tax counsel.

Like many good ideas, it was the consequence of necessity. Until the mid-1960s, the Merc had lost money year after year, so the Internal Revenue Service did not get any tax revenue from us, nor did they expect any. But by the end of 1969, the IRS suddenly realized that we had been profitable during the previous five years or so and claimed back taxes in the amount of some $5 million. It was all we had in the treasury and I wasn't about to give it up to the government. So I went to Marcus with a wild thought: Could we, I asked, avoid paying any taxes by putting our money in a trust for the benefit of the public? In other words, to be used as financial protection in the event of a clearing firm's failure. At first Marcus looked at me as if I had gone mad, then a diabolic smile crossed his lips. What a coup if he could pull this off. He did just that. We protected our $5 million, for which I had other plans.

To my knowledge, the Merc remains the only American exchange with such a nontaxable trust. It has grown dramatically over the years with a continuing flow of contributions from CME income.

When I looked back on my first year, it was hard to believe all that was accomplished. To say it had been a busy year is a classic understatement. *Change* was its underlying theme. It included the reformation of the Exchange rules, challenging corners and squeezes, the birth of a new image, a departmental organization, a membership committee restructuring, floor member participation in governance, completion of a new and expanded trading floor, a public relations overhaul, institution of a nontaxable trust, and the start of a process for product diversification. And still there was more.

There was no doubt in my mind. I was where I belonged. I had the Exchange's attention. The members were behind me. But just because I was their number 1 draft choice was no guarantee I would become the most valuable player. It was like playing a game of chess. There were so many moves to contemplate and strategies to consider in the face of growing competitive pressures. A good chess player doesn't anticipate an opponent's next move, but the next several. The key word is anticipation, whether you are trying to figure a market play or exchange strategy. There was something in the financial winds that I began to sniff in 1970. It was the smell of anticipation.

13

The First Milestone

One of the biggest opportunities for change came on November 6, 1969, the day when referendum Rule 206 was used for the first time. Ironically, it was a Board-initiated referendum requesting the membership to authorize the Board to proceed with a search and negotiations toward an eventual relocation of the Merc. True to my promise, I let the members decide. But not without politicking strenuously for this vote. I used to take a daily poll in my constant conversations with the members. Almost everyone knew that the present location had become too small and could no longer be expanded, thus I thought the members would support a move to new space.

This wasn't the first time the Merc considered a relocation or a new building. The idea had been simmering for several years and always provoked controversy. Past Boards had discussed it time and again, but never came to a decision. Sometimes feigned attempts were made at analysis of the issue, but these never culminated in taking action. I guess fear of change was always the prevailing reason; status quo is so much safer. And in retrospect, the disasters the Merc continued to encounter were reason enough not to take unnecessary risks. This time, I said to my inner circle who were unanimously behind me, it would be different: "Once and for all, we are going to bite this bullet."

But before I put the issue to vote, I knew I would have to confront the landlord of the Chicago Mercantile Exchange building which stood at the corner of Franklin and Washington Streets since 1928. I was reluctant to do so. He wasn't just any landlord. He was Colonel Henry Crown, the legendary tycoon who had amassed one of America's greatest fortunes.

Crown asked me to lunch so he could scare the hell out of me. We ate in his private boardroom on the top floor of the Merc building. There were just the two of us and a butler who privately attended to our meal. More than twice my age and the son of a Jewish Latvian immigrant, Crown had been through wars, depressions, and recessions, and had many millions to show for it. My claim to fortune was a new Corvette and a split-level home in Skokie, a middle-class suburb just outside Chicago. No doubt about it, he knew how to survive. He had begun humbly with a tiny sand and gravel company called Material Service Corporation, which he launched in 1919— ironically, the same year the Chicago Mercantile Exchange was founded. In a panic during the Great Depression, the Merc Board sold its building back to the insurance company that had financed it. It was bought from the company at bargain prices by none other than Colonel Henry Crown. A few years later, the Merc would pay the Colonel in annual rent what he had paid for the building.

"Melamed," he opened, "you are about to make a terrible mistake. What you are going to do could bring down the Exchange." He paused for effect. "There's a depression coming again." Here was the man who owned the Empire State Building and just about everything else dispensing his wisdom. I wasn't taking his ominous "tip" lightly. But I knew what I knew. I didn't come armed with a pile of flip charts, graphs, and statistical sheets, only with common sense and the knowledge that the Merc's trading volume had climbed 109 percent in 1969 over that of 1968. My every instinct foretold that this growth was only the beginning. I knew that we were the Colonel's main tenant and that we had outgrown our quarters. I knew that without new space the Merc was destined to remain second class forever. I knew that if we didn't take this first expansionary step, I could never advance my dream for the Exchange. I knew the membership was fully behind me. And I also knew that risk-takers take risks. I thanked Crown for the lunch and advice. I then told him we were going ahead with our plans.

Back at my office I got more pressure. Octogenarian L.D. Schreiber called to say the move was wrong, that we would inevitably exceed our cost projections and put the Merc in the red forever. At 6 feet 4 inches, Ludwig D. Schreiber was an imposing figure. Everyone knew him simply as L.D. or Barney. He had been city clerk of Chicago in 1932 and became CME chairman from 1933 to 1935. His firm's partner had been my technical guru— Elmer Falker, who was about half his size. They were dubbed Mutt and Jeff. But L.D. quickly rose from the ranks to become the role model trader—the first guy in the world to learn how to hedge eggs—and had everyone's respect. I listened politely. I then assured Mr. Schreiber that I would not allow a cost overrun. I would stay within the amount approved by the membership.

Of course, most of the old guard was against relocation. As Sol Rich said to me, "Lee, if you do this we will go broke. Just like when you expand a successful restaurant because it is too small; it never works." And the old guard was superstitious about the location at 110 North Franklin. It was where they had grown up and made their money. Any move was regarded as dangerous. But I knew they were in the minority, and I knew that without more space none of my long-range dreams would be possible. I knew the different views were generational; Milt Rich, Sol's son, was in favor of relocation.

Many a night I tossed and turned in a fitful sleep over Crown's pronouncement. What if he was right? What if another depression was coming? Would we have to sell the new building as the Merc had before? Would I go down in infamy? But the new building I was going to propose wasn't going to carry debt. It would be fully paid from our cash reserve of some $6 million. It was the money we had saved from getting into Uncle Sam's hands. That was my budget, and I wouldn't go a cent over it. I would not exceed that sum because I didn't believe in deficit spending or even financing.

In June 1970, we publicly announced our plans to search for a new building site and the interior design firm of Perkins and Will was hired to do a study of spacial and physical requirements. It was the same firm that had redesigned our present floor. The Merc Real Estate Committee headed by Dan Jesser considered some 200 locations before narrowing it down to the final one. I had put Jesser in charge because I could trust him. I had to be certain that the deal we made was the best for the Merc, and not for anyone else. Dan Jesser could never be bought. Still, I never left the committee's side and participated in its every decision. A hands-on approach with respect to all matters was the essential style of my chairmanship. It was how I got a "dictator" reputation, but it was grossly inaccurate. A dictator by definition does not need to respond to consensus. I always did. I met with Alan Goldboro of the Tishman organization, which was constructing office buildings in a complex known as the Gateway Centers. We agreed that the Merc needed two things: a trading floor and a building where its member firms could have their offices. Six million dollars, he stated, was not nearly enough to do both. He offered to build a "box" at 444 West Jackson that would house our trading floor while our member firms could use the connected 35-story tower at 222 South Riverside Plaza for office space. The Merc would own only the "box," but this gave us a measure of inflation protection. Jesser and I liked the idea. Although I realized that this might not be the ultimate solution for the Merc or give us the world-class image I dreamed of, it was the best we could do at this time. "But you cannot exceed $6 million," I warned. "I've got it," he replied.

Dealing with the Merc membership collectively required a different approach from facing individual adversaries in a trading pit where everything was an adrenaline rush and a spontaneous outburst. Outside the pit, I had to be deliberate and to plan, even to orchestrate as I did for the referendum. This too was to become one of the hallmarks of my administrative style: leave as little as possible to chance.

Perkins and Will prepared a slide presentation. I worked closely with the chief architect, Skip Rawlings, and could answer a wide range of questions thrown at me. The new premises would result in the most modern trading floor in the world. The day of the presentation over 200 members were in attendance. I had a coterie of my floor loyalists sitting in designated seats among the crowd with express orders about when to applaud. I put one of my staunchest partisans, Mike Sturch, in charge. Mike was pure diamond-in-the-rough. He grew up as a tough kid on the north side of Chicago and attended five different high schools before graduating—his family never moved out of their original neighborhood. But as early as age 12, he became exposed to commodities markets through his uncle, a CBOT member. The floor became his dream and life's goal. In 1964, he ended up at the Merc running orders for Bill Rankin of Bache & Co. From there he rose to the top of his profession as a currency broker and trader. As I explained to Sturch and the others, applause can be contagious. And it certainly was in this case as I rattled off the reasons why we needed a new building and why this was the best plan. The referendum received near unanimous approval with a vote of 320 to 21 in its favor. I always wondered about the 21 individuals who voted against this move, and I had a pretty good idea who they were.

On May 18, 1970, Lee Freeman arranged for the announcement of the new Merc Exchange to be made in Mayor Richard J. Daley's office. It was another coup for us. The Merc had begun its long journey to stardom. A year later, the building was topped out. The scheduled move was planned for the Thanksgiving three-day weekend in November 1972. To move an entire exchange is no small undertaking. We knew of no such previous moves, and we knew how many things could go wrong. I laid down the law: the Exchange must be fully operational the Monday following our move or heads would roll. I would have no disasters on my watch. John Geldermann was put in charge and every step of the relocation was conscientiously planned, programmed, and rehearsed. Glenn Windstrup was the project manager and carried out the myriad complexities entailed in moving into a new exchange. The move was made without a hitch and turned Windstrup into the singular expert in this field.

The traders were ecstatic over the new premises. It was as if we had left the dark ages and entered the promised land. Everything was modern, bright, brand spanking new, and in the right place. The psychological up-lift was nothing short of dramatic, giving everyone the feeling that they had left their second-class status forever. In the words of Lenny Feldman, "Everyone looks so clean . . . it's like we all came out of a shower."

We ended up with a square box of a building—43,665 square feet of space—modest compared with the retailing monument that would be built just down the block, the Sears Tower, the tallest building in the world. The new Merc building, however, fit our needs and pocketbook at the time. But not for long. The trading floor was nearly 24,000 square feet of columnless free space with a 34-foot ceiling. It was the biggest man-made cavern of its day, an enormous echo chamber where the sounds of capitalism reverberated off the walls.

Little did I know that a few years later, I would again assign Geldermann the additional complexities involved in expanding the Merc's trading floor over Canal Street. It couldn't be helped. No sooner had we made our move from the Merc's birthplace on Franklin Street than the space became cramped. The reason was clear. In 1970, when we instituted the plans for our new quarters at 444 W. Jackson, nobody had financial futures in mind. When we moved in 1972, the IMM had already been born—an infant of six months. A scant four years later, the successful new IMM contracts were pushing us against the wall. Not only didn't we have enough room to launch any of the new markets we had on the drawing boards, we could hardly manage existing business. Walter Kowalski, the Merc's statistician who had served the CME for nearly 40 years, threw up his hands, unable to keep up with the combined volume growth of our two exchanges. It brought us to the embarrassing conclusion, albeit one made with some perverse pride, that we had no choice but to either move again or expand the new premises.

To move again after only four years in the building was really out of the question—we couldn't afford it. But could we expand? The Chicago River made expansion to the east impossible. So our architects, Skidmore, Owings & Merrill, who had built the Merc's current structure, came up with the only solution. We could increase the trading area 40 percent by expanding the building to the west by 90 feet. Easier said than done. Such a solution required a major favor from the City of Chicago. We would need to purchase the air rights from the city in order to cantilever the present structure over the Canal street sidewalk, west of the Exchange. The Chicago Buildings Department rejected the plan out of hand. To build over a public sidewalk had been allowed only once in the history of Chicago, and that was for a hospital. The idea was dead in the water, unless his honor, Mayor Richard J. Daley, would be willing to override his own Buildings Department's veto.

I came prepped and rehearsed to the Mayor's office on the fifth floor of City Hall in the summer of 1976, bringing the architectural renderings and plans Skidmore had provided. Although he knew me, I was alone and very nervous. After all, I was in my early forties, hardly known outside of Chicago, while the Mayor was a world personality and a U.S. powerhouse. He had just been elected to his sixth consecutive term. Besides, I was there to ask for a personal favor, so to speak.

The Mayor listened quietly to my plea without interrupting, and when I was finished asked one question, "What will it do for Chicago?"

This was not the question I expected, but I thought I knew the right answer. "Mr. Mayor," I responded without hesitation, "if I am right about financial futures, the IMM will move the center of financial gravity of this country a couple of miles westward from New York."

The Mayor broke into a hearty laugh. "I like that," he said shaking my hand. "Go and expand your building."

We did, and my promise to Mayor Daley was fulfilled. Chicago became the capital of risk management, not only for the United States, but for the world. Without the Mayor's approval, it might not have been possible.

The expansion, although it again gave us only a temporary respite, allowed us to launch the next wave of financial contracts—the interest rates and the stock index futures—markets that insured the IMM's phenomenal success. It was also critical that the expansion resulted in a contiguous floor, which was primarily due to Billy Muno's insistence—at a $1 million price tag—that the architects remove the crossbeams from the building's outer wall before the new part was added. An uninterrupted floor is the most conducive to trading. Mayor Richard J. Daley died less than 6 months after our meeting in City Hall.

However, for Geldermann and his teammates, who by then, along with Windstrup, also included Tom Peak, the 1975 expansion was but child's play compared to the next and most critical test in the Merc's history. In the early 1980s, their accumulated expertise would become indispensable when my ultimate dream for the Merc—a building as big and prestigious as that of the Board of Trade—became a reality. But that was still a number of years away.

By now, I virtually ran the Exchange from the pork belly pit where I was one of the leading traders. It wasn't easy though, because the belly, hog, and cattle pits had attracted a lot of new talent; young, smart kids who had made it to the top step of the trading ring. Some, including Mark Millstein, Jimmy Kaulentis, Carl Leaven, John McGuire, Marshall Stein, and Mark Palmer had worked their way up, starting as runners or clerks. Some traders—Lonnie Klein, George Segal, Gerald Pam, Alan Mitchell, and Lou Schwartz—were introduced to the Merc by relatives or friends; and others, Walter Maxim, Milt Levine, Phil Karafotas, Ronnie Schiller, Jonathan Murlas, and Alan Miller were in families whose membership dated back to the CME's founding. Indeed, Schiller was a third-generation Merc member.

Ken Mackay and E.B. Harris would stand just outside the pit, catch my eye, and wait for me to take a break. Then we'd meet in between trading lulls right there on the trading floor. It went on for the four hours of the trading day, a steady flow of people coming to the pork belly pit to talk, and clerks handing me phone messages. I was never cut off from Exchange business just because I was trading. Besides, it was my ardent belief that the minds of traders, especially those who put their own money on the line, provided fertile ground for innovative thought. This was also the reason I encouraged many of my trading buddies to run for the Board. These were the people who knew what made a market tick. And because, as a trader, I had daily interaction with the others, ideas would quickly bubble up to the top. Today there are task forces, economic forums, economic departments, academicians, study groups, and electronic analysis probing the market to discover its secrets as if it were some laboratory specimen. But the best ideas came off the floor, out of the pits. The members themselves are the best experts.

For this reason, I always made myself accessible to members, to hear their thoughts, get their ideas, and listen to their complaints and their suggestions. Working the floor, however, was a two-way street; I massaged the members and they massaged me. I would plant ideas and lobby for what I wanted. And I could get feedback, learn what they would or would not support and why. I kept track of who said what on a stack of trading cards that accumulated in my pocket. Nothing was too small to get my attention. I was well aware that arrogance was an occupational hazard. That's the paradox of leadership: constituents are partial to their elected officials who seem both bigger than they are, yet are one of them.

Whether I held a group of 10 or 150 together, I was always talking, discussing, answering, explaining, educating, lobbying and listening. It was often a one-on-one process. It could be emotionally draining and time-consuming. And while it may have lacked all the finesse of managerial wizardry by current standards, in the end, it always worked. Once I gained the confidence of the membership, I could push harder. But I always stopped short of forcing my ideas without their approval. Consensus was critical. I was also an impassioned believer in education and logic. The members were smart, and if my ideas were good, they would support them. If I couldn't gain their confidence, my idea was probably faulty. I never wanted people to stop thinking critically. I needed to test my thoughts in a critical and intellectually honest environment. And when my ideas prevailed, I knew not to take full credit for the success. I always remembered to lavishly praise all participants and contributors.

By now my life was frantic. Besides the growing number of committee meetings I attended every day, I began speaking at an increasing number of special events from seminars on lumber or cattle to the dedication of the Poultry and Egg Building—the Merc's gift to the Lincoln Park Zoo in honor of the exchange's 50th anniversary. The gift idea—to build the Farm in the Zoo so that city kids could learn how chickens lay eggs—was Michael Weinberg's. The idea was a huge success. At the opening event, Secretary of Agriculture Clifford Hardin was the guest of honor, and I presented the

Merc's check for $50,000 to Chicago's Mayor J. Daley to cover the costs of the permanent exhibit.

When it came to the Exchange, I tried to put my personal passions aside. Take smoking, for instance. Like most teenagers of my era, I began smoking in high school, about a pack a week. Now I was running the Exchange on strong coffee and nearly four packs a day. I'd finish my first pack by 10:00 A.M. In spite of my smoking preference, I did not oppose a smoking ban, which came first in the pits and then on the Exchange floor. It was another case of the Board using Referendum rule 206. "You let me down," brooded Bill Katz, a heavy smoker like myself. Katz and I had by then become good friends, having long before buried the old hatchet. Indeed, from the mid-seventies on, Bill Katz supported my initiatives as if he were a Melamed patriot from the start. In turn, I became a Katz fan.

Although I tried to give up smoking many times, I knew it was nearly impossible because I believed it might affect my ability to play bridge. Bridge had become my passion during this period. Tournament bridge, or duplicate as it is called, was great therapy. It required total concentration. The game forced me to put the Exchange and the pit behind me for the duration of the game. But it didn't work without a cigarette, or so I thought. I began playing bridge as a conscious decision to give up chess. I had reached a level in chess where I could often beat my father, and consequently I found myself trying to lose. I didn't want to beat him. So I decided to switch to bridge and bought every book available on the subject. I began playing with Dan Jesser as a partner. Together we learned the rudimentary rules of the game, but I soon discovered that to get ahead in bridge one needs to play with a better player. As with everything else, my competitive urges drove me to win.

It is through bridge that I became acquainted with Carol (Mickey) and Bert Norton. They were both expert players, became my friends, and later, members of the International Monetary Market at its inception in 1972. Bridge is a subculture of civilization, with strict rules, codes, and mores. It has an untenable caste system, which is its worst feature. The better players, especially the life-masters, never even talk to the "wannabees" let alone teach them the game. As chairman of the Chicago Merc I was a bit of a celebrity, and I was treated as an exception to the bridge snob rule. Mickey Norton adopted me, bridge-wise speaking, and we made a deal: I would teach her to trade and she would teach me how to play bridge. Aside from Mickey becoming the first female pit trader, it was a good deal for both of us. I reached life-master, the highest standing in bridge, in something like record time (Mickey and I won many championships together), and she made enough money trading to ultimately become a part owner of the Chicago Bulls and the Chicago White Sox. Bert Norton eventually became my associate in a Class-B arbitrage firm, which I launched to advance currency trading at the IMM. He also made enough money so that he could continue being a full-time bridge player. On occasion, I would also play with my wife, Betty, who learned the game in self defense. To her credit, she became quite proficient. Much later, Brian Monieson became my regular partner. Together we capped our career by winning a national championship. And in 1975, we fielded a Chicago Mercantile Exchange commercial team in the National Championship tournament held in Chicago. In addition to Brian Monieson, Bert Norton, and myself, the team included Randy McKay, James Cordes, and David Joyce. We won handily, beating an IBM team in the finals.

Eventually, however, I had to give up bridge because the Merc demanded literally all of my time, and to stay on top of the bridge game required playing four or five times a week. As for cigarettes, I didn't get around to kicking the habit until 1984 when I traded in my Winstons for running shoes. When I finally kicked the awful habit, it was cold turkey—one of the hardest things I ever did.

Actually, I should credit my daughter Idelle for making me give up smoking. As soon as she was old enough to have an opinion, which in her instance was at the age of two, she was always on my case about smoking. All three of my children had an enormous impact on my life. Idelle came first, just after I graduated law school. We were living in a one-bedroom flat on the north side of Chicago at the time, and all our friends were having children. Betty and I followed suit, although by today's standards we were awfully young to raise a family. Betty was 18 when we got married and I was just two years older. I guess we grew up with our children. My daughter Idelle naturally became my princess, a common occurrence among fathers. Fortunately, my special love for her did not interfere with her inherent analytical ability nor detract from her innate wealth of common sense. She grew up to become an excellent lawyer (specializing in futures markets of course) following her father's footsteps at John Marshall Law School. She may yet pursue her law career, but for now it has taken a back seat to her desire to be the best mother in the world. Her intellect and analytical skills, however, have been put to good use in the suburban school system where she is very active and has become president of the P.T.A. Over the years, I have learned to seek her advice and opinions on every aspect of my life, and I utilize her talents as my personal confidante.

Naturally, Idelle met her husband Howard Dubnow at the Merc. The Dubnows are descendants of the famous Jewish historian Simon Dubnov. At the time Howard met my daughter, she had a summer job working as a runner for Dellsher, and he was a lowly board marker. It was love at first sight. Our four grandchildren, Joshua, Aaron, Jared, and Mara, are proof that the Merc can be a great matchmaker. Like so many others on the Merc floor, Howard Dubnow rose through the ranks as a broker and was elected by the Index and Options Market Division to the Merc Board where he served as governor for several years with distinction. According to Idelle, when he left the Board, it was to pursue his avocation as a coach for soccer, basketball, and little league baseball—after all, he and Idelle have contributed so many potential players. At the same time, Howard has pursued his full-time career as an expert broker in the Merc's demanding stock index pit.

Jordan, our first son, was born less than two years after Idelle. He was smart and very talented from the start, and highly competitive—like his father. After graduation from the University of Michigan, he quickly became successful as a trader and made good money. However, for Jordan, again like his father, trading was not enough. He wanted to prove himself in fields where his father's influence was not a factor. His interests were multifold, and his career goal was to be a film director. Before he embarked on his movie career, however, he talked fashion designers Marithé and Francois Girbaud into an exclusive license for the area and opened their first fashion store in Chicago. Later, after he began studying at the prestigious American Film Institute (AFI) in Hollywood, he and a partner opened a second Girbaud store in Beverly Hills. His 30-minute thesis film for AFI, which he wrote and directed, was about trading in the gold pit.

David was born four years after Jordan. He too was a smart child and extraordinarily observant. He received a bachelor's degree from the American University and grew up to be an extremely insightful adult. For instance, he has a well-developed sense of political perception and could easily become an excellent political analyst. David actually got some great political training by spending two of his college summers as an intern on the staff of senators on both sides of the political isle. He has also inherited his father's ability to use words and could probably transform that talent into a career in public broadcasting. But David's life ambition is to become a great futures trader. No easy goal. Still, to no one's surprise, he has soaked up an enormous amount of charting and economic knowledge over the years and is able to discuss the most sophisticated market complexity with experts.

With three children, a wife, a home in the suburbs, and an exchange to run that demanded all my time, my life was challenging, to say the least. I was torn apart in an attempt to do it all. Although I would come home exhausted from a day of trading, long meetings, speeches, press briefings, and the constant interchange with hundreds of members, I forced myself to give my family all my attention for whatever little time remained in the day. Often, I would rush home to arrive just in time to kiss the kids goodnight. Consequently, I made certain that the weekends were totally theirs. I tried to be with them throughout those days no matter what I planned to do, even if it was to go together to the drugstore. But more often than not, each weekend included a special feature, be it a movie, the zoo, or something unusual.

When they were old enough, Idelle and Jordy would sit with me at the dining room table, calling out the highs and lows from past records as I created yet another commodity price chart. Our weekend togetherness worked until outside activities and their friends began to monopolize them.

During the summers, once school was out, we always made a special excursion. Sometimes we simply rented a summer cottage in nearby Indiana or Michigan. I would come up on weekends and occasionally during the week. Once, our family traveled to Israel, Greece, and England. That was a unique and most memorable tour. Another time, after Jordan and David were older, we took them to Paris and to see the beaches at Cannes. For Jordan's eighteenth birthday, the two of us went to Monaco for the Grand Prix.

Other times we would plan extended car trips across the United States. Our plan was to take everyone to every part of the country. One year it was out west, another it was south, and so forth. We whiled away the hours spent driving by playing all sorts of car games we would invent, or by singing songs. The trips included all the usual and expected adventures of families on the road, including the unforgettable time I arranged for a special visit to the White House. Poor David had the stomach flu at the time and was suddenly struck with nausea. He threw up in the State Dining Room. I'll never forget the sight of Idelle sidling quietly away and pretending not to know us. Betty always chided David that he forced Pat Nixon to come down with a mop and a bucket to clean up the mess. All in all, those were wonderful summer trips. Jordy, however, likes to say that he got to know the location of every phone booth across the country. It's true. I would often pull over to call the market whenever we spotted a phone. It was the only way I could stay in touch with the market and monitor my position. There we would be, the car pulled over to the side of some highway, with me in a phone booth with the charts spread out on the ground.

Thus, no matter what we did or where we went, my life was connected to the market and the exchange which was always tugging at me, pulling me away from my family life. Betty understood my drive better than anyone and gave me the slack I needed. But I always felt guilty about my children, who were forced to share me with the futures world. I was working virtually three full-time jobs: one as a husband and father, the other as a trader, the third as Merc chairman. My days blended into the nights. I got by (and still do) on three to four hours of sleep. Because I could compartmentalize my responsibilities and actions, I could usually walk away from the pits after a trading session with a clear mind. Then I would plunge into

Exchange business with the same trader's intensity. Later, I would rush home to my family.

I never looked upon the chairmanship as a sacrifice or allowed its pressures to get me. I also refused to receive any remuneration for the position. I was prepared for 7-day workweeks. I even placed the development of my clearing firm, Dellsher Investment Co., low on my priority list; so low that I didn't get around to building it until nearly 25 years later. These, of course, were trade-offs. But as long as I could build the Exchange and move it forward, I satisfied a deep-seated inner goal to succeed. I knew that, in any event, I would also personally benefit in two ways: every new successful market I helped create was another trading opportunity for me, and larger volume would enhance the value of my membership. If the Merc prospered, so did I. But mostly what drove me was the intellectual challenge of building something new—a psychic satisfaction that had eluded me in the practice of law.

Yes, I was ambitious. Yes, I was idealistic. Yes, I was capitalistic. Yes, I liked the feel of being chairman with the power and ideas to shape something big. I wanted my persona identified with an important mission that could make a difference in the world. Just like Shloyme Mendelson had said I should.

14

The Maverick Idea

By 1970, I began to view the futures exchange as an ecosystem in which contracts competed for survival. Futures contracts that could not compete or find a niche disappeared like a species. But in nature, diversity takes over and an extinct species is usually replaced by another, either more efficient or more adaptable to the environment. And diversity, any scientist will tell you, is the logical outcome of evolution. So, if indeed these markets were going through some kind of evolutionary process, I asked myself, what would be the next stage toward diversity? I wasn't exactly sure what kind of futures contract that meant. It needed to be a serious contract in its own right, not another stepchild of agriculture.

The thought of a market in foreign exchange didn't come all at once. Nor was there any single event that caused me to wake up one morning and shout: *Eureka, I have a wonderful idea for a new market.* Rather, the idea was there, concealed as it were, within layers of past experience, in the flow of current events, in the undertone of discussion between friends and associates, and within the unceasing internal pressure of my mind to find something that would catapult the Merc to a greater destiny.

As a child transported from one border to another, I had my first peek into the mysterious realm of changing faces and values of foreign exchange. Within the short span of a year-and-a-half and before I had reached the age of nine, I had already lived with the Polish zloty, the Lithuanian lit, the Russian ruble, the Japanese yen, and the American dollar. A coin collection was something much more real to me than to most children my age. Then, still as a child, in the distant world of Japan, I had my first lesson in the fascinating black market arena of foreign exchange.

But my focus on the currency markets in the late 1960s and early 1970s stemmed from current events of the day. In 1967, the Bank of England jolted the world by devaluating pound sterling from $2.80 to $2.40, a move necessary to bring their currency unit closer in line with reality. It was the first of many steps destined to bring down to size the once omnipotent

169

British empire. Suddenly, foreign exchange and currency values were becoming recurring news items. There was an increasing flow of press stories about devaluations and revaluations on the business pages. There were articles on the deficiency of the Bretton Woods system. There were heated discussions about floating versus fixed exchange rates. There were assertions by renowned University of Chicago economist Milton Friedman on the merits of floating rates and the inadequacies of the present system. And there was my personal maven on currency trading, Richard Boerke, a close friend. With a sharp mind that cut deftly to the core, Boerke was a shrewd trader and fundamentalist who understood markets. Over coffee we would banter about world events and the international currency markets to which our attention was drawn. Boerke was the first in our crowd who had attempted to dabble in currency. He found it nearly impossible.

The Bretton Woods accord, hammered out in the small resort town in the silent mountains of New Hampshire after World War II, still existed and had tied the world's major currencies to the U.S. dollar. The agreement, signed by President Truman and representatives of most Western European nations, established a narrow band of fluctuations between world currencies and the U.S. dollar. The dollar, in turn, was pegged to the price of gold at $35 an ounce, and the United States pledged to sell it at that fixed price to governments that sought to hold gold rather than dollars. Thus, the official exchange rates of currencies were artificially fixed, shielded from the bids and offers of an open marketplace. Fixed, that is, until the pressures became too great.

There existed, also, a cash interbank currency market, but it was an exclusive club that operated in the shadows of international high finance. Behind the posted official exchange rates, banks traded currencies at slight fluctuations among themselves or for their big commercial customers, locking the public out of the market.

I had come across a newspaper article that reported an anecdote involving Milton Friedman who was turned down by the banks when he tried to trade British pounds. It was a curious piece that clearly showed the banks of the day limited the currency markets to commercial interests. They wouldn't deal with an individual, giving the feeble explanation that "individuals didn't have a commercial reason." It would encourage speculation, they said. Thus, individuals, no matter how high their net worth or station in life, were excluded from trading in the forward markets. If you were General Motors, you were permitted to trade currencies. But if you were Milton Friedman, you were banned from the marketplace. My buddy, Boerke, had also attempted to short the pound, anticipating a devaluation as had Friedman, but no bank would take his money either. Nevertheless,

Boerke was persistent and finally found a way, using his father's business connections. I talked often with him and others about the frustration of the situation and became emotionally intertwined with the topic. The opportunities were apparent.

For instance, it was clear that the British pound was out of line with reality. Either the British government would go broke trying to hold it, or they were going to have to let it go and devalue. To take advantage of this situation required a way to short sterling—or *cable*, as the professionals called the British unit. I also tried, but the banks refused to take my money. It made me wonder. Why shouldn't the individual have the same right as a corporation to trade currency? Doesn't economic opportunity apply to everyone? Doesn't the individual have a right to protect or enhance his personal estate?

These events and this line of reasoning led me to the obvious question. Why not create a currency market for everyone? But I was no economist. What did I really know about such things. So I posed the question to my currency expert, Dick Boerke: *Should I consider such a market for the Merc?* "Absolutely!" Boerke responded as if this were the most obvious question in the world. "It's a natural," he said, and passionately expounded on the subject. "It would be the greatest market of all times." Suddenly, it was there before me. Why not a futures market in currencies open to all participants big and small? It certainly would be a departure from our meat complex. The two of us discussed it again and again. I also talked to Harris and found him favorably inclined, but he thought that it was a nearly impossible concept. Boerke, however, thought so much of the idea that he took it upon himself to write a letter to E.B. Harris lobbying on its behalf. Harris didn't respond. Still, I was not dissuaded. I couldn't let it go. Here I was chairman of an exchange, desperately looking for diversification, and trying all these odd-ball and crazy contracts with dubious potential. Why not turn to finance?

I wasn't blind to the fact that by introducing a financial instrument to the futures world, I would be blazing a brand new trail. In the centuries-old history of futures markets—since the time when Japanese rice merchants began trading "rice tickets" in Osaka in 1650—these markets were exclusively the domain of agricultural products. Why hadn't anyone before considered finance, I wondered? Why not give business and financial managers the same risk transfer capabilities that their counterparts in agriculture had been using? Was there some fundamental reason that made financial products unsuitable to the mechanics of futures? I could think of no such reason. On the contrary, all my instincts told me that the world of finance could be better applied to futures markets than to the world of agriculture.

By March 1970, I was obsessed with the idea and determined to implement it. Harris was, by now, in lockstep. More important, Mark Powers embraced the concept fervently. This gave me heart since he was the only bona fide economist in my circle of friends. Clearly, Powers was the right person at the right time. One of 11 children raised on a Wisconsin dairy farm, Powers was 31 years old and had a doctorate in economics from the University of Wisconsin. He had written his dissertation on pork belly futures and I wanted an Economic Research Department. I needed someone to help us create new products and to write contract specifications. That someone was Powers, a thoughtful and articulate individual with a fertile mind. His resume had been given to me by Harris and I hired him in January 1969. To my knowledge, he was the first staff economist on any futures exchange and one of the few economists around who understood the mechanics of futures markets. It turned out that he was brilliant and never failed me in the revolutionary paths we would eventually take.

In his first year on the job, Powers reviewed some 30 prospects for futures contracts. We rejected most of them for one reason or another. Obviously, there weren't many to choose from. The CBOT had grain and all the grain by-products. We were locked out of that market. We already had the meat complex and were doing well. But where could you go from there? You can't invent another meat. Besides, meat was a single-line product and I was deathly afraid of leading the Exchange down the dependency path of a one product line. As a Merc brat, I had witnessed first-hand that such a policy was doomed. To succeed we had to diversify.

Still, I decided to walk slowly. First of all, I was fully conscious that the idea of foreign exchange was of such magnitude, of such a departure from the status quo, that it represented a near impossible dream under the best of circumstances. What we needed, and what every revolutionary idea needs before it's noticed, was validation from an unquestionably credible source. I needed someone of authority to tell me that I wasn't off-the-wall. I did not have to go very far. Under our very noses in Chicago was the answer to the credibility question: University of Chicago free market economist Milton Friedman, my economic demigod. Here was a world-renowned economist saying that the Bretton Woods system was archaic and had to be replaced with currency float. In such an environment, I knew a futures market in currency had a chance. Would Friedman agree? If he did, and would say it publicly, my idea would have international credibility.

Friedman's writings on free market economics had been like an irresistible magnet for me. I even used to sneak into his afternoon lectures at the University of Chicago to hear some of his words. (Since I wasn't a paying student, I proved somewhat of an exception to his famous rule that "there is no free lunch.") I also read most of Friedman's works, as well as a host of other economic textbooks. If Friedman believed the Bretton Woods system had to be changed, I had no doubt that it would.

What I learned served to confirm my belief that the different external and internal interests of the sovereign participants in the present system—their different rates of economic growth; their different fiscal and monetary policies, beholden to different forms of governments; their different workforce considerations; their different election timetables and political pressures—all would combine to destroy a system dependent upon a unified opinion regarding respective exchange values.

Milton Friedman knew this from the beginning. Here is how he put it:

> . . . from the time Bretton Woods became effective, it was inevitable it would break down . . . It tried to achieve incompatible objectives: freedom of countries to pursue an independent internal monetary policy; fixed exchange rates; and relatively free international movement of goods and capital . . . As one of the architects of Bretton Woods, Keynes tried to resolve the incompatibility by providing for flexibility of exchange rates through what he intended to be frequent and fairly easily achieved changes in official parities. In practice, this hope was doomed because maintaining the announced parity became a matter of prestige and political controversy. Countries therefore held on to a parity as long as they could, in the process letting minor problems grow into major crises and then making large changes . . .

So, I reasoned, if Bretton Woods were to fall apart, then a currency futures market would work. And the CME could provide this market with facilities, communications, public participation, and know-how. It could bring together buyer and seller. It could embrace both the commercial customer as well as the speculator. Considering size, what a gargantuan market currencies could become. This certainly fit my plans for diversification. It also fit the world I believed was coming. Forget about pork bellies, forget even agriculture, I told Powers; think money—the ultimate commodity—all kinds of money. I asked Powers to contact Friedman, economist to economist so to speak, to determine his reaction to the idea of currency futures. As I explained to Powers, if Friedman's answer was anywhere near affirmative, it would be the gateway to greatness for the Merc I so desperately sought.

We didn't have long to wait. Friedman's answer to Power's letter, which came a couple of weeks later was quite encouraging, although he admitted that he didn't know whether such a futures market would work. Of course he didn't know. No one knew. But it was encouragement enough for me. Indeed, it a screaming green light. Now I had to convince the CME Board.

I judged that it would take time for them to get used to the idea, so I tested the waters at one Board meeting. I remember there was a long moment of silence. Some of them no doubt held back their laughter. "Did you say for foreign currency?" asked Carl Anderson of Merrill Lynch, a bit bewildered. It was such a grandiose concept for our little corner of the world. Our history was butter and eggs, potatoes and onions, pork bellies and cattle. What the hell was this young Turk chairman dreaming about? Had he gone off his rails? Currency, indeed! Some of them gave it no more than a fleeting thought. Still, no one dared to openly oppose me. I had accumulated a pretty good track record by then, and everyone knew the floor crowd would be in my corner. I explained that it was still premature for this idea, given the realities of the world's fixed exchange rate system. We had plenty of time to prepare. But to underscore that I was serious, I admonished the Board, Harris, and Powers, under the threat of death, not to ever breathe a word of what we were thinking. I knew that ideas could not be patented. Others were bound to reach the same conclusion I had if we waited too long.

Sure enough, in April 1970, the International Commerce Exchange (ICE), the renamed Produce Exchange in New York, began offering futures contracts on currencies. My heart sank. It was just about the same time NASA's Apollo 13 mission ran into trouble. A couple months later, Harris and I flew to New York to take a firsthand look at this place. Somewhere in lower Manhattan, we came upon the scene of an old gasping Produce Exchange that had managed to turn itself into a glorified currency exchange. On one wall was a listing of the currency contracts; but the place was as quiet as a library reading room—it was deserted. There was no trading. To my relief, their contracts were tiny, geared for small-time gamblers. Their approach was rudimentary; the size of the contracts—$15,000 to $20,000— was not designed for commercial use. The ICE was no test for what I had in mind. Its idea was more a forward currency exchange than the financial futures market I thought was possible. Theirs was the wrong contract, with the wrong specifications, initiated in the wrong manner, at the wrong time.

I knew that, to succeed, the contract specifications had to be attractive to bank traders and corporate treasurers. The ICE contracts were just the opposite. This represented a fatal flaw. It was as if the ICE had not fully understood the idea. Successful futures contracts need, at a minimum, 20 to 25 percent commercial participation. You cannot have a market just for speculators. Nor did the ICE understand what this market represented. I would never dream of launching this new concept in a quiet way, as just another new commodity contract. A futures market in currency was as revolutionary an idea as futures markets themselves. It was either a real big deal or not worth doing. The plan I visualized required that the temples of finance take notice. We had to get world attention. We had to be taken seriously. And somehow we had to get support from officials of the U.S. government.

This would give us instant credibility. To succeed with so grandiose a notion as currency futures, there had to be drama.

I began to think about nothing else, and could hardly sleep at night. I had fallen madly in love with the idea. I knew that I was on the threshold of a rare moment in history. I could make my mark on markets for all time. And in the pit of my stomach, where I tested all my ideas, I knew it could work. But the more I thought about it, the more nervous I became. If I didn't act quickly, the idea might be usurped. Alexander Graham Bell and Elisha Gray independently invented the telephone practically at the same time. The fact that the ICE had knocked on the door of a currency market made me believe others were in the wings—perhaps with more ambitious plans. Perhaps the New York Stock Exchange or, even worse, the Chicago Board of Trade. I became paranoid.

Still, as Friedman had indicated, the timing was not right. The fixed exchange rate system would kill any chance of success. Indeed, the ICE's currency contracts soon quietly expired. So long as Bretton Woods was in effect, there wouldn't be enough business—or change in currency values—to keep a futures contract market alive. To me, it was axiomatic: to be successful, a futures market needs price movement in the underlying cash market. Hedgers need a reason to hedge, speculators a motive to trade. Under the current fixed rate system, day-to-day currency fluctuations were unlikely. The only time currency values changed was when finance ministers got together and devalued or revalued a given currency a hefty 5 or 10 percent in order to bring the rate into reality. At those junctures, overnight, there would be a whopping price change. But few could do anything about it beforehand. Even the ministers didn't know precisely when the shift was coming. After the one-day price upheaval, the situation would settle back to the normal fixed rate measured against the dollar.

The inadequacy of such a system was obvious on its face. The commercial world was at the mercy of finance ministers' decisions and then suffered a gigantic morning-after headache. They could do little to protect themselves from the impending change. The Bretton Woods system worked fine as long as there were few rate realignments, but the world of 1945, which had given rise to the system, had changed considerably. By 1970, the effects of the World War were gone. America was no longer the only industrialized nation in the world. Great Britain, Germany, France, and Japan had successfully reached a new commercial maturity. They had become our competitors. And the world was entering the Information Age, enabling everyone to know everything. While years ago it took days and sometimes weeks to learn about a foreign economic report or governmental action, now the information was available nearly instantaneously. This demanded immediate adjustments in foreign exchange relationships. No such mechanism existed.

As Friedman later stated, the forward markets in foreign currency among the money center banks in London, Zurich, and New York didn't have the breadth, depth, and resiliency or the wide-reaching communications apparatus necessary to make the market viable.

By the middle of 1971, the international currency markets had begun to shake beneath the feet of the world's finance ministers. As banker of the world, the United States had learned a painful lesson: the more currency the United States spent, lent, or gave away, the more the global economy became lubricated. But with more U.S. currency floating around the world, the less confidence other nations had in it, and the stage was set for an international financial crisis. Devaluations and revaluations began to occur with dangerous frequency. Eventually, unable to take the pressure any longer, West Germany and Japan cut their currencies' moorings to the dollar and allowed the mark and yen to float. In floating their currencies, the countries were in direct violation of the rules of the International Monetary Fund, the supranational agency that was the watchdog over the Bretton Woods agreement. Now it was monetary anarchy, and every country was out for itself, including the United States. The entire system was collapsing.

Suddenly, time became a critical factor. On August 15, 1971, President Richard Nixon stunned the international financial community when he announced the United States would no longer honor its pledge to exchange gold for foreign-held dollars. It sent a seismic shock around the world with vibrations that would be felt for a decade to come. The reasons for the President's action were multifold but primarily stemmed from a record deficit in the U.S. balance of payments that amounted to the value of all the gold left in Fort Knox. It should surprise no one to learn that Milton Friedman saw the problem coming three years earlier. In a private memorandum to the President-elect dated October 15, 1968, Professor Friedman urged Richard Nixon to close the gold window and outlined other necessary actions to be taken immediately. By the time the President followed Friedman's advice in 1971, the damage to the United States had already been done.

We began to move fast. I asked Harris to contact Milton Friedman and set up our first face-to-face meeting. Friedman was then at his retreat in Vermont, and arrangements were made for him to meet Harris and me in New York. On a warm Saturday morning in early November 1971, we met at the Waldorf Astoria. I asked Friedman if the new monetary order would be flexible, and if so, what he thought about us opening a futures market in currency. Friedman, never one to mince words, thought the idea for such a market was "splendid" and "imaginative." Later, he would reflect in an interview, "I also thought it was a courageous idea because we were betting on something that was going to have to happen, not on something that had already happened." There was something else about Friedman that endeared him to me. It was his view of Chicago. Unlike New York, where he had lived for a period, he saw Chicago as fertile ground for what he called "maverick" ideas that produced such unique concepts as the school of free market economics and the Chicago school of architecture, among others. Apparently, I had appealed not only to Friedman's intellect, but to the maverick in him as well.

Friedman did not know much about the Merc and its leadership when we met. But he knew a good idea when he heard one. I explained that to put the idea into action, I needed authentication from someone like himself. "Leo Melamed," I said, "was an unknown nobody. But Milton Friedman, now that's a different story. Will you write a paper for the Merc and state your views?"

Ever the capitalist he responded, "Of course, but you will have to compensate me for the effort." I was ecstatic. "How much?" I inquired, ready to pay almost anything. "$5,000," Friedman responded. It was more than reasonable. In effect, I had asked this great man to put his reputation on the line, and he was willing to do this, not so much for the Merc per se, but for an idea whose time had come. We have remained close friends since that day.

Three weeks later I had a rough draft of what he called "a possible article" on my desk. It was general, qualitative, and for the most part, avoided technical jargon. Like a fine-tuned stage performance, it didn't skirt the issue of interpretation. The title said it all: "The Need for Futures Markets in Currencies."

Friedman asked if we had any suggestions for changes. There were a few, but as I noted in my letter to him, they were not crucial to his paper. Could he elaborate his ideas for the Canadian dollar? Could he explain why a futures market would act as a stabilizing influence even if deliveries were affected? Could he further explain how the existence of a futures market in currency would ease the problem of executing monetary policy? Referring to the latter question, I noted that "this might make a most potent argument for the establishment of such a market, and an argument that might carry weight to the Federal Reserve Board and banking community."

I assured Friedman that even if he didn't respond to our suggestions, we would accept the article as he had written it. A check for $5,000—the best investment the Merc ever made—was enclosed for his work. And as we awaited the final draft. I was so confident of being on the right track that in closing my letter I told Friedman: ". . . we will begin our necessary moves for the establishment of this market and may in the near future make our official announcement with respect to the general concept—since, as you pointed out—time is of the essence."

Nixon's timing for us couldn't have been better. As the anonymous Latin saying goes, "Necessity is the mother of invention." This later became one of the advertising themes of the newly formed International Monetary Market of the CME. The closing of the gold window changed the psychology and manner of operation of American citizens, who would soon realize that the United States was no longer alone in determining the fate of its currency. The value of the dollar would grow more dependent on the relative value of the Deutsche mark or the yen. Outside world forces could even cause the almighty dollar to be devalued. Public awareness toward currency exchange rates would be heightened once the balance of payments story moved from the financial page to the front page then onto the television screen. Then, I assumed, citizens would begin to look for a way to get involved in this new internationalism by seeking investment and speculative opportunities in vehicles of an international monetary nature. Even more important, commercial interests would need a market to hedge their risk.

I wanted to organize a futures exchange that would deal exclusively in monetary instruments. The first instrument was to be the real thing—money. Instinctively, I knew there was a tremendous opportunity in this new contract—and something else: no one could squeeze and corner a currency market. Economics was going to dictate the market. Supply and demand was going to determine its values, nothing else. Government intervention, of course, could always be a factor since there would always be an effort by a government to prop up its currency. But because the currency markets were bound to become huge, a government was just another big player—like any trader—entitled to its view. I knew the market was bigger than anyone. And the governments knew it, too.

On December 13, 1971, the finance ministers of the leading industrial nations huddled in Washington's Smithsonian Institution to scrap the Bretton Woods agreement and hammer out a new plan. The United States agreed to devalue the dollar. Now an American would pay more for a Volkswagen, a German less for a roll of Kodak film. In effect, more U.S. goods would be sold overseas, and fewer foreign articles would be bought by Americans, thereby improving the U.S. trade balance. At least, that is the theory. For their part, the other nations agreed to adjust their currencies upward, making them worth more in relation to the battered dollar. The aim was to relieve pressure on the dollar in its reserve-currency role.

The 10 finance ministers at that meeting also made another decision, the most important one as far as I was concerned: to permit the exchange rates of the world's major currencies to fluctuate against the dollar by 2.25 percent above or below the official exchange rate. Bingo! Now currencies could fluctuate 4.5 percent instead of the 2 percent previously allowed under the Bretton Woods system. The wider range offered decent price action from a trader's standpoint, and the IMM was one step closer to reality. The Smithsonian Agreement was but the first in a series of steps leading up to the total collapse of the era of fixed exchange rates.

The following Monday, December 20, 1971, Friedman sent the revisions back and replied: "The suggestions you made were all very good, and I believe the changes that are enclosed will improve the memo. Delighted that you are moving forward on this."

Rushing forward was more like it. On that very Monday morning, I officially announced to the world our plans for a futures market in foreign currency that would trade seven contracts: British pounds, Canadian dollars, Deutsche marks, Italian lira, Japanese yen, Mexican pesos, and Swiss francs. "The anticipated monetary developments and the agreement to allow wider fluctuations of foreign exchange rates have made it imperative that we proceed with this new market as soon as possible, hopefully early next year," I stated in a three-page release from our Public Relations Department.

I also played my credibility card by disclosing that the Merc had retained Milton Friedman to analyze the feasibility and need of such a futures market. Excerpts from Friedman's paper were sprinkled throughout the release: "It is clearly in our national interest that a satisfactory futures market (in foreign currency) should develop, wherever it may do so, since that would promote U.S. foreign trade and investment. But it is even more in our national interest that it develop here instead of abroad. Its development here will encourage the growth of other financial activities in this country, providing both additional income from export of services and easing the problem of executing monetary policy."

Professor Friedman was not alone in his opinion. A number of notable economists concurred and, indeed, encouraged us. But clearly without Friedman's credentials on our team, the maverick idea might never have left the starting gate.

15

IMM Fever

There was no rest for me during the winter holiday season of 1971. Two days after Christmas, I met with the Merc's Board to discuss the plans for a member referendum to approve our concept of a new exchange and to accept the name we had selected. The name came from a list of five different options provided by Ron Frost for my selection. *International Monetary Market*—the IMM—immediately appealed to me because it said it all. The new entity would be incorporated as a separate and independent exchange, one not simply for the purpose of trading foreign currency, but for every kind of financial instrument.

Activities followed at a frantic pace: innumerable floor preparations, press statements, legal considerations, rules to be written, public relations and educational material to be prepared, committees to be established, and meetings with members. Jerry Salzman and I, together with the IMM Interim Committee composed of Richard Boerke, John Geldermann, William Goldstandt, William Henner, Barry Lind, Larry Rosenberg, and Michael Weinberg, were immersed in creating an entirely new set of bylaws for the new exchange. Although it was modeled after the Merc rules, the fact that it was *de nova* gave us great latitude to change old ideas or introduce new ones. Under the direction of Ira Marcus, our tax whiz, we also created the provisions for the public sale of memberships, while Barry Lind, my financial advisor, helped fashion new clearinghouse and financial rules for the IMM. "Leo," Lind had said to me, "we have to make a statement to the world so that there is no doubt that the IMM is as financially sound as the New York Stock Exchange." A rather lofty ambition at the time but it was a worthy goal. I formed a select clearinghouse subcommittee for this purpose and we began the process of deliberation. One of our first witnesses, my good friend, Dr. Henry Jarecki, nearly derailed the entire IMM project before it got started.

Henry Jarecki, the chairman of Moccatta Metals, a New York-based bullion dealer, whose intellectual strength and ever-present cynicism was an irresistible magnet for me, had become an instant enthusiast of the IMM concept and insisted that his credentials entitled him to a seat on the Board. It was a classic case of New York *chutzpa*, and its sheer audacity was enough to win me over. However, I had the presence of mind to require that Jarecki first become an IMM member, a investment that would cost him $10,000. This demand served to disclose the depth of Jarecki's ingenuity and the extent of his risk-averse nature. Somehow Jarecki got one of our members, Joe Siegel—the penultimate risk-taker who I would put on a par with Sky Masterson, the incomparable gambler in Damon Runyon's *Guys and Dolls*—to give him a one-year put on the IMM seat in question.

Although Jarecki and I became close friends from the first moment we met, on the day he appeared before our committee, for a second or two, I had some serious reservations. We never knew whether it was a sincere testimonial or a spoof, but Jarecki, together with his associate Sal Azzara, came prepared with a 1,300 foot long computer printout, which he explained categorically proved that the cumulative risk created by our new market in currency futures would someday "bring down Western Civilization!"

There was a moment of stunned silence as the members of our committee contemplated whether to laugh, cry, or ask Jarecki never again to show his face in Chicago. While Jarecki's dire prediction hasn't yet come to pass, I wouldn't count it out. However, in view of the magnitude of today's ponderous interbank and over-the-counter derivatives markets compared to our currency futures, I would suggest that if Jarecki's prediction comes true, the cause will be by virtue of the former rather than the latter.

But at the moment, I was less concerned about the financial condition of Western Civilization than I was about the financial integrity of the IMM. If this concept was ever going to work, I needed to attract as members the financial powerhouses of the world. Sure we had some of the Wall Street brokerage firms that had traditionally been clearing members of futures exchanges, but now we would need the banks and investment banks. Fat chance! The first question I was asked when I visited their New York offices was, "How do we know our money will be safe?"

Well, the truth was, no one knew for sure. Years before, when I questioned E.B. Harris about the safety of the Merc clearinghouse, he would shrug his shoulders and roll his eyes.

"Nobody knows, Lee, nobody knows." Theoretically, a failure by any one clearing member would be paid by the others.

"Has that principle ever been tested?" I asked.

"Not to my knowledge," E.B. admitted, "and I wouldn't push it if I were you. Next thing you know you'll scare Merrill Lynch out of their pants and they will resign from the exchange."

But it wouldn't let me rest. If we had to make the IMM as secure as the NYSE, as Barry Lind suggested, the world shouldn't have to guess about the safety of their money. We needed an iron-clad rule that was black and white in the bylaws. What better time than right now when we were writing a new set of rules. I made a simple proposal to our clearinghouse sub-committee which included our two attorneys, Salzman and Marcus, "Let's codify what has always been the unwritten principle. Let's create a common bond between all clearing members, one that guaranties the safety of everyone's money. If any clearing member fails, the others chip in."

This time, I had the immediate support of Ira Marcus. Salzman's reaction was also favorable. Lind, on the other hand had a practical concern, "What if the clearing members refuse to join?" he asked. "They won't." I responded confidently. I was far from certain, but this much I knew: without financial integrity, the IMM would never succeed. The committee went to work and as I knew it would, at the end of the day, we had fashioned what became known as the Good-to-the-Last-Drop Rule. In the event of a default of any clearing member firm, after all other financial remedies—including the CME Trust Fund—had been exhausted, the remaining unsatisfied default would be allocated among the clearing membership, taking into account each clearing member's capital, trading volume, and share of open interest. It made the Merc's clearinghouse one of the strongest in the world.

To say there was excitement in the air was the understatement of that decade. The delirium on the trading floor was infectious, and all the Board members had by now caught the IMM fever. In fact, I carefully tried to hold in check the surge of exuberance, since I wanted the anticipation to build over the next several months. The IMM wasn't scheduled to open until the following May. Timing of excitement over the launch of a new contract is as important as the contract itself. As every good politician knows, it can be fatal if your momentum peaks too early. And like every director of a great stage presentation, I laid out plans with my inner circle and Merc staff, which were designed to reach a crescendo on opening day. At the same time, I consistently cautioned everyone not to expect too much at the outset. I knew the IMM was not going to be an instant success; it was too revolutionary. The worst thing that can happen to a new contract is instant disappointment. Although I expected the floor members to give it their immediate support, I knew not to expect too much from the outside world. Privately, I hoped we could show some positive results within two or three years, but publicly, I cautioned that the IMM was a 10-year game-plan and should not be measured otherwise. Indeed, until the early 1970s, only a few hundred American companies transacted enough business overseas to be affected by currency fluctuations. But all that was about to change. With floating rates, thousands of firms that had never before used the foreign exchange markets would have to learn how. To explain this fact was to explain the IMM.

That we were tramping on innovative ground was evident from the fact that no one knew under whose regulatory eye the IMM was to come. The Securities and Exchange Commission had no jurisdiction over money trading and neither did the Commodity Exchange Authority. Both the Treasury Department and Federal Reserve Board had no rules on such matters. The market wasn't up and running, so it was impossible to know what, if any, impact there would be on the dollar. Of this, however, I was certain: the Merc couldn't launch currencies from a back pocket. If what we were about to do was meaningful, we had to make aware the movers and shakers of the financial world. I wanted people to salute the IMM, not decry it. But selling this idea was going to be harder than anything we had sold before. This wasn't a single commodity future for a single industry like, say, trying to involve ranchers in a cattle contract. This was the launch of a new era. This was an entire market—the International Monetary Market—with seven different currency contracts to be launched at once for users worldwide in a multitude of industries from finance to manufacturing. It was a new exchange—untried, untested, underrated, unknown, and every other "un" under the sun.

The pitch had to be more than mere razzmatazz, more than financial mumbo jumbo now that financial theory was becoming financial reality. I was advocating a new kind of futures exchange that was about to interact with a new monetary order. Private enterprise can work miracles for an economy, but an organized exchange is necessary to bring some kind of order between buyer and seller in their grapple with market forces. That was my message as I zigzagged the country dozens of times drumming up support for the market. I was an evangelist, a dreamer, a Don Quixote, half crazed with the belief that financial futures were an idea whose time had come. And I wanted everyone in the world to know it. I confronted big audiences and small; I spoke to influential domos and ordinary people; I lectured to commerce and academia. No one was excluded from the message I fostered; no one within earshot of my presence could escape my words. The reaction was mixed; there was a great deal of respect, there were many who applauded, but the vast majority was either skeptical, didn't understand, or didn't care. I persisted because I believed.

In the meantime, the IMM Interim Committee and I were in constant session, hammering out contract specifications. Mark Powers was remarkable: here was a pork belly expert, who, when I asked how fast he could write a set of currency specifications for contracts never before devised, had a draft of them on my desk by the next morning. As soon as he did, I ran smack into the age-old conflict between commercial and individual speculative interests. Commercial users always want large-size contracts. It is cheaper for a corporate user to buy or sell a contract worth, say, $100,000 than to buy or sell two contracts each worth $50,000, because a floor broker's commission charges and exchange fees are per contract. But individuals who trade markets want smaller contracts since they often don't want to assume larger risks. Similarly, exchange brokers prefer smaller contracts because they can generate more commissions. Then again, brokerage firms that specialize in commercial customers want large contracts, while those who cater to the retail trade want smaller contracts. Commercials are the hedgers and without them there can be no market. Of course, that is also true of speculators, therefore the equities have to be very carefully balanced. It is a never-ending conflict of many interests. As a rule, I sided with the commercial interests because, generally, speculators will trade an attractive market regardless of its size. Although I was far from certain, I once again stuck with my general principle. This time it turned out to be a mistake, but I didn't know that until after the market had begun.

By mid-January, we were back in New York courting the Wall Street brokerage houses. There were precious few that gave us their backing, with Merrill Lynch, E.F. Hutton, and Shearson clear exceptions. The rest of the financial community, those that had never used a futures contract—which was the vast majority on Wall Street—ignored us completely. Because I had started my commodity life at Merrill Lynch, the number one American stock house always had a soft spot in its heart for its former Chicago runner. Some months after the IMM was in operation, I was visiting the brand-new Merrill Lynch headquarters at One Liberty Plaza on Wall Street when I suddenly came upon a sight that choked me up and brought tears to my eyes. There, in their lower lobby, was a full wall-sized tote board for all the world to see, noisily clicking the changes in prices of IMM currencies. At considerable cost, John Conheeny, destined to head Merrill Lynch's futures subsidiary, decided that Merrill Lynch was bullish on the IMM.

Back in Chicago the major banks were used to dealing with the Merc and saw the IMM as an opportunity and a source for more Exchange business. Their long-standing relationship with futures markets had been profitable and had resulted in futures expertise. It was therefore easier for them to grasp the concept of a futures market in currency. It was fortunate that this was the case since I was desperately in need of their assistance. Happily, the four major Chicago banks, Continental Illinois National Bank & Trust Company of Chicago, First National Bank of Chicago, Harris Bank and Trust Co., and American National Bank & Trust Co., were very supportive of the IMM idea. In fact, Robert Abboud, executive vice president of the First National Bank of Chicago, became a director of the initial IMM board, and the bank became a clearing member, which meant it would deal with the new currency market on behalf of its own account. It was a breakthrough no one expected to happen for years. This tradition of assistance by Chicago banks, especially officials of First Chicago, continued through the years with my appointing William J. McDonough to the IMM board in 1975. He is now president of the N.Y. Federal Reserve Bank. And in 1983, I also appointed Richard L. Thomas, who later became chairman of First Chicago. Of equal importance was that Beryl Sprinkel, chief economist at Chicago's Harris Bank, also accepted my invitation to join the IMM Board. Dr. Sprinkel, who had national recognition and was destined to become chairman of this nation's Council of Economic Advisors under President Reagan, gave us instant credibility and became an invaluable ally who assisted me throughout the process of convincing Washington officials of the value of our IMM idea.

Of course, in 1972, the cooperation of the Continental Bank, then the largest of the Chicago banks, was critical. I couldn't even dream of a currency market unless I could make delivery (this was long before cash settlement would replace the need for physical delivery). It meant we needed a facility that operated around the world and would act as our delivery agent. In other words, if someone took delivery of Japanese yen, he had to be able to receive his money in Tokyo. If it was Swiss francs, then it had to be Zurich, and so on. In Chicago, only the Continental had a worldwide network. E.B. Harris knew its president, Tilden (Tilly) Cummings, who was a powerhouse in the city and part of the old-boy network. "I'll get us in, Leo; you explain it to him," Harris said to me.

Easier said than done. The chief of Continental's foreign exchange department was Robert Leclerc, who also happened to be that year's chairman of the Forex Association. The Forex dealers were a very elite group of global FX specialists who were happy with the way things were. The last thing they wanted was the IMM, as it might upset their profitable monopoly by making the prices of foreign exchange transparent. Leclerc told Tilly Cummings that I was poison. Fortunately, Tilly had a mind of his own and gave me a shot at convincing him. We sat in Cumming's posh Continental office on LaSalle Street as E.B. Harris watched me expound eloquently for 45 minutes about the virtues of the IMM. When I finished, Cummings called in one of his lieutenants.

"The Continental is going to act as the delivery agent for the IMM. Set up the machinery," the president of the Continental said. "We're going to charge for it, but we are going to do it."

As simple as that, and we were in business. I had to refrain from hugging him. It was one of those moments when I once again recognized how right my decision had been to keep Harris at the Merc. Without him, I could never have gotten into this office.

Now it was up to John McPartland, a Continental Bank officer who was assigned the job of devising the elaborate machinery for currency delivery around the globe. And this was well before there was a computer large enough to handle the complexities. McPartland did it. Armed with Scottish determination and an innovative mind, he singlehandedly devised a delivery system for foreign exchange and breathed life into the IMM. It was crude, by his own admission. In the early days, the Continental took an occasional risk when the bank would sometimes have to make delivery before it had the seller's payment in hand.

Six years later, in 1978, McPartland and the Merc's delivery specialist, Milton Stern, redesigned Continental's IMM delivery mechanism to make it completely secure. Milt Stern, whose son Will would later become a successful floor trader, knew nothing about foreign exchange delivery. But he knew a lot about cattle delivery, having devised the Merc's complex network of cattle delivery facilities. He simply transferred his knowledge to finance as did many of our traders. You see, to paraphrase Gertrude Stein, "A futures, is a futures, is a futures." McPartland and Stern's IMM's foreign exchange delivery mechanism functions to this day.

As expected, however, we didn't receive support from any of the major New York banks or other money centers. Not only did they question whether the IMM could really offer participants significant advantages over the existing network of banks and money dealers, they unanimously felt that Chicago was the wrong place for such an effort. After all, everyone knew that New York was the capital of finance. They were quite certain that the IMM idea would soon fall on its face. And if the IMM became successful, its detractors argued, it would incur the wrath of both the U.S. and foreign governments by fanning currency speculation and thereby disrupt legitimate exchange rates. Right there was the central nub of the problem I faced in launching a market in currencies that allowed, indeed, *invited* speculators to participate.

Long before the first major devaluation by the Bank of England in the late 1960s, it had became common in government circles to blame major currency changes on pressures caused by speculators. Speculators in general never have had much of a favorable image in the world of finance, and the genre money speculators were considered the worst of the breed. The speculator was pictured as those sleazy-looking characters who lurked about the financial centers of London, Zurich, and Frankfurt selling a pound here and a dollar there, buying a yen or a Deutsche mark, going short Swissy when it pleased them and so on. These utterly despicable characters then gleefully laughed up their collective sleeves when they earned a profit at the expense of the central banks. Money speculators—unpatriotic, greedy, irresponsible, no-good louts—became the rallying symbol of the central bankers who, in turn, were the good guys—patriotic, responsible, respectable, fighting bravely for law, order, and values for their currencies that they deemed proper.

When one took a closer look at this interplay of forces on the international stage and read some of the analysis by the likes of Milton Friedman, Otmar Emminger, Fritz Machlup, Robert Aliber, George Shultz, and so many other noted economists, one realized that there was much more to this story. In fact, upon becoming fully familiar with the complexities involved, one inevitably reached the conclusion that the very reverse of what the government officials were saying was true. First of all, the "bad guys," the speculators, were often corporate treasurers of multinational firms, bankers, sovereign nations, or highly regarded financiers. Moreover, the motivation of these people was not always personal gain, and often not gain at all. Rather, they were often motivated on behalf of the best interests of their companies, banks, or nations. Often, rather than seeking a profit, they were acting to prevent or minimize a loss. In sum total, their actions were based on what they believed to be prudent economic or business judgments.

But, by far, the most telling revelation came when one discovered that, by and large, the speculators were the ones who were telling the truth about currency values. Most often, it was the government or central banker that had political motivations for ignoring reality. It was futile anyway. In this day and age, a currency value, just like any other value, could not be determined in the secrecy of a closed meeting room. The communist world learned this truth the hard way. Only the free forces of the marketplace can make an honest evaluation.

I never polled the membership to determine the number of traders who really understood what the International Monetary Market would mean to the future of the Merc. But I knew they had faith in my judgment and were quite satisfied in the way the Merc was growing, as evidenced by the value of a Merc seat at the time: $100,000, far from the support price of $3,000 just a few years back. And they showed their faith on January 17, 1972, when the members voted 321 to 19 to approve the organization of the IMM as a separate exchange. It was an overwhelming personal vote of confidence.

Financially, it was also a good deal for them. Each Merc member got an IMM membership for a $100 fee. Actually, I had intended to give the new seats free to all existing Merc members, but Ira Marcus insisted that for tax purposes we had to establish a price. They made a $9,900 profit because additional memberships to the public were sold at the price of $10,000. But, in order to protect the new buyer, Merc members were obliged to hold their IMM seats for at least a year before selling it. Those of little faith did so as soon as they could take their profit. At first the price fell, dropping to a record low of $8,800. Twenty-two years later, an IMM membership would be worth better than three-quarters of a million dollars.

16

Who Were We

In my opinion, the critical component to our success was my insistence that the IMM be created a separate exchange designed exclusively for the trading of financial instruments. To my knowledge, such an idea had never before been attempted by an exchange. My strategy was to attract a new legion of traders who would fashion a financial image unencumbered by the history of agricultural futures. Indeed, some of the financial players and institutions I sought were repulsed at buying a "hog belly" seat. Besides, I needed young fresh blood, willing to take a chance on this new venture. The brave entrepreneurs I coveted would not have the money to buy a $100,000 Merc seat or a rich daddy to finance it. Most important, my fundamental reason for creating a separate exchange would be to limit the trading activities of its members to contracts provided by the IMM. In effect, they would be captives of the currency pits, forced to generate business there. Make it or break it. I knew that, otherwise, it was likely that the new members would gravitate to the successful cattle, hog, and pork belly pits where the activity was strong and where it was easier to make money. For the IMM to succeed, I needed traders who could do nothing else but trade currency or whatever financial contract we listed there for trade.

By any measurement, the element that most attracted the new breed of traders was that the IMM provided them with a dream—a dream of unlimited opportunity. Most of them had very little money at the start; most of them had even less formal training in finance or foreign exchange; most of them came from humble backgrounds. But those who were there at the start, tied their hopes to the IMM star and rose with it to heights they could hardly imagine. They were from different walks of life but they had a common-denominator: ambition. And if one randomly walked down the isles of the floor and stopped to listen, one inevitably found a different story with every member. I would do that from time to time, just to get the feel of who we were.

We attracted an assortment of young and aggressive entrepreneurs who covered a wide spectrum—from the average to the brilliant, from the students to the professionals, from doctors and lawyers to gamblers and adventure seekers.

For instance, guys like Tom Dittmer who had come to the Merc to be a clerk after he had served as a Marine Honor Guard to the White House. For extra cash on the floor, he would sell used watches. He soon realized that he had a inherent talent for finance and began to dream big dreams. For him the IMM provided a means to reach the highest rung on the American financial ladder. Working relentlessly to create REFCO, an international brokerage concern, he now rivals the old-line houses of Wall Street. To his credit, Dittmer never forgot his beginnings, our friendship, nor the role the IMM played in providing the opportunities to catapult him above the crowd.

In contrast, Yra Harris came to the floor under protest. He had received a Bachelor's degree in political science and economics from the University of Illinois and a Master's degree from the University of Wisconsin. He had his sights set on a political career and moved to Washington, DC to work for Idaho's Senator Frank Church. Yra Harris' father, Joey Harris, who was successfully doing silver coin arbitrage on the IMM floor, wasn't overwhelmed with his son's decision. And Joey Harris was no push over. He was a tough Air Corps veteran who had served as a navigator during World War II. To memorialize his wartime experience he used the letters A-R-M-Y to name his four children. Yra was the youngest. After Senator Church's Multinational Subcommittee didn't materialize, Joey Harris dragged his son, kicking and screaming, to the Exchange floor to do Class-B arbitrage with the American National Bank. It didn't take long for Yra to see the wisdom in his father's ways. Yra Harris became an outstanding and hugely successful IMM trader, a respected Exchange leader, and a permanent member of my elite floor corps.

Scott Gordon, on the other hand, came to the floor as a clerk for the Levy operation. Bright and ambitious, without ever having seen a Deutsche mark, he began a Class-B arbitrage shop for Rosenthal & Co., which led him up the executive ladder. He eventually was elected to the Board of the Merc where for many years he occupied my former office as CME secretary and then went on to become first vice chairman.

The history of Bill Shepard, Larry Shepard and Chuck Gilchrist offers as typical an IMM rags-to-riches tale as there is on the floor. In 1968, Larry Shepard was involved with some other kids in a high school prank on a river in New Jersey that ended up sinking a farmer's rowboat. The judges in those parts took that kind of crime seriously and Larry was given a choice: jail or the army. When he failed the army physical, Larry got scared, took his jeep and headed west. It broke down near Chicago. That night, in a short-order diner near downtown, Larry found himself talking to his waiter, Chuck Gilchrist. Gilchrist told him not to be fooled by his waiter's uniform; he was really a millionaire *wannabe* as a result of his daytime profession running orders on the Merc for Murlas Brothers. It was where Gilchrist predicted he would make his fortune. Without hesitation, the next morning Larry Shepard came to the Merc, where with some borrowed funds from his family he began to trade. He was a lot better at trading than row-boating. A few months later he wrote to his cousin Bill Shepard who was in a Viet Nam jungle at the time, that "Chuck Gilchrist and I will be millionaires in five years." Bill Shepard was nobody's fool. As soon as he was out of the army he went directly to the Merc floor to see what his cousin was talking about. He arrived on the very eve of the IMM, December 1971. Bill Shepard turned out to be an extremely savvy futures trader and became a respected lieutenant in my elite corps from the first day we met.

Then there were guys like Marty Liebman, who graduated as a psychologist from Roosevelt University and turned his back on a career in the professions, to guys like Jimmy Schneider whose family egg business helped start the Exchange and who left his chicken farm in Alabama to come back to the pits, to guys like Lenny Feldman, who left his dubious life as manager of Whisky-a-Go-Go, a nightclub on Chicago's fast moving Rush Street.

Liebman was thoughtful and kept mostly to himself. Schneider was quickly accepted to the floor; the Schneider family was an institution at the Merc; it was where Jimmy's grandfather had lived his entire life. Feldman was an extrovert whose extraordinary sense of humor instantly made everyone his friend. Once, during a particularly hectic trading session, Lenny Feldman's voice rose above the din: "Stop the trading, stop the trading," he shouted, as he threw his trading cards up in the air, "I think I'm broke." For a split second, some members actually hesitated to laugh before continuing their hectic trading pace. But only for a split second, for it is well known that trading in the pits stops for nothing. Not even the heart attack of a fellow trader who, as occasionally happens, is stricken in the pit. Minutes after he is transferred to a stretcher, the trading resumes as if nothing has happened.

Perhaps an even more poignant example of the single-mindedness of traders is the time *The Sting* was being filmed in Union Station beneath the new Merc building. Nancy Giles, an attractive young clerk, who knew the producer, was introduced to the film's stars, Paul Newman and Robert Redford. Giles, who eventually married Morrie Krumhorn, a very successful pork belly trader, had the presence of mind to call me to go down to the train station for introductions. It didn't take me long to convince the two superstars that they had to see the excitement of our pits. When

I proudly escorted them on to the floor, pandemonium broke out as the unprepared Merc membership suddenly saw, within their midst, two of the most known and beloved actors in America. The crush around us was immediate and all consuming. Suddenly, above the noise and excitement of the moment, I heard Bill Muno's voice shouting at the crowd from his perch in the pork belly pit: "Get those bastards out of the aisle; my runners can't get through with the orders."

These new IMM members quickly blended with the territory, and except for the fact that they were younger and traded only currency, you couldn't tell them from the original Merc line. We also got a large number of sons and daughters of Merc members, as well as clerks and runners who had been waiting for a chance in the big show. At the end of a year, we had sold 150 IMM memberships, and the issuance of new seats ceased. These original purchasers became my first IMM brigade in the battle for financial futures. They have remained my loyalists to this day, as did the original 500 members of the Merc.

There was no getting around it, however; to succeed with the new contracts, a part of the IMM had to be cut from a patch of the Merc. Getting Merc members who were used to making money trading the belly, hog, and cattle markets was at first tough. But most of them belonged to my elite floor troops who were loyal to the core. And they were bound by a common thread: a trader's instinct.

Marlowe King, my fundamentalist mentor, made the first IMM trade in the British pound—and he had never even seen what the currency unit looked like. I assigned Alan Freeman the responsibility for keeping IMM forward contract values in line with the current months. Freeman, who had begun as a clerk for Merrill Lynch at the CBOT when I began at the Merc, had never been out of the continental United States. Lou Madda, who cut his teeth running egg orders for Joe Siegel, never hesitated when it came to making a market in British pounds. Madda, a diamond in the rough, and I had established a special relationship, a sort of common bond in that we were both the product of Chicago's streets—never mind that his father made wine by stomping on grapes and my father wrote math books. Tommy Ricci, who knew nothing of FX, diligently devoted his time to providing liquidity to the new market. Ricci's father Tony was the right-hand man of Chuck Borden, the head of S.S. Borden & Co., an old-line Chicago dairy firm, which was a founding member of the Merc. Robert Schillaci was a charter member of my elite corps, who I loved for his inherent and right-on-the-mark understanding of the makeup and psychology of traders around us. We would often compare notes, and our assessments were inevitably in synch. Schillaci had graduated summa cum laude from the streets of the inner city of Chicago. He began his futures career in the meats, but instinctively developed an expertise on the Swiss franc. He has passed the IMM torch on to his son, Andrew.

Or take the three Levy brothers, Morrie, Mort, and Leonard, whose father was a prominent Chicago rabbi. They became the staunchest proponents of the currency futures. Morrie Levy had made his money as a spreader, taking a combination of long and short positions, in the various meat contracts. He knew there was a connection between the Deutsche mark and the Swiss franc, so he spread one against the other. In other words, the Levy brothers had transferred their trading skills from one commodity to another. There are countless similar stories of successful Merc traders who volunteered in the IMM army during the first few years of its wars. Some of them remained permanent citizens of the financial world, but most eventually returned to the meat pits.

The fact that our traders knew little of foreign exchange hardly mattered. In truth, most traders have never seen pork bellies even though they've been trading them for years. There is an old adage that a good trader walks on the floor, listens to where the noise is coming from, and that's where he goes to trade. It doesn't matter which contract, because markets go up and down for similar reasons no matter what product. And all pit traders want to do anyhow is go with the flow. Still, financial products were a much greater departure from the norm for us than any other new commodity in agriculture, and required a longer adjustment period. And clearly my pork belly crowd did not come from an international financial heritage. Bruce Johnson once confided to me that when some of his relatives from rural America came to visit him on the floor, they asked to be shown the pit where Swiss hot dogs were traded. It took him a minute to figure out they were talking about Swiss francs.

But my guys were fast learners. Logic dictated that unsophisticated pork belly, cattle, and hog traders could not long survive the treacherous waters of foreign exchange when pitted against seasoned Forex specialists. However, the odds were shortened by the simple fact that we were using our own money. Bank FX traders never risked their own capital. That singular difference spelled a trading discipline and a thirst for knowledge that became a winning combination for those CME members who came to the IMM's currency pits.

One additional benefit of a new exchange was that I could fashion its Board of Directors. I was conscious that the IMM image must portray itself as a serious player on the international stage. The Merc Board was composed solely of members elected by the membership, none of whom had financial credentials; the IMM provided me the opportunity to appoint a number of directors from the outside. (In 1977, after the merger between the Merc and the IMM, I would transplant this concept to the new Merc rules.) In fashioning the IMM Board, I first automatically appointed all sitting Merc board members,[1] then I added some well-known representatives from the financial arena including A. Robert Abboud, Frederick W. Schantz, Beryl W. Sprinkel, and Dr. Henry G. Jarecki; finally, I included two floor members, Richard E. Boerke and William E. Goldstandt, who had worked tirelessly to get the IMM off the ground but were not on the Merc Board.

I was elected chairman and Harris was chosen as president of the IMM. Both of us would be the only ones ever to hold those particular offices at both the IMM and CME because four years later, the IMM was merged as a division of the Merc. I soon relinquished my Merc title anyway, for two specific reasons: first because I wanted to concentrate on the IMM, and second, because I felt that the Merc chairmanship should not be held too long by any one individual. The Merc had suffered because of past abuses of power, and I fervently believed in Lord Acton's admonition: "Power tends to corrupt and absolute power corrupts absolutely." Besides, in my heart of hearts, I knew that control didn't necessarily rest with the chairmanship. From 1967 to 1969 as secretary of the Merc, I had virtually run the Exchange.

Still, one of the first rules I passed as Merc chairman limited a chairmanship to three consecutive one-year terms. In 1972, I therefore pressed for Michael Weinberg Jr. to replace me as Merc chairman while I took back my old position as Merc secretary. But, truthfully, since the activities of the IMM and the Merc were so often intertwined, in effect, I was leading both institutions.

Weinberg was a Merc blueblood, a third generation of Merc traders that began with his grandfather, Max, a charter member of the Butter and Egg Board and the Merc. His father, Michael Weinberg, Sr. had been president of the Butter and Egg Board and Merc chairman in the mid-1950s. Michael Jr. was a friend, a true loyalist, and an IMM advocate who had served on a half-dozen Merc committees and as secretary, treasurer, and second vice chairman. He was thoughtful and deliberate, and provided the Merc with many new ideas and worked with Harris and me in complete harmony throughout his two-year tenure.

The shift in leadership allowed me to devote all my energies to the totally consuming labor of marketing the IMM. I spent intense efforts over the next few years in getting the word out and sparring with the skeptics. Bankers, traders, journalists, and government officials all had their doubts, to say the least. Fighting skepticism, as I was to learn, is a difficult task.

---

[1] Michael Weinberg, Jr., Chairman; John T. Geldermann, First Vice Chairman; Daniel R. Jesser, Second Vice Chairman; Leo Melamed, Secretary; Barry J. Lind, Treasurer; Carl E. Anderson; Lloyd F. Arnold; Marlowe King; William C. Muno; Donald L. Minucciani; Robert J. O'Brien; Laurence M. Rosenberg.

There are those skeptics who, behind their egos, argue to show how much they know. There are the closet skeptics who seethe in silence as if they know something you don't, offering a nod here, a smirk there. Then there are the respectful skeptics who are willing to examine both sides of an issue. But whatever their posture, skeptics derive a perverse pleasure in quickly dashing ideas.

The line of IMM skeptics was long. And not only did they blast away at the idea, but the people behind it. "It's ludicrous to think that foreign exchange can be entrusted to a bunch of pork belly crapshooters," proclaimed a prominent New York banker on the eve of the IMM launch. *Business Week* echoed a similar sentiment: "The New Currency Market: Strictly for Crapshooters . . . if you fancy yourself an international money speculator but lack the resources . . . your day has come!"

These were some of the "sweet nothings" hurled at my colleagues and me as we made the rounds and read the papers that pegged us short of trying to commit financial anarchy. And it continued over many years. In 1976, at the opening of the new IMM interest rate market, the respected *Economist* had the following to say:

> Like Linda Lovelace, the girl with the deep throat, the International Monetary Market (IMM) of the Chicago Mercantile Exchange tries to make money by being more outrageous than its rivals. Now that its currency futures market is well established—it was opened in 1972 by women in fancy dress—the IMM has this month opened a trading pit in United States treasury bill futures. Bidding for the government paper takes place on the same floor as for pork bellies, live cattle, and three-month eggs.

And even a decade later, *Barron's* said the following about the new stock index futures market: "Like their lightning-paced video game counterparts, stock index futures offer instant gratification or instant annihilation depending on the accuracy of your impulses and the quickness of your reflexes."

Our detractors missed the point entirely. The IMM was not out to beat anybody and we were not trying to resurrect or *reinvent* something. This was pure *invention*—new market territory for an era in transition. I was trying to draw a map of the financial geography that lay ahead, trying to give business and finance the same risk transfer mechanisms that their agricultural counterparts had been using successfully for more than 100 years. And it was a tough sell.

Still, I did find allies. Indeed, there were many. Some in high places, like Arthur Burns, chairman of the Fed, or George P. Shultz, secretary of the Treasury, or Alan Greenspan, chairman of the Council of Economic

Advisors (CEA), or Paul Volcker, at the Treasury. Another was Illinois Senator Charles Percy, who was chairman of the powerful Senate Foreign Relations Committee and a strong Merc supporter who advocated free markets. He wrote a letter to then Federal Reserve Chairman Arthur Burns, noting that the IMM, ". . . could be of major significance to the foreign economic policy of the United States . . ."

Our attorney Jerry Salzman assured me that we did not require regulatory or other approval to launch currency futures, but my instincts told me otherwise. It was my belief from the start that there were compelling reasons to touch base with U.S. government officials and with foreign governments. First, I wanted to give the IMM the proper level of support and visibility; second, to gain a positive reaction that might be used in promoting the idea; and third, if the reaction was negative, to control any dissenting fallout. As it turned out, my instincts were right on target. In the years ahead, as financial futures took root, the fact that I had established support and rapport at the highest levels of American government was a critical component of our success. It also laid the groundwork for the eventual Washington lobby mechanism that we were able to construct. Fortunately for us, at the time of the IMM's birth, there were a bunch of free market folks in very high government places.

Harris and I paid a call on George Shultz, who became Secretary of the Treasury shortly after the IMM was launched. Only Harris was aware that this was my very first visit to our nation's capital. I didn't tell him, however, about the knot in the pit of my stomach and the goosebumps on my body when I entered the imposing structure of the Treasury Building for the first time. I felt a little of what Sholem Aleichem's Mottle described: *a nation of freedom, democracy, and opportunity.*

Shultz had been Milton Friedman's colleague at the University of Chicago and was the first government official to formally receive the Friedman paper, which I previously had sent to him. Unbeknownst to Harris, I had also arranged for Shultz to receive a private telephone call from Friedman before our arrival.

"Listen," Shultz said in a genial and reassuring voice, "I've read the notes and statements, and I know all about you. If it's good enough for Milton, it's good enough for me."

He was willing to accept the idea of currency futures, not because there was any law involved, but because he philosophically agreed. My stature rose with Friedman's. Indeed, Friedman had underestimated the benefit he had provided with his feasibility paper. We were flying on his coattails.

Shultz asked me all kinds of questions. Which currencies? What are the sizes of the contracts? I rattled off the currencies; the why was already explained in Friedman's paper, and all I did was verbalize in my own way and words about supply and demand in a free and open marketplace where bids and offers could establish true value. His eyes lit up. For Shultz, this free market tune was music to his ears. I knew then and there that coming to Washington was the right move—not to ask for permission, but to make sure—"my skirt was straight" and to make contact.

"It's an impossible thing that you're trying to do," Shultz said, "and your chances for success are near zero. But God bless you if you can make it work." In short, Shultz was saying "amen."

On the following trip, Harris, Powers and I met with the pipe-smoking Fed chairman Arthur Burns and Herbert Stein, chairman of the Council of Economic Advisers. In each instance, the response was similar to that of Shultz's: cordial, skeptical, and Godspeed. Even Paul Volcker who was at the Treasury at the time, although hesitant at first, warmed to the idea and told me it was an intriguing concept. Each trip to Washington left me further convinced I had done the right thing by making contact with the nation's power brokers of the day, none of whom told me I was tilting at windmills. By contrast, sometimes when I visited the offices of New York bankers, I would leave with the feeling that they didn't want me to get too close to them. Someone with such crazy ideas as currency futures might well be dangerous.

Although these government officials didn't do anything specifically to get the IMM on track, I made sure their voices were heard wherever I went. They became part of my chain link of credibility that started with Milton Friedman. In a hundred speeches from New York to San Francisco to Zurich to London, I would quote Friedman, Shultz, and Burns. First I explained how the market worked, then the need for the market. And I would always close with a tag line to the effect: "Look who's behind us. Look who also thinks it's a great idea." It was just the beginning of my romance with Washington, a relationship that would have its ups and downs over the next 20 years.

In February, two months before the IMM launch, and to celebrate its birthday, we hosted a monetary conference at Chicago's Palmer House, drawing more than 700 representatives of the largest U.S. and foreign banks, various industries, brokerage houses, academia, and Exchange members. It was a grand moment when I rose to publicly announce the IMM's creation and to introduce the speakers, which featured Paul Samuelson, Nobel prize-winning economist from the Massachusetts Institute of Technology, and included, among others, Paul Cootner, finance professor at Stanford University. Friedman's background paper was in everyone's hand. I had chosen Samuelson as the keynote speaker in an attempt to show how our idea was supported across the entire gamut of economic thinking, from the Monetarist, Friedman, to the Keynesian, Samuelson. It didn't quite turn out as I hoped. Although the evening was festive and very successful, to my utter disappointment, Paul Samuelson was somewhat of a downer, saying that although he didn't come to rain on our parade, he didn't give the idea of currency futures much of a chance. When I later told Friedman the story, he laughed, "What did you expect!"

Then in March, it was back to Washington where in the morning Harris and I met with Federal Reserve Board Governor James Mitchell and his staff at the Federal Reserve to discuss the economic impact of foreign exchange futures. We did a lot of guessing. A few hours later and a few blocks away, we met with officials at the Commerce Department. The roots of our promotional labors—and my Washington visits—were beginning to take hold. Now stories about the IMM were appearing not only in the Chicago newspapers but in *The New York Times* and *The Wall Street Journal*, as well as national magazines and wire services. The Reuters News Service, in late March, reported:

> The Treasury Department welcomes the establishment of a market for futures trading in international currencies in Chicago, department officials told a press briefing. They said there were no technical or legal problems involved in the establishment of the currency market. "We welcome a successful market," one official said, adding there was some growing need for a forward market. They said the currency market officials consulted with the Treasury before it was established.

After the symposia, seminars, press conferences, and reams of printed information were disseminated throughout the financial and banking community, the International Monetary Market opened for business on May 16, 1972. The era of financial futures was born. It was a momentous day, although only a few of us understood its full meaning. The 1990 Nobel prize winner in economics Merton Miller has often lamented to me that he missed not being on the trading floor to witness that historic event. In the years that followed, however, Professor Miller would contribute significantly to the success of this undertaking. He spurred modern academic theory to accept the principle of risk management as a necessary business regime, thereby assuring the use and legitimacy of financial futures within the temples of finance.

We opened with as much hoopla as we dared. We didn't want to be too irreverent about so reverent a matter as money. The guest speaker was William Dale, executive director of the International Monetary Fund, who reminded the audience it had been no accident that the IMM opened only five months after the Smithsonian agreement. "The wider bands," he said, "provided by that agreement indicate the usefulness of a market like the IMM in assessing risks and appraising the future." Such comments, especially from a Washington official, were sweet music to my ears. Milton Friedman finally had a market in currency he could trade.

I traded that first day along with hundreds of others. I didn't feel awkward at all in the currency pits. A trading pit was a trading pit, I told myself. Pork bellies, cattle, hogs, eggs, currencies; I could transfer my trading knowledge from one commodity to the next. Nevertheless, after time, my guys would tend to drift back to their old stomping grounds in the meat contracts; that's where the action was, and that's where they knew how to make a living. In the months following, I became an obsessed one-man enforcer—coercing, cajoling, admonishing, pleading with our Merc members to trade the currency markets. We needed liquidity, I begged. Everyone had to lend a hand. I could talk of nothing else day and night, and I would never leave the sight of the floor during trading hours. And for the most part, the floor responded to my pleas. These were, after all, my guys. At times I believed they would follow me anywhere.

For my part, I learned that the best way to teach is by example. I could not ask others to trade unless they saw me do it. This personal approach in the successful launch of new contracts, of which there were many over time, became my special trademark. Everyone knew that Leo put his money where his mouth was. I didn't ask someone to do something that I myself would not do. Unfortunately, it was sometimes very costly. As a trader, I am a better bear than bull. At the IMM's inception, I followed that instinct. I sold 10 Swiss francs contracts in a flurry of confidence. Unfortunately, it was the beginning of the dollar's first free fall. For the next five days, Swiss francs were limit up—the maximum price change permitted in a single trading session. I couldn't get out because there was no liquidity. Our limits were far below the cash markets. I was stuck in the market. It cost a fortune. It was a rough start, but I never denied that trading currencies could be tricky for even the most sophisticated traders. That was a given. It also established another maxim: an inventor must pay a special price for a successful invention.

In the first 21 days of trading on the IMM, some 22,455 trades were made—more than a 1,000 a day. It was only a beginning. There were many potential users of the market on the sidelines taking a wait-and-see posture. By year's end, a respectable 144,928 contracts traded on the IMM. Volume rose to more than three times that in the following year. It exceeded my wildest expectations. There was no doubt in my mind that the International Monetary Market was an idea whose time had come. My statement to the members in the 1972 Annual Report, the first to speak officially of its offspring the IMM, was not at all bashful in its assessment of what we had initiated and the potential I envisioned:

> The opening of the International Monetary Market on May 16, 1972, was as revolutionary a step as the establishment of the first organized commodity exchange when that event occurred . . .
> . . . we believe the IMM is larger in scope than currency futures alone, and accordingly we hope to bring to our threshold many other contracts and commodities that relate directly to monetary matters and that would complement the economics of money futures.

Of course, luck played its part. Indeed, if I could have ordained the perfect backdrop for the creation of a new financial futures exchange designed to help manage the risk of currency and interest rate price movement, I could not have done better than what actually happened. Within a year of the IMM's birth, economic disarray ensued that would dramatically change the world financial fabric for a long time to come. In October 1973, the oil embargo, oil price increases, and the Arab-Israeli War set in motion economic distortions and an era of financial turmoil rarely equaled in modern history. Over the next several years, the turmoil tested the very foundations of western society. The U.S. dollar plunged precipitously, U.S. unemployment reached in excess of 10 percent, oil prices skyrocketed to $39 a barrel, the Dow Jones Industrial Average fell to 570, gold reached $800 an ounce, U.S. inflation climbed to an unprecedented peacetime rate of 20 percent, and interest rates went even higher. These economic repercussions ensured that the IMM was indeed an invention based on the necessity of the times.

Not every trader who came to the IMM floor made it or became a millionaire. But those who were dedicated and had the guts were rewarded. Forget race, religion, or ethnic background. What mattered most was ambition. We were a quilt of many faces, a patchwork of dissimilar traits. But one thing remained constant: no matter where one looked on the floor, a similar dream could be found.

At the gala celebration of the IMM's tenth anniversary, I read to the audience a short poem I had penned for the occasion. It was entitled "Who Were We!" I think it captured the truth:

> Who were we?
> We were a bunch of guys who were hungry.
>
> We were traders to whom it did not matter—
> whether it was eggs or gold, bellies or
> the British pound, turkeys or T-bills.

We were babes in the woods, innocents,
in a world we did not understand,
too dumb to be scared.

We were audacious, brazen, raucous pioneers-
too unworldly to know we could not win.

That the odds against us were too high;
That the banks would never trust us;
That the government would never let us;
That Chicago was the wrong place.

17

Crusaders of the New Art

With the IMM up and running, I pushed harder than ever. Now I decided it was mandatory to trumpet our message on to the international stage. I authorized our Public Relations Department to hire Curtis Hoxter, a New York-based financial publicist who had taken great interest in our undertaking and wanted to help arrange for a grand tour of the European financial capitals. This IMM SWAT team, besides myself, would include eight Exchange officials: From the Board came all the IMM officers: John Geldermann, first vice chairman; Dan Jesser, second vice chairman; Robert O'Brien, secretary; Larry Rosenberg, treasurer; and Barry Lind, Merc treasurer, as well as E.B. Harris, our president; Mark Powers, our economist; and Ron Frost, our public relations officer. It was a momentous event in the history of the Merc and a special reward for those of us who had labored to bring the IMM into life.

Curtis Hoxter made the necessary arrangements, and in mid-June, I crossed the Atlantic with the contingent of senior IMM officials. Our goal was twofold: to pay our respects to each of the central banks whose currency we had listed for trade, and second, to create interest in the fledgling exchange among the European financial community.

We were crusaders of the new art of money trading, determined to put the IMM on the European corporate and monetary map. The two-week trip was to take us to London, Milan, Rome, Zurich, and Frankfurt. In each city we had scheduled three to four meetings a day. At each stop we delivered the same message we had to their counterparts back home: an explanation of how and why the new market was developed as an additional mechanism for reducing foreign exchange risk and how it might be utilized by those engaged in international trade, banking, and foreign exchange transactions. The IMM, we emphasized, was designed to supplement existing bank foreign exchange forward operations, not to supplant them, at a time when numerous European and U.S. companies had suffered losses as high as 20 percent of net income from currency fluctuations. The financial officers of such companies could hardly ignore the price protection gained by proper hedging.

As we met the Europeans, each of us had a specific assignment in the financial show-and-tell. I would give a rousing talk on free markets, outlining the new order of flexible exchange rates that had dawned and the IMM's philosophy of providing a marketplace to hedge the inherent risks. Harris provided the background of the Merc. Powers presented the contract specifications. Lind and Rosenberg fielded questions from a trader's perspective. Frost handled the press, dispensing brochures not only in English, but in French, German, Italian, and Spanish as well. I discovered that skepticism toward the IMM was universal. To my utter disillusionment, very few attended our meetings.

The expedition had actually begun on a rather high note. Curt Hoxter, who came with us, had arranged for The Bank of England to receive our delegation. We toured the bank, saw its boardroom, and were duly impressed with the history and grandeur of the place. The British were extremely gracious hosts and to our delight a luncheon was held within the premises of the hallowed halls of the Old Lady on Threadneedle Street. However, for a reason unbeknownst to us at the time, some of the central bank officials were missing and others had come quite late. During the luncheon, the Governor of the Bank explained that although the Bank of England was fully in favor of free markets, Britain could not really help our cause since its laws prohibited British citizens from trading currency futures. Then he toasted the IMM and politely asked if there was anything else they could do.

Not being bashful and ever mindful of the British sense of humor, I immediately wisecracked, "Yes, it would help us immeasurably if you would kindly float the pound."

The members of our Chicago delegation all chuckled, but I noticed that the Governor of the Bank of England didn't even smile, and the other British officials looked dismayed. Embarrassed, I guessed my joke had laid an egg and we quickly departed. The date was Friday, June 23, 1972.

The following morning we awoke in Milan. When our delegation got up for breakfast, the mystery was solved. I could hardly believe my eyes when I opened the English newspaper. *"Bank of England Floats the British Pound,"* the banner headline screamed. If this coincidence hadn't happened before my very eyes, I would not have believed it possible. Clearly, the reason the British officials didn't laugh at my joke was because, to them, it was no joke. They must have just returned from their secret executive session and no one in the public world had yet been advised of their historic decision on the pound. They could only conclude that through some unknown means I had learned of their action and was simply tweaking their nose. I figured that no matter what else happened on this trip, it was already an overwhelming success. For years following, I would tell this tale as evidence of the power of the IMM.

Thirty years earlier, military tanks had rumbled over the war-torn European continent, and now we were a think tank on the move, fighting our battles in the monetary wars. Unfortunately, from then on, our trip went downhill. By the time we got to Rome, where we were scheduled to meet with Dr. Carli, the highly regarded Italian central banker, most of our delegation was jetlagged, tired, and discouraged by the lack of audience wherever we held one of the seminars arranged by Hoxter and Frost. Indeed, it went from bad to worse. At times, Barry Lind and I would become giddy, desperately fighting to stifle our laughter, as we tried to explain in serious tones the beauty of the IMM to a room in which we outnumbered the audience. On such occasions, like children, one look between us would be enough to send us into uncontrollable convulsions. On top of that, the latest pig crop report had been a huge surprise, sending the U.S. meat futures into a tizzy. As traders, some of our contingent were losing a valuable trading opportunity. We decided to cut short the trip. Except for John Geldermann, Mark Powers, and Bob O'Brien, the rest of our delegation flew back to Chicago. The European trip only confirmed what we already knew: both the U.S. and foreign banks were distrustful of the IMM. To paraphrase an old Chicago adage about our city not being yet ready for reform, it seemed that Europe wasn't yet ready for free markets.

Upon return to the IMM floor from our European sojourn, I was confronted with reality. Although the Merc traders and their new IMM member counterparts were doing their best to trade currencies, their bids, offers, and prices were as if in a fantasy land—unconnected to the real prices of the interbank market. In short, the banks—even the Chicago banks— would not directly use the IMM. Our traders would read a report on the newswire and react to it by bidding up the Yen or offering the Deutsche mark down, but we never were certain that our prices were in line with real-world prices. Although I visited bank trading rooms both in Chicago and New York, met with bank officials, and made speeches, I could not persuade them to deal directly with our floor. They had a distrust of the futures market mechanism and did not consider our traders worthwhile counterparts to their commercial customers. For a while, I racked my brain to no avail. Suddenly I had the answer.

I had to go that extra step for the banks. I had to devise a means of connecting the IMM to the cash market. The answer, I thought, lay in arbitrage. Simply explained, it is an axiomatic principle that whenever two markets trade the same product, there are often price discrepancies between them. The arbitrageur was someone in position to take advantage of the price differences between these two markets. The application was age-old. The arbitrageur would simply buy the product in the market where its price was cheaper and simultaneously sell it in the market where the price was dearer. Not only would the arbitrageur thereby ensure a profit for himself, he would keep the prices of the two markets in line with each other and, most significantly, add liquidity to the marketplace. What the IMM needed, I decided, was arbitrageurs between our floor and the interbank market.

Easier said than done. The banks had little trust in the financial wherewithal of our individual members. To be an arbitrageur required some capital. Besides, how could the banks be certain that the arbitrageur would not use the arbitrage facility to speculate? For instance, by buying more yen for his bank cash market account than he would sell at the IMM. Then, if things went wrong, who would pay the loss? These were difficult questions, but I thought I had the answers to all of them. I again turned to my friends at the Continental Illinois Bank, and the bank's president came through once more. This time he directed me to Continental lawyers and we argued it out. They won everything they wanted to safeguard the system, and I got what I wanted—a direct link to the interbank system.

I had the IMM create a facility that became known as the Class-B clearing member. This clearing member could do no other business in this facility than currency arbitrage with a single selected bank. For financial safety reasons demanded by bank attorneys, each bank required a different Class-B firm. The Class-B arbitrageur would then open an account at the given bank for his own cash market activities while his IMM arbitrage trading would be conducted at his Class-B firm. The IMM would post with the bank a copy of all of the arbitrageurs' trading activities at the Exchange to ensure that all open currency positions at the Class-B firm were balanced with his positions in the cash market at the bank. The system was ironclad and would require no large additional capital from any of our members. Morrie Levy became the first Continental Bank arbitrageur. Later I also created a Class-B firm between my firm Dellsher Investment Co. and the Continental Bank to use as a showcase for others to follow. Bert Norton, my bridge-playing friend, became the arbitrageur for the new Class-B firm.

The idea was magical for the IMM. Among those first Class-B traders, who paid $50,000 for the privilege of arbitraging foreign exchange, were Morrie Levy, Gerald Hirsch, and Philip Glass. They would buy, for example, yen from the bank and sell yen futures on the IMM, or vice versa. The system, in effect, bridged the banks to the Merc trading floor—just as I knew it would. At last our prices were connected to the real world. Without Class-B, the IMM was like a loose cannon, sometimes near the prices of the real world, sometimes miles away. Once Class-B became established, one could trade the IMM with a measure of confidence that the prices were within a range of legitimacy. For our traders, it was a highly profitable situation. Every one of the arbitrageurs made good money, some of them a lot of money. I remember Bert Norton coming to me after his first week of arbitrage, showing me his trading cards, and saying that he didn't think he knew how to figure things out. According to his calculations, he had secured a $10,000 profit his very first week of arbitrage operations. He said, clearly, he must have misfigured. He hadn't.

At its height, there were probably some 35 different Class-B arbitrage firms in operation at the IMM with every major bank in the country. Not only was it profitable for the arbitrageur, it provided profit and new business for the banks. At long last, all the New York banks began to participate with the IMM. As Adam Smith taught us, a profit incentive can do wonders. So the IMM became connected to the interbank world and the interbank world began to look at IMM currency prices for hedging purposes. We were gaining respectability, volume, and credibility. Of course, as the IMM grew, Class-B arbitrage was destined to become obsolete. Once the major banks realized that dealing directly with the IMM was safe and profitable, they would eventually decide that they didn't need a middleman to act as arbitrageur. By buying an IMM membership, they could themselves act as the arbitrageur and make a profit at both ends of the market. It was precisely what I hoped would happen but that was still years away.

Class-B arbitrage was an exceptional concept, which the IMM era demanded. But there were other IMM innovations that the new market forced upon us. For instance, the cash market in currencies was moving so fast that our futures could not keep up with them. Futures had daily price limits, which determined how much the market could go above or below the previous day's close. That worked in agriculture where the Merc was the primary market. Once the futures contract was up or down the limit, trading in the cash market virtually stopped. But in currency, the IMM prices were secondary and followed the cash market. When the cash price exceeded the IMM allowable limit, our markets were out of business. There were times when it took 10 days before the futures caught up with the cash market. It was obvious to me that the old rules could not work in the new markets we had launched; we had to innovate. I called in Powers and told him that we would have to devise a new system to fit the new order. Powers was up to the challenge. He came up with a plan for flexible price limits in the currencies to allow our markets to quickly catch up with cash market realities. Flexible price limits are still in force today in the IMM currency markets.

My biggest mistake with the IMM was a result of my over-ambition. Seven currency contracts were launched at one time, something that

wouldn't be done today. What we did in one day in 1972 would now probably take several years. Perhaps I wanted my enthusiasm to become infectious, to lap over into the pits and trading rooms of banks and brokers, to
stream into offices of corporate treasurers, to replace the river of grain
with the river of money. I must also point out that I wanted to establish a
formidable beachhead on the world of finance. One or two currencies just
wouldn't do. Aside from that, FX trading is an interconnected enterprise.
We are dealing in relative values of one currency against another, and
every change in one affects all the others. The world would have ignored
an effort that didn't understand this basic reality.

My second mistake was in creating contracts so large that they discouraged the public's participation. In my anxiety to please the bankers and foreign exchange traders—the commercial interests—I was persuaded to agree
to very large contracts. In doing so, I had miscalculated. While the commercial users were comfortable with the bigger contracts, in the beginning,
there were precious few of them who would consider trading at the IMM.
And the size was far too large for the average speculator or even the floor
members. So the IMM contracts were lacking the central ingredient of success: liquidity—the amount of bids and offers that flow to a market. Fortunately, at the time I made the decision to go with the bigger contracts, I
knew a secret that has served me well over the years. If you err on the side of
too large, it is easy enough to cut a contract size in half. Someone who is
long one contract would now have two contracts—no disaster. But not so the
other way around. If you start with a contract size too small, you fall into a
trap. It is difficult to tell someone who bought one contract that he suddenly
owns only half a contract. As soon as I became convinced that the IMM
contract size was too large, I became like a bulldog with but one mission,
and I refused to listen to the commercial users' pleas to wait and see. I
quickly moved to cut the contract size by dividing it in two. That helped,
but eventually I pushed for another cut in half, bringing the size down to
about $100,000 per contract in order to make it attractive for speculators. At
that level, it worked.

Therein lies the frustration of building a new market—the tinge of insecurity one feels at the point of no return. Each time I attempted something
new, there was that vague fear I would become known as the quixotic chaser
of failed dreams. Then it was out there: my idea tested against the world.
There's no magic in a market, only realism. No one can will a market to
work. I had to wait it out, giving up control to dynamics until it either happened or didn't. Then, if there was a flaw that I could fix, I had to quickly do
the right thing—that is, if I knew what that was. It's a nail-biter.

If the futures markets had been keyed to a Richter scale, the meter
could easily have hit 9 not long after the IMM opened. That summer the

Soviet Union purchased massive amounts of American wheat to offset a disastrous grain crop. And the river of grain overflowed its banks. It was the greatest grain transaction in the history of the world, proclaimed Secretary of Agriculture Earl Butz at the time. The purchase set off a great bull market that denationalized commodities. Then as never before there was public sensibility and awareness of commodities on a global basis. Grains, meats, and metals became the focus of speculative fever across the nation, from the New York construction worker to the Peoria dentist to the Los Angeles barber. Everyone, it seemed, had an Uncle Harry who made a fast buck in a fast market.

With money pouring into these markets, there was none of the anxiety and insecurity common to many industries in the throes of dramatic change. Instead, there was more of an urge to innovate, to push fresh ideas. The financial world was changing too rapidly to lag behind in finding new and innovative tools that could cope with uncertainty. I wasn't about to sit around and wait for the business community to catch up with the IMM. I knew that the other exchanges also had new ideas.

A year after the IMM began, the Chicago Board of Trade, chaired by Fred Uhleman whose father had founded Uhleman Grain, spun off the Chicago Board Options Exchange (CBOE). Under the guidance of Joe Sullivan, the CBOE became the first exchange to trade puts and call options on stocks on an organized exchange. No small innovation. It became a permanent forum for the Black-Scholes model, the celebrated equation developed by Fischer Black and Myron Scholes to determine the fair value of an option.

Fortunately for us, the Chicago Board of Trade didn't yet bother with financial futures. This gave us the precious early IMM years all to ourselves, without competitors breathing down our neck. Actually, during the first few years of the IMM's life, CBOT officials viewed our attempt to enter into the world of finance not much differently from our New York brethren: *it was doomed to failure.*

Henry Hall Wilson was then CBOT President. He had been an assistant to President John F. Kennedy and was more interested in the securities market than in new futures contracts. I think his national credentials made him look down on us lesser trader-folk. Even as Merc chairman, I had trouble getting an appointment with Mr. Wilson. I then learned the power of knowing a person's secretary, a lesson I never forgot. If not for the fact that I was a personal friend of Sue Green, Wilson's secretary, I probably never would have met him.

The CBOT's view about financial futures was dramatically altered under Warren Lebeck, who followed him as CBOT President. Lebeck had learned his stuff as secretary and administrative assistant to Sewell Avery, the nationally known chief of Montgomery Wards, who in his final days had to be carried out of his office still sitting on his chair. Lebeck came to the CBOT in the 1960s and was made President in 1973. About a year later, he brought onboard Richard Sandor, a brilliant former finance professor from the University of California at Berkeley. Lebeck's move proved to be most propitious for the Chicago Board of Trade. In 1975, Sandor literally saved the CBOT by bringing it into the world of financial futures.

The early negative views about the IMM prospects, however, weren't necessarily shared by the CBOT rank and file. Traders operate on different instincts than do the mighty muck-a-mucks. Les Rosenthal, for instance, saw the activity at our place and didn't hesitate in becoming a member of the Merc. He immediately became a staunch IMM advocate. And the O'Connor brothers, Bill and Ed, who were a driving force behind the creation of the CBOE, bought some of the initial IMM public offerings. So did Lee Stern and Henry Shatkin, powerful forces at the CBOT, who influenced other CBOT members to do the same. My friendship with many of the Board of Trade members began with my takeover at the Merc, when Bill Mallars was their chairman. Even though the CBOT was viewed as our biggest competitor, I always respected their membership and was proud to have become a member of that exchange. Personal friendship with CBOT members paid many dividends during the decades that followed. Both Warren Lebeck and Rich Sandor became and have remained my close friends throughout the years. Some 20 years later, when Billy O'Connor became chairman of the CBOT, he and I—against all the odds and oddsmakers—hammered out a GLOBEX partnership between our two rival exchanges.

Many of the early CBOT purchases of IMM seats, resulted from the efforts of Les Rosenthal. After its initial year, when the IMM seat market was allowed to be freely traded, I didn't want to take a chance that the new exchange's image might be tarnished by a falling membership price. So I asked my buddy Rosenthal, who was a highly respected CBOT member, destined to become its chairman in 1980, to get some of his friends to support the IMM by buying memberships. As always, Rosenthal responded with gusto, "Sure, Leo, how many seat purchases do you need?" The IMM seat price held, and as a result, some of his CBOT friends made the best investment of their lives. Of course, I also used Merc buddies to help me hold up IMM membership prices. Glen Bromagen, one of the founders of Rufenacht, Bromagen & Hertz, provided some critical IMM price support. Bromagen, who had become one of my strongest allies, had been introduced to our markets when he worked at the Chicago stockyards at Swanson & Gilmore, a company owned by John Gilmore's father. Gilmore would become CBOT chairman in 1986. "How can I help, Lee?" Bromagen drawled, and I explained what I wanted. He responded by getting some of his cattle customers to buy

Leo Melamed with his parents in Humboldt Park, Chicago, 1945.

Betty and Leo Melamed, August 1953.

The Melamed children: Idelle, Jordan, and David Melamed with Leo's 1965 Corvette.

The CME trading floor, 110 N. Franklin Street, 1967.

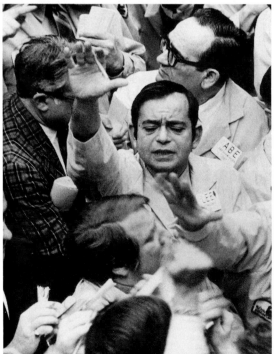

Chairman Leo Melamed trading in the Pork Belly Pit, late 1960s.

Nobel Laureate Milton Friedman opens T-bill futures, January 6, 1976.

Past Chicago Mayor Richard J. Daley opens a new market, November 24, 1976.

Speaker Tip O'Neill swaps stories with Leo Melamed, August 1980.

President Ronald W. Reagan greats Merc members, March 1980.

resident Li Xiannian of the People's Republic of China is introduced to capitalism at the erc by Brian P. Monieson and Leo Melamed, July 26, 1985.

Majority Leader Robert Dole meets Merc traders, March 14, 1988.

Chicago Mayor Richard M. Daley with Leo and Betty Melamed at Leo's retirement party, January 26, 1991.

The old high school gang: Jared Specthrie, Leo Melamed, Meyer Seltzer, Jack Bell at the American Jewish Committee presentation of the Human Rights Medallion Award to Leo Melamed, June 17, 1991.

The Board of Governors approve the launch of the International Monetary Market (IMM), 1971.

U.S. Trade Representative Clayton Yeutter shakes hands with Leo Melamed and Jack Sandner at the reception commemorating the opening of the Merc's Tokyo office, April 22, 1987.

Barry J. Lind roasts Leo Melamed at Leo's first retirement dinner, 1977.

IMM seats. Every one of them doubled their investment before they took their profit.

As the futures markets expanded, the Chicago politicians recognized their importance to the city—in jobs, taxes, overnight banking deposits, support services. (When the IMM began in 1972, there wasn't one foreign bank represented in Chicago; 20 years later, there were over a hundred foreign banks operating within the city.) In a historical first, Mayor Richard J. Daley declared the week of November 12-16, 1973, as Commodities Week. Eleven days later, I rang a replica of the Liberty Bell as a symbol of "Free Markets for Free Men" in an early-morning ceremony that marked the opening of our new Merc building at Jackson and the Chicago River.

The IMM was like money itself—it took on value because people had confidence in it. Markets, as E.B. Harris used to put it, represented the yin and yang of brooding economic forces; traders thrive on the instability of currencies, while governments struggle to keep them stable. And opportunity lurks in every market crevice as the arbitrageurs rush in to take advantage of the price differences in the same currency in different markets. The lure can be as small as 1/100th of a cent (as Henry Jarecki, the supreme arbitrageur, proved time and again) and the speed of execution makes all the difference: a quote that is a second old, is history.

At the end of its second year of operation, I began to feel a certain surge of confidence that comes with the first victories in a great war where the final outcome is still largely unknown. And I desperately wanted our members and the world to know that the outlook was good. In fact, things looked a lot better than I had dared to hope and certainly a lot better than anyone outside our close circle ever believed possible. I exuded confidence in my 1973 annual report to the members:

> . . . The new era also will afford us the opportunity to expand our potential into other areas within the monetary frame of reference. That was the essence of the philosophy that fostered the IMM; our new market was specifically designed to encompass as many viable trading vehicles in the world of finance as practicable. We must be willing and ready to explore all possibilities.

Indeed, as 1974 dawned, it provided us with the first opportunity to expand our market base. At long last, the United States was set to abolish the age-old law that prohibited Americans from owning gold. To me it meant that there would be a dogfight among futures markets for this coveted prize, but only one would win. The first problem was that the law would not take effect until January 1, 1975. This gave me an idea how I could get a jump on all the other exchanges.

London had for centuries been the capital of world gold trading. It was where the price of gold was "fixed" every day. But where was it written that

London was the only city that could establish a gold fixing? Why not Chicago? And since gold dealers were exempt from the prohibition against gold trading, why couldn't we establish a Chicago gold fix on the IMM floor immediately? If we could do that, then by the time it was legal for futures trading in gold, the IMM would have the upper hand. It was a guaranteed route to beat everyone in the gold derby. But there was a catch. To establish a gold fix in the United States, I needed permission from the Treasury Department. But not before I went to London to see firsthand how it was done. Then I went to my resident gold dealer expert, Henry Jarecki, and began the task of putting together the mechanism for a Chicago gold fix and some dealers to participate. We even established a special room where the fixing would take place. Finally, I arranged to meet with Paul Volcker, who was then an undersecretary at the Treasury in charge of this arena, to ask for permission.

"This isn't for trading by the public, so it won't violate the gold ownership prohibition." I said to the imposing Mr. Volcker, who is nearly seven feet tall.

I remember Volcker looking up at me from the desk and smiling. He had been friendly to the idea of financial futures. But this was something else, a way to get around the law and beat everyone to the punch in gold trading.

"Let me be frank; that's a tough one," said the undersecretary, who was destined to become one of this nation's most respected chairmen of the Fed. The way he said it I knew full well it would never happen in time. Still, he was honest with me and didn't give me a runaround. I appreciated that.

So I tried a different tack. In early August 1974, I met with Jack F. Bennett, the undersecretary for monetary affairs at the Treasury Department and gave what I thought was a compelling reason for the Treasury to modify its regulations to allow the opening of futures contracts in gold early—but with delivery to occur only after it became legal. The way the rule was written, it was unfair to U.S. citizens. I explained that if gold prices were to rise substantially between August 1974 and when it became legal for Americans to own gold in January 1975, the U.S. government would be sharply criticized by the public, I argued.

"It would be as if the Europeans and other non-U.S. citizens were given a sure bet at the expense of the American public," I said. "They can buy gold now and sell it at much higher prices to Americans."

I was hardly grabbing at straws because that's exactly what foreign speculators were doing at the time. A futures market in gold, I insisted, would solve the problem. Again, the idea was taken under advisement, and nothing happened.

Finally, on January 1, 1975, gold contracts began trading on the IMM. As I expected, we weren't alone. The COMEX, the New York-based futures exchange established long ago as the market for precious metals, started its gold trading at the same time. So did the CBOT and the Mid-America Commodity Exchange. The odds were in the COMEX's favor. Their ties to world gold dealers and their long tradition of metals trading made them favorites to win the gold futures market. I openly told our members that we had a very competitive fight on our hands and that the odds were against us. But the prize was worth the effort. Besides, I was ambitious and the COMEX didn't have my contingent of brave traders. If nothing else, we would give them a run for the gold, so to speak. We did.

Right from the start our members responded with vigor, and the volume on the IMM was actually better than at the COMEX. Our two exchanges left the others in the dust, and it became a battle between two warriors. The gold contract wouldn't actually pick up steam until nearly four years later when the world was in the grip of inflation, higher interest rates, and a sinking U.S. stock market. But the market had been in place to take advantage of the violently changing economic conditions. By 1980, at the height of world gold fever, the price of the yellow metal actually reached the phenomenal level of $850 an ounce. And during this run, both the IMM gold market as well as that of the COMEX flourished. Indeed, the fact that the IMM underdog had been able to sustain itself against its New York rival gave our exchange a permanent winning image and our members a feeling that they were invincible. I actually came to believe we would win. And I did everything I could think of to ensure that we did.

In an effort to better connect our exchange community to the London gold dealers, I even led some 30 IMM gold traders on a London junket in conjunction with the opening of our IMM office there. We held meetings, we partied, we turned old Londontown upside down. Imagine letting loose a bunch of cocky Chicago traders in dignified Britain. The resulting stories were enough to last a lifetime. The highlight of the events was a gala black-tie dinner in the prestigious Goldsmith's Guild Hall to which were invited the crème de la crème of London's financial world. I made a rousing keynote address, and Jack Sandner and Larry Rosenberg toasted the Queen.

Of course the best part occurred after hours. It all came about because Jack Sandner couldn't tie a tuxedo bow tie for the event and I had gotten Gerry Hirsch to exchange his clip-on bow tie with Jack. About 3:00 A.M., after the gala event, Jack and a few others were still enjoying a nightcap in my suite when the phone rang. It was Hirsch, a little tipsy, wanting his tie back from Jack and demanding to know my room number so he could come up and get it. At 3:00 A.M.? I thought that was a bit much and, to get even, gave him the wrong room number. I figured the worst that could happen was that he would wake up some stranger. About a half an hour later, there was a thunderous banging on our door. It was Gerry Hirsch, shouting and trying to break the door down. When the door was opened, Hirsch, red-faced and wild, lunged for me, with intent to maim. After two of the other traders held him down, he explained what happened.

"You see, when I arrived at room 607, the room number Melamed had given me, I saw a pair of shoes sitting outside the door to be polished. Assuming those were Melamed's shoes, I immediately zipped down my fly and made a night deposit in the shoes. Then I knocked on the door. To my utter dismay a seven-foot sleepy Englishman answered the door (Hirsch is barely five-and-a-half feet tall) and peered down on me still dressed in my tuxedo, holding his dripping wet shoes in my hands. I saw my life rush past my eyes, but thinking as fast as I could I immediately said, 'Sir, your shoes will be ready at 7:00 A.M.' I left without looking back, glad to still be alive, and now I must kill Melamed and everyone else in his room."

The IMM and COMEX remained in head-to-head competition for gold until about 1983. In the end, the COMEX won, proving what I firmly believe to be a unshakable market axiom: *the same futures product can't be successful at two exchanges within the same time zone.* Why did the IMM lose? There are a number of theories, some of them having to do with the belief that some unsavory practices were being committed in the Chicago pits. I never believed this to be the reason. Indeed, to believe that, I would have to assume that the New York traders were on a higher ethical plane than those of Chicago. Give me a break! My reason we lost the IMM gold market to the COMEX is much more complex, and much more substantive. It had to do with a tax deferral scheme known as "tax-straddles."

Through the use of futures markets, particularly highly liquid markets such as gold, one could conduct a spreading technique so that accumulated profits of one taxable year could be transferred to the next. It was a legal tax dodge, one of the many loopholes in the tax code. With a tax straddle, you could avoid paying income tax. For years, it was an "in-house" operation, that is, for local traders. But as our markets gained prominence so did the use of this tax dodge.

But there was a catch to tax straddles. Like all things in markets, they were not without economic risk. After one established the spread transaction—buying in one contract month while selling in another—one assumed a certain amount of risk because the price differential between the two contract months was constantly changing. At the COMEX, however, spread trading could be conducted in an "after-market" call, that is, when the real market was closed. Somehow, the COMEX members were able to ensure that in their after-market call, the price differential between contract months in gold futures remained remarkably stable. Not only that, it was much easier to establish a straddle while the market wasn't moving around. This after-market call was based on an old COMEX rule which made it legal. As a result, the COMEX was drawing huge tax-spreading business and the IMM was not. This greatly inflated their gold futures open-interest and transaction volume. While tax generated transactions had nothing to do with the relative success of our two gold markets, the world viewed the COMEX's larger open interest as proof that their gold market was more liquid than the IMM's. In reality, the after-market call at the COMEX was nothing but a subterfuge to facilitate a tax dodge. When I appealed to the CFTC to allow the IMM to conduct a similar after-market practice, the CFTC refused. When I protested that this was blatantly unfair and that the IMM would lose its gold market as a result, my pleas fell on deaf ears. The CFTC had neither the guts to stop the COMEX practice nor to allow the IMM to compete. The tax straddle controversy lasted for years. In the end, the U.S. Congress banned the practice altogether, but by then the IMM had lost the battle for gold futures. It was the only market we ever lost to another exchange.

18

The Feds Are Coming

The exact reason the Peruvian anchovies changed their mating habits was shrouded in some mystery. But there is no doubt that the consequences of their altered lifestyle resulted in huge shortages in the U.S. supply of fish meal used as feed for livestock. It also caused the quanay, a cormorant, to leave the coastline of Peru for more inviting skylines, dramatically diminishing the world supply of guano—the bird droppings rich in nitrogen— which are a mainstay of cheap fertilizer.

Believe it or not, these alterations by mother nature were critical factors in what became known in the early 1970s as "The U.S. Food-Price Spiral" and caused some bizarre as well as serious national repercussions. For one thing, it led to the price controls of 1971 under the hand of President Nixon—which culminated with President Ford's WIN (Whip Inflation Now) buttons. For another, it gave rise to legislation that resulted in the creation of the Commodity Futures Trading Commission, the federal agency that regulated futures exchanges, commonly known as the CFTC.

Nixon's price controls were predictably an unmitigated disaster. As a disciple of Milton Friedman's free market teachings, and as chairman of a fiercely free market institution, I became particularly exasperated by the stricture of price controls and led the Merc into battle for their removal. This controversy lasted for several years.

It began with Neal Smith, the contentious congressman from Iowa who found food price rises to be an ideal political platform. He chose commodity markets, particularly cattle trading, as a central theme of his election campaigns, claiming that these markets needed to be reined in. The underhanded shenanigans in the pits of Chicago, said Mr. Smith, particularly in cattle futures, were responsible for the rise in American meat prices, which were taking rightful profits away from the farmers of Iowa. Although Neal Smith did not have congressional oversight over commodity markets, he was chairman of the Subcommittee on Special

Small Business Problems and used this guise to hold hearings on the misuses and abuses of commodity markets. It offered me an opportunity to use my Yiddish stage oratorical skills and may have been the first time members of Congress heard so aggressive and spirited a defense of futures markets. But for Neal Smith, a sworn foe of futures, to make our markets his primary focus—well, it made all of us in the industry crazy. Unquestionably, he and the other enemies of commodity markets he attracted, could cause us a lot of trouble, especially if his hearings resulted in legislation over exchanges. To make matters worse, the congressman's accusations found an unfortunate echo in the current scandal caused by the failure of Goldstein Samulson Inc. of Beverly Hills, the nation's largest commodities options dealer. While options had nothing to do with futures markets at the time, the noise lumped us all together.

So we turned to Bob Poague, the powerful and legendary Texas Democrat, chairman of the House Agriculture Committee, which by tradition should have had jurisdiction over our markets. Poague knew nothing about futures and couldn't care less, but we gained his ear, if for no other reason than to stop Smith from poaching on his jurisdiction. In June 1973, chairman Poague delegated the commodity market issue to John Rainbolt, Associate Counsel of the House Agriculture Committee.

At that time, we were still apolitical, just babes in the woods when it came to Washington. There were congressmen who knew something about our markets, but there were more who thought the Board of Trade was a chamber of commerce, and if they had heard of the Chicago Mercantile Exchange at all, they assumed it was a bank. Consequently, our markets were virtually unknown and unregulated. Their oversight was technically under the CEA, the Commodity Exchange Authority, an insignificant department within the Department of Agriculture. This arrangement was fine with almost everyone in the futures industry. The fewer cops, the better.

But, suddenly, we were under attack, and it fell on John Rainbolt to save us from Neal Smith. Rainbolt talked it over with John O'Neil, the committee's chief of staff and some other staffers and Washington insiders, and it was decided that the Agriculture Committee had better hold hearings of its own. This is a fairly normal defensive tactic in D.C. Pretty soon Rainbolt got around to calling E.B. Harris, and Harris promptly pointed him toward Melamed.

Consequently, just after the Smith hearings, I again became a star witness, this time for the House Agriculture Committee for what were labeled "friendly" hearings. Although Rainbolt had started the hearings as a defensive maneuver, as often happens in Washington D.C., events took over, and the idea to create an independent federal agency to oversee commodity markets took on a life of its own.

I had mixed emotions on the subject. On the one hand, like everyone else in our industry, I opposed the idea of more federal regulation. Self regulation was our doctrine—we could be our own watchdog. But my rhetoric at the time was strictly diplomatic, and I publicly welcomed the CFTC. Human nature being what it is, I was willing to live with a federal agency, but not under an Orwellian shadow. I didn't want a cop in every pit, nor did I ever want to wait for the Feds to swoop down on us with a "close the still" mentality. We were legal, quasi-public, and certainly sophisticated enough to do our policing and self-regulating. We had come a long way from the days of the "squeeze-a-month-club" ruled by a handful of egg traders, the days when I once asked the CEA's Administrator Alex Caldwell to stand in front of the egg pit so it looked like he was watching. (Unfortunately, he never did). Those days were long gone.

But as I said, I had mixed emotions. I was aware that until we had a true federal agency, we simply wouldn't be respected as a field of business. By definition, as cynical as it may sound, any endeavor that can boast its own federal agency must be an important and legitimate national enterprise. Every successful industry had a federal counterpart whether it was banking and the Fed, or securities and the SEC. Besides, I had no doubt that our introduction of financial futures would cause substantial growth in the industry, increasing its prominence and notoriety. And a federal agency could act as a buffer between us and the enemies of futures markets, of which there were plenty.

In my opinion, therefore, federal oversight was unavoidable. And if that were the case, why not play a role in the process to help influence the outcome. Oddly, my first instinct was in favor of the SEC, a position I have since reversed 180-degrees. But in the early 1970s—well before financial futures, options, and derivatives took hold—agricultural commodities were king of the futures markets. The SEC didn't want any part of us. Who were we? Whoever and whatever we were, we definitely weren't finance. We were LaSalle Street, not Wall Street.

But most of all, buried deep in my head was a plan that only a federal agency could carry out: *remove the requirement of physical delivery in the mechanics of our markets.* Physical delivery was a straitjacket. By definition, this form of delivery excluded a vast array of products from ever being traded on a futures exchange. To put it simply, there are instruments that are intangible and cannot actually be delivered. One of these, suggested to me years before in a conversation with little Elmer Falker, was secretly tucked away in my head. Perhaps, I quietly contemplated, a federal agency would have the guts to open the gates of futures to a whole new ball game.

Toward the end of 1973, John Rainbolt, talked Poague into the creation of an ad hoc subcommittee for the purpose of writing the necessary legislation. The committee began its work, holding discussions with industry leaders, and even visiting the floors of the Merc and the CBOT. For some of them this was the first visit to a commodity exchange. With momentum building, some of us became immersed as special advisors during the process of drafting the legislation. Having discussed it with Merc attorney Jerry Salzman, as well as with our counterparts on the Chicago Board of Trade, I told Rainbolt that we could support the legislation under certain conditions. First of all, the legislation had to provide that futures contracts could be traded only on an authorized contract market (an exchange). Such a provision was fundamental in assuring the continued viability of exchanges. Second, the new agency should have exclusive jurisdiction. On this point, Rainbolt and I saw eye to eye. But in the final analysis, it took the CBOT's general counsel, Philip McBride Johnson of Kirkland & Ellis, to write the language to ensure that the CFTC would have exclusive rights over futures, and barring the SEC or regulators from the separate states from regulatory oversight of our markets.

Finally, we demanded that the new agency be given wide latitude in determining such issues as type of delivery (physical or otherwise), dual trading, self-regulation, the creation of a National Futures Association, and so on. It was our view that such complex matters could not be preordained and were best left for the agency to determine. Our reasoning, of course, was that since the exchanges had the experts in these matters, our thoughts should ultimately prevail. This did not always turn out to be the case. Of particular concern to me was to ensure that the agency not make *economic justification* a prerequisite to new contract approval. I was afraid that such a condition could stifle all future market innovation. With all that was involved, the bill finally drafted as H.R. 13113 grew to include five different titles.

New hearings were set, and in May 1974, I told members of the Committee on Agriculture, Nutrition, and Forestry that the Merc had no objections to a new commission nor to many of the provisions in the proposed legislation. However, I wanted the Congress to know that I had mixed feelings and some reservations. I was careful not to talk down to my listeners. The idea was not to alienate them, but to educate them; not to wow them with what I knew, but to calm them. The onion scandal had taught me that the size of a constituency doesn't necessarily have to be large to get Congress to take action. Since I was aware that the current issue was the food price spiral, and the constituency was both big and loud, the last thing I wanted was for Congress to blame our markets as in the case of onions.

My voice was genial and reassuring, my face a frown of concern, yet I wasn't dry or technical. My message was unique: "Mr. Chairman," I said, "there are no commodity exchanges in Moscow; there is no Peking Duck Exchange in China; there is no Havana Board of Trade. The farmers of those countries have no need for a vehicle that offers price protection. There the governments themselves establish the prices that they will pay for the farmers' products. Their system, however, is a failure. Only in the United States do the farmers produce more than we need to feed our nation." The words were calculated to appeal to Congress' free-market spirit and explain the value of our markets.

Marty Cohen, the Merc's talented advertising maven, was sitting in the hearing room. When he heard my words, he suddenly had a brilliant idea that got him that year's most coveted award in advertising. The ads depicting nonexistent exchanges in Moscow, Peking, and Havana asked the obvious question: How come no such exchanges exist in those places? The ads were colorful, attractive and offered a poignant message. The ads became famous Merc posters for which there is never a sufficient supply.

I also tried to clarify the role of our markets with respect to higher food prices. "To act like a messenger" is, in fact, one of the primary functions of futures markets. "Futures markets by their definition, must act to provide us with a glimpse of what is coming." If these markets had failed to predict the forthcoming high prices, they would not have functioned correctly. As a matter of fact, they did not fail.

Eventually, the Senate too did its thing, and the CFTC bill easily passed both the Houses of Congress. Then, Committee chief of staff John O'Neil and John Rainbolt tossed a coin to see who would name the new agency. O'Neil won, giving the agency its permanent CFTC moniker.

While all this was happening in our little corner of the world, our nation was in the throes of Watergate. President Nixon's days in the White House were numbered and Gerald Ford was about to take over. At the same time, Republican Secretary of Agriculture Earl Butz was of the opinion that we didn't need another federal agency and threatened to advise the President to veto the bill. Before he did that, Butz turned to John Damgard, one of his bright young staffers who actually knew something about our markets, and asked him to write a memo with the pros and cons of the CFTC legislation. After Nixon resigned and Gerald Ford took over the presidency, it was pretty well decided that the president would veto the CFTC legislation. In fact, Ford's press secretary, publicly announced to the media that the bill would be vetoed. It wasn't. Some supportive Republicans, at the last moment, prevailed on the President not to veto until he called his friend, Bob Poague, the chairman of the House Committee on Agriculture. Poague, argued in favor of the legislation on a personal level. John Damgard's memo now became pivotal to the process since it explained our industry to the President. With Damgard's memo in hand, Ford demanded that some of the bill's deficiencies be fixed and Poague agreed. Although he still had many reservations, Ford signed the legislation and John Rainbolt, its chief architect, received the presidential pen for his efforts.

What goes around, comes around. It was most appropriate that a few years later John Damgard would assume an important role in our industry by taking over the presidency of the Futures Industry Association, the FIA, when John Clagget, its founding president retired. Damgard made the FIA the respected trade association it is today.

So ended the CFTC legislation saga, and a new epoch dawned for our markets. The drama now shifted to the White House for the appointments of a chairman and four commissioners to the new independent federal agency. This became the primary responsibility of Beverly Splane who was an official in the White House personnel office at the time. Her recommendations to the President would most likely carry the day. Splane was proof to me that government can't be all bad. Here was one of the most intelligent, responsible, and articulate persons I had ever encountered, actually working for government. Besides that, as a native Chicagoan and a graduate of the University of Chicago, she was of a similar free-market philosophical bent as I. In Beverly Splane I saw a highly motivated and bright 31-year-old with a feel for the futures industry. The daughter of a tool and dye maker for General Motors who grew up in Flint, Michigan, she earned both a Bachelor's degree in Chinese and an MBA from the University of Chicago. Splane worked as a management consultant in Boston before joining the Ford Administration as a White House aide.

We had first met in the old executive office building next to the White House where among the issues we discussed were dual trading, margins, and the roll of the Exchange clearinghouse. She listened and took copious notes as I expounded in tutorial fashion. The meeting was cordial and I found Splane to be a quick study. From then on, every time she had a question, she'd call me and quickly became quite knowledgeable with respect to our markets. Splane reciprocated by serving as an invaluable ally, lobbying behind the scenes on some of the critical issues during the legislative process.

But unbeknownst to me, she harbored some dangerous secret thoughts which could have changed the course of my personal history. I was in Hawaii at the time, taking a long-deserved vacation with Betty at a national bridge tournament. At 4:00 A.M. one morning, I was awakened to hear Beverly Splane's voice: "Melamed, I have decided to recommend to President Ford that you be appointed as chairman of the CFTC."

Awakened from a deep sleep, I greeted that announcement with stunned silence. Finally, coming to my senses, I shouted, "Beverly, you're crazy!"

"Hell, I am," she replied, "it's all decided."

It was the last thing in the world I wanted. Here I was, just getting started with the IMM, bursting with ideas, energy, and plans to make that exchange the most successful in the world, and suddenly this Washingtonian bureaucrat wants to cut me off at the knees. The road to hell, I mused, really is paved with good intentions. I knew damn well that once the President officially asked me to serve, it would be most difficult to refuse.

"Beverly, listen," I implored. "At least don't do anything until you and I talk face to face. I'll get on a plane to D.C. immediately and be there as quickly as I can."

Reluctantly, Splane agreed, and Betty and I rushed to an airplane, leaving Hawaii in the middle of a bridge tournament—an unforgivable sin. Once in Washington, I used all my persuasive powers to explain to Splane that I could serve my country much better from the private sector by leading the Merc and futures industry. Mercifully, she saw the light and removed my name from the recommendation.

In March 1975, the President acted. John Rainbolt was duly appointed to the commission he helped create and later became its vice chairman. The other three commissioners were Reed P. Dunn, an old-line cotton trader and the Executive Director of the International Institute for Cotton; Robert L. Martin, a former chairman of the Board of Trade; and Gary L. Seevers, a member of the President's Council of Economic Advisors.

Although Seevers held a PhD from Michigan State University and taught agricultural economics at Oregon State University, he overcame this agricultural background to quickly become the new commission's inside expert on financial instruments. Seevers became my ally and helped immeasurably with respect to our eventual Treasury bill and Eurodollar contracts. Later, Seevers moved to Goldman Sachs, where he became a partner. In 1986, Seevers served as a director of the CME.

There is no accounting for fate though. Chairmanship of the CFTC went to William T. Bagley, a former member of the California State Assembly who had lost a close race for California State Controller, and who knew nothing about futures markets. Bagley, a graduate of the University of California at Berkeley and the Boalt Hall School of Law, was a politician. He was also a sweet guy, easy to befriend. An evocative gentleman who favored wide ties and suspenders, Bagley was coming to a new agency at a time when government regulation was beginning to lighten up. Bagley viewed the CFTC as an example of congressional initiative sparked by public demand. But he was quick to note that the agency hadn't been created as a result of industry scandal or industry demand. While he didn't understand our markets, he loved them instantly.

Bagley was the freeist spirit I ever knew, totally without inhibition. It was hard not to love him. His antics were legendary. Once, at a futures conference in London, I found myself at Mirabelle's, one of London's poshest restaurants; Bagley was a few tables away. As soon as he spotted me, without any hesitation, he got down on his knees, waddled over to where I was sitting, took my hand and kissed an imaginary ring on my finger. To the utter bewilderment of the stunned patrons of the restaurant— who stopped everything to watch in awe—the CFTC chairman spoke in a loud stage whisper, "Oh, godfather, how good of you to receive this humble servant!" It was vintage Bagley.

My buddy, Henry Jarecki, has an even better story about Chairman Bagley. When Jarecki and I served on the first CFTC Advisory Committee, we found ourselves on opposite sides of the options issue. Options on futures had been banned from U.S. markets, and Jarecki, a professional options dealer, wanted the ban lifted. I wasn't convinced, believing that while options on their face were useful and benign, they could grow to become complex and dangerous. The trading public, I knew, was not sufficiently sophisticated to use this vehicle of finance.

These personal doubts single-handedly delayed futures-options approval for a number of years. Eventually, I relented, since options became approved by the SEC for listing at rival securities exchanges. Options did in fact grow to become extremely complex instruments and, although highly successful and utilized today by a much more sophisticated trader than existed in the 1970s, I still harbor a suspicion that, for instance, imbedded options of the current exotic genre create dangerous financial risk in the marketplace.

However, at that time, Jarecki and I both agreed that professional dealers should be exempt from any ban, and we lobbied Bagley accordingly. Although Bagley tried to be helpful, he could not persuade congressional legislators. The exemption was rejected. Embarrassed by his inability to get the job done, the CFTC chairman asked Jarecki how much the ban would set him back.

"Oh, never mind," Jarecki responded.

"No, no," Bagley insisted, "I want to know how much the CFTC cost you with this ban."

"Okay, if you must know, $24 million," Jarecki said.

Without further ado, the chairman of the CFTC whipped out his personal checkbook and wrote a check to Jarecki for $24 million. Going along with the gag, Jarecki accepted the gift and put it in his suit coat pocket. That might have been the end of the story were it not that on the shuttle back to New York that evening, Jarecki's suit coat was accidently exchanged with someone else's. That someone turned out to be Joseph Kraft, the well-known syndicated columnist, who, to his amazement, found a $24 million check in his coat pocket to Henry Jarecki from the chairman of a government agency. Although the details of the prank were eventually sorted out, it first served as a hilarious piece in *The New York Times*.

One of the best things Bagley did upon becoming chairman was to appoint Beverly Splane as the CFTC's first executive director. This put a professional in charge of directing the new agency, creating its departments, and acquiring its staff. Splane's impressive results in putting the fledgling CFTC together were not lost on me.

At this time, Ken Mackay was ready to retire and I wanted to replace him with a newly created position of executive vice president. I needed someone who could help me run the Exchange in terms of the staff and organizational problems that came with quick growth. The obvious prospect to me was Beverly Splane. I met her in Washington and over dinner offered her the job. Our roles were reversed. A year earlier, she had been courting me to be chairman, and now I was courting her to work for me. Although she had served as the CFTC's acting executive director for only nine months, she accepted my offer.

It was no problem convincing John Geldermann, my good friend and new Merc chairman, that she was the best person for the job because Splane's conservative political credentials meshed with Geldermann's dyed-in-the-wool Republican views. I thought, however, it might be trickier convincing the Board. This was 1975, and there were precious few women in high offices within the financial world. In fact, Beverly Splane was about to become the first female executive vice president of any U.S. exchange. But any reservations the Merc Board members had were kept to themselves.

Splane's replacement of Mackay truly ended an era. He had been at the Merc for 48 years and had the longest institutional memory of any Merc employee. The Splane transaction was part of a major trade with the CFTC. Mark Powers, who turned theory into practicality by creating tradeable contracts in currency and interest rate futures, was calling it quits after a remarkable decade of service. I was successful in persuading the CFTC to appoint him as its chief economist—a newly created position at the agency. Talk about revolving doors. This appointment not only served as a stepping-stone in Mark's career, it was an insurance policy to keep the CFTC on track. And this was only the beginning of a pipeline that would deliver talent from the futures industry to government.

So ended an era. President Nixon resigned on August 9, 1974. Price controls became ancient history. Their legacy, the CFTC, was in our future. With the benefit of hindsight, if I were to make a judgment on the value and role played by the CFTC in the development of futures markets, I would unquestionably come down on the side of a favorable assessment. Sure, the agency often stood in the way of what many of us in the industry considered important to our continued expansion. There were many battles, some of which I led; some we lost, some we won. Indeed, there are those who would say our industry prospered *in spite* of the CFTC. But I would disagree with such an evaluation. A fair assessment must go beyond any individual issue, or any of the many petty squabbles, or the general anti-government attitude which often pervades the private sector. There were any number of critical junctures which could have spelled a limit to our potential and which were resolved in our favor, in large measure because of the CFTC. In sum total, the CFTC served our industry well and as a result served the best interests of the American financial service sector.

It must also be said that aside from leadership by its chairmen and commissioners, it took many talented staff people at the CFTC to produce the positive results achieved and, equally important, to protect the futures market turf from poachers at the SEC and other competitive forums. It is impossible to name them all but I know that professionals like Thomas Russo and Andrea Corcoran at the Division of Trading & Markets stand out in my mind; similarly, Howard Schneider, Jack Gaine, Marshall Hanbury, and Ken Raisler were highly effective in the office of General Counsel, as were Mark Powers and Paula Tosini in Economics and Education; and since no agency can be productive without an effective Division of Enforcement, I would single out the work of Dennis Klejna who functioned in this capacity for well over a decade. These professionals, and the others, who served the CFTC since its inception deserve a measure of our praise and, I for one, would judge their performance much higher than the overall image this federal agency has achieved.

When the dust settled, I penned this *Ode to Price Controls*, which I recited at one of our members' meetings.

> I wish to record, just for fun,
> How price controls happened in '71.
> The story can serve as a future lesson
> Should we with the economy go a messin'.
> So now that they're going some six feet under
> How did we make such a classical blunder?
> To future generations, this ode I christen
> Ladies and gentlemen, just listen:

Said the Democrats:
The next issue with which to contend
Are the rising prices and what they portend.
We need a remedy that will look good,
One that is appealing and understood.
"Price controls," of course, they fit the need!
A solution to the problem with instant speed!
Of course, they might turn out to be bad,
Cause shortages, disruptions, that would be sad.
But that should not be our main concern,
We'll create the issue, and then it's their turn.
The G.O.P. will never approve this solution,
It's against the free-market institution.
Then we can blame the rising prices
On Republican inaction in times of crises.

Thought the Republicans:
The Dems have created a clever trap,
An issue on which we could take the rap.
This could cost us many a vote
Inflation is at the public's throat
But we, too, can play this game of tag
In political know-how, we don't lag.
We'll turn the tables on their little scheme
We, too, will join the price control team.
Of course, they might turn out to be bad,
Cause less production, that would be sad.
But the President will never play this tune
And allow the country to go to ruin.
He'll ignore controls without any shame
And then nobody will be to blame.

Said the Media and Press:
To report the news is our obligation,
To seek the issues or their mutation.
Inflation has become a terrible woe,
We need a quick solution to keep it in tow.
Congress had enacted what sounds so good,
Why doesn't the President do as he should?
Of course, they might turn out to be bad,
Prove counter-productive, that would be sad.
But at least they would serve us for a time
The raising of prices would become a crime.

Thought the Labor Leaders:
Our workers have had it with rising prices;
Something must be done to end this crisis.
A free economy is good and well,
But not when our dollars are going to hell.
Controls on prices are what we need,

(But not on wages—heaven forbid!)
Of course, they might turn out to be bad,
Cause less employment, that would be sad.
But then we can blame the legislators
For being bad law perpetrators.

Espoused the Consumer Advocates:
Big business runs our U.S.A.
They make the little guy pay and pay.
To help the citizen is our job,
We're his saviors—the ignorant slob.
What we propose is a magic wand
To bring down prices with a wave of the hand.
Controls are the thing, they work like magic,
They'll stop the profits, and that's not tragic.
Of course, they might turn out to be bad,
Cause hoarding and panic, that would be sad.
But if they work like ancient voodoos,
Then we get the credit and take the kudos.

Said Business Management:
The crisis really must come to an end,
Our public image we must mend.
Controls will placate the public's mood
If we're for them, it will look good.
Of course, they might turn out to be bad,
Cause business slowdown, that would be sad.
But if we object too strongly,
It will be interpreted wrongly.
So let's hope they're what we need
To the free market economists, pay no heed.

Counseled the President's Advisors:
That controls are bad, there's no denial
But if we applied them for only awhile,
A sort of in-between election trial,
It wouldn't cramp our conservative style,
And maybe they wouldn't much harm compile.
Meanwhile we would derive a political mile
By quieting the housewife's growing rile.

Said the President:
I'm against controls in any form
They're not the answer to this storm.
They'll disrupt the economy of our nation,
Create shortages and cause us to ration.
They create bureaucracy like the O.P.A.
They cause inequities and disarray.
But wait—let's look at the facts

Controls were created by Congressional Acts.
The Dems and G.O.P. have had them adopted
To pass me the buck, they have opted.
The Press is for it, the Media too
The dissenters are quiet and very few.
Labor is pressing for action at once,
If I don't do it, I'll look like a dunce.
Consumers think it's a magic spell
Prices will come down at the ring of a bell.
Business is for it and they must know
What's good for the country to make it grow.
My advisors agree, if applied for a while,
They might not much harm compile.
How silly of me not to see the light,
If everyone's for it, they must be right.
They'll help diminish the public's ire,
They could break the rising spiral fire.
Maybe they are magic—you can't be sure,
Any action could be the right cure.
Of course, they might turn out to be sad,
But Congress passed the law, too, too bad.
This tale is funny, if it weren't so sad,
Ladies and gentlemen, we've been had.

PART THREE

The Future's Not What It Used to Be

19

Acid Test

If I had to pick the critical turning point in IMM history, it would be August 31, 1976, the date when the Mexican peso was devalued by 50 percent. It was a shocking event for the entire world, representing the worst devaluation during that era. The global foreign exchange markets became roiled beyond recognition and no one would quote a price for the Mexican peso. No one, that is, except the members of the International Monetary Market of Chicago. Our market remained in business and was fully operational. Suddenly we were center stage. Suddenly, the IMM peso market was the world's focal point for currency prices.

It was a glorious and pivotal moment in IMM history. For the first time, the world of finance recognized the enormous value of a futures market. The 1976 peso crisis proved to even the most stubborn doubters that a futures market could provide a price for the world of hedgers and speculators under any circumstances. The IMM was suddenly validated. However, no victory of this magnitude comes easy.

In the first place, I originally never wanted the Mexican peso listed for trade on the IMM. The whole point I had advocated for the market was for trade in instruments whose values would be determined by free-market forces of supply and demand. How then could we trade in a currency whose price was determined by government edict? By definition, we could not. Indeed, in the beginning, the Mexican peso was not on the IMM opening roster. It happened in a highly unusual manner.

A month or so before we announced the launch of our new currency market, I got a strange call from the State Department. They wanted an appointment to talk about our plans. Puzzled and a bit concerned about why the U.S. State Department would take an interest in our new IMM, I made the necessary arrangements.

"We hear you have no plans to list the Mexican peso for trade," the official stated after he was seated in my office on the fifth floor of the Merc building. "Is that true?"

Surprised, I explained we were hesitant to list a fixed currency. It was not conducive to the fluctuations of a free market. The official nodded thoughtfully, but then explained that the State Department feared that the government of Mexico would view this as an insult.

"You see," he said seriously, "you are listing the currency of Canada, our neighbor to our North, but ignoring the currency of our neighbor to the South. We think it could result in a diplomatic flap."

I didn't know whether to laugh or cry. I was flattered that the IMM had taken on such importance in world affairs; on the other hand, I was worried to hear that we had already done something wrong. The last thing I needed was a diplomatic flap. I decided that prudence was the better part of valor and called back into session the IMM Interim Committee. The Mexican peso was quickly added to the IMM scorecard. Years later, of course, we had to de-list the peso because of restrictive internal Mexican regulations that prevented delivery. Recently, after the 1994 crisis, the Mexican government finally freed the peso from government control and its currency unit is once again trading on the IMM.

But in 1976, four years after the IMM began, the peso was on my radar screen as an accident waiting to happen. In truth, the peso devaluation was not a surprise to most market observers; only its exact timing and magnitude was unknown. As I have always maintained, the markets know everything. Here's what I mean: From the very beginning of trading on the IMM, the forward price of the peso was discounted. In other words, the market was consistently predicting that the value of the peso in the future would be less than it was in the present. As the years went by, this forward discount became deeper and deeper. And this phenomenon made the peso a lucrative tax straddle. Simply stated, you bought the forward peso contract and sold a nearby contract. As time went by, the forward contract price would continue to rise, shedding its discount because on the day of maturity—when futures and cash prices converge—it had to be worth the official cash market exchange rate. If you held the forward position for six months or longer, you effectively converted your profit into a capital gain. Similarly, although it was much more dangerous, you could play this *sure thing* by simply going long the forward contract and holding tight for six months.

Word about this sure thing at the IMM began to spread in world currency circles and attracted a lot of big players. But, of course, it was no sure thing. As I once asked in a lecture to students at Northwestern University: *"Who do you think is selling the discounted futures price?"* A fool who is giving away his money? Of course not! The reason the price was discounted in the futures was that the market knew that the peso was worth less than the official rate. The market anticipated an eventual devaluation. In other words, commercial interests were willing to sell peso forward, at a lower rate, as a hedge against the drop in prices they expected. One of our IMM stalwarts, Eugene T. Mueller, was a smart trader who fervently believed the peso reckoning was coming and those short the market would be handsomely rewarded. Year after year, Mueller stayed short peso, shrugging off the large losses he had to take when nothing happened. "My day will come," he would tell anyone who would listen. Alas, there is a perverse old market law about those who stubbornly fight the market. It proved true again. Eugene Mueller had given up just before his long-awaited day came to pass.

As this moment of truth came closer and closer in 1976, some of us at the IMM became increasingly concerned. IMM margin requirements, as in all futures, were but a small fraction of the value of the contract. That's okay in markets where values adjust freely and the changes are paid for on a daily basis. But in a market like the Mexican peso, where a fictitious value is set, this system is fraught with danger. The normal margin requirements are grossly inadequate to protect against a sudden and severe devaluation. In such a case, clearing firms whose customers were long the Mexican peso might have insufficient capital to pay for the change in value.

Knowing that this danger existed, at first, Barry Lind, who was clearinghouse chairman, simply raised the peso margin requirement. "No way can we endanger our financial integrity," Lind lectured to our reluctant board. But after it was raised to about 10 percent of its contract value, we realized that to go any higher would close down the market. That would be bad for the IMM image. Still, if the devaluation was in the magnitude of 25 or 30 percent, the financial integrity of the Exchange was highly vulnerable. Some clearing members might fail. So I suggested an unusual protective measure. Barry Lind immediately embraced the concept, and together we forced the passage of a special rule requiring clearing firms with open positions in the peso contract to post with the clearinghouse—in the form of their own capital—an additional 30 percent of the value of the contracts held by their customers. It was a harsh demand and I could hear the clearing members' screams clear across Chicago. But as chairman, I knew I had written into the rules this kind of emergency authority.

Maduff & Co. had the largest long position in the Mexican peso. Sidney Maduff, the firm's owner, who had survived his penalties in the 1971 pork belly corner, screamed bloody murder when the new capital requirement was announced. He threatened to sue the Merc.

"The customer, who owns the Mexican peso positions on my books," Maduff shouted in my face, "has more money than the Chicago Mercantile Exchange. How dare you suggest that he won't be able to pay for his losses."

"Sidney," I countered, trying to stay calm, "I don't know who your customer is and I don't care. If you don't put up the capital, you'll be closed down." I pointed out to Maduff that the Exchange had no direct dealings with customers, only with its clearing members. Besides, if his customer was so wealthy, why couldn't Maduff get the required capital from him.

"Do you know who you are talking about?" Maduff yelled even louder. "My customer is Lamar Hunt." The mere mention of Hunt's name was intended to so shock me that I would instantly apologize to Maduff and rescind the requirement. After all, Mr. Hunt was the famous Texas billionaire, son of the late Texas oil tycoon, H.L. Hunt. At the moment, Hunt was playing the so-called sure-thing peso tax gimmick. Neither Lind nor I was impressed; nor did I shudder at Maduff's threat that Hunt would personally sue me.

Lamar Hunt and his attorney showed up at the Merc a few days later to confront Barry Lind and myself in the presence of Maduff. Hunt did the expected waving of hands and threatening, using very colorful language to make sure I understood who he was and what he thought I was. It's a funny thing about language, though; having grown up in Chicago's inner city and lived within the pits at the Merc, I could match most people in the use of the profane and was not embarrassed to do so. But it wasn't the right place or time, nor was it necessary. Hunt's lawyer calmed his client down considerably after Lind and I showed him the IMM emergency rule. We then suggested a solution to which all parties agreed. Hunt would be better off moving his Mexican peso positions to a clearing member that could afford the necessary additional capital. E.F. Hutton was chosen, and the positions were duly transferred.

Less than one month later, the peso was devalued by 50 percent. At the time, it represented the largest one-day swing in value between longs and shorts in the history of the IMM, $100 million. While that dollar figure pales by comparison to the $2.5 billion loss involved on the day of the 1987 stock crash, the amount was quite a shocker for that time. Nevertheless, because we had taken the precautionary measures, the Merc clearinghouse had the necessary capital from its members. There were no defaults. The strength of our clearing system had survived its acid test. This fact did not go unnoticed by the financial world. Indeed, it became a defining moment in IMM history. My biggest personal thrill was in being able to decline the emergency $100 million loan offered by Chase Manhattan "to save the Merc." Seldom was a "no thank you" so sweet.

This encounter with Lamar Hunt occurred a few years before he and his brothers lost most of their money trying to corner the world's silver market. The Hunt silver fiasco became a global event with serious financial reverberations that shook the very foundations of the New York Commodity Exchange (COMEX) where the silver contracts were traded. Although it was a failed venture, during the course of the corner the Hunts pushed silver prices to incredible levels. The high price ultimately resulted in bringing silver to the market from every householder who had a few silver bowls or spoons to spare, thereby causing the market to come crashing down. Congressional hearings followed. I testified in an effort to prevent the COMEX's debacle from causing permanent damage to the entire futures industry. The event led to the unraveling of the Hunt's financial empire.

The Hunt silver debacle also provided the setting for my worst trade. My company partner George Fawcett and I had become bullish on silver beginning in June 1978, when it was trading around the $5.00 an ounce level. We were right in the market, and silver prices moved higher. On and off over the next two years we each had accumulated sizeable long silver positions and kept "rolling" them over from contract-month to contract-month. In September 1979, silver reached the high price of $15.00 an ounce, and the profit we were each carrying was substantial. George and I had never before made that kind of money, it was truly a killing. We both started to get very nervous. How much higher could silver go? Wasn't it time to take the profit? Besides, the market seemed to be stuck in the same price range for many weeks. Large profits, as I learned, were even more difficult to handle than large losses.

I had a very good friend who was then a trading manager of a large and prestigious trading firm with special expertise in the precious metals markets. By happenstance, he was in Chicago and we were scheduled for lunch at the Metropolitan Club in Sears Tower. Since he knew I was long silver, I ventured to ask him his opinion. "Well, Leo," he responded, "you have done very well with your silver position and I really can't predict how much higher silver will go. But I'll tell you this, at $15.00 it is very expensive. On the basis of historical values, silver just doesn't warrant much higher prices." I never doubted that he gave me his honest and best opinion.

I transmitted this information to George and we decided that if nothing happened by the end of the week, we would liquidate our positions and take our profits. That's exactly what we did. This was in late October 1979. So why was this my worst trade when in fact it was the biggest profit I had ever made up to that time? Because, within 30 days after we got out of our position, the Hunt silver corner took hold. Silver went crazy, going up the permissible limit day after day. It did not stop going higher until it hit $50.00 an ounce in January 1980. George and I had been long silver for nearly two years, and had we stayed with our position for just another 30 days, we would have been "forced" to take a humongous profit. We both vowed never to calculate how many millions we left on the table.

The IMM's success in financial futures was bound to be imitated. The competition that I knew would some day come, was about to arrive. By

1975, there were signs that the CBOT, the competitor I feared most, had finally seen the light and was going to imitate the IMM's initiative by launching a financial product of its own. For me, it was surprising that we had been free of competition for as long as we had. Years later, the New York financial community would often lament that Chicago was the wrong place for the idea. Well, New York simply didn't want it. It would still be some five years before the New York exchange community would wake up to the new era of financial futures.

The New York Stock Exchange formed its New York Futures Exchange (NYFE) in 1978, but it did not begin trading its foreign currency, T-bill, or U.S. bond contracts until the summer of 1980. It was a frontal attack on Chicago—eight years too late. Actually, in the futures market, eight days can be too late. As I often declared afterward, "The first-eth with the most-eth, win-eth." NYFE chairman, Lewis Horowitz, as intelligent and honest a person as you can find, knew the truth. He privately admitted to me that they didn't have a ghost of a chance. He was quite right. The same year, the COMEX attempted to get into the financial act with a two-year Treasury note contract. It wasn't the same contract as that traded on the IMM, but it was too close. They had no chance either.

Indeed, the axiom about being first has stood fast no matter what instrument of trade or which exchange was involved. You pretty much have to be first with an idea if you are going to have a chance at success in futures. In 1981, the New York Mercantile Exchange (NYMEX) finally moved away from its traditional Maine potato market, which nearly ended its existence with one scandal after another. The NYMEX then launched a revolutionary concept by introducing so-called energy futures: contracts in heating oil and gasoline. These contracts became enormously successful, and when both big guns of Chicago, the CBOT and the CME, attempted to wrest those markets away from the NYMEX, we failed. Over the years, there have been similar attempts by various exchanges from time to time, also without success. The most recent example involves the Deutsche Termin Boerse (DTB) battle for the Bund contract which was launched by the London International Financial Futures Exchange (LIFFE). Since the Bund contract represents the German government bond market, the German-based DTB logically felt that it would win this market. Logic doesn't count. LIFFE launched the Bunds first, and to this date, it remains the dominant market for this contract.

In 1975, there were many instruments to choose from; the financial world offered nearly an unlimited array of untried products for futures trade. It made me feel like a kid in a candy store. But the answer seemed obvious. Since currency and gold were already spoken for, Mark Powers and I felt certain that the next direction would be toward a futures product tied to interest rates. The only real question was, which instrument? The yield curve represented a wide field of assorted attractions, and there were innumerable instruments tied to the fluctuation of interest rates.

Powers lobbied me strongly on behalf of a 90-day U.S. Treasury bill futures contract. The 90-day T-bill, he explained, was the benchmark for the short end of the yield curve. It would provide security dealers with a market in which to layoff their interest rate risk when they purchased and dealt in government debt. His arguments were very persuasive and I was inclined to bow to his economics expertise. But I did some covert investigation on the side. I had learned that at the CBOT, their new chief economist Richard Sandor was planning a mortgage-backed futures contract, or so-called Ginnie Mae (for Government National Mortgage Association). In contrast to the 90-day T-bill, the GNMA represented the long end of the yield curve. Before I made my decision on T-bills, I quietly invited Stanford University finance professor Roger Gray to the Merc for a chat. He was a friend of mine and had been a consultant to the CBOT on its Ginnie Mae contract. What he told me convinced me to go with Powers. While Professor Gray thought the Ginnie Mae contact was a neat idea, he had doubts about its potential for success. There was an inherent delivery problem, he believed, that would hurt the contract's use. I stayed with T-bills.

Now came the hard part. Unlike our listing of currency contracts four years earlier—which required no federal approval—this time around, new contracts required approval by our newly established federal regulator, the CFTC. That approval wouldn't come without some fancy footwork on our part.

It was deja vu. First, I recruited Beryl Sprinkel, now an IMM director, to set up a meeting with his former professor Arthur Burns, chairman of the Federal Reserve. That was pivotal to the approval process. The meeting that followed in the boardroom of the Fed, which also included Mark Powers, is forever ingrained in my memory and could make an interesting and funny short story. Both Burns and Sprinkel were heavy pipe-smokers, and I, of course, was still a chain-smoker. Between the three of us, the smoke was so thick we could hardly see each other.

"What a clever idea," said the chairman of the Fed after we explained what we had in mind. "Such a futures contract would be used by government securities dealers, investment bankers, all sorts of commercial interests as well as speculators, isn't that right?"

"Yes," Sprinkel and I agreed. "Its participants would include every segment of the commercial and speculative world." We talked further about the value of this contract, until the Fed chairman fell into his thoughts. Suddenly, he had a bright idea.

"In such case," Dr. Burns said, "this futures contract would become a terrific predictor of the direction of interest rates, isn't that right, Beryl?"

Beryl Sprinkel hesitated and looked to me for guidance. I didn't know the answer, so I looked up at the ceiling and watched the billows of smoke that had gathered there. Mark Powers too remained silent.

After an embarrassing pause, Beryl thought of a noncommittal response, "Well, Mr. Chairman, it will probably be as good as the Federal Reserve's own econometrics model."

"That," said the chairman of the Fed with a laugh, "isn't worth a shit." It was a refreshing bit of honesty.

That meeting with Dr. Burns evolved into a friendship after I discovered that he and his wife were Yiddishistin like my parents. At their request, I found for them the works of I.L. Peretz in Yiddish which Dr. Burns took with him when he became U.S. Ambassador to Germany.

Having survived this hurdle, I next sought and gained the support of Alan Greenspan, who at the time was chairman of the Council of Economic Advisors. The meeting with him was a shot in the arm. Before I could fully explain our plans for a futures contract in T-bills, Greenspan interrupted.

"What a great idea," said Greenspan, who was destined to become one of this nation's most admired Federal Reserve Board chiefs. He then proceeded to rattle off a dozen uses for such a market, some of which we hadn't even considered. In short, this meeting made him a friend, which he has remained throughout the years. Our friendship was of particular importance at the time of the 1987 stock market crash.

As I was leaving his office, I got a bonus by bumping into Herbert Stein, Greenspan's predecessor at the Council of Economic Advisors. Like any good evangelist, I immediately expounded on why we were there and asked his opinion. Without hesitation Stein quipped, "I don't oppose anything between two consenting adults."

I next turned to the CFTC. Commissioner Gary Seevers quickly understood the potential value of these new interest rate products and became a valuable ally. But now it was up to Bill Bagley, the CFTC chairman. I tried to impress Bagley with the fact that many federal officials were already aboard. But Bagley did not have any financial background and was afraid to take the responsibility for such a revolutionary decision.

"Leo," he implored, "I love you like my brother and want to do it, but I need someone higher up to give me an okay."

"How high up?" I inquired, thinking maybe he was looking for divine intervention.

"Well," Bagley responded, "aren't T-bills the property of the U.S. Treasury? Maybe we need approval, in writing, from someone like the Secretary of Treasury, William Simon."

A tall order. Simon was a fairly new name in Washington D.C. and E.B. Harris' connections provided me with no go-between. To go without proper protection seemed wrong. So I began to call around to some of the senior officials of our clearing members to see if anyone knew Bill Simon.

Sure enough, I hit paydirt. Sanford Weil, the chief of Shearson & Co., was a friend of the Secretary of Treasury. Weil was also a shrewd market analyst and sensed the great potential of our T-bill contract. He agreed to help. I then took one additional precaution. I called on Milton Friedman and asked him to again weave his magic. Friedman obliged by calling Simon and, by the time Sandy Weil and I appeared before him at the Treasury in winter of 1975, it was a done deal. He quickly agreed and signed the prepared approval letter to Bagley.

The T-bill futures specifications presented yet another tricky problem. The traditional method of trading stocks and commodities results in a bid that is lower than the offer. When a commodity or stock is bought and the price goes up, the purchaser has a profit. When the price goes down, he has a loss. Conversely, if he has sold short and the price goes down, he has a profit, and when the price goes up, he has a loss.

This is contrary to the trade of interest rates. In trading T-bills and other instruments that are quoted on a yield basis, it is normal that the bid is higher than the offer because of the inverse relationship of yield and prices. If the T-bill is to be sold at a greater yield, the price of the bill will go down, and vice versa. Thus, to trade interest rates as is done in the cash market, our traders would have to think inversely. It would mean that a bid would effectively have to be *above* the offer. That, I judged, would be difficult in pit conditions. The members might shun such a pit. What I needed were T-bill specifications that would conform to traditional methods of trading in futures and still be understood by professional cash money traders. To solve the problem, I turned to my T-bill Specifications Committee, which included Melvin Unterman, Philip Glass, William Goldstandt, and Atlee Kohl.

We brainstormed the problem for weeks, and it seemed there was no solution. But I refused to give up, and urged everyone to keep thinking. Then, over one weekend, Mel Unterman, who was a former banker, came to me with a brilliant solution: "We will trade the IMM index." His idea was based on the difference between the actual T-bill yield and 100.00 percent. Thus, a T-bill yield of 6.00 percent would be quoted on the IMM at 94.00. (If the bid price went higher, say 94.05, it meant the rate was a little lower, at 5.95 percent.) While this index did not change reality—higher prices still meant lower rates—it brought normalcy to the futures pit. A bid was again *below* the offer. When someone bought our contract and the IMM index went up, the individual will have made money. Of course, when a person expects interest rates to go up, he would be a seller of the IMM index since the price of the bill will drop as interest rates go up—just as it does in the cash market. On the other hand, if a person expects interest rates to fall, he would be a buyer of the IMM index since the price of the bill will rise as interest rates go down. We applied the IMM index not only for T-bills, but also for certificates of deposit (CDs) and Eurodollars. Unterman's idea was to become the standard for futures interest trade worldwide.

On January, 6, 1976, Milton Friedman did the honors, ringing the opening bell on the IMM's T-bill contract and ushering in the era of interest rate futures. Again I hit the marketing road. With each new product, I had to pay my dues all over again. I was feeling a bit like the newspaper man who writes a banner story one day only to be prodded the next by a hungry editor with, "What you got for me today?" Each futures product had to carry its own weight no matter how successful the exchange was as an entity. Just as the idea of currency futures had to be sold to banks, the idea of T-bill futures had to be sold to investment bankers. I knew if I could convince one of the premier investment bankers, then surely the others would follow. I targeted Salomon Brothers.

With some difficulty, I arranged to meet in New York with senior partner William Salomon. He listened carefully as I began. "T-bill futures," I explained, "will also become a good hedging device against rate volatility in instruments other than governments, such as commercial paper, bankers' acceptances, agency paper, and certificates of deposit. T-bills also offer a primary market of more than $3 billion and a secondary market with daily trading volume of up to $5 billion, making it a highly liquid market."

I could see in his face what I had seen in so many others when I first tried to sell currencies in the early IMM days: a look of doubt suffused with skepticism, and even a bit of fear that I might get violent. And each time I had to remind myself that there were only a handful of brave soldiers compared with the armies who viewed the idea of financial futures with disdain.

"This is not for Salomon," he said, giving me the clear impression that he didn't believe it would ever work. Then, as any good trader would do, Salomon hedged, "However, if you can prove it will work, rest assured Salomon will become your number one trader." I was then practically asked to leave the premises.

T-bills became one of those rare futures instruments: an instant success. After the first year, I got a telephone call from Tom Strauss, then executive vice president of Salomon Brothers, who had arranged the original meeting with his boss Bill Salomon.

"Are we persona non grata at the Merc?" Strauss sheepishly asked. I laughed. "Are you kidding?" Salomon Brothers was one of the biggest names in the business. It was a huge prize to make them an IMM member. "I hold no grudges," I said, and did even better. A year later, I appointed Tom Strauss to the IMM board. Strauss would eventually become president of Salomon Brothers. As promised, his firm became the number one user of our T-bill market and a friend of the IMM for all time.

Another important early user of T-bill futures was a Kansas banker named Wayne Angell. Directly after our T-bill contract opened in 1976, Dr. Angell, who was the owner of the Council Grove National Bank, read an account about the IMM's new market in the Wall Street Journal. It piqued his curiosity so he did a little investigating, called me by telephone for further information, and made some calculations. What Angell recognized was a profitable opportunity. He sold T-notes, bought T-bill futures of the same duration, executing an arbitrage that had little risk and resulted in 140 basis point increase of the Bank's portfolio yield. It provided a handsome profit. Wayne Angell, who was destined to become a member of the Fed Board of Governors where he served this nation with distinction, remained a staunch supporter of our markets.

It was just about that time that I uncovered the curious fact that very few of the American banks or investment bankers had ever actually used futures. Indeed, they were nearly devoid of knowledge about the open outcry system, its order-entry procedure, its floor practices, or anything else. They didn't even know that the futures market settled its open positions in cash on a mark-to-market basis at the end of every business day. I remember Tom Strauss's embarrassment when he had to ask me some rudimentary questions about our markets. This represented a serious problem, because, until that community understood our marketplace, they would avoid using it. I thought of a solution. I would have to assume my inherited occupation as a teacher.

My firm, Dellsher Investment Company, suddenly became a teaching institute. Over time, any number of the blue bloods in finance—such as Salomon Brothers, or Manny Hanny, or Chase Manhattan, or so many other Wall Streeters that I had enticed to the futures arena—had some of their first futures markets lessons under the tutelage of Valerie Turner, the chief operating officer at Dellsher. As soon as their formative lessons were over, I would literally push them out the Dellsher door. "You've graduated," I would to say, "now open your own clearing firm and bring your customers to the IMM." I knew that for the IMM to succeed, it was imperative that the New York financial community become our members and bring us their business.

240 THE FUTURE'S NOT WHAT IT USED TO BE

Over the next six years, Treasury bill futures would become the most actively traded contract at the IMM, providing security dealers with a huge security blanket and ensuring the success of interest rate futures. As interest-rate trading took hold, the CME became the home for the short end of the yield curve, and the CBOT for the long end. With the benefit of hindsight, we can now assess the decisions of that era. First, Professor Gray was correct that the GNMA contract would not become a great success. As he predicted, it ran into delivery problems. But neither Gray, Powers, nor Melamed could guess that Doc Richard Sandor would quickly realize the truth about the Ginnie Mae contract and transform his idea into the CBOT's hugely successful 30-year Treasury bond futures contract. As a result, Sandor not only brought the CBOT into the financial futures arena in a big way, he secured that exchange's future. Without long bonds, the CBOT would today be but a shadow of the market it has become.

Looking back, clearly I would have liked to have the long-term bonds at the Merc as well. But to go after the long end of the market, we would have had to take on a competitor when the field to an alternative instrument was wide open. The CBOT seemed to have the upper hand anyway because their GNMA contract, already trading there, was a long maturity instrument. On the other hand, we already had a successful contract at the other end of the yield curve, the 90-day T-bill contract. And Mark Powers, as well as the other economists who advised us, believed that the world was moving to the middle range of the interest rate spectrum rather than to the long range. They all liked the idea of listing a four-year Treasury note contract. Of course, this turned out to be a terrible mistake. The four-year contract bombed and, in fact, never had a chance. The 30-year bond contract was a huge success.

But there was an immense reward for staying with the short end of the yield curve. It was a thought that I kept carefully tucked away in the back of my mind and discussed only with E.B Harris, Mark Powers, and several members of my inner circle. I became convinced, after discussions with a number of international economists and bankers, that the ultimate short-term interest rate futures market would be Eurodollars—U.S. dollar deposits outside the United States held by individuals, companies, banks, and central banks. T-bills were a U.S. short-term instrument. But 90-day Eurodollars were the universal benchmark of short-term interest rates worldwide. Its pool of users dwarfed all competitive instruments, potentially making Eurodollars the all-time greatest futures contract. It was a prize worth coveting.

My strategy was simple and based on what I knew for certain: liquidity is the key to success of a market, and spreading is a key to liquidity. All short-term interest rate contracts had a strong correlation. I knew a trader could spread positions between T-bills and other short-term rate contracts, but wouldn't be able to spread between a short-term and a long-term interest rate instrument. Therefore, I knew that if the Merc secured the short range of the yield curve, it would go a long way toward guaranteeing the Eurodollar contract for the IMM. In other words, by continuing with the development of our 90-day T-bill market and later, for the same reason, a 90-day certificate of deposit (CD) market, it meant we would position ourselves to beat any competitor in a Eurodollar contest.

The strategy proved enormously successful. The domestic CD contract was contested by the CBOT as well as at the newly created NYFE. But because our members could spread T-bills against CDs, the IMM blew everyone away. By the time the Eurodollar contract was approved for trade several years later, no other U.S. exchange would dare to take us on. Thus, while Doc Sandor's 30-year T-bond contract saved the day for the CBOT, our 90-day T-bill decision secured for the IMM the short end of the yield curve and gained for us the greatest interest-rate prize of all: the Eurodollar contract.

I also knew that an exchange shouldn't launch too many products at one time. Launching new products requires a great deal of strategy, planning, money, and human resources. There are only so many traders to go around. So we had to plan very carefully and accept the fact that from time to time we would judiciously leave some products on the table. If an exchange bit off more than it could chew, it was going to choke on its ambition. Ultimately, not only would it hand over the market to a competitor, it would end up giving the institution a loser image. A bad image is a death knell to the future of an exchange.

There was yet another reward for the decisions of that period. If the Merc had beat the odds and won the long bonds, thereby keeping the CBOT out of financial futures, we would have been a loser in the long run. Alone in the unending confrontations with the CFTC or Congress, we might never have succeeded. It takes more than one exchange to make an industry. With the CBOT's successful entry into finance, the Merc suddenly had an influential and ardent ally when it came to the battles in Washington. Suddenly, our greatest competitor became our strongest confederate—at least when it came to the regulatory wars. We could never overestimate the value this represented. Together, time and again, we marshalled the clout and power to defend our Chicago market turf and turn back common competitors or enemies of futures. Separately, we might have failed.

20

The Grand Design

Of one thing I was certain by the mid-1970s: agriculture was never going to be the future. But finance was. If the Chicago Mercantile Exchange had any future, it was on the back of the International Monetary Market. But that was something I couldn't prove in 1975 because the currencies and financial futures still had a long way to go. One had to believe. And at the moment, the agricultural markets were still on top and in a boom. Meat market transaction volume was consistently at record levels and, by comparison, the financial markets looked like weak sisters. To believe in their potential, one had to see far beyond the immediate volume picture. After all, financial futures were only three years old.

The majority of the Merc membership went along with me. But not all. There were some, mostly the old guard, who had doubts. Times were good, and many of them thought the meats would go on forever. Why did anyone need a silly currency and a Treasury bill market? Futures were for agriculture not finance. These members had gone along with me merely for the immediate profit the new IMM seat would put in their pockets. They had, after all, received the IMM seat for a mere $100 and could now sell it for an $18,000 or $20,000 profit. Not a bad trade at all. There was, of course, a mirror image to this picture. There were CME members who believed so much in financial markets that they sold off their CME seats to remain solely IMM members.

I saw the rumblings of a problem in the making. The IMM was a separate exchange with its own bylaws and governing board, and once Merc members sold their IMM seats, they were no longer IMM members. Their loyalty was suddenly divided. They could no longer trade in the financial markets. Human nature being what it is, these non-IMMers began to look unfavorably at the IMM. In fact, as the IMM grew and its seat values rose in response, the sold-out IMM members looked foolish for having sold too soon. No one likes to make a bad trade. It served to increase their antagonism.

As more CME members took their IMM seat profit, the non-IMM contingent grew. As this group grew, so did its hostility. They were like a fifth column within our midst. They began to look at the IMM with hostile eyes. "Those IMM guys are using our floor." "They're drinking our coffee." To make matters worse, the ranks of non-IMMers were joined by another group of members, new CME seat purchasers whose seat privilege included only the agricultural markets. These CME members had never been IMM members and had no allegiance to the financial contracts whatsoever. This division within our ranks began to create tensions with respect to equitable use of floor space and facilities between the two exchanges. The lack of adequate space added to the problem. Much of the programmed expansion area in the new Merc building had been taken over by the IMM, and more space would be needed for the gold, silver coin, and T-bill contracts scheduled to be listed.

With each passing day, I recognized that this problem was getting worse. So far, the negativism was subdued and usually only spoken in whispers. After all, no one openly wanted to attack my "child." But it only takes a few rabble-rousers to cause a problem, and every now and then, the dissenting voices reached the boardroom. Some of the gripes had the ring of legitimacy. For instance, there was a demand to have the IMM pay for the use of the CME facilities. Of course, this was anticipated, and from the beginning I had arranged with our financial expert, Ira Marcus, to allocate certain charges to the IMM. But because the IMM was a fledgling exchange without money, the allocation was very favorable. If the IMM were forced to pay the full value for its use of Merc facilities, public relations, educational material, personnel, and so on, it would be bankrupt in no time. The potential of financial contracts might then never evolve and the future of the Merc might disappear into thin air.

And antagonism is a two-edged sword. IMM members also began to get hostile. They viewed the non-IMMer complaints as sour grapes and insincere: *they had sold their IMM memberships too soon . . . they were shortsighted.* To IMM members, there was no doubt that finance was the future of futures.

By June 1975, I began to believe that if this festering problem were left unattended, it would grow to rip the CME apart and create a civil war on the trading floor between Merc members and IMM members. "If this virus of bickering and squabbling is allowed to continue," I said to our Board, "it will spread to infect the entire Exchange and will, without fail, be the cause of the stagnation, if not the downfall, of our institution. We must prevent this at all cost." I meant every word. I saw what was happening at the Chicago Board of Trade as a result of its relationship with the Chicago Board Options Exchange (CBOE) in the 1973 spinoff. There was animosity between the sister exchanges that created a wall of independence, competition, and divided loyalty. From the start, the CBOE had been treated like a stepchild with its different markets and different players from those of the CBOT. The result was two separate cultures and growing antagonism, especially when equities were booming and commodities were at a lull. The schism remained, and each exchange existed as a separate entity, eventually housed in its own building. I didn't relish that prospect for the Merc and IMM. The CBOT experience and what it foretold reinforced what I had always believed: one can't transfer a culture, or superimpose it like some penciled plastic overlay on a map; one must live a culture. There had to be a better way than the CBOT's; a way of maintaining a unified culture under the same roof. But it would take more than pride and nostalgia to keep the markets separate *and* unified.

While the growing divisiveness problem was my priority, it was not my only concern. I often talked about the other difficulties we faced with my fellow board members. In the drive to make the Merc number one in the world, I knew that the CME was severely hampered because it had a limited number of members. Members are the most precious asset exchanges have—they are the bodies who bring life and liquidity into the trading forum. The more members at an exchange, the stronger its potential. When I took over the Merc, we were 500 strong. That's the limit of memberships prescribed in the CME charter. When the IMM was created, an additional 150 seats were sold, swelling our ranks to a total of 650 members. But the CBOT, our greatest rival, had more than twice that number. How could we compete or overtake our competitor when we were less than half their size. And our recent successes tended to make things worse. It led to higher membership prices, making it more difficult to add new members to the exchange. Membership values create vested interests, which are diluted when additional members are added. Members dislike dilution of membership values.

There was another problem that complicated everything. The CME members were concentrating their efforts trading cattle, hogs, and pork bellies. As a result, there were insufficient numbers to trade the other nonfinancial Merc markets we had been promoting, such as lumber, boneless beef, hams, milo, potatoes, and turkeys; or markets in the future, markets that were still only a hope and a dream—financial or otherwise. If the existing markets were underutilized, how could the Merc expect to promote new markets not yet listed? This problem could not be solved simply by adding new members, even if the rules would allow it. As E.B. Harris liked to say, "It is easier to keep a bicycle in motion than it is to get it going." I knew that whatever structure we devised for the Exchange, it had to force members to concentrate on certain products. This approach was proved three years earlier when the IMM was launched. The separate memberships we sold limited traders' activities to the financials. It worked. The new flow of

IMM traders gave the financial contracts continuous liquidity and a promising start. The zest for puffery to bolster a new contract could take us just so far. In the end, we needed bodies in a pit on a daily basis to keep the markets viable.

The best solutions are those that solve many problems. What I had in mind for the Merc went far beyond merger between the CME and the IMM. My plan would attempt to address all three of the fundamental problems we were facing. I formed a committee to focus on the reorganization and said to the members in a report I carefully crafted: "The fault in our structure is more pronounced than the figure of 500 would indicate. This limitation of members not only hurts the liquidity of the Merc's trading pits, it inhibits our future." At the same time I told the committee that reorganization must not shatter the Merc's original unity. As a French philosopher once said: "Break your chains and you are free, but break your roots and you die." It would take a carefully drawn blueprint keyed to the realities that existed to keep the Merc's roots intact.

The grand design I put forward was intended to serve both masters: unity and separation. It would create a divisional structure within a unified Merc. The CME and IMM would merge, with the CME as the surviving exchange. Divisional seats would be created to allow for trading *only* in the contracts listed within that division. The IMM would become the financial market division of the Merc, and IMM members would maintain their separate seats within this division. Existing CME seat holders as well as new CME purchasers would gain the privilege of trading in *all* Merc markets, including the markets listed in any of the divisions. A second division would also be created, tentatively called the Non-Livestock Market (NLM) division, whose members could trade only eggs, lumber, milo, butter, and frozen turkeys. (Not long after, the NLM was renamed the Associate Mercantile Market or AMM division. Ultimately, it became the Index & Options (IOM) division.) Although, to my knowledge, the concept proposed had never before been attempted at any exchange, I felt certain that it would work. (Years later, the CBOT basically copied this divisional design.)

I also believed that the plan would address the other issues we were facing. It was a formula to grow the Exchange by bringing it fresh blood, yet limiting activities to designated markets. And most important, it would immediately put an end to the divisiveness between our members. Since all CME members would be allowed to trade IMM products, the hostility stemming from allocation of space and facilities would end. And since the vast majority of Merc members still owned an IMM seat, the plan created an incentive for a sale or transfer of this seat to a new member who would be limited to financial contracts. This meant that, over time, as more IMM seats went into the hands of new members, the IMM membership ranks could grow to a total of 650. When you added that number to the original 500 CME members, the Merc would become double its premerger size. Add to that number the memberships to be issued in the NLM division, or other future divisions, and the Merc had the formula by which to continue to expand. In retrospect, it is now clear that the Merc's divisional structure was key to its ultimate success, enabling it to grow at a faster pace than any exchange in the world.

But the merger didn't come easy. First the plan had to pass the most difficult referendum in Merc history. It became a major controversy, and I lobbied as hard as I had lobbied for anything in my life. Many of the meetings were one-on-one. And each meeting was important because the Merc was at a critical juncture. I met with both sides: CME members and IMM members, those for the merger and those against. This was a merger for all seasons, but to be accepted, it had to be understood and explained. And once again I had to look beyond the here and now.

For Merc members, it was an easier case to make. They were getting their markets back, and they could now sell their IMM seats without losing trading rights. Corky Labkon, one of my loyalists, who came to the Merc from Arthur Andersen, said to me that "speaking as a lawyer and a CPA, I can tell you that this is a terrific deal for everyone." Corky was a hog trader and the merger would give him a chance to trade the financials. Similarly, Girard Miller, a staunch CME member who supported the merger, was tireless in his efforts on its behalf. But the IMM was asking, "Why are we giving them our markets?" "What are we getting in return?" It was a difficult concept to explain. The IMM contracts looked so promising to IMM members that it was hard for them to understand that this promise could never materialize without the complete backing of the CME. Potential has to have the right environment for fulfillment.

I remember my conversation with Randy McKay, one of the young, immensely successful IMM currency traders. He was an IMM blue blood who had come to the Merc with his brother Terry in 1970. They started as runners for Packers Trading Co., having been introduced to the floor by one of my lieutenants, Mike Sturch. Highly intelligent and ambitious, the IMM gave the McKay brothers a chance to shine, with Terry later using his trading profits to launch a successful career in real estate. They were both patriotic IMM members with influential voices who understood the IMM's immense potential. But Randy McKay was against the merger. He was among the IMM Turks who had absolutely no doubt that the IMM was going to be bigger than the Merc someday. I agreed, but only if the merger passed. I lobbied him hard because I knew a lot of people would listen to him. It was a hard sell, but finally I wore him down. It helped that he also believed in me.

"Leo," said Randy McKay in the end, "I'm going to vote for the merger and I don't even know why. I think you could sell refrigerators to Eskimos. I never thought it would happen, but I'm going to give you my vote."

The IMM members had to be convinced that they needed a unified community that included the Merc's infrastructure, real estate, clout, and money. After all, the IMM had been built on the back of the Merc, its resources, knowledge, and people, a fact that the naysayers had overlooked. Without the Merc, the IMM couldn't exist. At this point, it wasn't anything yet.

In early October, the boards of the Merc and IMM approved the reorganization plan proposed by the special committee. The referendum was to take place on November 3. The day before the vote, a meeting was held in the Bismarck Hotel to air the issues. There was a standing-room only crowd. A thousand eyes were focused on me as I spoke for an hour pointing out the problems and why the merger was imperative to the future of both exchanges. Antagonism and defiance crackled through the air.

Members' meetings were a sacred heritage at Chicago exchanges. They were much more than a ritual required in the bylaws. They represented a legacy that the citizens of this nation inherited from the early days of this republic, when the town hall meeting was the only means to publicly air a concern or confront an issue. A decade before, it was a members' meeting that provided me the opportunity to challenge the leadership of the Merc, thereby changing its course of history. And I had vowed that no matter how difficult such meetings were for the leadership or board of the CME, it was a trust that must never be broken. It represented the moment in time when any member could ask any question directly to the chairman. And more important, the member would have the opportunity for the entire audience to hear the question and the answer. Indeed, it was the latter consequence that was central to the process. At a meeting, the member's question—sometimes deeply embarrassing to the administration—was being addressed, not in the privacy of the chairman's office, or in private correspondence, or even in a memorandum disseminated to the entire membership (where responses can be carefully crafted), but in an open forum where all the members could hear the spontaneity of the answer, judge the honesty of the response, and have the ability to follow up immediately with another question. In other words, a members' meeting allowed debate, the lifeblood of a democracy—and of an exchange.

The us versus them tension at the members' meeting in November 1975 was typified by the granite-faced Izzy Mulmat, a Merc stalwart, who at that moment reminded me of a Tuscan gargoyle leering down

from the tower of a medieval church. Izzy epitomized the old guard who
had opposed the IMM from the outset. Indeed, Izzy even refused to put
up the token fee required to purchase an IMM membership. On the
other hand, his son, Maxwell "Buddy" Mulmat, was totally committed to
the IMM and the new era it represented. He paid the required $100 for
Izzy's IMM seat, which ironically served to be his father's nest egg after
its enormous appreciation over the years. Today, the Mulmats proudly
claim a third-generation Merc citizen, with Peter Mulmat, Izzy's grandson, as an outstanding IMM currency trader.

"What do we need the IMM for?" Izzy Mulmat demanded in a booming baritone voice. "They're using our space. They're using our chalk-
boards. They're breathing our air."

Indeed we were. The implication was quite clear: Melamed was using
the Merc's money and its infrastructure to nurture the IMM—a fact I
couldn't deny. What was the Merc going to get in return? *The markets of
the future.*

In contrast, Robert Swedlow, an IMM trader and patriot, defiantly
stood up to ask the opposite, "Leo, the IMM is giving new markets to the
CME; what is the CME giving the IMM in return?"

"Life," I replied. I meant it.

The CME voted 343 to 23 in favor of the plan and the IMM members
approved it 396 to 57. Thus the IMM was merged into the CME as a division. The merger gave the IMM a sound financial base for its future
growth, with all past debt forgiven. The CME, in turn, gained access to
the potential of the IMM, whose markets would become the world's most
active. In January 1976, after the election of the new CME board, I was
unanimously elected the first chairman of the reorganized—and unified—
Chicago Mercantile Exchange.

I wanted the chairmanship for a number of reasons. First, for historical
purposes: to be the first chairman of the newly merged CME and IMM exchange. Second, because implicit with this role was the opportunity to permanently fashion the new exchange in accordance with the way I thought it
should look and operate. I was particularly determined that the combined
set of bylaws replace some of the archaic CME rules with the modern rules
and concepts invented by the IMM. For instance, it was imperative to include the IMM's Good-to-the-Last-Drop clearing member bond so that the
financial strength of the combined clearinghouse would at least be equal to
that of its former sibling. To carry out this task, I established a special rules
committee and personally directed the process with Jerry Salzman constantly at my side. It took the better part of a year, but at the end of my term,
on December 21, 1976, the combined rules of the CME and IMM were
adopted. They formed the foundation for the modern Merc.

Still another reason for wanting to be chairman was to smooth the feathers ruffled by the merger referendum and to establish the framework for the Merc's permanent unification. My instincts told me that this must not be a merger in name only. The single most important element that had moved the Merc into the forefront of the futures industry was, in a word, unity. "It was a unique force of unity of purpose by our members which enabled the CME to innovate, to explore, to brazenly promote our ideas, and in the end, to succeed," I had said. To build a unified structure for the future was my mission. I spent the entire year working at it, talking to members of both divisions, getting their ideas, and feeling their pulse. Under the reorganization, the CME board was expanded from 12 to 18, with 4 new representatives from the IMM and 2 from the NLM. But it was equally important to merge the committee structure. Except in matters unique to agriculture, I wanted no separation in responsibilities. When members work on a committee together, they get to know and trust each other. It was strange but really not surprising that the members of the two divisions were remarkably similar—similar ideas, similar problems, similar solutions. Indeed, throughout the ensuing years, whenever a referendum was held, without exception, the majority of members in each division voted the same way.

In my view, one of the most significant post-merger innovations that I championed over objections by many board members and clearing members alike, was the rule that put a permanent bed-rock floor on the price of Merc memberships. It was no small accomplishment. I knew that membership values were the pride and joy of the rank and file, and under no circumstance would I participate in a exchange structure that put undue pressure on the value of these seats.

Under the rules, every clearing member of both the CME and the IMM had at least four memberships in the exchange, two CMEs and two IMMs. There were many who felt that with merger they could sell off two of the memberships. "Over my dead body," I told Everette Harris and Barry Lind at the time we wrote the merger rules. "From now on, every clearing member will need at least two memberships in every division the Merc creates, now and forever." I would not budge nor compromise. In establishing this principle, I was strengthening not only the financial integrity of our clearing members, I was ensuring that a large number of divisional memberships would remain permanently in financially-strong hands and off the market. This rule has remained the hallmark of the Merc clearinghouse and was later applied to the IOM when this division was created.

There is a footnote to the 1976 CME-IMM merger. The merger obviously occurred long before the financial markets matured into the King Kong they would become, eventually accounting for more than 95 percent of the Merc's volume. To reach this glory was precisely the purpose of the merger. But at that time, the CME members were kings of the hill. Their transaction volume was by far the dominant factor in the Merc's income and strength. We had to recognize this reality in allocating voting power between the CME and its divisions, otherwise we would never get the CME members' vote. I huddled with Barry Lind on this issue at great length and insisted that we establish a vote-weighting structure that favored the founding membership. I had looked upon the Merc as the parent, and the IMM and other divisions as its children. The rights commensurate with parenthood had to be permanently written into stone so that the children could never unfairly gang up on the parent. I called it my "covenant" with the CME. But the reverse had to be true as well: the CME membership should not be able to unfairly act against their offspring. What was needed was a perfect voting balance, and I asked Barry Lind to do the figuring; that was his expertise. "I think you are asking for the impossible," Barry said at first, but I knew he could do it. What resulted was a weighted system that would keep the parent safe from the children—and vice versa—in essence, preserving our roots. Every CME member got six votes, every IMM member got two votes, and every AMM (IOM) member got one vote. It also reflected their respective representation on the board. The 6-2-1 system was written into the foundation of the newly reorganized Chicago Mercantile Exchange.

At that time, I said to some of the more influential Merc members, including Joel Greenberg who was on the CME Board: "I'm going to give you this right, but you must never use it as a weapon because these children must be allowed to grow. The divisional members are going to need financing, and space, and promotion. The weighted vote is a means of control. But, don't use it as a sword, only as a shield." Greenberg understood, he was a strong friend and a highly successful cattle and belly trader. In fact, Greenberg had been instrumental in making the Merc "the house that pork bellies built." Greenberg was nobody's fool. Just because he had made his money and career in agriculture didn't mean that he couldn't visualize the huge potential of the financials. He and the others agreed. Ironically, two decades later, in 1994, this issue would resurface after the tables had been turned upside down, and the agricultural contracts were the weak sisters of the CME.

21

Power and Leadership

As 1977 drew near, a personal decision I had made remained firm. I would again step down from the office of chairman. I had thought about it countless times and always came to the same conclusion: my mission had been fulfilled—or so I honestly thought. Officially, I had been chairman of the Merc for three years (1969 through 1971), then chairman of the IMM another four (1972 through 1975), and again chairman of the Merc during 1976. In reality, it was even longer than that. I had led the CME from the years of takeover, beginning in 1965, which brought me to the Board in 1967. That would make it a full dozen years I had shaped the Merc. The time period represented the most significant epoch in the history of the Chicago Mercantile Exchange.

To say I was satisfied with my accomplishments would be an incredible understatement. Although I certainly did not do it alone—I had the assistance of many dedicated floor members, Board members, and staff—I had introduced financial futures to the world. With the help of my inner circle, my elite floor corps, and countless floor traders, I presided over the rebirth of the Merc, leading it from a dismal past and bringing it to the threshold of a bright future. And without exaggeration or conceit, I was certain that the majority of the members of the Chicago Mercantile Exchange and the futures industry would make a similar assessment about my years of leadership. E.B. Harris paid me the highest tribute by calling it the "Era of Leo Melamed."

There was also no doubt in my mind that if I chose to continue as CME chairman, I would be unanimously elected by the Board and have the full backing of the membership. But precisely for all those reasons, I thought it was time to step down. As every good actor will say, it is best to leave the stage while the audience is still wildly applauding. And like every actor, I wanted to be loved by everyone. But of course this is impossible. I knew that if I did not share the limelight with others, inevitably, over time, resentment would replace approval. It was human nature. Thus, my decision to step down was unalterable. But this left me on the horns of a terrible dilemma. What should I do about my future Exchange involvement. I was only 45. I could either leave the Board altogether, or run for reelection as another governor of the Merc as so many other chairmen had done before me. Neither alternative was acceptable.

To remove myself entirely from the governing body of the Merc was unthinkable. Too much of my blood flowed through its veins. On the other hand, to simply sit as another governor after my unique role seemed equally unsuitable. Nor did anyone on the Board want me to do that. I was, so to speak, the inventor of the game. Indeed, everyone I talked with, Board or floor member alike, wanted me to continue in an active leadership capacity. But how? I huddled with my inner circle, which at this time was made up of all my trusted friends: Barry Lind, Les Rosenthal, Henry Jarecki, Larry Rosenberg, Beverly Splane, and E.B. Harris.

The behind-the-scenes conversations led to a new idea. Why not create a special office to which I could be appointed by the Board. From such a post, it was reasoned, I could continue to serve in a leadership capacity, but would share the responsibility with a chairman who would be the titular head of the exchange. That solution would substantially overcome my objections to continuing in an exclusive role at the top. It sounded right. When the idea was tested with representatives of the membership, it received overwhelming approval. It seemed to serve the floor's desire to find a means to show its appreciation and keep me involved. The title we eventually settled upon was special counsel to the Board. My detractors would later say, "He was crowned emperor." In a sense, of course, it turned into a kind of super-chairmanship. I insisted, however, that the post require Board reappointment every two years since it would not require election by the membership. In this way, I reasoned, the Board reserved its right to change its mind.

I remember the last Board meeting in December 1976, when, over objections from most Board members as an unnecessary gesture, I insisted on leaving the boardroom so that the idea could be discussed freely outside of my presence. It was an immensely odd and uncomfortable feeling to be outside of the Merc boardroom while it was in session—the first time in over a decade. It was a feeling I did not again experience until I really did retire from the Merc in 1991. (As the members liked to say, "Leo has retired from the Merc many times.") The office of special counsel was unanimously created by the Board and I reentered the circle of leadership in a new capacity, one I held for the next 14 years.

But first, of course, in February 1977, the members held one of my (what was to become) ritual retirement parties. It was a roast with all the trimmings, sponsored by Larry Rosenberg, Dan Jesser, Joel Greenberg, and Beverly Splane. It was at this event that Beverly Splane first uttered the words "Melamed is a legend in his own mind." Barry Lind led the attack, and Morrie Kravitz played on his guitar something entitled "Melamdovich" with words that he wrote and sang in his raspy voice to the tune of the *"Ballad of Davy Crockett."* In addition, some of the Merc stalwarts gave me an inscribed Thank You plaque, the traditional gold watch, and put together a fund for a Melamed Prize in economics at the University of Chicago.

Although from that day forward I was never again chairman of the CME, our members soon recognized what is best explained by a Winston Churchill vignette. The great man had been invited to the house of a very prominent British socialite for a gala dinner. "Mr. Churchill," said the lady of the house when he arrived, "I want you to sit at the head of the table." Winston Churchill paused to look at his hostess and without hesitation replied, "Madam, wherever I sit is the head of the table."

My point is simple. Leadership is not something one attains by virtue of where one sits or the title one assumes. I didn't need the title for legitimacy. Although from the time I became special counsel, I would always work in harmony with the CME chairman—and share with him the responsibilities and spotlight—the world and our membership understood the reality and continued to view me as the leader of the Merc.

At the time I became special counsel, everyone wanted it to happen, but today looking back, it was probably a mistake. Over the years, as the membership changed dramatically, there was a stream of new members with a vague sense of Merc's history, who would look at me as sort of a dictator. I wasn't surprised that the wave of new traders in the late 1980s and early 1990s would sometimes wonder why I wasn't subject to the election process like everyone else. Many of them didn't know my history. They all knew a little of the past, but it was more like a legend. (The first comprehensive history of the Merc by Bob Tamarkin wasn't published until 1993, two years after I retired from official exchange duties.) I used to joke that I had to come on the floor every day to show the crowd that the legend really existed. Still, to the very end of my tenure, the majority of the Merc membership never wavered in its support of my status.

The CME chairmanship election process is different from the Board of Trade where the chairman is elected from the membership at large. At the CME, the chairman is chosen from those members elected to the Board. There are pros and cons with both processes, but the Merc's method allowed for continuity. Although I seldom involved myself with the jockeying that went on for other board positions, I was very careful about whom I would support for chairman. In a boardroom situation, one soon learns who the potential leaders are, whether they are honest, whether they have both feet on the ground, and whether they could be trusted to publicly represent the Merc. And as long as I was special counsel, any governor who ran for the chairmanship needed my full support to make it. While the voting process was in secret, the Board members faithfully followed my lead. Still, as I sometimes learned the hard way, mistakes can be made. I became mentor to a foursome that included John Geldermann, Larry Rosenberg, Jack Sandner, and Brian Monieson. Each had particular strengths I admired, and I felt comfortable with any one of them in the chairman's role. They, in turn, were happy to share the decision-making process and responsibilities with me.

In 1974 and 1975, I had backed John Geldermann as chairman. It was a time when his talents in communications and computers were particularly well suited for the Exchange. Although public speaking and charisma were not the long suit of this rock-ribbed Republican, Geldermann was straight as an arrow. It was this trait that attracted me most to him since I was still deathly afraid that the Merc might slip back into its sub-rosa ways of the past. As long as the chairman would protect the rules of the Exchange, I figured that I could continue to represent the Exchange in Washington and other public forums. It turned out to be the perfect combination. Geldermann and I became strong friends who worked in total cooperation. Neither of us ever had any doubts that our genuine interest was the betterment of the CME. I backed him again for chairmanship in 1989 and 1990.

After I became special counsel in 1977, Larry Rosenberg replaced me as Merc chairman. Rosenberg was vice chairman of my clearing firm Dellsher Investment Co., but our friendship went beyond business. He came to the Merc from the CBOT and I helped elect him to our Board. Our common Jewish and cultural backgrounds resulted in the Rosenbergs, Larry and his wife Joan, becoming close social friends to Betty and me. He was well educated, honest, and knew and understood the floor, making it easy for me to back him for Merc chairman after my departure. It was a good decision. Although he was much more private about his personal life than I, he took an avid interest in national politics and agreed with my agenda of active political participation for the Merc in order to build a Washington power base. His Democratic leanings didn't always mesh with my conservative bent, nevertheless we always found common ground with respect to CME issues. Rosenberg had two special qualities that held a particular attraction for me: his keen sense of humor and the fact that he always dressed with panache. The latter secretly made most of our Board jealous. We remained good friends during his tenure and often traveled around the world together preaching futures and expanding the Merc's internationalism. Rosenberg was Merc chairman from 1977 to 1979, and its vice chairman, first in 1976, then from 1983 through 1987.

Jack Sandner, who was president of Rufenacht, Bromagen & Hertz, Inc. (RB&H), followed Rosenberg as chairman in 1980 through 1982, and took the position again in 1986 through 1988 after serving as second vice chairman in 1978 and 1979. His initial election to the chairmanship was the only time that I encountered a serious political fight with another faction on the Board. Donald Minnuciani, a long-standing Board member, was backed for the chairman post by my old adversary Bill Katz. Minnuciani was a thoughtful and very decent fellow, but I had decided that Sandner's speaking ability would make him a better chairman. It was a critical test of my political strength on the Board, and I went all out to elect Sandner. The vote went my way, bringing Sandner to the attention of our membership and creating for him a slot in the hierarchy of the CME. Primarily because of my backing, Sandner was an officer of the CME in one capacity or another for a longer stretch than the others. As a result, he spent a great deal of time at my side.

Following Sandner's first tenure came my inner-circle bridge playing pal, Brian Monieson, who ran GNP Commodities, a futures commission merchant. He was the Merc's first vice chairman from 1980 to 1982, and chairman from 1983 to 1985. What attracted me to him was that he was market wise. Although unsophisticated in some ways, he had an innate sense of the world. What Monieson lacked in panache, he made up for in brains. He grasped complicated economic issues and could discuss with me new conceptual markets for the Merc better than anyone else on the Board. We also developed a common bond since he was one of the precious few on the Board who, like me, was a trader, someone with whom I could compare a trading opinion. "At least you and I know how the real world works," he would often say to me after a heated discussion with some others on the Board. Monicson's singular problem was that he was too trusting of people, a trait that eventually brought him serious problems.

I always accepted change as part of an ongoing process in building the Merc. And in that respect I didn't mind new executive talent. But continuity of leadership was a critical aspect of my strategy for the Merc because it showed the world we were stable. And that's why, over the years, to ensure continuity, I engineered a chainlink of positions that stretched into the 1990s and mentored each chairman of the Merc along the way.

Like most organizations, the Merc was a system with its own logic and weight of tradition and inertia. For nearly 25 years, I had provided a good part of that logic. It was continuity of leadership that enabled the Merc to sidestep the bureaucratic hold that often undermines most big organizations. I kept that thread of continuity taut. When Sandner, for example, stepped down as chairman in 1988, after having served the maximum number of consecutive terms, at his request I urged the Board to create a new position for him. We agreed on the title of senior policy advisor.

When he became chairman again in 1991, Rosenberg was elected to the senior policy post that Sandner vacated.

Each chairman had a particular strength: the athletic and affable Rosenberg was strong in marketing and public relations; the brainy Monieson knew technology and systems, as did Geldermann, who also oversaw our expansion operations; and Sandner was a tough-minded pragmatist with good negotiating skills.

They weren't a group of toadies by any means, and shared my vision and power. Naturally, I had worked closely with all of them. But it was Sandner I really took under wing. He was a scrabbler with street smarts who, as a tattooed 15-year-old kid, had dropped out of high school, dropped back in, went to college, then knocked on the door of Notre Dame's Law School and talked his way in, and graduated with honors.

In the late 1960s, Sandner had tried a couple of cases for Maury Kravitz's law firm. His first encounter with commodity traders ironically occurred at my firm's Christmas party in 1969, on the fifth floor of the Merc building. I didn't know him then, and he came to the party uninvited to meet my crowd. When Eddy Cahill and Wally Wizlewski confronted him at the party, words became harsh, and Sandner used his boxing skills to flatten the unsuspecting Wizlewski. Sandner then left. Although I was upset about the incident, I let it pass. My first official meeting with Sandner occurred later, while he was handling the books and acting as legal advisor for the Rittenhouse Brokerage firm, which had violated some Merc rules. Sandner accepted blame and promised me that the violations would be corrected. Two years later, he borrowed $80,000 and bought a Merc membership, keeping his law practice on the side.

In 1976, Sandner joined RB&H, one of the biggest commercial livestock operations in the nation. He donned a trading jacket, a pair of cowboy boots, and entered the cattle pit. He also became involved in exchange politics and, in 1978, was elected a governor. We would work closely in the years ahead, taking on some of the Merc's greatest challenges, and in the process bond as friends. Our friendship was the primary reason I would often invite him to accompany our delegation on official Merc trips even when he wasn't in office as chairman. We not only thoroughly enjoyed each other's company while traveling, but were close friends together with his wife, Carole, when at home. As chairman, he always waited for my decisions in Merc matters and followed my lead to the hilt. As he often acknowledged both privately and publicly, "Leo, you are my mentor."

As the years went by and the chairmen rotated, I remained the one constant. But every now and then, the burdens of chief troubleshooter would get to me, and the need to step aside became too great to resist. One such instance was November 7, 1984, when I dropped an organizational bomb on the Exchange. That day I sent a letter to the Merc membership once again announcing that I intended to sharply reduce my role at the Merc. The same old demons were nagging at me. I needed more time for my family, my business, and *The Tenth Planet*, a science fiction novel that I had begun writing.

I wasn't completely shunning exchange life. I intended to remain as special counsel, the unsalaried post I held since departing as Merc chairman seven years earlier, and serve the Merc on a federal level. But I thought that I would no longer attend board or executive committee meetings nor maintain a role in the ongoing Merc decision process. Brian Monieson, who was chairman at the time, described my new role as a change from "an operational manager to basically a strategic planner."

My partial self-exile lasted only five months. I quickly realized that what I was attempting to do was not possible. The Merc Board, its chairman, the president, and staff had for too long relied on my leadership to suddenly change their ways. As long as I was physically present at the boardroom table, my voice and opinion remained dominant. Thus, while I was pretending to be half-retired, I was more involved than ever. Bowing to reality, I sent another letter to the Merc membership, explaining that, "To paraphrase Mark Twain, news of my early retirement is grossly exaggerated . . . and, notwithstanding the chorus of I told you so's that this letter is bound to provoke, I thought it advisable to set the record straight. The truth, as most informed observers know, is that I was not allowed to withdraw from CME affairs as much as I had originally planned."

Forget withdrawing! By 1985, my functions and responsibilities had increased to a point that my special counsel title was a gross misnomer. In international waters, the title was even misleading. Clayton Yeutter, the Merc President at that time, once returned from Japan to tell me that Japanese officials interpreted *special counsel* as being a lawyer. I huddled with Yeutter, William Brodsky, CME chairman Brian Monieson, and other Merc officers to find a more appropriate title. The discussions led to a formalization of the true Merc hierarchy. The CME rules were amended to establish that special counsel would be chairman of the Executive Committee. Since the Executive Committee included all the Merc officers (including the Board chairman) and ran the Exchange when the Board was not in session, the title chairman of the Executive Committee reflected my true Merc role and required no further explanation.

The title also fit my modus operandi. Surely it was clear to me that once again I could have become chairman of the Merc. But the same rationale that prompted me to share the top honors since 1977—when I assumed the role of special counsel—were still valid. Above all, there was no practical need for the chairman's title. The Merc operated through a committee structure, and I was chairman of virtually every significant standing committee as well as many special committees. Whether it was the Financial Instruments Steering Committee, from which emanated all new financial products for the Exchange; or the International Steering Committee, which oversaw the Merc's foreign offices and operations; or the Strategic Planning Committee, which created and directed the Merc's long-range plans; or the CFPF, which administered our political action decisions; or the Legislation Committee, which directed the Merc's legislative agenda; or a host of other special committees, which functioned intermittently for a single purpose; as committee chairman, I was able to direct their agendas and activities. Since the composition of most of these committees included Board members and usually the Merc chairman as well, their recommendations were inevitably adopted by the Board.

So my responsibilities at the Merc remained all-inclusive and constant. But with constancy comes power. And power is a strange thing. While I sought it, I recognized that its dynamics were both enticing and dangerous. It can be an insidious trap. Power can seduce you to believe that you always know best. That you always know the truth. This was one of my singular concerns—not to let the power that emanated from my continuity overwhelm my senses. I often had to pause and ask myself one simple question: How am I going to test myself against the truth? The only way I knew was in open dialogue. I encouraged people to argue with me, to test me intellectually, to convert me to a fresh point of view. If they couldn't, then I usually stuck to my guns. But if they could, I would turn on a dime.

It is the reason I was continuously on the lookout for intellectually secure people to join the officialdom of the Merc. I knew that every leader's principal asset is the people who surround him. No one does it alone. Every organization must have officials who are smart, honest, and expert at what they do. Thus, when I interviewed new personnel for high offices at the Merc, I wasn't interested only in their credentials, which although important, don't tell the whole story. What I wanted to know was whether they could stand up to me and other high-level Merc officials and have the courage to tell us—in so many words—you are wrong. This is no easy trait to find. Nor is it always discernible during a job interview.

Once aboard, staff quickly learned that I would openly argue issues with them. Openly, that is, within the confines of Merc meetings. Jerry Salzman, our attorney, was the focus of any number of such open and sometimes heated discussions—over a wide variety of subjects that ranged from rule enactments to the creation of GLOBEX. I considered Salzman worthy of intellectual challenge. He was an astute individual whose grasp of the most complex subject was breathtaking. But for me, his single most important characteristic was his total and unabashed willingness to offer his version of the truth. Right or wrong, I could count on Salzman to offer his point of view and argue with me when he deemed it necessary.

Rick Kilcollin was another. He followed Fred Arditti, also an excellent economist. Kilcollin came to the Merc from the Federal Reserve where he had an outstanding record as a financial economist, but I liked him because he was stubborn and completely honest. As the chief economist of the Merc during some of its most innovative stages, Kilcollin provided the CME with an exquisite ability to analyze deep-seated and complex issues that were not always visible. And he was principled to a fault. Indeed, his single-mindedness, which was totally devoid of political considerations, could sometimes be embarrassing. For example, the time Sandner, Kilcollin, and I were in London with the chairman of the Rothschild Bank seeking his advice on how to bring a "gold-fix" to Chicago. From the heated debate that followed between Kilcollin and the chairman, one would have concluded that Kilcollin knew more about the subject matter than the legendary Rothschilds, the people who had founded the concept ages before. Still, I didn't lose sight of the fact that although Kilcollin's stubbornness could be exasperating, it represented an invaluable strength on which I could always rely. Kilcollin didn't always get his way, but we never had to doubt where he stood. I would elicit some of his provocative thoughts in front of the Executive Committee or within a smaller group of officials so that his ideas could be examined in a highly critical environment. Most of all, I relied on Kilcollin to tell me the truth. There are moments, such as in the aftermath of the 1987 stock crash, that this Kilcollin characteristic was the most critical for the destiny of the Merc.

Another outspoken star was John Davidson. He was first hired by the Merc in 1983 as domestic operations manager for the clearinghouse. It wasn't long before I began to have personal contact with him and discovered his intellectual honesty and intrinsic knowledge of clearinghouse matters. I embraced and wholeheartedly applauded his total candor about what was right and wrong at the Merc. Davidson rose through the Merc ranks at a meteoric pace, ultimately to become senior vice president of the clearinghouse. Just in time. The Merc was at a critical juncture in its trade clearing operations and desperately needed someone steeped in this expertise who wasn't afraid to take on sacred cows. I was happy to give him free rein. Under Davidson's direction, we innovated and changed our clearing procedures and operations so that when the 1987 stock crash occurred, I was confident of our capability to handle the unprecedented emergency, and certain that the statistical facts provided by Davidson would prove that the crash was not the Merc's doing.

Some CME officers, including Jerry Beyer, preferred the discussions between us to occur behind closed doors because of the sensitivity of the subject matter. Beyer, who for many years was in charge of CME compliance and regulatory matters, knew that rule compliance and regulatory CFTC issues could be explosive. He had come to the Merc from the Board of Trade where his talents were generally not perceived. But Jerry Beyer, a highly intelligent individual, had the ability to understand hidden motivations of people, and he was also perceptive about the consequential effects of regulations. He would take the time to press his conclusions on me, and I quickly recognized that he was completely trustworthy. As he told me, the Merc was his mistress, his love—as it was for me. This commitment to the Merc formed a strong bond between us. Most important, he complied with my demand to make me aware of the full nature of each subject under his command, irrespective of the consequences or whether I would like what I was going to hear. I trusted Beyer's judgment and nearly always followed his suggested directions.

Alysann Posner also liked to work behind the scenes and was similarly exceptionally competent and loyal. She came to the Merc from the Chicago Board Options Exchange where she was research analyst for new options products. In our first interview, when I asked her what she wanted to do at the Merc, she responded, "I want to be like you." What fascinated me most about this response was not its flattery but its audacity. As Beverly Splane had stated, *I was a legend in my own mind*, and here was this young thing, with hardly a proven record, who had the temerity to want to be like the legend. It was one of my most fortunate hires. Posner quickly rose to become my indispensable right-hand person. One of her exceptional values was to privately but unhesitatingly tell me when she thought I was wrong, regardless of the nature of the subject. It was sometimes frustrating, but always refreshing. Like Jerry Beyer, Posner was sensitive to the motivations of people and the nuances of their feelings, which were often invisible to me. Because of her direct access to my office and her outspoken approach, she was able to provide insights into the value of other Merc employees, of which I would otherwise have been ignorant.

Case in point was David Emmanual, an analyst sitting unrecognized in the CME's Research Department. No one paid much attention to Emmanual's talents, nor cared much about his invention of a system for evaluating options' risk. No one, until Posner brought it to my attention and coerced me to examine his work product. Emmanual was elated to finally demonstrate his innovation to someone who could understand its enormous value. The resulting SPAN, Standard Portfolio Analysis, is today the world's standard mechanism for evaluating performance bonds in the futures industry.

Aside from Posner's capacity to discern the landscape around me, so to speak, and keep me advised, she had a unique talent for organizing material and producing precisely the right documentation for the project at hand. She could transform into "hard copy" the imaginary innovations and ideas that I would verbalize. In this respect, Posner really did become like me. When the concept of GLOBEX was overwhelmingly approved by CME members—an electronic trading mechanism that should have been the equivalent of Darth Vader to the Merc's pit-orientated membership—I attributed a great portion of our success to the written and graphic material created by Alysann Posner, which each member received.

To be confronted by the opposition was also the reason I often appointed my harshest critics to important committees. It was the surest way of learning their views and to test them against mine. To outsiders, I may have come off as powerful and unyielding, but the Board and insiders knew differently. The most interesting phenomenon that resulted from such appointments was that our critics learned firsthand that the process by which decisions were made at the Merc was in a give-and-take fashion, and not the dictatorial manner as was the common view on the outside. Often, this discovery resulted in turning an enemy into a friend. The process fortified my belief that most people can be influenced through honest and open discussions.

Thus I learned that leadership is a combination of many things: to see, to hear, to prepare. Or as the great hockey star Wayne Gretzky of the L.A. Kings said, "To skate where the puck is going, not where it has been." But, primarily, leadership involves a search for the truth and the ability to influence others to believe in it.

22

The Merc Goes to Washington

There are a lot of things in life money won't buy, but have you ever tried to buy them without money? That little quip by humorist Ogden Nash came to mind when in 1976 I began to build the Merc's political base in Washington. I realized that money didn't buy votes, but it provided something else: access to the politicians who did vote.

The Merc was on the make. Our markets were growing and the prices were moving around, getting us plenty of attention. There was a bustle and excitement on the floor and a constant stream of stories in the press. The traders were busy and making money. Operational expansion among members, firms and the Exchange itself was widespread and extensive. New members were steadily joining our ranks and the word about our potential was spreading throughout the country. We were a boiling pot of new ideas and new demands garnished with a universal feeling of promise and strength. My days were spent in a dizzying whirl of meetings and speeches and discussions.

I had no written plan or blueprint to follow because everything was in my head. But the pieces were all there in my mind, aligned like the planets floating in some order. To make it work, I had to have control of committees, of people, of purse strings. I knew the kind of talent I needed and in what direction I was steering the Merc. I wasn't the product of a business school or a corporation, and much of what I was doing was instinctive, yet logical. The Merc was hurtling ahead and I had to make sure it didn't end up free-falling. Part of the control factor had to do with politics. Our new successes brought us national recognition; recognition brought us visibility; visibility made us political targets. And as targets we would be highly vulnerable, without influence. The Merc, I concluded, needed influence if it was ever going to reach its potential and be a major player in the world financial markets.

The U.S. futures markets had been around for more than 130 years, but with the currencies and other financial instruments, it was more like an emerging industry. Now we needed to explain ourselves within the context of the financial futures markets, to raise the level of consciousness among the lawmakers. The political friends we did have were mainly the congressmen from Illinois who understood—and appreciated—the exchanges and their impact. But that was to be expected; the congressmen from the wheat belt understood the farmer, and those from Michigan, the auto worker, and so on.

The entire futures industry was in transition: the exchanges were part of the rapidly growing service industry that was replacing manufacturing in America. And the financial markets would someday replace the agricultural markets as the dominant futures markets. I wanted to reach the breadth of Congress. If these markets were to grow, as I anticipated they would, we would have to change our relationship with the lawmakers. The only way to get inside their heads, I was convinced, was to get them inside the Merc. But first, to navigate the corridors of Washington and master the terrain of politics, I needed a guide.

Larry Rosenberg, who was the new CME chairman, the first to succeed me after the CME reorganization, agreed with my assessment about the need for a Washington office. He had recognized as I had, that our biggest weakness lay in Washington. "If we don't go there, they'll come after us," he joked. So we used the services of an executive search firm to seek the right candidate to open our window on Washington. They introduced us to C. Dayle Henington, who we brought to Chicago and hired on the spot. Dayle had spent 20 years in the U.S. Air Force, where he rose to the rank of major before serving as an administrative assistant to Representative W.R. Poage, the venerable Texas chairman of the House Committee on Agriculture. The son of a barber raised in Temple, Texas, Poage's hometown, Henington was glib and knew his way around Capitol Hill. As the first futures exchange to open a Washington office, my objective was clear and direct: to make the economic functions of futures markets better understood by legislators.

To say Poage was Henington's mentor was an understatement. Poage was his congressman when Dayle was seven, his friend from the age of 16, his boss at 40; and Henington lobbied Poage at 50. In 1978, Poage retired at 80, and Henington considered returning to Texas to run for Poage's congressional seat. We put on a show for Henington by flying him into Chicago aboard the private plane of Larry Rosenberg, who was also a pilot. Henington knew very little about the Merc, so we filled him in.

My concern, I told him, was over the kind of impact, if any, I was having in Washington. I'd visit a few people and then leave—always with the same feeling that I had eaten a meal and was still hungry. There was never any follow-up. If I'd call a few days later, more often than not, the Merc would be a vague recollection.

"What do you want me to do, Leo?" Henington asked.

"There's a corner between Longworth and the Capitol where all the members of Congress cross the street to vote," I said. "In fact, if you need to see a couple of people, you just go to that stoplight and wait for a roll call and you'd see everybody you'd need to see and save a lot of time. I just want you to stand on that corner and have everyone say 'the Chicago Mercantile Exchange.' "

"I know how to do that," Henington said, "but it's going to be expensive." Right there and then we started upping the ante with Henington. As Poage's administrative assistant, his salary was $22,000 a year. We offered him $60,000. And a few weeks later, Henington and a secretary were running the Chicago Mercantile Exchange's Washington office at 1101 Connecticut next to the Mayflower Hotel.

I wanted the Merc to find its voice just as do the Republicans and Democrats when they reach the Hill. The Merc stood for free and open markets. How does one explain that? I knew I could sell Washington officials the beauty of the market, but I couldn't do it in their D.C. offices with constituents waiting in the ante room, constant telephone interruptions, and their staff intermittently drawing away their attention. Besides, to fully appreciate the dynamics of our marketplace, a person had to witness it firsthand. That meant only one thing: we would have to bring Congress to the Merc.

After seven years as an administrative aide to Pogue, Henington had strong connections on the Hill. He was particularly tight with the Texas contingent. Shortly after he began working for us, Texas Democrat Jim Wright, who had just been elected majority leader by one vote, called Henington to congratulate him on the new job.

"If there's anything I can do for you, let me know," Wright said.

When I called Henington the next day I asked, "Who are we going to bring to Chicago first?"

"Well, why don't we start with the majority leader," Henington replied.

Wright came in for an evening. Over a three-hour dinner at the Ritz Carlton, the majority leader, Rosenberg, Henington, and I talked about politics, our backgrounds, and the markets. He understood the Merc and its potential and would become a champion of the industry. The bonding process with Wright had begun. It would lead to a relationship in which I could call on him directly with industry issues. I made certain that this newly developed rapport had continuity. Several years later, when Jim Wright became speaker of the House of Representatives, I arranged for him to meet our new CME chairman, Jack Sandner. The speaker complied, and Jack and I were privileged to lunch with him in his private dining room. This led to the discovery that the speaker, like Sandner, was a boxing aficionado, and once or twice traveled together to boxing events.

Henington taught me the importance of the congressional staff, even the secretaries. Henington knew everybody's secretary by first name. "They hold the keys to the kingdom," he explained. I had no problem following this lead and soon was a buddy to many key personnel. For instance, Marshall Lynam was the majority leader's right-hand man. There is a picture hanging in the famous Bookbinder's Restaurant in Philadelphia in which I am shining Lynam's shoes. Although it was a lark, it was one of Lynam's proudest photos. After that, I could do no wrong in his presence.

When it came to economics, I was a conservative, but a liberal on social issues. That was one reason I did well on both sides of the political aisle. When it got down to it, a lot of the rapport with congressmen was based on chemistry; you either liked one another or you didn't. Sure, I could be pals with Kansas Republican Bob Dole, but I also had a special relationship with Massachusetts Democrat Tip O'Neill, though we came from two different worlds. I had an intellectual upbringing with the idealistic focus on Jewish culture. O'Neill came out of the rough-and-tumble Irish political culture.

Even physically we were at extremes; I was of average stature, swarthy in complexion, with a neatly combed head of black hair. He was a big ruddy-faced man with big features, topped with a shock of white hair. We were almost caricatures of who we were. But the magic was there. Whenever we'd be in a room and he'd see me, he would stop, wave his hand toward me and say, "Stand up Lee." I was always thrilled by the fact that O'Neill knew my name. He conveyed a strong emotionalism, and he was a great showman; he strutted and had one of the hardiest handshakes around. I learned a lot from him by merely observing how he worked a crowd. He was both loved and respected.

During the celebration of our nation's 200th birthday, Henington arranged for a Merc party in Independence Hall in Philadelphia. As I waited to escort Tip O'Neill inside, I noticed that he was smoking one of his fat cigars. But smoking, for safety reasons, was strictly forbidden in the historic hall itself, and we had carefully cautioned all our guests about this. But who would tell Tip? His chief of staff glanced at me and whispered, "no one." Tip O'Neill was the only one who ever smoked inside Independence Hall.

Another time, we had invited a couple of hundred guests on a rented luxury yacht during the annual futures industry convention in Boca Raton. Our featured guest that evening was Tip O'Neill, and we planned a delightful cruise down the Intercoastal. I escorted the speaker to the ship, but Tip stopped short after seeing the boat. He pulled me to the side and said quietly, "Lee, I hate being trapped on boats. It means that everyone can press me on this or that. This boat doesn't leave the goddamn dock, right?" You bet. Tip O'Neill left no room for doubt. I told the captain that, under the penalty of death, not to move an inch from the shore that evening.

What I'm saying is that the political arena was not all that different from the trading floor, where an individual's background hardly makes a difference. We trade contracts and the lawmakers trade ideas, but in the end, it is performance that counts, that separates the winners from the losers. Only we tally our performance in dollars, the politician in votes, which cost dollars.

The futures industry had been around a long time, Henington mused, but it was just discovering that public policy was made in Washington. There was, of course, a trade-off. By trying to participate in the Washington process, as he put it, "You were really entering the fish bowl."

We were in one already. All you had to do was to peer down from the Merc's visitors' gallery on any given day to see that we had nothing to hide. We weren't dealing behind closed doors as do large corporations, shutting out shareholders and the press. Our business was out in the open. We were buying and selling our products in accordance with free-market capitalism. The Exchange itself was an open window on the world, reflecting what was happening in every quarter; it was a messenger bearing good and bad news. But just a messenger. And it was a self-correcting system that worked with a minimum of tampering.

I knew that a Washington office was only one piece of the puzzle. We needed national stature and political money as well. The Merc president, I realized, could be a great help if he were someone Washington could salute. Unfortunately, that wasn't 65-year-old E.B. Harris, who had been Merc president for 25 years. Harris was one of a kind, and I dearly loved him. He had a wide range of contacts and could make a couple of calls and ask a couple of favors, but he didn't know how to maneuver around Washington. How could he? That was never his job. While Harris was sort of my security blanket to the past, he seemed lost in the present. His interminable chatter, great enthusiasm, and homespun philosophy was wonderful in the 1950s and 1960s, but out of place in the internationalism of the 1970s. "Dress British, think Yiddish," he would privately tell me. It was cute, but its day was over. The future was my concern now. The IMM was the international key, the bridge to London, Tokyo, Singapore, Hong Kong, Frankfurt, and Paris. I needed someone not only with Washington contacts, but who could move in international circles as well. We were projecting a new and different image.

I think Harris knew this as well. He sensed that his day was over and would sometimes mention it to Beverly Splane who would shrug her shoulders and sigh. Then she would commiserate with me. Splane urged me to tell E.B. the truth, but I resisted, not wanting to hurt him. I wanted it to come from him. Then one day in 1977 Harris tested the water by muttering to me that maybe he should retire. I struck like a tiger, accepting his offer on the spot. Harris was somewhat taken aback by the immediacy of my reaction, but in a way he was relieved. We settled on a 1978 retirement date.

Rosenberg and I formed a presidential search committee, which I chaired. We retained the national executive recruiting firm, Spencer Stuart to do the search. Scott Shelton, a partner of Spencer Stuart was invaluable in designing our strategy, but from the start, I thought I knew who the next CME president should be. I had my eye on Clayton K. Yeutter. I had met Yeutter several years before, when he was an assistant secretary of Agriculture. He knew his way around Washington, and philosophically he was a free marketer. He had assisted in drafting the legislation that created the CFTC, so he knew a bit about our markets. A year or so earlier, I had brought him to the Merc for a visit and could read his reaction to the floor and our members. Our mutual conservative economic convictions and our similar disapproving views about big government made it easy to instantly take a liking to each other.

But it wasn't an easy sell. Yeutter didn't know much about the Merc, and he worried about tarnishing his reputation. The Merc's past history was a problem for him. Corners and onion debacles aren't exactly the stuff of which Washington careers are made. In Republican circles, he was a potential star and I knew he wouldn't remain at the Merc for a quarter of a century because he was too ambitious. An attorney with a PhD in agricultural economics, Yeutter, who was 47 years old at the time, had previously served as U.S. deputy special trade representative for President Ford. We both knew he had a political future.

When I offered him the job, he was hesitant. He told me that the only reason he wouldn't reject it out of hand was that he respected me personally and applauded the revolutionary markets I had introduced. He was certain that the Merc's future was in finance and that I had put it on the right track. It was enough to encourage me to keep lobbying. The two of us met twice at Chicago's O'Hare Airport during stopovers he had. We had extensive conversations. The first encounter got us nowhere, but by the end of the second one, I thought Yeutter had warmed to the idea.

At one of the small airport restaurants over endless cups of coffee, I spent a couple of hours discussing the job: the freedom he would have to wave the Merc flag and offer our message in quarters that didn't yet use futures, and to raise the level of our understanding in the international community. We would not demand that he act as administrator, since our executive vice president Beverly Splane would continue in that function.

As far as the members, I would take care of that. And above all, I promised I would ensure that the Merc never slipped into its past ways. As we spoke, I could see in his eyes the vision of opportunity: a chance to meet all types of financial figures throughout the world. As long as the Merc's stature would grow, so would his. I felt I had convinced him that the Merc position would be a boost for his career.

As he got up from the table, Yeutter complimented me, "Leo, you're a helluva lobbyist. You're the only one in the world who could have convinced me to take this job. I trust you and your judgment." I was truly flattered and we shook hands. The Merc had a new president.

Yeutter had lived on a public servant's salary, and we offered him substantially more. But he was never anybody who sold out for money. He would have turned the job down if he thought it would impede his potential rise in the American political system. And, of course, it didn't. After his stint at the Merc, Yeutter would go on to become U.S. Trade Representative, Secretary of Agriculture, and Chairman of the Republican Party. Yeutter had a streak of independence, yet his experience in the Washington culture taught him to be a team player and to take orders and directions. Shortly before he began his presidency in 1978, Yeutter said to me, "Listen, the Merc is yours. I'm just an interloper with a job to do." In other words, he never let his personal agenda overwhelm the Merc's, a characteristic I could readily identify with. We agreed that he would be "Mr. Outside," and I would continue as "Mr. Inside." It turned out to be a perfect marriage.

With a ready smile and forceful presence, Yeutter made an ideal emissary not only in Washington but in industry meetings across the United States and overseas. In the next four years, he would be constantly in motion, hopscotching the world and stopping at the Merc just long enough to update me on his progress. Yeutter was superb at verbalizing at the international level what the IMM and its markets were all about. The Merc benefited enormously and continued to grow. The same month Yeutter's appointment was announced, we opened our Washington office. At his first press conference as Merc president, he said he was going to be active in the Capitol because, as he put it, "that's where the action is." And having worked in government, he understood the hazards of bureaucratic red tape and wasn't afraid to speak out. "We won't kowtow to the CFTC," he told reporters. "If we have a problem, we'll tell them so, either formally or informally." Clayton Yeutter, turned out, as I expected, the best person possible at this juncture in CME history to be president of our exchange.

Later, we rounded out our Washington office by hiring Charles (Chip) Seeger as legal counsel to deal with the regulatory agencies and congressional legislation. Seeger worked in the Washington office of the

Nebraska-based law firm Yeutter had been a partner in. The firm specialized in administrative law.

Like Yeutter and Henington, Seeger was a political animal. The son of an Air Force career officer, Seeger and his siblings grew up traipsing around the world. Every three years or so, the family would uproot and Seeger learned to make friends quickly and wield his six-foot-three-inch frame with athletic prowess. His first job out of Johns Hopkins was on the reelection campaign of Congressman Charles Tieg. A California Republican, Tieg was on the House Agriculture Committee, which gave Seeger the opportunity to begin learning something about the futures markets.

Seeger endeared himself to me with one of his favorite Mark Twain quotations: "Clothes make the man; naked people have little or no influence in our society." The Merc had been naked long enough. Now I was about to dress it in a suit that was part pinstripe and part armor. If we hadn't implemented the Washington program when we did, there is no telling what would have happened to the Merc and the rest of the futures industry over the next three decades, what with lingering recessions, crashing markets, and changing administrations. With our own eyes, ears, and voice in Washington, we were better able to deal with those bureaucrats and politicians contemplating mischief and to create a little mischief of our own.

Now it was time to put the last component into place. I wanted to bring Washington's eyes and ears to the Merc. And for that I needed the stuff that made Washington work—money. In other words, no matter what I personally thought about money in the political process, I had better accept the view that "in politics, money is God." I got the idea of how to influence the political process from none other than the chairman of the CFTC, my good friend William Bagley. He sat me down some time in 1977 like a father about to tell his son the facts of life. In this case, it was the facts of life in our nation's capital. "Washington D.C.," he said, "is like a factory; there are bosses and workers. But it takes money to make it run." Bagley was saying that the pay was mediocre and the electioneering was expensive. "You guys will never have a voice in the process unless or until you have political muscle. For that, you need a political action committee."

It made eminent sense to me, and I thought I knew how to form one. First, as was my style, I wanted an authoritative voice. I asked Bagley if he would appear at a special members' meeting of the CME and repeat what he told me. The chairman of the CFTC obliged and came to the Bismark Hotel in Chicago where, at the specified time, I had gathered upwards of 500 Merc members. I introduced the topic, as well as CFTC chairman, who made a tough, down-to-earth pitch, explaining why the Merc needed a political voice in Washington and that this could not be achieved without money. That meeting allowed me to create the Merc's Commodity Futures Political Fund, the CFPF.

I modeled its operation after the United Jewish Appeal structure, which I knew firsthand to be enormously successful at raising funds. First, I created a board of directors comprised of respected members, from the Board as well as the floor. I was elected chairman of the CFPF, a position I served for the next 15 years. The board of directors worked in close harmony with a cadre of appointed ad hoc leaders. These were prominent members, who acted as the "precinct captains" of the floor and upon whose shoulders fell the responsibility of collecting voluntary contributions to CFPF from our membership. We would gather once a year to parcel out to each ad hoc leader some 30 to 50 Merc members' names, each of whom the ad hoc leaders had to contact for contributions. The CFPF structure was immensely successful, achieving about a 50 percent response from the membership during our annual campaigns, each of which lasted approximately two weeks. In most years, our goal was about $500,000, which quickly resulted in making the CFPF one of the strongest business PACs around.

In the beginning, deciding to whom and how much to contribute at election time was a new experience for everybody. Members of the CFPF board were like a group of frat brothers in a blackball session, spending hours vigorously arguing to whom the Merc ought to contribute, and why. We tried to choose candidates who at least had an open mind and who would listen to our message. But mostly we favored free-market thinkers. Naturally, our advisors Yeutter, Henington, and Seeger had a strong impact on who the CFPF favored. I signed the checks, so I made sure that I was politically abreast of developments in Washington, and directed Henington and Yeutter to provide me with briefings. The flow of money was important because I could see it building our alliances in Washington, where I was spending more time appearing at subcommittee hearings, expressing my point of view, meeting more lawmakers, and learning more about the nature of politics and politicians.

Over the years, the CFPF became one of the most effective business PACs in the nation. Other PAC money would usually follow our lead. And CFPF became central to the Merc's ultimate success. There were four ingredients to our success: our organizational structure; the political acumen of Yeutter, Henington, and Seeger; the role that I played in motivating the CFPF board, its ad hoc leaders, and the CME membership. This would require regular sermons at which I would emotionally and graphically explain the value of our PAC as an insurance policy against adverse legislation or other hostile actions by our political adversaries. And the fourth ingredient: the incomparable efforts of my ad hoc floor chairman, Harry-the-Hat Lowrance.

The Hat, as he was universally known, was a charismatic floor broker with a raspy voice and a street-learned intelligence that was difficult to match. He had earned his nickname in a Merc baseball game during which he wore a silly iridescent hat that lit up as he ran the bases. Harry Lowrance is as good a rags-to-riches story as there is on the Merc. In 1962, at the age of 16, he was a high school dropout working as a soda-jerk in a neighborhood drugstore. There he ran into Walter Kowalski, the CME venerable statistician, who took a liking to Harry and made him a "gofer" for the Merc's statistics department. But Lowrance quickly realized that success at the Merc required schooling and money—memberships at the time were at $9,000, which for Harry might as well have been a million dollars. Motivated, he quit his CME job to finish high school. Lowrance returned to the floor at the age of 19, already a father to a baby son (he had to get his mother's signature to get married because he was under age) and without a dime to his name. But he quickly talked his way into a job with Harold Heinhold, the legendary hog buyer who had become famous for his hog stations throughout Indiana. Heinhold was also the first to popularize commodity funds in futures markets. Lowrance soon held down two jobs by inventing the idea of "deck-holding" for Eddie Cahill and Dick Mosher, two brokers in the belly pit. It started a deck-holding tradition at all futures exchanges.

Meanwhile, at Heinhold & Rufenacht, where the Hat was officially employed, he struck up a friendship with Lloyd Arnold, one of the most beloved CME members who had a penchant for racing stables. In December 1970, Arnold's trip to Australia to buy horses presented Harry with an opportunity he could not resist. Lowrance convinced Arnold's son-in-law that Arnold had telephoned from Australia and authorized a $50,000 loan for Harry to buy a Merc membership. It worked. Afterwards, there was no way the Merc could reverse the transaction. It resulted in enactment of the so-called Lowrance regulation, which from then on required *written* permission from clearing members for any membership purchases. But it didn't take Lowrance long to become a broker par excellence and repay the *loan* to Arnold. It also didn't take Lowrance long to become my trusted friend and a charter member of my elite floor corps. Although at the time I got a lot of flack for it, the wisest appointment I ever made was that of Harry Lowrance as CFPF pit boss.

There was an added element to CFPF's success. As in most endeavors, there are unsung heroes and heroines who do the legwork and provide the administrative assistance without which nothing gets done. Joan Bush, a stalwart Merc employee, became my indispensable assistant in the CFPF effort. Bush knew every member by first name, knew who knew who, and knew which ad hoc leader would get the most money out of whom.

So now we were ready to begin to educate. In the beginning, we weren't up against a hostile Congress so much as a benign one. My job was to teach them about who we were and how markets worked. Henington's job was to contact and personally accompany them to the Exchange for a day trip. The Hat's job was to collect the money. Chip Seeger's job was to keep everything legal, and Joan Bush kept everything on track. It was a great team. When Yeutter was around, he was the topping on the cake.

In the early stages, Henington used his personal chits to get congressmen to Chicago. Once he brought them there, I took over. I believed in a personal approach to education. I would bring a senator or congressman to my Dellsher desk on the floor, write an order to buy or sell a given product while I explained what I was about to do. Then I would hand the order to my clerk who would run it into the pit to be filled while we all watched. It was live ammo in the trenches, and the Washingtonians ate it up. A minute later, the filled order came back to us as the officials followed the prices on the quoteboard to see if I made or lost. Inevitably, this exercise cost me money, but it was well worth the price. The congressmen learned firsthand how the process worked and how open and aboveboard it was. Years later, they would remind me of what I had taught them. The resulting rapport was invaluable.

Over objections from many on our board, I insisted that we run our program in conjunction with the CBOT. Everybody got more bang for the buck that way, and our combined muscle was much stronger. Besides, as far as Washington goes, I contended, the CBOT was not our competitor. The congressmen flew into Chicago and met with CME and CBOT officials at our respective exchanges. We would also invite governors and CFPF ad hoc leaders to ask questions and meet the dignitaries. Then the Washingtonians would tour the Exchange floors, give some brief remarks, and have lunch before returning to Washington. For the visit, a congressman received an honorarium of $2,000, each exchange putting up $1,000.

Eventually, we didn't have to do anything to solicit. Word of mouth did it. One congressman would tell another, "You ought to go with Dayle. It's a great trip. You'll learn a lot and enjoy it. And they put you on the PAC list." I bring this up as a point of reference. We ignored no one or anyone who would listen. And most of them would.

Over the next 15 years, the Merc would be visited by no fewer than 85 senators and nearly 200 congressmen. Henington accompanied every one of the senators. Many of them visited numerous times. The CFPF became an important part of my strategy, and the flow of funds depended on the political activity in a given year. In 1988, for example, the Merc distributed $20,000 to presidential candidates, giving donations to Republicans George Bush and Bob Dole and Democrats Richard Gephardt, Al Gore, and Paul Simon. In the previous year, 24 of 43 members of the House and Senate

Agriculture Committee—the authority over the CFTC—received hono-raria for appearances at the Merc and CBOT.

I never looked upon political spending as an offensive measure, but rather as a defensive strategy. Those who thought you could buy a congressman's vote with $1,000 or $2,000, were naive. In 1986, there was a congressional resolution to ban cattle futures. Fortunately, it lost, but many of the con-gressmen who had received CFPF contributions voted against the Merc and in favor of the ban. It was a "hometown" political issue that always took precedence. I respected that. All that a contribution could guarantee was the right to make our case. And that was a lot.

We could usually turn to our Illinois congressmen for a sympathetic ear. They understood our business, or at least the importance of the busi-ness to Chicago and the state. In the 1950s and 1960s, there were Senator Paul Douglas, who developed his free-market philosophy as a former Uni-versity of Chicago professor, and Senator Everett Dirksen, the downstate politician from the soybean belt who knew the value of hedging to the farmer. By the early 1970s, Douglas was replaced by his former student, Charles Percy, who had been chairman of Bell & Howell at the ripe old age of 28. As chairman of the Senate Foreign Relations Committee, Percy's clout often helped us connect with people we needed to reach in my early years as Merc chairman.

But it was much later, beginning in the 1980s, after our markets were be-coming big and boisterous and successful, that our needs in Congress be-came increasingly pronounced. No year would pass without some legislative issue or industry problem coming to the fore that would potentially impact the future of futures. Sometimes it was reauthorization of the CFTC, which led to problems regarding the agency's power, jurisdiction, or over-sight of exchanges. Sometimes it was the never-ending battle over a transac-tion tax on our markets. Often the issues seemed innocuous on their face, but that in itself was a trap. Minor issues have a way of accumulating and, when taken in the aggregate, can affect our markets in a major way. One of the major responsibilities of our Washington office was to stay alert for any issue, large or small, that could potentially impact the markets. And now and then the issues were very serious, involving legislation that would di-rectly bar or limit the right of futures markets to enter into certain arenas of business.

The trick was never to pawn ourselves off as victims, but as financial heros. My message to the lawmakers was direct and cautionary: Chicago was the futures capital of the world. Our exchanges had the foresight to change with the changes in the world. We had the guts to be innovative. And as a consequence, we brought world business to Chicago. But we were more than that. Our markets were an integral part of the financial services arena of our country. It should be no surprise to learn that other places around the world wanted to have markets like ours. So when the lawmakers were trying to make our markets better, I cautioned that they make sure they weren't putting us at a competitive disadvantage.

My friend Nobel laureate economist Merton Miller believes that innovative financial products lay like seeds beneath the snow waiting for some change in the environment to bring them to life—namely regulations and taxes. But those same elements can also drive business to other shores when you consider that money no longer changes hands, but screens. The Eurobond market, for example, grew in the 1960s out of U.S. regulations that placed a ceiling on the rate of interest that commercial banks could offer on time deposits. But eventually a 30 percent withholding tax on the interest payment of these bonds sold in the United States to overseas investors drove the market from New York to London where it still remains. I used his example time and again.

I didn't expect to win every fight. And when I lost a few, I carried no grudges against the lawmakers who disagreed with my viewpoint. In the fickleness of politics, yesterday's adversary can be today's power broker. I could virtually chart the Merc's influence by our annual Washington reception held every May. The yearly event began when Henington joined the Merc. "Well," said Pogue to Henington, "I suppose Herman (Talmadge) and I should give you a party to announce your new job to your friends. Of course, the Merc will pay for it." Only a few congressmen attended that first party in 1977. Rosenberg and I liked it and made it a tradition. Each year thereafter the guest list grew relative to our influence. By 1990, it was a big soiree drawing some 15 senators, 76 congressmen, plus cabinet members, regulators from the CFTC and SEC, and congressional aides, all schmoozing for a few hours in the House Agriculture Hearing Room filled with fancy food, fine wines, azaleas, and Washington gossip.

During the decades of the 1980s and 1990s, there were two Illinois officials who would act as our primary centurions, Senator Alan Dixon and Congressman Dan Rostenkowski. Senator Dixon had come up through the ranks of Illinois politics. He was smart, a quick study, and an expert on the State of Illinois. After several highly successful terms as Illinois Secretary of State, he ran for the Senate and won in a breeze. It was lucky for us that Dixon came to the Senate after a long-standing relationship with CBOT's Tom Donovan, which began during the years when Donovan was Mayor Daley's political point man. Now, as Senator Dixon, he became our market's strongest ally in the U.S. Senate. During his tenure, it was no accident that Dixon served on one or another of the two committees that materially affected the life of futures markets: the Senate Agriculture and the Senate Banking Committees. Tom Donovan helped convince Dixon that that was where he should be. Indeed, our futures market's influence with Senator Dixon proved, as nothing had before, how correct my insistence was that the CME work in unison with the CBOT when it came to PAC action or Washington lobbying. It was Tom Donovan who provided me with the earliest contacts with Dixon and made certain the senator knew to value my views and advice. Later, when Bill Brodsky became CME president in 1985, I was able to transfer to him this credibility with the senator.

Throughout the years and the many issues on which we beseeched Dixon's help, he would respond whenever Donovan and Melamed, and later Brodsky, made the request. His office was always open to us. Fortunately, Dixon was no mealymouthed politician who was just there for the glad-hand but did little to advance our cause. There were plenty of those kind of senators around as well. But in Dixon's case, he rolled up his sleeves and did battle. In fact, as a political pro, Dixon was a wheeler-dealer in the Senate who knew his way around and could trade votes and favors with the best of them.

In the years following the 1987 stock crash, when the Senate Banking Committee potentially became the operating room for the surgery on futures markets, as was advocated by the New York Stock Exchange, Senator Alan Dixon's office became our home. The stock crash was on the top of his priority list, and he was like a bulldog that would not rest until his neighborhood—our markets—were safe from prowlers. No materially damaging legislation in futures was ever enacted by the Senate during his watch. When Dixon lost in the 1992 election, it was a major blow to our Senate presence. But we were fortunate because in his place came Carol Moseley Braun. While Senator Braun did not come to the Senate with any background in futures markets, and it took her a while to develop Senatorial clout, she was extremely bright and very anxious to learn about our issues. Henington arranged for me to have dinner with the new senator on her very first night in Washington. Senator Braun has proved to be an important and effective ally and a staunch defender of Chicago's futures. In no small measure was this result due to the very effective political machinery our Chicago markets had built.

Although Dan Rostenkowski was an extremely close friend of Tom Donovan's, I had my own long-standing rapport with the congressman. In the 1970s, when I first showed up on the northwest side of Chicago at his office at Fullerton and Damen with a plea for assistance on some pending legislation, Rostenkowski stopped me short with one question, "Is this important for Chicago?" My affirmative response was all that was needed. Thus began a friendship that lasted the next two decades, a friendship built not only on the political needs of our futures markets. There was a kinship born of my Jewish immigrant background and the Polish immigrant ancestry of Rostenkowski's family. There was also the common bond forged between those of us who grew up during the 1950s on the streets of Chicago's northwest side.

Of course, Rostenkowski was not the only Illinois congressional friend of our industry. I can think of few more loyal to our issues than representatives Cardis Collins, John Porter, Dick Durbin, or former Congressman Marty Russo. Still, over the years, Dan Rostenkowski was the Chicago futures markets tallest and most effective soldier. No issue was too small or too big for him to undertake when it concerned the CBOT or the CME. And as dean of the Illinois congressional delegation, Rostenkowski also brought to our fold the other Illinois congressmen, Democrat or Republican. On November 28, 1983, at the celebration of the opening of the new CME building complex, Rostenkowski, the powerful chairman of the House Ways and Means Committee, came to say what he often publicly acclaimed about the futures markets of Chicago, *"The Merc is to Chicago what oil is to Texas or Oklahoma, what milk is to Wisconsin, and what corn is to Iowa."*

After Rostenkowski led us to victory in one particularly difficult legislative battle that stemmed from the 1987 crash, I purchased a bound copy of Thomas Babington Macaulay's epic poem, *Horatius at the Bridge,* and had every member of the Merc floor sign the book as a public thank you to Rostenkowski. The poem is about the Roman gatekeeper Horatius, who alone stood valiantly to defend *". . . the ashes of his fathers and the temples of his gods."* It was most appropriate since Dan Rostenkowski would often explain to our adversaries that, at the end of the day, after all the battles they had already faced, they would still have to face the chairman of the House Ways and Means Committee, who, like Horatius at the bridge, would stand to protect the temples of Chicago—our futures markets.

A word of caution: Political know-how, political capabilities, and political strength are obviously very important to the life of any major institution or industry. However, the political arena—national or local—can be a trap. To be recognized by the high and mighty, to know the movers and shakers of government, to hobnob with them, is an elixir that makes one feel good and self-important. But as every CEO knows, or should know, there is an inherent danger to this process; it can blind one's sensibilities and make one forget the priorities.

In politics as well as in cultural affairs, I tried never to lose sight that such activities were secondary to our real goals. Indeed, the primary efforts of our leadership had to be focused on growth, momentum, new markets, and innovation. Our political and cultural activities were to be used only to enhance the potential of our underlying objectives. These priorities must never be reversed.

23

Trading on the Run

Dayle Henington soon learned what my wife, our children, and our friends knew about me: the telephone was my constant companion. Henington once told Bob Dole that after he worked with me he knew where every pay phone in the Capitol was located. His point was well taken. To deal with me meant putting up with my trading habit. I almost never let anything stand in the way of trading the markets, no matter what part of the world I was in. In Singapore or Tokyo, I'd be up in the middle of the night trading Chicago markets from their opening to their closing. Then, with hardly an hour's worth of sleep, I would have to function normally during the following business day. In London and Paris, the time difference was better, but trading would still present problems.

My trading exploits would probably make a hilariously funny movie since I have made calls to the market from the strangest places and under the weirdest circumstances. No matter what, I would stay connected—from far-away islands where I would have to beg, or literally buy the telephone connection from a private operation; or from stores and hotel lobbies across the breadth of Europe. Whether it was from the side of a highway, or from a senator's office in D.C., or from the phone in a freezer of a small restaurant on a Caribbean island, I always found a way to get through to the pit. And in recent years, 30,000 feet up in the clouds never stopped me, as long as the plane had a phone. After quotations became available on portable machines, I would never travel without one. I would even place a QuoTrek screen, a portable quote gizmo that provides on-line quotations from FM frequency, on the table in front of me when I delivered congressional testimony. Often, the curiosity of senators and congressmen would get the best of them, and they would step down from their seats to come around to see what I was doing. After a time, it became my personal trademark, and eventually, the officials expected it.

But even with the quote machine, the phone was indispensable. One morning in Washington, long before the cellular phone made life a lot easier, Henington and I were scheduled to meet with New York Congressman Barber B. Conable, the number two person on the House Ways and Means Committee. He was a bigwig in the Republican party who headed the Republican Eagles and would go on to replace Robert McNamara as president of the World Bank. He was George Bush's "right-hand man."

We needed to speak with him regarding a technical tax issue. He was very difficult to reach, so we had to catch him on the run. Henington learned that Conable was going to speak at a breakfast meeting at the Sheraton Hotel sponsored by the Republican National Committee. And he knew Nancy Thawley, the secretary to the Republican party who arranging the breakfast. With a little fast talking, he managed to wangle me a seat next to Conable. People, Henington told me as we reached the hotel, were "killing" to get that chair.

The markets that particular morning were wild, and I had major positions. Outside the room were three pay phones and I was using all three. I couldn't leave the phones. Henington was inside stalling and was a bit embarrassed.

"Can you hold the chair, because Leo's on an important call?" he asked Thawley.

"If you don't take the chair now," she insisted, "I'm going to give it to somebody else."

"Leo, it's now or never." Henington urged.

Like a harried newspaperman on a hot story trying to scoop the competition, I dashed from the phones leaving them dangling by their cords to make sure the lines remained open. And I sat down next to Conable for 15 minutes or so. We covered the points that concerned me. Then I excused myself and was back on the phones.

I had long ago learned to trade in motion, using phone booths at a rate that would make Clark Kent envious. (Too bad I didn't have his x-ray vision.) There is a standing comment that follows me to this day: "Melamed is always on the telephone and always trading."

I did stop trading long enough in July 1979 to celebrate my daughter Idelle's wedding to Howard Dubnow. It was a gala black-tie affair with all the trimmings, the first of its kind where there were as many traders present as at the Merc's annual dinner dance. The traders were, after all, my family. Although it was held in the huge Guild Hall of the Ambassador West Hotel, Betty and I still had to limit the list of invites to three hundred. Those who didn't make the cut held a grudge for years. At the time, it was the social event of the season and was later compared to the wedding in Mario Puzo's *The Godfather*.

The wedding was everything Betty and I could ever have hoped for on such an occasion, but it contained one little-known incident that could have shattered the celebration. My daughter's in-laws, Herbert and Thelma Dubnow, were observant Jews, while my father, as I have explained, was not. The issue that surfaced was whether my father would wear the traditional skull cap under the *chupah*. As I suspected would be the case, he declined. After all, he had refused to wear one in the Bialystok Synagogue during a most foreboding hour at the outbreak of World War II. He rejected all my appeals and refused to budge, until I played my trump card. I spoke to him in Yiddish, saying, "Please, please, don't spoil the celebration for your only granddaughter." His love for Idelle momentarily overpowered his principles. It was a unique occurrence in the life of Isaac Melamdovich.

Fortunately, the wedding was on the Fourth of July while the market was closed. Otherwise, as my son Jordan would say, I probably would have called the market from the *chupah*. I remember during the heat of the gold market in 1980, I refused to let a gallbladder attack stop me. At 5:00 A.M. from my hospital bed, I telephoned my secretary, asking her to fetch my charts. When she arrived two hours later, I was propped up in bed, a cigarette dangling from my mouth, an oxygen tube in my nose, an intravenous-fluid needle in my arm and the telephone pressed to my ear, barking market orders to my floor clerk, Arthur Tursh. Tursh is my cousin and an extremely capable fellow. His father, Norman, and Norman's sister Janet, were the closest relatives my family had in the world and took us in when we first arrived in the States. Tursh used his experience as my quotation and order clerk to turn it into a career as an expert on the information highway.

When the hospital staff came to take me for tests, I refused to go until trading ended at 1:30 P.M. I can't recall if I won or lost that particular day, but I know I got out of the market just in case the X rays revealed something far more serious than a grouchy gallbladder. No operation was necessary. Just a change in diet and a little rest. I was back on the trading floor a few days later screaming at the top of my lungs. Before that, I'd have given odds that the first organ to go would have been my lungs, not my gallbladder.

I admit it. I am driven when it comes to trading, but I insist it is not because I'm a trading junkie. There are two valid reasons for my obsessive habit. To begin with, the markets don't know that I am away from the floor or, in later years, from the screen. They go up and down as the conditions dictate, whether or not I am there to see it. And I have found that for me and for most traders, one of the important elements of trading is to know the rhythm of the market. You have to have at least a mental picture of where the market has been and how it got to its current price level. While the telephone is, at best, a poor substitute for being there, providing only momentary glimpses of the market's movements, it is better than nothing. The more calls, the clearer the picture.

Second, as I have said, trading was my main source of income. There was no bonus for inventing the IMM or royalty payments. I didn't expect it. Compensation for my efforts wasn't what building the Merc was all about. I never approached it with a "what's in it for me" attitude nor intended to use the Merc as a jumping-off point to another job to further my career. Of course, I profited along with my fellow Merc members in the increased value of the seats as a result of the new markets, but that profit was not available as income.

Most people on the outside assumed differently. Once during dinner with one of this nation's top merger and acquisition specialists, he asked me if I would mind telling him what I was worth. Bemused, I inquired why he asked that question.

"Oh," he responded, "it is to satisfy a bet. It is a well-known fact that I am a billionaire and I bet that you are one as well."

I nearly fell out of my chair. "Where did you ever come to that silly notion?" I asked, unable to hold back my laughter. "Although I am well off, I'm nowhere near that kind of league."

"But how can that be?" my dinner companion persisted, "I know what I make when I participate in the launching of a new stock or a newly acquired company, and in your case, you invented an entirely new product line. Even if you received only 10 or 15 percent of the value produced to the Exchange, with the growth involved over the years, it would have to bring you billionaire status."

It was almost an embarrassment to explain that my invention was for free. But at least the conversation made a good story.

The Merc was a lifetime of careers rolled into one: business, finance, politics, and a dozen other disciplines shaping my role. But I still had to earn a living. And trading was my parallel career. I make all my own trading decisions and personally place them for execution by way of market orders, price orders, or stops, using a direct open speaker phone or private phone to a central Dellsher station on the Merc trading floor where my clerk Mary Ambrose flashes them into the pit for execution. The system is similar to the ones used by bank or investment bank traders who deal in the interbank and cash markets.

In the old days, just before entering the trading pit, I'd hastily review my hand-drawn price charts and then go at it, yelling and elbowing, sometimes to victory and sometimes to defeat. Today, I sit back (and sometimes pace) as I enter the information superhighway, where money changes on screens instead of in hands, and my trading landscape includes a Reuters SDS-2 communications system, which provides cash quotations as well as general information; an Aspen Net Graphics computer terminal, which operates on the basis of a variety of programs I devised; an array of daily, weekly, and monthly charts, which are updated every day; and a complement of internal MercQuote machines. This trading arsenal at my Chicago office is duplicated at my primary residence in suburban Chicago and my second home in Arizona.

The system I devised allows me to follow all the markets, to have quick access to the floor to place orders and execute them, and to have the flexibility to conduct a variety of official functions during the course of a market day. I am even able to handle phone calls and office appointments or meetings while trading, thanks to the mute button on my speaker phone. My trading method often bewilders visitors to my office as well as staff members who fall victim to my divided attention between themselves, the quote machines, and verbal orders I occasionally bark into the speaker phone.

During the course of my service to the Merc, I consistently rebuffed any attempt at compensation. When the issue would be brought up at Board meetings, an annual ritual, I would explain that serving the Merc was an honor, and that was compensation enough. I know that this may sound silly or square, but it was my honest opinion and I lived by it. As long as I could trade and earn a living that way, I was satisfied. The example I set, unfortunately, prevented other officers of the Board, particularly the chairman, from receiving any reasonable compensation.

Then things really changed. The Merc's fantastic growth created monstrous responsibilities for me as well as the CME chairman, and reached the point where it literally consumed all our business day and beyond. This problem was more severe for me because it seriously impacted my ability to trade. In 1987, in the wake of the stock market crash, the demand on my time was such that I could no longer trade effectively, regardless of the number of phone booths. Indeed, my increased responsibilities caused me to incur substantial trading losses. Brian Monieson, who was a trader like me and who as chairman had previously experienced the effects of the workload, insisted that the Merc redefine its compensation policy to reflect the realities of modern times. "Leo, you have to put your personal preferences to the side and accept reality. Running this exchange is a full-time job and the membership must be brought to understand this." After 20 years of no compensation except a token honorarium, I relented. A special Merc compensation committee, which included Donald Jacobs, Dean of Northwestern University's Kellogg School of Management, was created to examine what other exchanges were doing and make its recommendations to the Board. The resulting schedule approved by the Board established, for the first time, an annual $500,000 stipend for me as special counsel, and an annual salary of $250,000 for the chairman of the Exchange. While these numbers seemed fairly large after all the years of a "no-pay" policy, they were well below modern standards for CEOs of large financial institutions. Still, the CME membership was unprepared for the sudden change in policy, and when someone leaked news of it to the press before it was adequately explained to the floor, some members resented it.

At the time, the *Chicago Sun-Times* quoted Scott Shelton, partner of Spencer Stuart, as saying, "If they had to pay Leo Melamed $10 million a year, it would be a bargain." Nevertheless, a year or so later, it gave rise to an issue that caused a momentary blip in my otherwise uninterrupted love affair with the membership. The controversy was brought to the floor by my old nemesis, Douglas Bragan, and an old-line cattle trader, Emmet Whealen. They began pushing for a referendum that would prevent the payment of salary to any Merc board officer who was not elected by the membership. Ostensibly, it was not intended as a personal attack on me. Whealen publicly stated: "I and everyone else would elect Melamed as chairman and pay him as much as he wants, but we want everyone to run for office." The office of special counsel and executive committee chairman had for years been an office created and appointed by the CME board. While I didn't disagree with the spirit of the referendum, it upset me. Although the referendum was defeated handily, and although I realized that the incident reflected the views of a vocal minority, for the first time, I began to question whether my previous "no-pay" policy was wise after all.

Win or lose, the fact that I traded for a living had many applications in running the Exchange. Foremost, of course, was the fact that it gave me rapport with the trading community. I was one of them. I could not only discuss the markets with them on an equal level, but I understood what it took to make a product attractive to traders. This commonality of interest was the single most essential element in my ability to get the membership to assist me when it came to launching new products. I believe it was the Merc's secret weapon and the primary reason that the Merc's rate of success with new products far outdistanced all other exchanges. The S&P contract is still the last "large" contract successfully launched by any exchange. During its early months of life, I traded S&P full time.

Trading also provided me with an insight about new futures instruments that might work. Such information is not as valid when it originates away from the marketplace. Markets are a crucible of ideas. The good ones survive; the others are quickly relegated to the scrap-heap. And ideas are the springboard to new instruments of trade. It is how the idea for financial futures was born. And how the Merc's "Global Exchange," GLOBEX, evolved.

Being a trader also meant that I was fully acquainted with every aspect of futures markets applications, including its infamous tax straddles. When the futures industry was threatened with a change in the tax laws in the early 1980s, the issue fell on my shoulders as well as on the shoulders of my counterpart at the CBOT, Les Rosenthal, also a trader. Naturally, we went to Dan Rostenkowski with the problem and he pointed to Congressman Marty Russo as the guy to handle the issue. It was very complicated. The juggling of profit and loss through a so-called tax straddle as a means to defer payments of taxes was being challenged by the Internal Revenue Service. The futures industry contended that the practice was legal because there was an inherent economic risk to a tax straddle futures position. The risk was there because the differential between the contract months that made up the tax spread (short in one contract month, long in another) was always changing. Indeed, to minimize this open risk, the so-called butterfly straddle, involving three contract months, became popular. The butterfly spread stabilized the inherent changes between contract months and lessened the exposure.

Tax spreading wasn't small-fry. Especially after some of Wall Street's major firms—even the likes of Merrill Lynch whose chairman was Donald Regan and destined to become Secretary of Treasury under President Reagan—set up special departments for the purpose of conducting such tax trading maneuvers for their customers. You can't really blame them; tax straddles produced some fat commissions. It was rumored that even the Rolling Stones used tax straddles to avoid taxes. Perhaps, as Don Regan later claimed, he didn't know what some of the executives below him at Merrill were doing. Still, it was strange how, after he became Treasury Secretary, he took after our markets with a vengeance, trying to institute a transaction tax.

Les Rosenthal and I remained locked up for a full day in a rented room in the O'Hare Hilton with Marty Russo so that we could educate the Congressman on how futures markets worked and the complexities of tax straddles. Russo made an all-out effort. He proposed a bill that would have cracked down on the tax straddle for everyone, except futures traders. One of his key supporters was Tony Coelho, a California Democrat, who was chairman of the Democratic Congressional Campaign Committee in 1981. Coelho never let us forget his support. Russo's proposal was adopted by the House Ways and Means Committee and passed by the House of Representatives in July 1981. We had won half the battle. One could make a real good case that Russo was right: futures traders take an enormous risk in trading; this creates liquidity, which makes successful markets. But there are no guarantees that a trader will be profitable year after year. If a trader has a losing year after having paid the taxes for a profitable year, the trader will be out of risk capital with which to continue to make a market.

For a while, it looked as if Marty Russo had saved the commodity industry, and the CBOT crowed. But that was before the bill reached the

Senate side, where, although we also had friends, we couldn't win. Clout, even among friends, could take us just so far. Senator Bob Dole, a Kansas Republican, was certainly a free-market thinker, a friend of mine and of the Merc who had visited us six or seven times over the years. He could be acerbic, yet he was a compassionate person, quick thinking, smart, and straightforward. One day during the heat of the tax legislation controversy, Dole showed me a *sanitized* tax return in which an unidentified tax payer, a trader, had deferred $100 million in income without paying one red cent in taxes. (What the Senator didn't know is that I could have made a pretty good stab at who that trader was.) Dole showed this to me to prove that the tax straddle was going to lose in the Senate. I believed him. When the issue came to a vote on the Senate floor, New York Senator Patrick Moynihan spoke against tax straddles by exclaiming that, until then, he had assumed that *"A butterfly straddle must refer to a highly pleasurable erotic activity popular during the Ming Dynasty."* The Senate rejected tax straddles.

Before the legislation went to the Conference Committee to straighten out the differences between the House and Senate bills, Bob Dole called me into his office for a private meeting. Dole offered a compromise, one that I felt was eminently fair. Nevertheless, I could not accept his offer unilaterally; I needed industry-wide support. Although I lobbied for the compromise, the CBOT refused to budge, counting on the fact that Rostenkowski was to chair the Conference Committee and would hold strong for us. But Dole was also on that committee and this was Rostenkowski's first conference. Dole won. It was a stunning defeat for our industry. We were fortunate, however, to save something from the loss. The revised tax law carried favorable treatment for our traders. The maximum tax rate on trading profits was reduced from 70 percent to 32 percent and allowed traders to qualify for long-term capital gains rates even on investments held for less than six months. And it got even better. A few years later, at the urging of Tom Donovan and myself, Rostenkowski revisited tax straddles and successfully enacted a "grandfather" clause for traders who previously had conducted U.S.-based tax straddles. It saved many of our traders from the wrath of the IRS. In addition, it gave traders five years to pay the taxes they had deferred.

This had been my first serious encounter with Chicago Board of Trade intractability. This was an inbred heritage as a result of their being the oldest and biggest futures market in the world. It often bordered on an "our way or no way" arrogance. But then again, before the modern futures era, the CBOT was the only commodities market around. It had the clout and power to dictate its terms and get away with it. In 1981, I shrugged it off. Every great institution, I reasoned, had its faults. Besides, the CBOT had made an honest mistake; we all do that.

Over time, things changed. Financial futures came along to challenge the grain markets' dominance, and the CME challenged the CBOT's number one place in the sun. And while the CBOT's tough image remained, it learned to work within the futures community. I probably dealt with CBOT officials more than anyone else in the futures industry, and I learned a secret: The CBOT officials could be reasoned with and would compromise as necessary—if they trusted the person with whom they were dealing. Trouble was, its past reputation often frightened opponents and made them approach the CBOT in a cautious way. Distrust breeds distrust. Of course, back then, the CBOT's reputation made it easier for me to fashion a contrasting reasonable image for the Merc. It set the two institutions apart. Oddly, since my departure from Merc officialdom, I cannot help but detect that there seems to be a role reversal with respect to the public attitudes of the two Chicago exchanges. Maybe it's my imagination.

My relationship with the CBOT, its officials, and membership, however, remained strong throughout the years. It began, as I have stated, in the early seventies and continued through the current presidency of Tom Donovan and chairmanship of Pat Arbor. But the relationship was boosted considerably in 1979 during the tenure of CBOT chairman Ralph Peters, who, like me, was first and foremost a trader. Except that I was never in Peters' league. Indeed, if I had to single out the greatest futures trader I ever knew, I would have little hesitancy in choosing Ralph Peters. Because we were good friends, at the time of the S&P contract launch, I asked Peters to give us his support. He unhesitatingly did and bought 1,000 S&P contracts during the first week of trading. I think he held on to them for the next several years, making an enormous profit.

I was paid the ultimate compliment by rival CBOT when Ralph Peters, as CBOT chairman, offered me a directorship on its board. In turning down the offer, I wrote to Peters that it "was one of the highest plaudits anyone could bestow upon me." Because we were competitors, no doubt it would have posed a conflict of interest with my loyalty, obviously tilting toward the Merc. Besides, I was already on overload pouring all my thoughts and energy into Merc business. As special counsel, I attended every Merc Board meeting and countless ad hoc committee meetings. I was also chairman of the Merc Financial Instruments Steering Committee and a member of the Executive Committee, as well as the Real Estate Committee and several others. In addition, I was chairman of the National Futures Association and a director of the Futures Industry Association. And among it all, there was my trading.

I didn't, however, dismiss Peters' gesture lightly. Rather, I saw it as an opportunity to ease tension between the exchanges and to begin to lay the groundwork for an alliance for the future. In industry matters, I was convinced, a united front between the two biggest futures exchanges was imperative. In my letter to Peters, I assured him that his offer ". . . has had and will have some meaningful and lasting effects on CBOT and CME relationships." Then I sounded the trumpet of alarm:

> I need not tell you that we in Chicago are faced with formidable competitors in New York, not to speak of continuing altercations with Washington. Thus, it is incumbent that our two institutions coordinate our efforts in these regards and work closely and in harmony whenever possible . . . because our joint cause is beneficial to Chicago futures markets. I promise you that I will make myself available to you and the CBOT should any occasion arise where I could give counsel or undertake specific assignments on behalf of our mutual goals. Please convey these thoughts to the members of your Executive Committee.

That 1979 letter secured my favorable standing with CBOT members. Reviewing that letter today, it seems all the more remarkable given that it was written eight years before the stock market crash from which Chicago's futures industry would rise to challenge Wall Street's dominance of the financial markets and its influence in Washington.

Trading for a living also gave me ideas on how to best illustrate the beauty of our markets. Take the day in 1980 when I was escorting officials of the Bank of China through the Exchange. The chief of the delegation was a charming gentleman with a wonderful sense of humor who was visiting Chicago for the first time. We were on the trading floor and, as was my custom with official dignitaries, I wanted to show capitalism in action, to provide a textbook lesson in how markets work and people acquire wealth participating in them. I had done the exercise numerous times with senators and congressmen. I would buy one or several contracts and then have my guest observe the change in the prices. The idea was to make a profit on the trade. Get in and get out.

I bought five T-bill contracts that particular morning, not a very big trade. And promptly the market started to fall. I got out—with a loss. The Chinese official chuckled and whispered in my ear: "Hmm. No dessert for lunch." Dessert nothing! For what I had lost on that trade, I could have bought lunch for his entire entourage. It's one thing to have a costly lesson paid for by the student, but when the teacher had to shell out for the lesson, that's quite another matter. It was just another reminder that a market, like a lush rain forest, is filled with promise—and hazards.

Of course, that loss for me was a huge profit for the Merc. The Bank of China officials were so enamored with their visit that they kept in touch and several years later sent me a full-blown official invitation to visit the People's Republic of China—this was not long after Nixon and Kissinger opened the door to China and long before U.S.-Chinese relations really warmed up.

Since I wanted to share this opportunity with other exchange officers, I inquired whether I could bring along our chairman and other senior officials of the Merc. My offer was instantly accepted. In September 1984, I led a Merc delegation, which included CME chairman, Brian Monieson; first vice chairman, Larry Rosenberg; executive committee members, Girard Miller and Jack Sandner; and our spouses to the mysterious world of China for a week-long state visit. In some ways, this trip resembled our European outing a decade before, but this time we had a lot less to prove and were hosted by the government itself. We were treated to sights that at the time were still mostly hidden from the Western world, sights including the Forbidden City, the Great Wall of China, and Tiananmen Square with Mao Tse-Tung's tomb. Walking silently around his embalmed body gave me the same eerie feeling I had as a child when I saw the entombed body of Vladimir Lenin. It was a fabulous visit, giving all of us the privilege of seeing China in its last moments prior to modern reconstruction. It also confirmed what I always suspected: our government knew beans about China.

Prior to departure, an official of the U.S. State Department was sent to brief me on how to behave while in China. "Don't use the word *profit*," the official cautioned, "communists take offense at that word." Also he admonished, "Make certain to down your entire drink when you are toasted; it is an insult if you don't." There were several other such pearls that I have since forgotten.

Lo and behold, no sooner had we arrived when Bing Wong Xue (H.P. Wong), our official intermediary who, a decade later, would become the president of the Bank of China, asked us how much *profit* the average trader makes a year. So much for State Department intelligence. Then, at the state banquet, the governor of the Bank of China toasted me and our delegation, and watched in wonderment as I downed the entire cup of Chinese mai tai—the closest thing to jet fuel on this planet. When I was finished, I noticed that his lips had barely touched his drink. "You must like to drink," the bank official said to me with a wink. I could hardly respond. Betty had to carry me back to the hotel room.

There was a frosting on this cake, however. Upon return to the United States, I got the unbelievable news that the president of the Republic of China, Li Xiannian, had accepted my invitation to visit the Merc should he ever come to the States. The CME soon became a hub of frantic preparations. U.S. Treasury people, who guard heads of state, were all over us securing the premises. The big question was whether the Chinese president would tour the floor itself. If so, the T-men would require trained police dogs to sniff out any bombs that might be hidden in the vast array of members' stations. I hesitated with the answer. "What else will these dogs sniff out?" I asked. This was 1985 and lord only knew what *stuff* members might have hidden in their drawers. "The dogs would find everything," was the answer. Monieson and I huddled on the issue and tried to picture the headlines if any pot was found by the T-men. We decided that the president would view the floor only from the gallery.

On July 26, 1985, with machine-gun-totting T-men pacing the roof of our building, the President of the Republic of China arrived with his delegation. It amounted to an enormous public relations coup as Communism met Capitalism at the Merc. To my knowledge, we were the first U.S. institution to be so honored by the Chinese Republic. CME chairman Brian Monieson and I sat with Li Xiannian in the gallery, and together gave him a full-blown explanation of the trading, while the traders in the S&P pit below us gave him the CME version of a Wall Street ticker tape parade with thousands of trading cards tossed into the air. Afterward, when the State Department called me to inquire how we pulled this off, I explained that it took five T-bill contracts.

This visit not only was an unbelievable coup for the Merc; it set a pattern for all time. It established our floor us as a *must-visit place* when dignitaries came to Chicago. After all, it was so much easier to get a president, prime minister, or even a king to visit our floor when we could tell their public relations people that "the President of China paid us a visit last year." The value of free publicity generated by such high-level visits is impossible to estimate, as is the value of the morale it builds with the membership.

In the agricultural heyday of the Merc, the visiting dignitary was often a grand champion steer or a prize hog, but after finance came to the Merc, so did politicians. The modern tradition dates back to 1972 when I first invited Senator Edmund Muskie to pay us a visit during his campaign for the presidency. Muskie was a relatively small fish generating little attention, but it taught me how much the dignitaries love the media coverage these visits can attract. Such visits are also a colossal image builder for the Merc. So I kept reaching higher and higher on the social and political ladders with a variety of congressmen and senators. Then, in 1975, the highly regarded and eventual U.S. Vice President, Hubert Humphrey, came to view the workings of the new IMM. The resulting publicity spurred many other dignitaries to follow suit. Soon, the word was out: The Merc was *the* place to visit. This process of attracting dignitaries became easier when we established the Merc's Political Action Committee and insisted that officials see the market in action. In 1980, I was one of the early joiners of Ronald Reagan's presidential campaign and, as a consequence, arranged for his visit to the CME floor. To the delight of our membership, which gave him an overwhelming welcome, I made him an honorary Merc member. The Merc's CFPF contributed the $10,000 maximum allowed for each Reagan campaign; however, the total of individual member contributions was much greater. As president, Reagan remembered his trader friends at the Merc and came back for another visit. He did it again at his retirement in 1988.

Over the years, in an effort to share the spotlight, I established the policy that each high-level dignitary would be escorted onto the floor by a minimum of three Merc officials who, besides myself, usually included the Merc chairman and president. We also made certain that there were plenty of media about and that the official had ample opportunity to shake hands with members and clerks, as well as to have photos taken. In this fashion, the visits served a multitude of obvious purposes, including ingratiating the CME with the official and leaving him or her with a memorable experience.

All of this and the growing demands of running the place, of course, took a heavy toll on my floor trading and, eventually, I had to transform myself from a floor trader to an upstairs trader. It was a difficult adjustment, but my philosophical approach to the markets remained much the same. I am a short-term trader, jockeying for a long-term position. There were the practical adjustments as well. For one thing, I now rarely executed trades myself on the floor, and using floor brokers added a large expense to my occupation. For another, I was constantly being interrupted by telephone calls and appointments. A standing rule at the Merc and among my staff members over the years was to afford me as much free morning time for trading the markets. For years I fought on behalf of all traders and brokers who served on the Board or committees to prevent meetings from beginning until after market hours. I wasn't always successful in this quest.

Those few daily morning hours of trading isolation probably did more for me than a vacation every other week. I traded in one kind of stress for another. But there is a difference between trader stress caused by running after a market and the executive stress caused by running an exchange. Though I can't define it, I can feel it. After the market close, the market stress would end swiftly, but the business of the Merc was always hanging over me, seven days a week. Sometimes the only moments of quiet contemplation came at night when I barreled down deserted streets alone in my Porsche on the way home after a late meeting. From my youngest days, I learned that I possessed the same capability that James Clavell attributes to Dunross, the tai-pan in *Nobel House*. It enabled him to function under pressure and carry out a multitude of responsibilities without lowering the quality of his performance. Basically, it is an ability to compartmentalize one's focus. It is very much like closing a drawer and opening another. At no time do I allow the contents of the first drawer to influence my ability to deal with the contents in the next. Each subject matter would receive my undivided attention. This is an attribute necessary for all good bridge players. Without it, any mistake made in a previous contest affects the quality of play in the next. It is no different in running an exchange.

24

The Ultimate Contract

Before Eurodollars could become the supreme futures contract of the IMM, there was a big hurdle to leap. The problem was in the delivery mechanism. T-bills and CDs could be delivered because they were physical instruments. But Eurodollars were a different matter.

From time immemorial, the settlement of a futures contract was through delivery of the product. In fact, court precedent had established that the difference between gambling and futures was that futures "contemplated" delivery. In other words, without delivery, we were not much different from a gambling den—exactly what our detractors had been saying for years. Delivery was so ingrained in our definition that my father once told me that he always worried that someday someone would drive a truck to the building where we lived and ask him where they should deliver the carload of onions his errant son had purchased.

The truth was that deliveries occurred only a tiny fraction of the time. One was not supposed to use the futures market as a substitute for normal market channels in obtaining a product. Deliveries to settle a futures contract were intended solely to stop would-be corserers from driving prices beyond their intrinsic values. The threat of delivery acted as an enforcer, ensuring that if the prices of a futures contract and its cash market equivalent did not converge at the date of maturation of the contract, a seller had the option of making delivery of the product itself rather than offsetting his futures position. That was okay for farm products that could be squeezed out of line. But what about currency or interest-rate futures? To me, it was silly to worry about someone cornering, say, the Deutsche mark. So I reasoned that financial contracts did not need delivery.

Besides, futures markets were used as an insurance policy, not to actually take delivery. All a trader wanted was the difference—in cash—between the value of the instrument at the time it was bought and the time it was sold, or vice versa. In other words, never mind the Deutsche marks, give me the profit—in cash. As E.B. Harris always said, "Money talks, bullshit walks."

Eurodollars, unlike CDs or T-bills, were intangible; they were just the rate of interest. This reality not only escaped our regulators; it was not well understood by many of my colleagues—some of whom were on the Merc Board. Even Barry Lind, who was usually light years ahead of most of the other Board members in understanding how our markets worked, looked at me as if I had gone off the rails. "What do you mean, no delivery? How can you have a futures contract without delivery?" It was just as hard to describe what Eurodollars were. I remember in 1980 painfully explaining to the new Merc chairman Jack Sandner, who was from a cattle commission house, that Eurodollars were *not* simply dollars floating about in Europe, as many of our floor traders believed. Our proposed Eurodollar contract represented non-negotiable time deposits. This made the traditional delivery mechanism highly problematic. You can't deliver a rate of interest; instead, you can pay *in cash* the value of the differential in interest rates between the time of purchase and time of sale, or vice versa.

In other words, if the Merc was ever to have a Eurodollar interest-rate contract, it would first have to have *cash settlement*. But cash settlement was a new invention. The idea that on expiration day there would simply be a variation on margin payment based upon the final settlement price was untested. In the case of the Eurodollar contract, the settlement price would be determined on the last trading date by polling the London banks to determine the average LIBOR or London Interbank Offer Rate.

The concept to do away with the requirement of physical delivery did not come to me by virtue of Eurodollars. Indeed, when I first contemplated a market without delivery, it was before there was a CFTC. For me, the origin of this thought can be traced to a conversation I had with Elmer Falker long before—not about Eurodollars or cash settlement, but about stock index futures. Although I have often been credited with the idea of stock index futures, it wasn't my idea.

Elmer and I were once discussing new products for the Chicago Mercantile Exchange, a subject always uppermost in my mind. Suddenly, he became thoughtful, drew on the stub of his cigar, exhaled expansively, and spoke in a harsh whisper: "Listen, Lee, the ultimate contract is of course Dow Jones futures!"

"Dow Jones futures, wow!" I instantly knew what he meant and became enthralled with the idea. "Why hasn't anybody done it?"

"You can't make delivery," the little guy responded with finality.

I understood. Elmer said the idea had probably been around for a hundred years but no one would ever do it. After all, it was impossible to deliver a properly weighted portfolio with each of the stocks in the index. How indeed could we deliver 30 Dow stocks, what with splits and dividends and the constant changes in the list of stocks? But that conversation wouldn't let me rest. It stayed buried in my mind and haunted me for years. *What if someday we don't have to make delivery!* What if there was the ability to have settlement of futures contracts in cash instead of by delivery? Then, whammo, you could have Elmer's ultimate contract.

In 1974, when I began contemplating whether to support the creation of the CFTC, the thought hit me that only a federal agency could ordain the legitimacy of cash settlement. If it did, then the Merc could have stock indexes and lord only knows what else. Of course, cash settlement was not an early priority of the CFTC or even of the Merc. Our efforts toward cash settlement did not begin in earnest until 1977 after we had proved that interest rates were a successful vehicle for futures markets. Then, in 1979, the new CFTC chairman, James Stone, would not even hear of the idea. It wasn't until he was replaced by Phil Johnson in 1981 that Jerry Salzman, Mark Powers, and I began the difficult process of convincing the CFTC that cash settlement would not corrupt the market mechanism through price manipulation and that it wasn't a slick form of gambling. Commissioner Gary Seevers also played a pivotal role. Ultimately, I had one-on-one meetings with every CFTC commissioner, as well as Phil Johnson, the chairman. The weight of those personal discussions coupled with the legal arguments provided by Jerry Salzman finally bore fruit. I suppose that if ever the CFTC needs to prove its value to the marketplace, it can, above all else, point with pride at the innovation of cash settlement. I seriously doubt that our industry could have achieved even a fraction of the transaction volumes we have already experienced or plan for the potential that is still ours, without removal of the requirement for physical delivery from futures trade. That could never have happened without the CFTC. Phil Johnson said to me at the time that approval of cash settlement was the hallmark of his tenure as CFTC chairman. I certainly agree.

In 1981, principally as a result of my strong lobbying efforts, Phil Johnson became CFTC chairman. Oddly, because of a falling-out with the CBOT, Johnson did not have their full support. But with an excellent legal background and extensive expertise in futures, he was the perfect choice for CFTC chairmanship. I was tired of political appointees who knew nothing about our markets. As I anticipated, Phil Johnson did an outstanding job, streamlining the CFTC and its procedures, innovating, and breaking up the logjam of pending contract applications. Aside from cash settlement, Phil Johnson left our industry another legacy of immense value. Even before he was appointed CFTC Chairman, he had taken a nine-month sabbatical from his law firm to write a *Commodities Regulation* treatise. This comprehensive two-volume work, published by Little,

Brown and Company, became the industry's bible and is still today the definitive work on futures market regulation.

In 1981, the world took note of the Merc's Eurodollar contract as the first cash-settled futures market. Technically, however, Les Hosking, chairman of the Sydney Futures Exchange (SFE) in Australia beat everyone by launching a cash-settled U.S. dollar contract in 1980. Alas, that contract made little impact on the world at the time, but regardless, the era of index futures was now upon us. Ralph Waldo Emerson's simple truth kept echoing through my head, "Invention breeds invention."

I did not wait for approval of cash settlement to launch the strategy for Elmer Falker's ultimate contract in stock index futures. We had set our sights on the Standard & Poor's Corporation 500 Stock Price Index (S&P 500) as early as 1978, but didn't finalize a deal with them until 1980. That decision was the result of an excruciating internal Merc discussion, which ultimately led us to conclude, correctly as it turned out, that the S&P 500 index was the most likely stock index to succeed.

At the time, this represented the most controversial and difficult issue of that era. Every exchange, large or small, was preparing to launch stock index futures. The NYFE would obviously go with its New York Stock Exchange Index. The Kansas City Board of Trade (KCBT) ended up with the Value Line Index. And it was no secret that the Chicago Board of Trade had decided to go with the Dow Jones Industrial Average. Clearly, the Dow was the most popular and well-known index of the time. It was, as it is today, the way the public and the media measure the movement of stocks in the United States.

I was again faced with a similar issue as the one I had between short- or long-term interest rates. The Merc could either take on the CBOT and fight for the Dow, or go with the S&P 500, the only other index of renown. Our Economics Department provided an analysis that indicated that portfolio managers, who we reckoned would be the ones to drive the business toward futures, measured their annual results against the S&P 500. This indicated to me that the commercial hedgers would be attracted to the S&P Index rather than to the Dow.

But there was no empirical evidence on which to base a decision about which index would succeed. It was all feel, intuition, and guesswork. Our Stock Index Committee waited for my opinion, and I agonized and wrestled with it for months. I finally made up my mind in favor of S&Ps, but waited to hear Barry Lind's opinion. Lind, as a general rule, leaned in favor of contracts that appealed more to public participants, while I usually went with the commercial interests. This should have put us squarely on opposite sides of the index issue. But on this occasion, although Lind had previously vacillated back and forth, he agreed with me.

As history shows, the decision in favor of S&P was a most pivotal one for the CME. It ensured the Merc's position as the world's capital of stock index futures, bringing to our members an entirely new as well as huge source of business. Indeed, subsequent successes of the S&P contract have distorted the difficulty of this issue and clouded the fact that it was far from an obvious choice. Indeed, to this day, I believe that if the CBOT had been able to launch a Dow index contract, it would have been very successful. In truth, years later, we too unsuccessfully tried to make contact with the Dow Jones owners in an attempt to draw them into negotiations.

The way it turned out, the decision to go with S&P may not have been as important as the decision whether or not to pay for it. The critical error the CBOT made was not in choosing the Dow over the S&P, but because they decided that the Dow Jones index was public domain. In other words, the CBOT did not feel that they needed to get the rights from Dow Jones to use their index for a futures contract. As history bears witness, the owners of Dow Jones had a very different opinion on this subject. They took the CBOT to court and won in a decision by the Illinois Supreme Court. The Dow was ruled to be the private property of Dow Jones.

Later, in a locker room conversation at Chicago's East Bank Club, Illinois Supreme Court Justice Seymour Simon privately confronted me on this issue. Justice Simon was the lone dissenter from the majority opinion which refused to grant the CBOT rights to the index. Did I believe the CBOT should have been given the right to the Dow Jones index? I candidly replied that it was a close call.

But at the time we decided to use the S&P index, the issue whether such indices were public domain was still wide open. Our attorney Jerry Salzman believed as did the CBOT attorney, that these indexes had, over time, become "public utilities," and that the owners had lost their property rights. But Salzman was smart enough not to argue with me when I explained that, first of all, I wasn't convinced, and second of all, I didn't care. The point I made to Salzman was that my modus operandi was not to take unnecessary chances. I was not about to risk the future of the Merc's success in the ultimate contract by being miserly. Besides, Milton Friedman had taught me, first and foremost, to be a capitalist. I was prepared to pay a fair price for S&P index rights and not worry whether or not it was public domain.

Shortly thereafter, Jerry Salzman, Jack Sandner, and I were meeting with officials of Standard & Poor's Corporation to hammer out the contractual conditions. The negotiations were somewhat comical. To this day, I am not certain that Brenton W. Harries, president of Standard & Poor's Corp., or

George Baron, their general counsel, fully understood why we wanted rights to their index. At that time, futures contracts on the stock market must have sounded like an idea straight out of a science fiction novel by Isaac Asimov. Of course, none of us really knew what the rights were worth. The agreement we finally reached on February 28, 1980, for ten cents per trade with a set annual dollar amount as a cap, turned out to be far too low a price. Indeed, in 1984, I agreed with Ira Herenstein and Bob Andrialis, who were now heading up the Standard & Poor's Division of McGraw Hill, to tear up the old contract and renegotiate a much fairer deal for S&P and longer rights for us.

The CME was the first in line to apply for a *cash-settled* stock index contract, after the CFTC approved the concept of cash settlement. Technically this meant that the Merc would get approval before all the other applications for cash-settled stock index contracts. However, the first application for a stock index contract—before the concept of cash settlement was approved—was made by the Kansas City Board of Trade for its Value Line Index. This application was for physical delivery and contained a complex delivery mechanism. It didn't stand a snowball's chance in hell. Once cash settlement was approved, the KCBT quickly withdrew its physical delivery application in favor of a cash delivery equivalent. But this placed the KCBT behind the other applicants.

CFTC Commissioner Susan M. Phillips, who was destined to become the agency's chairperson less than a year later, called me with a very special request. The KCBT, she argued, was a small exchange, struggling to get a foothold in the financial arena; similarly the NYFE. Would the Merc, Phillips inquired, be a good Samaritan and not stand on the technicality if the CFTC approved the KCBT and the NYFE index contracts ahead of the Merc's? It would only be a difference of a few days, she promised. I agreed. I didn't think the Merc was giving much away since to me it was clear that our S&P contract would rule the index futures world. A favor of this kind to the CFTC would pay many dividends in the years ahead. Accordingly, the Merc's application was approved third in line, and our contract in stock market futures was launched on April 21, 1982.

I point all this out to illustrate that a market is more than a bright idea. It takes planning, calculation, arm-twisting, and tenacity to get a market up and going. Even when it's chugging along, it has to be cranked and pushed. And sometimes it has to be restarted.

The S&P futures contract started off with a bang and overtook the others shortly after the contract began trading, proving that good guys don't always finish last, contrary to what Leo Durocher proclaimed. But it was a gargantuan effort, and I gave it everything I had, working at a 24-hour-a-day pace in preparation. Not only did I personally speak with dozens of traders, but I prepared my elite corps on the floor to continuously turn up the "support-the-contract" rhetoric. We prepared innumerable workshops, seminars, and reference material for our members and potential equity participants. Leaving nothing to chance, I met with a number of large local traders and exacted assurances from them about how much they would trade on opening day and the days that followed. This was standard operating procedure for me. It was also normal for me to request open interest assistance from large traders. I usually got the help I needed. This latter procedure grew out of the explosion in new financial contracts and the competition for their national attention.

In the early days, before the IMM was born, the mission was simply to get the quotes into the newspaper—any paper. It was the only means to draw attention to the prices of a new contract: its daily high, its low, its close. Ron Frost and I used to spend days on end visiting and calling financial editors of newspapers around the country and even in foreign domiciles in an attempt to convince them that their readers desperately needed to know the closing price of March feeder cattle or December turkeys. In Chicago, the *Chicago Tribune* and the *Chicago Sun-Times* were key. *The New York Times* of course mattered; but to succeed nationally, you had to get the prices into *The Wall Street Journal*.

When the competition for new financial markets heated up, things really got difficult. The newspapers, particularly *The Wall Street Journal*, had only so much space available to devote to financial quotes and statistics. Every exchange competed for that block of newsprint. When this was unattainable, it became common to buy space on the financial page in order to quote the prices of new contracts. But that was an expensive proposition, and everyone's goal was to get the coverage for free. To determine who would get their quotes free and who wouldn't, *The Wall Street Journal* invented the open interest test. Open interest reflected the open long and short positions in a contract—theoretically, the higher the number of open positions, the more successful the contract. *The WSJ* arbitrarily declared that no contract would get free coverage until its open interest reached 5,000 contracts. Now the race was on. Every exchange with a new product wanted to be the first to hit that magic number.

The result was predictable. Traders at every exchange competing for a new market were urged to keep open positions on their books. The traders usually responded by instituting a spread transaction, going long one contract month and short another. In this manner, open interest was created with minimal risk to the trader. But in the case of new markets, the liquidity is sparse, and the likelihood of a spread transaction being executed quickly is minimal—unless, that is, a counterparty trader just happened to come along to take the opposite side to the differential. When an exchange was promoting a new contract and vying for increases in its open interest, it would encourage its traders to accommodate this need. The opening of the equity index contracts in 1982 was probably the last time that exchanges did so because the CFTC ordered this practice stopped. But until then, open interest assignments were common at all exchanges.

As a final insurance policy, I made calls on every major stock house, brokerage firm, and investment banker who was a CME member and called in the chits I had accumulated over the years: *Give us your business in the Spuz.* (The S&P futures contract was nicknamed "Spuz" by the members for its ticker symbol SPZ, representing the December contract.) Everybody pitched in, some more than others. My buddy James Cayne—whom I knew well from our days together in Chicago's bridge community—was now Ace Greenberg's right-hand man at Bear Stearns. Reputedly, Cayne had joined Bear Stearns years before at Ace Greenberg's request because Greenberg, a bridge enthusiast, wanted an expert bridge partner. Cayne didn't hesitate in responding to my call for help. Not only did Bear Stearns provide orders to the pit from day one, but on Cayne's own volition, his prestigious New York investment house took out a full-page *Wall Street Journal* ad supporting the Merc's S&P futures contract. Jimmy Cayne, of course has moved on to become chairman of Bear Stearns and one of the world's greatest bridge players.

I was feeling pretty smug—for about a month. My optimism had been premature, however, and our S&P trading volume began to lag behind that of our most formidable competitor, the New York Futures Exchange, NYFE. John Phelan was chairman of the New York Stock Exchange and his futures offspring, the NYFE, was led by his former specialist partner, Lew Horowitz. Phelan had visited me at the Merc several years before to witness firsthand, as he said, "how Leo made it happen." We spent some time talking and I showed him around the floor. Being an extremely competent guy, it didn't take Phelan long to figure out that there were two elements that made a difference: personal leadership and our traders. NYFE chairman Lew Horowitz also knew this.

I was in London at the time with Jack Sandner on a marketing visit to Keith Woodbridge who was in charge of our IMM office there. In 1979, Larry Rosenberg and I had opened the London office, the first American exchange to go overseas, as part of our efforts to internationalize the Chicago markets. But on this visit when our S&P volume started to sputter, I got very nervous. I couldn't concentrate, knowing that the S&P contract was in trouble. So we cut the trip short and hopped the next plane back to Chicago.

On the airplane, I had time to think. I decided that our floor crowd had become too complacent. We had gotten off to too fast a start. Having won so many competitive victories in recent years left the traders with a feeling of invincibility. And there was another problem. I realized that the new Index and Options Market (IOM) traders were far too inexperienced and undercapitalized to make a significant difference in our battle for trading volume. If we were to win this battle, it would be on the backs of our experienced CME and IMM corps. But asking experienced members to turn away from their own successful pits in the agricultural sector, currencies, or interest rates is always difficult, and nearly impossible when their own markets are extremely active, as they were at that time. What was needed was a special approach.

Suddenly, some 35,000 feet in the air, I had a brainstorm. It occurred to me that our guys would probably respond if I asked them for only a small portion of time each day. When we returned, we relaunched the S&P 500 contract with a brand new marketing campaign: "15 Minutes Please." I was dead certain it would work. Its thrust was directed at the old line members. Every member was urged to spend at least 15 minutes in the S&P pit during the course of the trading day. Jack Sandner and I stood at the door to personally hand to every trader a "15 Minutes Please" button. Not everyone, of course, took a shot. But enough did. It turned out to be the most successful marketing idea I ever had. Personally leading this counterattack, I never left the pit. I remember the traders' faces filling with pride as our volume began to bottom out and then surge forward.

Many of them, including Don Nadick, came over to me each day, as if to confirm that they had made good their time commitment. Nadick was a black belt in tae kwon do and kung fu. He loved sports and told me that to him "trading was like hitting a home run in baseball, a swish shot in basketball, or a touchdown in football." Nadick had his formative trader training at the Mid-America Commodity Exchange, the minor leagues of trading, as it were. The Mid-America Commodity Exchange, owned by the Chicago Board of Trade, traded half contracts of some of the CBOT products and was housed in the Merc's old building at Jackson and the Chicago River, which they had bought from us. It provided many with a cheap entry into the world of futures. It was where a good number of trading stars such as Rich Dennis got their starts and went on to make fortunes in the big leagues. Dennis, of course, became a national philanthropist who used his commodity profits to advance his philosophical causes.

Some traders, including Ted Kohl and Tim McAuliffe, came to do 15 minutes and remained to become permanent members of the S&P pit. Kohl was an old-line Merc trader. McAuliffe, on the other hand, was one of those tough-minded guys who loved to do battle. He had met some Merc members playing racquetball at McClurg Court, and soon $5.00 games began to escalate until they reached as high as $2,000 per game, with McAuliffe, a semi-pro, winning most of the money. One day in 1980, Sam Carl, a hog broker whose brother Howie was a former basketball star on one of DePaul University's strongest teams, told McAuliffe that with his kind of nerve he ought try his hand at trading. "That's where you'll find out what kind of stuff you're really made of." Tim McAuliffe took up Sam Carl's dare and instantly fell in love with the challenge of trading. As a result of our 1982 floor appeal, the S&P pit became his home—at least for a number of years—as it did for countless others who were attracted by the *Spuz* volatility once they found it. Soon, these traders turned things around. The S&Ps were off and running, never to look back.

Unlike the Byzantine politics and motives of many corporate executives, the culture of the Merc was one of shared values. The traders were the shareholders, and each had a vote that counted. There were no corporate rituals, no convoluted relationships between bosses and workers, professionals, and staff. I truly believe that I always got more response out of the membership at the Merc than did other exchanges from their members because like everyone else, I was a risk-taker, a trader reflecting the nature of the institution and its constituents. As the Merc was growing, so was my single-mindedness to build a world-class exchange. And while I could be relentless in pushing an idea I believed in, always in the back of my mind was the guiding tenet of my convictions: the Exchange ranked higher than any single member.

25

The Last Piece in the Puzzle

I never viewed the S&P contract as simply as another Merc instrument, say, like Swiss francs or even Treasury bills. From the day we signed the deal with Standard & Poor's, I knew it represented something really big, like the opening of financial futures itself. After all, it was the "ultimate" contract, one that would bridge futures markets with the mammoth business flows of the New York stock market. Not only would it help to legitimize the use of futures and bring them well within the temples of finance, but it was likely to change the face of our marketplace by bringing players and members who never before contemplated our exchange. And even more. While the Eurodollar contract was the Merc's first cash-settled *instrument*, the S&P's represented the first cash-settled *index* contract. To me it was obvious, once we began the journey on the index highway, we were on a road to contracts never before imagined—and transaction volume never before possible. Contracts in indexes for real estate, employment, inflation, insurance, energy, sentiment, and so forth, would now be possible. As would a variety of stock market subindexes in transportation, utilities, or technology and even in over-the-counter stocks.

Such reasoning again led me to the question of membership. The Merc didn't have enough. We could not hope to capitalize on the potential represented by index products with the current number of members. Add to that the fact that the CFTC was about to remove the prohibition on options. This would double the potential of contracts on futures exchanges. Who, I asked our Board, would service all these new contracts? The Merc's current membership was fully engaged in the markets we already traded. Clearly, without an influx of new members, the potential represented by the era just dawned would never be fulfilled.

The obvious answer to me was another new division for the Merc, specifically, an Index and Options Market division, or the IOM as it is known today. Once again, I believed we were at a pivotal juncture in the life of the CME. The idea for another Merc division was not new. It was a concept born with the launch of the IMM and imbedded in the 1976 merger between Chicago Mercantile Exchange and the International Monetary Market. But a new Merc division in 1981 was much more than expansion of members. In my head, a new Merc division also meant a new Merc building. It was what I called, "the last piece in the mosaic necessary to give the CME world-class status."

The first person I talked to about this idea was Barry Lind (this turned out to be somewhat of a diplomatic snafu since it neglected our tax counsel Ira Marcus). Lind was no longer on the Board, but he remained my most important inner-circle confederate. I explained to Lind that, according to Marcus, revenue from a sale of a capital asset was not taxable by the IRS—and that the S&P contract was a capital asset. It didn't take Barry long to figure out what I had in mind. If the Merc created a new division for trading in S&P contracts, the revenue generated from the sale of new memberships to this division would not be taxable. The money would be available to build a new Merc building. I remember Lind's grin as he enthusiastically embraced the idea.

There was no mystery about our need. This Merc was quickly running out of space. The box at Jackson Boulevard and the Chicago River which had been designed before the IMM was born—and then expanded at great expense to allow the new financial instruments to be launched—was bursting at the seams. Traders couldn't get into the pits to trade and runners couldn't get the orders to the brokers. The launch of the Eurodollar contract in 1981 left nearly no room for S&P futures. There was no way to contemplate further growth within those premises. The only answer was a new facility.

Lind and I began to play with some figures to arrive at the right numbers. How many seats should we sell? How many seats *would* we sell? And at what price to get to about $30 million—the amount we deemed necessary for the new building? By the time I went to Ira Marcus with the concept, I already had the blessing of Merc president Clayton Yeutter, Merc chairman Jack Sandner, first vice chairman Brian Monieson, and general counsel Jerry Salzman. They, too, immediately recognized the beauty of a solution that would give us new membership blood and at the same time provide us with the money for a new Chicago Mercantile Exchange. But none of this could be carried off without our financial counsel, Ira Marcus. I remember inviting Marcus to the Dellsher Investment Company Christmas party that December. It was being held at the East Bank Club, the plush athletic and social facility in Chicago, which is one of a kind in the nation. I wanted him there so that I could personally lobby for what I had in mind. Although he and I had initially discussed the concept, he was not involved in the deliberations. At first, Marcus was lukewarm, but he warmed up after I appealed to his sense of creativity; after all, I said, he had given the Merc its

"Non-Taxable Trust," something that no other exchange in the country has been able to accomplish. Once Marcus joined the effort, I knew it would happen.

Eventually, the IOM divisional structure and price of memberships was overwhelmingly approved by referendum; but not before there was a lot of jockeying between the Board and a faction of members led by Douglas Bragan, an IMM member. Bragan was one of those who was always spoiling for a fight. Most of the time, he represented a nuisance. Bragan and I had first crossed paths during the 1976 IMM merger issue. He opposed the merger and tried to torpedo the effort, going so far as to collaborate with another member, Les Bright, to pass out "Vote No," buttons. Their ignominious defeat guaranteed Bragan would remain an adversary. Over time, I tried to reach Bragan, once even offering him a seat on the CFPF board, but he refused, preferring the role of a spoiler. As Gerry Hirsch would always say, "different strokes for different folks." In the current issue, since the Board's proposal called for a two-tier sale—one price for existing members, the other for the public—Bragan's efforts were focused on lowering the price to existing members. Jack Sandner and I negotiated with Bragan, and eventually agreed that the price to existing members would be $30,000, while the price to the public would be $60,000. Overnight, not only did we earn a pile of tax-free money, the Merc's membership had grown by a ton. Existing members bought a total of 1,039 membership seats (who over time would sell or transfer them to new bodies), 125 were bought by the public, and 123 were created by conversions from the AMM division. Counting all of the divisional seats and conversions, the Merc membership rolls now swelled to a total of 2,724 members, 625 from the original CME division, 812 in the IMM, and 1,287 in the IOM. We were almost ready for the new era.

There was one more step to take, and Larry Levy, a savvy and ambitious real estate maven, knew the way. I first met Levy at a cocktail party at Joel Greenberg's house in the winter of 1979. What impressed me most was that he instantly grasped exactly what I had in mind when I told him that it was now time to put the missing piece into place.

"You mean," he ventured, "to achieve your ultimate vision for the Merc, you have to have your own building that is equal to the Merc's global stature and importance to Chicago."

I laughed, surprised at his perception.

He got it exactly right. "You bet," I countered, "or, at a minimum, of a stature equal to that of the CBOT's building."

I wasn't kidding. The CBOT's building, which dominated Chicago's financial quarters at the head of LaSalle Street, was a city landmark. I would never be satisfied until the Merc had one of its own. I had started to toy with the idea ever since CBOT chairman Ralph Peters broached the possibility of a common building for our two exchanges. We knew that a joint structure was the only certain avenue toward eventual merger between the CBOT and the CME, a grand design we had both flirted with. According to John Gilmore, who would later become CBOT chairman, Ralph Peters was so enamored with the idea that he privately told his associates he was willing to name the common building the Melamed Plaza in order to get it done. We even formed a joint real estate committee, but it went nowhere. The CBOT members and staff weren't ready to accept the Merc as an equal. The merger subject again came up when Les Rosenthal became CBOT chairman. The two of us also considered it a very worthwhile idea and pursued it briefly. Alas, the establishment within each exchange made it impossible to move forward. We still weren't equals. It remains one of those grand but illusive ideas which, now that the exchanges have reached equality, may some day become a reality.

In 1980, I knew that the time had come for our own permanent home. The first requisite was to find a real estate consultant, someone to pilot the Merc through the treacherous shoals of Chicago's downtown office market. There were many willing Chicago developers, including the Tishman people who had built our present structure at Jackson and the river. But from the time I had that conversation with Larry Levy, I knew he was our man. Levy, chairman of The Levy Organization, knew his subject matter and was a straight-forward guy. There was no doubt that he understood what I had in mind, as well as what it would mean for his career. The development of the multimillion dollar Merc project was a prestigious plum. He got his wish, and the deal proved its value, both for Levy as well as the Merc. Years later, after Levy's realty organization had grown to national status and his Levy Restaurant Organization operated 49 restaurants and specialty concessions throughout the country, he told me that development of the CME building was his greatest achievement.

We formed a real estate committee, appointed John Geldermann as its chairman, and laid down some requirements. Although there wasn't anyone in Chicago who I would have trusted more to chair this effort than Geldermann, this was to be the biggest undertaking of his career and I planned to stay on top of it. Once again we organized a team, putting Glenn Windstrup in charge. Of one thing I was certain, this had to be our final move. And that was the problem. The Merc's growth rate was something like 40% per year and at that pace we would easily outgrow any trading floor we built. Yet we couldn't keep building new buildings every few years. Our discussions led me to suggest that perhaps we should build a spare floor. Geldermann gave me a quizzical look, smiled, and agreed. It represented the only answer to the dilemma, and although novel and bold, we made it a prerequisite in our initial discussions with

Levy. It was much more difficult to convince our board. Bill Muno, during a heated discussion at a board meeting, once shouted "the spare floor will never be used." Yet in retrospect, that decision, at a construction cost of five million, saved the Merc untold millions and turned out to be one of our wisest decisions. In Levy's words, "the spare trading floor was a master stroke!" In 1995 when the CBOT decided that it needed another trading floor, the projected cost for the new building to house it was upwards of 180 million dollars.

In summer 1980, Larry Levy came to me with exciting news. Although he was in the midst of developing his 58-story One Magnificent Mile on Chicago's prestigious Michigan Avenue, he said he had a great idea for the Merc. He told me that JMB Realty Corporation, a Chicago-based real estate outfit that was run by a couple of local boys, Judd Malkin and Neil Bluhm, had just paid $30 million for a city parking garage on Wacker Drive, between Monroe and Madison. Although the amount paid for the property, at 300 dollars per square foot, was reputedly a record price, Levy said that the site was perfect for the Merc. JMB, together with real estate developers, Metropolitan Structures, were prepared to develop the property and put up two 40-story towers.

Levy's excitement was sincere and infectious. The site was indeed perfect from a point of view of prestige, one of my main missions. I viewed Wacker Drive at the Chicago River the equivalent to New York's Park Avenue, especially since the Sears Tower, the world's tallest building, was just down the street. The architects were to be Fujikawa Conterato Lohan and Associates, the successor organization to the prestigious Mies van der Rohe organization. The deal Geldermann, Sandner, and I hammered out with Larry Levy would give the Merc everything we wanted: The building would be known as The Chicago Mercantile Exchange Center—giving us permanent recognition; by owning 100 percent of the trading complex, we would control our own destiny; the construction price of $16 million for our trading facility not only fit our pocket book, it was a huge bargain; it would contain two column-free trading floors, one for our immediate use with 40,000 square feet, the other at 30,000 square feet as a hedge for the future; there would be favorable lease rates for the Merc and its member firms; there would be an underground garage for member parking; the exterior would be clad in granite—projecting the feel of security and strength.

And there was still one additional demand I had. I convinced the Board that we had to have equity in the project in order to have a strong voice in the building's operations. Negotiations ensued and Levy arranged an equity interest for the Merc—at *cost*. For a mere $800,000 the Merc became the owner of 10 percent of the South Tower, a fantastic investment. Finally, it was agreed that Levy's senior vice president, Holly Youngholm, would remain as the permanent Merc's real estate representative to handle all member leases and gripes. Ms. Youngholm took her liaison responsibilities so seriously that she even married one of our Eurodollar traders, Richard Duran.

On November 28, 1983, with the new Merc chairman Brian Monieson presiding, Chicago's Mayor Harold Washington officiated at the opening ceremony. The move had gone flawlessly over the Thanksgiving holiday thanks primarily to the planning and labors of John Geldermann and his crew. My last piece in the Merc puzzle had been put in place.

26

Coming of Age

In the last week of March 1982, just before the S&P launch, my son Jordan and I had planned to escape from Chicago's winter and catch a weekend of sun in Scottsdale, Arizona, at the beautiful Mountain Shadows resort. Just before we left, Bob Wilmouth, president of the CBOT, returned the call I had placed to him and insisted on traveling to Arizona with us. Our discussions, at the base of Camelback Mountain, had a meaningful impact on the direction of the futures industry.

Although my primary focus was always the CME, I was conscious that the Merc was only one slice of a much larger pie. We were part and parcel of the futures industry, and, to the greatest degree, the Merc's promise and potential depended on the destiny of futures markets generally. If the industry failed or its scope was limited, so would be the Merc's. I accepted this reality from the first day I became chairman of the CME over a decade before. And the industry always had some problems. But in the late seventies, these problems became critical: because of inadequate funds the CFTC was not capable of doing its job.

The federal agency's troubles had begun almost as soon as it was created in 1976. The combination of little expertise and very few funds was insurmountable. All the while, our industry was growing by leaps and bounds. Within a few years of its birth, the understaffed, underfinanced, and underappreciated CFTC found itself struggling for reauthorization. Under the law that created the agency, Congress had to decide its fate every few years. The dismayed CFTC vice chairman, John Rainbolt, complained that the reauthorization process had turned the agency and its staff "into lobbyists." In 1979, after a struggle, the CFTC won reauthorization, but Chairman Bagley lost his job and was replaced by the President Carter-appointee James Stone, whose expertise was in insurance regulation rather than commodities. CFTC Bagley's lament about the lack of understanding of the futures markets in Washington went from bad to worse. Hardly anyone in our industry talked to the new chairman, nor he to us—with Henry Jarecki and myself as perhaps the only exceptions.

But undaunted, the futures markets continued their unparalleled growth. By 1982, we had evolved into a sizeable industry. We encompassed 11 futures exchanges in four cities; 400 commodity brokerage firms or so-called futures commission merchants (FCMs); 55,000 salespeople and supervisors, who handled customer accounts; 5,700 floor brokers, who executed orders on the exchange floors; 1,500 people and organizations, which sold trading advice to the public; and 1,200 commodity pools.

Success has its costs. Unfortunately, unlike other regulatory bodies, the CFTC was not viewed as important enough to get more federal money. During the period just before the launch of index products, there was a concerted congressional push for an across-the-board per-trade tax on futures transactions to pay for regulation of our industry. We vehemently opposed such a transaction tax—an issue that continues to plague the futures industry to this day. However, Congress in 1981 was in no mood to pay us any heed. In spite of all our lobbying efforts, our industry was still perceived by most lawmakers as the Wild West, and, the trouble was, there was some truth to that image. There had been an explosion of new commission firms that were not members of any exchange. These *nonmember commission merchants* were not regulated by the exchanges. Their jurisdiction fell under the CFTC. But, our federal agency did not have the wherewithal to properly police them. The large sums of money these nonmember firms were receiving from the public represented a regulatory black hole. Failures of nonmember firms, such as that of Chicago Discount Brokers at the time, were occurring with alarming frequency. This threatened the image of our industry and put its future in jeopardy. Congress did not bother to differentiate a member firm from its nonmember counterpart. A default was a default, and our industry was the culprit.

Out of fear of increased federal control, I focused my attention on a solution that was available under Title III of the CFTC legislation. It was a plan that offered an alternative to additional federal regulation. The same act that gave life to the CFTC allowed for the creation of a self-regulatory body—the National Futures Association (NFA). Such an organization could theoretically regulate the off-exchange brokerage community and bring order to the chaos. I had first publicly mentioned the idea for a self-regulatory body in February 1978, during congressional testimony on CFTC reauthorization. It drew some mixed reviews from Congress. However, the NFA made a lot of sense to me and to some of the others in our industry, particularly John Conheeny, the head of Merrill Lynch futures. Fortunately, the two of us wielded considerable influence. Warren Lebeck, the influential former CBOT president, soon joined our team. The NFA, we reasoned, would give the futures industry the right of self-regulation and at the same time relieve some of the burdens on the CFTC. As we saw it, the NFA, with its own legal and investigative staff, would oversee the financial conditions, retail sales practices, and business conduct of futures commission merchants, commodity pool operators, commodity trading advisors, and introducing brokers.

We began to lobby for this concept. In spirited public discussions with Senator Dole, who was then chairman of the Senate Finance Committee, I persuaded him that it was a far better idea to let the futures industry regulate the mushrooming problem presented by nonmember firms than to depend on the CFTC. Senator Dole accepted my opinion and eventually agreed to utilize the existing legislation for the creation of the National Futures Association—as a counterpart to the National Association of Securities Dealers (NASD). However, to gain his support, we had to assure Congress that the NFA would obtain its budgetary funds through a self-imposed transaction fee. With the backing of John Conheeny, Warren Lebeck, and CBOT's chairman Les Rosenthal, this was agreed. In addition, I was able to convince Senator Dole that floor traders and member trades should remain exempt from the tax because the NFA was being created to protect nonmember transactions. It represented no small victory.

In September 1981, the CFTC approved the creation of the NFA. However, I learned that it was much easier to convince the federal bureaucracy of the need for self-regulation than it was to convince the futures industry of the need for regulation. Most of futures industry players didn't feel the need for another sheriff on the block. It was as if the last of the commodity robber barons of the world I had inherited in the 1960s were still clinging to their heritage of unregulated mayhem, a heritage where might made right and the money belonged to those who were clever enough to grab it. These forces never subscribed to my goal for the futures industry as a legitimate member of the U.S. financial service sector, nor did they want the regulatory framework that was implicit in this vision. The small band of NFA protagonists had a gargantuan lobbying effort on their hands.

Once again I had to become an evangelist. Indeed, in a sense, the problem had to do with religion—the religion of the trading floor. The floor was sacrosanct. The floor traders, particularly those of the CBOT and some of their New York counterparts, vehemently opposed the NFA for fear that this new regulatory body would strong-arm itself onto the exchange floors. No way would they allow any non-exchange entity to regulate or dictate their conduct. It represented a fundamental threat to their heritage. With these realities in mind, we organized the NFA Founding Committee. I was chosen as its chairman and John Conheeny its vice chairman. The balance of the committee included David Johnson, chief of E.F. Hutton futures;

George Lamborn, who headed futures for Shearson & Co; Warren Lebeck, the former CBOT president; Les Rosenthal, chairman of the CBOT; and Howard Stotler, head of Chicago-based giant Stotler Grain. This committee amalgamated the power brokers of the New York stock houses with the bosses of the Chicago exchanges and signaled a unification of purpose between the two centers of futures trade.

In the final analysis, however, the determining factor in the strategy to create an NFA was my friendship with the CBOT membership. In an unprecedented phenomenon, CBOT chairman Les Rosenthal arranged for the leader of the CBOT's greatest competitor to enter its hallowed boardroom in order to lobby on behalf of the NFA. It worked. In an emotional speech, I lectured the CBOT Board and its skeptical membership that our industry must grow up. That it was far smarter to police ourselves than to have government do it to us. NFA, I promised, would safeguard the integrity of the futures industry without ever stepping into the province of futures exchanges or interfering with the hallowed rights of its floor members.

I meant it and they bought it. More than that, I extracted from the CBOT a matching sum of $40,000 to equal the amount provided by the Merc toward the necessary NFA seed money. This was the first time that the Board of the CBOT witnessed my oratorical skills, such as they were. It was, of course, as I've mentioned, a talent born on the Yiddish stage, matured on the streets of Chicago, and honed in the courtroom. Over the years, time and again, my impassioned and fiery words to Merc members would serve to instill momentum and unity of purpose. It was my personal secret weapon, which I would sometimes unleash to motivate the Merc's membership. But to be effective, I had to first believe in the cause.

To face down similar NFA opposition in New York, particularly at the COMEX, I dispatched NFA's attorney, John Stassen of Chicago's Kirkland & Ellis, who had taken over from Phil Johnson and was contributing his time free of charge. Stassen did the job by pointing out to the New York traders that the leaders of the two big Chicago exchanges—Leo Melamed and Les Rosenthal—were both dyed-in-the-wool pit traders who would not break their covenant with the floor crowd. Said Stassen, taking some liberty with both our lives, "These two staunch supporters of NFA have authorized me to commit their promise—under penalty of death—that NFA authority would stop at the exchange walls." The New York exchanges capitulated and also contributed, albeit a much smaller sum, toward the creation of NFA.

It was about this time that Les Rosenthal called me to discuss the future of the CBOT presidency. Bob Wilmouth had been president of the CBOT since October 1977, when he took over from Warren Lebeck. Prior to coming to futures, he had a 27-year career in banking, beginning in 1950 at the First National Bank of Chicago. Wilmouth was president of the Crocker National Bank in San Francisco when CBOT chairman Ron Young offered him a way back to his hometown. The CBOT prospered under Wilmouth, but his tenure ran into trouble when the new building the exchange was constructing—behind its famous LaSalle Street landmark—came in grossly overbudget. Although it was uncertain who was to blame, as president, Wilmouth was generally held responsible by its membership. As a result, Rosenthal knew that Wilmouth's life at the CBOT was going to become increasingly difficult. He also knew that as chairman of the NFA founding committee, I now had the responsibility of creating an organization that would carry out the demanding requirements of my promise to Senator Dole. In other words, I needed a CEO who would organize and run the NFA. Would I make the indicated trade with the CBOT, Rosenthal inquired.

I agreed. Bob Wilmouth became NFA president and Les Rosenthal elevated their executive vice president, Tom Donovan, to the presidency of the exchange. Years later, John Gilmore, a Goldman Sachs partner who became CBOT chairman in 1986, would call this "the most artistic trade in the history of futures." He said that "it was vintage Melamed; a trade that made everybody happy." Donovan had come to the CBOT directly from Chicago's City Hall where since 1969 he had been Mayor Richard J. Daley's right-hand man. Chicago was known then, as it is today, as "the city that works." It still does under Mayor Richard M. Daley, the former mayor's son. But the fact that it worked under Richard J. was due in no small measure to the credit of Tom Donovan whose intellect, good sense, and administrative skill is second to none. Under the mayor's direction, Donovan assisted in the management of the myriad of complexities of a major U.S. city.

An exchange is much like a city—the members its citizens, the Board its governing council. When he came to the CBOT, Donovan knew little about futures, but he knew what it took to run a complex community. Within a few short years, he conquered the fundamentals of our markets and applied his administrative talent, amassed under the guidance of a Chicago master named Daley. Donovan also knew every Illinois and Chicago politician on a personal basis—some of whom owed their careers to his support. He also knew personally a host of national leaders, senators, and congressmen. After all, for years, Richard J. Daley's Chicago machine, administered by Donovan, was the most respected in the land. Donovan now used this vast accumulated store of knowledge and friendship to build the powerful Chicago Board of Trade Washington, DC lobby organization—a lobby machine from which I learned.

Donovan's talents were certainly not lost on me. Long before he became CBOT president in 1981, I took then Merc chairman Jack Sandner by the hand and together we offered Donovan the position of CME executive vice president. Donovan was surprised and duly flattered by the offer, but he had his eyes on a better trade. The creation of the NFA proved to be the opportunity he had been waiting for. Still, Tom Donovan's decision to stay at the CBOT did not deter the unusually strong friendship between the two of us, which grew out of mutual regard for our different backgrounds and talents.

For the NFA, Bob Wilmouth was perfect. Our NFA founding committee had been near desperation trying to find the correct avenue to its organizational structure. Not only did Wilmouth have the administrative experience and futures market expertise to get this job done, he wanted the appointment. The conversation I had with him over the weekend in Scottsdale, Arizona, established the framework for the creation of the NFA, its initial budget, its prospective executive personnel, and its underlying philosophy never to interfere with exchange regulation. Ultimately, Wilmouth put together a highly professional staff by bringing aboard Jean Tippens from the CBOT as vice president of administration, Dan Driscoll from the CFTC as vice president of compliance, Ken Haase from the CBOT as vice president of information systems, Joseph (Jeph) Harrison from Sidley & Austin as NFA's vice president and general counsel, and Dan Roth who later took over the office of general counsel.

The Chicago-based NFA began operating on August 2, 1982, as the only registered futures association in existence. It borrowed equipment and a quick-fix loan of several hundred thousand dollars from the Continental Bank. Once things got going, support rallied quickly, as did the responsibilities. By the early 1990s, the staff had grown from a dozen to 330 people, including 30 in a New York office, and a budget of $28 million.

The NFA made certain that futures industry members maintained high standards of professional conduct and financial responsibility. Its efficiency, coupled with its exemplary record in the safety of public customer funds, has earned the NFA applause from Congress, the CFTC, and other U.S. regulatory agencies, and has made it the model for similar regulatory bodies internationally. The NFA is also living proof of the cost-effectiveness of private sector self-regulation. Under the guidance of Wilmouth and NFA financial advisors, which included services of the Merc's Barry Lind, CBOT's John Gilmore, and Hal Hansen, chairman of Cargill Financial Services, the NFA per-trade fee has fallen by 57 percent. During the same period of time, all federal regulatory agencies have substantially increased their budgetary requirements. Indeed, it is a measure of NFA's success that the futures in-dustry, once opposed to its creation, today lobbies for additional NFA pow-ers. It is primarily to Bob Wilmouth's credit that the NFA became the highly regarded private sector self-regulator it is today.

I served as NFA's chairman from its inception in 1982 until 1990 (I have remained its permanent special advisor), with John Conheeny taking over the reins after my departure, followed by Hal Hansen, who is cur-rently its chairman. The NFA's highly diverse board—ingeniously devised by John Stassen so that everyone's vote counted—is comprised of over 40 representatives from every facet of the futures industry. For me, the NFA epitomized the coming of age of the futures industry.

27

Back Across the Pacific

I never agreed with the views of economist John Maynard Keynes when it came to fiscal policy. But there was one Keynesianism I heartily embraced: "The greatest difficulty in changing any enterprise lies not in developing new ideas, but in escaping from the old ones."

By 1982, I had escaped enough antiquated ideas to qualify as the Houdini of the futures business. Or at least to keep the skeptics at bay whenever I came up with a new notion. Now, instead of mockery, people listened—or they pretended to.

Along with a lot of energetic hope, I had sustained leadership strength by perceiving issues and developments. Leaving our agricultural market cradle was difficult, but youth and zeal can overcome most anything. The onset of federal regulation was easy to see. Building up the Merc's financial integrity by making sure no clearing firm defaulted was another priority, as were establishing a strong administration, expanding our membership base, diversifying the product line, developing a solid support staff to accommodate growth, and building a physical facility worthy of our stature and new potential. I thought of them as tactical moves, moves of anticipation rather than reaction.

The trick was never to be trapped by what Milton and Rose Friedman called *"the tyranny of the status quo."* It is so easy to stay with the successes you have achieved. Why take chances? If you do and are wrong, it can become awfully embarrassing. However, I knew an exchange was like a living being; it either grows or it risks demise. And it was nearly impossible for me to close my eyes to the reality of change.

There were internal changes to deal with first. In the spring of 1982, we began a search to replace Beverly Splane as executive vice president. Beverly wanted to distance herself from the daily rigors of exchange life and the Merc staff was sorely in need of reorganization. My choices for a replacement had narrowed down to William J. Brodsky, who knew little about our

313

futures markets and even less about the agricultural complex, cattle, and bellies, and such. But that didn't matter. As the 38-year-old executive vice president of the American Stock Exchange, his expertise was in stocks and options.

A graduate of Syracuse University law school, Brodsky had spent his career on Wall Street, following the path of his father, a veteran of the securities business for more than 60 years. Brodsky was pure New York City, born and raised there. You could hear it in his accent. What better time to bring an option-wise executive to the Merc than when the competition between LaSalle Street and Wall Street was heating up over financial contracts? The Index and Options Market (IOM) had been launched, and what we knew about options could have been written on a postage stamp, which meant we had to import the expertise from either the Chicago Board Options Exchange or American Stock Exchange, which were the centers of option trading. We needed someone from the equities world who understood both indexes and options.

I made a couple of attempts to get Brodsky. At first, he and his wife, Joan, also a New Yorker, were hesitant to resettle west of the Hudson. I didn't hard-sell nor did I make a promise that the position of executive vice president and chief operating officer would automatically lead to the presidency when Dr. Yeutter was ready to step down. All I could tell Brodsky was that it would be a strong possibility. I liked him from the start and, while I often met with Brodsky in the presence of Merc chairman Jack Sandner, I sensed Brodsky was attracted to my reputation. "Leo, you're the only one New Yorkers ever hear about," he told me. It was flattering, but more important were his experience and expertise. I think what did the trick for Brodsky was the creation of the IOM division, and the sale, over one weekend, of $30 million worth of new memberships. That accomplishment proved to him as nothing else the organizational strength of what we had put together in Chicago.

Brodsky accepted the position in August and began working with a $30 million budget. It took a year to restructure the departments and administrative staff, which had grown to 457 by 1982. Committees, of course, were important, but the old structure of committees running the daily affairs of the Exchange had long given way to a professional staff. The Board's complexion also had changed over the years. By now we had 18 directors (governors), who were Merc members; 3 public directors, and 3 industry representatives appointed from the Merc clearing firms.

One of the consequences of our successes was that I could, on a personal basis, attract to the Board people of stature. Their presence greatly enhanced the Merc's image and attracted others of equal prominence. Over time, it became prestigious for outsiders to sit on the CME Board. The directors were varied in their views and backgrounds.[1]

Suddenly, 10 years had passed. The idea that was given less than a slim chance of survival in 1972, had reached adolescence. On June 4, 1982, instead of the annual CME dinner dance, the Merc went all out to hold a black tie celebration commemorating the tenth anniversary of the International Monetary Market—the division that had made it a financial supermarket. I was master of ceremonies of this remarkable event with dignitaries from every corner of the world paying us tribute. We even prepared a bound historical review of the IMM as a gift for every member. But of course, the feature of the evening was our guest of honor, Professor Milton Friedman, who delivered the keynote address. We had sent a private plane to bring him to Chicago for this occasion. To tumultuous applause by the Merc membership for his friendship and assistance, Friedman offered some highly flattering remarks about me, and hailed the IMM as an innovation whose time had come.

I couldn't top his performance but I had prepared a surprise. It was a walk down memory land that I had penned, "It Seems Like Only Yesterday," which covered most of the events—sometimes bittersweet, sometimes funny—that we had endured in the process. It brought down the house.

We had won all right, but now it was a battle to keep the prize. Financial futures sowed their first international seed in London. The London International Financial Futures Exchange (LIFFE) opened its doors in 1982, and everyone in Chicago applauded. As the saying goes, imitation is the highest form of flattery. In a very real sense, this was good for the futures. Competition is the fuel for success. And another financial futures exchange would broaden the world's supply of market participants. So I did what I could to help LIFFE's principal innovator John Barkshire put the

---

[1]Among those appointed, some were former congressmen such as John White, who had been chairman of the Democratic party. Some were financial experts including Thomas W. Strauss, the former president of Salomon Brothers; Louis I. Margolis, also from Solly; Laurence E. Mollner of Dean Witter Reynolds; Robert B. Feduniak, Vice President of Morgan Stanley; Richard L. Thomas, president of First National Bank of Chicago; John J. Conheeney, chairman of Merrill Lynch Futures; Robert J. Birnbaum, the former president of the American Stock Exchange; W. Gordon Binns of the GM Pension Fund; Robert G. Easton, Chairman of Commodity Corp.; Donald Butler, president of the National Cattlemen's Association; and Fred Bogart of the Republic Bank. Others were academics like Donald Jacobs, Dean of Northwestern's Kellogg School of Business, and even Nobel laureates such as Merton Miller. Still others were from government, including Richard Lyng, the former Secretary of Agriculture; Richard Ogilvie, the former Illinois governor; Susan M. Phillips and Wendy L. Gramm, both former CFTC chairpersons; former Senator Rudy E. Boschwitz; former Federal Reserve Board governor Martha Seger; and Tom Eagleton, the former senator and Democratic vice-presidential nominee.

new enterprise together. Barkshire was a most engaging fellow. He came to Chicago to visit me in 1980 a number of times and brought a group of associates that included LIFFE's 1995 chairman, Jack Wigglesworth. On the outside, Barkshire was pure British: he had a lean build, a very British accent, and was immaculately dressed. But he was totally lacking in the conservative mentality that usually defines our U.K. cousins. He and his associates were ready to innovate. With a keen mind, Barkshire instantly grasped what made the IMM tick and asked me to help him copy the blueprint. While I was a bit nervous about that, there really wasn't anything I could do about it. Nothing we did at the IMM was secret anyway—one cannot patent ideas in financial services. Besides, Barkshire and I envisioned an eventual linkup between the IMM and LIFFE. Our imagined grand design was that, ultimately, our two exchanges could dominate the world's financial futures business. Indeed, the original contracts fashioned by Barkshire, Wigglesworth, and the other LIFFE pioneers were nearly carbon copies of the IMM's currency and Eurodollar contracts. At that time, I believed that the time difference between us and Europe would save us from becoming direct competitors. I soon realized that things were not going to work that way. In the first place, Michael Jenkins, a thoroughly knowledgeable and intelligent chap who followed Barkshire in running the London exchange, was first and foremost a fierce LIFFE patriot. He was more focused on Europe than the world. Although he too was willing to consider a linkup between our two exchanges, his negotiation demands on the IMM were beyond what we were willing to consider. His eyes were on the Eurodollar contract, and I didn't like what he was looking at. I recognized that LIFFE could become a serious competitive problem. Although their currency contracts never really got going, their Eurodollar contract was off to a fine start. Too fine. I soon learned why London was, for centuries, the financial center of Europe and beyond. A lot of it has to do with time zones.

All other things being equal, futures market participants will use the market open during their business hours. This meant that as long as our two markets were more or less equal in product line, liquidity, and so forth, traders based in Europe would use the LIFFE, while North American institutions would use the IMM. So far, so good. But for Far Eastern participants, we were not equals. The London time zone allowed LIFFE to open each day during the tail end of the Asian business hours—while in Chicago we were still sleeping. That made LIFFE very attractive to Asian bankers and other futures market participants. For the moment, the LIFFE advantage wasn't critical since the IMM's Eurodollar contract was so much more liquid. Traders tend only to use markets that are liquid. But the handwriting was on the wall. With every passing month, I could see the open interest in Eurodollars at LIFFE inching its way up toward the IMM's. Since from the outset I was certain that Eurodollars represented perhaps the most important futures contract of all time, LIFFE's time zone advantage made me very concerned.

And the problem didn't end there. Now that LIFFE proved the IMM blueprint could be copied, what was there to prevent an Asian market, say in Japan or Hong Kong, from opening its doors with a similar financial exchange and an identical Eurodollar contract—or anything else the IMM traded? The universe of futures was expanding across oceans and time zones, and I could feel the Asian world looking across the Pacific at our successes. The IMM's franchise was something to guard jealously, but there seemed to be no way. Still, I believed there had to be some kind of economic synchronization to enable us to compete internationally and protect our invention.

The only answer in 1983 was a linkup with a Far Eastern exchange with whom we could share the financial futures business and its growth. In the beginning, none of us actually envisioned the so-called mutual offset idea, since that was a bit far out. Mutual offset was a theoretical mechanism whereby an identical futures contracts traded at two separate exchanges could be used interchangeably. Currently, if someone was long Eurodollars on the LIFFE, for instance, and wanted to sell out that position after the LIFFE market was closed, the trader had no option other than to sell on the IMM, during our business hours. But this established a second position. It meant the trader was long at LIFFE and short at the IMM—a very costly and inefficient way to do business. The Mutual Offset System (MOS), eventually devised by the Merc, overcame this problem by making the two separate contracts completely fungible. With MOS, one could liquidate a long position established at one exchange by selling it at the second exchange. The result would be no position at either exchange. It was a highly revolutionary idea that had never been tested anywhere. But it was enticing. Surely, the cost saving and efficiency of such a system would dominate all other competitors. Still, in the beginning, I considered MOS a theoretical concept and a long way off.

I had gone to Hong Kong with Rosenberg and Sandner to find a possible link that would allow us to trade when our markets were tucked in for the night. Unfortunately, Hong Kong, where currencies flowed freely along with trade, was a disappointing prospect. The community was divided. The British didn't talk to the Chinese. The Hong Kong Chinese wanted their own exchange. The mainland Chinese were hidden from view. And the government didn't talk to anybody. Who were we going to talk to if we were going to take this major step in the evolution of our markets? Besides, no one knew what would happen when Great Britain's lease expired in June

1997, and Hong Kong was back in the hands of the People's Republic of China.

Everyone, of course, agreed that Japan would someday be the financial colossus of Asia. But at that time, Japanese laws prevented us from considering anything in Tokyo. Therefore, the only remaining option was Singapore, the tightly run city-state of Lee Quan Yew, which had ambitions to rival Hong Kong as a money center. The Monetary Authority of Singapore (MAS) was reexamining the role of the Gold Exchange of Singapore and organized a group of Singaporeans in the hope of tying in with an American futures exchange ahead of Hong Kong. In May 1982, CME chairman Brian Monieson and I arranged to visit Singapore and meet the so-called Singapore Working Party which had made strong overtures to do a joint venture with us. I invited Jack Sandner to come along because he had been with me during the Hong Kong fact-finding tour.

The Singaporeans were precisely what I was seeking. They represented the cohesive force composed of business and government that was absent in Hong Kong. But for me, it was Lim Ho Kee, an MAS official and the former chairman of the Singapore Gold Exchange, who represented the most important difference. Mr. Lim, who is now the executive vice president of the Union Bank of Switzerland in Southeast Asia, was the central figure and spokesman of the Working Party. He was an aggressive and articulate gentleman of slender build, a man after my own heart who understood futures markets and argued why things should work as opposed to why they shouldn't. And he spoke with the strong voice of the MAS. Lim convinced me that Singapore—not Hong Kong—was the logical location for a Merc connection. The next month, Lim Ho Kee came to visit me at the Merc, and from then on things began to gel. Until that moment, I was still considering some form of accommodation, but not mutual offset. The one-on-one conversation that I had with Lim led me to believe that maybe we could go all the way. He convinced me that if the Merc was ever going to take the revolutionary plunge with a Far Eastern partner, this was the time to do it and they were the people to do it with. But it was a dangerous step. Directly after the conversation with Lim, I sat down with Brian Monieson, and we privately discussed it for several hours, examining the concept from every angle possible. When we finished, Monieson said, "Leo, I am fully convinced that if we can pull this off, it will revolutionize futures trade." Monieson's support gave me the courage to proceed. I then met separately with Yeutter, Sandner, Rosenberg, and Lind to advance the idea. Everyone bought it.

Ideas are the fuel of revolutions, but individuals make them happen. And revolutions don't happen overnight. The Singapore connection simmered for two years. In May 1983, Lim Ho Kee came to Chicago with a contingent of 18 Working Party officials including Elizabeth Sam and Ng Kok Song, both of whom would later serve as Singapore International Monetary Exchange (SIMEX) chairmen. But when Lim suddenly advised me that although he'd remain in an advisory capacity, he was leaving the MAS to go into the private sector, I thought the project was derailed. It very well could have been, if it weren't for Ng Kok Song who took his place at the MAS. A strong chemistry had developed between the two of us, and I felt that with Ng's leadership, the Working Party would remain in capable hands. I was right. This was one of the most difficult agreements that I ever participated in and Ng Kok Song saved the day. He was sophisticated, reasoned, and methodical, and I learned to trust his deep intellect. Although his style was quite different from that of Lim Ho Kee, he was even more persuasive and equally passionate in his desire to achieve a mutual offset agreement. The Western-educated Ng Kok Song viewed the link as an important step in diversifying his nation's economy.

Hunched over the table, I led the relatively small CME negotiating team—one-third the size of theirs—which included Monieson, Rosenberg, Lind, Sandner, and our attorney Salzman. We scribbled notes on legal pads and peppered each other with questions in three days of marathon sessions that wound through a maze of such delicate issues as exchange independence, financial safeguards, trading regulations, and clearing mechanisms. It felt more like two nations in high-level trade talks trying to diplomatically work out a mutual course of events. In essence, we were. I needed to know that the Singapore government was behind us and that the MAS was willing to pass rules compatible with CFTC regulations. Ng Kok Song assured me it was. Both sides wanted mutual offset to happen, so compromise rather than veto set the tone of discussion. I thought so highly of Ng's efforts that subsequently I made certain he was featured in our 1983 annual report.

The practical considerations were awesome. Forget theory, how was this thing going to work? After all, it was going to allow investors to trade a futures position at the Merc or SIMEX and liquidate the resulting position at the same or other exchange. All the while, market prices would be moving in two time zones. The monetary consequences were frightening. The chance for fraud or failure was enormous. The CME was financially sound, but what about the SIMEX? It had no history whatsoever. What would the procedures be? How would the margining work? How could we ensure that the money flows for futures positions between the two exchanges would always be secure? Unanswered questions. The Merc Economics Department was working overtime, but every time they came back with a blueprint, our MOS committee shot it down. Then over one weekend, one of our economists, Michael Asay, came up with a complex, but brand-new approach. Asay and his buddy Roger Rutz had both come to the futures markets in 1980 from the Federal Reserve where they worked as staff economists. The Fed was a great training ground for us. Rutz went to the CBOT, where he quickly rose through the ranks to become chief of the CBOT's clearing facility, the Chicago Board of Trading Clearing Corporation. Asay came to the Merc, where in 1983, he invented the perfect mutual offset mechanism. I took it to Barry Lind and Brian Monieson to see if they could find any flaws. They couldn't. The three of us, working with attorney Salzman, then established a set of very stringent financial safeguards that had to be met by the SIMEX before we would proceed. While the Singaporeans at first balked, the demands became do or die. I refused to proceed unless the financial protection of the Merc, deemed necessary by my team of financial gurus, was in place. In the end, the deal was struck. The MOS system and its financial safeguards has worked flawlessly since its inception. It is a measure of pride that during the Barings Bank collapse in 1995, the MOS system kept the Merc clearinghouse safe and insulated from the London bank's financial disaster.

On September 7, 1984, four dancers circled the SIMEX trading floor, performing the oriental Lion Dance of good luck to herald the historic link between the Merc and the SIMEX. In my keynote speech to the Singapore business community at the gala birthday celebration, I saluted the members of the SIMEX and wished that "the IMM torch burn brightly on the Singapore shore."

In trying to do everything to make this innovation succeed, I assigned Beverly Splane as the Merc's liaison in Singapore, where she lived for the next two years working with SIMEX officials and traders to provide advice and direction. As I expected, Splane was an important component in making the new mutual offset connection work. So was Koh Beng Seng who took over at the MAS. What was of the greatest significance was that our special purpose for listing the Merc's Eurodollar contract in Asia—as a defensive weapon against the growing London LIFFE threat—worked like a charm. From the moment the SIMEX opened its doors, we could actually watch the open interest in Eurodollars at LIFFE begin to falter. A few years later, its officials gave up the fight and delisted the contract entirely. The Merc-SIMEX connection made Singapore the financial futures beacon of Southeast Asia, and allowed the IMM's Eurodollar contract to become the greatest futures contract in history.

However, in futures, life is complicated and doesn't always follow a straight line. In the midst of our SIMEX negotiations, the battle for stock index futures heated up once again. The Board of Trade, after licking its wounds over the loss of the Dow contract, went back to the drawing board and came up with another idea: an index on the over-the-counter (OTC) stock market. It was a helluva idea, but our Economics Department had the same notion. The only prominent index in existence for this market was the one operated by Nasdaq itself, and both Chicago Exchanges scrambled for its rights. We sent Brodsky to New York to negotiate with the Nasdaq officials. It was to be his first experience with the rough-and-tumble world of Chicago's futures exchanges. I felt his strong equities credentials coupled with the Merc's enormous success in the S&P stock index contract would put us over the top. But it was a baptism of fire for Brodsky. The CBOT won. They convinced Nasdaq that at the Merc their contract would play second fiddle to the S&P market, that the Merc's members' trading attention would be spent creating liquidity in the Spuz. The argument rang true to Nasdaq, and it left the Merc high and dry.

But all was not lost. We could not give up the fight because, if the CBOT were successful in developing a Nasdaq futures market, it would shatter the image of the Merc as the exclusive capital of U.S. index futures. Besides, the OTC equity market looked like a comer. I brainstormed with Merc chairman Brian Monieson and our chief economist Rick Kilcollin. In desperation, we came up with a thought: perhaps we could go to Standard and Poor's and convince them to create a new over-the-counter stock index. It might not win the OTC index market for us, but it would surely muddy the water for the CBOT.

The ensuing war between the Merc's SPOC (S&P Over-the-Counter) Index and the CBOT's Nasdaq Index was, to that date, the most competitive in the history of our two exchanges. We pulled out all the stops. Each exchange spent some $4 million on preparations, public relations, and advertising. Our respective memberships, like two armies preparing for war, were fired up to a maximum frenzy. Every conceivable gimmick was applied, including banners on our buildings as well as on the streets of Chicago. The CME even made an attempt to reach Leonard Nimoy, Mr. Spock of *Star Trek*, to ring the opening bell on our SPOC contract. Alas, he wanted too much money. A large portion of our budget went to Louis Rukeyser, who became our leading equity voice in national advertisements. He also taped an explanatory how-to cassette for portfolio managers. Rukeyser subsequently even taped his *Wall Street Week* television program from the floor of the CME. In addition, a picture of all the Merc traders, myself included, standing tough and ready to do battle on behalf of liquidity in stock index futures, was used as a major advertising piece in every leading newspaper and periodical. I personally spent morning after morning trading in the SPOC pit (losing a bundle in the process) in an attempt to attract our floor traders. The amount of money spent, the ferocity of competition, and the rancor engendered were surpassed only by the eventual battle between the two Exchanges' respective electronic trading systems, GLOBEX and Aurora.

The OTC battle ended in a standoff with neither contract succeeding. Perhaps in 1985 it was still a bit too early for the *"market of the next hundred years."* But of this I am certain: without interference by the CME, the CBOT's Nasdaq market would have had a very good chance. It was unquestionably the better of the two OTC index contracts. So, although it never became a successful contract, SPOC served its primary purpose of preserving the CME status as the center of index futures.

Shortly before the SIMEX began to operate, Betty and I, along with our youngest son David, took a long weekend at our Arizona home. On the way, I happened to catch a news story on the radio that reported that Bill Brock was stepping down as U.S. Trade Representative to take over as Secretary of Labor. The idea struck me like lightning: Clayton Yeutter, who had championed our free market cause around the world, would be perfect as Brock's successor. Yeutter had often told me privately that the USTR post could lure him back to Washington.

I immediately called him. "Clayton, I am hesitant to say this, but if you've ever thought about going back to Washington, this is the opportunity. Reagan has just appointed Bill Brock as Labor secretary and the Trade Rep job is open."

Dr. Yeutter instantly agreed it was the opportunity of a lifetime. But here it was a Friday morning, and in a few hours he was scheduled to catch a plane for Germany where he was to give a speech at an international conference. How could he put it all together?

I wasn't looking for Clayton to leave the Merc by any means. To the contrary, I thought he was doing an outstanding job as president, and my respect for Yeutter couldn't have been higher. His tireless efforts on behalf of the Merc were producing excellent results. During an era of globalization, Yeutter had proved to be the perfect person to serve as our representative throughout the financial centers of the world. He could speak, he understood futures, he knew the territory, and he knew countless financial movers and shakers from around the world. His Mr. Outside role played perfectly against my role as Mr. Inside. So I certainly didn't want to lose him, but neither did I want to stand in the way of his career. He belonged at the Merc. But he also belonged in the service of an American president who could appreciate his dedication and the international communication skills he developed as our globe-trotting ambassador.

Trade representative, it seemed to me, was a perfect fit. Dr. Yeutter had wit, sophistication, and an authoritative presence, yet there was that homespun Nebraskan charm just beneath the surface that he could turn up or down, depending on who was present. And he understood international trade. I really thought he was a valuable asset for the nation. And so did he.

"You handle it," urged Yeutter. "I'll get Jim Lake to do what he can in Washington, and you put together the private sector. The two of you can do it. We'll keep in touch."

The vacant post was sure to draw a host of top candidates. But if Jim Lake, White House advisor and media consultant to President Reagan, and I could get Yeutter's name on the short list of candidates under consideration, I was certain Yeutter could do the rest himself. His own credentials would win the day.

As soon as I hung up with Yeutter, I began to dial the wheel of influence—the telephone. Over the next 48 hours, my son, David, who sat with me throughout the process, got a firsthand lesson in the art of lobbying. And how influence works. In a cyclone of telephone activity during which I worked with my assistant Sue Green who was now working for me and operating from my office in Chicago, the Yeutter lobby unfolded.

Once again Betty became a business widow as so often happened in the course of my service to the Merc and the futures industry. One of my wife's greatest attributes is that she very seldom complains, and is always ready to accept the realities dictated by my priorities in business life. Again and again, she would suffer the disappointments of a missed holiday or outing that, without warning, was postponed or cancelled. But as a true trooper and full partner in my career, Betty would lend her total support and assist the process in any way she could. Sometimes, this would mean making arrangements, or doing some research, or help in the writing of a document; sometimes it meant simply being there, or merely offering "tea and sympathy;" and other times it was as a confidante or someone with whom to discuss a difficult issue in the decision-making process. Sometimes it was to share the joy of a victory or the sorrow of a defeat. Whatever the cause, whatever the mission, Betty never failed to be there and do her part.

Jim Lake and I strategized, putting together a battle plan. The trick was for us to strike fast. In D.C. politics, if a prospective appointee takes too long to make a move, the enemy sharks will eat him alive. We had this weekend and no more. We made up a list of people whom we had to energize for support and divided it between us. Lake took the job of pulling the political strings from the inside while I lobbied the business community. Over the next two days, I contacted 35 major chief executive officers of corporate America around the country, asking each of them to personally call their senators and the influential officials they knew. Clayton Yeutter, I explained, was this nation's perfect candidate for trade representative. Word like that travels fast. I only got one turndown.

In some instances, Lake and I agreed that we both had to make the pitch, which was the case with respect to Republican Senator Bob Dole, who was critical to any appointment process. I knew that historically Dole wasn't a big fan of Yeutter's. He had tangled with Yeutter over issues going back to Yeutter's days at the Agriculture Department. Lake called him first, catching the senator as he was about to go to a meeting with Don Regan, the White House Chief of Staff. My call followed on Lake's heels, and together we managed to persuade Dole to put the past aside. Senator Dole agreed to weigh in on behalf of Yeutter for trade rep. It was a key victory. I also called Dan Rostenkowski, who although a Democrat, could be helpful with his friend President Reagan.

Another critical call was to my friend Beryl Sprinkel who had been an IMM director and was now President Reagan's Chairman of the Council of Economic Advisors. Sprinkel was close to Donald Regan, who would most likely make the final recommendation to the President. I was able to track down Beryl Sprinkle in Germany where he too was attending an economic conference. Sprinkle's staff made the international connection for me, proving once again the importance of rapport with staff. Sprinkle agreed that Dr. Yeutter was perfect for the job and took it upon himself to call Donald Regan.

Then I got lucky. When I called John Phelan, chairman of the New York Stock Exchange, I learned that Don Regan would be visiting the NYSE that following Monday. Phelan, a buddy of Regan's from his Wall Street days as chairman of Merrill Lynch, agreed to give Yeutter a boost with the President's chief of staff. Things were clicking.

Jim Lake and I must have talked a dozen times as we briefed each other, comparing notes and mapping additional strategy. Several times I talked with Yeutter from Germany. The weekend effort paid off. Dr. Yeutter ended up on the short list. By the time he returned from Germany, he had an appointment with Donald Regan in Washington. And as I expected, Clayton Yeutter, being a consummate political pro, did the rest by himself. He was appointed by President Reagan to the highly prestigious ambassadorial and cabinet level post of U.S. Trade Representative. From there, Yeutter could continue higher up the political ladder. It was not only a great accomplishment for Yeutter, it was a great public relations victory for the Merc. The trade rep position gave both Yeutter and the Merc a huge boost in credibility in the international waters. This effect was later accentuated when Yeutter was appointed Secretary of Agriculture under President George Bush.

But now we had to fill the empty slot at the Merc. I went to bat for Bill Brodsky to get him the presidency and found that not everyone on the Merc's Executive Committee was in his corner. There was a strong inside view that Brodsky wasn't of the stature the Merc deserved. He was virtually unknown outside the Exchange and was clearly a far cry from Clayton Yeutter's national credentials. The committee urged me to conduct a search for someone with more international credibility. I refused to budge, insisting that Brodsky had the smarts and professionalism to grow into the job. My principal argument was that the Merc was in good shape internationally and now needed strong internal rule. Brodsky had shown his expertise in this respect. Eventually, I wore the opposition down, and personally negotiated a handsome contract on his behalf. Bill Brodsky succeeded Dr. Clayton Yeutter as president of the CME on June 1, 1985. History has proved my stubbornness correct.

Before Yeutter left, he and I talked about the future of the Merc. We both agreed that a role reversal for me would be necessary. With his departure, I would have to turn my attention to leading the Merc to the outside world, especially on the international front. The SIMEX connection, we agreed, was a step in the right direction, but it was only the beginning. The Merc had to continue its global march. Indeed, what I was seeing on the international horizon made me quite concerned. Financial instruments now dominated the markets. Interest rate, equity, and currency contracts had soared from 18 percent in 1980 to 59 percent in 1985. There was no doubt in my mind that this trend would continue and, to the extent possible, we now had to protect the Merc's business flows from anticipated international competition. We again looked to the Far East.

In May 1985, the Merc took its initial steps toward Japan, the financial colossus of Asia. I was invited by Arthur Andersen to act as keynote speaker at the inauguration of their Financial Futures Center in Tokyo. This represented my official return to Japan, and the beginning of many trips to the country which had provided my parents and me an escape route from the horrors of the Holocaust. But this event afforded yet another first. Milton Friedman was the featured speaker at this conference. He was somewhat of a demigod in this country, having been a valued advisor to the Bank of Japan. He spoke macro-economics while I spoke futures. Sharing the stage, so to speak, with the world's most renowned economist, provided me with an introduction to the Japanese community that money could not buy.

On the same trip, I concluded negotiations, begun by Clayton Yeutter, with the Nihon Keizai Shimbun organization for an exclusive license to their Nikkei 225 stock index. The CME thereby gained the right to list a futures contract based on the Nikkei stock index which tracked the Tokyo Stock Market. It was an enormous coup—Japan represented the second largest stock market in the world. A week later, I spoke in Hong Kong at the IMF's International Monetary Conference, the first time futures were represented. A few years later, on September 2, 1988, I would cut the ceremonial ribbon at the opening of the Nikkei 225 futures contract at the Osaka Securities Exchange and made the pilgrimage to the Kobe area where I had briefly lived as a child.

Arthur Andersen's 1985 venture in Asia to establish itself as the expert in futures markets was no accident. It represented a continuation of its long-range strategic plan that began almost from the inception of financial futures a decade before. This enormously successful strategy was primarily the work of Mitchell R. Fulscher, one of AA's brightest young officials. Fulscher and I met in the early 1970s and we instantly developed a close personal and intellectual friendship. Fulscher grasped what financial futures could mean for his career, and I understood how the wherewithal of a major accounting organization could advance the cause of futures markets. In a manner of speaking we became partners, finding commonality of interest which served our respective goals. It was a partnership that lasted throughout the years.

The Merc had begun to spread its global wings both east and west, and I sat down with the Merc's chief of Marketing, Barbara Richards, to discuss the idea of an annual Merc symposium program. The CME, I explained, had to be dressed in international clothing. Richards was smart and an extremely quick study who was well liked and well connected throughout the financial community. She intuitively understood what I had in mind and expertly laid the groundwork for symposia that began in London in November 1985 and were later extended to Tokyo. At my behest, Richards also instituted European and Asian Financial Instrument Advisory panels to which selected experts from our global clearing member community were appointed.[2] Not only did these panels provide prominent visibility to up-and-coming managers and economists—the outstanding economist David Hale, from Kemper Financial Services, for instance, got his first international exposure through this forum—it gave the Merc special entrée to their ideas and criticisms and made for us a lot of friends. Over the years, these seminar programs, which continued throughout my Merc officialdom, were overwhelmingly successful and became a major factor in achieving the Merc's global stature. In time, the symposia were regarded as the standard for other exchanges to follow, and much later these programs were conducted in partnership with the CBOT. However, the Merc's head start

---

[2] Among those included were: Gary P. Brinson of Brinson Partners Inc.; Max Chapman of Kidder Peabody & Co.; Myra Drucker of International Paper Co.; Fred Grauer of Wells Fargo Investment Advisors; T. Brett Haire of First Boston Corp.; Kekichi Honda of Bank of Tokyo Ltd.; Robert L. Isaacson of Futures Funding Consultants; Moez Jamal of Credit Suisse; Sheldon Johnson of Morgan Stanley; Frank Jones of De Zoete Wedd; Aki Kamiya of Mitsubishi Bank; Peter Karpen of First Boston Corp.; John Kelley of Chase Manhattan; Morton Lane of Discount Corp.; Bernard J. Lind of Midland Montague; Edward McCartin of J.P. Morgan Futures; Wm. Michaelcheck of Bear Stearns; Bruce Osborne of Harris Trust and Savings; Waite Rawles of Continental Bank; John Richards of Merrill Lynch; David Schoenthal of Shearson Lehman; Myron Scholes, Professor, Stanford University; Didier Varlet of W.I. Carr Futures; and Naoki Yokoyama of Nikko Securities Ltd.

in this arena and Richard's expertise gave us an image no other exchange enjoyed.

In 1986, we returned to Japan, this time to appoint Takeo Arakawa as managing director of the CME's new Tokyo office. Arakawa, a former official of the Japanese Ministry of Finance (MOF), had been recommended to me by none other than Makoto Utsumi, special advisor to the finance minister of the MOF. Over the years, I had become sort of an unpaid and unofficial MOF advisor with respect to futures markets in Japan. This role began with my friendship with Utsumi and was carried forward by Toyoo Ghyotan (currently chairman of Bank of Tokyo/Mitsubishi, the world's largest bank) when he was the MOF's special advisor. As a consequence, I got to know many Japanese officials on a personal basis. Utsumi, an extremely erudite and highly intelligent person, and I developed a friendship that was absolutely critical in later years, one that enabled me to win approval from the MOF for GLOBEX to operate in Japan. It was a mission nearly everyone believed impossible to achieve.

But then again, impossible missions are the stuff dreams are made of. The speed of our growth, the breadth of our impact, the expanse of our plans, comprised a heady elixir, the kind of fuel that made no mission seem too wild or unthinkable. Clearly, I knew that not all my dreams would come true, but the safety of status quo had no appeal to me whatsoever, and the futility of tilting at windmills was not a frightening deterrent. Without impossible dreams, there can be no vision, and without vision there is no futures market. My fondest gift, still hanging on my office wall, was the one I received from our general counsel, Lee Freeman—it was a sculpture of Cervantes' hero, Don Quixote.

PART FOUR

Machines, Markets, and Minds

28

GLOBEX

In May 1986, precisely 14 years after the birth of the IMM, Merton H. Miller, Distinguished Service Professor of Finance at the University of Chicago, nominated financial futures as "the most significant financial innovation of the last 20 years." Professor Miller, who went on to become the 1990 Nobel Laureate in economics, not only bestowed upon us this unparalleled honor, but also left us with a heavy burden: how to keep the IMM on top?

The futures industry of 1986 was in no way, shape, or form the same industry that gave birth to the innovation Professor Miller singled out. In 1972, when financial contracts were introduced, the mechanics of futures trade were still pretty much the same as when these markets were established a century before. Indeed, in an article I wrote for the *Hofstra University Law Review* in 1977, I sang the praises of the open outcry system. The pit, I said, was the only way liquidity could be achieved. Electronic trading would never work. Period. I was, of course, writing from the vantage point of that era. That was before satellites, microchips, and fiber optics lifted the geographic security blanket from U.S. financial markets and made us vulnerable to international competition. Then, there were no such things as personal computers; Bill Gates was still in college; windows were something to look into or out from; and an apple was something to eat. Things change. Now, a decade later, I had to rethink my position. To do so, I had to come full circle in my beliefs and take on the status quo once again. But that metamorphosis didn't happen overnight. It represented my acceptance of an evolving reality caused by an ever-changing world.

During the past decade, our markets went from a strictly domestic profile to international breadth, and the Merc grew sevenfold—from a 1976 volume of approximately 37 million contracts to a 1986 volume of 216 million contracts. Financial futures had become the standard tools for risk management around the world; their applicability extended to new products, new techniques, and new users. With this success came competition.

New exchanges were popping up on every continent and threatening the CME's dominance of futures markets.

The Merc-SIMEX link—14 hours and 9,400 miles apart—had shown that exchanges, like nations, can transcend culture, oceans, and time zones to form strong alliances that are mutually beneficial. But everything was changing. Nothing was constant. Or safe. Japan, once it got its futures markets in gear, might overwhelm the Singapore futures market. There was also a flood of new over-the-counter competitors to our contracts, hybrid off-exchange futures products being developed by banks, investment banks, and boutique-type operations, not to mention the competition we felt from the interbank market and EFPs, the so-called Exchange for Physicals markets.

The fundamental influence driving all of these changes was the technological revolution. And it wasn't about to end; rather, it was about to make everything obsolete. Walter Wriston, the former chairman of Citicorp, said it well: "We are witnessing a galloping new system of international finance . . . one that differs radically from its precursors," in that "it was not built by politicians, economists, central bankers or finance ministers . . . it was built by technology . . . by men and women who interconnected the planet with telecommunications and computers . . . ." As a result, Wriston suggested, the world had replaced the gold standard with the "information standard." Indeed it had.

I viewed this transformation with awe and trepidation. Because information could now flow freely at the speed of light, it had become the dominant force of the international financial system. The impact of this reality on futures markets was extraordinary. In alerting our membership, I was straightforward: "The marriage of the computer chip to the telephone," I explained, "has changed the world from a confederation of autonomous financial markets into one continuous marketplace. No longer is there a distinct division of the three major time zones—Europe, North America, and the Far East. No longer are there three separate markets operating independently of external pressures by maintaining their own unique market centers, products, trading hours, and clientele."

Today, users of our markets come from around the globe as news is distributed instantaneously across all time zones. When such informational flows demand market action, financial managers no longer wait for local markets to open before responding. Rather, they have the capacity to initiate immediate market positions—a capacity that has come to be known as "globalization." With globalization, each financial center has become a direct competitor to all others, offering new opportunities, challenges, and perils. In the face of this dramatic metamorphosis, we had to determine how to prevent our market share from shrinking. A strategy was needed to meet the demand, one based on a global scale that involved sophisticated systems and political maneuvering as well. The process would involve a lot of tough soul-searching since the use of high-tech computerized technology could surely threaten the Merc's most sacrosanct ground: open outcry.

To bolster our efforts, I did two things. As chairman of the Merc's Strategic Planning Committee, I placed on top of its agenda the responsibility of finding an answer to the effects of globalization. Second, I put a new Merc staffer, Kenneth Cone, in charge of our committee's deliberations. Ken Cone, a Stanford University-trained economist, had taught at the University of Chicago Business School, and had also been a management consultant at Booz Allen Hamilton. It didn't take but one conversation with Cone for me to figure out that he was the guy for this job. He was brilliant, thorough, and would tell it like it is. Cone, along with Todd Petzel, Eric Wolf, Carl Royal, and Eileen Flaherty represented the next generation of Merc officials whom we recruited or promoted from within. These professionals, in the same vein as the early CME staffers, were experts in their fields, possessed strong independent minds, and would not hesitate to speak out. Petzel, an economist recruited from the Coffee, Sugar and Cocoa Exchange, would in time become the most respected and senior of the Merc staff. Wolf stood out because of his supreme expertise in market surveyance. Royal and Flaherty were extremely competent attorneys. Indeed, I became so enamored with Eileen Flaherty's legal expertise and capabilities that in subsequent years I sought her out to become the general counsel for my firm, Sakura Dellsher, Inc.

The Strategic Planning Committee was the nerve center of the CME. Organized earlier for the purpose of examining the fundamental problems the Merc was facing, I became its chairman and Brian Monieson its vice chairman. The committee members were some of the most influential of the Exchange. Its recommendations, which were invariably accepted by the Board, would have far-reaching effects on the direction of the Merc. I knew that in the case at hand, our recommendations could very well change the course and history of futures markets.

Of course, the Merc wasn't alone in perceiving the competitive danger our markets faced from globalization. The Board of Trade also viewed the coming Japanese market as a potential threat to its financial jewel, the 30-year U.S. Treasury bond. U.S. bonds had an extremely liquid cash market that traded nearly 24 hours a day around the globe. It would not be too difficult for the Japanese to open a new financial futures exchange in Tokyo to trade the U.S. bonds and draw the Asian long interest rate business to its domicile. This was business that the CBOT banked on for continued growth. To combat this competitive threat, the CBOT did the obvious. They opened a night futures session for U.S. bonds, beginning at 6:00 P.M. to coincide with the opening of the Japanese business day in Tokyo. With this defensive maneuver, the CBOT reasoned, it would attract Japanese and other Asian business to its pits in Chicago rather than to a potential exchange in Tokyo.

It was a fairly novel idea, and I gave the CBOT high marks for recognizing that they faced a serious competitive problem and taking action quickly. But I gave the CBOT a failing grade for the defense they utilized. To me, a night market—for a couple of hours each evening—was like trying to hide from a tornado in a cardboard box. Night trading addressed only a small portion of the hours of the foreign business day—it was highly unlikely that such an after-hours session could be extended the full 16 hours necessary to protect the other two time zones. Besides, the night session, at best, could be applied to selective instruments of trade; it might work for bonds, but it would become increasingly more difficult as additional products were attempted. And after all was said and done, I deemed it highly doubtful that night sessions in the United States would dissuade a foreign community from launching its own exchange, in its own domicile, during its own regular trading hours. Indeed, the Tokyo International Financial Futures Exchange (TIFFE) opened for business in 1989.

But, frankly, the CBOT saw no other choice. It was a captive of the open outcry system. It would be nothing short of heresy for it to consider, say, automation in response to globalization. And in fairness, the CBOT was much like almost every other exchange in our industry. Pit trading was all we knew. Any movement toward electronics or even the adoption of technological advancements was advancing the "black box," the "Darth Vader" of our world. No futures exchange anywhere in the world had yet dared to take such a step.

Let's face it—even though organized futures markets had been in existence since the Osaka Rice Exchange in 1730, even though they had left their agricultural cradle, even though they had shed their straitjacket of physical delivery, one thing had remained constant: open outcry. With good reason. The open outcry trading system was the only proven mechanism for achieving the degree of liquidity necessary to produce and maintain a viable market.

Still, the world and our markets were dynamic. And the threat to our markets wasn't only from international sources. New competitive forces from domestic securities exchanges, from OTC markets, from nonregulated entities, and from new technologies were mounting enormous competitive pressures. If we ignored the sea change around us, we risked being left behind. To assume that pit trading would always be the end-all was to create a false sense of security that could be fatal. Rather, I believed, in order to preserve the viability of open outcry, we had to examine whether this transaction system could meet current demands, and, if not, what to do about it.

Nor did I view the Mutual Offset concept I championed a few years back between the Merc and the SIMEX as an adequate response to the competitive challenges of globalization. While MOS was working successfully and proved that markets in separate time zones could be linked to provide both markets the advantage of the other's nonregular trading hours, such linkages had serious limitations. It was at best a partial solution. Although MOS worked for Eurodollars, it did not succeed with other financial products. More important, the regulatory complications we encountered in creating our MOS system were a nightmare. I doubted if this could be undertaken on a worldwide basis. No single linkup could cover the entire 24-hour trading period, and some of the financial centers we feared didn't want a MOS connection.

The way I saw it, the technological revolution of the past several years was dictating an entirely different response to our competitive problems. To me, those who had not seen the handwriting on the wall were blind to the reality of our times. To survive domestic pressures, we had to embrace the new technologies and to determine whether we could integrate them with open outcry. To compete globally, we had to admit that telecommunications was fashioning a global marketplace that would encompass electronic trading mechanisms. Those who dared ignore these realities, at best, flirted with being relegated to a secondary position in world markets, and at worst, faced extinction.

The answer I sought was simplicity itself: To extend the trading hours for our futures and options contracts through the facility of an electronic screen—after our regular trading day ended. These screens would be available through the facilities of Merc members, would offer our contracts in every part of the world, and would make Merc markets open virtually 24 hours a day. Such an electronic system would represent a comprehensive response to the demands of international competition and put the Merc on the information standard in a big way. In effect, an after-hours screen-based system would combine the elements of MOS linkage with those of night trading and integrate them with open outcry. For certain, it would deter our foreign competitors from listing Merc contracts for trade on their own trading floors. In addition, by embracing computerized technology, we liberated our market environment and opened it to a multitude of modern capabilities and innovations. When I first explored the idea with Rick Kilcollin, he immediately embraced it. "I love it!" he exclaimed and called it "a conceptual leap," which left traditional responses to globalization far behind.

I was taking a cue from what was happening around us. In 1976, the New York Stock Exchange launched its small order execution DOT (Designed Order Turnaround) system, followed by Super-DOT in 1984. The same year, the idea of INTEX, an international electronic order matching system for futures products, was announced. It had no chance since it was without exchange sponsorship and was intended to replace the present auction system. In 1985, the Chicago Board of Options Exchange initiated its Retail Automated Execution System (RAES) for stock and index options. The New Zealand Futures Exchange announced an experimental electronic trading system the same year. Then, in 1986, the London Stock Exchange, in what became known as the "Big Bang," closed its trading floor in favor of SEAQ, an automated stock quotation system. And there were other technological rumblings all around us.

Just as I had done in 1972 when I entered the murky waters of currency trading with the IMM, I was now asking the futures industry to follow me on yet another odyssey, over oceans, across continents, and through the channels of high technology. I had learned long ago that if my goals weren't big, then neither was my vision. After all, what is vision other than imagination extended to the future. Take the science fiction novel I wrote, *The Tenth Planet*, in which the central character is Putral, an all-powerful computer that runs five planets in its galactic world. I began writing the novel in 1983 and finished it in 1986, just at the time I fostered the concept of GLOBEX, a kind of Putral of the futures world as I had envisioned it. The connection was obvious: life had been imitating science fiction since Jules Verne voyaged to the moon—and before that. Computers will some day run the whole show. *The Tenth Planet* was published in 1987. Writing it had been the perfect therapy from the pressures of the market. It also kept me technologically current. The novel was started in longhand and finished on the PC. In airports, on vacations, in the early hours of the morning, I would lose myself on my laptop.

But I knew that of all the things I had undertaken, electronic trade was to be the most difficult. The futures market establishment was extremely powerful and could be expected to fight automation with Luddite zeal. As historian Barbara Tuchman said, "Men will not believe what does not fit in with their plans or suit their prearrangements." To have a chance in a members' referendum, the plan would need some very special attractions. I went back to strategize with my inner circle of that day: Barry Lind, Brian Monieson, Jack Sandner, and John Geldermann.

I think Sandner loved the idea from the start because it would illustrate how much more progressive the Merc was than the CBOT. "This will leave the CBOT's night session in the dust," Jack confided to me and later expressed those same views to the media. But it was Barry Lind who became the most avid proponent and my trusted advisor in the development of GLOBEX. Instantly embracing technology as a must for the CME, he gave me the courage to proceed, saying, "Leo, I rate the move toward electronics as high as your original IMM idea." And putting his money where his mouth was, Lind soon adopted a high-tech strategy for his own brokerage firm.

In conversations with Ken Cone and also Rick Kilcollin, I explained that for the Merc membership to accept the introduction of electronic trade, we would have to devise a package that included three central components. First, as was my standard approach with respect to revolutionary concepts, we had to find a highly credible expert who would join this effort and provide us with the technological credentials we did not have. Ken Cone and Rick Kilcollin quickly proved to me that Reuters Holdings PLC, the giant international quotations firm, was our most likely partner and was very interested. Reuters had already taken steps toward automated trading when they purchased *Instinet*, an order matching system for stocks, and with their introduction of a *Dealing FX* system for foreign exchange. And Reuters was far and away the most well-known international name. It seemed to me that Reuters could play the credibility role for automation as Milton Friedman had done for financial futures a decade before.

The second component I needed was to remove any fear that electronic trade could ever become a threat to members' livelihoods during open outcry hours. Merc chairman Jack Sandner, who was ex officio of strategic planning, and I agreed that we would guarantee our members that without their permission the screens would never operate during CME regular trading hours for competitive products.

Next, I reasoned, the plan had to provide for a monetary reward to Merc members. Our traders were first and foremost capitalists, and they had to be offered a profit motive. It was not difficult to devise. Clearly, the trades accumulated by this new electronic system would be charged a transaction fee. These fees would ultimately produce a profit, and that profit could be paid out as a dividend to our members. I proposed a 70-20-10 split which was agreed to by Monieson, Lind, Sandner, and Geldermann. Seventy percent of the profits would go to members, 20 percent to clearing members, and the remaining 10 percent would go to the Exchange for running the new system. Long range, I speculated, there could be some other great profit opportunities. The same global competitive problems facing the Merc were also being faced by every other exchange. Why couldn't we eventually invite other exchanges to join our electronic system and list their own instruments of trade? But that was a long way off.

The final component of the proposal would be in its presentation. In my mind, this had two parts. Until we were ready to disclose the idea, its rationale, and all its provisions, it would have to be kept super secret. I was adamant on this subject. I was fully aware how the smallest leak could create erroneous impressions and speculations and give our detractors an opportunity to distort the concept. It would surely destroy any chance of its passage at the required referendum. If this concept was going to have a chance at all, it had to be presented to the membership in its full scope at a special meeting, where we were in control of the unveiling. Jack Sandner and I had threatened death to anyone on the Board or staff who breathed a word of what we were doing. Equally important, the written information that would be distributed to every member at the presentation had to be prepared in a manner to ensure a most favorable impression. I delegated this responsibility to Alysann Posner, who was our ultimate in-house professional when it came to written and graphic presentations. Indeed, the final brochure, entitled *The Future of Futures* was as much an element in the overwhelmingly favorable response by the membership as any of the other components.

Getting Reuters aboard the venture was actually easy. When I met with their officials at a special Reuters board meeting in New York, I found them anxious and very willing to become a partner to an electronic trading system that would give them virtual exclusivity as a vendor of after-hours futures quotations. I needed no assistance convincing them that the future would be dictated by technology and that the Merc had to embrace this reality. For the opportunity to break this ground with us, they agreed to build the system at no cost to the Merc and to operate it for us on a per-transaction fee basis. Some weeks later, subject to membership approval, the CME and Reuters Holdings PLC entered into a long-range agreement that would create a global electronic automated transaction system for the trading of futures and futures options before and after regular U.S. business hours.

Over 1,000 Merc members came to the meeting held in September 1987 on the Merc's still unused spare trading floor; it was the largest member attendance in our history. The feeling was electric. I could sense a collective holding of breath by the entire membership. The secrecy surrounding the Merc's proposal was so tight that in the week prior to the members' meeting, the *Chicago Sun-Times* predicted that the Merc would follow the CBOT with an open outcry after-hours market. To a hushed, standing-room-only crowd, we unveiled P•M•T. This was the working name of the system that I had insisted on in order to underscore the fact that the concept would be a Post-Market-Trade and allay any fears that it threatened open outcry. To my chagrin, we quickly learned that the same initials were also used for other purposes; in the United Kingdom, for instance, it described premenstrual tension. We soon changed the name to its permanent designation *GLOBEX* (Global Exchange), chosen by the Board from a computer-generated list of names.

From the moment the special members' meeting began, I was certain that the vast majority of our members approved the idea. I could see it in the rapt attention they gave to the long presentation; I could hear it in their applause at just the right moments; and I could sense it in the way they took the written material as they filed out. Andre Villeneuve and John Hull, the officials sent by Reuters to the meeting to personally assure our members that Reuters was ready to be the Merc's exclusive partner, were absolutely fabulous in their remarks. The credibility card worked like magic. And although Sandner and I spent many hours lobbying the members prior to the referendum, I never really had a doubt about its outcome. On October 6, 1987, our members overwhelmingly approved the concept, and once again, the Chicago Mercantile Exchange changed the course of futures markets forever.

The Merc's announcement sent a seismic shock throughout the futures industry worldwide. CBOT chairman Karsten Mahlman later described GLOBEX as an H-bomb that threatened the life of open outcry. But to everyone's surprise, the fact that the CME—with its strong history of innovation—had been the one to take this monumental step, coupled with the fact its membership had so fully approved of it, put a highly favorable spin on the concept. The media loves technology and regarded this revolutionary announcement as a signal that we at the Merc were again brave innovators to be saluted and admired. GLOBEX and its technological partner Reuters had precisely the right ingredients to receive instant credibility and praise from the media—just as I had planned and hoped.

And, almost on cue, the GLOBEX pronouncement resulted in a virtual torrent of electronic systems, devised either to extend existing trading hours or to conduct the entire transaction process. The following year, the Tokyo Stock Exchange, the Osaka Securities Exchange, the Copenhagen Stock Exchange, the Danish Options & Futures, the Swiss Options & Financial Futures Exchange, and the Tokyo Grain Exchange all launched automated electronic systems. The next year, the Irish Futures and Options Exchange, the Tokyo International Financial Exchange, the London International Financial Futures Exchange, and the Sydney Futures Exchange initiated similar systems. By the end of 1991, 10 more exchanges followed suit, including the Deutsche Termin Boerse, the London Futures and Options Exchange, the Swedish Options Market, the Finnish Options Market, and Mercado Espanol de Futuros Financieros.

To the world, GLOBEX represented more than an idea whose time had come; it was an official endorsement by the futures market establishment that automation was a necessary adjunct to its infrastructure. The Merc once again was the darling of the U.S. financial services industry. Alas, there was no way I could envision what actually happened. I had no way of knowing that it would be nearly five years before GLOBEX would become a reality. As Robert Burns said, *"The best laid schemes o' mice and men gang aft a-gley."*

29

Early Warning

Early in 1987, I remember the uncomfortable, almost hilariously funny conversation between Susan Phillips, chairperson of the CFTC, and me. "Let me get this straight, Leo. You, of all people, want a *daily price limit* in S&P? Frankly, I don't believe my ears."

Susan Phillips, a free-market economist and a former professor of economics at the University of Iowa, knew me very well. I had actively supported her candidacy for the chairmanship of the CFTC and had extensively explored her views on our markets. We both felt strongly about the beauty of a market economy and were of a common mind against artificial restraints to market movements. For me to suddenly suggest an arbitrary barrier to the free flow of prices was completely contrary to everything I stood for, and she knew it. It must have been nearly impossible for Phillips to understand my sudden turnaround. Did Melamed lose his balance? Well I hadn't, but it was impossible for me to explain to the federal regulatory chair of our industry that I feared a stock market crash. Such a conversation could itself initiate a crash.

Of course, I wasn't alone in the belief that the stock market had gotten too high. There were others who thought as I did and saw the vulnerability of the Dow and the S&P Index. Among them was John Phelan, chairman of the NYSE. In various speeches, Phelan voiced his fear over the possibility of a "market meltdown." He also threw in his "cascade scenario" as a result of the adverse reaction between index arbitrage and portfolio insurance—a futures market hedging strategy.

What worried me was that on the day of reckoning, our S&P contract would be the first to signal the bad news to the world. And I knew what people did to messengers with bad news. So, in desperation, I initiated a bold attempt to insulate our markets from the storm that I knew would follow. There was only one way. If our S&P contract had a prescribed daily price limit that it could not transgress, then our market could fall only so far on any given day. If a stock market meltdown occurred, futures market prices would remain well above the cash market levels. Then our markets could not possibly be blamed. Although I couldn't get it done, I got close.

To Susan Phillips' everlasting credit, she bit her lip and agreed to my request under certain conditions. "Leo, only because it's you would I ever consider supporting such a request before the CFTC. But, since it is you, I will agree that we propose it on an experimental basis. But Leo, you know the industry will scream bloody murder. They'll never stand for price limits. How are you going to overcome that?"

Before rule changes were adopted by the CFTC, they were subject to the weight of opinions of the institutional community that used our market. I knew that if during the "comment period" the CFTC got a deluge of letters opposing the experiment to institute a daily price limit, the CFTC would not be well placed to override these objections. It was a battle we would have to face. I told Phillips that I would test the water by placing the issue before the industry at the upcoming FIA Annual convention in Boca Raton.

"Susan," I said, thanking her for supporting my idea, "if it doesn't fly in Boca, I'll relieve you of the burden."

Daily limits in futures were nothing new. All commodity markets had them. They were a consequence of the comparatively small margin (security deposit) required for initiating a market position. However, while price limits worked for agricultural markets, they posed serious problems for financial contracts. Our new market participants were not used to artificial limits to price movements. A chorus of institutional users, especially our stock index participants, argued that daily price limits were a serious impediment to the success of index futures and contrary to our avowed free-market philosophy. Besides, I recognized that in finance, unlike in agriculture, our markets were competing with strong underlying cash markets that had no price limits. Indeed, we had successfully lobbied all the futures exchanges to petition the CFTC to eliminate price limits on financial contracts. Although the S&P contract began life with a small daily limit, with CFTC blessing, it was soon expanded, and eventually eliminated.

Suddenly, in February 1987, I was contemplating a 180-degree about-face. My motive, of course, was to save our markets from a worse fate, but I could not verbalize this view. As the leader of the world's most prominent stock index market, I felt constrained from speaking publicly about a market crash. And I knew I would get no support from the institutional users of our index market. Lou Margolis, an executive of Salomon Brothers who was serving as a director to the Merc Board, was a lone exception in this respect. He had independently embraced the idea of a daily limit for the same reason I did.

I huddled with Barry Lind, Brian Monieson, and Rick Kilcollin. I explained my concerns and the remedy I was considering: "Let's remove the possibility of futures blame by limiting how much our market can fall in any given day." Together, we weighed the pros and cons carefully. Lind and Monieson, no differently than I, thought a day of reckoning was coming and that the price limit idea would work. "The day of disaster is coming just as sure as we are standing here," Monieson said. The only question in Lind's mind was the amount of the price limit and whether it could be implemented in time. We all agreed that the downside was that futures would be out of the play during the crisis, but felt that this was a small price to pay for survival. Jack Sandner soon also joined this effort and accepted my view that we form a special committee to forge a recommendation to the Merc Board for the establishment of a daily price limit for the Spuz. I chaired the committee which included Sandner, Margolis, Lind, Monieson, and Rosenberg, and we settled on a 12-point daily S&P limit, a recommendation ultimately approved by the CME Board. This was the easy part of the battle.

I next called John Damgard, the FIA president, to schedule a session on price limits for stock index futures on the convention agenda. But before the convention, I had one more difficult mission. I knew my mentor, Milton Friedman, Mr. Free Market himself, was bound to hear of my initiative. Clearly, Friedman would react against any form of infringement on market movement. But then Friedman wasn't running a futures exchange and wouldn't have to contend with the political aftermath that I envisioned, if what I anticipated happening, happened. With extreme trepidation, I called Friedman and spent a trying hour on the telephone giving him the rationale for my idea. The thrust of my argument had to do with the amount of resting orders found in brokers' decks that act as a cushion during extreme market movements. The further away from the norm—what is called standard deviation—the fewer resting orders are found. In other words, whenever there is a highly unusual price movement, there are fewer and fewer standing orders to absorb the shock of incoming at-the-market orders. At some far-out point, there are theoretically no more resting orders, and the market can go into free fall—something I desperately wanted to avoid. I don't know whether I ever fully convinced Friedman, but I did get him to understand that for me there were considerations that transcended pure economic ideology.

The entire exercise was to no avail anyway. I was nearly stoned to death when I placed the idea before the equity industry representatives who had gathered in Boca Raton at the FIA's annual convention to hear my proposal. Again, Lou Margolis was the only person that I remember from the New York contingent who had the guts and foresight to support the idea. Alas, Margolis' voice, even coupled with mine and a few Merc traders who understood what was at stake, was far from enough. I called Susan Phillips to tell her I had lost. She was off the hook. In the months that followed the 1987 stock market crash, I often reflected about how close I came to saving our markets from the criticism that ensued—a barrage that at times looked like the end to futures markets.

Our markets were victims of an anti-index futures sentiment that stemmed mainly from two seemingly enigmatic market applications: *index arbitrage* and *triple witching*. While these two futures market operations were separate and independent of each other, together they provided our antagonists with proof of the villainous nature of our markets. As stock index futures grew, so did the attacks against them. Every drop in the Dow was blamed on index arbitrage. Every so-called triple witching expiration was considered an unnecessary disruption to the market. And together these futures-related effects were accused of creating uncontrollable volatility, which self-appointed equity mavens proclaimed was "frightening away the small investor."

It was mostly nonsense. There is nothing mysterious about the technique known as index arbitrage nor is it some new evil on the investment scene. It is no different in its application than any other form of arbitrage; it is a market operation that has been around ever since there were two or more markets for the same or similar product. In stock index arbitrage, a firm monitors both the stock market and a stock index future such as the S&P 500 futures contract. If futures are expensive compared with the underlying stocks, for example, a short position is established in futures and a portfolio of stocks is bought. When futures are relatively inexpensive, they are bought and stocks are sold. As long as the price differential exceeds the costs of trading in both markets, a certain arbitrage profit is possible.

To a trader or specialist in New York, this arbitrage selling (or buying) looks like the root cause of the price change, but the root cause actually lies in the investor sentiment that generated selling or buying pressure in the futures. The Merc's Kenneth R. Cone minced no words in his rebuttal: "Blaming index arbitrage for market-wide price movements makes as much sense as blaming snowplows for blizzards. Snowplows move snow around, but they cannot create a blizzard. Arbitrage traders buy in one market and sell in another to transfer demand pressure across exchanges, but (they) do not create the net pressure that moves prices in equity products as a whole." As Alan Greenspan, chairman of the Federal Reserve Board of Governors, explained in testimony before the U.S. Congress, futures markets routinely react more rapidly to new information than do cash markets, and "arbitrage activity acts to ensure that values in the cash markets do not lag behind."

Index arbitrage was the rallying cry of our detractors, but there was a much more fundamental reason for their attacks. Stock index futures represented something new, a stark departure from the past, and almost everyone had a secret longing for the simpler days of times gone by. Everywhere we looked, someone seemed to call for a return to those "good old days" before there were stock index futures, before there was program trading, before index arbitrage. Of course, everyone overlooked the fact that in those good old uncomplicated days, the average daily volume on the NYSE was a mere 11.5 million shares, large block transactions accounted for 15 percent of reported volume as opposed to the current 50 percent, stocks were bought solely on the basis of inherent individual stock values, mutual and pension funds had not yet complicated things by introducing market performances comparisons based on indexes, asset allocation was virtually unknown, fixed commissions were still legal, and globalization of markets was but a futuristic notion. Those good old days were long before we were so dependent upon and competed for foreign cash, before we cared what other stock markets were doing and they could do little about ours, long before LBOs, zeros, or junk bonds, and eons before unbundled stocks.

The antagonists could be divided into two main groups: those who genuinely didn't understand the function of index futures and feared the unknown, and those who had a secret agenda. The latter were primarily fund and money managers (such as Neuberger & Berman, who were prominent in its vocal opposition to our markets) who oversaw the investments of billions of dollars for mutual funds, pension funds, and wealthy individuals by picking investments in selected stocks. These money managers viewed the growth of stock index investing as a competitive trend that threatened their selective stock-picking investment philosophy. It was a trend, however, that was on a very strong growth path since the 1960s and our futures markets, which quickly became an important tool of index trading, assisted the trend. As a friend of the enemy, we became the enemy.

After the 1987 crash, SEC Chairman David S. Ruder explained the issue well:

> To understand what happened in the U.S. securities markets in October 1987, it is necessary to understand changes in institutional trading strategies that took place during the last decade. During this period, the increasing size of many institutional portfolios made it difficult for portfolio managers to trade in the stock of a single company without unduly affecting the price of that stock. In addition, modern portfolio theory gained increasing acceptance. As a result, many portfolio managers began to shift emphasis from individual stock selection toward trading the market as a whole.

Or as SEC Commissioner Joseph Grundfest put it:

> Some participants in the policy debate have a perfectly rational incentive to continue to confuse the message with the messenger in order to forestall technological progress that threatens traditional trading mechanisms that

generate substantial rents for certain market participants. Put more bluntly, some people are making money off the system as it operates today, and measures designed to make our markets more efficient by improving information, expanding capacity, and enhancing liquidity are not necessarily in everyone's financial interests.

To combat this growing anti-futures movement, which I knew represented an incredibly dangerous impediment to our continued viability, I organized an Index Trading Coordination Committee which, aside from CME officials, included CBOE Chairman Alger "Duke" Chapman, its President Chuck Henry, and its Executive Vice President Arne Rode; from the CME were Tom Dittmer of Refco, Lou Margolis from Salomon Brothers, Jim Porter of First Options, and Gary Seevers from Goldman Sachs. The strategy included a rare meeting with members of our New York-based community. That community had been profitably and extensively using our index markets, but were generally silent in its defense. Either they didn't recognize the problem or needed a push. I wanted to gain their formidable support, energize their voices, and organize their public response in an attempt to correct our damaged image.

The meeting took place on September 30, 1986, at the offices of Salomon Brothers. It brought together the most prominent members of the New York-based community, all protagonists of index trading and prominent users of our markets. There was a total of 27 officials present representing the AMEX, CBOE, CME, NYSE, Bear Stearns, Drexel Burnham Lambert, First Boston Corp., Goldman Sachs, Kidder Peabody, Merrill Lynch Capital Markets, Morgan Stanley, PaineWebber, and Salomon Brothers. To his credit and my immense gratitude, Richard Grasso, now Chairman of NYSE, was present at this meeting and totally in support of its purpose. His enlightened remarks set a positive tone and gave testimony to the fact that our markets were inextricably linked and were jointly providing the American investor economic benefit.

I spoke for about 30 minutes, offering some graphic examples of the contentious views reported in the media about our markets, and painted the mural of the negative environment in which index futures found themselves. This was followed by some strong comments by Bill Brodsky who, after all, had been part of this community; then others took turns to making comments and offering suggestions. Everyone seemed ready to do his part, and there was general consensus that a counterattack was warranted. I concluded with an impassioned appeal to those in the room: "Your voices, your expertise, your knowledge about index futures must be heard. You represent our primary source of credibility."

The second most contentious problem—triple witching—was treated by the media as if it were an evil disease brought to mankind by index futures and options. Triple witching happened four times a year, on the third Friday of every quarter. On that day, the current contracts of stock index futures, futures options, and security-based options and index options expired at the same time. And there could be no doubt that on the days of expiration—as a consequence of cross-currents of complex strategies in both futures and options markets—unusual volatility was created. It became the focal point of unceasing criticism.

Near the end of SEC Chairman John Shad's term, he and his commissioners had begun to figure out ways to handle big swings of triple witching. I welcomed Shad's interest since I too was very concerned about this problem. Shad had compared the situation to a gigantic mobile that when pulled on one part by traders the rest adjusted "incredibly efficiently and almost instantly." Shad's point was obvious: the market would adjust to any dislocation, as opposed to regulators taking disruptive action. But his opinion was in the minority.

Except for those who advocated doing away with index futures entirely, there were two points of view. The first claimed that there wasn't much anyone could do about the expiration phenomenon and lobbied for retention of the current "Friday close" approach; the second advocated that we close trading on the third Thursday prior to settlement, with settlement to occur on the morning after the contract expired.

The fact that the specialists at the NYSE were actively in favor of a "morning after" settlement naturally made me suspect that idea. Indeed, most Chicago experts were in the camp advocating retention of the present procedure, claiming that the suggested change would be to the disadvantage of the CME. Sensing that this issue could get out of hand, I again organized a special committee to tackle the complex subject. What I needed was a body of experts on whom I could rely for the Merc's ultimate decision. The committee was loaded with talent. Aside from the Merc Board officers, I chose people who would provide an honest but diverse point of view. I especially needed people who would speak out with authority. Joe Ritchie was that type of guy. As the CEO of Chicago Research & Trading (CRT), at the time the nation's largest and most successful options trading firm, he had a strong opinion. "Leo," he told me, making no bones about how he felt, "if we move to a Friday settlement, Chicago's blood will flow eastward."

Bob Zellner, a thoroughly erudite and knowledgeable member, was another I trusted. Zellner, I knew, did not come to the meeting with a preconceived notion and would provide a balanced and thoughtful opinion. From Merc staff, I included Bill Brodsky, CME president; Mike Apatoff, the Merc's EVP; Galen Burghardt, our director of research who had a good head on his shoulders; Rick Kilcollin, CME's chief economist; Alysann Posner, our VP of special projects; and Jerrold Salzman, our general counsel.

But beyond the foregoing, I also wanted an expert academic view that would provide us with an unbiased, studied analysis of the subject. For that purpose, I turned to Hans R. Stoll, the highly regarded economist and professor at Vanderbilt University. Professor Stoll had written extensively on the triple witching subject and was respected throughout academia and the markets.

The committee's decisive meeting, held at the Metropolitan Club in the Sears Tower, occurred on October 29, 1986—a full year before the crash. I opened the discussion by emphasizing that although the controversy occurred only four times a year, it was "our most vexing problem and used by adversaries and the press to lambast futures throughout the year."

Professor Stoll provided us with his extensive data and analysis, enabling us to clearly inspect the consequences on expiration days. A comprehensive discussion followed that lasted many hours, but from which a clearer picture of the problem emerged. It produced a very surprising result. A majority of the committee, including CRT's Joe Ritchie, concluded as I did: that the NYSE point of view was probably correct.

In an historic move, one that was then taken as a signal of cooperation between our two markets, we proposed to revamp our settlement procedure. After federal regulatory approval was received in June 1987, the Merc and the NYSE carried out a coordinated shift in futures market settlement for expiring contracts to occur *after trading ceased* on the third Thursday of the contract month. The settlement price would be established the following morning based on the Special Opening Quotation procedure at the NYSE. Basically, it gave NYSE specialists more time to resolve large order imbalances and substantially reduced the volatility caused by expiring contracts. Since then, nearly all world markets (the CBOE is a major exception) have adopted this U.S. procedure for final settlement in stock index-related products.

These efforts notwithstanding, I wasn't so naive as to think that the controversy over the economic value of our markets had been put to rest. I knew better. Once my attempt to move our markets out of harm's way in the event of a stock market crash had failed, I knew that we would most likely get the blame if anything really went wrong. We did. And although in the final analysis our markets were completely vindicated and gained enormous stature as a result, it took about two years, tons of studies, an immeasurable amount of brainstorming and planning, unending appearances before congressional committees, an incalculable number of media interviews, reams of reports, an inestimable amount of time in conferences and discussions, and hours upon hours of meetings and telephone conversations with regulators and government officials. And during all of that, it was anybody's guess how it would end.

30

Black Monday

It was a perfect fall day that Monday, October 19. I don't remember how fast I was driving along the Edens Expressway, but the colors of the trees had blurred into an autumnal palette. Everything raced that day: my mind, my heart, the markets.

Shortly before 6:30 A.M., my car phone rang. On the other end of the line was New York Stock Exchange Chairman John Phelan, Jr., and I knew he wasn't calling to chitchat.

"Leo, have you heard the news? It looks like we're in for a very bad day," he vexed.

I thanked him for the call and we talked a bit, both agreeing to stay closely in touch.

Phelan was alerting me to news I had anticipated. He told me that an inordinate number of sell orders were gathering on the NYSE, set to hit the market. Our conversation took place more than two hours before the NYSE was to open. Normally, the Exchange did not see that kind of order flow that early. I realized it was going to be a rough day, picking up where it had left off on Friday when the Dow Jones Industrial Average sank 108 points, pushing the market to the edge of an abyss.

I never denied that the world I grew up in was a volatile one and remains so. And since the markets reflect the world beyond its economic chaos, it's only natural they too should be volatile. But in the fall of 1987—on that Black Monday—America's financial community was ill prepared for the worst stock market crash in history.

I leave the analysis of the crash to the economists, who always seem to find the traces of tinder amid the ruins of a burned-out market. There are a thicket of causes that turn a market from a robust bully into a frail weakling. There were as many theories as there were theorists for this crash. Among the more notable was the hypothesis that it was the result of so-called portfolio insurance, a futures-related hedging strategy devised by the two Berkeley economic professors Hayne Leland and Mark Rubinstein, and promoted by their LOR (Leland, O'Brien, Rubinstein) investment firm. Another was that it was the fault of "computerized program trading on automatic pilot," as some pundits were quoted in the media. Both of these contentions were debunked after the crash. Still others blamed it on the NYSE specialist system, judged by many as an antiquated system, inadequate to meet the onslaught of sudden selling in a global marketplace. On the other hand, Treasury Secretary Jim Baker blamed the Germans for raising interest rates and the Democrats for proposing a tax hike. The Democrats blamed the President for opposing a tax hike and for not controlling federal spending. But whatever exacerbated the crash, none of those reasons produced the conditions necessary to create the panic in the first place. Suffice it to say that the stock market had been spiraling upward for years, and nothing goes up forever. Overlooking that fact (or because of it), the United States was an overextended threadbare trillionaire; the market was overvalued, overbought, and overwrought. And the crash served as a stark reminder: markets wane as easily as they wax with a power to change minds—and empty pockets in a flash.

One thing is certain. The crash was not a random event. Most informed observers agree that its cause can be found in the underlying economic conditions of that time frame. Alan Greenspan, chairman of the Federal Reserve Board would later testify before congress that the 1987 crash "was an accident waiting to happen." There were, of course, more than one who had seen it coming.

"How bad do you think it will be," asked Martin Feldstein, the former chairman of the Council of Economic Advisors (CEA) under President Ronald Reagan. It was about a week or so before the crash, and Feldstein had come to my office to chat. He too feared market conditions and agreed with my assessment that we might be in for a bad time. "I don't know for sure," I responded, "but I would buy some insurance." Feldstein smiled, "Oh, I already did; I bought OEX puts at the CBOE." It turned out to be a very wise move.

Another who saw it coming was Beryl Sprinkel, who was steeped in the Chicago school of economics and had served as one of the initial directors of the IMM. In 1987, Sprinkel, the current chairman of the Council of Economic Advisors (CEA) under President Reagan, was one of the precious few at the highest levels of government who understood the supply and demand fundamentals that made financial markets move up and down. And what he was seeing made him very nervous. U.S. monetary policy was definitely too tight in Sprinkel's view. U.S. financial markets could buckle if things didn't change.

Sprinkel recognized that the tightening wasn't as much the doings of Alan Greenspan, the newly appointed chairman of the Federal Reserve, as it was of Jim Baker's, the Secretary of the Treasury. Sprinkel respected Alan Greenspan and knew that his economic credentials were solid. Jim Baker, on the other hand, had no formal economic credentials. Baker was a smart guy and had been an outstanding chief of staff at the White House, but when the President agreed to the game of musical chairs with high government officials, it spelled trouble. Jim Baker became Treasury Secretary and made a deal in Paris with the Germans, the so-called Louvre Agreement, to defend the dollar and stop its fall.

Sprinkel knew the agreement was fatally flawed and spelled danger for financial markets. He wasn't alone in this view. My respected friend, Allan Meltzer, chairman of the Shadow Open Market Committee and professor at Carnegie-Mellon, publicly proclaimed the need for the U.S. Treasury to "cease efforts at targeting the dollar's exchange rate" and allow market forces to work. In the long run, such efforts were hopeless anyway. In today's global markets, where daily capital flows measure in the trillions of dollars, it is ludicrous to attempt to manage the value of the U.S. currency. And that was precisely what Baker was doing when he coerced the chairman of the Fed to tighten U.S. monetary policy in order to influence the value of the dollar.

Such undertakings are not new or unique. In fact, there are always some bureaucrats who dream about a return to Bretton Woods and fixed exchange rates. They love the power they could have in determining how much the Deutsche mark or yen should be worth in relation to the dollar. A year or so earlier, because of chronic weakness in the dollar, this idea began to gain ground. Even some Washington heavyweights joined the movement and advocated a return to active management of currency values. Beryl Sprinkel called me at the time to make sure that I did not ignore this development.

"Leo, it's a slippery slope, and you never can tell where it will end. You better get some people together to nip it in the bud."

I took this as marching orders, and immediately called Milton Friedman. He too saw the movement for a return to fixed exchange rates as dangerous and suggested that I lead an effort to stem the tide. First, I organized the American Coalition for Flexible Exchange Rates (ACFX). The ACFX represented over one hundred of the most prominent American economists and businessmen rounded up by our Washington attorney Charles (Chip) Seeger. They gladly joined the endeavor to make a public statement against any form of fixed exchange rates. In my essay entitled "Fixed Exchange Rate Foolishness" which was published on the editorial page of *The Wall Street Journal* in January 1986, in so many words I said that the exercise was foolishness, that market forces would undo the manipulations of the G-5 or any other artificial system that attempted to dictate the relative value of the dollar.

Milton Friedman also encouraged me to act as editor of an anthology, *The Merits of Flexible Exchange Rates*, which was published subsequent to the October crash by the George Mason University Press. Again, it was Chip Seeger who was invaluable in putting the material together and coordinating the project. The anthology, with an introduction by Friedman, included several of the classic writings on the subject by renowned scholars Harry Johnson, Fritz Machlup, Gottfried Haberler, as well as Milton Friedman. It offered perspectives from the Federal Reserve Board, with Governor Henry Wallich and Chairman Alan Greenspan; from the International Monetary Fund, with Jacques de Larosiere; and from the Council of Economic Advisers, with Chairman Beryl Sprinkel and member Michael Mussa. It presented important thinking by a number of today's leading scholars, including Martin Feldstein, Rudiger Dornbusch, and my good friend, University of Chicago Professor Jacob Frenkel, who was destined to become the governor of the Bank of Israel.

The anthology also published for the first time Milton Friedman's confidential memorandum to President-elect Richard M. Nixon, which provided Nixon with a bold prescription for resolving the U.S. balance of payments problem created during President Johnson's era. Alas, it took the Nixon administration three years to carry out Friedman's recommended action and by then it was too late.

But as October 1987 approached, Beryl Sprinkel became increasingly frustrated. The first meeting he had with the President and the relevant government officials to warn of the negative effects of the Louvre Agreement had not produced any changes in U.S. tight monetary policies. In his view, time was running out. Of special concern to him was the fact that soon he would be leaving the chairmanship of the CEA. An illness in the family (Sprinkel's wife was very ill) had forced him to submit his resignation to the President. At first President Reagan refused to accept it. But Beryl insisted that he had served the nation faithfully for a number of years and that he must now be relieved of government responsibilities. Reluctantly, the President accepted Sprinkel's resignation and his departure was announced to the media, although no specific date had been set.

Thus, Sprinkel went to Howard Baker, President Reagan's new chief of staff, and told him that a second meeting had to be held right away. "The President must be made to understand the urgency of the situation."

Howard H. Baker, Jr., a former United States Senator from Tennessee and an exceedingly smart politician who knew his way around Washington, was no expert in economics. But Howard Baker knew that Sprinkel had the President's ear and made the arrangements. The meeting was held in the Oval Office at the White House on October 16, 1987—the Friday before the stock market crash. When President Reagan arrived, all the government movers and shakers of the American financial system were present: Jim Baker, the Secretary of Treasury; Alan Greenspan, chairman of the Federal Reserve; Beryl Sprinkel, chairman of the CEA; Howard Baker, chief of staff; as well as Baker's deputy chief of staff.

According to Sprinkel, Howard Baker called the meeting to order. "Mr. President," Baker said, "at Dr. Sprinkel's request, we have again gathered to review the situation in the U.S. financial markets." He then asked Jim Baker to offer his assessment. Baker assured the President that the U.S. financial markets were stable and that he saw no reason to be concerned. The Louvre Agreement on foreign exchange, which he had fashioned, was taking hold. "The dollar has stabilized," he said, and the recent drop in the U.S. stock market was nothing to be concerned about.

Sprinkel said Baker then turned to the chairman of the Fed and asked, "Alan, do you agree with this assessment?" At the time, Alan Greenspan was the new kid on the block. He had only been in office several months. According to Sprinkel, it seemed that the Fed chairman was not prepared to fight openly with the Treasury secretary so early in their official relationship, and offered some "Fedspeak," the noncommittal Esperanto language of all central bankers, which Greenspan ultimately perfected during his tenure as Fed chieftain.

Sprinkel was disappointed. He had hoped that Greenspan, of the same economic and philosophical persuasion, would come to his assistance. When Howard Baker asked Sprinkel whether he agreed with the assessments made, Sprinkel adamantly demurred.

"Mr. President, no, I do not." Sprinkel reasoned that he might as well speak out since he had nothing to lose anyway; he was soon to leave Washington politics. "We shouldn't have made the Paris agreement in the first place. The resulting tight monetary policy of the Federal Reserve, forced by the Treasury, has put the financial markets in a very precarious situation from which there could be a perilous fall."

The meeting went on for a while longer, but nothing was decided. The President would take things under advisement. Greenspan was scheduled to leave for Texas to give a speech to the American Bankers Association. Everyone else prepared to leave for the weekend. It was too late anyway—all hell was about to break loose. The following week would begin with Black Monday, October 19, 1987.

On that fateful October morning, well before John Phelan's call, I knew it was going to be an awfully long—and painful—day based on what had already occurred in the overseas markets. I had been following the markets in other parts of the world, and the news was dismal. That morning in Tokyo, the Nikkei 225 Stock Average, Japan's equivalent to the Dow Jones Industrial Average, fell 2.5 percent. Panic struck the Hong Kong Stock

Exchange where the Hang Seng index dropped 133 points in the first 40 minutes of trading. The FTSE index in London—which was six hours ahead of Chicago—had slipped 10 percent by midday. From all indications of the activity in the London market when I was awakened by the radio at 5:00 A.M., traders were estimating the Dow Jones Industrial Average 200 points lower on the NYSE opening, an unprecedented expectation. The large U.S. brokerage firms with overseas branches knew that further selling by foreign investors was on the way to both the cash and futures markets back in the United States, not to mention the overbought American pension funds and institutions. As it turned out, it was grimmer than anyone expected.

Upon reaching the Merc, without hesitation, I called an emergency meeting of the CME Executive Committee for 10:30 A.M. For all practical purposes, it remained in session until 6:30 P.M. the following evening. I then called Merc chairman Jack Sandner to tell him what was afoot because he normally did not get to the office until after 9:00 A.M. He had not yet heard the news.

Before the opening, I went into the pit to get a pulse on the market and give some comfort to the broker community that was brave enough to take the deluge of sell orders that were coming at them. They all gathered around me. There was anxiety in their eyes. No one was certain how much lower the market would open, but things looked bad. We would have to hear where the buyers would be willing to buy. It was the scariest moment of my life. Brokers are responsible for the prices they report on executed orders. If they miss an order, execute it incorrectly, buy instead of sell, fill at the wrong price, or do any one of a hundred other things that can go wrong in the stress of a pit situation, they are held responsible. And on that morning, errors would mean many thousands, even hundred of thousands of dollars. Some brokers and traders elected to stay away. Still, the bulk of S&P traders, like very brave soldiers ready for battle, were there. I remember the brief conversation I had with John Oberman, an old-hand S&P broker and a stand-up guy.

"What do you want us to do, Leo?" he asked, as if I had a magic solution. I knew pandemonium was about to break loose.

"Do the best you can," I quietly responded, our eyes meeting for a brief second in mutual understanding of the difficult situation.

As expected, long before the opening, sell orders were piled high in both stock and futures markets. On the NYSE, the huge order imbalance overwhelmed the specialists, the dealers who buy and sell stocks from their own inventories against orders from the public or other broker-dealers. The specialist has a franchise on certain stocks, and in return for that monopoly, pledges to maintain a fair and orderly market. But there was no orderly market that Monday morning. In fact, there was hardly a market. Oh, the NYSE opened, all right; that is, an opening bell sounded, and the lights were on, but few prices ensued. The sell orders were so great that specialists either couldn't or wouldn't make a market. For a majority of stocks on the NYSE, there were no prices. Those that were reported were sometimes hours behind the actual last sale. And often during that Monday, the prices used in calculating the DJIA or S&P Index were the last available quotes from the previous Friday's close. Thus, for the better part of the morning, the Dow Jones Industrial Average reported a price that had no real relevance to the actual price of the cash market.

The big difference between a futures market and the stock market is that our market always opens at the prescribed time and always provides a price from the opening bell. Our market makers have no monopoly on the market and must compete with everyone in the pit. The buy and sell orders find each other and a price is established the moment the market opens. Unfortunately, if there are more sell orders than buy orders, then the price is lower—and that's precisely what happened that morning.

The S&P futures market opened on time at 8:30 A.M. CST, and a price between buyers and sellers was instantly established. It wasn't a pretty price and at first I even had trouble understanding what it was showing. *How much lower is that? My God, is that possible?* The SPZ (December) futures contract had opened at 261.50, down 20.75 points from Friday's close. In Merc terminology, the market was down over 2,000 points. None of us had ever seen anything like it. But my reaction was more than shock. It was genuine fear.

For the rest of the day, nothing was certain. It was like living in a nightmare with events happening in nonsequential fashion, except that there was an eerie connection between each of the scenes as they unfolded. The first emergency session of the executive committee met as called at 10:30 A.M. Monday. The boardroom became a warroom with 26 people, including staff members, sitting around a huge table with reports from the fronts. I reported my conversation with John Phelan and other industry officials dealing with market conditions. Bill Brodsky reported his conversations with industry officials. There followed a normal progression of reports by staff members detailing such matters as margins, volume, and the fact that due to the unusual market conditions a special intraday call for settlement money was already made on 13 clearing members for a total of $290 million.

Don Serpico, the Merc's MIS chief reported that because of heavy trading volume, "Condition Red" clearing procedures went into effect by which a special out-trade session for S&P 500 and Eurodollar futures and options was scheduled for 11:30 P.M. that evening. Merc staff agreed to continue to maintain an open dialogue with the officers of the CBOT and the CBOE; Brodsky would remain in touch with the AMEX. Although we listened to each of the reports, the atmosphere was trancelike, with everyone's eyes glued to the overhead screens that surrounded the CME mahogany board-room table. The screens, tuned to the Merc's in-house quotation system, provided an on-line price report of what was happening on the real front—the floor below. I adjourned the meeting at 11:05 A.M. and reconvened two hours later.

The markets had been disconnected, but the telephone lines between the Merc, the NYSE, and Washington were entangled as we traded tissue-thin information on our respective markets. For the next four hours, we fought the market forces: more reports of conversations with government and exchange officials, more calls for settlement variation, and more re-ports from clearing members and floor traders.

In between each of the adjournments, I would rush to the S&P pit to touch base with the traders and brokers who were dealing at a frantic pace. Each time I came to the floor, I was instantly encircled by a swarm of members, beseeching me with questions and searching my eyes to see how bad things really were. They were bad, but like the commander of a ship caught in a hurricane, I knew it was imperative to keep the crew from pan-icking. I would smile, "everything will be all right."

Unbeknownst to me, at that very moment, the Washington muck-a-mucks were again meeting with President Reagan, but this time in emer-gency session. The markets were in free fall and alarm bells were sounding around the world. The plunge that had begun in the Far East with the Tokyo markets had spread like a viral disease to London, and now had in-fected New York and Chicago. The discussion centered on the question of whether the financial markets should be closed down. Richard Darmen, the Deputy Secretary of the Treasury, made the case in favor of closing.

Beryl Sprinkel exploded: "Mr. President, that's crazy. If you close the markets down, you will lose the ability to interpret what they are telling us. The markets must be left open."

Greenspan had not yet returned from Texas although he had cancelled his speech and was on telephone hookup. He emphatically agreed with Sprinkel. The emergency meeting ended with two objectives: keep the markets open, and pump money into the system. Beryl Sprinkel took on the assignment to deal with the Chicago markets, and Howard Baker agreed to handle New York. Sprinkel relates how Alan Greenspan became a cool hand under fire and knew precisely what he must do. "Financial gridlock as a result of lack of funds must be avoided at all costs," the Fed chairman told everyone. Greenspan then used the considerable powers of the Federal Reserve working in conjunction with Gerald Corrigan, presi-dent of Federal Reserve Bank of New York, to orchestrate injections of liq-uidity into the American financial system.

There is a footnote to this history. At the end of the week, Howard Baker stopped by to see Sprinkel. "Beryl, the President told me that he changed his mind; he cannot accept your resignation. The President asked me to tell you that if you remain, the chairmanship of the CEA will be raised to cabinet level."

It was a huge vote of confidence and an admission that Sprinkel's assessments about the vulnerability of the markets had been correct. Before Beryl Sprinkel could make up his mind, Treasury Secretary Jim Baker telephoned. "Beryl, you must stay. The President would be very unhappy if you left."

This was a gracious call to show there were no hard feelings. It was too much to resist. Beryl Sprinkel remained in office until the end of the Reagan administration.

By the time the Executive Committee reconvened at 1:15 P.M., the December 1987 S&P contract was down 5,125 points. I again reported on my conversations with Beryl Sprinkel, John Phelan, Tom Donovan, and Kalo Hineman, (who had been appointed CFTC acting chairman after Susan Phillips left in July to await her appointment as a governor of the Fed), as well as a host of other government and industry officials. Jack Sandner and Bill Brodsky offered their reports as well: A second intraday call for settlement will be made for about $670 million later in the day . . . trade submission deadlines to the Clearinghouse were extended for the first reconciliation . . . the Cleared Trades by Brokers Report would be available at 6:00 A.M. . . . and on and on. The meeting was adjourned at 1:40 P.M. and reconvened at 2:30 P.M.

As we filed out of the boardroom, I felt as a ship's captain navigating during *force ten* gale conditions. Will the ship survive? Mercifully, from an operational standpoint, as we learned the following morning, the Merc held up, which was no small credit to John Davidson, the CME's clearinghouse chief, ably assisted by Mary Murphy, Director of Operations. As the CFTC would conclude in a post-crash report, "The order routing, trade execution, and clearing procedures employed by member firms and the CME performed well during this period. . . ."

Throughout the day, the knot in my stomach remained. It was made up of two main concerns: the immediate fear about the gigantic settlement call to square the pays and collects between longs and shorts, and the distant fear about the aftermath of the tragic event—the recriminations and the blame. Because ours had been the first market on the American shore to actually open, we had the unenviable duty of flashing the bad news to the U.S. investor. If past is prologue, the messenger had a real good chance of becoming the culprit. I wasn't wrong.

What actually happened was that most of the traditional markets were operating on a technological standard equivalent to the steamboat, while those who make market decisions were using the jet plane. The decision-making power in finance had become compressed: huge sums of capital in fewer hands. Large capital pools, of course, offered the small investors a chance to profit along with the institutional pros. Unfortunately, the traditional market mechanisms, particularly in stocks, were simply not structured to accommodate the massive and sudden money flows these managers commanded.

Time also was a factor. Europe, North America, and the Far East had become a continuous market reacting to news instantaneously and reaching across all time zones. Markets that had been separate rivers had suddenly combined to become oceans. We weren't a part of the market revolution; we were the revolution. We had overthrown old technology, old ways of looking at market plays, old notions of time and place. And when everything kicked in at once, the markets became a monster frothing at the mouth and trampling anything in its way until the rampage ended.

On that October morning, the specialist system at the NYSE had been overwhelmed by waves of orders that eventually also caused the Designated Order Turnaround (DOT) machines at the stock exchange to break down. And because there were many unopened bellwether stocks at the NYSE, it meant that no one in the world could accurately gauge the Dow or the S&P Index, upon which our futures prices were based. This meant that the futures on the Merc's S&P contract, the Major Market Index (MMI) on the CBOT, the NYFE contracts at the NYSE, or the Value Line contracts in Kansas City, as well as options on the Chicago Board Options Exchange and other exchanges were cut loose from the NYSE and the AMEX cash markets. The surfeit of sellers and scarcity of buyers had put tremendous downward pressure on both the stock markets and futures markets. But futures markets got the brunt of the early selling because we had a market. And by any comparison, futures markets were technologically more advanced and had no problems bringing orders to the brokers in the pits. As large discounts developed between futures and stocks, those investors who could switched from selling futures to selling stocks. But to the consternation of many investors, often their equity account executives in securities wouldn't or couldn't answer their telephone calls.

On October 19, 1987, both the stock and index futures markets suffered their worst single-day declines in history. The Dow plunged 508 points, a 22.6 percent drop. This was nearly double the previous record of 12.8 percent drop on October 26, 1929, and nearly equalled the two-day drop on October 28 and 29, 1929, of 24.5 percent. More than $500 billion in paper value—a sum equal to the entire gross national product of France—had vanished in a sea of orders totalling a record 608 million shares. In Chicago, the derivatives markets took a beating down the line. The Merc's

S&P 500 futures contract fell 80.75 points, a 28.6 percent decline. The CBOT's MMI index future, composed of 20 stocks—17 of which were in the Dow Jones Industrial Average—sank 24.38 percent. And the most popular index option for retail investors, the CBOE's S&P 100 Index (OEX) contract, lost 21 percent of the value of the underlying index.

The crash was a global event in its fullest meaning. Although the United States suffered the largest single one-day drop among the major markets, Japan dropped by almost 15 percent, the United Kingdom dropped by 11 percent and 12 percent on consecutive days, Sydney exchange prices plummeted nearly 25 percent, and in Singapore the Nikkei futures contract for a mad moment seemed without a bottom for lack of liquidity. In Hong Kong, the decline caused far more dramatic consequences than in any other market. On October 19, the Hang Seng Index plunged 420 points or 11.3 percent, the biggest one-day fall in its history, with many investors unable to meet margin calls. The probability of worsening conditions and the possibility of massive defaults caused the Hong Kong Stock Exchange to close for the remainder of the week. The futures market followed suit the day after the close. Closing the exchanges turned out to be the debacle one would expect. When it reopened the following Monday, October 26, there was a further 33 percent drop in prices. It took a $4 billion government-sponsored rescue plan to resurrect the Hong Kong financial marketplace.

But numbers never convey the emotions behind them. Throughout the day, mind and machines battled the one thing impossible to program for on a microchip: fear. Retreating on a broad front, stocks, options, and futures were inextricably linked through strategies, all coping with a market in denial. In the end, the market, as it always does, had its way with the small and big players alike.

When Monday's final bell sounded at 3:15 P.M. CST, I said a silent prayer. I didn't know whether we had survived, but at least the market couldn't go any lower that day. The pain would stop for a little while. As I looked down on the S&P pit from the balcony, there were hundreds of jarring human portraits, a sea of traders and their clerks in a state of disarray, confused and anxious over dreaded out-trades, those trades that do not match between buyer and seller. They milled about the S&P pit with dazed expressions caused by a war of nerves in a market skewed and fragmented.

Through some twist of fate, we had previously scheduled yet another meeting for the evening of October 19, a dinner meeting that included myself, Sandner, Brodsky, Rick Kilcollin, Ken Cone, and executives of Reuters Holdings PLC, Andre Villeneuve, and John Hull, to discuss the launch of GLOBEX, our joint venture electronic system. But that night over our 10:00 P.M. dinner at the Metropolitan Club high in the Sears Tower, we were in no mood to begin mapping plans to globalize futures trading on a 24-hour basis through a Merc-Reuters computer hookup. Our minds were elsewhere.

Just before midnight, our weary group of Merc officials nervously returned to the CME building to see if it was still standing. A bleary-eyed Pat Reiffel, my secretary and faithful assistant who dutifully stayed on guard in my office on the 19th floor, handed me a record number of phone calls that included Fed Chairman Alan Greenspan; Chairman of the CEA, Beryl Sprinkel; Senator Don Riegle, ranking Democrat on the Banking committee, calling on behalf of the committee chairman William Proxmire; and Kalo Hineman from the CFTC. It occurred to me that this array of calls from the highest levels of government was certain proof of the Merc's arrival as a major player on the American financial scene. It wasn't the way I wanted to arrive.

With sweating hands, I returned Greenspan's call first. We had known each other many years, ever since he supported my plans to introduce Treasury bill futures in 1976. He knew I had great admiration for him because just before his Fed appointment as chairman, I had invited him to sit as a director of the Merc. Alas, he had bigger things in mind. During the course of October 19, on more than one occasion, I silently thanked the Lord that he was in charge at the Fed rather than a director at the CME. I had little doubt that someone of lesser competence might not have been up to the challenge of this critical moment in our nation's history. Greenspan's voice was calm, conveying to me the impression that things would be all right. Of course, that was his normal demeanor. His first question, however, revealed the true danger of the situation.

"Will you open tomorrow morning?" he asked, both of us understanding that this was the most crucial question.

As long as the Merc's trades cleared, as long as all the market positions were paid to the previous day's closing settlement price, as long as buyers and sellers got their money, the Merc would open the following morning on time. But there were an awful lot of ifs. Unlike the securities industry, which had five business days to clear a trade, the futures industry operated on a pay-as-you-go system. All accounts had to be settled in cash—every winner had to be paid by every loser—before trading resumed the following business day. And John Davidson, our clearinghouse chief, told me that the settlement sum for October 19 was a tremendous record: a total of $2.53 billion, versus $120 million on a normal trading day. In other words, as a result of the crash, the longs owed the shorts some $2.5 billion. *"My God!"* I thought silently and shuddered, *"That's more money than the gross national product of some countries."* Even as Davidson said the amount, we both recognized the bizarre nature of the moment. No one had never imagined that such a day was possible.

But while the trades miraculously cleared, neither Davidson nor I could guarantee that the money from the longs would come in—and in time to open the next day. If the money didn't come in and the shorts didn't get paid, then the Merc could not open. If it didn't open, not only would it cause a dysfunction in the U.S. market system, which was inexorably connected between cash, options, and futures, but the world would suspect that someone within the United States financial structure had failed. Perhaps someone big had gone broke. And I didn't mean a local trader (there were some of those too), I meant any one of a hundred major institutions, maybe more than one. The unknown is much more feared than the known. This could result in financial gridlock, where institutional players hesitated to pay one another for fear they wouldn't get paid themselves. Such an environment easily leads to panic, which could quickly spread to individual investors. Panic is what causes a run on the banks, which is precisely what happened in 1929.

The chief U.S. banker, the chairman of the Fed, was asking me if that was going to happen. He knew I fully understood the gravity of the moment and he knew I was sitting in the eye of the hurricane.

"Mr. Chairman," I responded in a hoarse whisper, my stomach in knots again, "I don't think we have a problem, but to tell you the truth, it's too early to tell."

"I understand . . . . did your trades clear?"

"Yes."

We talked some more. He assured me that the Fed was doing everything necessary to liquify the financial system. It was good they did since that was one of the primary actions that saved the financial system. As we anticipated, by morning, rumors were everywhere of huge losses by major market dealers, and banks were reluctant to provide credit to even well-established customers. Financial chaos was knocking on the door. This was probably the finest moment for the Fed. Gerald Corrigan, president of the Federal Reserve Bank of New York, coerced the banks to use aggressively the liquidity that Greenspan had provided. Without Corrigan's untiring and forthright admonishment not to withhold credit, gridlock might have set in and the situation could have ended in disaster.

At the end of our conversation, the Chairman of the Fed asked me if there was anything else I could think of that he should be doing. Even the question frightened the living daylights out of me. The second most powerful person in the Western world was asking me if there was anything else I could think of. Then I remembered something we had discussed in the boardroom. I asked, "Alan, will you keep the Fed wire open all night?"

The Fed wire was the special Federal Reserve secured banking communication system that guaranteed money flows between the banks. Normally, the Fed wire closes with the close of business hours. But on this night, if the Merc was going to have a chance at getting $2.5 billion, we needed the benefit of the entire night.

"Good idea," the Chairman of the Fed responded, and told me that his telephone line would also be open to me all night should I need to reach him.

For the next hour or so, I attempted to return the remaining calls and, although it was well past midnight, most of my calls were answered. Beryl Sprinkel briefed me on how the officials in Washington were handling the crisis, and we talked at length about what might yet be in store. We tried to cheer each other up. The remainder of the night I camped out in the Merc Clearinghouse, joined by John Davidson, Barry Lind, Bill Brodsky, Jack Sandner, and clearinghouse staffers. Tension from the long torturous trading day carried into the night with the mechanics of the clearing process. I remember my private conversation with Barry Lind in the middle of that night. Lind was chairman of the Clearinghouse committee and I tried to find comfort in his expertise during this crisis. "What do you think, Barry, will we make it?" I asked him after we were alone, and looked deep into his eyes to read his answer. He hesitated, then whispered, "I don't know, Leo, but if we don't open tomorrow morning, all bets are off!"

Wall Street's major investment bankers had been among the biggest players that day. The Merc owed $670 million to Goldman Sachs and $917 million to Kidder Peabody on one side of the equation. On the other side, Morgan Stanley owed the Merc some $1 billion. This ultimately became a source of great anxiety for the clearing operation. It wasn't that Morgan Stanley wasn't good for it, but could it pay by 7:20 A.M. the next morning? With such huge numbers at stake, settlement banks became extremely cautious and slowed the credit approval process significantly. The Chicago banks such as Continental Illinois were unwilling to complete transactions from member firms until they had verification that funds had reached Chicago from the New York banks involved.

At about 3:00 A.M., Davidson told me he suspected there might be a delay in the payment by Continental because Morgan Stanley's money was slow to come in. It scared me half to death. I told Jack Sandner that before I called Alan Greenspan to tell him of our concern, perhaps it would be prudent for someone to call Richard B. Fisher, then president of Morgan Stanley. We divided the tasks. Jack would call Fisher and I would handle Greenspan. But Jack was hesitant; he wasn't quite sure how he could explain the situation in the middle of the night to a guy at the other end of the phone who wouldn't even recognize his name. I agreed to be at his side and listen to the conversation. We made the call. It would have been funny if it wasn't so serious. There I was, whispering in Jack Sandner's ear with Davidson and others standing behind us, as he woke the president of one of this nation's most powerful investment banks in the middle of the night to tell him that he owed us $1 billion. I can only imagine Fisher's thoughts.

Later that night, Rick Kilcollin told me that Sandner's call might not be enough. We discussed again whether I should call Greenspan, but decided that first Kilcollin would get in touch with Steve Thieke at the Federal Reserve Bank of New York. He had been in constant contract with us. Thieke agreed to follow up with Fisher. It turned out that none of these efforts worked. I never doubted that Morgan Stanley was good for the funds, but if they caused a delay in our opening, all hell would break loose.

At 6:00 A.M., just after dawn in Chicago, the Executive Committee was back in session to review the numbers in the S&P contract from Black Monday. They were staggering: the December S&P contract had closed off 8,075 points; total S&P 500 futures volume was 162,000 contracts, nearly one-fourth of the total exchange volume for the day; open interest in the contract had jumped from 146,000 to about 172,000; out-trades were about 8 percent, and total margin required was $3.9 billion. We also reviewed the bids and offers on seat prices, which were pretty far apart and reflected distress sales.

Just before 7:00 A.M., a half an hour or so before the opening, I left the meeting to call Wilma J. Smelcer, Continental Bank's financial officer in charge of the Merc's account. I had to know the answer to Greenspan's critical question, would we open. If the news was bad, my next call would be to the Fed chairman. I asked Smelcer where we stood in the collection of pays and collects. She responded that we were still short some $400 million. She couldn't tell me who was causing the shortfall because of the bank's confidentiality rules, but of course I had a pretty good idea who the customer was.

"Wilma," I said, "you mean we're down to $400 million from $2.5 billion? That's pretty damned good."

"Yes, Leo, but not good enough."

"Wilma," I responded, getting agitated, "I am certain your customer is good for it. You're not going to let a stinking couple of hundred million dollars cause the Merc to go down the tubes, are you?"

"Leo, my hands are tied."

"Please listen, Wilma; you have to take it upon yourself to guarantee the balance because if you don't, I've got to call Alan Greenspan, and we're going to cause the next depression."

There was silence on the other end of the phone as Wilma hesitated. She was the "Lady or the Tiger" of the moment. I hated to put this kind of pressure on Smelcer who was a responsible officer of Continental and had worked on the Merc account for years. Besides, given the situation, who could blame her? She felt she didn't have the authority to underwrite that kind of money, especially under the current dangerous circumstances. Suddenly, fate intervened.

"Hold it a minute, Leo," she shouted into my earpiece, "Tom Theobald just walked in." Theobald was then the chairman of Continental Bank.

A couple of minutes later, but what seemed to me like an eternity, Smelcer was back on the phone. "Leo, we're okay. Tom said to go ahead. You've got your money."

I looked at the time, it was 7:17 A.M. We had three full minutes to spare before the opening of our currency markets when I signaled John Davidson that we were all right. The world never knew how close we came to a serious problem. The money from Morgan Stanley actually came into Continental about 20 minutes later. But in reality there never should have been a problem. The money was always there but tied up in positions at another exchange. It was one of the most important lessons of the crash: to make the settlement banks aware of all the customers' positions at other markets. There were many other lessons to be learned from this episode in history. But the value of these lessons would come much later, when we could contemplate the future by learning from the past. During the course of the storm, I wasn't so sure that there would be a future. Was this the end of our futures markets, I sometimes wondered silently, or the end of the world?

Years later, Jens Carsten Jackwerth, a post-doctoral visiting scholar, together with professor Mark Rubinstein, (who received the International Association of Financial Engineer (IAFE)/SunGard Financial Engineer of the year award in 1995), would offer incontrovertible proof that October 19, 1987, didn't happen. According to their probability formula, (published in 1995) the likelihood for the crash to have occurred was 10^{-160}. In other words, "Even if one were to have lived through the entire 20 billion year life of the universe, and experienced this 20 billion times (20 billion big bangs), the probability that such a decline could have happened even once in this period is a virtual impossibility." I wish I had known this comforting piece of wisdom at the time of the crash.

31

Free Fall

On Tuesday, at 8:30 A.M. CST, the Spuz market opened on time again, but unlike Monday's straight down action, Tuesday would prove to be a roller coaster. The Continental Bank payment incident was but a precursor of what came next, and it was touch and go all the way. October 20 turned out to be—by any measurement—the most difficult day in my tenure as leader of the Merc. It was also the most critical moment in the history of the Exchange.

Notwithstanding the enormous overnight falls in foreign markets, we expected Wall Street to open on the up side, and this, I hoped would provide a good tone for our futures as well. It did, with our market opening up sharply higher—up 23.50 points and then a rally of another 16 points from there. The Dow opened strong as well, following through with a 200-point rally. But the Dow rally evaporated just as quickly as it started. At the Merc, the selling pressure developed within an hour or so. As soon as it did, the knot in my stomach returned. I knew that the market kickback had been temporary and that those sellers who had not sold on Monday or on Tuesday's opening would begin to pound the market. It happened just as I suspected, and the market started down with a vengeance. Sell orders poured into the Merc and NYSE, hitting our market and kicking down the blue chips. Many of the secondary stocks never even saw the benefit of any buying in the first place.

By about 11:00 A.M. CST, I began to get reports that the large-capitalization stocks at the NYSE were inundated with sell orders and the specialists could not make a market. I was told that due to order imbalances in some 140 NYSE major stocks, most of them part of the S&P Index, trading had been halted in those stocks. Donald Stone, an expert old-line specialist, whom I got to really know and admire during the crisis, later told me that it was the scariest moment of his life. After the opening rally on Tuesday, he said there were no bids and the NYSE was receiving hundred of thousands of sell orders at the market. "Leo," he stated, "it was like having your head inside a cannon, with the cannon ball coming at you." In Chicago, our pit also went into what looked like a free fall.

It was just after 11:00 A.M. CST and the situation had turned really dicey. Bill Brodsky had called to confirm that both the Chicago Board Options Exchange and American Stock Exchange had officially closed their markets. It sent shivers down my spine. We were quickly becoming the only functioning market. All morning long, the Merc had been under enormous pressure. Prices on the CBOE didn't exist from the start, and many of the stocks on the NYSE and AMEX either never opened or closed as soon as the selling overwhelmed the specialists. Although the Board of Trade's MMI index was technically open, its contract was too small and illiquid to count for very much. None of the other futures markets counted at all. So, for all practical purposes, the only two exchanges still open that mattered were the NYSE and the CME. Even that wasn't really true with so many of the stocks in New York no longer trading. But at least there was the public perception that New York was still open. As long as that was the case, I was prepared to tough it out.

Just then, I was advised by the CFTC what I feared most: the NYSE had informed the SEC that it was considering closing the Exchange. One thing I knew for certain: if the NYSE closed, uncontrollable panic would follow. In such a case, if the Merc was left open, the world would dump on us. Under no circumstances could we allow that to happen.

It was the third time I had talked to Phelan that morning. This time the call was on a squawk box in Bill Brodsky's office off the boardroom. I was there with Sandner, Brodsky, Kilcollin, Salzman, and Jerry Beyer. We held our collective breath.

I told Phelan that we had heard rumors that the NYSE was about to close. Was that true, I wanted to know.

Phelan's voice sounded like death warmed over. "It's getting close to that," he responded. "There are no buyers . . . we are going into a meeting to decide. We may very well close."

At our end, everyone looked at each other. There was virtual certainty that the NYSE was about to close. And Phelan did not say that he would advise us before they acted on a decision to close. "There is no way they're going to tell us anything," Sandner confided to me. Our market was about to be left alone in the world.

We had left the Executive Committee meeting to make the call, and everyone was waiting for us to return. Before we did, we held a brief conference. I stated that if the NYSE closed without telling us, which, under the circumstances, all of us suspected was likely, panic would ensue, forcing all the selling to our floor. In such case, before we could act, there would be a lag of some 15 to 20 minutes to make the necessary decision and announcements; during that interim, there was no telling to where the price of Spuz would be driven. There was no time to lose. Even if word got out that the NYSE was *considering* a close, it would be enough to send our market another thousand or two thousand points lower, the equivalent to 10 or 20 points on the S&P 500 stock index.

In my mind, there was only one protective measure we could take, and we had to act fast. We had to call for a temporary halt of our market until the NYSE made its decision. Sandner and Brodsky agreed, and the Executive Committee unanimously approved the move. We prepared the necessary announcement, making certain not to give much warning so that no one could take advantage. Brodsky advised the CFTC, and I called Beryl Sprinkel at the White House and Tom Donovan at the CBOT. I explained the situation and that, if possible, the halt would be temporary. Simultaneous with the announcement I went to the pit to personally explain it to the traders; Jack Sandner came with me. It was approximately 11:30 A.M. As we entered the pit, the bedlam subsided. The traders stopped in their tracks as if in a game of "statue" so that they could hear what we had to say.

Although my mind was on fire, my voice was calm. In my most confident tone, I explained that the trading halt was temporary to determine whether the NYSE was closing. "We cannot be left alone for everyone to dump on us," I stated. Most traders nodded their heads in agreement. We would advise them of the NYSE's decision as soon as we knew for certain. There were no questions. A few of the traders thought that this was the beginning of the end for the Merc and ran to sell their membership.

We went back to Brodsky's office to wait it out. About 15 minutes later, we placed the call again. Phelan sounded much more confident. The NYSE hadn't yet closed. His voice told me everything I had to know. My decision to reopen was instantaneous. The Executive Committee agreed, and the announcement was made. About 35 minutes after our temporary halt, the S&P contract reopened for business. The crisis had passed.

Phelan's voice had told me—without any of the words being spoken out loud—that the corporate buy-back program, which I had been hoping for all morning, had begun to take effect. Initiated as a result of aggressive suggestions by Washington officials, dozens of companies announced share repurchase programs, a trend that continued for the rest of the week. That buying power was the most influential factor in generating the blue chip recovery on Tuesday and sending buyers into the futures markets. Later, it also helped when the SEC suspended its rule that barred corporations from buying their own shares during the last half hour of the day. Word of the buy-back program was the single most important element in stopping the NYSE from closing.

In reality, whether or not the NYSE closed officially, the Merc was the only market operating. As the figures would bear out in the post-crash analysis, for the first two hours on the morning of Black Monday, when the first wave of panic selling hit, the Merc was the only big market in existence where that selling could come in. If we hadn't been there for that, the NYSE might never have opened that day. Of course, in fairness, no mechanism was in place to cope with the massive volume at a moment of panic. Neither the NYSE specialists, nor the NYSE automated systems, nor the options market, nor the over-the-counter markets, nor even the futures markets were built for panics. Communication lines were jammed, technologies were strained, and, at times, the entire financial system looked as if it were going to fold. Still, by any comparison, the S&P 500 pit held up quite well during the tumultuous trading days.

There were big winners as well as big losers, those who retired wealthy and those who ended up selling their seats to cover losses. But most traders came out shaken, yet solvent. The smaller traders who had left the pit on Monday began to return on Friday when everyone was exhausted. There were many temporary pains, many permanent rifts, and many stories to tell, enough to fill memories for a lifetime or to write a thousand books. There were the stories of traders who became millionaires in a matter of hours, sometimes in minutes. There were stories about harrowing errors, some that made brokers rich, others that brought ruin. And there were stories about the hits, the misses, and the near misses.

One of the most celebrated tales centered on the altercation between George Soros, the charismatic and penultimate successful money manager, and Shearson & Company, the venerable Wall Street brokerage firm. As reported in the November 2, 1987, issue of *Barron's*, George Soros "was part of the maddening crowd in the October 19 week." The story had many versions and resulted in a lawsuit filed in the U.S. District Court in Chicago on behalf of Quantum B.V.I. Mutual Fund, owned and operated by George Soros. The amount of the suit was for reimbursement of $60 million in losses as well as $100 million in punitive damages.

The lawsuit contended that on Thursday, October 22, Shearson, 3 of its floor brokers (Larry Israel, Michael Mullins, and Douglas Young), and about 100 other traders and brokers conspired to sell 2,400 Spuz futures held by Quantum at artificially low prices when the fund entered a large sell order through Shearson. What apparently happened was that the Soros fund decided to sell out its entire position on the opening bell Thursday morning. On the bell, the Shearson broker offered 1,000 lots at the going price. According to *Barron's*, "The pit traders, picking up the sound of a whale in trouble, hung back but circled the prey. The offer went from 230 down to 220 to 215 to 205 to 200. Then the pit traders attacked. The Soros block sold from 195 to 210. The spiral was ghastly. As soon as the order was filled, the market bounced back to 230 and the local buyers sold out at a tremendous profit." One anonymous pit trader is quoted as saying that "the Shearson execution was one of the worst we have ever seen."

Shearson denied the accusations. According to some reports, the lead broker had pleaded with the fund manager not to place so large a market order, but rather to put a price limit on the order. In any event, the lawsuit never went to trial and was settled for a minor amount.

Out of the ashes of the October crash came a deep chord of disquiet, an interminable number of studies, analyses, pronouncements, and recriminations. Of all the examinations, the most prominent and influential was the one appointed by President Reagan, the Presidential Task Force, chaired by Nicholas F. Brady, who was to become the next Secretary of Treasury. Brady, co-chairman of Dillon, Read & Company and a former U.S. Senator from New Jersey, was a venerable Wall Street pro, but knew very little about futures. I would not have been surprised if he harbored many of the myths about our markets that were prevalent with Wall Streeters. Without question, there were those within the Brady contingent who initially looked at the Merc as the prime suspect. The first thing the Task Force no doubt did was to examine the trading records of all market officials. I expect that my trading activities were put under a high-powered microscope and examined by the FBI, CIA, Interpol, and Nixon's plumbers—if they were still around. I can only imagine what thoughts would have been confirmed if Brady had discovered that special counsel to the Board and chairman of the Executive Committee of the Merc had been short the market and made a killing. Instead, I privately chuckled at their consternation when they found that coming into Monday, October 19, I had no market positions whatsoever.

Normally, getting out of a short position directly before the market tanks is the kind of thing that makes a trader want to eat razor blades. But as it turned out, getting out the Friday before the crash was what I liked to call the best trade I ever made.

Throughout the years, I meticulously avoided a conflict of interest between my personal trading and my Merc leadership status. Oh, it was perfectly legal for me to trade, but I made certain not to hold positions in situations where I would be involved on an official basis. This meant that, sometimes, when I faced a controversial issue, I would lose trading opportunities and get out of the market just to be on the safe side. In 1987, I got mysterious help from above.

Early in 1987, I had turned bearish on the stock market. But the market kept going higher and higher. I was stubborn and continued to believe that stocks were overpriced and the market was due for some kind of correction, so I stayed with my contrarian view and kept selling the S&P 500 index as it moved higher. My losses piled up. But by July, my strategy began to pay off as the market turned erratic. The five-year bull market peaked in August. Little by little, as the market turned down, I began to make my money back. Tight monetary policy by the Fed and a rash of negative economic factors around the world were pressuring the market, and investor confidence was waning. By October, I was again in the black for the year.

No one, of course, knew for sure that the market was going to crash, or if so, when. But the week prior to the crash there was very heavy selling. By Friday of that week, the market had taken a huge plunge; it was the worst week for stocks in recent memory, and I made a lot of money. Since I was now well ahead for the year, I decided to cash in and take my profit rather than hold my position over the weekend. I expected the market to eventually go lower, but I hoped for a rally first. What I didn't know was that the intensity of market fear would galvanize over that weekend—to a large extent because the national media used that weekend to play up the similarities between 1929 and 1987. As I read Sunday's newspapers over breakfast, I already knew that I had made a big mistake covering my short position. That weekend, a majority of investors around the world decided to take some profit on Monday. The rest is, of course, history.

Had I held my short positions instead of covering them the previous Friday, I clearly would have cleaned up on Black Monday—it would have been worth a ton. But by getting out of the market, I walked away with something far more valuable. There could be no accusation of conflict of interest to impair my ability to act on behalf of the Merc and the futures industry. Indeed, ultimately, I think Nick Brady learned to trust us guys in Chicago.

I remember his first official visit to the Merc and his observation that what he feared most was the next shoe to fall.

"How much will it fall on the second round?" he asked.

I think what impressed him most is that I didn't even hesitate in responding, "I don't think it's going to fall any further."

"How can you be sure?"

I shrugged my shoulders. "I think all the excess water is out of it."

He smiled. "Hope you're right."

Then he asked how fast we could give his Task Force the records of the trades on the Merc for the week of the 19th. "Will 60 days be enough time?" he wanted to know.

Sandner, Brodsky and I looked at each other and smiled. "How about if we give them to you before you leave?" Brodsky responded.

Brady didn't hide his surprise. It was difficult for someone used to Wall Street procedures to grasp that but a scant week after the crash, we already had a complete record of every trade made by all participants. Indeed, we had that information the day after the crash. At the NYSE, it took months.

The executive director of the Brady Task Force, Harvard professor Robert R. Glauber, summed up the most salient lesson of the crash: "From an economic viewpoint, what have been traditionally seen as separate markets—the markets for stocks, stock index futures, and stock options—are in fact one market." That's right. These markets are linked by financial instruments, trading strategies, market participants, and clearing and credit mechanisms. Although it was essential that the Brady Task Force highlighted this "discovery," and to the Brady people this may have been a revelation, to us in Chicago—and I daresay market professionals in New York and elsewhere—the fact that the markets were linked, not only in the United States but worldwide, was old news.

Linked but woefully uncoordinated. This deficiency became the primary focus of the markets after the crash. But first the market became an object of public contemplation. Millions of stockholders suddenly were awakened to the reality of another market, the futures market, a derivative market. And though they may not have understood it, they knew it was important because suddenly the Wall Street establishment was blaming it for the greatest stock market crash in history. How could a market that had so little public awareness be something so powerful, so influential as to account for such a heartbreaking financial toll? The futures market—the Chicago Mercantile Exchange in particular—was sharing the headlines with the almighty New York Stock Exchange. If we were to believe the NYSE at the time, the Merc caused the problem because of so-called index arbitrage. Presumably, the crash started with selling in the futures market in Chicago, causing big discounts in the S&P futures contract, which in turn were transmitted to the cash markets in New York through index arbitrage. I didn't buy that for a second.

Indeed, in the final analysis, the evidence was clear and the eventual reports unanimous that those accusations were unfounded. Both markets were hit with enormous selling volume at the same time. If anything, the trouble pointed to the specialist system on the NYSE where some undercapitalized market makers withdrew from their obligations. Futures markets were no more the cause of the crash on Monday than they were the source of the turnaround on Tuesday. Nor did the panic psychology end by virtue of the CBOT's Major Market Index pit or because the NYSE shut down program trading. And, contrary to popular myth, there were no secret federally directed purchases of stock index futures contracts at Goldman Sachs or anywhere else. There is no mystery about it. The Federal Reserve's release of liquidity to the market and the corporate buy-back of stock, combined with an exhaustion of panic selling, turned the situation around on Tuesday.

But try to explain that to a world whose financial landscape had been roiled and whose denizens were looking for a scapegoat. It was as if I had to once again face the challenge I had as a child when I came to the plate. But this wasn't softball; it was hardball—and the major leagues. Yet the ghost of Elmer Falker and his three-decades-old omen about the success of futures markets as a messenger had risen in my memory: "If the truth is too bad and too loud, they'll close us down."

Well, nobody was going to close down the Merc. I lost no time putting together a strategy. On the Saturday following Black Monday, I called together a strategy team. I found myself cooped up in Alysann Posner's small office just outside the Merc boardroom with Rick Kilcollin, Jerry Salzman, and Posner, downing endless cups of hot coffee and slices of cold pizza, and brainstorming into the early hours of the next morning. Salzman was there to make sure I didn't step into any legal morass; Kilcollin, with indisputable statistics, was there to prove what I knew to be true: the technical weakness exposed in the financial markets by the crash was neither the fault of futures markets nor machines. Posner's role was to coordinate and put together our product.

For me, Kilcollin's authentication of my gut feelings was an immense relief. It was one thing to believe we were not at fault, quite another to have the facts. I was desperately afraid of being stroked by Merc officials in order to make me feel good. I needed Kilcollin there that Saturday morning because, of everyone on the Merc staff, he was one of the few I could rely on to give me the truth. For me, facts from Kilcollin were ironclad.

Years later, Rick Kilcollin would tell me that what amazed him throughout the Black Monday episode was my instant certainty that Chicago selling did not cause the NYSE collapse. My strong and immediate opinion in this regard, he said, gave him and other Merc staffers the confidence that the CME would survive the vicious attack led by the New York financial community, aided and abetted by the media, which automatically assumed the Wall Streeters to be the *true* financial mavens.

"How did you know?" Kilcollin asked me that Saturday morning as he proudly confirmed that the statistics completely authenticated my view that there was little transference of Chicago stock-index selling to the NYSE.

It was gut instinct coupled with logic. By watching the pit and talking to traders, I had a sense that the buyers in the early hours of the Monday morning collapse were not arbitrageurs buying Chicago in order to sell to New York, the process by which index arbitrage is executed. This belief was corroborated by the logic of the situation. In order to carry out index arbitrage, one has to know the cash market index price and needs a ready buyer at the NYSE. I was certain that on Monday this was not possible. Index arbitrage was in dysfunction. My instincts proved to be right on the mark. On the morning of October 19, the order imbalances at the NYSE opening were so widespread that the specialists could not make a market in many of the stocks most heavily represented in the S&P index. In fact, one hour after the opening bell, more than one-third of the Dow stocks, including IBM, Sears, and Exxon had not opened. No arbitrageur in his right mind would attempt index-arbitrage under such circumstances. Throughout that day at the NYSE, there was a total of 187 opening delays, 7 trading halts, and 3 stocks that did not resume trading after halts. Most of Tuesday morning, October 20, was the same. On that day, there were 92 opening delays at the NYSE, 175 trading halts, and 10 stocks that did not resume trading. Clearly the NYSE specialists, who had limped away from Monday overloaded with large inventories of stocks, were tapped. "There was virtually no market-making ability left after Monday," noted Joel Cohen, the general counsel of the Brady Commission.

Aside from the foregoing, arbitrageurs rely on the NYSE's DOT system, the automated order execution system. Cohen eventually reported that "the DOT system broke down on Monday afternoon because the massive volume overwhelmed the system. Orders got backed up, and order execution was so unreliable that arbitrageurs did not know when their orders were going to be executed or at what prices orders had been executed." Then on Tuesday, October 20, the NYSE prohibited the use of DOT completely for index arbitrage.

The Saturday morning the four of us met to map the Merc's strategy, Kilcollin was able to confirm with certainty that, on Monday, only about 20,000 contracts were purchased in index-related arbitrage transactions—the equivalent of about 50 million shares of stock. In other words, Kilcollin could prove that less than 10 percent of the NYSE's record 605 million share volume was caused by S&P futures-related selling on the NYSE, just as the CFTC and SEC studies later confirmed. To put it another way, contrary to all the Wall Street accusations, on Monday, over 90 percent of the total shares traded on the NYSE had nothing to do with futures activity at the CME. Instead, it turned out the Merc absorbed about 150 million shares or 25 percent of total stock market volume. These initial sales at the CME would have gone to the NYSE had it been open. Merc speculators, including our "locals," relieved the institutional selling pressure, just as we claimed from the outset.

Out of that Saturday marathon session, I developed a series of position papers in the form of booklets produced under the auspices of Kilcollin's

Research Department, Salzman's legal guidance, and Posner's organizational skills. These booklets were presented over the next six months and dealt with every aspect of our markets as it related to the October crash. The first, produced two weeks after the crash, was entitled *October 19, 1987: The Facts.* It was distributed to hundreds, perhaps thousands, of people in the financial community, government, and media. The second booklet, *Studies on the Effect of Stock Index Futures and Options on Stock Market Volatility,* presented a host of previously published material relating to program trading and index arbitrage, and was intended to rebut accusations that futures market-related activity was detrimental to the cash market and created unusual volatility. The final booklet, *The Role of Futures "Margins,"* provided a comprehensive description of the difference between the role of "margins" in futures versus stock margins.

Most important, I was conscious that the Merc membership was reading the newspapers just as everyone else in the world was and no doubt feeling the burden of the attack against us. I knew the membership represented a powerful army that would defend the Merc's domain if properly led. Morale of the troops is of the highest priority. It was therefore imperative to provide the members with guidance and the facts; those are unparalleled weapons in the fight that was about to unfold. I made certain that on Monday morning, October 26, our membership understood that we weren't going sit quietly as the world assailed us unfairly and illogically. On every desk of every Merc member was an official Merc statement drafted that Saturday. It set the tone for the counterattack. The statement provided our members with the facts and offered no doubts that the Merc and its Spuz traders performed flawlessly during the crash. It became the Merc's party line.

Then with the *Fact Book* in hand, Brodsky, Sandner, and I took to the road. We held press conferences in Chicago, New York, Washington, Paris and London, explaining—and defending—stock index futures, program trading, portfolio insurance, margins, and index arbitrage. There were also a series of meetings with editors of *The Wall Street Journal, Fortune,* and *Newsweek,* along with many radio interviews and television panels. Clearly, we were defending the defensible.

Meanwhile, practically new on the job as SEC chairman was David Ruder, former dean of the Northwestern University Law School, who knew a lot about the SEC and virtually nothing about the futures markets and derivatives. Our initial impression about Ruder's views on our markets was based on his first public speech shortly after he became chairman in August 1987. He chose Chicago—his hometown—to speak to the Bond Club. The subject: market volatility.

On the second Sunday following the crash, I and a CME delegation met with SEC chairman David Ruder, who, we discovered through some super counterintelligence spade work, would be spending the weekend at his home in Evanston, a northern Chicago suburb. We hastily arranged an appointment to meet the new SEC chairman for the first time. We were all conscious that Ruder's statements about the crash would have great significance. The SEC was highly regarded in Washington, certainly much more so than the CFTC, which didn't even have a permanent chairman at the time. While these perceptions were far from the truth, in politics, perception is reality.

Attending the late afternoon meeting along with me was Merc President Brodsky, Rick Kilcollin, and Donald Jacobs, a colleague of Ruder's from Northwestern University and dean of its Kellogg Graduate School of Management. Don Jacobs was serving as a Merc outside director at the time. By lending his prestige during this first critical audience with the SEC chairman, Jacobs provided us with an immeasurable boost in what was otherwise a very difficult encounter. It was soon painfully evident that Ruder, a decent human being, had little understanding about our markets. For the next two-and-a-half hours, I led a review of the hectic week of the crash, beginning with a formative lesson on how futures markets worked, what their function was, and how they were different from the securities world. That was followed by a breakdown of the preliminary statistics of the crash gathered by our research department. Ruder took copious notes and asked questions as if he were one of the law students he had lectured just a few months before. Nevertheless, I left the encounter with the distinct feeling that Ruder had not changed his mind that futures caused volatility.

The meeting with Ruder confirmed what we all knew. Things would get a lot worse before they got better. I could feel the earth beneath the Merc's building shudder as enemy forces gathered to invade. We were about to enter the battle of our lives. We were too fat a target to be ignored by government or press. This was the kind of fodder that turns mild-mannered editors into terrorists. This was financial civil war between the states: the state of futures and the state of stocks. It was to be our most difficult hour. I knew for certain that things would never be the same. With the NYSE leading the charge in the East, I had no choice but to counterattack. It would result in the defining moment of the Merc.

32

Boomerang

Long before the week ended, they were rounding up suspects. Although the financial community—and the exchanges—had gotten through the week of the crash intact, there was confusion and almost a sense of disorientation. Perhaps that's why so many were so quick to point a collective finger of guilt at the Merc. A market panic is a complex situation, but there are always those who think there are simple answers. We were being viewed as a bunch of speculators taking book on the stock market.

When emotions hold dominion over the mind, logic drifts and people stop thinking straight. A crash is a series of small rebellions against fear, the kind of fear that threatens the well-worn path of habit, which in the case of markets means profits and performance. The NYSE pointed westward to Chicago and the media accepted the accusation. In the meantime, the Merc, out there alone, looking for a comrade-in-protest was hoping to garner support from the major Wall Street investment bankers who had used stock index futures to hedge client portfolios. We got silence.

The market crash was a big story, an economic story, a political story, a story with sound bites and cyber bytes, a story in which, perversely, technology was the monster. It became a conspiracy of computers. The media really didn't have to try very hard to create a turf war. The Hudson River, it seemed, was the dividing line. New York and Chicago at odds in the razzle-dazzle world of finance with the Washington lawmakers poised as referees, gave the story a spark. Indeed, much of the controversy in the post-crash days reflected the politics of finance.

"The War of Two Cities," screamed the headline in the May 30, 1988, issue of *Time* magazine, bringing issues of risk management and modern global markets down to political basics. Quoting a Donaldson Lufkin & Jenrette stock trader, "I have nothing nice to say about Chicago," and the retort by Chicago's Richard Dennis, "The gulf between us is large, and the stakes are even larger," *Time* offered a simplistic setting for what are sophisticated and complex issues. And while the foregoing may be explained

on the grounds of human interest, its bias in favor of New York and Wall
Streeters was unforgivable. My protest to the editor, subsequently published by *Time*, tried to put it into context.

> One need not take sides in this complex controversy to know that for *Time* to
> resort to a cliche-esque description of the 'warring' cultures—New York:
> 'tradition-bound, analytic, fraternal, relatively restrained' versus Chicago:
> 'young, brash, speculative, unabashedly noisy'—is crass stereotyping and a
> throwback to views of an era at least 50 years ago. And, in case anyone missed
> the point, the *Time* writers assured the reader that: 'Certainly in terms of ap-
> pearances, everything about the Chicago traders' style makes them look
> more like hockey fans than financial professionals.' It is a mild understate-
> ment to say that such characterization of the two markets is blatantly unjust.

No question about it, this was to be a mean, uphill battle. FIA president
John Damgard characterized it correctly when he depicted the NYSE as
an "800-pound gorilla that was motherhood and apple pie in the eye of
Congress." And in the eye of the media, as well. I knew we were in danger
and I wasn't about to let the Merc become a refugee in the land of finance.
There was the feeling that we were isolated, a dot of an island unattached
to any group of islands in the vast Pacific. It wasn't a new feeling. I had
been there before, scrambling to sell the IMM and currencies to a skeptical financial world. I could still remember the blank stares and grimaces
that had greeted me 15 years earlier.

Today, so many years after the 1987 crash, it is nearly impossible to re-
capture the charged atmosphere that permeated Washington, New York,
and Chicago at that time, or to adequately describe how close it came to
prompting legislation that would ban or cripple stock index futures
specifically and restrict the growth of futures markets generally. The
fact that our markets were so efficient, so in touch with modern communications capabilities and computers, played against us. Indeed, our markets were *too* efficient. Critics cleaving through the waters of despair
were saying that index futures made the markets too complicated and too
volatile. For years, the world did fine without computers. Why did we
need them now? The headlines after the crash explained it all: *"The
mindless computers on automatic pilot. . . . Technology had outdistanced its ef-
fectiveness . . . Efficiency needs a brake pedal!"*

It made my blood boil. I never could dance fast, and in any case I'd
rather dance the way we did in the fifties. But I didn't blame John Travolta
for spreading *Saturday Night Fever* and the disco rage in the seventies. The
world changes. It globalized, and markets now demand an ability to react
instantaneously to information and has the tools that can do that. The
stock index futures market is one of those tools.

One of the most succinct comments came from an unknown source and was reported in the *Washington Post:*

> Before the politicians and the regulators go on a witch hunt to slay the beast called computerized trading, it might be useful for them to learn what the term means. In essence, it refers to Wall Street applications for two familiar features of the computer revolution: high-speed electronic communication from one computer to another, and high-speed number crunching. The computers can be programmed to ring bells or flash lights to signal the optimum time to sell a particular contract on a certain exchange. But these inhuman machines don't decide when to buy or sell, any more than an alarm clock decides when you should wake up.

But a witch hunt it was. University of Chicago Professor Merton Miller publicly warned that "Computer trading is going to get the blame. Yet this was the same as in 1929, and there was no computer trading then. There always has to be a villain. In '29 it was margin buying; now it's computerized trading. This is simply a panic, like a classic bank run."

Miller's words and those of other brave souls who attempted to counter emotion with logic were lost in a storm of accusatory nonsense that pervaded the written and electronic media. Instead, the words "futures are turning the United States into a casino," as some proclaimed, was a much catchier sound bite and had more immediate mass appeal. So did the cry "Ban futures."

Edward J. Markey, the Democrat from Massachusetts, whose House subcommittee on Telecommunications and Finance had jurisdiction over the SEC, immediately called for hearings, and didn't even wait until the corpse was cold before he visited the CME during the week following the crash. His mind was made up even before he came to Chicago.

On the Thursday following the crash, Markey was already certain of the findings and the penalty. "Program trading was caught red-handed as the chief villain behind the meteoric velocity of the decline," he was quoted in the *Washington Post.* "Monday signaled the end of program trading . . . this is it . . . it's over."

Feverish agitation always revved up the competitive juices in my blood and sent me barrelling forth to fight the good fight. At the first Markey hearings, scheduled barely 10 days after the crash, facts in my hand, I gave no quarter in my testimony: "Because our markets are different, shall we be forced to become the same? Because we have advanced into the information standard, shall we be forced to retreat to a less technological past? Because we have succeeded in an arena that some have viewed as the exclusive domain of New York, shall we be forced to relinquish to them our market share?"

The late Senator John Heinz, a Republican from Pennsylvania, was among a number of congressional officials to call for margin on stock index futures to be hiked to 50 percent to match the margin for stock. This concept, or *harmonization* of margin, as it came to be called, picked up steam when Don Regan at the White House supported the idea. The issue became one of our greatest nightmares. It is one of those ideas that sounds so right and is so wrong.

The difference between margin in futures—which is simply a security bond to protect the nearest movement in price—and margin in stocks, which is partial payment for the securities purchased, is all the difference in the world. Jack Sandner delivered an outstanding explanation of the difference between the two types of margins when we testified at a congressional hearing on the subject, graphically describing to the congress how much safer our system was. For some, the demand for margin harmonization was based on lack of understanding. For others, it was based on sinister competitive motivations. For us, said Merton Miller, "the margin issue is a code word for killing the futures markets." Merton, as always, hit the nail on the head.

Meanwhile, like a shrink doing tedious analysis of a patient's inner self, the markets were probed, pinched, poked, and examined in detail in a series of reports that poured forth out of the cup of analysis. The Merc was put under a microscope, and if we had any warts, they would be exposed. Knowing full well that some of the planned studies were under the direction of our antagonists, we decided to launch a study of our own as a counterbalance. However, I made certain that the CME Committee of Inquiry, which was organized to examine the events surrounding October 19, 1987, was composed of people whose credibility was hard to question. To chair the blue-ribbon committee, we called on University of Chicago economist Merton Miller, who three years later would win a Nobel Prize for his research in finance theory. Then we included Yale School of Management economist and Dean Burton Malkiel, author of *A Random Walk Down Wall Street;* Stanford University finance and law professor Myron Scholes, codeveloper of the Black-Scholes widely used options pricing model; and attorney John D. Hawke, Jr., former general counsel for the Federal Reserve System, who specialized in regulation of financial institutions. Their report was released on December 22, 1987, and served as a model for the reports that followed. As I anticipated, no one dared to take on the conclusions of this panel.

All in all, there were some 77 different reports and studies about the crash. Collectively, the various reports became the historical context for a short period when psychic jitters took over the markets. But markets are not like, say, war-torn cities left unrebuilt and uninhabited; the vacuum of neglect is quickly filled by those who see market sell-offs as opportunity.

And the market began to rebound well before the last crash report was completed. The CFTC interim report was released on November 9, 1987 (and a follow-up on January 6, 1988); the Nicholas deB. Katzenbach report, commissioned before the crash by the NYSE to study program trading, was released December 21, 1987; the General Accounting Office (GAO) report came on January 26; it was followed on January 29 by the CFTC's final report; and by early February, the SEC issued its final report. Each report was different, and to my satisfaction none of the reports blamed futures markets for the crash. The CFTC report commended futures exchange decisions and performance throughout the crash and rejected the contention that index arbitrage and portfolio insurance interacted to cause the crash. The SEC report corroborated these findings and concluded that institutional stock selling was the single direct factor responsible for the initial opening declines on October 19.

One of the most comprehensive reports came from the independent study conducted by Professor Richard Roll, Allstate Professor of Finance, UCLA. His conclusions exemplified those reached in virtually every other academic study and went a long way to still the uninformed angry voices against futures: First, the crash was a global event; the United States market was not the first to decline sharply, and out of 23 stock market comparisons, the United States had the fifth smallest decline. Second, since the United States was the only country with a highly developed index futures market, it nullified the notion that derivative markets were somehow a cause of the crash. Third, automated quotations, forward trading, transaction taxes, limits on price moves, and margin requirements all had no perceptible influence on the extent of the crash. Fourth, computer-directed trading such as portfolio insurance did not exacerbate the crash; indeed, the average decline of five countries in which computer directed trading was prevalent was 6.6 percentage points less than the average decline of the 15 countries where it was not prevalent. And finally, in an examination of 10 characteristics empirically associated with the extent of the price decline, options and futures trading were unrelated to the extent of the crash.

The Brady Report was submitted on January 8, 1988, to the President, to the chairman of the Federal Reserve Board, and the secretary of the Treasury. While favorable to futures in many respects, it contained two highly negative recommendations. It was in favor of harmonization of margins and a single regulator for both the stock and futures markets. The latter recommendation was widely supported by some key senators and congressmen, the NYSE, and the SEC chairman, David Ruder. Everyone in futures was of a common mind on this issue. Falling into the SEC regulatory hands might be the end of futures innovation and expansion. The SEC knew stocks, but not futures. Until that agency considered our markets equal to the equity markets, we wanted no part of them. Jerry Salzman summed it up succinctly: "The futures industry resists SEC regulation because of the certain knowledge that the SEC regards the NYSE as its first-born son and the CME as the bastard daughter of a nubian slave taken in battle."

I met individually with many members of the various oversight committees. The message we imparted was simple: they were dealing with highly complex mechanisms that had made the U.S. financial service sector number one in the world. Unnecessary legislation was not in America's best interests. Some of them had received CME honoraria and PAC contributions, but I wasn't foolish enough to think that this meant they would automatically be on our side. To gain their support, they had to believe in our markets, and to do that, they had to understand them. Our supporters were on both sides of the political aisle. Among our strongest allies were Senators Alan Dixon, Bob Dole, Phil Gramm, Donald Riegle, and Christopher Dodd. With several of them, like Bob Dole and Chris Dodd, I had developed what amounted to a personal relationship based on trust and mutual respect. But none of them would have joined our side if our cause was fallacious, if we were really the villain.

Still, relationships in Washington often count more than reason, and many of the people we met had visited our floors over the years and had learned to trust our judgment. "Chicago has been much more active and much more sophisticated politically than any exchange in the country," said Arthur Levitt, then chairman of the American Stock Exchange and a longtime member of the New York financial establishment. Levitt, an astute political observer if there ever was one, was ever so right. The Merc was a politically sophisticated exchange, the result of our recognition early on that a strong presence in Washington was a mandatory imperative of survival. Thanks too to the likes of Bill Bagley, Clayton Yeutter, Dayle Henington, Chip Seeger, and our CFPF.

On February 10, David Ruder took a dramatic step to bring the leaders of the two warring camps together. It was a brilliant idea and an enormous contribution toward solving our differences. The SEC chairman had invited Phelan and me, along with CFTC acting Chairman Kalo Hineman, to an informal meeting at his Washington office in an effort to work out a system of trading halts, or so-called circuit breakers that would slow down the markets in a volatility crisis. The meeting served to begin the dialogue. We immediately found common ground in that Ruder and Hineman agreed with Phelan and me that the exchanges, not the regulators, had to solve the problems. With respect to circuit breakers, however, we had some difficulty. For me, circuit breakers was simply a fancy name for price limits, which I had contemplated long before the crash. To Phelan, it meant interfering with the free movement of prices, something he was reluctant to embrace. "If you have a real crescendo of selling, anyone who thinks you're going to get it to stop with a systemic pause is crazy," Phelan said.

Philosophically, I wholeheartedly agreed with Phelan, but I argued that a measured "cooling off" procedure of short duration, preordained, and well publicized could do some good. "It is a compromise we can both live with," I argued. My good friend former SEC Commissioner Grundfest would later chide me that I, of all people, should know better. "When the system is ready to lay an egg, the system will lay an egg regardless of any trading halts," he said.

While Phelan and I did not resolve the issue there and then, we left that meeting in an upbeat mood and agreed to keep the dialogue going. On April 14, Congressman Ed Markey achieved what he set out to do. He had invited John Phelan and me to testify before his House Telecommunications and Finance subcommittee. His hearing room became the focal point of the aftermath of the crash. It was crammed with reporters and TV cameras. Our testimony, remarks, and agreements or disagreements would be covered by everyone in the media and spread across the pages and screens of America. But Phelan and I wanted no public controversy or recriminations. Instead, we had agreed to privately meet over breakfast at the Four Seasons Hotel in Washington shortly before we were to appear at Markey's hearing. We talked about markets, timing, volatility, and agreed on a 90 day timetable in which to improve the communications between the CME and NYSE and to devise a new circuit breaker system.

That afternoon the two of us appeared front and center, sitting side by side before Markey's subcommittee to explain the steps each of our institutions had already taken in response to the crash and what we planned for the future. I testified that among the measures the Merc already instituted was raising margins on stock index futures contracts and implementing temporary daily price limits. Phelan told the congressmen that the NYSE also was working on technological enhancements and creating safeguards that would avoid the kind of gridlock that took place on Black Monday. The two of us offered an absolutely marvelous performance—some said a love fest—providing neither the press nor the Congress with any public acrimony to legislate or write headlines about.

The *Washington Post* subsequently reported, "The turning point occurred on April 14, when Phelan and Melamed met for breakfast at the Four Seasons before appearing together at a hearing of the House Telecommunications and Finance subcommittee chaired by Rep. Edward Markey (D-MA). The deal they reached that day would help quell concerns about volatility caused by computerized trading while showing Congress for the first time that the exchanges could work toward a solution on their own."

But to achieve a coordinated result with the securities markets, the futures market also would need a united front. That clearly meant that the CBOT had to be included. Once again it was fortunate that I had a close relationship with CBOT officials. However, the CBOT and the NYSE had a history of distrust that was difficult to overcome. When Phelan invited me and other CME officials to sit down for talks with him and NYSE officials, at first he didn't mean the CBOT. But I held my ground and made certain the CBOT was invited. Ultimately, CBOT President Thomas Donovan and Chairman Karsten Mahlmann joined Brodsky, Sandner, and me in a meeting with Phelan at the New York Stock Exchange. Alas, the age-old animosities between the NYSE and the CBOT again came to the surface, resulting in a clash of egos, and little was accomplished.

Nevertheless, in between press conferences and congressional testimony—and unbeknownst to the media—my dialogue with Phelan continued. Over time, we talked by telephone and met privately, sometimes in New York, sometimes elsewhere. While the press continued to play up our differences, accentuating New York versus Chicago, Phelan and I rejected that conflict. We fully understood and respected each other's position. He was damn well going to prevent blame from ending up on the specialists' doorstep, and I was ready to die before I would allow the futures markets to become the culprit. We were two emissaries, each with our own constituents and concerns back home, but we recognized that ultimately some kind of agreement had to be forged. And above all, we both loved our markets and understood that they complemented each other. Under no circumstances did either of us want government intrusion into the marketplace. Exchanges had to prove they were capable of solving mutual problems; that was our common ground. At the end of the day, we knew we would get together, compromise our differences, and provide this nation with a coordinated market structure. For me, one of the most rewarding results of this difficult period was that Phelan and I came out of it good friends. Indeed, at his retirement party from NYSE chairmanship in 1990, I was the only one from the futures arena that Phelan invited.

But peace did not come quickly or easily. In fact, during the early part of 1988, things went downhill. One of the most difficult challenges was to get our New York-based member community to speak out publicly on our behalf. I knew that the media would never be stilled until the people they considered expert came to the defense of futures markets. But I was mostly unsuccessful. The New York members of our markets were under orders from above. The old-line brokerage firms and investment houses made most of their profit from stocks and other securities; futures were only a small portion of their bottom line. Why should they endanger their pocketbooks? Why should they anger their customers, stockholders in corporate America who generally didn't understand or trust futures markets?

The media was merciless in its continued quest to nail the culprit of the crash. The witch hunt was in full gear and index arbitrage remained the target. In January, Shearson proudly advertised during the Super Bowl that it had stopped using index arbitrage. Reports, facts, logic do not count when a demon is hunted. The witch hunt gained momentum—and an impressive following. It reached its zenith on May 10, 1988, when several of the most prestigious U.S. investment banking firms bowed to the nonsensical pressure and announced their withdrawal from proprietary index arbitrage. It represented a singularly sad day in the annals of American finance.

It was just about then that I asked for an appointment with the Fed chairman. Although Greenspan and I had talked on the telephone, we had not had a face-to-face meeting since the crash, and there were a number of things I wanted to say. He asked me why I hadn't come sooner, and when I told him that I didn't want to bother him, he responded, "My door is always open to you, Leo." I judged he meant that sincerely. After we were settled in his office—one-on-one—he quietly asked: "Leo, why are you guys in Chicago taking such a beating? Where are your friends? Where are all the Wall Street investment bankers who so successfully use index futures? Why isn't anyone of substance speaking out in your defense?"

I looked at my respected friend and didn't hesitate in my response. "Mr. Chairman, our friends are out there all right, but they are afraid to talk. And they will continue to be afraid and silent, until someone with authority, someone with expertise, someone with credibility, someone, maybe, high up in government speaks out first."

There was a moment of silence as we looked at each other, each of us fully appreciating the meaning of his question and of my answer.

On May 19, 1988, Fed Chairman Alan Greenspan testified before Edward J. Markey's House subcommittee on Telecommunications and Finance. Greenspan's words will forever be burned in my memory because they proved to be the turning point in the battle on behalf of our markets.

Said Chairman Greenspan:

> What many critics of equity derivatives fail to recognize is that the markets for these instruments have become so large not because of slick sales campaigns but because they are providing economic value to their users. By enabling pension funds and other institutional users to hedge and adjust positions quickly and inexpensively, these instruments have come to play an important role in portfolio management.

Greenspan then went on to explain why futures tell the truth:

> It is also worth noting that we routinely see the futures markets reacting to new information more rapidly than the cash markets. Some have concluded . . . that movements in futures prices thus must be causing movements in cash prices. However, the costs of adjusting portfolio positions are appreciably lower in the futures market, and new positions can be taken more quickly. Hence, portfolio managers may be inclined naturally to transact in the futures market when new information is received, causing price movements to occur there first. Arbitrage activity acts to ensure that values in the cash market do not lag behind.

The testimony of U.S. Treasury Undersecretary George D. Gould followed. He was a man who spent better than 30 years as a Wall Street investment banker, but he also knew the truth: "Much public criticism of index arbitrage," he succinctly stated, "is a classic case of wanting 'to shoot the messenger' that brings the bad news of selling on the CME to the floor of the NYSE . . ."

I had been introduced to the undersecretary by my good friend Michael R. Darby, who was then assistant secretary of the Treasury for Economic Policy. Darby, an economist who was a member of the crisis-management team following the October 1987 stock market crash, was thoroughly conversant with futures markets, knew we needed help, and rolled up his sleeves to lend a hand. By the time he shepherded me into Gould's office at the Treasury, the undersecretary was well prepared to accept me as a good guy. And Gould gave me hours upon hours of his valuable time to learn how futures worked and why we were messengers not culprits. Coincidentally, Michael Darby went from the Treasury to become undersecretary of the Department of Commerce for Economic Affairs where he provided the CME with immeasurable assistance by convincing Commerce Secretary Mosbacher to help me receive permission from the Japanese Ministry of Finance for the introduction of GLOBEX terminals into Japan. Darby is today a professor at the University of California at Los Angeles and director of the John M. Olin Center for Policy.

After Greenspan's and Gould's clear and unequivocal testimony to Congress—and I made certain that their words were transmitted and disseminated to every nook and cranny of the financial world—it was as if Moses had come down from the mountain. Suddenly, all kinds of New York-based financial experts came to the defense of futures markets. Suddenly, our markets provided economic value. One by one, the moguls of Wall Street began to publicly admit that, maybe, just maybe, what Robert R. Glauber said in the Brady Report was true: we were one market and we needed each other. Bob Glauber followed George Gould as U.S. Treasury undersecretary.

On June 14, Sandner, Brodsky, and I met with Phelan and other NYSE officials in New York. Over dinner that night, we discussed some of the Brady Commission's key recommendations. In the October crash, the markets for stocks and futures had disconnected, and we never wanted that to happen again. In an unprecedented show of cooperation, the Merc and NYSE agreed to institute coordinated circuit breakers and "shock absorbers" that would allow tumultuous markets to catch their breath. The agreements forged between Phelan and myself, and adopted by our two exchanges, are still the underpinning of present market procedure in the event of another market fall.

By now, Fed Chairman Alan Greenspan had made it clear that the Federal Reserve wasn't interested in overseeing the futures exchanges. Ruder, however, a member of the Presidential Working Group of Financial Markets, held to his view that the futures industry was underregulated compared to the securities industry and pressed for higher margins in futures as a means to curb volatility. But newly appointed CFTC Chairperson Wendy Gramm saw no need for such action. Gramm was a dyed-in-the-wool free-market economist who staunchly stood her ground on behalf of our markets; she would not give an inch. The result was a line in the sand between the SEC and CFTC; it was a good old intra-agency standoff.

Late in 1988, the futures industry showed its political muscle when President Reagan appointed Mary Schapiro to fill a vacancy as an SEC commissioner. Schapiro had been an assistant to former CFTC chairperson Susan Phillips, which provided us with an opportunity to get to know each other. I went to bat on her behalf. Schapiro's futures background proved to be extremely valuable in our continuing battle to defend against SEC jurisdictional takeover. However, Richard Breeden, who took over the chairmanship of the SEC from David Ruder, violated the assurances he had made to us and joined forces with the new Secretary of Treasury Nicholas Brady to again heat up the jurisdictional battle for oversight of our markets.

Our congressional influence prevailed in spite of Breeden and Brady. What helped immensely was that, pursuant to the agreement I forged with Dick Grasso, the NYSE stayed out of the issue. Ultimately, by virtue of an aggressive Merc, CBOT, and futures industry lobbying effort, the congressional bill to transfer stock index futures jurisdiction over to the SEC never made it out of committee. It was one of the defining moments of the futures industry's power in Congress, a consequence of labors, friendships, and alliances of many years.

I had thus overcome the clash of egos, the clash of cultures, the clash of cities in making peace with the NYSE. On January 5, 1989, as John Phelan's special guest, I was invited to address the NYSE board of directors. It was an historical first and an unprecedented honor. I had crossed the Hudson from the West and offered a similar invitation to Phelan to come to Chicago and visit the Merc. He accepted.

In 1993, Arthur Levitt became SEC chairman and by then Mary Schapiro was a highly regarded SEC commissioner. So much so, that when Levitt requested my recommendation for a nominee to the chair of the CFTC, I unhesitatingly pointed to Schapiro. He balked. "Too valuable for me to lose," he told me. But later, Levitt relented, and in 1994 Mary Schapiro was appointed by President Clinton to chair the CFTC. Now, of course, she has become the chief regulator of the NASD.

As in many profound dramas, there was an epilogue to the crash. In a way, the NYSE wanted the last word. Before the rather significant rule changes and new coordinated market procedures that grew out of the 1987 crash became imbedded in the infrastructure of the American marketplace, the NYSE wanted a forum in which to legitimize the process. Toward that purpose, as if to put the issues to bed and make recommendations for the future, the NYSE formed the Market Volatility and Investor Confidence panel. Roger B. Smith, chairman and CEO of General Motors Corporation was chosen by the board of directors of the NYSE to act as the panel's chairman. Included on the panel, which was intended to be independent of the NYSE, were 19 people, representing individual and institutional investor communities, listed companies, member firms, academia, and stock and futures exchanges—a who's who of corporate America and American financial markets.[1] Theoretically, the NYSE could have launched this panel without representation from futures markets. But if it did, it ran the risk

---

[1] Serving on the NYSE Panel were: Chairman Roger B. Smith, Chairman and CEO, General Motors Corporation; Robert E. Allen, Chairman and CEO, AT&T; Rand V. Araskog, Chairman and CEO, ITT Corporation; John S. Chalsty, President and CEO, Donaldson, Lufkin & Jenrette, Inc.; James Cloonan, President and Chairman, American Association of Individual Investors; Benjamin F. Edwards, III, Chairman, CEO and President, A.G. Edwards, Inc.; John A. Georges, Chairman and CEO, International Paper Co.; S. Parker Gilbert, Chairman, Morgan Stanley Group, Inc.; Frederick L.A. Grauer, Chairman and CEO, Wells Fargo Nikko Investment Advisors; John H. Gutfreund, Chairman, President and CEO, Salomon, Inc.; Thomas W. Hayes, Treasurer, State of California; Leo Melamed, Chairman, Dellsher Investment Co., Inc.; Merton H. Miller, Graduate School of Business, University of Chicago; Philip J. Purcell, Chairman and CEO, Dean Witter Financial Services Group; John G. Smale, Chairman of the Executive Committee, Proctor & Gamble Co.; Sherwood H. Smith, Jr., Chairman/President, Carolina Power & Light Co.; Donald Stone, Senior Partner, Lasker, Stone & Stern; Stephen B. Timbers, Senior Executive Vice President and Chief Investment Officer, Kemper Financial Services; and Dennis Weatherstone, Chairman and CEO, J.P. Morgan & Co. Inc.

that any criticism or recommendation regarding futures in its report would be subject to skepticism and ridicule. So it chose just two representatives from our markets: Nobel Laureate Merton Miller, and Chairman of Dellsher Investment Co. Inc. Leo Melamed.

Over the five months of its discussions, the panel addressed concerns about the impact of market volatility and the need to maintain a strong market for all participants. The panel met monthly and consulted with experts in business, government, and academia, and reviewed the major changes that took place in the financial markets since October 1987. The panel submitted its report to the NYSE Board on May 24, 1990, and made eight recommendations. The recommendations covered the full scope of market action from such items as coordinated "circuit breakers" to a request that the SEC ease existing restraints on the ability of corporations to repurchase their own common stock to education of the media about program trading to enhanced capabilities for detection of market abuses.

Professor Miller and I kept a watchful eye during the discussions, doing everything in our power to protect the interests of futures markets. I relied heavily on Miller's intellectual depth and he took comfort in my unabashed faculty to speak out. We got some welcome and unexpected help from Morgan Stanley, and James Cloonan, president and chairman of the American Association of Individual Investors, and occasionally other representatives. On the whole, I believe we were successful, warding off negative views, sentiments, and wording. However, at the end of the process, two contentious recommendations were made at which Miller, Cloonan and I vehemently balked. First was a recommendation that "regulatory authority over the U.S. equity and equity derivatives markets should be consolidated under one federal agency," and second, that "a majority of the panel believes that margin requirements for U.S. equity and equity derivative instruments should be set by the exchanges with government oversight consolidated in one federal agency."

Those were recommendations that Miller and I could never accept. We were joined by several others, and angry, loud arguments ensued. In the end, Merton Miller and I (joined by James Cloonan), told panel Chairman Roger Smith that we would not sign the final report unless it included our written dissent, to the foregoing two recommendations. There followed a lot of behind-the-scenes discussions. Roger Smith wanted a unanimous report without dissenters, but we would not budge. He had to decide whether to go without us or give in to our demands. We won.

Thus, after nearly three years of pain, recriminations, and soul-searching, the 1987 stock crash was finally put to rest. It did not produce the result one might have expected. "Use adversity as stepping-stones of opportunity," Everette Harris used to lecture me. We did. Instead of being an instrument of our demise, the crash had become a stepping-stone to a higher degree of credibility for our markets than we ever before attained. The imbroglio had cast the Merc into the national spotlight. Futures markets had become important and valuable and regarded as an equal partner in the American financial service sector. It represented a monumental turning point in our history.

There were a thousand lessons. But for me, of all the lessons learned, none was more meaningful than what I wrote in the *Anthology on Flexible Exchange Rates*, which was published following the crash: "Tinkering with free market forces in a significant way creates unnatural economic conditions that may beget unnatural economic consequences." This simple truth was obvious to Milton Friedman, Beryl Sprinkel, Merton Miller, Allan Meltzer, Martin Feldstein, and so many others right from the beginning.

33

Here Come the Feds, Again

Chicago winters have always reminded me of that Siberian chill I had felt so long ago. Rattling winds whip off Lake Michigan. The air is raw. The snow is heavy. The ice lingers. A landscape in turmoil—the kind of winter it was in January 1989.

It was also a festive one. I was in Washington attending the inauguration of President Bush when on that night, January 18, a storm of federal agents with subpoenas in hand, descended upon the homes of some 40 futures traders from both the CME and CBOT. The surprise visits were the culmination of a two-year investigation in which four FBI agents, posing as traders with hidden tape recorders, penetrated the trading pits of both exchanges. The investigation, the biggest ever to hit the Chicago markets, was a sting designed to catch traders who were allegedly defrauding customers.

As part of their arsenal, the feds used RICO—the Racketeer Influenced and Corrupt Organizations Act—to pry pleas from the traders or to get them to testify against others. The RICO Act was designed as a tool in the war against organized crime to confiscate homes, cars, boats, and other assets acquired by ill-gotten gains. No one was taken into custody that night, so technically the traders did not have to be represented by counsel. The government had staged its midnight raid to cause fear and confusion.

The RICO raid seemed unreasonably harsh. *The Wall Street Journal* would later agree in an editorial that criticized the strategy: "Whatever the alleged crimes, these tactics violated the Justice Department's own guidelines prohibiting RICO threats 'solely or even primarily to create a bargaining tool.' Coerced pleas under these circumstances raise credibility problems."

The night of the raid, Chicago's exchange leadership was in Washington. Along with me were Brodsky, Sandner, and John Geldermann, the Merc's newly elected chairman. Tom Donovan and Karsten Mahlmann of the CBOT were also in Washington, DC. It didn't occur to me until much later that the raid was probably timed to start while all the top leaders of the Chicago Exchanges were away. The strategy seemingly employed by the FBI added to the confusion of our members.

The TV in our hotel room was tuned to CNN as Betty and I were in the process of putting on our formal attire for the gala inauguration ball, when to my utter consternation the newscaster made a flash announcement of the raids in Chicago. Among the things the announcer stated was that I, as well as Sandner and the other Merc officials, had received subpoenas. The fact that this was false on its face not only infuriated me, it also made me think that maybe the whole thing was some sort of comedy of errors. CNN later retracted its ridiculous assertion and apologized to me.

Chicago awoke the next morning to a *Chicago Tribune* banner headline that blared: "U.S. Probes Futures Exchanges." At first reading, it sounded pretty grim. Traders were alleged to have engaged in widespread cheating of customers, market manipulation, fraud, and tax evasion involving millions of dollars—all under the nose of an exchange surveillance system that was badly flawed—if we could believe the report.

For nearly two years, the FBI had used undercover agents, so-called moles, on the trading floors of both the CME and CBOT. (The FBI's investigation at the Merc was code-named "Operation Hedgeclipper" and "Sourmash" at the Board of Trade.) The moles recorded conversations in the trading pits, in bars, restaurants, health clubs, in the homes of traders they befriended. It was an elaborate and very costly piece of espionage, the most ambitious financial sting in FBI history, the authorities said.

I had hardly unloaded the burden of the stock market crash and now the emotional sparring started again. My thoughts flashed back to the Bialystok syndrome—my mother's fear of something bad lurking around every corner. How right she was. Initially, I couldn't fathom the situation. This smacked of the big time crime-busting aimed at the mob or the drug cartel or some kind of organized underworld crime network. The allegations of an intricate web involving hundreds of traders conniving and stealing in a free-for-all crime spree was an outrageous accusation. I knew that such contentions were off the wall.

Nevertheless, the media—and Justice Department—had a field day. The FBI's nighttime swoop, as *The Wall Street Journal* put it, was "sentence first, trial later." And for a while it seemed that way. Before we could sort things out, we had to face the usual gauntlet of indignities. By the first week in February, *Business Week* had already pronounced judgment: "The exchanges will be forced to change their arcane, century-old trading system, and scores of go-go traders could find themselves gone-gone to jail."

It didn't take me long to figure out what might be behind this sting operation. The FBI investigation of the Chicago futures traders came during the wave of heavily publicized indictments and convictions of Wall Street's insiders. New York-based U.S. Attorney Rudolph Guiliani, the terror of Wall Street's insider traders, got a helluva lot of political mileage out of his white-collar crime attack. The scandal, involving hundreds of millions of dollars, rocked New York and caught traders who were manipulating the stocks of target companies in merger deals. First snared was Dennis Levine, a Drexel Burnham Lambert investment banker, who had pleaded guilty in 1986 to profiting from insider trading. The authorities then got Levine to implicate Ivan Boesky, a Wall Street speculator, who was fined $100 million and sentenced to three years in jail. Boesky in turn helped prosecutors pursue Michael Milken, Drexel's junk bond king of the eighties. In March 1989, Milken and two of his colleagues were indicted on numerous counts of criminal racketeering, securities fraud, and other crimes. Drexel Burnham Lambert paid a record $650 million fine for securities fraud and other felonies, subsequently leading to the demise and disgrace of the 152-year-old firm—the biggest failure in Wall Street's history.

The rationale was simple. If that kind of megabuck underhanded dealings went on in New York's securities markets, there must be at a minimum the same kind of megabuck rot in Chicago's futures markets. Of course, it didn't turn out that way, but not because the Justice Department and the FBI didn't give it a college try. The Chicago press even began comparing U.S. Attorney Anton Valukas to his counterpart in New York, who was able to turn such high-profile cases into political currency and eventually won the mayor's seat of New York City. Indeed, the manner in which the Justice Department handled prior investigations, including the Wall Street insider trading scandals, appeared to have become the model for the Chicago sting. The use of undercover agents and moles wired with hidden recording devices in the investigation was similar to the FBI's approach in so-called Operation Greylord, a probe of Chicago's Cook County justice system that had taken place five years earlier. In that case, people were pressured to "roll over" or snitch on others in return for leniency. It resulted in a slew of convictions of judges, police officers, lawyers, and court officials of federal crimes from fixing traffic tickets to bribing judges in drug cases.

Both local and national media were relentless, and, just as in the stock market crash, the Merc was showered by a fuselage of accusations, rumors, and innuendoes. Hordes of print and television reporters and cameras descended on the exchange. Many of them were unfamiliar with futures markets. I issued a statement that "the allegations were unfounded and unwarranted," but the difficulty of not knowing what information our adversary had became a constant impediment in our denials. No doubt that was part of the FBI strategy, to create the fear that they had uncovered something really big, when in truth, what they had was fairly small, and what they were on was a fishing expedition. But none of us knew that in the beginning. The innuendoes, the headlines, the subpoenas, and the night-time tactics threw everyone off balance. I kept insisting that the vast majority of our members were law-abiding, and couldn't bring myself to believe that any undetected major crimes had been perpetrated on our floors. Still, we had to couch our words very carefully just in case there was some bomb out there we knew nothing about.

In an attempt to quell anxieties among members, the Board issued a letter on February 13, stating, in part:

> . . . it is imperative at this juncture to make it absolutely clear that the Chicago Mercantile Exchange, as an institution, is not the focus of the federal investigation. This should have been clear from the outset. However, the relentless media coverage has created an environment of confusion and misinformation . . . As a consequence, the damage already inflicted on the futures industry may outweigh the good that may yet be achieved by the ultimate exposure of wrongdoing by some Exchange members . . . Indeed before a single indictment has been issued—before anyone has been brought to trial, let alone found guilty—this media frenzy has unjustly cast doubt on all futures business, the Commodity Futures Trading Commission (CFTC), as well as the self-regulatory process. It has resulted in a delay of CFTC reauthorization and instigated at least one Congressional probe . . .

The press kept hammering. Soon there was the clatter of skeletons as old stories of the legendary robber barons who once cornered markets were dredged up and highlighted in sidebars to spice up copy and remind readers of the nefarious characters who used to inhabit the pits—as if they were still directing the current trading culture. The *Chicago Tribune*, which had broken the story, milked it with Pulitzer Prize zeal, playing it on page one for two weeks straight. The headlines made it out to be a bigger story than the greatest stock market crash in history. And much bigger than the New York insider trading scandal. Every time subpoenas were issued, reporters would hit the streets and the phones to randomly interview traders whose names were culled from newspaper articles, directories, and other sources. It appeared that the government had used the press to its advantage by providing the necessary leaks to keep the story alive and to create a kind of Pavlovian reflex among some reporters. An editorial in the March 1989 issue of *Chicago Lawyer* summed up the situation: "Together, the *Tribune's* telephone calls and stories produced an atmosphere of panic and paranoia that may have been calculated by Justice Department leakers to frighten traders into cooperating in the investigation, a tactic used in previous sting operations."

David L. Protess, a professor at Northwestern University's Medill School of Journalism, instructed his students to do a content analysis of the first 10 days of coverage. His observation was damning to the media:

"What began as a government leak (to the press) swiftly became a torrent of intrusively gathered news stories that were frequently misleading and sometimes inaccurate."

Subsequently, in an article written for the *Columbia Journalism Review* on the press coverage of the sting, Protess would conclude, "All the stories had one common characteristic: none of the allegations was attributed to anybody with a name . . . almost two-thirds of all information contained in the stories was attributed to anonymous sources."

The CBOT's Tom Donovan and Karsten Mahlmann sent letters to the editors charging the *Chicago Tribune* and *Chicago Sun-Times* with slanted coverage. "Continuous front-page stories in your newspaper," they stated, had fostered "a presumption of guilt of individuals, businesses, and institutions in the futures industry that only have been subpoenaed for information . . . The news reports are based on unofficial and unverified allegations from unnamed sources."

Nevertheless, the media blitz was taking its collective toll. Paranoia became part of the daily routine in the pits. Rumors about alleged statements made to the FBI, or arrest warrants issued, or wires being worn by this or that trader or clerk spread through the floor like wildfire. Market rumors are part of the daily routine of traders. The market often feeds on stories that are gossip or garbled information, and traders learn to act and react to such stories. These are usually sorted out during the course of a trading day, with the facts ultimately rising to the surface. But in the case of the sting operation, no one knew what the facts were. So the innuendoes and rumors built on each other, becoming a gigantic pyramid of fear and confusion. It didn't take long for the normal trader banter to dissipate out of fear that the guy standing nearby might be a mole or might be wired. And the vivid horror surrounding the FBI's night raids, widely reported by the press, exacerbated these fears and heightened the anxiety of the floors. How many moles were there in the pits? Who could we trust? As Jim Oliff, a British pound broker and member of the Board said to me, "It isn't like I have anything to fear, but I've become afraid to talk to anyone. Who knows what some FBI mole will make out of what I said." Oliff hit the nail on the head. Everything within the arcane world of futures—with its unique practices and language—could look suspicious to an outsider trolling for scandal. Jim Oliff would later become the Merc's first ethics training instructor, a required classroom activity for members—one of the positive results of the sting operation.

It is difficult to describe the emotional impact to one's senses that results from a continuous FBI sting operation which seemingly is conducted in partnership with the media. The unceasing barrage of public allegations are calculated to spread fear to everyone. And it can work.

After a time everyone gets rattled. On January 25, some 20 traders were called to testify before a grand jury. Among them was David Horberg, co-chairman of the Merc's yen pit committee, who cleared his trades through my firm, Dellsher Investment Company. At that point, on the advice of Merc counsel Jerry Salzman who had interviewed Horberg, I summarily severed my clearing relationship with Horberg. I had buckled to accept guilt by accusation. Unfortunately, it made *The Wall Street Journal*. Horberg was never accused of wrongdoing and was back trading at another firm by mid-March.

By now I had cancelled plans to visit Australia, where on January 27, Sandner and I were scheduled to speak at a new building dedication for the Sydney Futures Exchange. Brodsky made the trip on our behalf. I always looked at setbacks as temporary. But this situation by its nature promised to drag out for months, perhaps even years, what with more subpoenas, then indictments, and trials to come. Once again, I braced myself to take on the harrumphers, needlers, and enemies of the futures markets. It was precisely the kind of situation that could earn me steadfast friends and bitter enemies—at the same time. And, once again, it delayed my thoughts of retirement. During the 1987 crash, on more than one occasion, I had contemplated taking a breather after the Merc was back on an even keel. Now with the sting operation in full force, I again felt the responsibility of staying at the helm and doing whatever was necessary to overcome the problem and keep the Merc on course. But secretly I vowed to leave the Merc officialdom as soon as this latest disaster ended.

The media was tireless in their attack, looking in every nook and cranny for some dirt. Clearly, the FBI wanted to find a trail to the Merc's and CBOT's big shots. That would be their big prize. No doubt they presumed that just like in the New York insider scandal, the chain of wrongdoing would lead up the ladder and implicate the futures exchanges' leadership. It is easy to understand how a bureaucrat or investigator would conclude that if the guys in the pit made some underhanded money, surely the guys on top made a lot more. Indeed, during the sting epoch, in an attempt to get something going against the past and present Merc hierarchy—including me—news stories appeared that were laden with innuendo, and prompted rumors to circulate.

Merc Chairman John Geldermann became, as Professor Protess put it, "one of the first victims of the journalistic excess." And I was another. On the evening of January 19, Cable News Network reported that three brokerage firms, including mine, and one "owned by" Geldermann had been subpoenaed. In fact, no subpoenas had been issued to any of the firms, and Geldermann had only a minor interest in the firm CNN said he owned. CNN retracted the story the following evening.

Former Chairman Larry Rosenberg was falsely victimized by the dredging up of a previously discredited media accusation about conflict of interest. CNN had, months before, incorrectly reported that Rosenberg had accepted the position of presidency at LNS Financial, a Merc clearing firm, while he was chairman of the CME Business Conduct Committee that was in the midst of conducting hearings of alleged rule violations by an officer of that firm. In truth, as Merc attorney Salzman told CNN, Rosenberg immediately reported to the Merc that he had received such an offer and voluntarily disqualified himself from the Business Conduct hearings. Rosenberg's actions were exemplary.

Similarly, the *Chicago Tribune* and *The Wall Street Journal* had begun to circle Jack Sandner, who had been CME chairman during the two years under investigation. Numerous negative stories about him and his firm, RB&H, began to appear in the press, giving him a bad time and some bad publicity, particularly about the firm's past sales programs. Sandner tried to defend his actions, but was quoted as admitting that "in hindsight, maybe we'd do things differently." It prompted Thomas Russo, the former highly respected deputy general counsel for the CFTC who became its first director of the Division of Trading & Markets, and today is managing director and chief legal officer of Lehman Brothers, Inc., to say, "I don't think the industry is doing enough" to monitor its hiring practices. That hurt, and raised serious perceptions about the Merc's ability to police its firm's practices.

A constant source of problems were the floor rumors and allegations that Sandner was financially connected to one or another of the so-called broker groups, a subject that had become very controversial at the Merc. The *Chicago Tribune* ran a comprehensive report with the headline "Broker Rings Legal—But Can Lead to Abuse." In the story, John Troelstrup, former head of the Merc's Compliance Department was quoted as saying, "The potential for abuses is enhanced, because brokers are controlled by the people who brought them into the group." *The Wall Street Journal* later published a report that Sandner had profited from his "especially close relationship with ABS Partners, the most influential group of brokers at the Merc."

Broker associations, formed in the late 1970s, were a group of floor brokers who together could better service our clearing firms in their need for order-execution coverage throughout the floor. As such, broker groups provided a legitimate service to firms and offered very competitive commission rates compared to "independent" brokers who were not members of any group.

The allegations by and perceptions of many members were that broker groups used questionable trading practices, and because of their large numbers, had achieved undue influence in Merc affairs during Sandner's tenure as chairman. The broker groups were particularly unpopular with traders and brokers who weren't in them. Among the complaints was the allegation that members of the groups traded within their respective associations without exposing their orders to the entire trading pit, as required by the Merc's open outcry trading rules.

I never confronted Sandner on these rumors and gave him my sympathy and support. The press was trigger-happy, looking to implicate the big shots, and taking potshots at anything that smacked of scandal, with the Justice Department prodding it on. I refused to give credence to such tactics, or to bow to rumor or innuendo. Our world was confused and caught off balance. The FBI sting had hit the futures world and the Chicago Mercantile Exchange with tremendous force. Trading volume was down nearly 25 percent in the week following the news of the investigation. Indeed, the FBI investigation overwhelmed everything we did for the next year and a half, just as the crash had done in the prior two years. Between 1987 and 1990, the Merc estimated it spent from 5,000 to 10,000 labor-hours dealing with congressional hearings and federal officials.

From the beginning, U.S. Attorney Anton Valukas made it clear that neither the Exchange, its officers, nor member firms had been implicated in any wrongdoing associated with the federal investigation. That was helpful, but it put the Exchange in a very difficult position; clearly, the Merc and the CBOT had no choice but to cooperate fully in the investigation. But in doing so, we gave the perception to the membership that we were against them. It left me walking a tightrope between acquiescing to the authorities and standing up to them in defense of the membership, whom I maintained were not guilty of the accusations. In the process, many Merc members were angered and sometimes denounced the Exchange leadership for not coming out with a clear-cut defense. But we had the responsibility of being on the side of law and order, and we never knew what the Feds might have up their sleeve. Throughout the difficult process, no matter how the members interpreted my actions, I had my eye on one mission: the Merc must survive.

And there was another set of problems. The Merc's political base in Washington was strong, but with the CFTC up for reauthorization and the SEC jurisdiction looming in the background, there was a fear of legislative retaliation. Now our ability to regulate ourselves was called into question. At this point, the Board agreed to hold nothing back and to tighten surveillance procedures in order to bolster investor confidence and preserve our rights of rule enforcement.

The CME record of penalties for rule violations for the period 1984 through 1988, under the direction of Jerry Beyer, showed that our Rule Enforcement Department increased its enforcement and fines as business activity expanded. For instance, in 1984, a total of $750,000 of fines was assessed, $1,499,000 in 1985, $1,969,000 in 1986, $3,517,000 in 1987 (the year of the crash), and $1,762,000 in 1988. Indeed, compared with other major futures exchanges, the Merc had been the most active in rule enforcement, as the U.S. General Accounting Office (GAO) would note in a report submitted in September 1989 to the Senate Committee on Agriculture.

Still, it felt as if the integrity of the institution was now on the line. All that I had worked for since the 1960s flashed before me. I grew a bit melancholy and felt I was pushing that old boulder up the hill again. The FBI allegations had challenged two of our sacred cows: self-regulation and open outcry. While the CFTC was the futures industry's regulator, the exchanges were the initial level of regulation. But now the federal investigators claimed that traders routinely ignored trading rules and that violations of the Commodity Exchange Act had gone undetected.

As a result of a conversation with Henry Jarecki and Tom Russo directly after the sting operation first broke, I decided on the strategy with which to best protect the Merc's integrity as well as its self-regulatory capabilities. I went to Brodsky and Geldermann with the idea. They both immediately recognized its value and wholeheartedly agreed. "It will give us instant credibility," Bill Brodsky said. We proceeded to create a Special Committee to Review Trading Practices. Launched on January 25—a week after the FBI sting was made public—it became known as the Merc's Blue Ribbon Panel and proved to be an outstanding defensive maneuver that, in the long run, kept the Merc's integrity intact. The Blue Ribbon Panel idea was not new; it is a concept that has been used time and again by private sector institutions as well as governments whenever a problem demanded the creation of an "independent" review board or commission. One of the most well-known of this genre is the Warren Commission formed to investigate the assassination of President Kennedy.

The essential key to success of such special commissions is that the credibility of their appointed members be beyond reproach. They have to be of such high integrity—literally, squeaky clean—so that even the most cynical of media reporters will not be able to deny the panel's wholesomeness. If it is less than that, the panel's results will be meaningless, and the effort will look like an attempt at a whitewash. At the same time, these panels must have a high degree of expertise in the subject matter involved. This was particularly true with respect to the arcane world of futures markets.

In huddling with Brodsky, we were able to structure the Special Committee with just the right balance. To provide internal Merc expertise, it was right to have CME Chairman John Geldermann, whose integrity in my mind was never in question, to act as chairman of the panel. I would be co-vice chairman and act as the panel's executive director, while Susan Phillips, the former CFTC chair, was perfect as my co-vice chair both for her futures expertise as well as her unquestionable credibility. Bill Brodsky, as CME president, automatically had to be a member of the panel; Donald Butler, a public Merc governor and the former president of the National Cattlemen's Association would represent agricultural interests; Louis Margolis, also a Merc-appointed governor was managing director of Salmon Brothers and would provide financial market representation; John Wing, president and CEO of the Chicago Corporation, a former SEC attorney, was highly regarded in our community and was an excellent choice as the industry-wide representative; and Robert Wilmouth, president of NFA, our private sector regulator, would serve as special advisor to the panel.

So far so good, but now I was faced with a dilemma of two parts: Jack Sandner, who was serving as chief policy advisor to the CME board—a post I helped create for him after his term as chairman had expired—and former Senator Thomas F. Eagleton, who was a sitting public director of the Merc. Sandner came to me and pleaded to be on the panel. His reasons made sense. If I overlooked him, he argued, the obvious conclusion people would draw was that the rumors, allegations, and negative media reports about him were true. With Brodsky and Geldermann on the Special Committee, Sandner's absence would be conspicuous. In his view, it could ruin his career. Jack's rationale was valid but it was the very reason I had a problem with his appointment. Not that I couldn't trust him or benefit by his help. But with the whole world looking over our shoulder and with the media cloud over Sandner, I didn't want to take any unnecessary chances by having someone on the Special Committee who might taint its credibility. I had just spent the past 15 months fighting to recast the Merc's image in the wake of the 1987 crash, swinging both the lawmakers and public back to our side. And this was a crucial period not only for the Merc, but for the entire futures industry with the CFTC up for reauthorization. How would it look to a cynical media if the Merc's Blue Ribbon Panel included someone whose past record the press had questioned so aggressively?

Still, Jack and I were good friends of long standing. He had always been supportive of my actions at the Merc and often stood at my side in the battles. I could never turn my back on a friend. So I opted to face down the criticism of the media, but under one condition: I had to know the truth.

"Okay Jack, tell me straight up," I said. My throat was tight and I had to swallow hard. "Are you connected to any broker group? I have to know because broker associations are bound to be one of the critical issues the Special Panel will consider and I don't want any conflict of interests. Do you have any financial or other interests in any broker group as the rumors say you have? I've got to know so that I'm not blindsided."

He looked directly at me and swore that he had no connection to any broker group. That was good enough for me. I put him on the Special Committee, giving him the credibility he needed to face his critics while I took the heat from the media.

Senator Eagleton presented the opposite part of the dilemma. He didn't want to serve on the Special Committee, and I wanted him there in order to enhance the panel's plausibility. When the news of the FBI sting broke, Eagleton reacted with deep frustration and embarrassment. I didn't really blame him. There he was, a former U.S. senator and past Democratic nominee for vice president of the United States, sitting as a public director of an institution whose membership was accused by the FBI and Justice Department of all kinds of heinous trading practice violations. He was extremely upset and said so publicly. It was all I could do to keep him from resigning from his CME post in protest and demanding an independent investigation by the U.S. Senate and the world court. His presence on the Special Committee would clearly raise its credibility. Without him on the panel, its value would be put in question and he could act as a loose cannon. Fortunately, Eagleton trusted me and, maybe, even liked me. At the CME's November 1988 London Finance Symposium, Senator Eagleton introduced me to the audience by stating: "While Churchill might quote Disraeli or Lord Hume, and John Kennedy might quote Tennyson, Leo Melamed quotes . . . Leo Melamed. But that is okay. You see, Leo Melamed is as smart as Henry Kissinger *thinks* he is."

So I convinced Senator Eagleton that if he served with us on the Blue Ribbon Panel, there would be no holds barred. "Everything that is connected with floor practices will be on the table," I told him. I assured him that everyone on the panel was beyond reproach. He could ask any questions he chose to, request the appearance of anyone he wanted, and wouldn't have to sign the final report and recommendations unless he was completely satisfied.

Upon announcement of the Blue Ribbon Panel, Tom Russo called it "a major step forward." And so did many in the press, stating that "the move may lead to a stronger market." It was the first bit of favorable publicity we received, and it represented a short respite in the blizzard of negative comments and accusations. I always felt that the CBOT had made a mistake in not launching a similar independent review board.

In the weeks ahead, our internal investigation involved a review of the compliance system in the same way an accounting firm does an audit. The panel had scheduled weekly meetings through mid-March in both Chicago and New York. Three meetings were held to receive testimony from and to question more than 40 expert witnesses. Scores of meetings were held for deliberations. It was a top-to-bottom review in which customers, representatives from the FCM community, the legal community, a diverse group of users, broker groups, the academic community, and the CME's floor broker and trader community were interviewed in detail.

Trading practices were scrutinized and enforcement procedures thoroughly examined. Witnesses were encouraged to testify on any topic, but were expressly requested to provide input on specific issues such as dual trading, broker associations, customer pressure for guaranteed prices, market openings and closes, fast markets, electronic surveillance; as well as disciplinary matters, including committee composition and minimum sentencing guidelines. In addition to the oral and written testimony provided by the witnesses, the committee also received extensive written testimony from other experts within and without the industry. In short, it was as comprehensive a review of Merc trading rules and practices as any exchange had ever undertaken.

Of course, the process didn't always go smoothly. Eagleton was constantly looking for any weakness in the Merc's resolve to reform its trading practices. He thought he found such an instance when U.S. Attorney Valukas objected to the Merc's internal investigation of rule violations which was running parallel to the one the Justice Department was conducting. Merc attorney Jerry Salzman countered by pointing out that the CME would be in violation of CFTC regulations if it ignored its federal mandate to continue its internal vigilance and investigatory procedures. Indeed, Salzman was correct, and the CFTC did not suspend the requirement. But Eagleton, a former U.S. attorney himself, didn't trust the CFTC either and took Salzman's response to represent an underhanded maneuver by the Merc staff to interfere with the Justice Department investigation. It resulted in an embarrassing shouting match between Salzman and Eagleton during one of the panel's meetings and caused a permanent rift between the two. This rift had meaningful ramifications down the line.

In the meantime, the Justice Department continued to keep its investigative heat on high. The near panic conditions that hit our members in the early days of the sting operation had now assumed a sort of permanent condition of nervousness. Normal trade conversation was kept at a minimum and was replaced with facial expressions. Everyone meticulously followed every trading rule to the letter of the law. Rumors continued to persist and an air of distrust and fear permeated the pits. Floor humor, always spontaneous and right to the point, spurred some traders to begin wearing lapel buttons depicting a microphone with a red slash through it to assure colleagues that they were not wired for sound. To add to the anxiety factor, the Merc's trading records from January 1, 1983 to January 18, 1987 were subpoenaed. The computerized printouts handed over to the authorities totaled about 100 boxes. We cooperated to the hilt. But this appeared to me as another fishing expedition by the Justice Department, which had invested millions of taxpayer dollars in its investigation and could ill afford to come up empty-handed.

Mysteriously, during this time, I began to receive diabolical anonymous letters that accused me of secret wrongdoings that were going to be exposed to the world. These increased in intensity and frequency as the months passed. "Soon the membership will know that you are the Boesky of futures," one of the letters stated, and vowed to tell all to the CFTC. I officially advised the CFTC and the Merc's attorney of these slanders. The CFTC did indeed receive some of them, as did the media. But for the most part, as best as I could, I ignored the taunts and threats, shrugging them off as the work of some evil kook, either a disgruntled member or a demented being set off by all the press coverage. Over the years, I had on more than one occasion received threatening or goofy letters from anonymous sources—I got used to it. But now, as the threats became more and more menacing, I decided to turn them over to an investigator to see if he could find the source. It came down to a number of possibilities, none of them conclusive. But some of the possibilities had a sinister undertone. The most obvious was that this was an attempt to either specifically take the investigative heat off someone in particular, or to generally divert the FBI sting operation from its natural course. My investigator also accumulated many facts and statements from members and attorneys who had some definite opinions about the source of the anonymous threats. None of it had any material effect on me or the course of the sting operation, and the anonymous letters just as mysteriously stopped after I retired from office.

My frustration with the media was lessened only by the one bright spot that I knew would outlast their negative blitz. Several dozen times each day, countless radio listeners heard Alan Crane, WMAQ's principal news commentator, say "and now the latest financial news from the floor of the Chicago Mercantile Exchange." I was certain that no amount of money could buy us that kind image value, nor could any amount of negative publicity take it away. That plug was initiated about a year earlier in 1988 when David Goldberg, General manager of radio station WMAQ, called me to discuss the establishment of a second all-news radio station in Chicago. Group W (Westinghouse Electric), which owned radio station WMAQ, had shown interest in becoming a competitor to WBBM, Chicago's current all-news radio station of the Columbia Broadcasting System. WMAQ wanted to know whether I thought it would be possible to broadcast the news from the Merc. "The floor of the Merc," Goldberg said, "would give the show special attraction and veracity." He explained that he had come to me because, in his words, "as an innovator you would understand." It didn't take me 10 seconds to recognize the opportunity this represented, both for

WMAQ and the CME. I rebuffed the objections from some board members and drove home approval to spend the $80,000 required to build a news booth in the fourth floor visitors' gallery overlooking the trading floor. The show, which began broadcasting from the CME in March, 1988 became an overnight success and is now a permanent fixture on Chicago's airwaves. In the beginning, we even arranged for Hayami Shiraishi and Yumi Koyama of our CME Tokyo office to broadcast the financial news direct from Tokyo. Later, I made sure that Alan Crane was assigned a permanent booth on the floor so that he could write some of his reports from where the action was taking place. To his credit, Crane studiously avoided the use of his program to ever injure the Merc's image during the sting operation.

Around mid-April, our Blue Ribbon Panel presented its findings. Even Senator Eagleton was generally satisfied, although he had some dissensions. In a congratulatory letter to me he stated, "These recommendations and the investigation which preceded them mark a milestone in the evolution of the commodity futures self-regulation. The Special Committee's study was more intense and far-ranging than any previously conducted by a commodities exchange."

Of much greater relevance was the *Chicago Tribune* editorial of April 26, 1989. The editors were downright flattering, first in their approval of the creation of the Special Committee and, second, in its recommendations.

> Leo Melamed, architect of Chicago's financial futures market, is an outspoken champion of self-regulation, and it's easy to see why. With Melamed as its chief policymaker, the Chicago Mercantile Exchange has been a consistent industry leader in new products and services while remaining largely free of heavy government interference. But Melamed knows that self-regulation is a right that can disappear rapidly if an institution doesn't act responsibly. Faced with increasing global competition and a government investigation of industry trading practices, he's fighting hard to preserve that right.

Among the sweeping reforms we proposed were the ban of dual trading in all highly liquid contract months, a number of critical restrictions concerning broker groups, doubling the Merc's 10-person surveillance staff, picking up trading cards every half hour, and appointing nonexchange members to all major Merc disciplinary committees. We had even gone so far as to recommend the installation of video cameras that would zero in on individual members in the pits suspected of wrongdoing.

They were potent recommendations. They had to be. As the *Tribune* correctly indicated, if we lost self-regulation, we would lose the other side of the coin, too—innovation. "We cannot afford to lose," I recall telling a reporter at the time.

The ban on dual trading was as critical a reform as any the Special Committee proposed. It represented a revolutionary departure from the norm for futures markets where it was always legal for a member to simultaneously be a trader for one's own account and to act as a broker for a customer. Such dual trading is standard procedure in virtually every futures market worldwide, as well as within most securities exchanges (for certain classes of members on the floor), and throughout the cash markets; it also is a widespread legitimate practice at most major securities brokerage firms. Indeed, there is nothing inherently evil about such duality of functions, and it has been argued that dual trading benefits market liquidity. However, dual trading, by definition, can create a conflict of interest, and it provides opportunity for hanky-panky by the unscrupulous. And in the tumultuous environment of a futures pit, the opportunities for such trading abuses are heightened. Consequently, dual trading has always given our markets a bad image, and it has been a source of interminable accusations that the practice leads to customer abuses. In my view and the view of all the other committee members, there was more to be gained from a ban on dual trading than would be lost in market liquidity.

In 1987, just before the crash, I had encouraged the Merc in its first experiment with limiting dual trading. The process began with a petition to ban S&P dual trading initiated by four members: Bill Shepard, Ed Charlip, Cliff Kabumotto, and Joel Stender. They and many other members were concerned that alleged dual trading abuses were endangering the sanctity of index futures at the Merc. Their petition led to the creation of the so-called Top Step Rule, which limited the top step of the S&P pit to floor brokers and prohibited all top step brokers from trading for their own accounts. This rule affected about 90 percent of S&P public business and went a long way in correcting the perception of front running and other alleged pit abuses. The rule is still in force and has been a model for the futures industry.

Before the implementing a floor-wide dual trading ban, the Board first created a dual trading committee which was headed by IMM governor Steve Wollack—who later became a contender for the Merc chairmanship. This committee held floor hearings and eventually endorsed the Blue Ribbon Panel's recommendation. In subsequent referenda, the majority of Merc members consistently voted in favor of the dual trading ban. The Merc is still today the only futures exchange with such a ban in place.

The Special Committee recommendations pertaining to broker groups also represented dramatic reforms. The committee tried to balance the constructive values of broker associations with their potential for abuse and undue influence. Among the most consequential recommendations were: the prohibition of members of broker associations from trading for their personal accounts with others in the same association; a 25 percent limitation on the amount of customer orders that a member of a broker association could execute with another broker of the same association; and the establishment of a registration procedure to identify the membership of all broker associations.

It was the latter rule that resulted in an unexpected event. During the broker group registration process, Sandner officially advised the Merc that he had a financial interest in the ABS Partners broker association. It meant that Sandner had served on the Special Committee to Review Trading Practices with a connection to a broker group—contrary to what he had sworn to me prior to his appointment. In doing so, he had put the credibility of the Blue Ribbon Panel in jeopardy. Although he didn't commit a rule violation, he violated my trust and endangered the Exchange. I was furious.

One late afternoon, we faced off near the elevator bank that separated the RB&H and Dellsher offices on the 19th floor of the south tower of the CME Center. It was a shouting match. And I stormed away from him. He followed me back to my office to apologize. He was sorry, he said, that he had jeopardized the process but he was afraid for his career. He said all the things he should have said up front, but didn't.

I let it drop. To make a public issue over it would have reignited the flames of the government's investigation. More important, it might have injured the very positive results of the Special Committee. We were the first futures exchange in the nation to recommend such sweeping measures. I decided that it was far better to preserve the reforms achieved than to dwell on Sandner's indiscretion. But the issue didn't go unnoticed by the press. In the October 2, 1989, issue of *The Wall Street Journal*, it was reported that "John F. Sandner received investment income from one of the Chicago Mercantile Exchange's most active broker groups while serving on a 'blue-ribbon' panel that was convened this year to recommend rule changes affecting Merc floor broker groups and others." The report added: "The apparent conflict between Mr. Sandner's investment and his role on the special panel could stir controversy." I had to fend off a barrage of media criticism.

During the process of implementation of the reforms, Senator Eagleton again became disenchanted with the futures industry. The reform process did not come as quickly or as smoothly as Eagleton would have liked. In July, he sent me a letter saying, "You have an enormously difficult job. You have genuinely—at times, valiantly—tried to lead the cause for constructive reform of trading practices and constructive reform of self-regulation . . . but your troops, by and large, don't want any reform." Then, in a flash of the exquisite humor the Senator was known for, he said, "Leo, you are worse off than General Custer. At least he had a few troops and a couple of sympathetic historians." It gave me a laugh, but needless to say, I did not agree with his sentiments.

Throughout 1989, I spent endless hours in Washington, together with Geldermann, Brodsky, Donovan, and Mahlman explaining to lawmakers why we thought self-regulation was working, while the federal investigation moved toward a wave of promised indictments. Over eight months, FBI agents issued some 500 subpoenas, conducted about 500 interviews, and reviewed more than a million documents. It turned out to be a colossal waste of taxpayers funds.

On a sunny but muggy August 2, with the press poised in the Everett Dirksen Federal Building—ironically named after a friend of the futures exchanges—the first round of indictments was handed down at 2:00 P.M.: 46 people—45 of them traders and one a trader's clerk—were indicted on a total of 608 charges for alleged illegal trading practices at the Merc and CBOT. From the Merc were 21 Japanese yen traders and three Swiss franc traders, and from the CBOT were 19 soybean traders and 3 bond traders. Eighteen of those indicted were charged with RICO or RICO conspiracy violations, which carried penalties of up to 20 years in prison, forfeiture of trading seats, and any other assets that may have been derived from illegal transactions.

Valukas piously told the press, which included correspondents from Japan, France, Great Britain, and Canada, "We are talking about hundreds of customers and thousands of trades. We are not talking about technical violations. It can be described as wide-ranging activity." Yet as the *New York Times* reported the next day, "Many brokers and traders who were interviewed said that they thought the indictments pinpointed a few corrupt individuals and that the intense scrutiny of any industry would reveal a comparable level of corruption." After two years of intense investigation of the more than 6,000 brokers and traders at the Merc and CBOT, 46 people had been identified by Valukas as participants in the "systematic theft of customer funds on customer orders."

The accusations seemed all the more serious given the appearance of Valukas's boss, Attorney General Richard Thornburgh, who came to Chicago from Washington along with FBI director William Sessions and CFTC Chair Wendy Gramm to announce the culmination of the two-year investigation. It was an unabashed publicity grab. In his comments to the press, Thornburgh emphasized that the indictments did not implicate either the two exchanges or brokerage houses. "This probe is part of an expanding Department of Justice crackdown on white-collar crime from Wall Street to LaSalle Street to Main Street with all stops in between," he said. "The activities at these exchanges, the largest of their type in the world, cannot be tolerated."

Given the importance the media attached to the indictments and the publicity attendant to their announcement, it could have been a heavy blow to the image of the Merc. To minimize the damage, the following day, August 3, the Merc held a press conference in its boardroom. Pounding my fist on the table, I intoned, "We will put the fear of God in anyone who breaks the rules of this Exchange." While the intensity of my statement was mostly for effect, I meant it, and we were prepared to back it up. My single-minded goal was to safeguard the Merc's future.

Once again, Eagleton was on the attack. This time it had to do with the fact that GNP, the clearing firm of former CME Chairman Brian P. Monieson, had been accused by the CFTC of inadequate supervision when two of its salesmen allegedly violated customer trading rules. The CFTC had finally found something they could sink their teeth into that involved a former Merc big shot and they were going to play it to the hilt. Ironically, the alleged violations were not related to floor practices and had nothing to do with the sting operation. What set Eagleton off was when he learned that Jerry Salzman had received Merc permission to be privately hired by Monieson as defense attorney. Eagleton went ballistic. He publicly announced that that was "the last straw"; he resigned as a Merc public director, and went on to state that "Self-regulation is the Chicago mirage," and that the CFTC was "a sleeping pygmy."

I was of course upset and sorry about the incident. Eagleton and I were on a different wavelength. When Brian Monieson, a close personal friend who had continuously served within my inner circle and who had been Merc chairman during some of Clayton Yeutter's term as CME president, asked me to testify as character witness at his forthcoming CFTC hearing, I readily agreed. Although there were some members at the Merc who criticized me, as an officer of the CME, for accepting such a request, I ignored these criticisms without even a second thought. Friendship to me is holy. But to everyone's surprise, U.S. Secretary of Agriculture, Clayton Yeutter, also accepted Monieson's request. It was a rare insight to the man's strength of character.

For me, the character and moral values of individuals are best examined and verified under stress. It is easy enough to be a friend to someone when he is on top, but it is more telling when things have gone awry. As Henry Jarecki later said to me, *"Amicus certus in re incerta scernitur"* (the sure friend proves himself in the unsure situation). Even more telling is the part of the story few knew about. Yeutter received a letter strongly criticizing his decision from two powerful U.S. Senators, J. James Exon and J. Robert Kerrey. Without beating around the bush, the senators said that Yeutter's testimony on behalf of a friend was in conflict with his official position as Secretary of Agriculture. In one of the finest examples of moral fortitude, Clayton

Yeutter never even flinched. In his response to the senators, Yeutter stated simply: "Life is too short for us to avoid or ignore our responsibilities to our fellow man. If that conflicts with my position as Secretary of Agriculture, then I would give up the position before I would shirk my responsibility as a human being."

To its credit, the *Chicago Tribune* ran an editorial that put the matter into proper focus. "Testifying for former friends in such proceedings is done all the time in other industries. And Eagleton, who had been a public governor since 1987, had said he planned to step down at the end of this year anyway." In a subsequent letter to Clayton Yeutter, I told him that even though our character references were of no help in the ultimate outcome of the proceedings (the penalties against GNP and Monieson were harsh), his appearance on behalf of Brian Monieson was a magnificent tribute to the American system of government and made him 10 feet tall to our members.

The CFTC had no choice but to show a tough side at a time when it was up for reauthorization. And to prove that they weren't biased against Chicago, in May the CFTC and the Manhattan branch of the U.S. attorney's office—with the aid of the U.S. Postal Inspection Service—issued subpoenas for the records of a number of New York traders as well as the four New York futures exchanges in a criminal and civil investigation of trading practices.

The New York investigation had no connection to the probe of the Chicago exchanges, but it did strike yet another blow to an industry reeling from negative publicity. Even Senator Patrick Leahy, a Democrat from Vermont, and sponsor of the CFTC reauthorization bill, who was a good friend of mine and Henry Jarecki's, and fully recognized the importance of futures markets, became worried. He told the press he viewed the New York investigation as an indication "that concerns about floor trading practices are not limited to Chicago, but rather are industry-wide." Privately, Senator Leahy, Henry Jarecki and I commiserated over the possible damage to our industry as a result of the investigations.

In mid-October 1989, the two Chicago exchanges were back before the Senate Agriculture Committee in Washington, pleading the case against a pending bill intended to end open outcry trading. Illinois senators Alan Dixon and Paul Simon both made special appearances to speak on behalf of the Merc and CBOT. Such legislation, they argued, would cripple one of Chicago's and the state's most important industries. Citing a study published by the Commercial Club of Chicago in 1987, they stated that our two futures exchanges—along with the CBOE and Chicago Stock Exchange—were of enormous economic value to the Illinois community. Perhaps even more meaningful was the help provided by Senator Rudy E. Boschwitz, a

Republican from Minnesota, who had come to the Senate from the private sector and was an outspoken advocate of open and competitive markets. Boschwitz eventually became a Merc public governor.

Of course, if the stock market was any indicator, scandals had little impact on investor attitude. In New York, after Dennis Levine, Ivan Boesky, and a band of colorful bankers and brokers were nailed for insider trading schemes, the market shrugged off the negative implications and surged to a record high on August 24, 1989. A similar reaction seemed likely in Chicago. Barry Lind's firm, Lind-Waldock & Co., by then the largest discount futures company in the nation, conducted a private investor confidence survey in April 1989. The questionnaire was sent to 4,353 individual investors, with 1,142 responses (26 percent). Only 12 respondents stated that they stopped trading as a result of the government investigation. Nearly 70 percent of the respondents believed the trading pits at the exchanges operated efficiently and honestly.

On April 24, 1989, a CME membership sold for $554,000, a record high.

34

A Farewell to Arms

Although the sting operation was extremely disruptive, life moved on. Times were changing. The CME's turf was no longer Chicago but the world, via the GLOBEX flying carpet. And I encouraged everyone to come along on the ride. "Those who ignore the march of science and technology will soon be history," I exhorted. "GLOBEX will offer the world a transaction capability as far-reaching as the future itself."

Not everyone saw that at first. Two years earlier, when the Merc's GLOBEX introduction was first made, it did not, to say the least, generate wild enthusiasm down the street at the CBOT. Rather, we were immediately labeled as traitors to the sacrosanct concept of open outcry. Were it not that the idea of a 24-hour electronic transaction system was so obviously right and the rest of the world's futures community was so roundly applauding GLOBEX, the CBOT might have dug in its heels. But when all was said and done, the Board of Trade had to admit the truth and knew precisely what it had to do. As CBOT Chairman Mahlman put it, "You can't defend against atomic warfare without an H-bomb of your own." So they went back to the drawing board and came up with Aurora, an alternative electronic trading system to GLOBEX. Aurora, they claimed, would be better because it would be their own electronic system, not owned by Reuters, and would carefully replicate the pit. What followed was the greatest competitive battle between the Merc and the CBOT in our entire history. Again, all stops were pulled, and both exchanges spent huge sums to advance their respective electronic systems. At stake, both exchanges realized, was the future of futures.

By then, I had persuaded the Merc Board to transform the GLOBEX concept into an international system, a sort of futures market utility, so that we could invite other major exchanges of the world onto our system. As I saw it, every exchange wanted to offer its products internationally around the clock and needed an after-hours electronic system to do it. Reuters was of course delighted with the idea. We devised an elaborate

GLOBEX structure that would include a separate board of directors; I was made its interim chairman, and we made presentations to the other exchanges to join our system. The CBOT followed suit, claiming its system could do it better and for less money. The race was on, each of us wooing all the other exchanges around the world. We had even each retained expert public relations firms for the battles. The climax came at the Boca Raton annual FIA conference in March 1989, when the CME and the CBOT made high-tech presentations of their respective electronic systems to a standing-room-only audience. It was the show of shows for the futures industry—a battle of its titans.

But we were winning. Our strategy—which included promoting that we were first with the concept—had the full force of my personal credentials behind the effort, offered the world a single unified after-hours transaction system, and had the credibility provided by the Reuters name. It proved to be an invincible combination of factors. Jack Sandner and I quickly became a two-man GLOBEX sales team and entered into negotiations with a number of American and foreign exchanges for whom the concept had great appeal. In my mind, the turning point in our competitive fray came with the announcement in Boca Raton that the *Marché a Terme International de France* (MATIF), had joined GLOBEX. As in most things in life, it was the chemistry of personalities that made the difference. From the moment we met, Gerard Pfauwadel, the chairman of MATIF, an extremely bright and erudite Parisian, and I developed a mutual respect, friendship, and rapport that was unshakable. He embraced the vision of a universal after-hours global trading system for futures and options as passionately as I had. It not only fit his own image of tomorrow's world, it gave him entrée to what he viewed as an imperative technological capability for his exchange. Pfauwadel knew that in his battle for European futures market dominance—a battle in which his main competitor the British LIFFE had an upper hand—GLOBEX could play a critical role. The MATIF remains today the strongest user and proponent of GLOBEX. Its favorable decision gave the Merc the upper hand in our war with CBOT. But more important, it provided us an opportunity to emulate the Cold War, which at the time was thawing, and embark on our own era of *glasnost*.

In my heart of hearts I knew that the fight between the CME and CBOT was stuff and nonsense. And a huge waste of money. The CBOT had already spent some $25 million developing Aurora and my information was that their costs were about to escalate. By contrast, the Merc's costs were merely a couple of million dollars for administrative necessities. The arrangement that I had negotiated with Reuters provided that they would build the system, irrespective of what it cost. That turned out to be an incomparable advantage for Merc members, since the ultimate GLOBEX system reputedly cost Reuters some $100 million. The plan we fostered from the start was one that Barry Lind, Brian Monieson, and I discussed endlessly—the key was the CBOT. It was a strategy based on logic and reason: after GLOBEX was successful in bringing aboard one or two other futures exchanges and after the costs to the CBOT in developing Aurora became prohibitive, they would recognize the value of being a partner to our system. Once we made the deal with the CBOT, we could sit and wait for the globalization process to evolve. It seemed clear to me that the attraction of being on the same global electronic after-hours system that included the world's two largest exchanges would eventually become an irresistible magnet for most, if not all, the other world's exchanges. The beauty and cost-efficiency of a unified world system was too obvious to argue. In time, we could even extend GLOBEX to include securities options trading, and, above everything, Chicago would be assured of its status as the capital of futures markets. The principal element for success of this goal was to bring the CBOT and the CME together on one system. I relied heavily on the logic that there was no rationale for the two Chicago exchanges to compete when our competition was global and not on the American shore.

With MATIF as a partner, I thought the time was ideal to take the first step at reconciliation with the CBOT. In all delicate matters of this nature, I knew timing to be as important as substance. I discussed the strategy at length with officials at Reuters and with CME Chairman John Geldermann who was totally in step with the goal but did not believe that I could ever convince the CBOT. Nevertheless, he agreed that we had nothing to lose in making the attempt. Since he was about to leave on a prescheduled trip, we agreed that Jack Sandner would join me at the outset. I then called Tom Donovan at the CBOT and arranged for him and their chairman Karsten Mahlman to meet with Sandner and myself for informal discussions. So as not to arouse the press, the meeting took place in the conference room of my firm, Dellsher Investment Company. The four of us talked for about an hour. The key ingredient was our offer to create a joint system in which the two exchanges were *equal* partners. I knew that CBOT pride, coupled with the fact that their financial futures volume was about the same as the Merc's, would make equality a mandatory provision of any agreement between us. The result of that meeting was a preliminary understanding, subject to approval of our respective boards, that the Merc and the CBOT would form a special committee to examine the possibility of unification of our different electronic systems. It represented yet another impressive milestone in the history of futures. The odds against the two Chicago arch-rivals ever getting together on so radical a concept were "astronomical," as John Geldermann told me privately.

Of course, our understanding was but a preliminary handshake; the real agreement was nearly two years away.

It became our highest priority, suspended all other negotiations, and overwhelmed all our other endeavors. I chaired what amounted to an intensive year and a half of negotiations between a special team of representatives from both exchanges. It was an experience probably on a par with a peace mission between the Hatfields and McCoys, except we were successful. Our negotiations went into high gear when my friend of many years William O'Conner took over the chairmanship of the CBOT. O'Conner's global vision and belief in technology was in synch with my own. Early in the process, we agreed that GLOBEX would be the surviving entity for both our exchanges. However, the myriad technical questions, the system's specifications, its upgrades and priorities, coupled with the structural considerations of how a unified GLOBEX, owned jointly by the CME and CBOT and operated by Reuters would function and operate, were enormous. It required John Hull and David Silverman of Reuters who had devised the original system to join the negotiation process. On our side of the fence, I relied heavily on Scott Gordon who led our technology committee and the advice of Barry Lind, as well as that of Bill Shepard, whom I had appointed to the committee. The CBOT also had some very skilled representatives of its own, but its strongest advisor was Burt Gutterman who was a technological expert and extremely demanding that Reuters provide us the best system possible.

There were some who thought that the CBOT was playing a Machiavellian game to delay the process and thereby stymie GLOBEX. I never believed that for a moment. Rather, I saw Tom Donovan and Bill O'Conner consistently press forward and assist me in compromising issues wherever possible. Although the process took much longer than I had hoped, it resulted in a monumental accomplishment: a long-range agreement between the CME, the CBOT, the MATIF, and Reuters. It was as historic a moment as the original GLOBEX announcement in 1987. We had changed the course of futures market history, again. The GLOBEX corporation was formed, I was elected its first chairman, and Merton Miller and Beryl Sprinkel its public directors. To a majority within the futures world, it represented a near miracle. While GLOBEX was still a long way from being operational, for me, Tom Donovan, and a few others, it seemed that the era of common goals between our two exchanges had dawned.

Indeed, it was a sign of the times. In Washington D.C., the Merc and the CBOT had fought side by side to further our interests and those of the futures industry; we were together in the shadows of the FBI sting and the impending trials of our respective traders; on a technological front several years before, we had jointly undertaken to develop Computerized Trade

Reconstruction; and recently, in a joint undertaking we had created AUDIT, the Automated Data Input Terminal system of handheld electronic trading cards. The two exchanges had even agreed to begin discussions on a unified clearing system which would produce the largest, most secure clearing organization of its kind in the world. *Glasnost* was breaking out all over the world.

By early 1990, I was feeling a bit worn, but the better for it. I had guided the Merc through its development of financial contracts, its rise to equality with the CBOT, its internationalization, and recently through its crucial periods of the 1987 crash, the FBI sting, and the introduction of GLOBEX. Thoughts of retirement were again surfacing in my mind and I began to seriously consider the possibility. A quarter of a century of dedicated service to any one institution is a lifetime of work. And I was still young and energetic enough to do what I had neglected for so long, perhaps to build my small Dellsher firm into a world-class financial futures and options organization, perhaps again to concentrate on trading, perhaps to travel, to do things with our children, play with our grandchildren, and perhaps write more books (I had already started a sequel to *The Tenth Planet* called *Cousins*). Whatever I did, I knew I would never be bored in my pursuit of other matters. But I didn't know how long it would take to officially wean myself away from the institution that was as much a part of me as a family member. After months of deliberations with family and friends, I had reached a decision that could not be altered. In December 1989, I had already resigned as chairman of the National Futures Association, a clear indication that I was winding down. But my retirement announcement from Merc affairs caught a lot of people off guard. I carefully prepared for the announcement in secret, working with Alysann Posner who readied over a thousand faxes to be simultaneously sent out. On March 5, 1990, at a meeting of the Merc board of governors, I announced that decision: to retire at the end of the year. This was followed by a special news conference, attended by the entire business media corps in Chicago. "There comes a moment in everyone's career when he knows in his heart it is time for a change," I stated in a letter sent to the membership timed to my announcement. "After 23 years at the leadership of the Chicago Mercantile Exchange, that time has come for me."

My retirement coincided with dramatic global changes of an unprecedented nature. Within the span of several short years, those citizens of planet Earth, fortunate enough to have been present at the tail end of the twentieth century, were privileged to have witnessed some of the most monumental events of this era, events equal to any celebrated milestone in the history of mankind: the fall of the Berlin Wall, the unification of Germany, the end to the Cold War, the disintegration of the Communist empire, the liberalization of Eastern Europe, and the end to apartheid. Indeed, we were ring-side spectators at a near-global insurrection that unshackled the chains of political and economic systems that had threatened the sanctity of world peace and enslaved a full third of the world population.

What a magnificent triumph of democracy and freedom—a monument to Winston Churchill, Andrei Sakharov, Mikhail Gorbachev, Lech Walesa, and Nelson Mandela. What a glorious victory for capitalism and market-driven economic order—a majestic tribute to Thomas Jefferson, Adam Smith, and Milton Friedman. What a divine time to be alive.

Not that the world will now be free of strife or tyrants. Utopia, I am afraid, has not yet arrived. Indeed, the Gulf War and the war in Bosnia were stark reminders that my mother's Bialystok Syndrome is alive and well.

But for my father it represented the last curtain. It was almost as if he had waited until the last vestige of the tyrannical epoch that he despised, that had been party to the rupture of the glorious potential of Yiddish and its culture, that had helped destroy Jewish civilization and sent him and his family into the Diaspora, had finally disintegrated. On October 14, 1990, after two years of failing health, Isaac Moishe Melamdovich passed away. For me it was like the second crash. It was the first crash in the lives of my children, Idelle, Jordan, and David, who were extremely close to their grandfather. He had given them the same deep feelings for Yiddish and for the equality of mankind that he had instilled in me.

It was standing-room only at the funeral where what remained of Chicago's Jewish cultural sphere came to pay their last respects. A large contingent of futures market representatives both from the Merc and the CBOT came as well. Professor Nathanial Stampfer of Spertus College presided. As my father would have demanded, his services were a departure from the norm. In his honor, I read in Yiddish a poem by Kalmen Liss entitled *Is Gefalen a Demb* (*A Giant Oak Falls*), that epitomized my father's stature in the Yiddish cultural forest and the vacuum that would be felt by surrounding trees as a result of his passing. Idelle and David offered some poignant personal reflections, and Jordan delivered a moving tribute at the gravesite. As part of the eulogy, Danny Newman, my father's friend and Lyric Opera publicist, heralded him as one of the last pillars of Chicago's Yiddish culture. On October 31, 1990, the City Council of Chicago introduced an official resolution commemorating Isaac Melamed's contribution to the Jewish community of the city.

Three years later, on February 20, 1993, my mother, Chay Faygl Melamdovich, née Barakin, would join her beloved husband. To the end of her life, she continued to bond with my wife, our children, and her grandchildren, offering them the warmth, understanding, and sensitivity that was her specialty. Betty, our children, and I conducted a similar funeral ceremony on her passing as we did for my father. Jordan delivered a poem he had written, entitled *Bobie Taught Us to Fly*. Indeed, an era had passed.

Perhaps fate saw fit, in commemoration of my father's passing, to invite me back to the part of the world from which our family stemmed. At the invitation of the Soviet government, in the last week of October 1990, I agreed to lead a delegation of senior officials from the Merc and CBOT to Moscow. We had come to sign a commodity market cooperation agreement with the city of Moscow, the Moscow Commodity Exchange, and the Federation of Russia. From the Merc, I was accompanied by our Chairman John Geldermann and his wife Jane, and Bill and Joan Brodsky. From the CBOT were Chairman William O'Connor and his fiancée, Mary Jane Callans, and CBOT President Tom Donovan and his wife Vita.

I was returning to Moscow, the city that had been so crucial in my escape 50 years earlier. Then I took a train through its back door; now I entered through its front aboard a streamlined jet. It was a far different Moscow from the one I experienced as a child, although physically it looked the same. The childhood luster that had aroused my senses was now replaced by an air of gloom. You could feel the tension brought on by the creaking pillars of central planning about to topple. Although Gorbachev was still in power as president, we had arrived within earshot of the breathtaking revolution that was sweeping like wildfire across this part of the world.

In an attempt to save the Soviet Union, President Gorbachev had reached for the tenets of capitalism, knowing full well it would take more than a few market reforms and the transfer of state-owned companies into private hands. Earlier, he told the Soviet Congress of Peoples Deputies, "We must get down to creating a full-blooded domestic market . . . Steps to create first commodity and then stock exchanges will become necessary in this respect." He wanted to succeed without bringing his own rule down. But he didn't.

The KGB had yet to come in from the cold, as witnessed by our official government guides who steered us away from the proletariat. "Who better knows Moscow than the KGB," said Serge, the guide personally assigned to me, a man with a quick wit, intense blue eyes, and a stiff-backed demeanor. "I know New York, too," he confided. "I had 21 missions to the United Nations."

The Soviet markets were only cash auctions, or barter markets covering a variety of items such as building materials, computers, and other consumer goods. I was given the honor of ringing the bell at the official opening of the Moscow Commodity Exchange. The first trade: an exchange of a million Marlboro cigarettes for a personal computer.

Then it was off to the Kremlin where we spent an hour with Leonid I. Abalkin, Gorbachev's economic minister. To become a modern economic state, Abalkin agreed, Russia had to transform its ruble into a convertible currency. That would not happen soon from what I had seen. During our tours and visits to the well-known stops, I sensed an air of desperation. Everywhere I looked there were acute shortages of consumer goods from apples to vodka. Everyone we talked to seemed worried, cynical, and depressed. "We pretend to work, and they pretend to pay us," was a well-known saying that aptly described the Russian economic order. The infrastructure, too, left something to be desired, as I learned firsthand. There I was, in the Kremlin, the nerve center of a superpower that had balanced half the world on its shoulders for 70 years, and I had one modest request: to use the telephone. I wanted to place an order to the stock index futures pit at the CME. It would have been a first in Russian history, a pure capitalistic transaction by a private party from within the Kremlin walls. But it wasn't to be. Even from the Kremlin, apologized Abalkin, the telephone connection to Chicago would take several hours to make. It would have been comical if it weren't so sad. In typical communist fashion, comrade Abalkin suggested that I take a photograph with a phone in my hand and pretend I made a trade. To pretend, I explained, would be a violation of CFTC rules.

I may have achieved an historical first anyway when, on November 1, 1990, as keynoter, I delivered an impassioned capitalistic speech in the Kremlin to over 500 guests who had come to hear the free marketeers from Chicago. To my delight, in the question-and-answer session following, I was asked how soon GLOBEX would be operational in Russia.

But the highlight of my Moscow trip occurred on the last night of our visit at a farewell party. We were the guests of the Federation of Russia along with some 40 officials from the Russian equivalent to the CFTC and SEC. On that cold November evening, we had gathered at the famous Writers' Union, the exclusive club of the Communist party. A light snow fell outside and a huge fire crackled brightly in the banquet hall that was a scene out of John LeCarre's *The Russia House*, "Dark timber, splendid food, respectful menials, the atmosphere of a baronial lodge."

Spirits ran high that night and the vodka flowed. For every toast one of the Russians made, custom called for a member of our delegation to offer a toast in return. A Russian toast, Serge explained, is anything that comes to your mind. I was worried that our side might have a problem keeping pace. Fortunately, Pepsi-Cola was available for some of the teetotalers. In their toasts (translated to us by Serge) the Russians told stories about their childhoods, about their grandmothers, about their philosophies of life, and so on. Late in the night, I knew we were in trouble when Billy O'Connor returned a Russian toast with a roaring tribute to the squeaky hinges on the banquet hall door. Donovan and I exchanged glances—it was time to go.

I turned to Serge for advice. The celebration, he said, could end any time I called for the last toast. So I rose to do the honors. By now everyone in the room knew my personal history and of my escape route through Moscow that led to freedom. Serge stood beside me to translate.

"As everyone in this room knows," I said, raising my glass, "I had been to Moscow as a small child, exactly 50 years ago." Everyone raised his glass and nodded in agreement.

"What you don't know was that at that time I took a secret oath to return in 50 years—and here I am." The Russians applauded.

"And tonight," I continued, "I have taken another oath—*not* to return for another 50 years."

It brought down the house. The Russians, if anything, were cynical enough to appreciate the meaning of my toast.

Upon my departure, as we were standing in the airplane terminal, Serge politely requested a copy of *The Tenth Planet* as a farewell gift for his labors. I was somewhat surprised that he knew about the book, and I assured him I would send him a copy immediately upon my return to Chicago.

"No need to wait," he smiled, pointing to my baggage. "You have a copy in that suitcase." He was right. I had forgotten; indeed, a copy of *The Tenth Planet* was in my suitcase. I guess once KGB, always KGB.

As planned, I left Moscow to meet Betty in Paris where we were guests of Charmaine and Gerard Pfauwadel, the chairman of MATIF. While there, I delivered a talk to the Alumni Association of Ecole Polytechnique, Pfauwadel's alma mater and perhaps the most distinguished institution of higher learning in all of France. It represented my first assessment of what I had just learned from our visit to Moscow at the dawn of post-communist rule. Our Parisian visit was also an opportunity to catch up with Samuel Pisar, the famous international attorney and fellow Bialystoker, and his wife Judith. Pisar's life history was parallel to mine. However, Pisar, unlike me, did not escape Nazi enslavement. Nevertheless, he survived Auschwitz and at the age of 16 began his difficult climb back to life and ultimately achieved world fame and acclaim. In his well-known autobiography *Of Blood and Hope*, he admits that like me, my father, and so many others who survived the Holocaust, he at first refused to return to those places where, as he says: "I saw my world, my people, my family, my school friends, my identity systematically destroyed, where I myself barely escaped physical obliteration as a captive of the Soviet empire and a subhuman of the Third Reich." Those were precisely my father's sentiments when year after year I suggested that we do a pilgrimage back to Poland. He categorically refused, saying that for him there was nothing left to return to. That was painfully true. But like all survivors, Samuel Pisar and I found a strong bond based on a common heritage and history.

My informal remarks in Paris were a practice run for my formal address in London at the Merc's sixth annual symposium the following week. To an audience that attracted more than 300 industry people from all over Europe, I offered a rather depressing assessment of Russia. It was a rude awakening to a world generally euphoric about the new *perestroika* that was emerging from Moscow. While I too was exceedingly elated that free-market forces of supply and demand had finally overwhelmed the centrally planned economic order based on communist rule, my Moscow visit provided a large dose of firsthand realism.

"To say the country is bankrupt is to misconstrue the actual desperation of the situation," I told the audience both in Paris and London, which was eager to learn how quickly they could invest in the new Russian economy.

> Stalinist command economy and rigid central control has molded an obedi-ent, passive labor force that is plagued by heavy absenteeism, idleness on the job, poor-quality work, low morale, and serious alcoholism. Cheating and fakery is an accepted way of life. Decades of central planning, decades of dependence on the state, have obliterated most incentives in the average Russian. If the average worker had a choice between the free market and a guaranteed salary, he is apt to choose the guarantee. For the great masses of Soviet people, capitalism is still a dirty word. Thus, it is bound to be a painfully slow process. I am afraid it is generational. I am afraid things will get much worse before they get better.

But in the United States, as well as in Chicago, things were looking up. January 1991 brought good news both from Desert Storm as well as opera-tions Hedgeclipper and Sourmash. In the Middle East, the United States and its United Nations allies used a rapid-fire stream of deadly technology to rebuff Saddam Hussein's aggressions in a 100-hour rout of Iraq. In Chicago, federal jurors provided a favorable close to the dark chapter in fu-tures markets created by the FBI sting operation. There are some 6,000 members of the CME and CBOT. Of the 48 individuals indicted two years earlier, 36 had been convicted or pleaded guilty, many to minor infractions, 10 faced a retrial on remaining charges, and 2 were acquitted. That's all there was to it. At the CBOT, in spite of all the federal allegations, only 10 soybean traders were convicted of defrauding customers through illicit trades. At the CME, in the case of 12 Japanese yen traders, the jury reached a verdict on March 13 without any convictions. The jurors had voted not guilty on more than 100 commodity, mail, and wire fraud counts. Two of the yen traders were cleared of all charges and the jury failed to reach ver-dicts on 80 counts against the other 10 traders. The judge was forced to de-clare a mistrial. Previously, in the case of three Swiss franc traders from the Merc, one of the traders was convicted of 20 charges, another of one charge, and a third was acquitted of violations of commodity law.

In the end, all the hype from federal authorities and the media implying the futures game was fixed proved hollow and shameful. Eighteen months after the sting surfaced, the *Chicago Tribune*, which had broken the initial story and was the most strident in its coverage, concluded: ". . . the multimillion-dollar federal probe has hardly lived up to its billing, and the mixed jury results may make other traders less eager to cooperate."

But long before the trials were over, the world judged the Chicago exchanges as being sound markets. Merc trading volume had soared as an indication that what we were doing for the world was important, providing economic value for our users. While the Justice Department's investigation on trading floor practices had cast a shadow on Chicago's futures industry and provided an incentive in establishing stricter trading rules and enforcement procedures, the integrity of the CME and CBOT never came into question.

I felt extremely satisfied leaving the Merc's helm when I did. My history of over two decades spoke for itself. And, as a final contribution, I thought I had put the Merc membership on a solid footing for its next step toward the twenty-first century by bringing GLOBEX to its doorstep. No one could shortchange the growth of the Merc under my stewardship. When I first became chairman in 1969, annual volume stood at 3.8 million contracts; at the close of 1990, the Merc had topped 100 million contracts. Another measurement was the phenomenal rise in membership values. Perhaps Brian Monieson's hyperbole dramatized it best, "Leo Melamed," he said, "had single-handedly produced more millionaires than any other person in the world." It wasn't a single-handed result by a long shot, but it is true that Merc members of 1972, as well as the initial IMM purchasers and others who became members early on, did fabulously well with their membership investments. In fact, at my retirement, a calculation was made that the cumulative value of one original Merc membership in 1969 (worth about $100,000), was worth on that day upwards of $1.5 million when the present value of the IMM distribution and other seat dividends over the years were counted.

The accolades followed. The board of governors awarded me the title of chairman emeritus. The Chicago Mercantile Exchange-endowed chair at the University of Chicago was renamed the "Leo Melamed Chair." And there were the goodbye bashes. My friend Tom Dittmer threw an extravagant farewell party for me at his house with a copy of *The Tenth Planet* at each table. The guests were asked to volunteer their thoughts about my service to the industry. These thoughts were then included in a bound volume and presented to me. There were many poignant remarks that are memorable. For instance, Clayton Yeutter's comment that "no one else's departure from a leadership role in the futures industry will leave such a gigantic trench to fill," was extremely touching.

But the eloquent words of Jack Sandner, my friend and compatriot of so many years to whom I now passed the torch of leadership, were the most noteworthy, particularly in view of the unexpected turn of events after my departure. Wrote Jack:

> To the world you have given an idea, just as Newton, Galileo, Copernicus, Euclid and other great thinkers and innovators did before you. Your idea, ultimately, like theirs, has and will continue to spawn many others that will have an immeasurable impact on the world. In our lifetime, because of you, we will see international trade burgeon, time zones disappear, and cooperation between countries, small and large, flourish. Most importantly, the world will be a better place because of you, your idea, your persevering spirit, your continued vision and your indefatigable energy to see it all through.

The Merc transformed its annual member's dinner dance into a gala retirement tribute held on January 26, 1991, in the Grand Ballroom of Chicago's Regency Hotel. It was a kind of "This is Your Life" coda of family, friends, and associates who had helped me achieve some of my goals over the years. It attracted the who's who of American and international finance.

Among the nearly 2,000 guests at the black-tie affair were domestic and foreign government officials; city and state officials; representatives from academia, commerce, and industry executives; civic leaders; and officials of the futures industry and its clearing member firms. The former Secretary of Agriculture, now chairman of the Republican Party, Clayton Yeutter was there, as was CFTC chairperson Wendy Gramm. Over the years, the Gramm's strong free-market beliefs served to draw us close. Indeed, Senator Phil Gramm, on May 5, 1992, read into the *Congressional Record* the speech I made in Tokyo entitled, "Protectionism: the Scourge of Markets." Nobel Laureates Milton Friedman and Merton Miller came and were featured speakers. Mayor Richard Daley, who like his father was a friend of mine, also came and announced that he had proclaimed January 26, 1991, to be "Leo Melamed Day in Chicago." Every major foreign futures market was represented: from Paris, came Gerard Pfauwadel; from London, David Burton; from Singapore, Elizabeth Sam and Ang Swee Tian; and from Australia, Leslie Hosking. My old friend and former Merc President E.B. Harris came, as did Beverly Splane. From the American markets, Dick Grasso, soon to become chairman of the New York Stock Exchange came, as did Mary Schapiro who would become the next chairperson at the CFTC. My greatest joy was that my mother was there to see the tribute to her immigrant boy who had made good. Bill Brodsky acted as master of ceremonies and Jack Sandner led the toast to me as his "friend and mentor."

The festivities also included a lighthearted video montage of my life at the Merc, poking fun of me in and out of the pit. Of all the speakers that evening, Barry Lind, in the introduction to the video presentation, captured the can-do spirit I had brought with me when I first arrived at the Merc in 1954 as a wide-eyed runner.

"Remember those old Judy Garland and Mickey Rooney movies," Lind said, "where one moment they are sitting in a barn in Indiana saying 'let's put on a show' and within 10 minutes they are opening on Broadway? It made great entertainment but it really wasn't plausible. Well, imagine Leo walking around an ailing Butter and Egg Exchange telling some guys who just found out that pork bellies were bacon that someday we would be members of the greatest agricultural and financial exchange in the world with a cast of thousands. Just as implausible, but then he went and did it."

Barry had nailed it. He knew from personal experience. Over the years, he had been one of the faithful beside me in the trenches during my battles on behalf of the Merc. I walked away that evening knowing in my heart that I had made a difference in pursuit of a mission. The farewell editorial of the *Chicago Tribune* on March 23, 1990, was entitled, "Leo Melamed, Father of Financial Futures." It paid me the highest tribute by comparing my accomplishments to some of the great American entrepreneurs: "Some may say it's too early to anoint Melamed a financial wizard and visionary, but there's no doubt he has made his mark, and Chicago is the better for it."

35

Tilt

In my first conversation with Milton Friedman after my retirement, the great man tried to warn me. "You won't like what the leaders do after you depart," he said. "You were a creator; that was your mission; that won't be *their* motivation."

At first, I could only guess at what Friedman meant. Oh sure, I knew that it would take me a little while to become uninvolved. After all, the Merc had been my body and soul. I also realized that I would not always agree with Merc decisions. Still, I vowed not to become a Monday morning quarterback. (On the anniversary of my departure, I actually sent the Board a letter of congratulations for a job well done.) Although my age was still far from real retirement status, I was prepared to assume the role of senior industry statesman pursuant to my new title of chairman emeritus. I expected the new Merc leadership, with Jack Sandner as chairman, to want to establish their own credentials, and I did not want to get in their way. If they made mistakes, I vowed they would have to live with them. Hopefully, none would be critical. Besides, as chairman emeritus, I would be there to offer advice. The fact that I would no longer attend board meetings would not change my willingness to come when invited. Sandner said as much shortly after he became chairman when he told a reporter, "I have always looked at Leo as a mentor and a teacher and a brilliant strategist, and I would be foolish not to adopt many of the policies and attitudes he represents. I would also be foolish not to call on him regularly to check my thinking with his." Well, it sounded good on paper, but over time, I learned what Friedman's prescient words foretold.

There was plenty to keep me busy. John Wiley & Sons, Inc. had contracted me to publish a collection of speeches I had made during the two decades of my Merc tenure. Alysann Posner and I became absorbed in the preparation of *Leo Melamed on the Markets*, published in 1993. Additionally, a good deal of my time was devoted to preparing for the merger between my firm Dellsher Investment Company and the financial giant

The Sakura Bank Limited, to form a new global futures firm, Sakura Dellsher Inc.

But I also became immersed in an entirely different endeavor, one that I considered holy. After my father's death, Benjamin Meed, one of the council members of the U.S. Holocaust Museum, planted an idea with me that wouldn't let me rest: "To honor your father's memory, you ought to get involved with the Museum . . . As a survivor, you owe this debt." His words had a deep impact on me and I immediately set about the task. In 1992, President Bush appointed me to the council. I quickly became a member of its executive committee, throwing my body and soul into the work involved. Directly after the museum opened, Chicago's Mayor Daley and I led a delegation of over 1,000 prominent Chicagoans to Washington D.C. for a commemorative celebration and a visit to the museum.

It wasn't long before I realized that one of the primary objectives of the Holocaust Museum had not yet been fulfilled. One of the sacred goals of Elie Wiesel when he chaired President Carter's commission, which gave rise to the creation of the National Holocaust Memorial Council, was to establish a permanent Committee of Conscience at the Museum. Unfortunately, 12 years previously, the attempt to create such a committee became tangled in politics, and failed. This now became my mission, and I formally reintroduced the concept. The idea was that the Holocaust Museum must use its powerful voice to *"alert the national conscience, influence policy makers, and stimulate worldwide action to confront and work to halt acts of genocide or crimes against humanity."* By speaking out against potential genocides, we would ensure that the Holocaust victims did not die in vain. During the following year, I worked in unison with Miles Lerman, the chair of the U.S. Holocaust Memorial Museum, Ruth Mandel, the council's vice chair, Hyman Bookbinder, a former U.S. congressman who had spearheaded the original effort, and several other council members to achieve the objective. On June 14, 1995, the Committee of Conscience became a permanent instrument of the U.S. Holocaust Museum.

Still, most of my life revolved around the markets and my first year of retirement ended on a high note. On the morning of December 11, 1991, President George Bush visited the trading floors of both the CBOT and Merc. In a speech before hundreds of Merc traders and prominent Chicago business people, he singled me out, referring to me as the "Babe Ruth of the futures industry."

His previous visit to the Merc had been in 1979 as a congressman. Ironically, it was Bush's Justice Department that had declared war on the Merc and CBOT and his administration that had pushed for stiffer regulation of our markets. And now here he was, olive branch in hand and presidential election around the corner. As the *Sun-Times* summed it up: "Nearly three years after the news that FBI agents had infiltrated the Board of Trade and Chicago Mercantile Exchange, Bush spent the morning praising the exchanges and declaring that "Chicago-style capitalism is the nation's best hope for the future."

Certainly, his appearance that morning was a vote of confidence for the Chicago futures exchanges. "The Merc has become a bellwether of the future because it never, ever lost the inventive spirit of its founders," Bush stated. "You defied the doomsayers when you pioneered that risk-pool management through the Exchange Trust. You established the first financial futures market, the International Monetary Market. You saw an international marketplace and established offices overseas before most exchanges even thought about setting up domestic branches. And you created the Eurodollar futures a decade ago—and I know you celebrated its tenth anniversary yesterday, and you should be very, very proud of this world leadership . . . ."

Afterwards, the President invited me, Sandner, Brodsky, and others to join him for cheeseburgers at the Billy Goat Tavern, a lower Michigan Avenue hangout for Chicago journalists. Amid all the risk takers, it was only fitting that, after the meal, Bush flipped a coin to decide who would pay the bill. He called heads. It landed tails. The restaurant owner insisted on picking up the tab.

But most of my efforts were spent as chairman of GLOBEX, putting the final details together on this momentous undertaking between the CME, the CBOT, and Reuters. To me, GLOBEX represented the markets of the future, whether it would take 10 or 50 years to get there, and whether it would be called GLOBEX, grandson of GLOBEX, or any other name. This electronic system was the perfect hedge against the future. Either open outcry would continue unabated forever, or it would operate in conjunction with electronic after-hours trade, or someday it would be replaced completely by an automated system. Whichever occurred, GLOBEX ensured that the franchise represented by futures markets remained securely in the hands of the members of the Chicago exchanges.

On June 25, 1992, GLOBEX was finally launched. It was five years in the making and long overdue. Indeed, it had missed the right "timing" window by a good two years. By now, every exchange in the world could boast of some form of electronic trade, either for their entire trading environment or to augment their open outcry session. From being first conceptually to becoming the last in real terms, GLOBEX had lost much of its glamour and would have an uphill battle to prove its merit.

Still, GLOBEX was the only international trading system around, all the others were no more than glorified local area networks. Its future was made no less brighter by its delayed implementation. Proudly, I made certain—by entering a "highball" order to buy 10 Japanese yen at 80 cents—

that I would make the very first GLOBEX transaction. And Nobel Laureate Merton Miller made sure he was among the guests at the opening celebration on the Merc floor. "I missed the launch of financial futures by not being there when the IMM opened," Miller confided in me, "so I made damn well certain to be there for the opening of electronic trade."

The launch went without a hitch; however, the seed of discontent for GLOBEX had already been planted, and it had nothing to do with its technical capabilities or its delayed implementation. It had to do with a revision to its governance structure. The structure of its governing body had been agreed upon by all concerned during the previous two years' of deliberation. There would be a GLOBEX Joint Venture (JV) Board, with seven representatives each from both the CME and CBOT, and two representatives from the FIA; I was elected chairman for a two-year term, with the CBOT to gain chairmanship for the following two years in rotating fashion.[1] All decisions pertaining to GLOBEX would be made by this governing JV Board. We were ready for the new age.

After becoming Merc chairman, and in a totally unexpected turn of events, Jack Sandner suddenly had a change of heart about the governance of GLOBEX. Milton Friedman's warning was beginning to come true. The Merc chairman demanded that all decisions by the JV governing board would have to go back to their respective exchange boards for approval before implementation. Sandner said that he was acting on behalf of the Merc Board in order to preserve its control over GLOBEX decisions. It was a paper-thin excuse. The representatives to the JV were chosen by the Merc and CBOT boards in the first place; a majority of them had to be directors of their respective exchanges; they served the JV at the pleasure of their exchange chairmen. Consequently, their actions were, in effect, always controlled by the exchange boards and there was no need for further controls.

On the surface, it looked like a fairly harmless modification. The *Chicago Tribune*, for instance, saw it simply as an issue over "power and money, not to mention prestige." What they missed was that it was an issue over the very destiny of GLOBEX, one that could materially diminish the potential of the after-hours system. For me, Sandner's reason was

---

[1] The other six representatives from the Merc included Jack Sandner, John Geldermann, M. Scott Gordon, Barry Lind, Gordon McClendon, and William Shepard. From the CBOT, the seven representatives were Bill O'Connor, John Benjamin, Charles P. Carey, David J. Fisher, John F. Gilmore, Jr., Burt Gutterman, and Neal Kottke. In addition, Thomas H. Dittmer and John J. Conheeny were selected to represent the FIA; and Bill Brodsky, Tom Donovan, as well as the chairman of the FIA would serve on the board in ex officio capacity. I appointed Gary Ginter, a former partner of Chicago Research and Trading (CRT), as GLOBEX managing director and chose Tyrone Fahner, of Mayer, Brown & Platt, as GLOBEX general counsel.

obvious: it was meant to personally assure him the upper hand in controlling the destiny of GLOBEX. While I could understand the motivation from a purely political point of view, it undermined the functionality of the GLOBEX system.

It is not difficult to understand what I foresaw. GLOBEX, a system correctly described by the *Tribune* as "a one-of-a-kind network that some have likened to the space shuttle for its complexity," had to have hands-on management to succeed or even to survive. It would be impossible to run GLOBEX—with the myriad decisions that would be necessitated in the course of its global implementation, its ongoing negotiations with world exchanges, and its around-the-clock operation—if approval by the CME and CBOT boards had to be obtained before any action could be taken. The JV board would be required to act on issues involving highly technical matters, which sometimes required hours upon hours of expert explanations, followed by hours of discussions by the JV board representatives. How would the knowledge or expertise gained during such processes be transmitted to the exchanges' boards of directors for approval? Realistically, how timely could the exchanges act on the matters involved, considering that their boards had many other priorities on their agendas in the day-to-day running of an exchange?

Without any doubt, the revision represented a cumbersome and inefficient procedure that decimated the power of the JV board. But even more sinister was the fact that it gave the CME and CBOT chairmen (although Bill O'Conner never sought this power) virtual dictatorship over the destiny of GLOBEX. With this procedural change, either of them could thwart any JV decision they did not personally agree with by delaying or not bringing the matter to their boards in a timely fashion; or they could accidentally or purposefully distort the facts involved on any given issue during board presentations; or they could use any number of other tactics to guide their boards' decision to their liking. In short, the revised procedure was a prescription for failure.

Subsequently, on more than one occasion, Tom Donovan admitted to me that the CBOT had made a terrible mistake letting Sandner get away with these changes. But by then it was too late. And it turned out just as I believed it would. In a very real sense, that revision changed the course of Chicago market history. From the moment the rules were altered, I privately decided to leave the GLOBEX chairmanship as soon as I carried out the early critical responsibilities I had undertaken. I realized, of course, that this may have been precisely what Jack Sandner had hoped for, as my departure would give him the chairmanship of GLOBEX for the balance of the term assigned to the Merc. But I wasn't interested in the prestige or salary this office represented (by resigning I would forfeit the $200,000 annual chairmanship stipend), and I refused to be party to the potential tragedy created with the change in governance.

Nevertheless, during the months that followed, I directed all my energies at those components of GLOBEX I believed were critical to its future, namely its actual launch, the contract with Reuters, and the approval of GLOBEX by the government of Japan. With respect to the latter assignment, there were many who bet that it couldn't be done. Japan was not ready to approve the type of trading freedom within their borders that GLOBEX screens would allow. But I got it done with the assistance of some powerful friends. Help came first from David W. Mullins, Jr., assistant secretary of the Treasury for Domestic Finance. I had convinced him that GLOBEX represented a trading mechanism that was in the best interests of the financial service sector of the United States. As a result, he placed GLOBEX on the agenda for formal discussions between the U.S. Treasury and Japan. Help came second from the offices of my good friend Makoto Utsumi, the special advisor to the Finance Minister of the Japanese Ministry of Finance.

Having brought GLOBEX to three continents and three time zones, I was ready to step down at the end of my first year in office. There were many who tried to dissuade me. High on that list was Pat Arbor, who became the CBOT chairman at the beginning of 1993. Arbor was a friend of mine dating back to the early IMM days. He was also an ardent proponent of the CME-CBOT joint venture and totally committed to its implementation. In fact, Arbor was in synch with the era of common goals and wanted to continue the discussions I had begun with his predecessor Bill O'Connor about a merger of our two exchanges' clearing facilities.

Similarly, Tom Donovan valiantly tried to change my mind. Donovan confided that life between the CBOT and the CME without my presence—whether with respect to GLOBEX or other matters—would become much more difficult, if not impossible. "You have achieved a trust factor with our board and membership that no one else holds," he told me. I respected his sentiments, as well as similar ones from a host of officials at both exchanges, including the personal appeal from my good friend John Damgard, president of the FIA, and that of Reuters permanent representative to GLOBEX Rosalyn Wilton. But my decision was final. I simply would not lead a venture whose procedural setup was shortchanging the members of both our exchanges, something I could not countenance. I stepped down as the first chairman of GLOBEX on May 31, 1993.

It didn't take too long before my worst fears began to materialize. As Donovan predicted, the CBOT and the CME began to squabble. At first it was nonsense stuff: which exchange does more volume, which exchange is smarter. Both exchanges actually put ribbons around their buildings to claim their dominance. To the outside world, these were childish actions that made both exchanges look bad. Then things turned serious. The road to a unified clearing system, a virtually unanimous goal of our clearing member community, was scrapped—a victim of the deteriorating climate between the leadership of the Chicago exchanges. Then things went from bad to worse. GLOBEX became a political football. The GLOBEX agreement that was due to be renewed with Reuters had reached an impasse. The Merc and the CBOT were on a collision course over three or four issues, and neither exchange would budge. The trust factor between the exchanges had been wounded by acrimonious actions and statements, which had even reached a point of public recriminations. The most intractable issue had to do with the theoretical right of the CBOT to continue in its attempt to do a mutual offset system with another exchange just as the Merc was doing with the SIMEX. The Merc refused to grant this right to the CBOT. To me, it was more a symbolic issue than a real concern. No functioning new mutual offset system had been implemented since the CME-SIMEX connection, and it was highly doubtful it would ever be done again. I felt the issue was not material to the well-being of the system. Nevertheless, the two exchanges were heading for an irrevocable rupture, and GLOBEX would be the clear loser. If the Merc did not budge and the CBOT left GLOBEX as it threatened to do, the grand design that we had instituted years before would disintegrate. And with it would come an immeasurable diminishment to the potential of GLOBEX. I tried to intervene with Reuters behind the scenes using the assistance of Henry Jarecki who was on the CBOT board, but to no avail. I tried to talk one-on-one with all the principals involved, but I achieved nothing. While I didn't absolve the CBOT from blame in this altercation, in my opinion, the underlying problem was that the CME chairman really didn't mind if the CBOT left. Finally, the inevitable happened: the CBOT officially announced its departure from the GLOBEX joint venture with the CME.

In a last ditch effort and seeing no other choice, I decided to go public. I would appeal to the court of last resort: the membership of both the CME and the CBOT. On April 22, 1994, I wrote an open editorial directed to the members to be published in the *Chicago Tribune*.

Suddenly, Sandner and Brodsky called to meet with me again. It was a stormy meeting in Brodsky's office with heated words. I read the proposed editorial to them, and they were adamant that I not publish it. "It will serve to further confuse the public, which is already confused on this issue," Brodsky stated. We compromised. I called the *Tribune* and asked them to withdraw indefinitely the publication of my letter. As a result, my editorial was never published. In return, it was agreed that I would appear before the Merc Board to make a final appeal for reconciliation with the CBOT.

I did. I spoke for over an hour. I offered my view of the issues involved and why they should be resolved. I used many of the words I had written in the editorial.

> There is no comfortable way to phrase it. The recent collapse of the agreement between the two Chicago futures exchanges in GLOBEX is to the detriment not only of the system itself, but to the memberships of both the Chicago Mercantile Exchange and the Chicago Board of Trade, the member firm community, as well as Reuters. What's more, it represents an incredible loss to the City of Chicago because GLOBEX goes a long way toward assuring Chicago's continued dominance as the global capital of futures markets and the center for risk management. This is an achievement that took decades of planning, innovation, and vision by both Chicago exchanges. The result has made Chicago the envy of every other city in the world, copied and emulated by every center of finance. It is folly to endanger this prize. In addition, the era of common goals has been materially affected with this squabble. The negative fallout may be felt for years to come, all to the advantage of our competitors.

There were questions, there was discussion. But basically, most board members felt that the CBOT was the main culprit and that the Merc had done all it could. In fact, Tim Lankford, one of the governors, suggested that I make the same appeal to the CBOT. I agreed to do so but left the meeting feeling discouraged.

I did appear before the CBOT board the following week. But it was far too late to do any good. The breakup altered GLOBEX's attraction. As I had feared, within days of the CBOT-announced departure from GLOBEX, LIFFE advised the Merc that it too had decided to reject the offer of joining the GLOBEX system. Now there was no reason for the CBOT to reconsider its decision. The rupture was complete. Alas, it was predictable. As I had anticipated, the CBOT eventually launched its own electronic system, Project A, and began discussions in earnest with LIFFE to create a trading accommodation between the two exchanges. It ultimately led to an agreement between them. The seed sown by virtue of Sandner's governance revision had produced the fruit I feared.

In spite of everything however, I remained committed to GLOBEX. In the long run, I was still optimistic. Although it had been injured and its potential would take longer to achieve, I firmly believed that GLOBEX represented the way that the markets of tomorrow would function. It was still central to the Merc's future.

Having done all I could, I once again retreated to my other responsibilities, withdrawing from Merc affairs almost entirely. Indeed, I vowed not to involve myself in CME matters unless they were of the utmost urgency or I was specifically requested to by the CME leadership. In view of the recent altercations between me and the Merc chairman, I knew full well that this was unlikely to happen.

But in the fall of 1994, a situation began to brew at the Merc that in the long run I again couldn't ignore. A plan advocated by Jack Sandner—and supported by the Board—called for the merger of the CME and IMM, ostensibly to give traders of financial contracts the same voting rights as full exchange members. In other words, to remove the 6-2-1 weighting of votes that existed between the CME, IMM, and IOM. I was never quite certain of the true motivation for this proposal. On its surface, it sounded right. After all, financial futures accounted for 95 percent of the Merc's volume, but traders of the financial products had only one-third the voting power of full Merc members, who were mainly agricultural traders. Under the plan, the exchange was to make one-time payments of between $60,000 and $80,000 to compensate each full member. These payments represented roughly the difference between the cost of a full CME seat and an IMM seat. But in doing so, the CME divisional members would forever give up their controlling right over the destiny of the Merc. The IMM division would then merge into the CME and be extinguished. The members of the surviving entity would have equal weight in votes. This was considered a constructive result because in the Board's view, "We want a unified CME, without divisions."

When I thought about it, I realized the whole proposal was nonsensical. When the 6-2-1 weighting for divisional voting rights was established, it was written into the structural foundation of the Exchange. Indeed, I believe the divisional structure, its voting system of checks and balances, its ability to bring new members to our fold—approved in 1976 by the entire membership in the original merger referendum between the CME and IMM—was a supreme piece of constitutional design on which much of the Merc's strength has been achieved. The CBOT and other exchanges copied this formula. Ironically, when the structure was first devised, the voting rights were balanced so that the CME could not take unfair advantage of the fledgling financial division. Now, two decades later, the financial contracts were dominant and, if the merger was adopted, agricultural members would lose all their influence at the Exchange.

I was absolutely certain that Sandner would not have dared to suggest such a proposition were I still sitting at the boardroom table. But was it worth my effort to enter into the issue? After all, the CME's board of directors approved it and the membership seemingly found no problem with it. My inclination was to refrain from offering an opinion and stay removed from the issue. Until, that is, Joel Greenberg and a few other members appealed to me.

Joel Greenberg was a good friend of many years and one of the strongest proponents of agricultural markets. His opinion carried weight with me, and his strong appeal caught my attention. "Leo, you know the proposed merger is breaking a covenant written in stone," Greenberg stated. "When the CME divisional members were given the six voting rights, you warned us never to use them as a sword against the IMM, only as a shield in the event our rights were in jeopardy. We have kept our word. But now the Merc Board is threatening our rights. You know that if this referendum passes, it will bury the agricultural sector of the Merc."

Everything Greenberg said was true. "But what do you want me to do Joel?" I asked. "The membership seems not to care."

Greenberg, looked up at me and said, "The membership has no leadership. Leo, you are the only one who can stop this nonsense. Don't let them do this."

When I asked Greenberg how many others wanted me to intervene in the issue, he said he would show me. Within half an hour of our conversation, with the help of Joe Gressel, Thomas Bentley, Harvey Paffenroth, Bob Schillaci, and Mark Adrian, I was presented with a copy of a petition to the board of governors signed by more than 200 brokers and traders, asking me to address the membership and offer my opinion on the issue.

I prepared two letters to the 3,000 members of the Merc and held several standing-room-only members' meetings. In addressing the issue, I acknowledged that the IMM had been the driving force behind the Merc's phenomenal success and that IMM members were indeed entitled to equal representation on the Board. But this could be achieved by a board vote, without cost, and without tampering with the entire structure of the Merc. Indeed, IMM representation had already been increased once before in the foregoing manner.

As far as the weighted vote, I noted, "It was carefully structured to ensure that the founding CME division—whose ideas launched the revolutionary new contracts and upon whose infrastructure and finances the new divisions were built—would remain the controlling factor on core Exchange issues." Moreover, I continued, the vote issue was a "red herring" in that the weighted vote never had any material impact on the Merc's direction. Indeed, the majority of members in each division had always voted the same. There were also tax implications that had not been addressed in the proposal in view of the Merc's not-for-profit status and the question of whether the Merc should deplete its treasury in this manner. After all, one should always retain a reserve for a rainy day.

As far as the divisional structure, I told the members that I found no logic in the argument that there was a need to unify CME divisions to strengthen the institution. How could the Merc have been stronger without its IMM division—the IMM name and image was world renowned. Why tinker with this spectacular success? To do so called to mind one of the biggest marketing fiascos in recent years when someone decided to replace classic Coke with a new taste. That effort also failed thanks to a demanding public.

Last, there was no doubt that the Merc's agricultural sector needed new blood. It was a critical matter that had to be addressed. But the proposal at hand would do nothing to achieve this objective; rather, it would dramatically reduce the agricultural voice of the Exchange.

Jack Sandner, Bill Brodsky, and other officers of the Merc Board didn't like what I was saying. They went all out in their effort to win the proposition. I mean *all out.* They needed a two-thirds majority to win, and every FCM was contacted and cajoled for their vote. Virtually every member was also called and lobbied. It was unprecedented. Of course, over the years, I had done my share of campaigning in favor of or against many issues before the Merc membership. Indeed, I was no shrinking violet when it came to politics, and I campaigned hard in this controversy as well. But in my long history of Merc referenda, I had never participated or seen the kind of arm-twisting that I saw this Merc administration undertake to win this referendum.

All for naught. On Tuesday October 25, 1994, the membership voted to reject the Board's merger proposal. The 6-2-1 voting allocation held. And because of their all-out campaign, the loss turned out to be a huge embarrassment for the Merc administration.

It could have been avoided. During the members' meetings, more than one member asked the obvious question, "Leo, you are chairman emeritus of the Merc, so how come the Board didn't bother to ask your opinion on this issue?"

Good question. I could not come up with any rational answer. Logic would have dictated that the Board use every resource at its disposal—particularly the opinion of the Merc's chairman emeritus—before deciding to launch a critical restructuring of the CME. Maybe I could have dissuaded them, or offered some changes that would have made the proposal palatable. I wasn't asked.

On the morning following the referendum, Irv Kupcinet, who is "Mr. Chicago" himself and who for decades has authored the famous and newsworthy "Kup's Column" for the *Chicago Sun-Times,* reported that "Leo Melamed, founder of the Chicago Mercantile Exchange, and Jack Sandner, now head of the exchange, went mano-a-mano on the bitterly contested membership issue in an election Tuesday. Melamed, known as the father of the Merc, defeated Sandner, once known as his protege."

Similarly, the *Chicago Tribune* played up the story as "a major rebuff to Chicago Mercantile Exchange Chairman John F. Sandner" and as a "dramatic victory" for me. Now the press was portraying me as Sandner's intense rival. "I think the vote is a victory for the institution and the membership," I commented. "The proposal was flawed from the very beginning and injected a terrible divisiveness among members that had not been there before."

Suddenly, there was a constant call from many members for my return. I declined, stating: "The vote does not mean that I am returning to Merc politics. The simple fact is that after 25 years of service in building this institution into one of the world's leading financial markets, I could not walk away from or ignore a proposal that was harmful to the Merc."

As a footnote to this event, the incident resulted in my being asked by Sandner to serve as an advisor to many of the Merc's special undertakings. And I found it ironic that within a year of the failed attempt to unify the Merc on the pretense that "divisions were no longer necessary," the Merc Board launched yet another new division—the so-called GEM, the Growth and Emerging Market Division. I thought it was a good idea and gave it my support.

I also thought it was a good idea to take some time off, to think, to write, to reflect on the rush of years, the struggles I faced, my accomplishments, the future. I took Betty's hand and we headed for Scottsdale, Arizona, where we maintain a winter retreat. I left in full comprehension of Milton Friedman's warning.

36

A Call from the White House

The lights of Phoenix flickered below as the 727 began its descent. The flight from Chicago had been a welcomed breather. Three hours without phones or faxes. Just me, Betty, and my Game Boy. *Tetris* assured that my hand-eye coordination was on par with Joshua's, my 10-year-old grandson. I seldom sleep on planes, even on the long trips to China or Japan. A long flight is a good time to work on things: speeches, business plans, trading strategies; I even wrote *The Tenth Planet* in assorted airplanes and airports around the world.

Once we arrived, I had my battery of trading tools—charts, software programs, economic projections, and so on—at my fingertips as the computer screens zeroed in on various markets. I never go anywhere without them. As I've said, trading for me is a priority, and always has been. For me, it represents life's ultimate challenge. It provides a new adventure every day, a quest, a mystery to solve. The competition is fierce, the rewards can be great, the punishments even greater. Everything else seems to pale by comparison, all other professions seem humdrum, as I make my way through the technological landscape of a global financial world in search of the answer to the same question millions of people ask daily: Will the market go up or down?

Not that long ago, it seemed, the answer came easier. When I began trading in the 1960s, my competitors were around me in the pit. I could touch them, hear them, see the whites of their eyes, and, when the trading really heated up, I could even smell them. I knew who they were and their exact tolerance for financial pain, the size of the position they could take, how much loss they could afford, and at what point they would retreat from the market. If I was clever enough, I could preempt them and push them. It was all part of the game plan. Even then, pit trading valued speed, strategy, and finesse over muscle, wealth, or pedigree. And aside from that singular goal of making money, they also shared one denominator: survival. It was a lesson I learned long before I got to the pits.

Things change. While, in the early days, there was a flow of business from the outside, it was the heat of competition within the pits that had an immediate impact on market swings. But technology changed all that. It made competitors invisible. There are still pit traders and brokers, but now there is also a faceless army of "upstairs" traders, off-the-floor speculators, fund managers, financiers—some with the minds of mathematicians and physicists—moving in and out of markets on the blip of a computer screen. Among them are institutional investors, commercial hedgers, corporate treasurers, and money managers—major competitors who move the market with their deep pools of capital—who primarily trade financial instruments such as futures contracts on foreign currencies, Eurodollars, Treasury bonds, Treasury bills, and the S&P 500 index. The institutional investor long ago replaced the dentist in Des Moines as the primary user of the futures markets. Today, a fund's entry in the market is an enormous undertaking and there is no way to determine how much business, how much flow, how many buys or sells it will represent. The worst part is that the market is a chain, in that one fund's move triggers that of another fund, and everybody follows. No one dares stand in the way of the market because there is no way to estimate a competitor's tolerance.

And the computer has spawned a vast array of new market instruments, that is, OTC derivatives, that impact the market in ways that cannot be precisely gauged. Many of these instruments represent unknown dangers to both traders and the marketplace. Although I agree with the assessment of Federal Reserve Board chairman Alan Greenspan, who told Congress "the Board believes that the array of derivative products that has been developed in recent years has enhanced economic efficiency," I recognize that we do not know all their effects. As Mr. Greenspan pointed out, "Even if derivatives activities are not themselves a source of systemic risk, they may help to speed the transmission of a shock from some other source to other markets and institutions." For one thing, the failure of a major derivatives dealer could impact its counterparties. This represents the chain reaction peril that many observers have verbalized. For another, there are the unknown dangers created by a wide assortment of over-the-counter financial options and, to an extent, even exchange-traded options. There is also an emerging genre of contingent options where payment is a function of multiple possibilities. These contingent options create risks that cannot be perfectly hedged, therefore the resulting risks normally need to be managed through a process of dynamic hedging—an inexact science that can heighten price movements and produce unknown consequences.

The new traders use these new strategies and new technologies, and I had to go with the times. I had no choice. The computer has facilitated the business flow from everywhere to markets anywhere. The flow isn't just from Iowa or New York anymore, but from anywhere in the world, day or night. The world has shrunk and people are trading around the clock. We live in the information age. There are a multitude of services that provide a trader with instant information flow: Reuters, Knight Ridder, Bloomberg, Dow Jones, Telerate. I am never disconnected, no matter where I am or what I am doing. The tangential benefit of being a trader is that it forces you to stay informed and in touch. The negative side is that you never relax.

But the most important effect of trading is that it keeps me linked to reality and truth. The beauty of the markets, and for me their quintessential characteristic, is that they are the final determinant of veracity. As Elmer Falker taught me, "the markets tell the truth." Washington policymakers, Tokyo or Berlin ministers, officials of governments the world over can try to tell the world whatever they want, but the markets tell the world the truth. It's that simple; no one can fool the market. Universally, government officials insist that their personal value judgment about the level of interest rates or the rate of their currency is the correct interpretation of the facts, but their opinion doesn't count a tinker's damn unless or until it is endorsed by the market.

Once during those early years when I was criss-crossing the world as the lone evangelist on behalf of financial futures markets, I was asked to meet with a former governor of the Bank of Japan who was traveling through Chicago. He had heard of the new exchange, the IMM, and wanted to meet me. We had lunch at the Metropolitan Club in the Sears Tower and I immediately went into my spiel. He understood and spoke English quite well, so I spared nothing in offering the reasons why the idea of a financial futures exchange was important. When I was finished with my tirade, the old gentleman smiled and nodded.

"You have given many good reasons for such a market, but you still have not given the most important reason."

Dumbfounded, since I had used every persuasive argument in my arsenal, I asked him what I had missed. His answer gave me compelling ammunition that I used time and again during the years that followed. With a twinkle in his eyes, he asked: "Do you know how it is when a congressman walks out of his house of parliament, be it Washington, DC, London, or Tokyo, and he stops on the steps of his government building and the reporters of his country gather around him with notebooks and microphones. Do you know how that is?"

"Yes," I nodded, "I do."

"Do you know how it is when this congressman waves a paper with his hand in the air and tells the reporters that the measure he just proposed in his parliament or congress is a wonderful idea that will greatly benefit the people of the nation. Do you know how that is?"

"Yes," I nodded again.

"Well, in such a case," he said, "let there be a public market that the following morning can loudly exclaim *bullshit!*"

Indeed, that may very well have been the best reason for the creation of the new futures market that I fervently advocated. That is not to say that markets do not sometimes become distorted as a consequence of misinformation or phony interpretations, or even manipulations and the like, but these aberrations are infrequent and usually correct themselves swiftly, sometimes violently. The trick to trading successfully in today's global age is not only to be connected, but to be able to decipher the truth from the information received.

Telling the truth can be rewarding, but it can also be punishing. Since time immemorial the futures markets' compulsion to tell it how it is have caused them to be plagued by skepticism and scapegoatism. I have seen it all: derogatory comments, defamatory innuendoes, inflammatory jokes, false accusations, misleading opinions, half-truths, out-and-out lies. The examples were endless. During the 1972 food price spiral, a group of Chicago homemakers marched on the Chicago Mercantile Exchange to protest *high* prices for food products. Five years later, U.S. farmers drove their tractors to the Chicago Board of Trade to protest *low* prices on their products. Somehow it was not illogical to blame futures for both high as well as low prices. And why not? As the ancient saying goes: "Behead the messenger of bad tidings." Futures have often been a lightning rod for those who seek a convenient culprit, a place to lay blame; futures occupy a place shrouded in mystery and misunderstanding—the ideal scapegoat.

And why not? Read the headlines, the stories. Someone is always making a killing in those markets; clearly something dastardly must be going on. Look at the members, the brokers; they're rough, boisterous, undignified. "Cowboys," some are called for their quick-draw antics and their hellbent bravado.

Many of the innuendoes and much of the finger-pointing over the years have come from competitive market quarters, from those who do not understand the nature of futures, or from those who have a hidden agenda. They always paint futures speculation with a scarlet S. I have spent my entire adult life fighting this brand of scapegoatism, as witnessed during the 1987 stock market crash and the FBI sting.

And wasn't it just the other day that the First Lady, Hillary Rodham Clinton, who dared to speculate in futures, became the object of a similar reproach? The media had suddenly focused on the First Lady's speculative venture in the cattle futures market 15 years ago. On that venture she had been a winner, a big winner, turning a $1,000 investment into nearly a $100,000 profit in 10 months.

Unfortunately, the media did not believe that she could do this without some hanky-panky. So suddenly the White House called me. Would I examine the records of her trading and offer an opinion, they asked. Could I help them explain to the world how a novice trader in the treacherous futures business could legitimately make that kind of money. As former chairman of the Merc—where cattle futures are traded—and founder of the IMM, I could provide both credibility and expertise. As for political objectivity, I was on safe enough ground there, too. While I have voted for candidates on both sides of the political aisle, my philosophical bent on behalf of free markets and fiscal conservatism is considerably closer to the Republican point of view.

My involvement with the Clinton trading episode began when Rahm Emmanuel, the former lieutenant to Chicago's Mayor Richard M. Daley and now a political assistant to President Clinton, called in early April 1994 to alert me that John P. Podesta, assistant to the President and White House staff secretary, was going to call me about Mrs. Clinton's cattle trading. Would I please do him a favor and take the call? Emmanuel was a good friend, and I knew Podesta from his days with House Committee on Agriculture. He was a straight-up guy whom I respected and with whom I always got along. I agreed to take the call.

An hour or so later Podesta's call came in. The gist of his inquiry was whether I would do the White House a big favor by examining Mrs. Clinton's cattle trading records of a decade and a half ago. "The White House needs expert advice, Leo. Can you help us?"

My immediate inclination was not to get involved. In late March, Mrs. Clinton's trading records were released by the White House. Although there was no documented evidence that she had received favoritism from the brokerage firm that handled her account, the news reports were very skeptical and had painted a pretty bleak picture. The implications were that the First Lady must have violated a host of regulations to turn $1,000 into big money or that someone had handed her the profit. The issue grew even murkier when the White House initially said that Mrs. Clinton learned to trade by reading *The Wall Street Journal*. With all due respect to that paper, it is impossible to believe that anyone can learn about futures trading simply by reading that publication.

The White House quickly backed away from that response and provided the facts: Mrs. Clinton had been advised by James Blair, who was then the outside counsel to Tyson Foods, the big Arkansas-based poultry processor. It was a situation that sent Clinton critics circling like a school of sharks. Conflict of interest, influence peddling, favored treatment were among the phrases bandied about by the Washington wags. In late March, however, Mrs. Clinton's trading records were released by the White House and there seemed to be no documented evidence that she had received favoritism from the brokerage firm that handled her account.

Even if I were willing to give Mrs. Clinton the benefit of the doubt, I didn't need the embroilment of controversy and the publicity that accompanies it. I had more than my share of it leading the Merc all those years. I told this to John Podesta. I also advised him that I had received a similar request from Leslie Stahl of CBS. She had called a few days earlier to ask if I would act as a guide and explain how the futures market worked for the next *60 Minutes* broadcast. The broadcast was to deal with Hillary Rodham Clinton's cattle trading and would be filmed from the floor of the Chicago Mercantile Exchange. My immediate reaction to Stahl's request was negative, although she assured me that I would not be asked to comment on Mrs. Clinton's trading practices. My instincts, however, dictated that this could become a politically nasty matter from which the Merc should stay away. I told Stahl I would think about it.

Within minutes after Stahl's call, I contacted Bill Brodsky to discuss the request. In the old days, the decision would have been mine, but as chairman emeritus I was no longer in the policy-making loop. I told Brodsky I was inclined to turn down the request. He agreed with me, reasoning that there would be no benefit to the Merc having *60 Minutes* film from the trading floor. "Leo, I wouldn't touch it with a ten foot pole; it is a no-win situation for the Merc," he said.

The next day I politely turned down Leslie Stahl's request, explaining that the Merc did not wish to get involved in what was a politically charged issue.

But before I knew it, there was a change of mind. The Merc would do it, and Jack Sandner would be Stahl's guide. Neither Brodsky nor anyone else at the Exchange explained to me why the Merc was so opposed one moment, so willing the next. I guess the decision hinged more on *who* would be the Merc's guide for the broadcast, than whether it was good for the Exchange. So Stahl got her tour.

I explained to John Podesta that I had similar misgivings about his request. Podesta, however, was insistent. "The White House is not CBS, Leo," he protested. "Let us simply overnight Mrs. Clinton's records to you so that you can examine them and tell us what they show. If you decide not to help us after you see the records, we will accept your decision."

It was difficult to refuse such a reasonable request from the White House. Politics and party labels did not seem to count. Besides, the accusations against Mrs. Clinton sounded similar to so many unfounded rumors

I had heard over the years. So I agreed to review Mrs. Clinton's trading records, with several caveats: my conclusions would be strictly with respect to the buys and sells involved, drawn solely from the records provided by the White House. I would make no assessment as to how Mrs. Clinton's trading decisions were made nor would I delve into any relationships between her and Mr. Blair. I would also reserve the right to say nothing.

As promised, the records came the next day. I rolled up my sleeves and asked my chief operating officer, Valerie Turner, and marketing director, Alysann Posner, to assist me. We carefully analyzed the buy and sell orders that made up Mrs. Clinton's trading account in 1978 and 1979. The analysis was made in the context of the highly volatile market conditions at the time.

Indeed the First Lady had a fast start. On a $1,000 investment she made $5,300 on her very first trade. That is a big profit, but those were the days when the cattle markets had wide price swings. Within a year, for example, beef prices had risen from 47 cents per pound to 80 cents per pound. That meant that a $1,200 investment in early 1978 would have produced a $13,000 profit one year later on just a single futures contract. Of course, Mrs. Clinton didn't just simply buy and hold, she traded, moving in and out of many positions and many commodities over the course of some 10 months.

After all was said and done, from the records that were provided, our analysis concluded that Mrs. Clinton appeared to have been a relatively modest trader. She had paid normal commissions. On many trades she made a profit; on some she sustained a loss. On balance she had done extremely well. In my opinion, she must have received well-educated advice to which she had every right. This advice, as the press reports indicated, was most likely provided by James Blair, who was an expert futures market trader in addition to being Hillary Clinton's friend and lawyer. Although I could not tell for certain, I also assumed that she had discretionary trading executed on her behalf by Mr. Blair.

But by far the most important fact I discovered was something totally missing from all press reports. Out of some 32 separate transactions, all but a few had been so-called overnight trades. The distinction between overnight trades and day trades is significant. If one is going to allocate favorable trades, it is highly likely that it would be done in the course of a day trade. With an overnight trade, the control of profitability is given up to the market. In other words, an overnight trade will be a winner or a loser as a consequence of the next day's market movement and little else. And one cannot control the next day's price movement. Since most of Mrs. Clinton's trades were overnight positions, she had assumed the market risk in the bulk of her transactions.

Podesta was relieved by my report. "Would you be so good as to come to Washington to provide your opinion to the White House Staff?" he asked. "We really have no such expertise around here."

Clearly, there was no harm in giving the White House staff a firsthand opinion on what I had found. I said I would come to Washington with my assistant Alysann Posner.

The next day I found myself at the White House before a bevy of staff people and officials. Besides Podesta, there were at least 20 White House staffers in the room including David Gergen, White House counselor; George Stephanopoulos, senior presidential adviser; Lisa Caputo, Hillary Clinton's press secretary; and David Kendall, Mrs. Clinton's attorney. I verbally etched a 30-minute report carefully looking for puzzled faces and changes of expressions. But there were none. Apparently, what I had said made sense to everyone in the room.

"Would you be willing to give what you just stated as an official independent report?" David Gergen asked.

"Now wait a minute," I exclaimed. "That was not the deal."

David Gergen apparently had found a comfort zone serving a Republican administration as Ronald Reagan's press chief, and was now in a Democratic administration in a similar capacity. Though the press had tagged him as a spin doctor, Gergen had been recruited out of their ranks. A strapping man with a Yale law degree, Gergen was a former political columnist for *U.S. News & World Report*, and was sensitive to the demands of a story. I always liked and respected him. He had experience, intelligence, and depth. He didn't strike me as the kind of journalist who turns himself into a skilled technician of illusion once he becomes a spokesperson for an organization. His style wasn't to stonewall. Nor was mine. Over the years I had learned to spar with the press, to deal with pack journalism and point-of-view journalism. Sometimes I took lumps; other times I gave them. But I never retreated over an issue I believed in.

"I'm not even a true blue Democrat," I protested.

David Gergen laughed. "Do you think, I am? I'm asking you to do it for the United States."

Gergen had pushed the right button, but I doubt that he realized it. Patriotism was my Achilles heel. As flag-waving as it may sound, I've always had a huge debt of gratitude to the United States. There are all sorts of people who honor gratitude in quiet ways. For instance, I have a friend who was a child during the Second World War, but to this day he will do anything for veterans. Why? Because he sees their generation as having sacrificed their lives to keep the world free for his generation. He says he will always be indebted. That's how I feel about the United States.

Thus, it was nearly impossible for me to reject a serious request based on patriotism. I agreed to provide a report for release to the public on the basis of what I had found. I requested and received a private office with a personal computer so that I could prepare a statement. Before we knew it, Posner and I were planted in front of a PC in a White House room. And some two hours later we had drafted a statement that was released by the White House on April 11, 1994. In short, it stated that there was nothing in the records I examined that reflected any trading violations on the part of Mrs. Clinton.

As for the firm she had traded with, that was a another matter. As my statement indicated, Mrs. Clinton's trades were made some 15 years ago when exchange rules and federal regulations were different, as were enforcement procedures. For instance, there were questions surrounding Mrs. Clinton's margin, the money put up as a security deposit on each contract. The margin on a futures contract is set by the exchange. It is determined by the volatility of the market and the possible change in daily price movement. My analysis revealed that, at times, Mrs. Clinton's account had been thinly margined and, on occasion, she had traded with insufficient margin. Her first transaction was clearly undertaken with insufficient margin on deposit. But margin inadequacies are not a customer violation. Rather, margin insufficiency is a violation of the rules of the exchange by the firm at which the customer account was held.

In 1979, the firm through which Mrs. Clinton traded, Refco & Co. (Ray E. Friedman & Company), was found by the Chicago Mercantile Exchange to have committed many trading violations. Although Refco neither admitted nor denied any wrongdoing, the alleged violations involved hundreds of the firm's customers. Hillary Rodham Clinton's account was so small that it wasn't even on the radar screen in the multitude of accounts involved. I know because I was instrumental in making certain that the Merc levied a $250,000 fine, the biggest fine in its history up to that time, against Refco for repeatedly violating margin requirements, for a lack of discretionary account authorization, for improper order entry procedures, and for exceeding position limits.

Is there more behind Hillary Rodham Clinton's cattle trades than the records reveal, as some suggest? I could find nothing. Jim Blair's help for the First Lady was important, but he was, after all, a pretty decent trader who had made many millions in the markets. And providing trading advice or even directing another's trading activities is no crime. In any event, I wasn't asked to be a political analyst or a psychiatrist. The request for my assistance focused strictly on what I could deduce from the transactions themselves. And from what I examined in the records, she did nothing wrong. In fairness, Hillary Rodham Clinton was not the first person who took a risk in commodity markets and made a bundle.

There are innumerable tales of rags to riches in our markets. It has happened time and again. Take Bruce Kovner, for instance. This legendary currency speculator started as a taxi driver and made untold millions in futures. He began trading by borrowing $3,000 on his MasterCard. Or take Gene Cashman, a Chicago policeman who pyramided a $5,000 position into a $100 million fortune during a hot soybean market. Many others started on a shoestring and made a fortune in commodity markets. I know many of these stories. But then, futures are an arena of opportunity, and we are a nation of risk-takers.

George Washington and his fellow colonists took the ultimate risk in defying the British. The American pioneers who left everything behind to settle the West were nothing short of high-risk rollers. When this nation opened its doors to immigrants from every sector of the world and consequently gained enormous benefits, it did so at risk. Our farmers risk the weather and a hundred other variables every year in order to plant their crops. Our nation's financial service sector is number one in the global marketplace primarily because the American financial community dares to innovate and is willing to assume risk. Indeed, risk is a four-letter word that has historically served our nation well.

There is an additional by-product of market risk that is seldom recognized. Since risk is assumed for the potential reward it offers, the process tends to create an environment that makes no distinction between race, knows nothing about ethnic origin, and is indifferent to gender. The floors of futures markets and the offices of member firms are proof of it. Religious discriminations of past eras are virtually nonexistent; race barriers still put up elsewhere are down; ethnic distinctions of consequence in other endeavors are meaningless. In the futures markets we fashioned in Chicago, the trophy goes not to the Catholic or to the Jew, not to the white or black, not to the man or woman; it goes to the one who understands the economic principles of supply and demand. It is not what one is, but whether one can figure out which way the market is headed. All members and employees soon learn that the market rewards people when they are right or when quality is high and service is good, and punishes them when they are wrong or quality is bad and service inferior, no matter who their fathers were, what they did for a living, or where they came from. Futures markets are far from utopia, but I know of no other private sector establishment that is more free of human prejudice than are futures markets, especially the ones in Chicago. Risk and reward are the controlling factors.

After the White House release of my findings, after the *60 Minutes* airing, and after Mrs. Clinton's press conference, the controversy continued to smolder. Eventually, David Kendall, Mrs. Clinton's attorney, called me to say that the White House was going to ask the Chicago Mercantile

Exchange to release Hillary Clinton's trading data contained in the so-called trade register of the exchange for the period covering her trading, October 11, 1978, through July 20, 1979. He stated that Mrs. Clinton wanted to go the last mile to prove she had nothing to hide. He then asked if I would review the Merc's records and issue another statement on what they showed.

Again, I felt beholden to the process. I reviewed the Merc's records and issued a second statement released by the White House on May 26. It substantially repeated what the first statement had concluded: Hillary Clinton did not herself violate any Chicago Mercantile Exchange rules. A few weeks later, Mrs. Clinton, who had accompanied President Clinton on a European trip to commemorate the 50th anniversary of the D-Day invasion in Normandy, called me from Rome to again thank me personally for my efforts.

From my office window I could see Camelback Mountain—the highest point in Phoenix—basking in a blaze of late morning light. Hummingbirds flitted among the bougainvillaea, and shards of light glistened off the pool's surface as I dangled my feet in the tepid water. I felt drained, too tired to sleep. I needed to blank out, to do nothing for a few days, to clear the fog that had settled in my mind—and perhaps to contemplate a bit. It's times like this when I try to look forward *and* think back, with detachment, like a film dissolve in which the present fades . . . into my childhood . . . and beyond. I had come a long way since reaching the United States in 1941 as a child refugee escaping Nazi persecution. That took strategy, too. And risk. Survival always does.

Epilogue

Wake Up Call

These remarks were presented at the annual meeting of the International Association of Financial Engineers, New York, New York, on November 9, 1995, and were reprinted in the December 1995 issue of the *Journal of Financial Engineering*.

We are at an unprecedented moment in the evolution of finance and markets. We find ourselves at the vortex of three primary crosscurrents that have converged to create some turbulent waters and whose resolve is still uncertain. The rush of these currents has been extremely rapid and they have advanced upon the world at nearly the same time. Their remarkable history is quite recent and still very fresh in our memory.

First: globalization. Walter Wriston, the former chairman of Citicorp, sensed it early. In 1985, he told us we were witnessing a "galloping new system of international finance," one that was not built by politicians, economists, central bankers, or finance ministers, but by men and women who interconnected the planet with telecommunications and computers. As a result, Wriston stated, the world had replaced the gold standard with the *information standard*.

Indeed it had. Our separate financial existence was transformed into one interrelated, interdependent world economy. Geographical borders that once could limit the flow of capital are history. Internal national mechanisms that once could insulate a population from external price influences are increasingly impotent. Financial markets have become virtually unencumbered, continuous, and worldwide. A company located anywhere in the world can use resources located anywhere in the world, to produce a product anywhere in the world, to be sold anywhere in the world.

Second: political. As Nobel Laureate Milton Friedman and his wife Rose predicted, the free economic precepts of Adam Smith combined with the principles of political freedom espoused by Thomas Jefferson have resulted in an unmitigated triumph of market-driven economic order over central planning, of capitalism over communism, of democracy over dictatorship.

445

The world experienced the incredible might of these two ideals as together they seemingly overnight forced the unification of Germany, the liberalization of Eastern Europe, the fall of communism, the collapse of the Soviet Union, and the dissolution of apartheid.

This political/economic transformation has propelled virtually every nation in the world to move to a market-driven economic order. It is a unique historical occurrence. For the past 20 years when we spoke of a global economy, we were only talking about 25 percent of mankind—mostly North America, Western Europe, and Japan. As recently as 1988, almost 70 percent of mankind was living under Marxist or socialist economic systems. Suddenly, there are 3 billion more participants in the capitalist system. Suddenly, every country on the planet is a competitor in the global marketplace.

Third: microdynamism. This is a word I made up to explain that the world has moved from the big to the little. In physics, we traveled from general relativity to quantum mechanics. We went from contemplating atoms to inspecting their nucleus and discovering quarks and leptons. Particle physics was upon us. Similarly, in biology, scientists migrated from examining individual cells to peering within their structure and ushering in the era of gene engineering. Molecular biology was born.

This microdynamism and downsizing can be seen in every aspect of our lives. Today's personal computer, small enough to be stored in a briefcase, can do much much more than the UNIVAC, the world's first computer, which required an entire room to be housed. We wear much lighter material that is warmer and stronger than the bulky clothing of previous eras. Fiber optic cables are replacing mountains of copper wire. Transistors transformed the radio and a myriad of other electrical appliances into handheld devices. Microprocessors miniaturized the entire technological world and keep getting smaller and smaller. And on and on.

In markets, the evolution was strikingly similar. When advancements in computer technology were applied to established investment strategies, the result was remarkable. Just as it did in the sciences, market applications went from macro to micro. Intricate calculations and state-of-the-art analytical systems ensued, offering financial engineers the ability to divide financial risk into its separate components. Derivatives—the financial equivalents to particle physics and molecular biology—were born. Investment methodologies were transformed from all-encompassing traditional strategies to finely tuned modern portfolio theories. Long-term hedging evolved into continuous on-line risk management.

The foregoing three primary crosscurrents, coupled with a swarm of secondary flows, have converged to create our present financial market environment. It is unique to history. It is still undefined and not understood. It is volatile and dangerous. At times the whirlpool is smooth and easy to anticipate. Suddenly it is vicious and unpredictable. Markets go up with unrelenting force, only to turn without warning and collapse without end. Participants find inventive ways to cash in, only to be caught in unsuspecting savage traps. Rogue traders unearth ingenious techniques to deceive or cheat as traditional controls are found antiquated or woefully inadequate. Market regulators, along with business managers, seem helpless and off guard.

What will the world do? Condemn the events that produced the turbulence? Curse the reality of the present? Outlaw the markets? Restrict price movement? Ban derivatives? All of the above?

We can neither expunge the history that brought us to this fate, nor prevent its ultimate resolve. We are in the midst of a great transformation. We are negotiating an unknown expanse between a world we knew and the one we know not. We are on a gigantic bridge between past political arrangements, past economic orders, past technical capabilities, past market applications, past internal controls, and a new reality.

We are yet insufficiently conversant with the new order, its dimension, its demands, its potential, to write the rules. If we act in haste to severely harness the currents, rigorously restrict its flow, or sternly direct its course, we take the risk of creating conditions far more dangerous than what is naturally in store for us. If we so fear the computer that we adopt a Luddite philosophy, if we so recoil from Procter & Gamble, Orange County, Metallgesellschaft, Barings Bank, Daiwa Bank, or similar debacles yet unknown that we enact Draconian rules to prevent their occurrence, if corporate boards shrink from the use of derivatives because of fears of consequential losses to their corporate bottom line, civil actions by shareholders, or sanctions by regulators, then at best corporate profits are headed south, and at worst Western civilization has hit its top.

At this juncture in the transformation, while we dare not ignore the dangers it has engendered, we must not cower in its presence. Just as we found it impossible to curtail the developments in gene engineering, so we will discover that financial engineering also cannot be stopped. Instead, we must be prudent and vigilant. We must set standards, benchmarks, and especially internal controls. We must heed the lessons we have learned and adopt the prescriptions that are warranted. We must enforce the recommendations of such forums as the Group of Thirty, The Windsor Declaration, and the FIA Global Task Force on Financial Integrity. We must observe and learn and intensify our education process. Risk management implicitly must include risk enlightenment.

And, above all, we must be realistic. There are but two certainties. Neither is surprising. First, that the metamorphoses I described is unending—by definition, evolution is a continuing process, whether in physics, biology, or markets. Second, that the unmistakable common denominator of recent crosscurrents has been technology. Indeed, throughout the ages technology has consistently been the foremost force in dictating fundamental and revolutionary change in the political and economic landscape of our planet. In the past decade, the technology of telecommunications forced a stark, uncompromising examination of political and economic systems, bringing down state-controlled economics and racial inequalities, while the technology of computers enabled physicists, biologists, and financial engineers to peer into the smallest detail of our structure and manipulate its makeup.

Clearly, the introduction of fire brought about a profound change in the life of our species, as did the invention of the wheel, electricity, and the printing press, or the onset of the industrial revolution. But events speeded up. The technological revolution of recent years is of a larger magnitude and came upon the world in a shorter time span than ever before experienced. At an unprecedented pace that continues to accelerate, technology has produced, and continues to produce, fundamental changes that reverberate through every facet of our civilization, but nowhere more than in financial markets where the transformations have been spectacular, global, and absolute.

There are still within our markets those who would ignore these realities. These souls are simply following historian Barbara Tuchman's prediction that "men will not believe what does not fit in with their plans or suit their prearrangements." Pity! For no longer is there a valid debate on the subject. Anyone who is still skeptical about the direction we are headed is simply deaf to the thundering maelstrom of the technological avalanche around us. Anyone who has not seen the handwriting on the wall is blind to the reality of our times.

One can no more deny the fact that technology has and will continue to engulf every aspect of financial markets than one can restrict the use of derivatives in the management of risk. The markets of the future will be automated. The traders of the future will trade by way of the screen. Those who dare ignore this reality face extinction. Round-the-clock electronic information in stocks, futures, options, and mutual funds is now commonplace. Real-time spreadsheet capabilities that display, analyze, and monitor current financial data with electronic on-line datafeeds are old hat. Portfolio information management systems designed to document and control transactions, provide real-time positions, P&L, and credit limit updates are routine. Electronic alerts, predetermined target prices, complex option spreads, currency conversions, and volatility cones are now standard trading applications. Software products providing a host of complex analytical calculations, multidimensional charts of theoretical preexpiration curves, historical comparisons, projections, regressions, and exponential smoothing from single or multiple databases are abundant. Risk analysis modules providing a snapshot of the portfolio under varying market circumstances are standard. Support programs for exotics such as average rate, chooser, corridor, digital, double-digital, dual, lookback, quanto, and trigger/barrier options are available. There are even computer trading systems that anticipate and incorporate the human thought process of traders, so-called artificial intelligence. And there is much more. The information standard has become the information superhighway. There are many millions of users of the Internet on the North American continent alone.

In the 1970s and 1980s, futures markets led the way. We recognized that to survive competitive pressures we had to embrace new technologies and integrate them with open outcry. To compete globally, we recognized that telecommunications was fashioning a global marketplace that would necessitate electronic trading mechanisms. Proudly, in 1987, the Chicago Mercantile Exchange membership overwhelmingly approved GLOBEX. It was the first embrace of an electronic screen-based system for futures anywhere in the world. And almost on cue, the GLOBEX pronouncement resulted in a virtual torrent of electronic systems devised either to extend existing trading hours or to conduct the entire transaction process.

The following year, the Chicago Board of Trade, the Tokyo Stock Exchange, the Osaka Securities Exchange, the Copenhagen Stock Exchange, the Danish Options & Futures Exchange, the Swiss Options & Financial Futures Exchange (SOFFEX), and the Tokyo Grain Exchange all launched automated electronic systems. The next year, the Irish Futures and Options Exchange, the Tokyo International Financial Futures Exchange (TIFFE), the London International Financial Futures Exchange (LIFFE), and the Sydney Futures Exchange (SFE) initiated similar systems. By the end of 1991, 10 more exchanges followed suit, including the Deutsche Termin Boerse (DTB), the London Futures and Options Exchange, the Swedish Options Market, the Finnish Options Market, and the Mercado Espanol de Futuros Financieros (MEFF). Indeed, except for Brazil's BM&F and the MATIF in Paris, all new derivatives exchanges built since 1986 are fully automated.

Alas, in recent years the process toward technology in futures markets seems to have come to a screeching halt. Suddenly, our market establishment reverted to establishment ways. The evidence to support this conclusion is overwhelming. While GLOBEX volume statistics are growing, they are still pitifully small and the system itself has become enveloped in politics. It still accounts for only 1 percent of the Merc's annual volume. That is about the same percentage as the ACCESS system of the NYMEX. The LIFFE APT system does a little better with about 3 percent of its annual volume and the MATIF has done much better. Its GLOBEX volume has grown from 5.5 percent in 1993 to a 8.7 percent in 1995, proving that technologically the system is sound. Similarly, Sidney's SYCOM system has grown from a 5.1 percent of its volume in 1993 to a 1995 total of 8.9 percent. In contrast, the evening session of the CBOT is losing volume from 1.6 percent in 1993 to a projected 1.1 percent in 1995.

The low level of screen-based transaction volume on after-hour exchange systems gives testimony to a lack of understanding by many futures exchanges that—like it or not—a screen-based transaction process is in their members' future. While it is comforting to know that the mass of futures liquidity is still on the floor today, it represents a false security blanket. Foreign exchange, a market institutionalized by futures exchanges, offers a stark and sobering comparison between electronic-driven volume and open outcry. The average daily FX turnover measured in U.S. dollars was approximately $200 billion in 1986 compared to $1 trillion in 1995, a 500 percent increase. According to figures recently released by the Bank for International Settlements (BIS), the turnover figures for major Forex centers in cash markets between 1992 and 1995 shows whopping increases of between 30 percent and 60 percent. However, CME foreign exchange contracts did not benefit from this growth. It registered a mere 9.5 percent increase in volume in 1993 and another 6-plus percent increase in 1994. While admittedly some of this OTC volume can be attributed to exotics not traded on the exchange, one must accept the fact that OTC screen-based technology is an extremely attractive medium for FX market transactions. The global trading day begins in Tokyo and Sydney and is virtually unbroken 24 hours a day, as it moves around through Singapore and Hong Kong to Europe and finally the United States before starting again in Japan. How can the open outcry hours of any single exchange hope to capture a significant portion of such business?

While I do not advocate turning off the lights on existing trading floors—that would be unforgivably stupid—it is equally suicidal not to seriously prepare for a technological tomorrow. Whatever progress there has been in recent years has been at a snail's pace. In almost every critical area of advanced technological competence, exchanges with trading floors have fallen behind. For instance, LIFFE is the only exchange with real-time clearing capabilities. Futures exchanges are far behind securities exchanges in automatic order routing. No futures exchanges have advanced capabilities for floor communications with brokers and have limited capabilities for handheld price reporting. Only the CBOE has developed a system for handheld terminals. No futures exchanges are developing automatic small-order execution systems. Use of electronic books in the transaction process can only be found at securities exchanges.

And everything within the technological revolution of the last two decades—which produced the present information standard and transformed the world into what we know today—is about to become old if not obsolete, for technology is poised once again to take a quantum leap. The computers that Walter Wriston wrote about and that wired the world in the mid-1980s, are about to go wireless in the mid-1990s. Satellites will soon allow wireless communication from anywhere on the planet. When this wireless transformation goes into high gear—over the latter half of this decade—we will transfer information literally over thin air.

Today's cyberwizards have combined the magic of electrical and electromagnetic waves, and propelled them at the incredible speed of 300 million meters per second, about three-quarters of the way to the moon with every second. In doing so, they have produced an invisible wave of energy that can carry a computer command, the human voice, or virtually any program including market information, quotations, analysis, and orders from anywhere to anywhere. The new technology will create a world which will result in not just a series of new technological marvels, but in a spectacular lifestyle emancipation.

By unplugging us from existing infrastructures, networks of information, and communication hookups, we will suddenly have many more choices about where we live, work, or how we trade. This new freedom of wireless communications can be best illustrated with how the simple pager is already transforming our lives. So-called alphanumeric pagers with small LCD screens can show not only a phone number, but a complete message. By the end of this year, a so-called bidirectional pager will enable us not only to receive e-mail, but to acknowledge these messages by choosing one of the 100 set responses. Think of the possibilities for trading, if the response is buy or sell and is linked into an automated trading system.

Nor will we be limited to the telephone boundaries of today's cellular capabilities. New phone networks, operating by way of satellites, will begin providing round-the-globe service later in this decade. Without the limitation of land-based antennas, everyone on the planet, and especially market traders, will be able to trade from places never before thought possible. Are today's exchanges preparing for this world?

Futures markets take heed! Complacency is the enemy. Tomorrow's futures traders grew up with Nintendo and Sega. They were given a keyboard for their fifth birthday; their homework was done on a computer; their recreation time was spent in video centers; the World Wide Web is their playground; Cyberspeak is their language.

When the current transformation process has been completed, when we have crossed the bridge to the new reality, when the new set of rules has been written, derivatives will still be the primary way to manage financial risk, but it will be carried out on the information superhighway. Tomorrow's traders will likely execute a complex set of trades from an interactive multidimensional wireless communication system representing the coalescence of key communications technologies: television, telephone, personal computer, and laser storage systems. The only question remaining is whether those trades will still be transacted on our futures exchanges.

Index